NIGERIAN POLITICAL PARTIES

POWER IN AN EMERGENT
AFRICAN NATION

BOOKS FROM
THE CENTER OF INTERNATIONAL STUDIES

WOODROW WILSON SCHOOL OF PUBLIC AND INTERNATIONAL AFFAIRS
PRINCETON UNIVERSITY

✦

Gabriel A. Almond, *The Appeals of Communism*

Gabriel A. Almond and James S. Coleman, editors, *The Politics
of the Developing Areas*

Robert J. C. Butow, *Tojo and the Coming of the War*

Bernard C. Cohen, *The Political Process and Foreign Policy:
The Making of the Japanese Peace Settlement*

Percy E. Corbett, *Law in Diplomacy*

Charles De Visscher, *Theory and Reality in Public
International Law*, translated by P. E. Corbett

Frederick S. Dunn, *Peace-making and the Settlement with Japan*

Herman Kahn, *On Thermonuclear War*

W. W. Kaufmann, editor, *Military Policy and National Security*

Klaus Knorr, *The War Potential of Nations*

Klaus Knorr, editor, *NATO and American Security*

Klaus Knorr and Sidney Verba, editors, *The International
System: Theoretical Essays*

Lucian W. Pye, *Guerrilla Communism in Malaya*

James N. Rosenau, *National Leadership and Foreign Policy: A Case Study in the
Mobilization of Public Support*

Rolf Sannwald and Jacques Stohler, *Economic Integration:
Theoretical Assumptions and Consequences of European Unification*,
translated by Herman F. Karreman

Richard L. Sklar, *Nigerian Political Parties: Power in an Emergent African Nation*

Glenn H. Snyder, *Deterrence and Defense*

Sidney Verba, *Small Groups and Political Behavior:
A Study of Leadership*

Myron Weiner, *Party Politics in India*

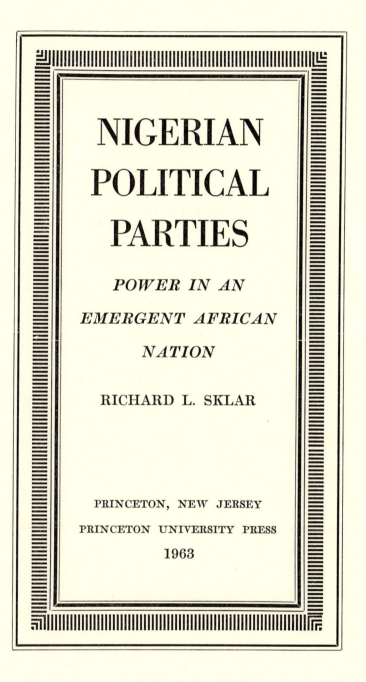

NIGERIAN
POLITICAL
PARTIES

POWER IN AN
EMERGENT AFRICAN
NATION

RICHARD L. SKLAR

PRINCETON, NEW JERSEY
PRINCETON UNIVERSITY PRESS
1963

PREFACE

THE present study is concerned with the development of the Nigerian party system during the final decade of British colonial rule. The core of its analysis is the social composition and construction of those parties which stood at the forefront of the movement for independence.

A portion of the study is deliberately cast in narrative form, the better to reveal the interplay of three converging social forces, namely, the thrust of nationalism, the persistence of cultural particularism, and the crystallization of emergent class interests. Nonetheless, I have shied away from any rendering of Nigerian politics which imposes a burden of interpretation on the actual data beyond what they can reasonably sustain. For the most part, I have been content to set forth the pertinent data and documentary evidence in the hope that their accuracy will survive the test of further research.

I am pleased to express my appreciation to Professor William Ebenstein, for his wise supervision of the doctoral dissertation on which this book is based.

I am greatly indebted to many persons for their encouragement and counsel, notably Professor C. S. Whitaker, Jr., Professor Hugh H. Smythe, Dr. Eme O. Awa, Professor Paul J. Bohannan, Professor Harwood L. Childs, Professor James S. Coleman, Professor Harry Eckstein, Mr. Lawrence Ekpebu, Mr. Thomas Hodgkin, Professor Elie Kedourie, Dr. Jean H. Kopytoff, Professor Ruth Schachter Morgenthau, Mr. Ayo Ogunsheye, Professor Kenneth Robinson, Professor John D. Sly, Dr. Mabel M. Smythe, Professor Harold H. Sprout, Professor Morris Watnick, and Mr. Herbert F. Weiss.

Among those who read the manuscript at various stages and contributed to its improvement, I am especially grateful to Chief H. O. Davies, Mr. V. Olu Sanu, Malam Isa Wali, and Mr. Howard Wolpe.

My research in Nigeria was supported by the Ford Foundation Foreign Area Training Program; supplementary assistance was provided by the Penfield Fund of the University of Pennsylvania and the Princeton University Center of International Studies. Appreciation is expressed to Professor Klaus Knorr, Director of the Center, Mrs. Jean McDowall, Secretary, Mrs. Jean Pasley, and other members of the Center's staff. An acknowledgement is due to Mr. John B. Putnam and Mrs. Gail Filion of the Princeton University Press. The index was done with the help of my wife, Eve.

PREFACE

Acknowledgements for assistance during the initial phase of my research in England are due to Mr. T. F. Betts of the Fabian Commonwealth Bureau, Hon. Fenner Brockway, M.P., Mr. J. A. Hutton of the Colonial Office Library, Mr. Joseph Iyalla of the Nigerian Commissioner's office, and Mr. David Williams of *West Africa*.

As a matter of propriety, I will refrain from expressing personal thanks to people who were prominent in Nigerian public and professional life, employed in the government services or in the field of communications, or active in political affairs, many of whom figure directly or indirectly in these pages. But I would like to record my indebtedness to a group of Nigerians whom I regard as being the unsung heroes—an American might say the Jimmy Higgins'—of the nationalist movement. They are the full time workers of the political parties who do the paper and leg work of "political mobilization." Some of them went to great pains in taking me around and showing me the ropes. I am grateful to Mr. C. C. Anah, Mr. E. D. O. Iloanya, Mr. Mbazulike Amechi, Mr. Michael Ugoala, Chief Gogo Abbey, Mr. Fred Agugu, Mr. D. O. Akoma, Mr. Joseph Bolumole, Mr. R. A. Kumuyi, Mr. R. K. B. Okafor, Mr. S. E. Onyiah, and Mr. H. A. S. Uranje of the NCNC; to Mr. S. T. Oredein, Mr. Olatunji Dosumu, Mr. O. Agunbiade-Bamishe, Mr. J. O. Ogunyanwo, Mr. S. A. Adeniya, Mr. Lasisi Ajimobi, Mr. S. L. Ayeni, Mr. R. A. Babalola, Mr. A. A. Folorunsho, Mr. A. Olomola, Mr. J. O. Oloronyolemi, Mr. Ayo Oshunremi, Malam Mmah Sanssan, and Mr. S. J. Umoren of the Action Group; to Malam Habib Raji Abdallah, Malam D. A. Rafih, Malam Abubakar Tugga, Malam Garba Abuja, Malam Yusufu Dantsoho, and Mr. S. Ade. Lawal of the NPC; to Malam Tanko Yakasai, Malam M. R. I. Gambo Sawaba, Malam Ibrahim Heebah, Malam Usman Ango Soba, and Malam Tanko Waziri of the NEPU. To those of their fellow workers unnamed, and to the "honorary" secretaries of local party branches, this book is appreciatively dedicated.

CONTENTS

CONTENTS

Maps on pages 5 and 7 by R. L. Williams

LIST OF TABLES

TABLES

NIGERIAN POLITICAL PARTIES

POWER IN AN EMERGENT
AFRICAN NATION

CHAPTER I
PROLOGUE: THE SOCIO-POLITICAL
SETTING

NIGERIA is situated at the eastern end of the Gulf of Guinea between the 4th and 14th parallels (North). Its total area is approximately 356,000 square miles, slightly more than the combined areas of France and both Germanys. Its name is derived from its main inland waterway, the river Niger, which flows some 2,600 miles from the hills of Sierra Leone into the enormous fluvial complex of the Niger Delta.

Geographers distinguish three principal zones of vegetation: "the swamp forests of the coast-belt, the high forests of the humid south, and the savannas of the subhumid Middle Belt and north."[1] There are two major seasons—a wet season (April-October) when rainfall in the coastal sector varies between 100-140 inches, and a dry season (November-March) when it lessens to 20 inches at the coast and zero in the north. By and large, temperatures vary between 70-80 degrees F. in the morning and from 90-100 degrees F. in the afternoon. The lower temperatures are recorded during the dry season, when a dust-driving northeasterly wind, known as the harmattan, sweeps across the northern plain. Occasionally night temperatures dip below 40 degrees F. on the Jos plateau of central Nigeria, which rises to an altitude of more than 5,000 feet above sea level.

The population of Nigeria, estimated at about 35 million in 1959, exceeds the combined populations of all other states in the West African region south of the Sahara. Among the nation-states of the African continent, the Nigerian population is most nearly approached by the 27 million of the United Arab Republic (Egypt), followed by the 16 million of Ethiopia, the 14.6 million of the Republic of South Africa, and the 13.6 million of the Congo. When the Federation of Nigeria became an independent member of the Commonwealth of Nations on October 1, 1960, the total population of United Kingdom dependencies the world over was reduced by about 45 percent.

The Federation of Nigeria consists of three political regions—the North, the East, and the West. The Northern Region comprises over three-fourths of the area and contains about 54 per cent of the population of the country. Each region is said to have a dual cultural

[1] K. M. Buchanan and J. C. Pugh, *Land and People in Nigeria* (London: University of London Press, 1955), pp. 33-34.

3

makeup: a territorial "nucleus" inhabited by members of a cultural majority and a "peripheral zone" inhabited by cultural minorities.[2] Majority and minority groups include both tribes and "nationalities." James S. Coleman has defined these terms thus:[3]

Tribe: "... a relatively small group of people who share a common culture and who are descended from a common ancestor. The tribe is the largest social group defined primarily in terms of kinship, and is normally an aggregation of clans."

Nationality: "... the largest traditional African group above a tribe which can be distinguished from other groups by one or more objective criteria (normally language)."

In each region, a single "nationality" group of culturally related tribes is numerically preponderant—the Hausa in the Northern Region, the Ibo in the Eastern Region, and the Yoruba in the Western Region. Nigerians speak "approximately 248 distinct languages."[4] These include ten languages that are spoken by groups of more than 350,000; the Hausa-speaking people of the North number about 9½ million, while Ibo and Yoruba are spoken by more than 5 million people each.[5] English is the official language in every region (Hausa is a second official language in the Northern Regional Legislature); it is the principal language of commerce and the primary linguistic link between peoples of different nationalities. In 1953 some 10 per cent of the population was recorded as officially literate in Roman script; but an indeterminate large number of people can speak English with varying degrees of fluency. In the Northern Region, where approximately 72 percent of the people professed the Islamic faith, literacy in Arabic script was higher than that in Roman script (5.4 to 2.1 per cent). English literacy was higher in the Western and Eastern Regions (17.3 and 15.6 per cent respectively) owing to the intensive activity of Christian missionaries in these areas for nearly a century. In the Western Region, Christianity and Islam have an approximately equal number of adherents; in the Eastern Region, where Christianity is the exclusive modern religion, denominational differences are politically salient.

[2] Ibid., p. 94.

[3] James S. Coleman, *Nigeria: Background to Nationalism* (Berkeley and Los Angeles: University of California Press, 1958), pp. 423-424.

[4] Ibid., p. 15.

[5] Demographic information in this chapter is taken mainly from the census of 1952-1953. A new census, in preparation at the time of writing, is expected to reveal significant growth in the populations of all major linguistic groups.

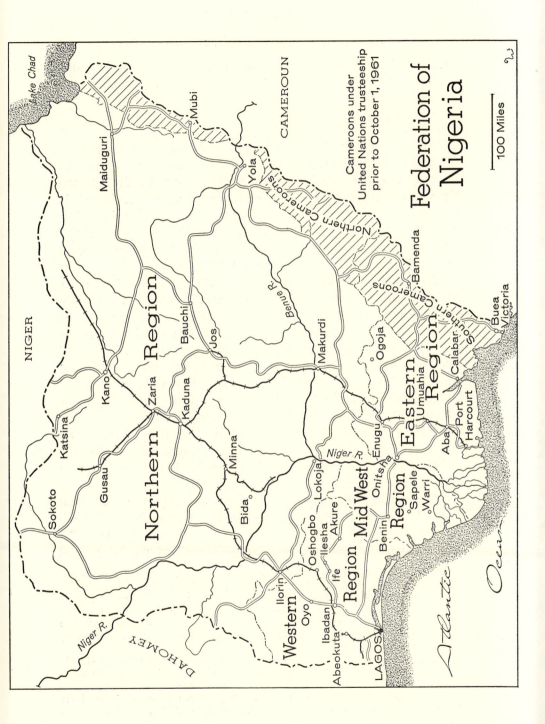

Federation of Nigeria

100 Miles

Cameroons under
United Nations trusteeship
prior to October 1, 1961

NIGER

DAHOMEY

CAMEROUN

Northern Cameroons

Southern Cameroons

Lake Chad

Maiduguri

Mubi

Yola

Benue R.

Bauchi

Jos

Makurdi

Bamenda

Ogoja

Buea
Victoria

Calabar

Port
Harcourt

Aba

Umuahia

Enugu

Onitsha

Eastern
Region

Sapele
Warri

Benin

Mid West
Region

Niger R.

Lokoja

Oshogbo
Ilesha
Ife
Akure

Oyo

Ibadan
Abeokuta

Ilorin

Western
Region

LAGOS

Atlantic
Ocean

Niger R.

Bida

Minna

Kaduna

Zaria

Kano

Gusau

Katsina

Sokoto

Northern Region

3

A Synopsis of Nigerian Culture and History

Only the barest outline of Nigerian culture and history[6] is provided in this chapter to assist readers who are not generally familiar with the relevant background.

Peoples of the Northern Region

More than two-thirds of the 17 million Northern people in 1953 belonged to the six largest nationality groups, as follows: 5.6 million Hausa, 3.1 million Fulani, 1.3 million Kanuri, 800,000 Tiv, 500,000 Yoruba, and 350,000 Nupe. The remaining 5 million people include about 220 linguistic groups, most of whom inhabit the southerly half of the Northern Region where Hausa culture does not predominate. The Hausa nationality includes a number of tribes that are related by the Hausa language, the Islamic faith, and roughly similar physiognomic traits. M. G. Smith defines Hausa to mean "the entire settled Moslem, Hausa-speaking population."[7] Two principal subdivisions need to be distinguished: the indigenous Habe and the "settled" Fulani, who have intermarried extensively with the Habe, assimilating their language and customs. Apart from the "settled" or "town" Fulani, there are two other Fulani groups: pastoral nomads, called Bush or Cattle Fulani, and an intermediate group that is semi-pastoral and semi-agricultural. Each of the remaining major nationality groups of the Northern Region is identified with a particular territorial subdivision, thus: the Kanuri of Bornu Province, the Nupe of southern Niger and eastern Ilorin, the Tiv of Benue Province, and the Yoruba of southern Ilorin and western Kabba. (See Map 2)

The original Habe states, seven in number, appear to have been established in the territory of modern Hausaland about the tenth century. During the twelfth and thirteenth centuries, they were "at least partially within the sphere of influence" of the Islamicized

---

[6] For a chronological outline and survey of historical sources, see Thomas Hodgkin, *Nigerian Perspectives* (London: Oxford University Press, 1960), pp. 1-52. A good, lively introduction is Michael Crowder, *A Short History of Nigeria* (New York: Praeger, 1962). See also Sir Alan Burns, *History of Nigeria* (Fifth edition, London: Allen and Unwin, 1955), and J. D. Fage, *An Introduction to the History of West Africa* (Second edition, Cambridge: Cambridge University Press, 1959).

[7] M. G. Smith, *The Economy of Hausa Communities of Zaria* (London: H.M.S.O., 1955), p. 3. Elsewhere, M. G. Smith has written: "Hausa is a linguistic term which distinguishes Hausa-speaking Muhammadans from other major linguistic and cultural groups quite adequately; it is misleading in other contexts." "The Hausa System of Social Status," *Africa*, Vol. XXIX, No. 3 (July 1959), p. 240.

6

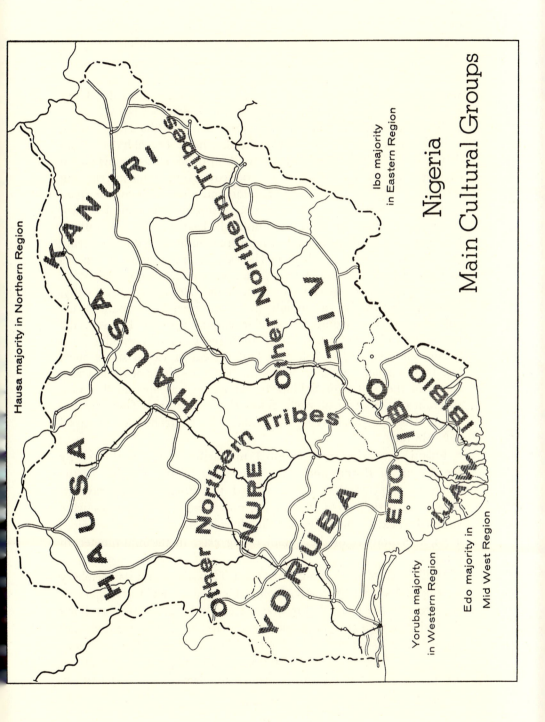

Nigeria
Main Cultural Groups

Hausa majority in Northern Region

Ibo majority
in Eastern Region

Yoruba majority
in Western Region

Edo majority in
Mid West Region

kingdom of Kanem-Bornu, "unquestionably the dominant state in the central Sudan."[8] Islam was introduced into Hausaland in the fourteenth century by Negro believers from the western Sudan. Shortly thereafter, Fulani tribesmen, migrating from the west, were welcomed as allies by the factional and periodically embattled kings of the Habe states. In time, many of the Fulani denizens forsook their nomadic customs and settled permanently in the Habe towns.

In 1804, a learned Fulani clan head, Shehu (Sheikh) Usuman dan Fodio, rebelled against the persecution of Muslims by his pagan overlord, the King of Gobir. He rallied devout Muslims, among whom the settled Fulani were predominant, and proclaimed a *jihad* or holy war against the Habe rulers. Assuming the title of *Sarkin Musulmi* (Commander of the Faithful), he bestowed flags of authority upon his zealous lieutenants who were commissioned to prosecute the *jihad* throughout and beyond Hausaland. His militant emissaries subdued pagan and Islamic communities alike, for they identified genuine piety with the cause of the *Sarkin Musulmi*. Subsequently, Usuman dan Fodio, a humble man in principle, renounced his political power, dividing his secular empire between his son, the first Sultan of Sokoto, and his brother, the Emir of Gwandu. Each became the overlord of a loosely knit system of vassal states ruled locally by virtually autonomous emirs. Thus the Emir of Zaria was a vassal of the Sultan of Sokoto, by whom he was appointed, and a suzerain of the Chief of Keffi. Similarly, the Emir of Gwandu was suzerain to the *Etsu* (King of) Nupe, who controlled lesser vassal states in turn.

Fulani expansion was arrested militarily in the northeast by the Kanuri of Bornu, and in the southwest by the Yoruba. In the southeast impenetrable terrain barred the Fulani mailed cavalry. Along the periphery of the empire, non-Muslim communities were suffered to exist, sometimes for the ulterior purpose of slave-raiding, a common practice of the Fulani ruling class in the mid-nineteenth century.

While each of the leading emirates in Hausaland and its periphery developed its own distinctive political system, certain principles of emirate rule are general. First, emirate rule is theocratic, involving the fusion of political and religious authority. Secondly, it is dynastic; normally, emirs are chosen by traditional electors subject to conditions that are peculiar to particular states, e.g., as the presumptive heir of a single royal dynasty (Kano), from a number of royal dynasties in

[8] Hodgkin, *Nigerian Perspectives,* pp. 4, 23.

rotation (Bida), from alternative dynasties subject to the approval of an overlord (Zaria). Thirdly, emirs rule through aristocracies of birth and rank, most of the higher offices being restricted to men of noble birth. As M. G. Smith has observed: "Status is conferred by birth and is a prerequisite of eligibility for rank, but rank and office, as the Hausa say, is the gift of Allah."[9]

Finally, emirate rule exemplifies the principle of clientage, defined by M. G. Smith as "an exclusive relation of mutual benefit which holds between two persons defined as socially and politically unequal, which stresses their solidarity."[10] In the pre-colonial era, clientage was basic to the system of territorial organization. Fief-holders residing at the capital of an emirate were clients of the emir; in turn, they were patrons of subordinate agents through whom they administered and exploited the subject communities within their jurisdictions. The emirs conferred both territorial and non-territorial titles upon members of Fulani families, fewer non-Fulani retainers, and senior functionaries of slave status. Major titleholders were empowered to create subordinate titles which they allotted to clients within their jurisdictions. During the colonial period, many new offices, created for the conduct of administrative functions, e.g., education, agriculture, forestry, etc., were absorbed into the title system and "converted to the traditional purposes of *sarauta* [the Hausa term for titled political office]."[11] Consequently, the modern elite of Hausaland has evolved mainly within the framework of traditional authority and value.

Elsewhere in the Northern Region, traditional forms of government vary widely. Kanuri and Nupe institutions resemble those of Hausaland. In the lower North, indigenous systems of authority vary from the divine kingships of the Igala and the Jukun to the egalitarian if not anarchistic polity of the Tiv. Nearly all of the 4.3 million Animists and 550,000 Christians of Northern origin live in this southerly zone, called the "middle belt."

Peoples of the Western Region

Over 70 per cent of the 6.1 million people of the Western Region (1953) belong to the Yoruba nationality. Nine tribal or territorial sections have been distinguished, eight in the Western Region and the Federal Territory of Lagos, the ninth in neighboring areas of

[9] Smith, *The Economy of Hausa Communities of Zaria*, p. 93.

[10] M. G. Smith, *Government in Zazzau* (London: Oxford University Press, 1960), p. 8; see also S. F. Nadel, *A Black Byzantium* (London: Oxford University Press, 1942), pp. 123-124.

[11] Smith, *The Economy of Hausa Communities of Zaria*, pp. 107-108.

the Northern Region.[12] Non-Yoruba peoples inhabit the two south-eastern provinces of the Region, termed the Mid-West. The greater number are Edo-speaking people; these include the Edo of Benin Province and the Urhobo of Delta Province. Ibo-speaking peoples inhabit easterly areas bordering on the Niger River; the Ijaw and the Itsekeri live mainly in the creek areas of Delta Province.

The Yoruba are believed to have migrated from northeastern Africa into their present homeland about a thousand years ago. Ile-Ife is the "cradle" of Yoruba culture; but political pre-eminence was acquired by the city-state of Oyo which, by the late fifteenth century, had become the capital of a Yoruba empire. To the south, Oyo power was checked by the extensive but centralized kingdom of Benin.

Tribal legend ascribes the origin of the Yoruba to a deity, Oduduwa, who is said to have reigned at Ife where he created the earth and its inhabitants.[13] The principal royal dynasties or lineages of the main tribal sections are purported to have been founded by the deified grandsons of Oduduwa. Minor royal lineages are ramified from the Oduduwan branches and there are numerous kings, great and petty, in Yorubaland. *Oba* is the Yoruba term for king, but most kings have titles which are unique to their chiefdoms. *Obas*, unlike the theocratic emirs of the North, are innately sacred because of their putative descent from Oduduwa and their identification with the mystical essences of their states.[14] The pre-eminent spiritual *Oba* is the *Oni* of Ife; it is indicative of the vigor of tradition in the modern Western Region that in 1960 the incumbent *Oni* was designated as its first African constitutional Governor.

Certain features of political organization are typical of the traditional Yoruba states. The basic element of the Yoruba political system is the patrilineage, an exogamous descent group whose members venerate a founding ancestor.[15] In general, superior title holders are

[12] Daryll Forde, *The Yoruba-Speaking Peoples of South-Western Nigeria* (London: International African Institute, 1951), pp. 2-3.

[13] J. O. Lucas, *Oduduwa: A Lecture* (Lagos: 1949); S. O. Biobaku, *The Origin of the Yorubas* (Lagos: 1955), p. 15.

[14] Archdeacon Lucas, an authority on the traditional religion of his people, observes that all Yorubas, not merely the royal families, are regarded as *Omo* (children of) Oduduwa; but *Obas* or kings are *Omo* Oduduwa in a "special sense" because "they are regarded in Yorubaland as 'incarnate souls of the nation or their respective tribes.'" *Op.cit.*, p. 20.

[15] On the Yoruba lineage and related political institutions see P. C. Lloyd, "The Yoruba Lineage," *Africa*, XXV (July 1955), pp. 235-251; "The Traditional Political System of the Yoruba," *South-Western Journal of Anthropology*, 10, No. 4 (Winter 1954), pp. 366-384; and *Yoruba Land Law* (London: Oxford University

chosen from among the lineage elders. Specific titles may be vested in particular lineages, but the process of appointment involves both selection by the lineage and confirmation by the *Oba* (king). Customarily, the sacred *Oba* of a Yoruba state is chosen from a royal lineage or clan (related lineages) by a council of traditional chiefs, or "kingmakers."

The classic illustration of Yoruba government is the kingdom of Oyo.[16] All decisions of the *Alafin* (King) of Oyo required the approval of his council of chiefs. In former times, a gift of parrot's eggs from the leader of the council was a sign to the *Alafin* that his death was desired by the chiefs and the people. Invariably the *Alafin* complied by taking poison, so the threat of a dread gift was a safeguard against tyrannical rule. As remarked in an authoritative study, the proscription of this custom by the British "dislocated the checks and balances of the old constitution."[17] In theory and in practice, the powers of the Yoruba kings were regulated by custom and limited institutionally by countervailing organs of the state. Unlike the Northern emirates, the Yoruba monarchies were constitutional rather than despotic; fear of authority does not appear to have been a normally important factor in tribal government. Great kings lived in the midst of their people, and lesser chiefs, like the titled lineage heads who controlled the election of kings, were necessarily close to the people. Government was a communal interest and at some point every adult had a say.

In recent years the Yoruba institution of chieftaincy has been modernized and adapted to the requirements of democratic, representative government. Socially, it has become the supreme symbol of achieved status. The traditional authorities regularly bestow "honorary" or "courtesy" titles of chieftaincy upon wealthy and otherwise

---

Press, 1962), pp. 38-47. Also William B. Schwab, "Kinship and Lineage Among the Yoruba," *Africa*, XXV, No. 4 (October 1955), pp. 352-374.

[16] An authoritative description of Oyo political institutions is found in Samuel Johnson, *The History of the Yorubas* (London: George Routledge and Sons, 1921), pp. 40-78.

[17] Margery Perham, *Native Administration in Nigeria* (London: Oxford University Press, 1937), p. 172. Another convention of the traditional constitution, which has been long since abandoned, required the execution of the *Aremo* or eldest son of the *Alafin* at his father's funeral in order to discourage parricide and to ensure that the council of chiefs would be able to exercise its free choice in the selection of a successor by eliminating an otherwise powerful claimant to the throne. A failure to observe this custom precipitated a war between Oyo and its satellite state of Ijaye in 1860, when the chief of Ijaye rebelled against the abandonment of tradition and refused to recognize the new *Alafin*. Saburi O. Biobaku, *The Egba and Their Neighbors, 1842-1872* (Oxford: The Clarendon Press, 1957), p. 64.

prominent men and women in recognition of their personal achievements and contributions to community development and welfare.

It is a basic cultural trait of the Yoruba for lineages to cluster, forming politically unified towns.[18] Members of the lineage in town live together in compounds or multi-dwelling residential units which normally house more than 100 people.[19] Farm lands surrounding the towns belong to lineages, and many persons divide their time between the "family farm" and a lineage compound in town.

Probably the proportion of urban dwellers in Yorubaland is higher than among any other people in tropical Africa. In 1953, nine of the eighteen cities in Nigeria with populations exceeding 50,000 were predominantly Yoruba communities of pre-commercial origin. This traditional pattern of urban organization appears to have minimized the amount of social disorganization produced by secular forces.[20] Yet the two principal cities of Yorubaland, Lagos and Ibadan, have not been spared the social traumas of modern urbanization. In both cities large cosmopolitan communities, populated mainly by Nigerians who are not sons of the soil, have arisen beside the traditional settlements. The juxtaposition of conflicting cultural value systems in the brisk urban setting has been an active spring of political competition.

The political institutions of Benin differ from those of the Yoruba in fundamental respects, despite the fact that the royal dynasty of Benin is derived from the Yoruba dynasty of Ife.[21] Benin chieftaincies, including the sacred kingship, are inherited by primogeniture and

[18] William Bascom, "Urbanization Among the Yoruba," *American Journal of Sociology*, LX, No. 5 (March 1955), pp. 446-454.

[19] W. R. Bascom has defined the compound as "a residential unit housing some 200-300 individuals and occupied by part of a clan, their wives and children, and usually a few outsiders." "Social Status, Wealth and Individual Differences Among the Yoruba," *American Anthropologist*, Vol. 53, No. 4, Part I (October-December 1951), p. 498, n. I. A detailed description of the Yoruba compound may be found in W. R. Bascom, "The Sociological Role of the Yoruba Cult Group," *American Anthropologist*, 56, No. 1, Part 2 (Memoir 63; January 1944), pp. 11ff; and Lloyd, "The Yoruba Lineage," *loc.cit.*, pp. 263ff. The constituent houses of a compound are occupied by extended families. When a compound becomes overcrowded some of the members will establish another one elsewhere in town, so that a prosperous lineage may have numerous non-contiguous compounds in a single town.

[20] " . . . The disintegrating and unsettling consequences of modern urbanization have been minimized in Yorubaland as a result of the pre-existence of structured urban communities based upon lineages. Yoruba city dwellers could absorb the characteristic aspects of urbanization without being physically uprooted. In short, the new economic forces resulted in the commercialization and adaptation of a relatively homogeneous and structured community, with minimal changes in social stratification, political authority, and place of domicile." Coleman, *op.cit.*, p. 75.

[21] See R. E. Bradbury, *The Benin Kingdom and the Edo-Speaking Peoples of South-Western Nigeria* (London: International African Institute, 1957).

non-heritable titles are bestowed by the *Oba* irrespective of lineage considerations. Traditionally, the powers of the *Oba* of Benin are more absolute than those of a Yoruba king. Titleholders, in particular the senior town chiefs, do influence the *Oba* but they have no traditional rights of opposition. Elsewhere in the Mid-West, among Edo, Ibo, and Ijaw-speaking peoples, traditional forms of government are conciliar, with age-grades and title associations playing an important part.

In the Western Region, in 1953, 37 per cent of the population professed Christianity, 33 per cent espoused Islam, and 30 per cent followed indigenous animistic creeds. Over 96 per cent of the Muslims and 84 per cent of the Christians were located in Yorubaland where the two faiths coexist in amicable rivalry. Such interfaith tension as exists is largely a consequence of the superior educational and political opportunities which have been enjoyed by Christian elements in the past.

Peoples of the Eastern Region

Among the 7.2 million people of the Eastern Region in 1953, about 5 million or 61 per cent belonged to the Ibo nationality which comprises some 30 territorial sections. Non-Ibo peoples inhabit the southern and eastern sectors of the region. The largest groups are the Ibibio and the Annang who jointly total some 15 per cent of the regional population. The 75,000 Efik people of Calabar in the Cross River Estuary have given their name to the language of the Ibibio-Annang who are classed, with peoples of the Cross River Basin, as Efik-speaking. Ijaw people, numbering about 265,000, inhabit the coastal creeks of the Niger Delta, while the easterly Ogoja Province presents a linguistic medley which is yet undocumented in its entirety.

Most of the region is thickly forested and densely populated—269 persons per square mile is the average density as compared with 148 in the West and 67 in the North. In the Ibo heartland, population densities average about 450 to the square mile. Largely as a result of population pressures on the land, many Ibo people have migrated to urban areas in all parts of Nigeria. Of the five major urban centers in Iboland, only the Niger River city of Onitsha has a traditional nucleus of any political importance. Port Harcourt, the second seaport and petroleum capital of Nigeria, Enugu, an administrative and coal mining center, Aba, and Umuahia are all essentially non-traditional cities.

As a rule, traditional systems of authority and land tenure among the Ibo are based on patrilineal kin groups. Typically, the Ibo village chief is the head of a specified lineage; the chief of a senior village in a group may "preside" at meetings of the village-group. In some cases, village-group heads enjoy great prestige, but their authority never extends beyond the village-group. Indeed there are parts of Iboland where chieftaincy is virtually unknown and "tribal government is thought of as the collective rule of the senior age grades."[22] The dispersed power system of the Ibo is characterized by a high degree of popular participation in the making of public decisions.[23] Ibo culture magnifies the value of individual achievement; yet the Ibo people are known for their cooperative propensities as well, exemplified both by their enthusiasm for community development[24] and by the multitude of voluntary improvement associations, e.g., town unions, clan unions, divisional unions, etc., that provide loans to businessmen, scholarships to youths, electoral support to politicians, and perform many other services of a political and communal nature.[25] Ibo women's organizations are probably unexcelled on the African continent in their cohesion and ability to exert political influence.[26]

[22] G. I. Jones, *Report of the Position, Status, and Influence of Chiefs and Natural Rulers in the Eastern Region of Nigeria* (Enugu: 1957), p. 44.

[23] "In pyramidal systems of government the chief is the law-maker, though he very often merely pronounces what is the general will of his council. But not until he has made the order or pronouncement does it become law. In the segmentary societies of the Eastern Region it is the other way round. The usual pattern here is for public matters to be discussed at a general meeting at which every able-bodied male who is a full member of the community has a right to attend and to speak if he so wishes. After a general discussion the elders retire to consult and when they return a spokesman announces their decision to the meeting who either accept it by general acclamation or refuse it. The community, particularly in the Ibo area, is not prepared to surrender its legislative authority to any chiefs, elders, or other traditional office holders. . . ." *Ibid.*, pp. 10-11.

[24] I. C. Jackson, *Advance in Africa* (London: Oxford University Press, 1956), pp. 20-21.

[25] Simon Ottenberg, "Improvement Association Among the Afikpo Ibo," *Africa*, XXV (January 1955), pp. 1-27.

[26] The "meeting," a kind of folk investment institution based on subscriptions to a common fund from which benefits are paid to the subscribers in rotation, is particularly vigorous among Ibo women. See M. M. Green, *Ibo Village Affairs* (London: Sedgwick and Jackson, 1947), pp. 44-48; Women's demonstrations have been highly effective in the East and rather difficult for the authorities to control. The Aba Riots of 1929 against the "Warrant Chief" system and the riots of 1958 against the re-introduction of primary school fees are leading examples. See C. I. Meek, *Law and Authority in a Nigerian Tribe* (London: Oxford University Press, 1937), pp. ix-xi, 332; Perham, *op.cit.*, pp. 206-220; *Memorandum on the Origin and Causes of the Recent Disturbances in Owerri and Calabar Provinces* (Lagos: Government Printer, 1930); *Sessional Paper of the Nigerian Legislative Council*, No. 28 of 1930; also, see Phoebe V. Ottenberg, "The Changing Economic Position of Women Among the Afikpo Ibo," *Continuity and Change in African Cultures*, ed. W. R. Bascom and M. J. Herskovits (Chicago: University of Chicago Press, 1959), pp. 205-223.

Finally, the Ibo people are famous for their exceptional "receptivity to change."[27]

There are two culturally marginal Ibo groups that merit special mention in this account because of their extraordinary influence on recent Ibo history. First, the Onitsha indigenes, numbering about 10,000 people, who live mainly in the traditional sector of that great Niger River metropolis. The Onitshas are thought to have migrated from Benin in the 17th century; their traditional ruler, the *Obi* of Onitsha, is a sacred chief whose traditional political status in the eyes of his people is probably unmatched in Iboland.

Twentieth-century Onitsha is the leading market town on the Niger. Men of initiative have flocked to Onitsha from the Ibo hinterland. Diocesan headquarters were established there by the Anglican and the Roman Catholic missions; schools flourished, and education became the order of the day for Onitsha youth. Today non-traditional boom towns have outstripped the Onitshan rate of growth, but the city on the Niger remains the cultural capital of Iboland and its educational eminence is unexcelled. The proverbial Onitsha lawyer has earned an auspicious niche in the political history of Eastern Nigeria.

Another group, the Aros, are thought to have migrated from the North to their homeland in Enyong Division adjacent to the Ibo and the Ibibio. Some Aro people affirm Ibo nationality while others deny it. K. Onwuka Dike observes that Aro power emerged during the period of the slave trade which they dominated by establishing colonies along the trade routes and procuring hapless Ibos for sale as slaves to the chiefs of the coastal city-states, who sold them in turn to European traders.[28] The Aro system was based on an oracle known as *Aro Chuku* (God of the Aros) that was feared and respected throughout Iboland as a sacred court of appeal. Dike writes:[29] "The Oracle, directed by the Aros, was the medium through which the slaves exported from Delta ports were largely recruited. As the highest court of appeal, this deity was supposed to levy fines on convicted individuals and groups. The fines had to be paid in slaves which were believed to have been 'eaten' by Chukwu (the Oracle), although in fact they were sold to the coast middlemen. This recruiting campaign, carefully staged under conditions of awe and reverence, was rarely attended by violence."

[27] Simon Ottenberg, "Ibo Receptivity to Change," *ibid.*, pp. 130-143.
[28] K. Onwuka Dike, *Trade and Politics in the Niger Delta, 1830-1885* (Oxford: The Clarendon Press, 1956), pp. 37-41, 45.
[29] *Ibid.*, p. 40.

Lesser oracles in the various Aro colonies supplemented the main oracle and the Aros employed certain warrior tribes to coerce those intransigent groups who did not bend to their authority. Following the suppression of the Aro oracle by the British in 1900, the Aro people and their warrior allies transferred their energies to other pursuits, achieving signal success in the fields of legitimate enterprise and education.[30]

Title-taking is common among the Ibo and non-Ibo peoples alike. Most titled men have attained mature ages and respectable levels of personal wealth. In some communities, specific titles are vested in particular lineages. Titled men form societies which require the payment of initiation fees that are too great to be taken lightly either by the initiates or by the general public. At local government levels, title societies and "secret societies" of a religious nature are influential in the formation of public opinion.

According to the 1953 census, about one-half of the Eastern population is Christian; most of the others are Animists. The four largest Christian denominations are the Roman Catholic, the Anglican, the Methodist, and the Church of Scotland Presbyterian in that order. Roman Catholicism is strongest in the Ibo area, while the Church of Scotland is based mainly in Calabar, where it was established in 1846.

From European Penetration to Independence

In the fifteenth century Portuguese explorers established diplomatic relations with the King of Benin; missionaries and traders, especially slave dealers, followed. Subsequently England, France, Holland, Denmark, and other European powers joined in the exportation of slaves from Africa to the colonies of America. J. D. Fage estimates that some fifteen to twenty million slaves were imported into America between the sixteenth and nineteenth centuries.[31] British merchants dominated the West African slave trade for at least a century before it was declared illegal by the British Government in 1807.

Recent scholarship has been concerned with the effects of the slave trade on various aspects of West African history.[32] Professor Dike has suggested that the abnormally high population density of the Eastern Nigeria forest belt is attributable in part to an influx of people from the west and north, seeking to escape the raids of

[30] For example, the Ohaffia tribe, a military ally of the Aros during the period of their ascendancy, has produced five Ph.D.'s since 1940.

[31] Fage, op.cit., p. 82.

[32] An illustrative study is C. R. Newbury, *The Western Slave Coast and its Rulers* (Oxford: The Clarendon Press, 1962).

slave chieftains in more open country.[33] In Yorubaland, incessant strife was fomented by slave raiding and the related insecurity of tribal states.[34] Portuguese slave dealers established their main base of operations on a Yoruba coastal island, and by 1840 the island of Lagos had become a principal depot for slaves and other export commodities in the Bight of Benin. For reasons that were partly humanitarian and partly economic the British made a determined effort in the 1840's to suppress the traffic in slaves.[35] Ultimately the British decided that a stable administration at Lagos was required in order to secure the abolition of the slave trade and to promote legitimate enterprise. In 1861 Lagos was annexed; thereafter the main commercial houses established their headquarters in the sea-coast colony which was destined to become the leading port on the West African coast and the capital of an independent Nigeria.

In 1879, Mr. George Goldie Taubman (later Sir George Goldie), the empire builder of British West Africa, accomplished the amalgamation of all British trading companies in the Niger Basin area into a single company that was strong enough to exclude French competition.[36] At the Berlin Conference of 1885, British claims to the Niger Basin were conceded by other European powers, whereupon a British protectorate was established in the Niger Delta (the Oil Rivers Protectorate, later renamed the Niger Coast Protectorate) and Goldie's enterprise was granted a royal charter to administer all territories in the Niger Basin, after the fashion of the famous

---

[33] Dike, *op.cit.*, pp. 27-28.

[34] Saburi O. Biobaku, *The Egba and Their Neighbors, 1842-1872*, pp. 13ff., 96f.

[35] Professor Dike has pointed out that the abolitionist cause in 19th-century England had every prospect of success because the economic basis of slavery had disappeared:

"At the end of the 18th century a predominantly mercantile epoch was being succeeded by a predominantly industrial age. In Britain, where the industrial change was greatest, the slave trade which had fitted perfectly into the scheme of mercantilist economics, was being rendered obsolete by the rapid technological advance of industrial production. Abolition of the slave trade was therefore only one manifestation of the major changes of the era of mercantilism to that of the industrial revolution and aggressive free trade.

"The humanitarianism so widely advertised at the time was, in one sense, the reflection on the ideological plane of changes taking place in the economic sphere. . . . The change-over was gradual, yet it was this mounting economic change which reduced slave interests to manageable proportions and enabled the abolitionists to attack it successfully. On the other hand, had it not been for the spirited and inspired attack of the Christian humanitarians such as Wilberforce and Clarkson, slavery and the slave trade might have lingered on—as indeed other decadent systems did linger on—long after they had outlived their usefulness." Dike, *op.cit.*, pp. 11-12.

[36] See John E. Flint, *Sir George Goldie and the Making of Nigeria* (London: Oxford University Press, 1960).

East India Company. In 1900 Protectorates were proclaimed for Northern and Southern Nigeria, and in 1906 the Colony of Lagos was joined to the Protectorate of Southern Nigeria. From 1900 to 1906 Sir Frederick Lugard, former army officer and agent of the Royal Niger Company, was High Commissioner of the Protectorate of Northern Nigeria.[37] There he established the practice of administration through emirs and chiefs that became known as indirect rule or the Native Authority System.[38] In 1912 Lugard was appointed to the governorship of both Northern and Southern Nigeria, and in 1914 he was designated Governor-General of the amalgamated territories called the Colony and Protectorate of Nigeria. In 1923 provision was made for a Legislative Council comprising a majority of official members (representing the Government), half as many nominated unofficial members (both African and European), and four elected African members (three from the Colony of Lagos and one from the eastern township of Calabar). Inasmuch as Northern members were not included, jurisdiction of the Council was limited to the Colony and the Southern Provinces. For a period of twenty-two years thereafter, the Northern and Southern Provinces were linked tenuously in law and through the person of the Governor; their distinctive political identities were preserved by the maintenance of separate administrative establishments. In 1939 Southern Nigeria was reorganized for administrative purposes into two groups of provinces —the Eastern and the Western.

The Second World War ushered in a new era of militant nationalism based on the ideals of racial equality and national self-determination. Effective political action by Nigerian nationalist leaders required an artful blend of agitation for constitutional reform and maneuver for partisan advantage. Three constitutions were ratified in the eight-year span 1946-1954.[39] The Constitution of 1946 was promulgated by the Colonial Government without consultation and was deeply resented by nationalists for that reason among others. It converted the Northern, Eastern, and Western Provinces into governmental regions, and provided for the creation of three non-elective regional legislatures. For the first time, an all-Nigerian Legislative Council was formed, comprising a majority of unofficial members chosen

[37] Margery Perham, *Lugard: The Years of Authority, 1892-1945* (London: Collins, 1960).

[38] The classic work on indirect rule is Lord Lugard, *The Dual Mandate in British Tropical Africa* (Fourth edition, London: William Blackwood, 1929). Other literature is reviewed by Perham, *Native Administration in Nigeria.*

[39] See Kalu Ezera, *Constitutional Developments in Nigeria* (Cambridge: Cambridge University Press, 1960).

mainly by the regional legislatures. This constitution was not acceptable to the leaders of nationalist opinion, who demanded nothing less than the introduction of a democratically elected, responsible government. In 1947 the National Council of Nigeria and the Cameroons sent a protest delegation to London under the leadership of its President, an American-educated journalist, Dr. Nnamdi Azikiwe. Subsequently, a general review of the constitution was initiated by the Nigerian government leading to its replacement in 1951 by a new constitution that provided for the appointment of African ministers in both the regional and the central governments. Three major political parties emerged, each of which acquired governmental power in one of the regions. But the system of government itself remained essentially unitary until 1954, when a new constitution (framed by two all-party conferences) provided for a genuinely federal form of government. Thereupon the leaders of the major parties became regional premiers: Alhaji Ahmadu (later Alhaji Sir Ahmadu Bello) the Sarduana of Sokoto, a lineal descendant of the founder of the Fulani empire and leader of the Northern Peoples' Congress, became Premier of the North; Mr. (later Chief) Obafemi Awolowo, a barrister and leader of the Action Group, became Premier of the West; Dr. Nnamdi Azikiwe, leader of the National Council of Nigeria and the Cameroons, became Premier of the East. Simultaneously, the United Nations Trust Territory of the Southern Cameroons, which had been administered as part of the Eastern Region, was granted a separate government in response to Cameroonian demands, and constituted as a quasi-federal territory.

Elections to the Federal House of Representatives were held in 1954, after which ten federal ministers were appointed as stipulated by the Constitution: three from the party in each region having a majority of the seats in the Federal House from that region and one from the Southern Cameroons. It was expected that in each region the dominant party in the Regional Legislature would emerge victorious and send three members to the Federal Council of Ministers. But the National Council of Nigeria and the Cameroons (NCNC) won a majority of seats in the West as well as in the East and was entitled thereby to a total of six federal ministers. The Northern Peoples' Congress (NPC), which won an overwhelming majority in the Northern Region, emerged as the largest single party in the Federal House and provided three ministers. These two parties (the NCNC and the NPC) then formed a governing coalition.

The Constitution was revised and amplified by another conference in 1957. Internal self-government was granted to the Eastern and Western Regions—a step taken by the Northern Region in 1959—and the status of the Southern Cameroons was altered virtually to that of a region; however, the right of the people of the entire Cameroons Trust Territory (Northern and Southern) to self-determination was affirmed. The office of Prime Minister of the Federation was created and, in September 1957, Alhaji Sir Abubakar Tafawa Balewa, Vice President of the Northern Peoples' Congress and leader of his party in the Federal House of Representatives, was designated Prime Minister. He formed a national government, including all major parties, which lasted until the federal election of December 1959. At a Resumed Constitutional Conference in 1958, the Secretary of State for the Colonies announced that if the next Federal Parliament passed a resolution for independence, the British Government "would introduce a Bill in Parliament to enable Nigeria to become a fully independent country on the 1st October, 1960."

In the federal election of 1959 the Northern Peoples' Congress and independent candidates supporting that party obtained 142 of the 312 seats in the House of Representatives, followed by the National Council of Nigeria and the Cameroons with 89 and the Action Group with 73. Another NPC-NCNC coalition government was formed by Prime Minister Abubakar Tafawa Balewa. Dr. Azikiwe assumed the office of President of the Nigerian Federal Senate, Alhaji Sir Ahmadu Bello, the Sarduana of Sokoto, remained as Premier of the North, and Chief Obafemi Awolowo became Leader of the Opposition in the Federal House of Representatives. When Nigeria attained its independence, the Cameroons Trust Territory was separated from it pending the outcome of a plebiscite under United Nations supervision. In 1961 the Northern Cameroons voted to rejoin the Northern Region of Nigeria, while the people of the Southern Cameroons chose to become part of the Cameroon Republic.

Sociological Aspects of the Economy

It has been estimated that 78 per cent of the adult labor force of Nigeria is engaged in agriculture, forestry, animal husbandry, fishing, and hunting.[40] The vast majority live in areas of traditional habitation, i.e., in rural areas and traditional towns where communal values based on tribal identity generally prevail. In 1952, the percentage of the total population living in urban centers of 20,000 or more varied

[40] The National Economic Council, *Economic Survey of Nigeria, 1959* (Lagos: Federal Government Printer, 1959), p. 106. (Hereafter this work is cited as the *Economic Survey of Nigeria, 1959.)*

from 26 percent in the Western Region to 8 percent in the Eastern Region and 3.5 percent in the Northern Region. Yet the Eastern Region showed the greatest increase in urbanization (688 percent) between 1921 and 1952.[41] As noted above, most urban dwellers in the traditionally rural East are new urban dwellers, engaged in modern commercial and other non-agricultural occupations, while the urban populations of the West and the North include a majority of urban farmers, i.e., persons who till family land in nearby rural areas, and others who are involved in the "native economies."[42] In 1958 there were some 480,000 employed workers in Nigeria comprising about 1.5 percent of the total population. About 63 percent of them were employed by public authorities, including local governments and public corporations; somewhat less than one-half were members of trade unions. Minimum wages for daily-rated labor varied from 2s. 1d. paid by the Northern Government, to 2s. 7d. by the Federal Government, and 5s. by the Eastern and Western Governments.[43] In all regions male persons of sixteen years or over were required by law to pay a general tax or local rate of several pounds or less according to local determination and assessment. The average per capita income for Nigeria as a whole in 1956-1957 was estimated at £25-£29.[44]

All regions have embarked upon roughly similar courses of economic development involving balanced programs of public, private, and foreign investment. Of course, the major sustaining economic institutions are those related to the agricultural sector of the economy which "occupies the majority of the male working population and provides at least 50 percent of the national product and 85 percent of the country's exports."[45] The principal export crops are palm produce, mainly from the East, cocoa from the West, and ground nuts from the North. Most agricultural exports are handled by regional marketing boards which prescribe minimum prices for the purchase of controlled

[41] Coleman, op.cit., p. 76.

[42] Professor Daryll Forde has distinguished three main components of the "Native Economies": the subsistence or home-consumption economy, the internal exchange economy, and the external exchange economy. "The Rural Economies," The Native Economies of Nigeria, ed. Margery Perham (London: Faber, 1946), pp. 32-33.

[43] Overseas Economic Surveys, Nigeria: Economic and Commercial Conditions (London: H.M.S.O., 1957), p. 160.

[44] Economic Survey of Nigeria, 1959, p. 17. In 1952-1953 the per capita regional products were reported as £34 in the West, £21 in the East, and £21 in the North. International Bank for Reconstruction and Development, The Economic Development of Nigeria (Baltimore: Johns Hopkins Press, 1955), p. 616.

[45] Economic Survey of Nigeria, 1959, p. 22.

crops from producers.[46] The boards appoint qualified firms as licensed buying agents who are authorized to purchase controlled crops from the growers either directly or through middlemen. Prior to the establishment of the marketing-board system following the Second World War, the lucrative produce trade was monopolized by European firms, notably the United Africa Company.[47] It has been the policy of all marketing boards under African control to license African buying agents and the latter have now acquired the major portion of the trade. Furthermore, funds accruing to the regional marketing boards have been used by and large in consonance with recommendations by the International Bank for Reconstruction and Development to finance research and development.[48] The regional governments have established development corporations, which undertake agricultural and industrial projects independently or in partnership with other agencies, governments, and private interests; regional finance corporations and loans boards extend credit to African businessmen, facilitating their entry into the produce trade and other spheres of commercial activity. In the 1950's both the Eastern and Western Regional Governments invested funds derived from their respective marketing boards in private banking institutions which were enabled thereby to provide additional credit facilities to African businessmen. Possibly the most imaginative of all government policies involving the utilization of marketing-board funds is the arrangement made by the Eastern Marketing Board to set aside £500,000 annually for ten years to finance the new University of Nigeria.

Among the economic interest groups that figure prominently in the political sphere, financiers and pioneer industrialists are pre-eminent. In 1958 there were five African banking institutions in Nigeria; the two largest banks have since been acquired by the Western and Eastern Governments respectively. Building contractors and civil engineering firms constitute politically important groups in every region and in the Federal Territory; their number and influence is least in the Northern Region. All regions have their road transport magnates and their general merchants engaged in the export-import trade.

[46] *Ibid.*, pp. 41-44; the outstanding general discussion of the Nigerian export trade and the Marketing Board system is P. T. Bauer, West African Trade: *A Study of Competition, Oligopoly and Monopoly in a Changing Economy* (Cambridge: Cambridge University Press, 1954), pp. 195-434.

[47] See J. Mars, "Extra-Territorial Enterprises," *Mining, Commerce, and Finance in Nigeria*, ed. Margery Perham (London: Faber, 1948), pp. 58-59, 76-88; David E. Carney, *Government and Economy in British West Africa* (New York: Bookman Association, 1961), pp. 44-46.

[48] International Bank for Reconstruction and Development, *op.cit.*, pp. 88-89, 118.

The internal market system is highly complex; its nature is indicated by this excerpt from the *Economic Survey of Nigeria, 1959*:[49] "This system of village markets is universal and of long standing. It is, however, more highly organized in the densely populated and intensively cultivated areas of the South. No estimate of the total number of such markets is available, but almost every village has its own market and most towns are served by a ring of several. These markets, the more busy of which function daily, range from the small village type, comprising a dozen or so temporary stalls, to permanent concrete constructions extending over as much as 200 acres and having daily attendances in the region of 15,000, such as at Onitsha, Kano and Ibadan. In the South women traders predominate in the marketplaces but in the Moslem North trading is mainly confined to men."

Politically, the most important group of market women has been the Lagos group, estimated conservatively as 8,000 in 1951.[50] The former Lagos Market Women's Guild is said to have constituted the financial backbone of the first nationalist party (Nigerian National Democratic Party) from the mid-1920's until the early 1940's.

Nigerian trade unions are weakened by a pattern of organizational fragmentation that is called the "house" or "company" union system, according to which membership is limited to single companies or government departments.[51] There were 298 trade unions registered with the Federal Department of Labour in 1958 with a total membership of about 237,000, including eight unions with memberships exceeding 6,000;[52] all but two of the latter consisted exclusively of employees of government departments or public corporations. In 1958 there were two central labor federations of roughly equal membership.[53] The

[49] *Economic Survey of Nigeria, 1959*, p. 41.

[50] Suzanne Comhaire-Sylvain, "Le Travail des Femmes à Lagos, Nigeria," *Zaire*, V (February 1951), p. 183.

[51] Thus there were eight separate railway unions in 1954. See J. I. Roper, *Labour Problems in West Africa* (London: Penguin Books, 1958), pp. 70-71.

[52] The eight largest trade unions in 1958, with membership totals and the year of latest report were as follows:

1. Nigerian Union of Teachers: 37,153 (1955)
2. Western Region Production Development Board African Workers Union: 19,999 (1956)
3. Public Utilities Technical and General Workers Union: 16,793 (1956)
4. Nigerian African Mine Workers Union: 13,200 (1958)
5. Railway and Ports Workers Union: 11,022 (1955)
6 Cameroons Development Corporation Workers Union: 10,220 (1953)
7. Nigerian Civil Service Union: 6,812 (1956)
8. Nigerian Association of Local Government Staff Employees: 6,309 (1956)

[53] In 1956, the National Congress of Trade Unions of Nigeria was formed by

cooperative movement is particularly vigorous in the Western Region, where more than 600 produce-marketing societies are active; central organizations buy produce from these societies and propagate the cooperative idea.

Professional groups, including lawyers, doctors, engineers, clergymen, administrators, and teachers, are dominant in the articulate advanced echelon of political leadership in southern Nigeria and their ascendancy in the social and political life of Lagos is unmistakable.[54] The professional element is similarly prominent in the main urban centers of the East and West, but much less so in the North where the western canons of prestige and social status are not supreme.

THE STRUCTURE OF GOVERNMENT

The Federation of Nigeria is one of the few federal governments in history to have evolved from unitary foundations. In 1954, Lord Milverton, an architect of the 1946 "Regionalist" Constitution, declared its purpose to have been a "Unitary State with wide local government centers in the Regions."[55] The quasi-unitary, quasi-federal Constitution of 1951 authorized the regional governments to legislate in specified areas only, subject to approval by the Central Executive Council, but the Constitution of 1954 was a decisive federalist departure: the Federal House of Representatives was empowered to legislate on specified subjects; other subjects were enumerated as concurrent; residual powers were retained by the regions. This essential pattern has survived but the federal system was tightened by constitutional conferences in 1957 and 1958, and a potentially strong federal government appears to have emerged.

---

a group which split away from the All-Nigerian Trade Union Federation. The new group favored affiliation with the International Confederation of Free Trade Unions, while the older body opposed affiliation with any non-African international. The two groups recombined briefly in 1959 but divided again in 1960 as the Nigerian T.U.C. and the T.U.C. of Nigeria respectively.

[54] Hugh H. Smythe ranks the professional elite in the second grade of the Nigerian social hierarchy, just beneath the holders of high public office, many of whom are professional men by occupation. Within the professional category his ranking is as follows: senior civil servants, the bracket of medicine, law, and senior university faculty members, high churchmen, engineers, and the bracket of assistant secretariat officials in the civil service and schoolteachers in that order. "Social Stratification in Nigeria." *Social Forces*, Vol. 37, No. 2 (December 1958), pp. 159-170. See also Hugh H. Smythe and Mabel M. Smythe, *The New Nigerian Elite* (Stanford: Stanford University Press, 1960).

[55] Lord Milverton, "The Future of Nigeria," *The English and National Review*, 143 (October 1954), p. 269.

Most of the crucial powers of government are enumerated in the Exclusive (Federal) and the Concurrent Legislative Lists; thus external affairs, immigration, citizenship, defense, external trade, monetary exchange control, customs and excise duties, currency, communications, and the power to borrow money abroad are among the Exclusive List subjects, while public order, prisons, labor relations, welfare, higher education, and industrial development are among the Concurrent List subjects. In all matters of concurrent jurisdiction, the supremacy of federal law is asserted.[56] The Federal Supreme Court is empowered to hear appeals on questions involving both constitutional interpretation and the constitutionality of acts passed by the federal or regional legislatures. Furthermore an extensive declaration of fundamental freedoms, based largely on the Convention for the Protection of Human Rights and Fundamental Freedoms, is embodied in the Nigerian Constitution and the Federal Supreme Court is empowered to interpret these rights and to hear appeals involving questions of their denial or enforcement.[57] Ultimate control of the police force is vested in the federal government, while the regional governments participate in operational control.[58]

The nature of the revenue system is a revealing guide to the relative strengths of the regional and federal governments. The latter has exclusive jurisdiction in respect of taxes and duties on imports and exports, excises, sales taxes, company taxes, mining royalties, and mining rents, while the regional governments have basic jurisdiction over personal income taxes. During the decade prior to independence, the principles governing revenue allocation among the regions occasioned frequent controversy. In 1954 public revenues were regionalized to a maximum extent in accordance with the principle of "derivation." But in 1958 a principle of national integration was vindicated with the creation of a distributable pool to foster the balanced economic development of the Federation.[59] This fund, financed by 30 percent of mining revenues and import duties may prove to be a unifying factor of great strength.

The Federal Parliament is bicameral, comprising a popularly elected House of Representatives and a Senate which consists mainly of an equal number of members from each region, chosen by the regional governments subject to confirmation by the regional legis-

[56] *Nigeria (Constitution) Order in Council, 1960*, Section 64(4) (5).
[57] Federation of Nigeria, *Report by the Resumed Nigeria Constitutional Conference, September and October, 1958* (Lagos: 1958), pp. 3-8, 28.
[58] *Ibid.*, pp. 8-10.
[59] See Colonial Office, *Nigeria: Report of the Fiscal Commission*, Cmnd. 481 (London: 1958), pp. 31-33.

latures. The Senate is empowered to delay non-monetary bills for six months only. Since Nigeria has affirmed its allegiance to the British Monarch, the nominal Heads of State are the representatives of the Crown, styled Governor-General for the Federation and Governor for each region. The executive authority of the Federation is exercised by a Council of Ministers, appointed by the Governor-General on the advice of the Prime Minister, who must be a member of the House of Representatives. Each of the three regional legislatures is bicameral, consisting of a House of Chiefs and a popularly elected House of Assembly. Only in the Northern Region is the House of Chiefs a coordinate chamber, although monetary bills are required to originate in the House of Assembly. The Western and Eastern Houses of Chiefs are empowered merely to delay the passage of non-monetary bills for six months. In each Region, there is an Executive Council consisting of the Ministers of the Government, headed by a Regional Premier.

The judicial power of the Federation is exercised by a chief justice who presides over the Federal Supreme Court. There are regional high courts and a High Court of Lagos, over each of which a chief justice presides; the chief justices of the regions are *ex-officio* members of the Federal Supreme Court. Two systems of inferior courts exist in each region: magistrates' courts and customary or native (in the Northern Region) courts. Magistrates are appointed by the regional governor upon the recommendation of a Judicial Service Commission. The members and assessors of customary courts are appointed by the Judicial Service Commission in the West, by the Minister of Justice in the East, and by local authorities in the North. Customary courts have primary jurisdiction in cases involving native law and custom; in addition, they are empowered to enforce statutory law in a wide range of civil and criminal cases.

Every government of the Federation has its own civil service establishment, within which appointments are made by the Governor-General or Governor, as the case may be, upon the recommendation of a Public Service Commission. Superior positions in the local government service are filled by the Local Government Service Board in the West, by the Minister of Local Government or the local authority concerned upon optional advice of the Local Government Service Board in the East, and by local authorities in the North.

Local government in the Northern Region has developed within the framework of the pre-colonial authority system; the principal units are still termed Native Authorities. Until 1960 the most important emirs governed their domains through councils which they were obliged to consult but could override subject to the intervention of a higher authority. They have since been restricted to a casting vote in the event of a tie. Major emirs preside over councils comprising "traditional" members and others nominated (co-opted) by the council itself. They are also advised by larger bodies representing subordinate councils and important interest groups. In lesser chiefdoms the trend has been toward election, and some 50 percent of all native authority councils now have elected majorities. All subordinate and advisory councils at the village, town, district and Native Authority levels are required to have elected majorities, and taxpayer suffrage is the rule.

A two-tier structure obtains in the West: local and district councils are elected directly and divisional councils are elected by and from the members of the lower-tier councils. Invariably, the party in control of a lower-tier council will elect the specified number of its members to represent that council in the divisional council. At both levels, instruments establishing the councils may prescribe the inclusion of "traditional" members, either specified by title or elected for stated terms of office by specified colleges of recognized chiefs. The traditional membership must not exceed a maximum of one-fourth of the total. Normally councils have a traditional president and an elected chairman. If there is no single pre-eminent traditional chief in the council area, the presidency will rotate among the leading chiefs. Ideally, divisional council areas correspond to the spheres of authority of paramount *Obas*. In several divisions where there is no paramount chief, the system of government is single-tiered.

Native administration had never been a successful form of local government in the Eastern Region, since it was difficult to reconcile with the dispersed power system of the people. In 1948 the terminology itself was rejected as obnoxious by a select committee of the Eastern House of Assembly. Ever since, regional authorities have grappled with the task of reconciling the multitude of traditionally cohesive local units with the necessity of centralization at effective levels of local authority. At present a two-tier system obtains: local councils form district councils, each of which is administered by an officer of the regional government. Above this level, deliberative bodies, called Provincial Assemblies, are constituted by the representatives of local councils while the twelve provinces of the region are administered by political agents of the regional government (Provincial Commissioners),[60] all of whom were regional legislators

[60] Provincial Commissioners were also created by the Northern Regional Government in 1962 to facilitate central supervision of the Northern Native Administrations.

at the time of writing. In all regions, local government efficiency is buttressed by officials of the regional public service styled Local Government Adviser in the West, Local Government Commissioner in the East, and in the traditional form, District Officer, in the North.

Local revenue practices have evolved in conformance with the varying patterns of local authority. In the North, Native Authorities are empowered to levy and collect a general tax and a cattle tax. The Native Authority will assess each district within its jurisdiction on the basis of population; the district, village, and ward authorities in turn apportion tax liabilities on the basis of ascertainable incomes. Thus, in 1958 the incidence per taxpayer in Zaria Division varied from 28s. to 46s. 6d. In the West, all male persons of sixteen years of age or above are liable to pay income rates imposed by local government authorities on the basis of a graduated scale. Such persons are assumed to have a minimum income of £50 per annum; at Ibadan the minimum rate in 1958 was £3.5/-. Incomes are assessed by committees appointed by the rating authorities and allegations of unfair assessment frequently have political overtones. Persons who earn £300 or more are subject to a regional income tax levied by the Department of Inland Revenue. The Eastern Government taxes the income of male persons over the age of sixteen and female persons above that age who earn more than £100 per annum in wages or salaries, as well as women traders who earn more than that amount in the principal urban districts of the region. Responsibility for collection is vested in an internal revenue commissioner acting through the local government commissioners. Eastern local councils are permitted to levy special rates and license fees only.

Evolution of the Electoral System

The electoral principle was introduced in Nigeria in 1923 with the concession that three unofficial representatives from Lagos and one from Calabar should be elected by residents of those towns who had minimum incomes of £100 per annum. No extension of the franchise was made by the Constitution of 1946 which prescribed the selection of unofficial members of the Regional Houses of Assembly by and from the Native Authorities (conciliar bodies of local government); the Houses of Assembly in turn selected a minority of the membership of a central Legislative Council. Under the Constitution of 1951 the Regional Houses of Assembly were elected indirectly through a system of electoral colleges; there were three stages in the East and West (termed the primary, intermediate, and final electoral colleges) with taxpayer suffrage at the primary level; in the North there were four or five stages initiated by open voting in about 20,000 village and ward areas at the primary stage. Every final college elected one or more persons to the House of Assembly by secret ballot. Final colleges were relatively small groups of several hundred or less and the members were vulnerable to the temptations of bribery. One candidate to the Eastern House of Assembly in 1953 has recorded his observations at the meeting of a final electoral college as follows:[61] "On the morning of the election some leaders of the clan or agents would wear special large overflowing native robes with specially designed large pockets. These pockets would be filled with folded currency notes and the carrier [sic] rolled luxuriously to the polling station. He would take a stand directly opposite the voters but on the side of the fence which was built to keep off the intruders. He would take a fixed glance at a voter and signal him off to see him. He would greet him by shaking one of the folded notes into his hands and bidding him goodby and, naming the candidate, would ask him to call out the next on his bench. That process was repeated until the whole people were met and instructed. . . . the last minute [bribes] . . . usually carried more weight than thousands of pounds already spent."

The significance of the "dash" was reduced substantially by the subsequent introduction of direct election systems.[62] But candidates of weakly organized parties in competitive constituencies have been obliged to assume heavy financial burdens. A parliamentary contest may cost the candidate £2,000-£4,000, a good part of which may be attributed to transportation expenses and much of the remainder to "good will" or "treating" mostly in the form of drink.[63]

[61] A. Nwoke, "Memoirs of Three Elections in the Eastern Region, Nigeria" (a memorandum prepared for the writer).

[62] "The sort of small-scale bribery and 'treating' that have been mentioned can never be eliminated by law; as has been said, they are not of any great political significance. 'Cola', 'dash', and other synonyms for tips and 'rake-offs' still play a very large part in public and private life. Sometimes the dividing line between them and outright bribery and corruption is obscured. This is an evil of which people in all walks of life are aware, and efforts are being made by various private associations to stamp it out. 'Leagues of Bribe Scorners' and similar bodies often make their presence felt." Philip Whitaker, "The Western Region of Nigeria, May, 1956," *Five Elections in Africa*, ed. W. J. M. Mackenzie and Kenneth Robinson (Oxford: Clarendon Press, 1960), pp. 101-102.

[63] W. J. M. Mackenzie states that in Britain "some county elections in the 18th and early 19th centuries are said to have cost each candidate over £100,000 at prices then current." And see his observation on the practice of "treating" in British public-houses before the parties "in effect finally agreed on 'disarmament.'" *Free Elections* (New York: Rinehart, 1958), pp. 154, 156.

In the Northern Region, special techniques were devised to weight the vote in favor of traditional and conservative elements in early elections. In 1951 every Native Authority, typically an emir, was permitted to "nominate" a number of persons equal to 10 percent of the final electoral college who were "injected" into the college. It was understood that these nominees included the choices of the emir, and various pressures operated to induce the members of the final colleges to vote for them. Thus in Kano Emirate not one of the twenty persons elected to the House of Assembly by the final electoral college had been elected by the voters at a lower stage; in fact, ten of them had been defeated in the earlier balloting. On the other hand, four candidates of the radical Northern Elements Progressive Union who had been successful at the intermediate stage were defeated in the final college by previously defeated nominees who were injected into the college by the Native Authority under the 10 percent rule.[64] Consequently, no members of the Northern Elements Progressive Union were elected to the 1952 House of Assembly which served as an electoral college for the House of Representatives. For the federal election of 1954 the regulations were altered to permit any ten members of a final college to nominate non-members as candidates. In Kano Emirate sixteen of the eighteen successful candidates were so nominated.[65] Once again no members of the opposition party were returned to the House of Representatives. Direct elections based on taxpayer suffrage were introduced in the Northern Region for nineteen specified urban electoral districts in the regional election of 1956, eleven of which were won by the government party, including all four in Kano.

Universal adult suffrage was introduced for the first time in Nigeria in the Lagos Town Council election of 1950. Outside of Lagos, it was employed for the first time in a parliamentary election in 1954, in the Eastern Region, to elect members to the Federal House of Representatives by plural voting in multi-member constituencies; the

[64] Memorandum of Northern Elements Progressive Union to the Secretary of State, July 1952. (Mimeographed.)

[65] "It is the experience of the N.E.P.U. that their candidates who won at the primary and intermediate stages have to contest at the final stage against their defeated opponents. This happens because the Electoral Law of the Region provides that any person whether or not he had gone through the first two stages may be nominated to stand at the final stage by anyone who has passed through the primary supported by *Nine* other members of the same Final Electoral College . . . This also makes it possible for any person who may never have fought the elections at all to be nominated at the final stage as a candidate even in his absence." Memorandum of the Northern Elements Progressive Union Delegation to the Secretary of State for the Colonies, December 19, 1955. (Mimeographed.)

same system was used for the Eastern Region election of 1957.[66] A single-member constituency system with direct and quasi-universal, quasi-taxpayer suffrage was introduced in the Western Region for the federal election of 1954; the West adopted a virtually universal franchise for the regional election of 1956, including the right of a person to vote in his "home" constituency based on the principle of "nativity."[67]

The federal election of 1959 was conducted on the basis of universal adult suffrage from single-member constituencies in the Eastern Region, the Western Region, and in Lagos, but adult male suffrage was adopted in the Northern Region. While the NCNC, the Action Group and the Northern Elements Progressive Union were committed in principle to female suffrage in the North, the Northern Peoples' Congress refused to modify its orthodox stand on this issue. Otherwise, the franchise was extended to all British subjects or British protected persons of twenty-one years of age who were "ordinarily resident" in Nigeria. Under the Constitution, a qualified voter could be nominated as a candidate for Parliament from any constituency in the Federation, provided he, or his father, had been born in Nigeria, or he had lived there for a continuous period of three years immediately preceding the date of election. In the Northern Region, however, only male persons were eligible for nomination. At the Constitutional Conference of 1958, it was agreed that the qualifications for voters in regional elections would henceforth be the same as in federal elections, and that members of the regional Houses of Assembly would, in the future, be elected directly from single-member constituencies.

By 1958 local government elections in the East, West, and in Lagos were conducted on the same basis as parliamentary elections: universal adult suffrage and simple plurality voting in single-member wards. In the North, taxpayer suffrage was the rule for subordinate local councils, including district, village, and town councils. In all

[66] On the mechanics of plural voting in multi-member constituencies of the Eastern Region see J. H. Price, "The Eastern Region of Nigeria, March 1957," *Five Elections in Africa,* ed. Mackenzie and Robinson, pp. 115-119.

[67] Under the Western Region Parliamentary and Local Government Electoral Regulations, 1955, Section 10, an individual qualified as an elector in one of two ways: by residence in the constituency for a continuous period of two years prior to the qualifying date during which time he must have paid such taxes and rates to which he may have been liable; by virtue of his birth or the birth of his father in the area of the constituency provided he is twenty-one years of age or has paid a tax rate for the preceding financial year. See Whitaker, *op.cit.,* pp. 104-105, for a criticism of the "native qualification."

TABLE I Nigerian General Elections, 1951-1961

Election	Method of Voting*	Candidates per Constituency	Qualifications of Electors	Number of Persons Registered	Number and Percentage of Those Registered Actually Voting	Total Seats
Eastern regional election of 1951	3-stage electoral college system	Multi-member constituencies	Taxpayer suffrage at the primary level			84
Western regional election of 1951	3-stage electoral college system; direct voting in Lagos	Multi-member constituencies	Taxpayer suffrage at the primary level; universal adult suffrage in Lagos			80
Northern regional election of 1951	4- or 5-stage electoral college system	Multi-member constituencies	Taxpayer suffrage at the primary level			90
Eastern regional election of 1953	2-stage electoral college system	Multi-member constituencies	Taxpayer suffrage at the primary level			94
Federal election Eastern Region, 1954	Direct, secret ballot	Multi-member constituencies	Universal adult suffrage		1,039,551	42
Federal election Western Region, 1954	Direct, secret ballot	Single-member constituencies	Taxpayer suffrage			42
Federal election Northern Region, 1954	2- or 3-stage electoral college system	Multi-member constituencies	Taxpayer suffrage at the primary level			92
Federal election Southern Cameroons, 1954	Indirect	Multi-member constituencies				6
Federal election Lagos, 1954	Direct, secret ballot	Single-member constituencies	Universal adult suffrage			2
Western regional election of 1956	Direct, secret ballot	Single-member constituencies	Virtually universal adult suffrage	1,899,520	1,291,174 (68%)	80
Northern regional election of 1956	2- or 3-stage electoral college system in rural electoral districts; Direct, secret ballot in urban electoral districts	Multi-member rural district constituencies; single-member urban district constituencies	Taxpayer suffrage at the primary level			

					Plural voting	
Eastern regional election of 1957	Direct, secret ballot	Multi-member constituencies	Universal adult suffrage	1,767,008	(46.78%)	84
Federal election of 1959	Direct, secret ballot	Single-member constituencies	Universal adult suffrage in the East and the West; universal male suffrage in the North			
Total				9,036,083	7,185,555 (79.8%)	312
East				2,598,234	1,929,754 (75.3%)	73
West				2,653,188	1,887,209 (71.2%)	62
North				3,640,284	3,258,520 (89.4%)	174
Lagos				144,377	110,072 (76.2%)	3
Western regional election of 1960	Direct, secret ballot	Single-member constituencies	Universal adult suffrage			124
Northern Regional election of 1961	Direct, secret ballot	Single-member constituencies	Universal male suffrage	3½ million		170
Eastern Regional election of 1961	Direct, secret ballot	Single-member constituencies	Universal adult suffrage	2,712,598	1,554,420 (57.3%)	146 in 135 contested constituencies

* The simple plurality, single ballot system has been used in all Nigerian elections. In multi-member constituencies, voters have been permitted to cast a ballot for as many candidates as were to have been elected. While the electoral college system was in effect, voters in the primary and intermediate colleges normally balloted by a show of hands; in final colleges, voting was by secret ballot.

Sources: Federation of Nigeria, Report by the *Ad Hoc Meeting of the Nigeria Constitutional Conference Held in Lagos in February 1958* (Lagos: Government Printer, 1958), Part IV, sections 14-29, Annex IV: Election (House of Representatives) Regulations, 1958, Annex V: Amendments to Draft Electoral Regulations; *Report by the Resumed Nigeria Constitutional Conference Held in London, 1958* (Lagos: Government Printer, 1958), Part XVII, sections 73-76, Annex III: Federal Electoral Regulations (Amendments); *Report of the Constituency Delimitation Commission* (Lagos: Government Printer, 1958); *The Constitution Orders*, sections 9 and 38, *Supplement to Official Gazette*, No. 4, 15 January 1959, Part D, pp. 20, 33; *The Northern House of Assembly (Elected Members) Electoral Regulations, 1956*, N.R.L.N 240 of 1955, Amended by No. 20 of 1956, No. 41 of 1956, No. 208 of 1956, No. 314 of 1956; *The Eastern House of Assembly Electoral Regulations, 1955*, E.R.L.N. No. 9 of 1955; "Report of the First General Election to the Western House of Assembly: General Elections, 1951," Colonial Reports—Nigeria, 1951, pp. 117-125; *Report on Local Government Elections in the Western Region of Nigeria, 1958*, Sessional Paper No. 7 of 1958; *Report on the Holding of the 1956 Parliamentary Election to the Western House of Assembly, Nigeria*; *Report on the General Election to the Eastern House of Assembly, 1957*; *Report on the Nigeria Federal Elections, December 1959* (Lagos: 1960).

The following commentaries contain valuable information: P. C. Lloyd, *Report on Eastern Nigeria General Election, 1961* (Enugu: 1962). "Some Comments on the Election in Nigeria," *Journal of African Administration*, IV, 3 (July 1952), 82-92; W. J. M. Mackenzie and Kenneth Robinson, *Five Elections in Africa*; J. R. V. Prescott, "A Geographical Analysis of Elections to the Eastern House of Assembly, March 1957" (Department of Geography, University College of Ibadan, Research Notes, No. 10, June 1957), pp. 8-15; Philip Whitaker, "The Preparation of the Register of Electors in the Western Region of Nigeria, 1955-56," *Journal of African Administration*, IX, 1 (January 1957), pp. 23-29; M. J. Dent, "Elections in Northern Nigeria," *Journal of Local Administration Overseas*, I, 4 (October 1962), pp. 213-224.

parliamentary contests, all local government elections in the East and the West, and in town council elections in the North, votes are cast secretly by the insertion of a ballot paper into a box that is marked with the name of the candidate, an optional photograph, and the symbol of the party. In rural areas of the Northern Region, open voting is still used. The electoral rules of a typical district council stipulate: "The returning officer shall call upon electors to cast their votes by grouping themselves behind the candidate of their choice and the two candidates who have the highest number of votes shall be declared duly elected."

Recently the secret ballot was introduced in a few district councils; its adoption is expected to become widespread in the near future.

TABLE II

Election	Party	Vote	Percentage of Total Vote	Seats
Eastern Regional election of 1951	National Council of Nigeria and the Cameroons (NCNC)			65
	United National Party			4
Western Regional election of 1951	Action Group			45
	NCNC			30-35 (approximately)
Northern Regional election of 1951	Northern Peoples' Congress			Indefinite, but an overwhelming majority
Eastern Regional election of 1953	NCNC			72
	National Independence Party			9
	United National Party			3
Federal election, Eastern Region, 1954	NCNC			32
	United National Independence Party			4
	Action Group			3
	Independent candidates			3
Federal election, Western Region, 1954	NCNC			23
	Action Group			18
	Commoners Liberal Party			1
Federal election, Northern Region, 1954	Northern Peoples' Congress (NPC)			79
	Middle Zone League (allied to NPC)			2
	Idoma State Union (allied to NPC)			2
	Igbirra Tribal Union (allied to NPC)			1
	Middle Belt People's Party			1
	Action Group			1
	Independents			4
Federal election, Southern Cameroons, 1954	Kamerun National Congress			5
	Kamerun People's Party			-
Federal election, Lagos, 1954	NCNC			1
	Action Group			1
Western Regional election of 1956	Action Group	623,826	48.3%	48
	NCNC	584,556	45.3%	32
	Nigerian Commoners Party	5,133	0.4%	
	Nigerian People's Party	3,029	0.2%	
	Dynamic Party	4,841	0.4%	
	Nigerian Commoners Liberal Party	5,401	0.4%	
	Independent Candidates	64,388	5.0%	

Election	Party	Vote	Percentage of Total Vote	Seats
Northern Regional election of 1956	Northern Peoples' Congress			100
	Independent candidates allied to the NPC			7
	Rival wings of the United Middle Belt Congress			11
	Northern Elements Progressive Union—Bornu Youth Movement Alliance			9
	Action Group and Ilorin allies			4
Eastern Regional election of 1957	NCNC	63.26%		64
	Action Group	10.75%		13
	United National Independence Party	6.32%		5
	Independent Candidates	19.67%		2
Federal election of 1959				
Totals	Northern Peoples' Congress	2,027,194	28.2%	134
	National Council of Nigeria and the Cameroons/ Northern Elements Progressive Union Alliance (NCNC/NEPU)	2,592,629	36.1%	89
	Action Group	1,986,839	27.6%	73
	Others	578,893	8.1%	16
East	NCNC/NEPU	1,246,984	64.6%	58
	Action Group	445,144	23.1%	14
	Small Parties and Independents; Niger Delta Congress (NPC ally)	237,626	12.3%	1
West	Action Group	933,680	49.5%	33
	NCNC/NEPU	758,462	40.2%	21
	Northern Peoples' Congress	32,960	1.7%	-
	Small Parties and Independents	162,107	8.6%	
	Mabolaje of Ibadan			7
	Independents			1
North	Northern Peoples' Congress	1,994,045	61.2%	134
	Action Group	559,878	17.2%	25
	NCNC/NEPU	525,575	16.1%	8
	Small Parties and Independents	179,022	5.5%	
	Igbirra Tribal Union (NPC ally)			1
	Independents (declared for NPC)			6

Election	Party	Vote	Percentage of Total Vote	Seats
Lagos	NCNC/NEPU	61,608	55.9%	2
	Action Group	48,137	43.8%	1
	Northern Peoples' Congress	189	0.2%	
	Small Parties and Independents	138	0.1%	
Western Regional election of 1960	Action Group			79
	NCNC/NEPU			33
	Mabolaje of Ibadan (NPC ally)			10
Northern Regional election of 1961	Northern Peoples' Congress and allies			156
	Action Group/UMBC			9
	NEPU/NCNC			1
Eastern Regional election of 1961	NCNC	901,887	58.02	106
	Action Group	240,075	14.44	15
	Dynamic Party	68,007	4.38	5
	Small parties and independents	344,451	22.16	20

PART I

THE RISE OF POLITICAL PARTIES

CHAPTER II: NATIONALISM
AND THE ROOTS OF PARTISANSHIP
IN SOUTHERN NIGERIA[1]

ORIGINS OF THE TWO-PARTY SYSTEM IN LAGOS

IT WAS the natural destiny of Lagos, the leading port, administrative capital, and commercial center of Nigeria, to have been the cradle of its political party system as well. European civilization had an earlier impact of magnitude on this Yoruba town than on any other traditional community in Nigeria. Missionary-sponsored education flourished in Lagos; Africans who could read and write were employed by governmental agencies and firms. The rapidly growing number of settlers included many non-Nigerian Africans who did not, as a rule, readily identify their own interests with those of the indigenous Nigerian people. Among them, however, were many of the journalists, barristers, and other professional men who were prominent in early nationalistic political movements that were "African" first, "Lagosian" second, and "Nigerian" as an afterthought.

The earliest political associations in Lagos are reported to have been organized in protest to the tax and land policies of the British administration.[2] The People's Union of 1908 appears to have been the first; it was formed in the wake of protests against the imposition

---

[1] The political history presented in this chapter is selective and limited to observations on the origins and antecedents of contemporary political parties. With few exceptions, the topics discussed are widely known. In addition to James S. Coleman, *Nigeria: Background to Nationalism* (Berkeley and Los Angeles: University of California Press, 1958), valuable sources of general relevance to this chapter include Nnamdi Azikiwe, *The Development of Political Parties in Nigeria* (London: 1957); Raymond Leslie Buell, *The Native Problem in Africa*, Vol. I (New York: Macmillan, 1928), pp. 645-777; T. O. Elias, "Makers of Nigerian Law" (reprinted from *West Africa*, November 19, 1955-July 7, 1956; London: n.d.); Margery Perham, *Native Administration in Nigeria* (London: Oxford University Press, 1937).

[2] Professor Coleman has chronicled five instances during the period 1895-1913 when concerted protests were made by groups in Lagos against policies of the Government. *Op.cit.*, pp. 178-182. He concluded that: "In general, membership in the early political associations in Lagos was limited to a few leaders who sought to defend what they considered the natural rights of Africans, and their acquired rights as British subjects, against the policies of a colonial government in the first phase of expansion and development. Such associations were primarily instruments for achieving a united front in protesting against particular grievances, and little effort was made to build them into permanent associations. Once the grievance was disposed of, the organizations either became moribund or split into hostile factions."

41

of a general rate to finance a new water scheme. In 1909 local opinion was agitated by the introduction of a sedition act, limiting freedom of expression, and in 1910 strong feelings were aroused by a decision of the Supreme Court of Southern Nigeria to the effect that the ownership of land in Lagos had been transferred to the Crown by treaty at the time of the annexation.[3] In 1911 the Lagos Auxiliary of the Anti-Slavery and Aborigines Protection Society was formed at the instance and with the support of the parent body in Great Britain. When the British government appeared to contemplate the advisability of assuming formal control of all lands in Southern Nigeria, as under the prevailing system of land tenure in the North,[4] the Lagos Auxiliary of the Anti-Slavery and Aborigines Protection Society spread the alarm of an impending threat to customary rights and sent a delegation of protest to London.[5]

At this time the most outspoken critic of the British Administration in Lagos was Herbert Samuel Heelas Macaulay, a civil engineer by training, surveyor by occupation, journalist and politician by inclination.[6] Macaulay campaigned vigorously against the water scheme of

[3] *Attorney General of Southern Nigeria v. John Holt and Co.* (1910), known as the *Foreshore* case; see Elias, *op.cit.*, p. 28; the Treaty of Cession, 1861, made by King Docemo and his chiefs under duress, is reproduced by Sir Alan Burns, *History of Nigeria* (London: Allen and Unwin, 1955), pp. 305-306.

[4] When the Protectorate of Northern Nigeria was proclaimed in 1900, the Northern emirs and chiefs ceded all their rights in land to the Crown. It has been suggested that this cession was not regarded primarily as an absolute transfer of ownership, which might have entailed grave social consequences, but as an act "incidental to the abdication of sovereign powers possessed by the Emirs and Chiefs." In 1910 the Northern Nigeria Lands Committee issued a report which led, in 1916, to a legislative declaration that all lands in the North were "under the control and subject to the disposition of the Governor." Lord Hailey, *Native Administration in the British African Territories*, Part III (London: H.M.S.O., 1951), pp. 89ff.

[5] The London delegation (1913) of the Lagos Auxiliary of the Anti-Slavery and Aborigines Protection Society, protesting the appointment of the West African Lands Commission by the Colonial Office, included "both educated Lagosians and chiefs from such interior centers as Abeokuta, Ibadan, Ijebu-Ode, Ilesha, and Ife . . . although the whole episode was based upon fear, rather than the actuality of some new imperial coercion or deprivation, it resulted in the political mobilization of new elements of the population and brought together for the first time educated Lagosians and chiefs from the Interior." Coleman, *op.cit.*, p. 181; see also Buell, *op.cit.*, pp. 770-771; and Herbert Macaulay and S. Herbert Pearse, *Views of the Lagos Auxiliary of the Anti-Slavery and Aborigines Protection Society upon the Present Policy of His Majesty's Government with Regard to Lands in Lagos and the Rights of the White-Cap-Chiefs and Private Owners* (Colonial Office Library, London; West African Pamphlets, Vol. III).

[6] Herbert Macaulay was born in Lagos in 1864, the son of Reverend Thomas Babington Macaulay, founder of the Church Missionary Society Grammar School, Lagos, and maternal grandson of the Right Reverend Samuel Ajayi Crowther, first African Bishop of the Niger Territory. His paternal grandfather had been captured by slavers but liberated and settled at Freetown, Sierra Leone. His parentage,

1908 and the Sedition Law of 1909; he fomented opposition to a proposed ban on the importation of alcoholic beverages on the ground that the resulting loss in revenue would oblige the Nigerian Government to impose additional taxes; and he was a leader of the Anti-Slavery and Aborigines Protection Society protest against the threatened extension of the Northern land system to Southern Nigeria.[7] By 1914 Macaulay and John Payne Jackson, editor and publisher of the militant *Lagos Weekly Record*, were the leading exponents of nascent nationalism.[8] Their immoderate aims and allegedly demagogic methods earned them the antipathy of prominent leaders of the respectable African elite no less than the hostility of the Government.[9]

Macaulay became a pre-eminent political leader during the historic Apapa Land Case of 1921. Briefly, Chief Amodu Tijani, the *Oluwa* of Lagos, claimed compensation from the Government for lands at

---

therefore, was Yoruba, but he belonged to the set of educated Lagosians with non-Nigerian and Western cultural orientations.

From 1881 until 1890, he was employed as a clerk in the Public Works Department, when he was awarded a government scholarship for higher education in England; there he qualified as a civil engineer and was elected to membership in several learned societies. Upon his return in 1893 he served as Surveyor of Crown Lands for the Colony of Lagos, until his resignation in 1898 after which he began private practice as a licensed surveyor.

He is reputed to have been an accomplished violinist, and his home, Kirsten Hall in Balbina Street, Lagos, was the scene of frequent musical evenings which were attended by Africans and Europeans. It was named for a "young German pianist" who spent most of his leisure time over a two-year period in Mr. Macaulay's house playing "on the only Bechstein Boudoir Grand in Lagos." Isaac B. Thomas, *Life History of Herbert Macaulay* (Lagos: n.d.), pp. 1-15; see also Peter Enahoro, "Wizard of Kirsten Hall," *Sunday Times*, November 9, 1958, pp. 12-13.

[7] Macaulay's biographer reports that in 1913 he addressed the new Governor-General, Sir Frederick D. Lugard, on the subject of customary land tenure "for 105 minutes without notes." Thomas, *op.cit.*, p. 17.

[8] For a portrait and appraisal of John Payne Jackson see Coleman, *op.cit.*, pp. 183-185.

[9] Three conservative opponents of Herbert Macaulay and John Payne Jackson are honored by contemporary nationalists for their contributions to Nigerian political development. Dr. Henry Carr was a student of mathematics and physics who qualified as a barrister and joined the Nigerian civil service. In 1918 he was appointed to the post of Resident of the Colony of Lagos, the highest office ever attained by an African at that time. Sir Kitoye Ajasa was a close friend of Governor Lugard and publisher of the conservative Nigerian Pioneer, which was inaugurated in 1914 to counter the radicalism of Jackson's *Weekly Record*. Dr. John K. Randle was a founder of the People's Union in 1908; the People's Union appears to have expired in 1916 when its leadership supported the Government during a renewal of agitation against the Lagos water scheme. See *West African Pilot*, May 9, 1944 for a portrait of Henry Carr; also Joan Wheare, *The Nigerian Legislative Council* (London: Faber, 1950), pp. 76-77; Sir Kitoye's career is discussed by Coleman, *op.cit.*, pp. 184-185, and Ernest Ikoli, "The Nigeria Press," *West African Review*, XXI (June 1950), pp. 625-627.

Apapa (Lagos) which had been acquired compulsorily. His petition was denied by the Nigerian Supreme Court but granted on appeal to the Judicial Committee of the Privy Council on the ground that the Treaty of Cession had not annulled "communal" rights in land.[10] Few matters are more crucial to a traditional African community than its landed interest,[11] and Chief Oluwa's cause was supported universally by the chiefs and people of Lagos. Herbert Macaulay astutely served Chief Oluwa as his secretary and interpreter during the latter's appellate journey to London. As a gesture of his support, Chief Eshugbayi, the *Eleko* of Lagos, head of the ruling House of Docemo, entrusted his silver staff of office to Macaulay. The staff had been given to the *Eleko's* father, King Docemo, as a token of recognition by the British monarch at the time of the cession of Lagos in 1861; in later years, Macaulay gloried in the assumed title "Minister Plenipotentiary of the House of Docemo." During the course of a newspaper interview in London, Macaulay was reported to have made exaggerated claims about the status of the *Eleko* to which the Nigerian Government took grave objection.[12] Irate officials advised the *Eleko* to telegraph for the return of his staff and to repudiate Macaulay. When the *Eleko* refused to comply, the government withdrew its recognition of the stubbornly proud chief and terminated his salary. Macaulay responded by publishing an essay in London on "the moral obligation of the British Government to the House of Docemo."[13] Shortly after his triumphant return to Lagos, he inaugurated the first genuine Nigerian political party.

Macaulay's organizational base before the *Oluwa* mission had been a quasi-political association known as the *Ilu* (town) Committee, comprising town elders and prominent men who advised the *Eleko* on matters affecting the welfare of the community. The *Ilu* Committee

---

[10] *Amodu Tijani v. the Secretary, Southern Provinces, Law Reports*, A.C. 1921. See Elias, *op.cit.*, pp. 28ff, and Buell, *op.cit.*, pp. 755-756.

[11] "Land and all that appertaineth to land are matters of life and death with the Natives of West Africa. . . . The shortest and easiest way to start a conflagration in West Africa is to make an attempt at depriving the Native of his land, or inherent rights thereto." Memorandum of Proposals placed before the Under-Secretary on behalf of the Nigerian Democratic Party, *West Africa*, April 10, 1926, p. 415.

[12] It seems that the Governor of Nigeria was informed that Macaulay had stated that the *Eleko* was acclaimed by all Nigeria as King, and that the natives "rightly regard" the revenues of the Dependency as his personal income. However, R. L. Buell discovered that Macaulay had referred to the *Eleko* as "merely the king of Lagos, acclaimed as such by the seventeen million people of Nigeria." *Op.cit.*, p. 664.

[13] Herbert Macaulay, *Justitia Fiat: The Moral Obligation of the British Government to the House of King Docemo of Lagos* (London: 1921).

was formidable in terms of traditional prestige and was buttressed in addition by the support of the majority faction of the Muslim congregation of the Central Mosque of Lagos. Here we touch upon one of the crucial underlying factors of Lagos politics which is paralleled in many cities of Yorubaland. The vast majority of indigenous people, mostly traditionalist in outlook, are followers of Islam, while the overwhelming number of settlers, especially the commercial and professional groups, are Christian. Macaulay was a Christian but his mass support was derived from the indigenous community, and he worked closely with the leaders of the Muslim Congregation. When the *Jam'at* (congregation of the Central Mosque) split on issues of doctrine and secular politics, probably in 1916,[14] the majority faction rallied to the leadership of Macaulay and his associate, Joseph Egerton-Shyngle. The latter, a Gambian by birth and a prominent barrister, participated in the historic inaugural meeting of the National Congress of British West Africa at Accra in 1920, and served as a member of the Congress delegation to London which petitioned the Colonial Secretary for the introduction of representative government and other democratic reforms in West Africa.[15]

[14] According to R. L. Buell, the *Jam'at* controversy erupted in 1914 because "the head *Lemomu* (Chief Imam) who came from the North, had stricter ideas than the Yoruba Moslems." The *Lemomu* and Alli Balogun, a wealthy Muslim who was associated with Macaulay's opponent, Dr. J. K. Randle, supported the Government's water rate. At this juncture, the *Eleko* of Lagos appointed Muslim opponents of the *Lemomu* to certain traditional offices which were then held by the Lemomu's followers. Alli Balogun and the *Lemomu* led their minority faction out of the *Jam'at* and founded a separate congregation which ultimately built its own mosque. It was natural for those who opposed the water rate and the doctrines of the *Lemomu* to accept the leadership of Macaulay. See Buell, *op.cit.*, pp. 665-666, where these matters are discussed in part.

[15] See National Congress of British West Africa, *Resolutions of the Conference of Africans of British West Africa, Accra, 11-29 March 1920*; *The Humble Petition of the National Congress of British West Africa* (to King George V) *by its Delegates now in London*, 19 October 1920; George Padmore, *Africa, Britain's Third Empire* (London: Dobson, 1949), pp. 201-204; Martin L. Kilson, Jr., "The Rise of Nationalist Organizations and Parties in British West Africa," *Africa Seen by American Negroes*, ed., John A. Davis (Paris: Présence Africaine, 1958); pp. 45-50. J. S. Coleman observes that Herbert Macaulay also played a "prominent role behind the scenes" in Congress affairs while in London with Chief Oluwa in 1920 (*op.cit.*, p. 456, n. 48). A Nigerian section of the National Congress of British West Africa was formed in Lagos, in which non-Nigerians were most prominent. At a meeting of the Nigerian Council in December 1920, Governor Clifford denounced the Congress group as both unrepresentative and unrealistic; subsequently he gave encouragement to the formation of a group known as the Reform Club by "a few gentlemen of high standing," apparently to counteract the Congress group. In addition to these groups there was at this time in Lagos a branch of the Universal Negro Improvement Association (Garveyites). *Ibid.*, pp. 182, 191ff, 452, n. 36.

In 1922, the so-called Clifford Constitution conferred the right of franchise on a restricted Lagos electorate (about 3,000 male taxpayers with an income of £100) to return three members to the Legislative Council every five years. On June 24, 1923, Herbert Macaulay and his associates inaugurated the Nigerian National Democratic Party (NNDP), and Egerton-Shyngle was elected president.[16] The stated aims of the NNDP included the attainment of municipal status and local self-government for Lagos, the provision of facilities for higher education in Nigeria, the introduction of compulsory education at the primary school level, the encouragement of non-discriminatory, private economic enterprise, and the Africanization of the civil service. In addition, the party was committed to cooperate with, and to support, the program of the National Congress of British West Africa.[17] During the entire period of its history as an independent political association (1923-1944), the NNDP was virtually confined to the Lagos political arena and mainly concerned with local matters, in particular with elections (to the Legislative Council every five years and to the Lagos Town Council every three years) and with the fluctuating fortunes of the House of Docemo. Indeed the NNDP was practically reared on the traditional foundation of that popular dynasty. Chief Oluwa's case had gained Macaulay the devoted support of the so-called "White Cap" Chiefs of Lagos,[18] and it was not difficult for him to secure the adhesion of the religious leaders of the *Jam'at* as well as the socially cohesive

[16] The initial planners of the party are reported to have been Thomas Horatio Jackson, editor of the *Lagos Weekly Record* following the death of his father J. P. Jackson, and Mr. Bangan Benjamin in addition to Macaulay. See the "Presidential Address to the NNDP by C. C. Adeniyi-Jones," *West African Pilot*, June 13, 1938. See also Thomas, *op.cit.*, p. 120.

[17] J. C. Zizer, a leading member of the NNDP, edited a Congress weekly, *West African Nationhood*, in Lagos. In 1930 the Congress held its fourth session in Lagos, but the Nigerian section expired when Zizer departed in 1933 (Coleman, *op.cit.*, p. 195). For a summary of the aims and objects of the NNDP, see *ibid.*, p. 198, and the "Address to the NNDP by Herbert Macaulay," *West African Pilot*, June 13, 1938. One of the most comprehensive statements of the political philosophy and program of the NNDP is contained in the "Memorandum of Proposals placed before the Under-Secretary on behalf of the Nigerian Democratic Party," and "Notes of an interview between African leaders of Southern Nigeria and the Colonial Office mission headed by Mr. Ormsby-Gore, Under-Secretary." Among the topics covered in the memorandum and discussion are the handling of native produce, objections to the system of plantation agriculture, and policies relating to land, commerce, education and the administration of justice. "Cards on the Table," *West Africa*, April 10, 1926.

[18] The "White Cap" Chiefs include the heirs of the traditional landowners and certain other chiefs whose titles were created by former kings. See J. B. Losi, *History of Lagos* (Lagos: 1921), and Burns, *op.cit.*, p. 34. There were said to be 21 in 1958.

organized market women. Both groups were traditionalist in outlook, loyal to the *Eleko*, and socially distant from the Westernized, Christian, professional set that predominated in the opposition to Macaulay. Moreover, the influential *Ilu* Committee, comprising the town elders and leaders of traditional societies, was incorporated into the new nationalist party.

At its inception, therefore, the NNDP embodied a stable coalition of radicalism and traditionalism based on an expedient division of political spheres of interest. The bedrock of the party was its component of chiefs, Imams, and market women leaders; this group, which was largely non-literate and included a few wealthy merchants, dominated the party executive and controlled the selection of candidates to the Legislative Council. From 1923 to 1938 they bestowed candidatures upon a small group of Christian and non-Nigerian professional men who monopolized all elective offices in Lagos. Among the latter were genuine progressives of outstanding ability, including Egerton-Shyngle, Dr. C. C. Adeniyi-Jones (Sierra Leonian), second president of the NNDP and a leading member of the Legislative Council, barrister Eric O. Moore (Nigerian Yoruba), legislator and Vice-president of the NNDP, J. C. Zizer (Sierra Leonian), editor of *West African Nationhood* and a member of the Lagos Town Council, and T. A. Doherty (Nigerian Yoruba), member of the Legislative Council, of the town council and a founder of the National Bank of Nigeria. Macaulay's position was unique; he identified himself wholly with the traditional groups and enjoyed their absolute confidence. Probably his political reputation was enhanced by the fact that his devotion to the party's cause could not be rewarded by an elective office inasmuch as a criminal record of two convictions, once for the misapplication of trust funds at an early stage in his career and again for the publication of a libelous falsehood in 1928, barred him from contesting any election. In fact the latter offence was committed in connection with his ultimately successful campaign for the restoration of the *Eleko*, who was deposed by the government and deported from Lagos in 1925.[19] Within the Democratic Party,

[19] Eshugbayi *Eleko* was "deposed" by a faction of the Docemo family in 1925, an action that was sanctioned by the Government, which then deported the *Eleko* and recognized his replacement. At bottom, the *Eleko's* deportation reflected a continuing struggle between Macaulay and the conservative elite, of which Dr. Henry Carr was the most illustrious representative. Carr had been Resident of the Colony when Eshugbayi refused to renounce Macaulay, and the replacement of the *Eleko* was an object of Carr's policy, although it was actually carried out a year after his retirement. At the height of the excitement in 1925, Macaulay inaugurated his *Lagos Daily News* and published the notorious "Gun Powder Plot" story, alleging a conspiracy to assassinate Eshugbayi's supporters. Three years

the personal rule of Herbert Macaulay was acknowledged by his intellectual peers, and his power of decision was subject only to the concurrence of the important Imams, elders, and chiefs.

The Era of the Nigerian Youth Movement

Two currents of opposition to Macaulay and his Democratic Party are discernible in the 1920's. His conservative critics revived the People's Union, which had been defunct since 1916, while a group of younger progressives organized the short-lived Union of Young Nigerians.[20] The latter may be regarded as a forebear of the first genuinely national political party. From about 1929 to 1934, the political consciousness of the Lagos intelligentsia was stimulated by a controversial government scheme to increase the number of Nigerian technical and medical assistants through vocational education of a sub-professional quality. In the eyes of the professional and educated elite, the government proposal represented a potential diversion of talent from liberal to vocational studies and was objectionable on two counts: first, it seemed to be a reversion to the despised theory that the African should be educated along "his own," i.e., inferior, or non-liberal lines; secondly, it evoked the image of a prolonged future during which Africans would be confined mainly to inferior jobs under European specialists.[21] When the government inaugurated

---

later he served a six-month prison sentence for having circulated a malicious libel. Yet he persevered indefatigably for the restoration of his patron and his efforts were rewarded in 1931 when a newly appointed Governor, Sir Donald Cameron, reinstated the *Eleko*. The following year the *Eleko* died, and Macaulay, at the zenith of his prestige and influence, was instrumental in the selection of his successor, Prince Falolu Docemo, by the chiefs. See Buell, *op.cit.*, pp. 662-667, for details of the *Eleko* controversy until 1926. The discussion is carried further by Perham, *op.cit.*, pp. 264-271 and Elias, *op.cit.*, pp. 39ff.

[20] Dr. Nnamdi Azikiwe writes that the People's Union "was said to be controlled by Dr. J. K. Randle, Dr. Orisadipe Obasa of Ikeja, Sir Kitoye Ajasa, Dr. R. Akinwande Savage, Sir Adeyemo Alakija and others" (*op.cit.*, p. 5). Despite the conservatism of its leading members, the People's Union did attract a class of potentially radical professional men with progressive ideas, e.g., Ernest S. Ikoli, Nigeria's leading journalist and a founder of the Nigerian Youth Movement, was its last secretary. However, the People's Union never posed a serious challenge to the NNDP. It expired in 1928 shortly after the death of its founder, Dr. J. K. Randle. The Union of Young Nigerians was formed in 1923 by barrister Ayo Williams, Dr. J. C. Vaughan, and Ernest Ikoli, then editor and publisher of the *African Messenger*; it was active for five years during which time it contested elections without success. *Ibid.*, p. 6; Coleman, *op.cit.*, p. 217.

[21] An Administration plan to replace the Oxford and Cambridge school certificates with a Nigerian certificate provoked Nigerians to form the National School Committee in 1929 which had as its object the raising of £10,000. When the National Union of Students met to convene a national political front in 1944, an unsuccessful appeal was made to the trustees of the National Education Fund

the Yaba (Lagos) Higher College as a vocational institution authorized to confer Nigerian diplomas, the critics responded with a demand
for government scholarships to finance the education of deserving
students in the United Kingdom. In order to propagate their ideas
on educational policy, a number of young men, mainly students and
graduates of Nigeria's premier institution, King's College (Lagos),
formed the Lagos Youth Movement in 1934, which in 1936 was
renamed the Nigerian Youth Movement. The founding members were
Dr. J. C. Vaughan, Ernest Ikoli, H. O. Davies and Samuel Akinsanya.[22] In 1937 the Youth Movement was strengthened by the
return to Nigeria of Nnamdi Azikiwe, after nine years as a student
in the United States and three years as a newspaper editor in the
Gold Coast.

Nnamdi Azikiwe was born in 1904 in Zunguru, Northern Nigeria,
where his father was employed as a clerk in the Nigerian Regiment.[23]
His ethnic heritage is Onitsha Ibo; however, the indigenous people
of Onitsha town trace their descent to Benin. In his early youth
Nnamdi Azikiwe spoke the Hausa language, but his parents sent him
"home" to Onitsha at the age of eight to acquire the language of his
people. Subsequently he attended primary schools conducted by the
Roman Catholic and Anglican (Church Missionary Society) missions
at Onitsha, the Wesleyan Boys' High School in Lagos, and the
Hope Waddell Training Institute in Calabar. As a student in Lagos
he added fluency in the Yoruba language to his linguistic competence.
During these impressionable years, he claims to have been inspired
by the "Black Zionism" of Marcus Garvey, the teachings of the Rev-

---

to contribute the £1,600 which had been raised by the Committee of 1929 to a
revised National School project. *West African Pilot*, June 12, 1944; Azikiwe,
op.cit., p. 9; Coleman has discussed the symbolic stigma of inferiority which the
nationalists and professionals attached to Nigerian diplomas, *op.cit.*, pp. 123ff, 217;
frequently the professional Nigerian owed his sense of personal and racial dignity
to his attainment of European qualifications. It was his proof and promise of racial
and national equality.

[22] Dr. J. C. Vaughan (Yoruba) was a medical doctor; Ernest Ikoli (Ijaw)
was a distinguished journalist; Samuel Akinsanya (Yoruba) was a trade unionist;
Hezekiah Oladipo Davies (Yoruba) was then a government employee; he studied
economics under Harold Laski at the London School of Economics where he
compiled a distinguished record as a scholar and a student leader, serving as
President of the West African Students' Union in the U.K. and as representative
of the University of London on the Executive Committee of British Universities.
He returned to England for legal training in 1944. In 1959 he was appointed one of
the first two Nigerian Queen's Counsel. In 1961 Chief Davies became Chairman and
Managing Director of the Nigerian National Press.

[23] This sketch of Nnamdi Azikiwe's early life is drawn mainly from his auto-
biographical articles in the *West African Pilot* from July 26, 1938 to June 1939,
entitled "My Odyssey."

erend Dr. J. E. K. Aggrey (an American-trained African minister) and W. M. Thayer's biography of James A. Garfield, "From Log Cabin to the White House." In the course of his brief, unsatisfying experience as a junior clerk in the civil service in Lagos he resolved to go to America for higher education and one day to establish a university in Africa.[24]

Eventually, with parental assistance, he journeyed to America and enrolled, at the age of twenty-one, in Storer College, a two-year preparatory school at Harper's Ferry, West Virginia. There his fellow students gave him the nickname "Zik," by which he is widely known throughout Nigeria and abroad. His early years in America were difficult; he took various laboring jobs and he suffered the commonplace indignities of racial prejudice. One night, at a point of extreme depression and absolute penury, he attempted to commit suicide by lying cross-wise over a tramway in Pittsburgh. His own memoir of the event records that an unknown person dragged him from the path of the oncoming tram and reproached him kindly that "only God can take life away." The conductor of the tram reassured his passengers "that it was only a young Nigger who wanted to die"; but Azikiwe's unknown benefactor gave him $5 and notified a white minister, who visited the youth in his YMCA lodging and helped him to secure temporary employment. Ben (his Christian name, which he discarded legally some years later in reaction to a racial slur in England)[25] Azikiwe—he went by the name of Ben Zik —worked as a dishwasher, mill hand, coal miner, and road gang laborer, before his matriculation at Howard University in Washing-

[24] *West African Pilot*, August 13, 1938.

[25] In 1934, Nnamdi Azikiwe spent a memorable summer in England en route to Africa from the United States. He applied to compete in the British Empire Games "for Nigeria" in the mile and one-half race and the high jump. In America he had been a successful collegiate athlete and he was confident that he could do the mile in less than 4:30. But he was barred by the London Amateur Athletic Association following protests from the South African team. Thereupon he decided that if he was an "extraneous element" in England because of his color, he could do without his English name; he discarded his Christian name "Benjamin" and changed his name legally in a London publication to Nnamdi Azikiwe (*West African Pilot*, June 14, 1939). In later years he became a patron of sport in Nigeria and President of the Nigerian Amateur Athletic Association. His observations on his lessons from athletics may not be without political significance:

"From athletics I learned how to suffer in silence. I learned how to let the other fellow suffer with me as soon as I decided to apply the pressure. I learned how to act as if I was helpless even though I was as powerful as an ox. . . . I have always looked at most of my life's problems as problems which confront a Miler in a Mile Race. . . . Boxing taught me to cultivate capacity to absorb punishment and to bid for my time so that when I struck I could knock out my opponent." *West African Pilot*, August 1938.

ton, D.C. Financial pressures caused him to leave Howard and enroll in Lincoln University, in Pennsylvania, where he completed his undergraduate education. Subsequently, he obtained a certificate in journalism at Teachers College, Columbia University; he edited the *Columbia University Summer Session Times* (1930), achieved an M.A. in political science at Lincoln University, where he was employed as an instructor, and an M.Sc. in anthropology at the University of Pennsylvania.[26] At the age of thirty he realized with "mortification" that despite his academic qualifications, he was "a serf, from the point of view of practical economics," and he applied in vain to the education departments of four colonies, to missionary societies, and to the governments of Liberia, Ethiopia, and Turkey for a suitable position. Finally, in 1934, he accepted an offer to edit the *African Morning Post,* a new daily newspaper in Accra, Gold Coast.

In 1937, Azikiwe and his associate editor, the noted trade unionist I. T. Wallace-Johnson of Sierra Leone, were prosecuted for the publication of a seditious article. Following the reversal of their convictions on appeal, Azikiwe returned to Nigeria. He resolved to establish a high-class daily newspaper in Lagos and solicited the assistance of well-to-do and nationalistic Nigerians for that purpose. On November 22, 1930, the first issue of the *West African Pilot* appeared; its masthead featured the motto: "Show the light and the people will find the way." Azikiwe inaugurated his personal column, "Inside Stuff" by listing twenty-five principles of public policy for which the *Pilot* stood, ranging from governmental ownership and control of all railways, mines, financial institutions, and communications facilities to Africanization of the civil service, compulsory education, compulsory military training, and radical constitutional reform. In format and style, the *West African Pilot* showed evidence of Azikiwe's training in the American art of popular journalism, and for nearly fourteen years thereafter "Inside Stuff" by "Zik" treated the Nigerian reading public to pungent, incisive, sometimes malevolent, but always informed commentaries on Nigerian and world affairs.[27]

[26] Dr. Azikiwe became a Fellow of the Royal Anthropological Institute at the suggestion of Professor Bronislaw Malinowski of London University who was in attendance when the Nigerian student reported to a seminar at the University of Pennsylvania. *West African Pilot*, March 20, 1939.

[27] James S. Coleman in his portrait of Nnamdi Azikiwe (*op.cit.*, pp. 220-223) has drawn attention to the universalist and racially conscious quality of his writings: "His first two published works, *Liberia in World Politics* and *Renascent Africa*, were written with the basic preconception that the struggle of the future was racial, between black and white. In propagating his ideas, Azikiwe was just as much at

In 1938 the Nigerian Youth Movement won the election to the Lagos Town Council and all three elective seats in the Legislative Council, thereby putting an end to the fifteen-year electoral rule of the Democratic Party in Lagos. The results could not be taken as a reflection of popular opinion, owing to the restrictive property franchise—the total vote was only 792—but it did indicate the political leaning of the upper strata of the Westernized elite. In preparation for the elections, the Youth Movement chose an executive committee of about a dozen members and officers, including Azikiwe. All but two of them were Yoruba or non-Nigerians with strong Yoruba family ties—one only was a Muslim; at least one-half of the officers were King's College alumni.[28] Without exception they were men of substance, engaged in business, law, medicine, or journalism. Despite its elitist character and predominantly Yoruba complexion in Lagos, the Nigerian Youth Movement was not exclusive or sectarian in conception. Branches of the Movement were established in urban areas throughout Nigeria, and the theme of inter-tribal amity as a condition of national unity was emphasized by the *Youth Charter and Constitution* of 1938.[29] In Lagos, however, the multi-tribal character of the Movement depended largely upon the membership of Azikiwe, to whom the growing community of non-Yoruba—particularly Ibo—settlers in Lagos were devoted.

In retrospect it appears that the Youth Movement embodied a congenital weakness of conflicting interests that were partly ethnic

---

home in Accra as in Lagos or Onitsha. Lynchings in America, pass laws in South Africa or boycotts in the Gold Coast (now Ghana) received just as much attention in his newspapers as did the problem of creating an independent Nigerian nation-state."

[28] The officers and executive members of the Nigerian Youth Movement in 1938 were as follows: Dr. Kofororola Abayomi, President; Mr. Ernest Ikoli, Vice-President; Mr. H. O. Davies, Secretary; Mr. Hamzat A. Subair, Treasurer; Mr. O. Caxton-Martins, Legal Adviser; Mr. Paul Cardozo, Editor of the "Service," then a quarterly magazine; Dr. Akinola Maja; Mr. Nnamdi Azikiwe; Mr. Jibril Martins; Mr. Bank-Anthony, and Adjutant Jones. *West African Pilot*, January 19, 1938. Other leading members were H. S. A. Thomas, Obafemi Awolowo, S. L. Akintola, J. A. Tuyo, F. Ogugua-Arah, S. O. Shonibare, and L. Duro Emmanuel. N. Azikiwe, *op.cit.*, p. 8. Identified by the writer positively as non-Yoruba are E. Ikoli (Ijaw) and N. Azikiwe (Ibo); J. Martins was a Muslim. Coleman observes that "the average age of the leaders of the Youth Movement was forty." *Op.cit.*, p. 229.

[29] Extracts from the Nigerian Youth Charter have been reproduced by Obafemi Awolowo in his Autobiography, entitled *Awo: The Autobiography of Chief Obafemi Awolowo* (Cambridge: Cambridge University Press, 1960), pp. 121-123. Chief Awolowo reports that Chief H. O. Davies, then editor of the Daily Service, was "the sole author and genius of the 'Youth Charter.'" *Ibid.*, p. 155. Cf. Coleman, *op.cit.*, pp. 225-226; Azikiwe, *op.cit.*, p. 7.

and partly economic. Before the appearance of Azikiwe's *West African Pilot*, Ernest Ikoli, Vice-President of the Youth Movement, was the acknowledged leader of Nigerian journalism.[30] Although the *Pilot* espoused the cause of the Youth Movement, it was an independent commercial newspaper and the principal Youth Movement leaders decided to publish an official party organ. In 1938 they launched the *Daily Service*, advertised as "the official journal of the Nigerian Youth Movement," with Ikoli as publisher and editor, and H. O. Davies as business manager.[31] Azikiwe, whose financial resources were limited, appears to have resented this intrusion of friendly competition for the comparatively small reading public.[32] Early in 1939 he resigned from the executive of the Youth Movement for compelling "business" reasons,[33] and in 1941 he broke with it finally and dramatically. At that time a crisis within the Movement was precipitated by the resignation of Dr. K. A. Abayomi from the Legislative Council. Ernest Ikoli, then President of the N.Y.M. sought the party's nomination for the vacancy. He was opposed by Samuel Akinsanya, Vice-President of the N.Y.M. and Secretary of the Nigerian Motor Transport Union. The selection of Ikoli led to allegations of tribal discrimination: Azikiwe and Akinsanya charged that the latter had been rejected only because the dominant group of Lagos Yorubas would not countenance the nomination of an Ijebu

[30] Ernest Ikoli served his apprenticeship on the *Lagos Weekly Record* under Thomas Horatio Jackson. In 1922 he founded the *African Messenger* which supported his party, the Union of Young Democrats. In 1926 the *African Messenger* was absorbed by the *Daily Times*, a newspaper company founded that year by seven directors—six prominent European businessmen and barrister Adeyemo Alakija. Ikoli served as editor of the *Daily Times* from 1926-1930; in 1933 he became editor of T. A. Doherty's *Daily Telegraph* and in 1938 he founded the *Daily Service*, which he edited until 1944.

[31] In the latter part of 1938 the assets and liabilities of the *Daily Service* were acquired by the Service Press Limited, under a directorate comprising seven leading members of the Youth Movement. The original subscribers of the Service Press Limited were: Samuel Akinsanya, a founder of the Youth Movement and secretary of the Nigerian Motor Transport Union, Dr. Akinola Maja, an executive member of the Movement and a director of the National Bank of Nigeria, barrister Jibril Martins, an executive member of the Movement, Hamzat Adisa Subair, Treasurer of the Movement and an accountant and director of the National Bank, Dr. O. A. Omelolu, a medical practitioner, O. I. Akinsan, a businessman, S. O. Gbadamosi, manager of the Ikorodu Trading Company, Ernest Ikoli, and H. O. Davies.

[32] See Coleman, *op.cit.*, p. 227.

[33] *West African Pilot*, February 2, 1939. Prior to Azikiwe's resignation from the executive of the Movement, the Zik Press was involved in a nuisance action brought by barrister (now Chief Justice) Adetokunboh Ademola and compelled to move its publishing plant to another site. The plaintiff's counsel was O. Caxton-Martins, legal adviser of the N.Y.M. *West African Pilot*, February 24-25, 1939.

Yoruba. Certainly there had been a tendency on the part of the Lagos elite to look down at their brethren from the provinces, a kind of snobbishness that elicited resentment. But Ikoli was an Ijaw, not a Lagos Yoruba, and his candidature was supported by another prominent Ijebu Yoruba, Obafemi Awolowo, then secretary of the Ibadan branch of the N.Y.M. and assistant secretary (to Akinsanya) of the Motor Transport Union. Adamantly, Azikiwe and Akinsanya insisted that anti-Ijebu prejudice was the underlying motive at play, and they resigned from the Youth Movement. Akinsanya stood as an independent candidate against Ikoli, with Azikiwe's support, but he was defeated.

At bottom the Youth Movement controversy of 1941 merely crystallized antagonisms that were bound to mature. Neither the Yoruba elite nor the non-Yorubas who followed Azikiwe were directly involved, but partisans of both groups entered the dispute on a question of principle and the ensuing struggle was fatal to the Youth Movement.[34] We cannot with certitude offer a single-factor explanation for the deterioration of Azikiwe's relationship with the Youth Movement. He may have resented the commercial competition of the *Daily Service* and he may not have been content to remain a subordinate political leader. It is undoubtedly true that his impetuously dramatic, highly personalized type of leadership was not palatable to the elite group that controlled the Youth Movement, among whom were the professional and intellectual luminaries of Lagos. Possibly he sensed or imagined a veiled hostility to the "pushful Ibo-man." In Lagos, as in other urban centers, an ever-increasing number of industrious Ibos from the densely populated East had settled in quest of economic opportunities. Invariably their presence created new social tensions. As a group, they were highly resourceful, disposed to support political nationalism, and possessed of an intense psychological need to overcome their comparatively late acquisition of Western education.[35] It is significant that the first Ibo doctor,

[34] It is not at all likely that a nomination controversy alone could have produced as grave a consequence as actually followed. The N.Y.M. was a turbulent party and controversy among the leadership was nothing new. Thus Dr. K. A. Abayomi, President of the Youth Movement after its reconstruction in 1938, was replaced a year later and is reported to have resigned from the Legislative Council partly as a result of having fallen from favor within the party. In 1941 the split might easily have been averted since the death of Olayimka Alakija had created a second vacancy in the Legislative Council that was contested that same year. Obafemi Awolowo has reviewed the controversy from a partisan standpoint and attributed the fall of the N.Y.M. mainly to the tactics of Nnamdi Azikiwe. Awolowo, *op.cit.*, pp. 133-159.

[35] The extent of the Yoruba lead over other tribes in the field of Western

Sir Francis Ibiam (later Governor of Eastern Nigeria) did not return to Nigeria until 1935, and the first Ibo lawyer, Louis Mbanefo (later Chief Justice of Eastern Nigeria) returned in 1937. Azikiwe was the first great Ibo leader of the twentieth century.[36] Notwithstanding his constant affirmation of non-tribal African values, he could not be unmindful of the fact that he was identified by his people (the Ibo) with their own national pride. His career typified their growing assertiveness in Nigerian affairs; his clash with the elite leadership of the Youth Movement was both a sign of latent Ibo-Yoruba tension and a major contributing factor to the ethnic hostility that erupted later.

But the social division of Lagos was not fundamentally tribal; at least, tribalism was not the sole fundamental factor. We have seen that the Yoruba population was politically divided on class or quasi-class lines. By and large, the traditionalistic, predominantly Muslim, indigenous masses followed Macaulay and the Nigerian National Democratic Party, while the Westernized, predominantly Christian, cosmopolitan (i.e., drawn from several provinces—Ijebu, Abeokuta, Oyo, and Ondo—in addition to the Colony) rising class followed the N.Y.M. Indeed the N.Y.M. in Lagos relied upon the "detribalized" working class, many of whom were Ibos, for its mass support. Azikiwe's defection virtually destroyed the multi-tribal character of the Lagos section of the Nigerian Youth Movement, as most of the Ibos and many of the Ijebu Yorubas turned to the NNDP. His break with the Yoruba elite set the stage for the political fusion of the Ibo and Yoruba masses of Lagos, which took organizational form in 1944.

The Birth of the National Council of Nigeria and the Cameroons

The Second World War, as Thomas Hodgkin remarked, "was a forcing house of new political movements in West Africa."[37] The right of self-determination, as proclaimed in the Atlantic Charter, was interpreted by the nationalists of British West Africa as a promise of self-government. James S. Coleman has examined in detail the wartime gestation of militant nationalism, and it is not necessary to review that crucial phase of Nigerian history in this limited account

education and its consequences are discussed by Coleman, *op.cit.*, pp. 142ff, 246; see also his section on "the Ibo awakening," *ibid.*, pp. 332-343.

[36] *Ibid.*, p. 224.

[37] Thomas Hodgkin, "Political Parties in British and French West Africa," Information Digest, Africa Bureau, No. 10 (London: August 1953), p. 14.

of party origins.[38] It suffices to mention in passing that the West African Students' Union of the United Kingdom took the lead in demanding both constitutional reform on a territorial basis and inter-territorial unity. In 1943 a West African Press delegation to London, under the auspices of the British Council and the leadership of Nnamdi Azikiwe, requested the Secretary of State for the Colonies to initiate a fifteen-year program for independence in West Africa: ten years of "representative" government followed by a final five-year term of limited tutelage with fully "responsible" government. This proposal had been formulated by Azikiwe in 1942; it was the outcome of deliberations by a small study association known as the Nigeria Reconstruction Group, which also concluded that the time was ripe for partisans of independence to create a unified national front.[39] These efforts culminated in the Ojokoro Youth Rally of November 1943, which was attended by members of the Nigerian Youth Movement, the Nigerian Youth Circle (an association of study groups under the leadership of H. O. Davies), the Nigerian Reconstruction Group, and the Nigerian Union of Students (N.U.S.).[40] It was the last-named (N.U.S.) which ultimately took the initiative in forging a national front.

In March 1944, student action was precipitated by the notorious King's College strike. Three years earlier the student dormitories had been turned over to the army and the boarders were obliged to occupy disagreeable lodgings in town. When their petition for re-establishment in their quarters was denied the students went on "strike" to emphasize their grievances.[41] Seventy-five senior boarders were apprehended, tried for disorderly conduct, and expelled by the school authorities for their breach of discipline; eight of the student leaders were conscripted immediately into the military service. This incident aroused both the ire of the Lagos intelligentsia and the latent militancy

[38] Coleman, op.cit., pp. 230-267.

[39] Azikiwe, op.cit., pp. 8-9; Coleman, op.cit., pp. 262, 464, n. 20. See also N. Azikiwe, Political Blueprint of Nigeria (Lagos: African Book Co., Ltd., 1943).

[40] The Ojokoro Youth Rally appears to have been the most concrete manifestation of wartime unity moves prior to June 1944. "Many militant nationalists look back upon the Ojokoro Youth Rally as the occasion on which their enthusiasm for political action was first aroused." Coleman, op.cit., p. 263. An attempt to unify the N.Y.M. and two factions of the Democratic bloc (the NNDP and the Union of Young Democrats) in a joint council for electoral purposes collapsed in 1944 in a wrangle over nominations to the Lagos Town Council. West African Pilot, June 3, 1944.

[41] The student petition complained about the physical hardships and study problems created by congestion, filth, and "factors of a degenerating moral character" in their temporary quarters. West African Pilot, March 8, 1944, and subsequent issues.

of the N.U.S.[42] Student leaders forthwith decided that a central organization was required to coordinate the political endeavors of existing associations, including political parties, trade unions, professional organizations, and tribal unions. On June 10, 1944, the N.U.S. convened a mass meeting in the Glover Memorial Hall, Lagos, to consider (1) the King's College strike, (2) the possibility of raising funds for a national school, and (3) the immediate formation of a representative national committee.[43] The venerable Herbert Macaulay presided and resolutions were passed favoring the organization of a "National Council or Committee" and the establishment of a national school.[44] Pressing its initiative, the N.U.S. issued a "call from the youth," inviting all patriotic associations to attend the inaugural meeting of the National Council of Nigeria on August 26, 1944.[45] Over forty organizations, including political parties, tribal unions, trade unions, literary associations, professional associations, religious groups, social clubs and women's organizations were represented, and a resolution was adopted expressing the determination of the National Council "to work in unity for the realization of our ultimate goal of self-government within the British Empire."[46]

From the outset, leaders of the Nigerian Youth Movement remained aloof, for they viewed the National Council as a stratagem by Azikiwe and Macaulay to seize control of the entire nationalist movement.[47] Ultimately these two were elected General Secretary

[42] The Nigerian Union of Students was inaugurated in March 1940, by students of the Abeokuta Grammar School at the prompting of their principal, Reverend I. O. Ransome-Kuti, founder of the Nigerian Union of Teachers. Its primary purpose then was to counteract tribal separatism among students; however, study groups were set up to consider the public problems of Nigeria and practical means for their solution. See address by Mr. C. O. Bamgboye, General Secretary of the Nigerian Union of Students, at the inaugural meeting of the National Council, *West African Pilot*, August 29 and 30, 1944; also N. Azikiwe, *The Development of Political Parties in Nigeria*, p. 9, and Coleman, *op.cit.*, p. 264.

[43] *West African Pilot*, June 7, 1944.

[44] The students were unsuccessful in their attempt to persuade the trustees of the National Education Fund set up in 1929 to contribute that fund (*supra*, p. 48 n. 21) and the project was never carried out. The June 10 meeting, including remarks by speakers and resolutions adopted, was reported by the *West African Pilot*, June 12, 1944.

[45] The students are reported to have termed their effort the "Youthgrad," which recalled to the *Pilot* the example of Leningrad and the revolutionary effort of "emancipated Russia." *West African Pilot*, June 28, 1944.

[46] *West African Pilot*, August 28, 1944. The chairman of the inaugural meeting of the National Council was Duse Mohammed Ali, an Egyptian who founded and edited the Lagos *Comet*. See Coleman, *op.cit.*, p. 202; Azikiwe, *The Development of Political Parties in Nigeria*, pp. 9-10.

[47] At the meeting of June 10, 1944, a spokesman for the N.U.S. reported failure to reach agreement with the N.Y.M. *West African Pilot*, June 12, 1944; the

and President respectively of the National Council of Nigeria;[48] Dr. Akinola Maja, President of the Nigerian Youth Movement, and his associate, Oluwole Alakija, are reported to have declined the subordinate offices of Vice-President and Legal Adviser.[49] Both the Nigerian National Democratic Party and its dissident satellite, the Nigerian Union of Young Democrats,[50] affiliated with the National Council, so that the net effect of its creation on Lagos politics was the complete polarization of local political groups. By January 1945, the National Council comprised 87 member unions[51] including three Cameroonian groups, for which reason its official title was changed to National Council of Nigeria and the Cameroons. Membership was organizational only, and affiliated branches were defined by the constitution as "coordinations of member-unions" in various towns and districts.[52]

Within a few months of its formation, the NCNC was embroiled in the opening phase of its postwar struggle for constitutional advance. It lies beyond the scope of this discussion to explore the intentions or effects of British colonial policy. Scholarly critics have discerned its dual tendency: on one hand the British recognized the right of democratic action toward the accepted end of self-government; on the other, they supported institutions and fostered policies of an undemocratic nature.[53] In March 1945, Sir Arthur Richards (later

---

N.Y.M. was listed, perhaps erroneously, as one of 43 organizations in attendance at the inaugural meeting of August 26 (*West African Pilot*, August 28, 1944); Coleman, *op.cit.*, p. 265, reports that it declined to send representatives.

[48] See Azikiwe, *The Development of Political Parties in Nigeria*, p. 10, for the names of officers elected by the third meeting of the Inaugural Session on September 10, 1944, and for the names of the constitution drafting committee. Also, *West African Pilot*, October 3, 1944.

[49] Kolawole Balogun, *My Country Nigeria* (Lagos: 1955), p. 29.

[50] The Nigerian Union of Young Democrats was organized in 1938 by professional and "middle class" supporters of the Democratic Party who were dissatisfied with the accommodationist and parochial outlook of its old guard leadership. Its first President was Chief Ayo Williams, a barrister and former leader of the Union of Young Nigerians. Azikiwe, *The Development of Political Parties in Nigeria*, p. 6; *supra*, p. 48, n. 20.

[51] Among them were about 60 tribal unions representing Ibo, Yoruba, Edo, Efik and other Southern Nigerian Nationalities, but only the Tiv Progresssive Union from the North. Coleman has noted the failure of trade unions to affiliate at this stage, owing possibly to conservatism of the leadership or government pressure (*op.cit.*, p. 265); only two are listed by the *Pilot*, but one is the Trades Union Congress of Nigeria, a central body which claimed 86 affiliates. A comprehensive list of 105 member-unions of the NCNC in 1945 was published in *African Affairs*, Vol. 44, No. 17 (October 1945), p. 165.

[52] *The Constitution of the National Council of Nigeria and the Cameroons* (Lagos: 1945).

[53] Dennis Austin has drawn attention to the inner contradiction of British

58

Lord Milverton), the Governor of Nigeria, submitted constitutional proposals, which fell far short of nationalist expectations, to the Nigerian Legislative Council. Their content reflected a dilemma in British colonial thought which has been analyzed incisively by James Coleman.[54] The "Richards Constitution" established a Legislature in each of three regions, based on elections from the undemocratic organs of local authority known as the Native Administrations. The regional legislatures, in turn, sent representatives to a central legislative council. In short, the official planners linked their concessions in the sphere of representation to their interest in preserving the authoritarian system of indirect rule.[55] Nigerian nationalists, including members of the NCNC and the Nigerian Youth Movement, demanded elective representation and responsible government, with the participation of African ministers; but Youth Movement leaders were more conciliatory,[56] and disinclined to support the militant tactics of their political opponent, Azikiwe, and his party.

Fortunately for the militants, the same session of the Legislative Council which approved the objectionable constitution enacted four ordinances, respecting land, minerals, and the position of chiefs, which were easily if unfairly depicted as inimical to the interests of the indigenous people and contrary to traditional laws and customs. The NCNC urged all chiefs, elders, local councillors, and members of Native Administrations to protest the implementation of the "obnoxious ordinances"; simultaneously it initiated a campaign throughout

---

colonial policy in West Africa: "There was always a hidden conflict, a constitutional tug-of-war, between Indirect Rule—which tended to accentuate differences within and between Regions—and the developing system of Crown Colony Government—which, in the reforms of 1922-1954, had to reconcile such conflicts at the centre." *West Africa and the Commonwealth* (London: Penguin Books, 1957), p. 82. Coleman concluded his study of nationalism in Nigeria with the observation that "Nigerian nationalists forced a change [in] the general assumption underlying British policy . . . that British control would endure for a long time." *Op.cit.*, p. 409. David Apter offered another interpretation from the perspective of functional analysis: "One of the important contributions of indirect rule was the creation of this marginal group [of nationalistic Gold Coast Africans]. By failing to turn over substantive authority to these newly created segments of the population in advance of their expectations, and by allowing them to coalesce into an effectively organized national organization, indirect rule created an awareness of national membership which overrode the limits of local traditional affiliation." *The Gold Coast in Transition* (Princeton: Princeton University Press, 1955), p. 275.

[54] Coleman, *op.cit.*, pp. 271-284.

[55] A revealing exposition of official thought is Sir Bernard Bourdillon, "Nigeria's New Constitution," *United Empire*, XXXVII (March-April 1946), pp. 76-80.

[56] Coleman, *op.cit.*, p. 281; one feature at least of the Richards Constitution, namely regionalization, was approved by most of the N.Y.M. leadership. *Ibid.*, pp. 277, 465 n. 10.

Southern Nigeria for the public repudiation of those African members of the Legislative Council who had voted in favor of the ordinances and the Constitution. A decision was taken by NCNC leaders to tour the entire country in order to obtain mandates from the chiefs and people for a delegation that would present the nationalist case to the Colonial Secretary in London.[57] In June 1945, nationalist agitation erupted on a new front when seventeen trade unions, representing 30,000 public employees, decided to strike for higher wages and allowances required by the rising cost of living.[58] Azikiwe's press gave full support to the striking workers in the face of a threatened ban on publication.[59] In the eighteenth day of the strike, "Azikiwe's two Lagos dailies, *West African Pilot* and *Daily Comet* were banned [for 37 days] by the government for misrepresenting facts relating to the general strike. . . . A week later Azikiwe wrote his 'last testament' and then fled to Onitsha, where he went into hiding."[60] It was alleged by his supporters and widely believed that government officials had planned to assassinate him. These allegations were denied vehemently by officials, and Azikiwe's political opponents charged him with the deliberate perpetration of a "colossal falsehood." Yet the incident gave an enormous boost to his stature as a national hero, evoking the sympathy of thousands in Nigeria and many persons abroad.

In April 1946, the NCNC pan-Nigeria tour was begun under the

[57] Dr. Azikiwe has disclosed that proposals for the pan-Nigeria tour originated with a recommendation from leaders of the Nigerian Youth Movement in October 1944. *The Development of Political Parties in Nigeria*, p. 12.

[58] Coleman, *op.cit.*, pp. 258-259; the strike lasted 37 days and resulted in the appointment of a commission of inquiry. *Enquiry into the Cost of Living and the Control of the Cost of Living in the Colony and Protectorate of Nigeria*, Col. No. 204 (London: 1946), pp. 9-10. See also the tabulation of economic events in *African Affairs*, Vol. 44 (October 1945), pp. 139-141.

[59] Under an Emergency Powers Act the Governor was empowered to prohibit any publication in Nigeria and to prosecute editors and proprietors. Upon the receipt of warnings the *Pilot*, on successive days, published blank editorial columns on its front page with maxims and quotations on freedom of the press inserted. Editorial columns on inside pages were left blank. Thus on July 8, Zik's personal column, "Inside Stuff," entitled "If I were Governor of Nigeria," began: "From September, 1939, to December, 1944, the cost of living had increased with no corresponding increase in wages; I would make an analysis and recommendations as follows:" (blank spaces followed).

[60] Coleman, *op.cit.*, pp. 285ff; Azikiwe, *Suppression of the Press in British West Africa* (Onitsha: 1946); *Assassination Story: True or False* (Onitsha: 1946). On August 16, 1945, the *Pilot* reappeared with a "Resurrection Edition" (after a 37-day ban) and on August 21 Zik began a series of fictitious tales entitled, "Fugitive from an Assassin's Bullet." On September 3rd he began a series entitled, "History of the General Strike," which ran intermittently for a period of over three months. See also *Nigeria Legislative Council, Debates,* March 18, 1946, p. 21.

leadership of Herbert Macaulay, Nnamdi Azikiwe, and Michael Imoudu, President of the Railway Workers' Union and a principal leader of the 1945 general strike.[61] In the third week, while the touring party was in Kano, Macaulay fell ill and returned to Lagos where he died at the age of 82. His last words were:

"Tell the National Council delegates to halt wherever they are for four days for Macaulay and then carry on.

"Tell Oged [his son] to keep the flag flying."[62]

The NCNC team toured Nigeria for eight months, obtaining written mandates from 153 Nigerian communities (24 in the North, 48 in the West, and 81 in the East, in addition to the endorsement of the *Oba* of Lagos), and raising some £13,500. In order to refute allegations by the Governor to the effect that the NCNC did not truly represent the Nigerian people, members of the delegation stood for the three elective Lagos seats in the Legislative Council on the platform of the National Council's local affiliate, the Nigerian National Democratic Party (NNDP); they were returned with overwhelming majorities.[63] These three elected councillors personified the social basis of the NCNC/NNDP in Lagos: Nnamdi Azikiwe, who was backed solidly by non-Yoruba elements and was enormously popular among the Yorubas; Prince Adeleke Adedoyin, who was the son of an important Ijebu Yoruba chief, a barrister, and president of the Nigerian Union of Young Democrats; Dr. Abu Bakry Ibiyinka

[61] See N. Azikiwe, *The Development of Political Parties in Nigeria*, pp. 14-15. Michael Artokhaimien Omiunus Imoudu became President of the Railway Workers' Union in 1940 and led a successful campaign for increases in the cost of living allowance, which were granted in 1942. Subsequently the Government invoked the Emergency Defence Regulations against Imoudu and deported him from Lagos to his native Auchi, Benin Province, as a potential threat to the public safety. He was released in time to play a leading part in the general strike. See P. I. Omo-Ananigie, *The Life History of M. A. O. Imoudu* (Lagos: 1957).

[62] *West African Pilot*, May 8, 1946; Herbert Macaulay's funeral was an event of civic mourning in Lagos. The market women closed their stalls for two days as a token of respect; Nnamdi Azikiwe delivered the principal oration. Thomas, *op.cit.*, pp. 68f, 77ff. In his last years, Macaulay served the cause of nationalism with unsurpassed zeal. From June 1944 until his death he worked in nearly perfect harmony with his "political son," Azikiwe, and played a leading role in the campaign against the Richards Constitution and in behalf of the 1945 strikers. At the same time he fought as vigorously as ever for his old ally, the Lagos Market Women's Guild, during the latter's protest against regulation. When Azikiwe began his career in Lagos he looked upon the NNDP as an ideologically destitute electoral machine and supported the N.Y.M. Subsequently he perceived that its mass membership could be elevated to serve the cause of Nigerian freedom, an object to which Macaulay was wholly dedicated.

[63] A reduction of the income qualification from £100 to £50 enabled many more persons to vote than heretofore and each of the successful candidates polled well above 3,000 votes, while the sole opposing candidate polled a mere 308.

Olorun-Nimbe, who was a Lagos Yoruba, Muslim, medical practitioner, and leader of the Lagos Ratepayers Association.

At a post-election mass meeting of the NNDP, the elected councillors were instructed to boycott the Legislative Council until such time as the Constitution had been amended to provide for responsible government.[64] Seven delegates were chosen to put the case of the NCNC to the Colonial Secretary in London: Chief Nyong Essien (Ibibio), member of the Legislative Council, later first President of the Eastern House of Chiefs; Malam (later Zanna) Bukar Dipcharima (Kanuri), a businessman, later Federal Minister of Commerce and Industry; Mrs. Funmilayo Ransome-Kuti (Yoruba), a teacher, the founder and President of the Nigerian Women's Union; Paul M. Kale of the Cameroons (Bakweri), an educator; and the three elected members of the Legislative Council. Prior to their departure, Azikiwe was elected to succeed Macaulay as President of the NCNC;[65] enroute to London, he visited Storer College, West Virginia, which conferred a D.Litt. on its distinguished alumnus, as had Lincoln University, *in absentia,* the previous year.

In London, the NCNC delegates' request for immediate constitutional reform was denied by the Secretary of State for the Colonies who "advised them to return to Nigeria and cooperate in working

[64] The boycott resolution was moved by the chairman, Chief Amodu Tijani, the *Oluwa* of the celebrated Apapa land case. It was seconded by Chief Olayemi Aluko *Onikoyi* and supported by various chiefs, Imams, and leaders of the Market Women's Guild. An enumeration of the speakers and important people reported present indicates the extent to which the NNDP was based solidly on the social structure of the Lagos indigenous community. The speakers were well-known political personalities: Chief Yesufu Oniru, Chief Ayo Ajala of the Young Democrats, J. H. Willoughby, a foundation member of the NNDP, Madam Ogundimu of the Market Women's Guild, Miss Aduni Oluwole, Oged Macaulay, A. J. Marhino and the three elected members. The White Cap Chiefs present were *Oluwa, Onikoyi, Oniru, Eletu, Washe, Olumegbon, Onitolo, Shashore* and *Oloto*; Imams present included Murano, Ledija, Alphayat, and Sadiku. *West African Pilot*, March 19 and 21, 1947.

[65] In his Presidential address, he stated: "I want you to make it plain to me that you are ready for the type of militant leadership I envisage—a leadership that will not accept the crumbs of imperialism in order to compromise issues. . . . Today, I might be with you, but that is no guarantee that I would not be prepared to suffer heavy blows from the enemy; you must be prepared to make sacrifices in order to guarantee for Nigeria a nobler heritage . . . as from today, under my leadership, you must be prepared for the worst." Nnamdi Azikiwe, "Before Us Lies the Open Grave," a Presidential address, May 7, 1947. (Printed as a pamphlet.) Other officers of the NCNC were elected as follows: Magnus A. O. Williams, Vice-President; A. K. Blankson, Vice-President; Adeleke Adedoyin, General Secretary; Dr. A. B. Olorun-Nimbe, General Treasurer; Ogedengbe Macaulay, Assistant Secretary; M. C. K. Ajuluchuku, Assistant Secretary; Oyesile Omage and Mr. Ojokwei, Auditors; and F. U. Anyiam, Financial Secretary. *West African Pilot*, May 8 and 13, 1947.

the Constitution which they had discredited."[66] Furthermore, there was disharmony among the delegates themselves involving personality conflicts and differences of opinion.[67] Early in 1948, the NCNC rescinded its boycott of the Legislative Council and in April the first National Assembly of the NCNC, now designated the first Annual Convention, was held at Kaduna. The memorandum on constitutional reform which had been submitted to the Secretary of State for the Colonies was adopted, with amendments, by the Assembly as the "NCNC Freedom Charter." Dr. Azikiwe was elected Federal President for a three-year term and given the power to appoint all other officers of the National Council.[68] In his address to the Assembly,

[66] Azikiwe, *The Development of Political Parties in Nigeria*, p. 15; see the "Memorandum Submitted by the Delegation of the National Council of Nigeria and the Cameroons to the Secretary of State for the Colonies on the 11th August, 1947." (Mimeographed.) It was the view of the NCNC that the Secretary of State for the Colonies "treated our National Delegates and the national cause we sent them to present, in a most summary, unpleasant, unfavourable and disappointing manner which we regard as a great insult to our entire Nation." Quoted by N. Azikiwe in his presidential address to the Kaduna National Assembly of the NCNC. *West African Pilot*, April 7, 1948.

[67] Adeleke Adedoyin and Dr. Olorun-Nimbe contend that the memorandum and constitutional proposals submitted to the Colonial Secretary were drafted by Azikiwe alone, a charge which assumes credibility in the light of its similarity to other documents, e.g., the *Political Blueprint of Nigeria*, and various press commentaries. Possibly, the memorandum went further than members of the delegation had anticipated in setting forth a program for full independence in fifteen years. Upon their return to Nigeria, the rift between Azikiwe and the two other Lagos elected members became more pronounced; Adedoyin and Olorun-Nimbe, General Secretary and Treasurer of the NCNC respectively, were actually expelled along with the Vice-President, M. A. O. Williams, at the First Annual Assembly in April 1948. But Adedoyin and Olorun-Nimbe were the standard bearers of the party in Lagos and their expulsions were neither permanent nor effective. Press critics alleged that the funds of the delegation were not handled properly, but this was never proved, and seems not to have been the case. Yet Lord Hailey, in a cursory review of the activities of the NCNC, remarked with condescension:
"It attained in 1947 and 1948 a position far greater than that hitherto reached by any political association in Nigeria, but has since then lost some of its influence, for a variety of causes, among which is the inevitable charge of misuse of funds by some of its leaders." *Native Administration in the British African Territories, III* (London: H.M.S.O., 1951) p. 22. There is not a shred of evidence adduced to support this aspersion although it reflects scandalously on all the members of the delegation, all of whom are eminent people in Nigerian public life today.

[68] The Federal Cabinet of the NCNC chosen by Dr. Azikiwe following the Kaduna National Assembly of April 1948 was as follows:
Nnamdi Azikiwe, elected Federal President; Ibo, Onitsha, Protestant, journalist.
O. N. Ojugun, elected Federal Auditor; manager of the African Continental Bank.
Eyo Ita, Vice-President; Efik, Calabar, Protestant, educator.
F. O. Blaize, Vice-President.
A. K. Blankson, Vice-President; Ghanaian, Protestant, journalist.
Malam Sa'adu Zungur, Federal Secretary, Bauchi Habe, Muslim, Government dispenser and Koranic scholar.

Dr. Azikiwe referred to the NCNC as a party, but press reports indicate that the members of the National Assembly and their supporters viewed the NCNC as an alternative government, or dual state.[69] However the Freedom Chapter was never fully implemented by the NCNC for its own organization; as James Coleman observed, from 1948-1951 the NCNC "as an organization, was virtually moribund."[70] It languished while the colonial government undertook an extensive program of constitutional review, and the nationalist initiative was assumed by ethnic group associations and radical factions that were incapable of sustained political action.

THE IBO AND YORUBA NATIONALITY MOVEMENTS

Various studies have drawn attention to the social and political importance of voluntary associations based on kinship or territorial affinity—e.g., clan, village group, district, or tribe—in the new towns of West Africa.[71] Settlers in these burgeoning communities

---

E. D. A. Ojaleye, Federal Treasurer.

Oged Macaulay, Field Secretary; Lagos Yoruba, member of the Zikist Movement.

F. O. Coker, Publicity Secretary; Yoruba, Labor unionist.

Ladipo Odunsi, Legal Adviser; Yoruba, barrister.

Arthur Prest, Legal Adviser; Warri, Itsekeri, barrister.

Jaja A. Wachuku, Legal Adviser, Aba/Ngwa, Ibo, barrister.

Luke Emejulu, Assistant Federal Secretary.

Nduka Eze, Assistant Publicity Secretary; Asaba, Ibo, trade unionist, member of the Zikist Movement.

Assistant Field Secretaries:

L. A. Namme, Cameroons.

D. O. E. Essessien, East.

Adenipekun Adegbola, West.

Mal. S. G. A. Zukogi, North, Nupe, member of the Northern Elements Progressive Association.

S. A. George, Permanent Under-Secretary; Cameroons.

Mal. H. R. Abdallah, Permanent Under-Treasurer; Igbirra, member of the Zikist Movement.

M. A. O. Imoudu, Edo, Auchi, trade unionist.

Cultural nationalities as follows:

Six Yoruba, five Ibo, three Edo, two Bakweri, one Hausa, one Ibibio, one Nupe, one Efik, one Itsekeri, one Igbirra. *West African Pilot*, June 19, 1948.

[69] Thus the *West African Pilot* referred to the NCNC as "a Cabinet of the Commonwealth . . . fully empowered to implement the Freedom Charter." The Charter was praised for its recognition of cultural and linguistic sections of the nation which have historic similarities and would be permitted to enjoy limited autonomy in government. Provision was made for villages and towns to elect representatives to annual assemblies. Such are "the pillars on which our New Nigeria is speedily arising." *West African Pilot*, April 17, 1948.

[70] Coleman, *op.cit.*, p. 295.

[71] See I. Wallerstein, "Ethnicity and National Integration in West Africa," *Cahiers D'Etudes Africaines*, No. 3 (October 1960), pp. 129-139. The nature of

include men and women of entrepreneurial, professional, and managerial status in addition to clerical and manual workers. Their values and social perspectives are largely non-traditional, and ethnic group associations or "tribal unions" of their creation were among the principal centers of enlightenment and political ferment in Nigeria during the growth of nationalism. Many such urban groups maintain affiliations with parent bodies in the home towns and villages of their members. These organizational connections, as Thomas Hodgkin remarked before the advent of independence, "provide a network of communications, entirely under African control, through which ideas, information and directives can be diffused from the great towns to the bush."[72] Among the major Nigerian ethnic groups, only the Hausa do not as a rule form tribal unions, which may reflect the primacy of Islam as an integrative factor in Hausa society. The highest level of ethnic group organization in Nigeria is the pan-tribal or nationality association which unifies ethnic groups on the basis of their widest cultural and linguistic affinities. All such associations are devoted to educational advancement; a few of them have become highly politicized.

The first pan-tribal or nationality association was formed in 1928 by prominent representatives of the Ibibio-speaking people of the Eastern provinces, mainly for the purpose of educational advancement. During the 1930's, all-Ibo unions were formed by the members of Ibo clan and tribal unions in certain towns, notably Port Harcourt and Lagos. The Ibo Union of Lagos, organized in 1934, was a pillar of strength for the NCNC at the time of that party's inauguration in 1944; in that year, leaders of the Lagos Ibo Union organized an Ibo Federal Union, encompassing local Ibo associations throughout Nigeria.[73] In 1945, a parallel movement for the unity of the Yoruba people was initiated by a group of students in London.

Two salient factors which appear to have motivated the movement for pan-Yoruba unity were the desire of enlightened leaders of the Yoruba people to overcome their sectional antagonisms which date

---

kinship and tribal associations in Nigeria is discussed by Coleman, *op.cit.*, pp. 213-216; other literature is cited at *ibid.*, p. 459, n. 27.

[72] Thomas Hodgkin, *Nationalism in Colonial Africa* (London: Frederick Muller, 1956), p. 87.

[73] See Coleman, *op.cit.*, pp. 340-341. In June 1944, the Lagos Ibo Union petitioned the Governor for an increase of Ibo representation in the Legislative Council from one member to six, on the ground that a single member for four million inhabitants of the Ibo Division was a gross example of malapportionment. *West African Pilot*, June 19, 1944. The decision to form the Ibo Federal Union was taken at about this time.

from the inter-tribal wars of the 19th century and their desire to reform the authoritarian system of government which had been imposed on the Yoruba states by the British following the amalgamation of Northern and Southern Nigeria in 1914. Because the principal Yoruba chiefs ruled over large traditional states, British administrators thought it would be feasible to apply the principles of Native Administration, which had been evolved in the Northern Provinces, to the Yoruba states. But the traditional system of Yoruba government was unlike that of the Fulani emirates. The government of a Yoruba state was genuinely conciliar, with a high degree of participation by representatives of the lineages; in short it was incompatible with the appointment of any chief as a "Sole Native Authority" after the fashion of the North. The widespread discontent produced by this autocratic innovation did not end with the abolition of the Northern style in the late 1930's, since certain chiefs were reluctant to amend their unorthodox arbitrary habits. However, a new class of democratically-minded reformers, including teachers, professional men, businessmen, and educated persons generally, were anxious to restore the traditional balance between chiefs and their communities by affirming the right of the people to depose autocratic chiefs and by educating the chiefs themselves in the ways of traditional and modern democracy. By and large, the social horizon of this new class was non-parochial, i.e., non-local, and its leading representatives were determined for political, cultural, and economic reasons to overcome the historic antipathies of the Yoruba tribes.

The motivating personality of the pan-Yoruba movement was Obafemi Awolowo, an Ijebu Yoruba, born in 1909 at Ikenne, Ijebu-Remo Division. His father, an ardent Christian, was a farmer and a sawyer of moderate means who died when the lad was eleven. He attended various denominational schools and was employed as a school teacher in Abeokuta for two years. Subsequently, he qualified as a shorthand typist; he served as the clerk of Wesley College, Ibadan, and as a correspondent for the British-owned *Nigerian Daily Times*. In keeping with his determination to study law, he undertook several business ventures—money-lending, public letter-writing, taxi proprietorship, produce-buying and motor transport —which failed to produce the necessary funds. Yet he never deviated from the path of self-improvement and in 1939, at the age of thirty, he passed a matriculation examination for the University of London and began correspondence studies in Nigeria for the Bachelor of Commerce degree which he completed successfully. Meanwhile, he became secretary of the Nigerian Motor Transport

66

Union and an influential member of other important associations —namely, the Nigerian Produce Traders' Association, the Trades Union Congress of Nigeria, and the Nigerian Youth Movement, which he served as Western provincial secretary.[74] At length, his efforts as a food contractor for the army and the generosity of his friends produced the wherewithal to finance legal training in England, which he commenced in 1944.

The following year he wrote a critical book on the administrative policies of the British in Nigeria in which he advocated, among other things, the right of ethnic nationalities to "home rule," the introduction of a federal system of government in order to unite several states that should be founded on the principle of ethnic affinity, and the restoration or innovation of popular control over the institution of chieftaincy. Cogently he argued that pan-tribal unity was a necessary condition for political advance: "The barriers of tribalism and clannishness within each ethnical unit," he wrote, "must be totally destroyed."[75] In his view, pan-tribal unity presupposed the leadership of the Westernized elite: "The educated minority in each ethnical group are the people who are qualified by natural rights to lead their fellow nationals into higher political development. Unless they desire a change it would be futile to impose it upon their group."[76]

In 1945, Mr. Awolowo and several others inaugurated a pan-Yoruba cultural society in London, called the *Egbe Omo Oduduwa* (Society of the Descendants of *Oduduwa*—the culture hero and mythical progenitor of the Yoruba people).[77] Mr. Awolowo returned

[74] Chief Awolowo's contribution to the development of the N.Y.M. has been disclosed by James S. Coleman, *op.cit.*, pp. 228, 261-262. See also O. Awolowo, *Awo*, pp. 152-159.

[75] Obafemi Awolowo, *Path to Nigerian Freedom* (London: Faber, 1947), p. 35.

[76] *Ibid.*, p. 64.

[77] This writer has identified the original founders of the Egbe Omo Oduduwa in London in 1945 as Dr. Oni Akerele, President (a medical practitioner), Obafemi Awolowo, Secretary, A. B. Oyediran (later Secretary to the Nigerian Commissioner in the U.K. for student affairs and Chief of the Nigerian Liaison Office in Washington, D.C.), Abiodun Akerele (later Balogun of Oyo and a barrister, in partnership with Mr. Awolowo), Mr. Akin Reis, S. O. Biobaku (later Secretary to the Executive Council of the Western Region and Vice-Principal of the University of Ife, Victor Munis (later a barrister), C. O. Taiwo (later Principal, Edo College, Benin City, and Inspector of Education, Western Region). In addition, Akintola Williams (later a chartered accountant) and Ayotunde Rosiji (later a barrister and Federal Minister of Health in the National Government of 1957-1959) are listed by Chief Awolowo among the founders of the *Egbe Omo Oduduwa* in London. *Awo*, p. 168.
The society lapsed when Mr. Awolowo returned to Nigeria in 1946 but it was revived by students in London in 1947, including S. L. Akintola (later a barrister, Federal Minister, and Premier of the West), Ayo Ogunsheye (later Director of Extra-Mural Studies, University College, Ibadan), Ayo Okusaga (later a barrister and Regional Minister), and Dr. Akerele, the first President.

to Nigeria in 1946 as a barrister; he established a highly successful law practice at Ibadan, and assumed a leading role in the movement for Yoruba unity. His activities in that regard were generally approved by the Yoruba professional and political elite of Lagos, many of whom were deeply troubled by the meteoric rise of Azikiwe, by the latter's unprecedented popularity among politically conscious Nigerians, and by the growing militancy of the Ibo settler community of Lagos which supported its "favorite son" to a man. In February 1948, the *Egbe Omo Oduduwa* was advertised as a non-political, cultural organization for men and women of Yoruba nationality, comparable to the Ibo Federal Union.[78] In June a conference of Yoruba notables met at Ife, "the cradle of all Yorubas," to inaugurate the society formally. Sir Adeyemo Alakija, a distinguished barrister, former President of the Nigerian Youth Movement, former member of the Legislative Council, and an incumbent member of the Governor's Executive Council, was elected President of the *Egbe Omo Oduduwa*; Mr. Awolowo was chosen General Secretary; most of the officers and executive members were professional and businessmen resident at Lagos.[79] A constitution was adopted setting forth nine aims and objects which attest to the progressive, nationalistic, and non-traditional implications of Yoruba pan-tribalism.[80]

[78] "A Statement to the Nation" by Ajani Olujare, pro-tem Administrative Secretary of the *Egbe Omo Oduduwa, West African Pilot*, February 14, 1948.

[79] The inaugural officers of the *Egbe Omo Oduduwa* were as follows:

Sir Adeyemo Alakija, (Brazilian-Yoruba) President; Vice-Presidents: Yekini Ojikutu (Lagos, businessman), S. A. Akinfenwa (Ibadan, businessman), I. O. Ransome-Kuti (Abeokuta, educator), Alhaji Shoye (Ibebu-Ode, businessman), Dure Adefarakan (Ife), Chief Otun Akinyede (Ondo), S. O. Gbadamosi (Ikorodu, businessman), Dr. Akinola Maja (Lagos, medical practitioner and banker); Dr. K. A. Abayomi (Lagos, medical practitioner), Treasurer; Obafemi Awolowo (Ijebu-Remo, barrister), General Secretary; Legal Advisers: Bode Thomas (Oyo, barrister) and H. O. Davies (Ekiti and Oyo, barrister). In addition there were 44 executive members; of the 35 identified positively by the writer, 23 were resident at Lagos and 9 at Ibadan. Records of the *Egbe Omo Oduduwa*, Ibadan.

[80] The aims and objects of the *Egbe Omo Oduduwa* as set forth in its constitution are as follows:

AIMS AND OBJECTS

(A) Yorubaland

(i) "To study fully its educational problems; to plan for the improvement of educational facilities both in content and extent, to encourage in every way possible especially by means of Scholarship awards by the Society, the pursuit of secondary and university education by Yoruba boys and girls, to explore the means of introducing, and as soon as possible to introduce, or cause to be introduced, mass and compulsory education among the people of Yorubaland, and to foster the study of Yoruba Language culture and history.

(ii) "To combat the disintegrating forces of tribalism, to stamp out discrimination among the Yorubas, *inter se* and against minorities. To unite the various clans and

Although the *Egbe Omo Oduduwa* did profess to be neutral in party politics, it was viewed from the first by partisans of the NCNC as an overt political threat, and a vigorous campaign to discredit the *Egbe* was conducted in the columns of the *West African Pilot*.[81] In mid-June 1948, Yoruba supporters of Azikiwe and the NCNC formed a Yoruba Federal Union in an undisguised attempt to counter the *Egbe*'s appeal.[82] *Egbe* spokesmen responded with allegations to

tribes in Yorubaland and generally create and actively foster the idea of a single nationalism throughout Yorubaland.

(iii) "To recognize and maintain the monarchical and other similar institutions of Yorubaland, to plan for their complete enlightenment and democratisation, to acknowledge the leadership of Yoruba Obas and to establish a firm basis of entire cooperation between the Yoruba people and their Obas in the political, economic and social affairs of Yorubaland.

(iv) "To study fully its political problems, to plan for the rapid development of its political institutions, and to accelerate the emergence of a virile modernized and efficient Yoruba state with its own individuality w/in the Federal State of Nigeria.

(v) "To study its economic resources, to ascertain its economic potentialities, and advise as to the wisest utilisation of its wealth, so as to ensure abundance and prosperity for its people.

(vi) "To promote the social Welfare of Yorubaland, combat the evils of superstition and ignorance, spread the knowledge of medical relief and stimulate the provision of hospitals, maternity homes and suchlike amenities.

(B) Nigeria

(i) "To cooperate in the fullest manner with the other regions to see that the Aims and Objects set out in (A) in so far as they are applicable to such regions are achieved throughout the whole country.

(ii) "To encourage and aid in every way possible the creation and continuance of associations similar to the Society, among the other ethnical groups in Nigeria.

(iii) "To strive earnestly to cooperate with existing ethnical and regional associations and such as may exist hereafter, in matters of common interest to all Nigerians, so as thereby to attain unity in federation."

[81] See, for example, the articles by Oged Macaulay, *West African Pilot*, February 12, 1948, and June 30, 1948. At first the *Egbe* eschewed overt political action, and its main initial project, stipulated in its constitution, was the promotion of an Endowment Fund to finance the higher education of "Oduduwa scholars." See *Egbe Omo Oduduwa, Monthly Bulletin*, Vol. I, No. 2 (November 1948), and subsequent editions which published the names of individuals who made promises to the Endowment Fund, the amounts promised and the contributions actually made. However, the *Monthly Bulletin* also featured sharp criticisms of Dr. Azikiwe and the NCNC. In 1949 the London branch of the *Egbe* is reported to have passed a resolution for neutrality in national politics, an idea that was never seriously contemplated by the founders of the society. In retrospect it appears certain that the initial object of the *Egbe* was political. At the 10th Annual Conference, Oshogbo, 1957, Chief Awolowo is reported to have said that "the *Egbe* was formed ten years ago to end the distrust and misunderstanding between Yoruba Obas and their subjects. Another reason was to save the Yoruba people from the 'destructive role' played by Dr. Nnamdi Azikiwe on his return to Nigeria in 1937." *Daily Times*, November 9, 1957.

[82] *West African Pilot*, June 14, 1948. J. Olumide Lucas was chairman of the first meeting and A. A. Olowu was Secretary; others mentioned included Oged Macaulay and S. D. Ogunbiyi.

the effect that the Yoruba Federal Union was an Ibo-dominated front group, designed specifically to keep the Yorubas divided politically while the Ibos were united in support of Azikiwe.[83] Throughout July and during most of August, the rival newspapers (the *West African Pilot* and the *Daily Service*) published diatribes of unprecedented virulence with overtones that were disturbingly tribalistic.[84] Ibo and Yoruba groups in Lagos held mass meetings that were notorious for the use of strong language but there were no actual breaches of the peace.

In December 1948, a pan-Ibo conference was held at Port Harcourt "to organize the Ibo linguistic group into a political unit in accordance with the NCNC Freedom Charter."[85] This conference produced a new association, the Ibo State Union, the membership of which was open to the clans and towns of Iboland. The founders of the Ibo State Union were no less politically motivated than were the organizers of the *Egbe Omo Oduduwa*; at least nine of the thirteen inaugural members of the Union's Provisional Committee rose to high office in the NCNC and seven of them have attained ministerial rank in the Eastern, Central, or federal governments.[86] Nnamdi Azikiwe was

[83] *Daily Service*, June 14 and 17, 1948.

[84] Azikiwe wrote a series of *ad hominem* attacks on the leaders of the *Egbe*, the Youth Movement, and his former colleagues, Adeleke Adedoyin and Olorun-Nimbe, entitled inoffensively "Political Reminiscences, 1938-48." Notwithstanding their highly partisan coloration, these columns by Azikiwe displayed his unsurpassed knowledge of Lagos politics and his ingenuity in pressing that knowledge to an advantage. In mid-August, the *West African Pilot* (August 18, 1948) announced that Azikiwe had agreed to discontinue publication of his "Reminiscences" in deference to pleas from leaders of the Muslim community.

[85] *West African Pilot*, January 4, 1949. The Freedom Charter provided for the organization of Nigeria into states based on cultural and linguistic affinity, and the founders of the Ibo State Union did anticipate the future organization of the Ibo country as a member state of the Commonwealth of Nigeria. *Ibid.*, January 5, 1949.

[86] The members of the Provisional Committee of the Ibo State Union, elected December 1948, were as follows:

President, Nnamdi Azikiwe (President of the NCNC, later Premier of the East and Governor-General of Nigeria); Deputy President, A. C. Nwapa (later Central Minister of Commerce); First Vice-President, R. A. Njoku (later Federal Minister and Second Vice-President of the NCNC); Second Vice-President, M. O. Ajegbo (later Attorney General Eastern Region); Third Vice-President, H. U. Kaine (later a Federal Judge); Principal Secretary, J. A. Wachuku (later Chief Whip and Secretary of NCNC Parliamentary Parties, Speaker of the Federal House of Representatives and Federal Minister); Permanent Undersecretary, B. O. N. Eluwa (later an executive with the Nigerian Broadcasting Corporation); Treasurer, M. I. Onwuka; Political Adviser, Nwafor Orizu (later a member of the Eastern House of Chiefs and Federal Senator); Economic Adviser, Mbonu Ojike, (later a minister in the Eastern Region and Second Vice-President of the NCNC); Cultural Adviser, K. O. Mbadiwe (later Second Vice-President of the NCNC

elected to the presidency of the Union, an office that appears to have been thrust upon him by the Ibo leaders.[87] In time his occupancy of the top position in the Ibo State Union proved to be a source of acute embarrassment to the NCNC as it was cited by opponents to substantiate the allegation that the NCNC was "Ibo-dominated."

It should not be inferred that Ibo-Yoruba friction in 1948 fractured the bi-national (Ibo-Yoruba) foundation of the NCNC in Lagos. Hostility and verbal aggression was confined mainly to the level of the educated and politically astute elite groups of the rival NCNC and N.Y.M. Nearly all of the Yoruba indigenes of Lagos, including their customary and religious leaders (the White Cap Chiefs, Imams, and Ratibis)[88] who had been loyal to Herbert Macaulay, followed his "political son," Nnamdi Azikiwe. When Azikiwe quarrelled with his Yoruba lieutenants in the Democratic Party, the Chiefs, Imams, and elders of Lagos always counselled reconciliation.[89] It was not until 1949, with the accession of Adeniji Adele as *Oba* of Lagos, that the ties between the NCNC/NNDP and the indigenous community were weakened. Oba Adele II, a former civil servant, was a supporter of the Nigerian Youth Movement, a member of the *Egbe Omo Oduduwa*, and an advocate of pan-Yoruba unity. The NNDP tried in vain to prevent his installation,[90] and there is good reason to believe that the subsequent defection of the majority of the Lagos

---

and a Federal Minister) ; Medical Adviser, F. A. Ibiam (medical practitioner, later principal of Hope Waddell Training Institute, Chairman of the University College, Ibadan, and Governor of Eastern Nigeria) ; Educational Adviser, E. I. Oli (later a minister in the Eastern Regional Government). *West African Pilot*, January 4, 1949.

[87] The writer reached this conclusion as a result of interviews with several knowledgeable persons.

[88] Each of the major divisions of the Muslim community of Lagos has its Imam; Imam Ratibis are district prayer leaders. See note 18 (*supra*, p. 46) on the White Cap Chiefs.

[89] Thus, in August 1948 it was reported that the Chief Imam, Ahmed Tijani Ibrahim, and thirty Ratibis met with Azikiwe urging him to reach a settlement with Prince Adeleke Adedoyin and Dr. A. B. Olorun-Nimbe. *West African Pilot*, August 18, 1948.

[90] It has been noted above that Herbert Macaulay virtually founded the NNDP upon the bedrock of the House of Docemo. Adele II was not a descendant of King Docemo and his installation was a setback for the NCNC/NNDP. For years the NNDP refused to acknowledge the legitimacy of Adele's succession and resorted to legal proceedings in an attempt to dispossess him of the traditional palace. Adele was defended by prominent barristers associated with the *Egbe Omo Oduduwa* and the Nigerian Youth Movement, including Sir Adeyemo Alakija, first President of the *Egbe*, H. O. Davies, Bode Thomas, and F. R. A. Williams. His right to the *Iga* (traditional palace) was finally sustained by the Privy Council in 1957.

indigenes from the NCNC/NNDP, apparent by 1953, was largely attributable to Adele's efforts in behalf of the pan-Yoruba cause.

Throughout the Yoruba provinces, leading chiefs were persuaded to become patrons of the *Egbe Omo Oduduwa*. They embraced the *Egbe* either because they responded to its cultural appeal of pan-Yoruba unity, or because they were impressed by the political and economic power of the pan-tribal elite. Leaders of the *Egbe* began to mediate disputes among chiefs or between chiefs and their communities. Similarly, in Iboland (Eastern Nigeria) the Ibo State Union assumed the role of a conciliator and pacifier. Both associations were created by representatives of the new and rising class—lawyers, doctors, businessmen, civil servants, and certain far-sighted chiefs —who perceived that the locus of economic and political power was not local but regional and national.[91] Their values were fundamentally non-parochial, non-traditional, and nationalistic, and the pan-tribal associations of their creation signified an advance in social and political integration. Yet it was probably inevitable that the nationality movements would be politicized—indeed they were politically inspired—and for several years, cultural nationalism of a partisan nature threatened to engulf the nationalist ideal of Nigerian unity.

ZIKISM AND RADICALISM

The Zikists of 1946-1950 were the angry young men of postwar Nigeria. They were inspired by a patriotic idealism that could not be reconciled with the tribalistic and self-seeking tendencies of the middle-class nationalists to whom they looked for leadership. Their alternative to tribalism, regionalism, and gradualism was a militant program of positive action,[92] to which they gave the name "Zikism."

Zikism was the conception of A. A. Nwafor Orizu, a Nigerian student in the United States during World War II.[93] His book,

[91] See Richard L. Sklar, "The Contribution of Tribalism to Nationalism in Western Nigeria," *Journal of Human Relations*, Vol. 8 (Spring and Summer 1960), pp. 407-418. For valuable discussions of the "new middle class" in the Yoruba areas see Peter C. Lloyd, "Cocoa, Politics, and the Yoruba Middle Class," *West Africa*, January 17, 1953, p. 39, and "The Integration of the New Economic Classes into Local Government in Western Nigeria," *African Affairs*, Vol. 52, No. 209 (October 1953), pp. 327-334. See also Martin L. Kilson, "Nationalism and Social Classes in British West Africa," *The Journal of Politics* (May, 1958) pp. 368-387.

[92] On the strategy of Positive Action by nationalists in the Gold Coast (now Ghana), see George Padmore, *The Gold Coast Revolution* (London: Dobson, 1953), and his *Pan-Africanism or Communism* (London: Dobson, 1956), pp. 178-185; also Kwame Nkrumah, *Autobiography* (Edinburgh: Thomas Nelson, 1957), pp. 110-122.

[93] Prince A. A. Nwafor Orizu is the son of the *Obi* of Nnewi (Onitsha Division) in Iboland. He was one of twelve Nigerian students who went to the United

Without Bitterness, called for a modern awakening of the African people in the spirit of Azikiwe's earlier manifesto, *Renascent Africa.* In addition Orizu espoused the political utility of a revolutionary social myth: "Like Georges Sorel, I believe that human society must have an all-embracing myth that can arouse whole communities of men into action . . . however, the kind of myth I am thinking of need not be catastrophic or violent. . . . There is one social myth upon which Zikism should grow and spread its branches. That myth is *African Irredentism* . . . the redemption of Africa from social wreckage, political servitude, and economic impotency; it must also mean extricating Africa from ideological confusion, psychological immaturity, spiritual complacency, and mental stagnation."[94]

Orizu's specific social philosophy was non-dogmatic, embracing pragmatism, mild socialism, and liberal democracy. His choice of the term "Zikism" was not intended to create a personality cult around the figure of Azikiwe; the latter was merely an "exceptional character" whose life was a source of inspiration to others. "Zik," he explained, is derived from the "African name Azikiwe . . . which can be translated: 'The Youth is overwhelmingly indignant,' or 'The New Age is full of revenge.' . . . The man . . . is unmistakably the embodiment of a new thought—the propounder of a New African philosophy. That is why the author has chosen the word 'zikism' to represent the New Philosophy of the New Africa he has in mind. The author is but little concerned with the personality involved."[95]

The Zikist Movement was inaugurated in Lagos in February 1946; it was expanded by the adhesion of a Kano section in 1947 and soon became a nationwide association of radical youth, affiliated

---

States for higher studies in 1938 and one of three who published books on the subject of African Nationalism: A. A. Nwafor Orizu, *Without Bitterness, Western Nations in Post-War Africa* (N.Y.: Creative Age Press, 1944); Mbonu Ojike, *My Africa* (N.Y.: John Day, 1946) and *I Have Two Countries* (N.Y.: John Day, 1947); K. O. Mbadiwe, *British and Axis Aims in Africa* (New York: Malliet, 1942).

Orizu studied political theory at Lincoln and Harvard Universities. He returned to Nigeria in 1945 with a scheme to promote American education among Nigerian youth and formed the ill-starred American Council on African Education to provide scholarships. In 1948 he was among the founders of the Ibo State Union and in 1951 he was elected to the Eastern House of Assembly. In 1959 he was appointed as a special member of the Eastern House of Chiefs; subsequently he became a Federal Senator.

[94] Orizu, *op.cit.,* pp. 304-306.

[95] *Ibid.,* pp. 293, 297; the writer was also informed that Azikiwe is a construct of the Ibo words *Az* meaning "present generation" and *iwe* meaning "ire" or "frustration."

with the NCNC as a member-union.[96] In 1948 leaders of the Zikist Movement decided that a revolutionary political drive was required to stem the rising tide of tribalism and revitalize the NCNC. To that end the Central Committee of the Zikist Movement plotted an illegal action which they hoped would result in the imprisonment of Azikiwe. Then, they imagined, the nation would arise to positive, revolutionary action, the jails would overflow with political prisoners, and the government would be obliged to grant a more democratic constitution. This "revolutionary" program was initiated by Osita C. Agwuna, Deputy President of the Zikist Movement, who delivered an address on October 27, 1948, in the Tom Jones Memorial Hall, Lagos, entitled "A Call for Revolution." Agwuna did not advocate violence, nor was there any danger that his speech would cause a breach of the peace; it was not intended to have that effect. The Zikists wanted to provoke the British to take action against Azikiwe, who was not informed because they anticipated that he would not cooperate. Subsequently, Nduka Eze, a Zikist leader, wrote that the revolutionary movement needed Azikiwe because "thousands of people in the country looked up to Zik as the Joshua of Nigeria." The Zikist Central Committee wanted to use his person to arouse the people; by going to prison, "Zik might become the Nehru of Nigeria."

"We in the Central Committee decided that whether Zik liked it or not, the struggle would be spearheaded by him but we miscalculated for we did not know that we were dealing with someone who was intuitively cleverer than ourselves. We decided to pay our tax into the NCNC, recognize the NCNC as the only Government of Nigeria and invest Dr. Zik with all gubernatorial powers. . . . Agwuna delivered a 'Call for Revolution' as the Deputy President of

[96] The Zikist Movement was actually initiated in Lagos by four staff members of the *Nigerian Advocate*: M. C. K. Ajuluchuku (Ibo), Abiodun Aloba (Edo), Kolawole Balogun (Yoruba) and Nduka Eze (Western Ibo). Balogun became pro-tem President when the Movement was formally inaugurated on February 16, 1946. Nduka Eze, in his highly informative unpublished manuscript, "Memoirs of a Crusader" wrote that the choice of Balogun as President was intended to counter allegations that the movement was Ibo dominated, although a majority of the inaugural members appear to have been Ibo. Eze reports that Herbert Macaulay declared himself a Zikist, although he had some reservation about the use of that term. Earlier, in 1945, two young nationalists in the civil service at Kano, Malam Habib Raji Abdallah (Igbirra) and Osita C. Agwuna (Ibo), formed the African Anti-Colour Bar Movement. In 1946 A. A. Nwafor Orizu persuaded them to merge with a broader national front and the following year they attended a general meeting of the Zikist Movement in Lagos. H. R. Abdallah was elected President of the Zikist Movement, O. C. Agwuna, Vice-President, and M. C. K. Ajuluchuku, Secretary. As a result of his connection with the Zikist Movement and the Northern Elements Progressive Association, Abdallah was dismissed from the government service and took an appointment as field secretary of the NCNC.

the Zikist Movement . . . exhorting the nation to pay their taxes to the NCNC as the new People's Provisional Government. Feeling that Zikism was becoming too racialist and commercialist, he projected the adjunct philosophy of 'youth internationalism.' "[97]

O. C. Agwuna admonished the nationalists to be prepared to endure physical sacrifice, even death, for the sake of freedom. He advocated "progressive revolution, beginning with civil disobedience without violence, or non-cooperation."[98] Both Agwuna and the chairman of the meeting, Anthony Enahoro, a non-Zikist and editor of the Lagos *Daily Comet* (Zik Group), were arrested on charges of sedition. The NCNC Cabinet resolved to stand by the Zikist Movement during the crisis and gave its approval for a mass meeting on November 7. However, all members of the Cabinet save three Zikists stayed away from the meeting at which Malam Habib Raji Abdallah, President of the Zikist Movement, declared himself to be a free citizen of Nigeria, holding no allegiance to any foreign government and bound by no law other than Nigerian native law and the law of nations.[99] In addition, he reiterated Agwuna's crucial proposal: "Pay no more tax to this Government because if you pay they use that money to perpetuate their domination over you."

Swiftly the government brought to trial ten of the Zikists, eight of whom were convicted.[100] Azikiwe appears to have regarded their

[97] Nduka Eze, "Memoirs of a Crusader," Chapter 2 (typewritten).

[98] "With a deep sense of responsibility and reverence to God, and with allegiance to no constituted political authority alien or national . . . besides the NCNC," O. C. Agwuna advanced thirteen specific proposals for "positive action," of which refusal to pay tax alone was an illegal proposal. The "Call for Revolution" was published by the *West African Pilot*, November 9, 1948.

[99] Part of H. R. Abdallah's speech of November 7, 1948, as submitted to the court during his subsequent trial for sedition is as follows:
"We have passed the age of petition. We have passed the age of resolution. This is the age of action—plain, blunt and positive action. . . . This iniquitous British Government is determined to keep us slaves for ever and the only way out, as I see it and as I know it, is for every one of us to declare himself free and independent and be resolved to stand by that declaration and damn the consequences. I have nothing against the person of George VI of England. But I hate the crown of Britain with all my heart because to me and my countrymen, it is a symbol of oppression, a symbol of persecution, and, in short, a material manifestation of iniquity. . . . I hate the Union Jack because, save in Britain, wherever it goes, far from uniting, it creates a division. It feeds and flourishes on confusion and dissension. We must, therefore, have no more place for it in our hearts—this ugly representation of that satanic institution, imperialism." *West African Pilot*, February 10, 1949.
Those members of the NCNC Cabinet who attended the November 7th meeting, in addition to H. R. Abdallah were Nduka Eze and Oged Macaulay. Malam Sa'adu Zungur, the Federal Secretary, was ill, while the other members, including Dr. Azikiwe, had engagements elsewhere.

[100] H. R. Abdallah refused to enter a plea and was sentenced to a prison term of two years. He served 16 months and became President of the Freedom Movement

conduct as irresponsible and yet his attitude was ambiguous.[101] His principal organ, the *West African Pilot*, defended the right of the Zikist Movement to pursue its own policy, but criticized that policy severely and disassociated the NCNC from Zikist activity. In turn, the Zikist-controlled *African Echo* attacked Azikiwe for having disavowed the militant youth. At the Second Annual Convention of the NCNC in April 1949, Azikiwe made critical observations on the conduct of the Zikists which the prisoners and their supporters deeply resented and which they have never entirely forgiven.

In November 1949, the focus of nationalist agitation shifted dramatically from the political to the trade union field. Earlier, the Nigerian Trades Union Congress had split on the issue of continued affiliation with the NCNC. When a majority voted to withdraw, a "left" section under the leadership of three members of the NCNC Cabinet (M. A. O. Imoudu, President of the Railway Workers, F. O. Coker, Secretary of the Posts and Telegraph Workers, and Nduka Eze, Secretary of the Amalgamated Union of the U.A.C. African Workers—abbreviated as UNAMAG) formed a "dual" central organization, the Nigerian National Federation of Labour. Eze, in his early twenties, was acting President of the Zikist Movement and a member of the NCNC Cabinet. His object since 1946 had been to link the labor movement to the Zikist Movement for revolutionary action. At the Third Annual Conference of the UNAMAG in November 1949, Eze's faction obtained decisive control of the union executive and took a decision to strike against the largest of the British mercantile firms. At this point the conscience of the country was suddenly aroused by a melancholy incident in the Iva Valley coal mines of Enugu.

Historians may conclude that the slaying of coal miners by police at Enugu first proved the subjective reality of a Nigerian nation.

---

in January 1951. Later he became the principal organizing secretary of the Northern Peoples' Congress. O. C. Agwuna challenged the competence of the court to try his case and was sentenced to a term of three years. Later he became NCNC member of the Federal House of Representatives for Awka Division. S. O. Ebbi, an editor of the *African Echo*, was sentenced to a term of one year for publication of a seditious article; his co-editor, J. J. Odufuwa, was acquitted. Oged Macaulay and F. U. Anyiam were each sentenced to one year. The latter is now National Publicity Secretary of the NCNC. A. Enahoro served six months; his distinguished career is noted elsewhere. Ralph Aniedobe and O. Dafe were fined £25 for seditious utterances. Nduka Eze was acquitted and appointed Acting President General of the Zikist Movement.

[101] Azikiwe's critics allege that he did not want to be the "Nehru of Nigeria." On the other hand, he is said to have disapproved action which might have incurred government reprisals against the NCNC at an inopportune time.

No previous event ever evoked a manifestation of national consciousness comparable to the indignation generated by this tragedy. Eze's
emotive description of the reaction, written three years afterward,
conveys the drama of the impact, although it exaggerates the effects:[102] "The radicals and the moderates, the revolutionaries and
the stooges, the bourgeoisie and the workers, sank their differences,
remembered the word—'Nigeria' and rose in revolt against evil
and inhumanity."

It mattered little that the miners, striking for the redress of
grievances and an increase in pay, were misled by their union secretary and by a Zikist-controlled newspaper, *New Africa* (not a
Zik Group publication). Their misapprehensions had been reinforced
at any rate by the misguided statements of a government official.
A large quantity of explosives were stored in the mines, and the
Chief Commissioner of the Eastern Provinces decided that the
explosives should be removed to ensure against theft by political
agitators. The miners, who occupied the premises, believed that once
the explosives had been removed, the management would effect a
lock-out and force them into submission. A police contingent, sent
to remove the explosives, fired on the miners at the order of a
European officer, killing 21 and wounding 51 others.[103]

Within a week serious riots, involving three deaths, flared in Aba,
Port Harcourt, and Onitsha. All of them seem to have been instigated
by Zikists and were directed mainly against foreign mercantile establishments. In Lagos, three prominent supporters of the NCNC
—Mbonu Ojike, formerly General Manager of the *West African
Pilot*, K. Ozuomba Mbadiwe, and Mokwugo Okoye, general secretary of the Zikist Movement—met with Dr. Akinola Maja,
H. O. Davies and other leaders of the Nigerian Youth Movement to
explore the possibility of forming a united front and a national
political party. Consultations resulted in the proclamation of a National Emergency Committee with the immoderate slogan: Self-Government for Nigeria Now. Dr. Maja, President of the Youth Movement, was elected chairman of the N.E.C., Mbonu Ojike became
secretary and Dr. J. Akanni Doherty of the Youth Movement, treasurer. Azikiwe, who was in England when the shooting occurred,
having attended meetings of the Council of Peoples Against Imperialism in London and Moral Rearmament in Caux, Switzerland,[104]

[102] Eze, *op.cit.*, Chapter 3.

[103] *Report of the Commission of Enquiry into the Disorders in the Eastern
Provinces of Nigeria, November, 1949* (London: H.M.S.O., 1950).

[104] Dr. Azikiwe told the writer that his association with Moral Rearmament
began coincidentally in 1949 in England. He and Malam Sa'adu Zungur, Federal

returned to Nigeria, but left shortly for engagements in the United States.

The Colonial Office promptly appointed a Commission of Inquiry, including two African judges, which conducted hearings in Enugu during December and January 1950. The commissioners found no evidence of collusion between the miners and political agitators, and concluded that the "active employment" of the police had been without justification. Yet their report was so patently biased against legitimate nationalism *per se* that sober nationalists renewed their efforts to create a united front. Indeed the National Emergency Committee was an impressive demonstration of inter-tribal unity in Lagos and the fact that it was a working-class tragedy which impelled the unity movement strengthened the bonds between laborites, leftists, and the bourgeoisie.[105] From the Enugu hearings of December 1949 to the United Africa Company (U.A.C.) strike of August 1950, professional men from Lagos and other towns devoted their services unstintingly to labor causes.[106] Nevertheless the united front collapsed

Secretary of the NCNC, attended a meeting of the Council of Peoples Against Imperialism, a group led by Hon. Fenner Brockway, M.P., and contemplated visits to Prague and Moscow. As the Russians were signatories to the Berlin Treaty of 1885, partitioning Africa among European powers, they might be persuaded to raise the Nigerian case in the United Nations on the basis of treaties between the British and the Nigerian chiefs. However, technical difficulties and second thoughts intervened; Azikiwe and Zungur cancelled their plans and accepted an invitation from Moral Rearmament instead to spend a few days at the Caux, Switzerland, retreat. Since then Azikiwe's relationship with MRA has been cordial and the latter has claimed to exert influence on his political thought and practical policies. In this case as in others, MRA claims have been prone to exaggeration, as confirmed by Dr. Azikiwe himself in 1961. See *West African Pilot*, May 20, 1961.

[105] During this period, socialistic elements in the Zikist Movement and the "middle class" nationalists of the National Emergency Committee issued equally strong condemnations of the exploitative and monopolistic practices of European firms. See *Report of the Commission of Enquiry into the Disorders in the Eastern Provinces of Nigeria, November, 1949*, p. 45. For a scholarly exposition of such practices see J. Mars, "Extra-Territorial Enterprises," *Mining, Commerce, and Finance in Nigeria*, ed., Margery Perham (London: Faber, 1948), pp. 43-136.

[106] Prominent barristers who represented the Colliery Workers, union officials, the National Labour Committee, and the National Emergency Committee before the Commission of Inquiry included: F. R. A. Williams, H. O. Davies, H. U. Kaine, J. A. Wachuku, G. C. Nonyelu, M. O. Ajegbo, G. C. Nkemena, G. C. M. Onyiuke, C. D. Onyeama, J. M. Osindero and M. O. Ibeziako. *Report of the Commission of Enquiry into the Disorders . . . ,* pp. 4-5. Nduka Eze, commenting on the U.A.C. strike of August 1950, wrote that lawyers associated with the Nigerian Youth Movement, including S. L. Akintola, F. R. A. Williams, H. O. Davies, G. B. A. Coker, and Latunde Johnson, offered their services to striking employees of the U.A.C. without charge. Of the doctors, he remarks, only Dr. Maja, President of the Youth Movement, gave the "revolutionary" strikers free treatment. "Memoirs of a Crusader."

within a year and a portion of the blame may be attributed to chronic dissension within the volatile labor-left and to the inability of the radicals to work within the main body of the nationalist movement. This facet will be reviewed briefly before we consider the failure of the National Emergency Committee itself.

In 1949, the labor-left was a melange of bickering cliques. There were two rival factions of trade unionists, grouped respectively in the rightist Trades Union Congress and the leftist Nigerian National Federation of Labour. Closely allied to the leftist labor wing, with whom they were partially identical, was an accretion of militants and intellectuals: the pure Zikists, who were racialist and revolutionary, the revolutionary Zikists who espoused socialism or communism, and the non-Zikist Marxian socialists. An early penetration of Zikism by radical socialism was discernible in O. C. Agwuna's proposal of "youth internationalism" in his celebrated "Call for Revolution" of October 1948. But the pure Zikists resisted Marxian leadership, while the latter extended their influence through uncoordinated study groups in various towns.

Meanwhile the organized Zikist Movement under the leadership of socialistic Zikists, including Nduka Eze and Mokwugo Okoye, intensified its program of positive action. Copies of the "Call for Revolution" and other radical tracts were circulated throughout the country and on February 18, 1950, Chukuwonka Ugokwu, a twenty-four-year-old, 2s. 8d. a day laborer of the Posts and Telegraphs Department, attempted to assassinate the Chief Secretary to the Government, Sir Hugh Foot. The government reacted swiftly; agents searched the homes of Zikists in several towns, and it was alleged that seditious literature and plans for revolutionary action were uncovered.[107] Mokwugo Okoye, Secretary of the Movement, was convicted of sedition for having in his possession revolutionary pamphlets and sentenced to 33 months in prison.[108] Over 20 more Zikists

[107] At the trial of Francis Ikenna Nzimiro, secretary of the Onitsha branch of the Zikist Movement and an official of the UNAMAG, seized documents were produced, alleged by the Government to project a revolutionary triple alliance of the Zikist Movement, the Nigerian National Federation of Labour, and the UNAMAG. *West African Pilot,* March 8, 1950. Nzimiro was sentenced to nine months.

[108] At his trial Mokwugo Okoye refused to plead on the ground that "the matter was between Britain and Nigeria." He spurned the judge, an African, as "a symbol of that imperialist machinery," and refused, "as a Zikist," to concede the right of the court to try his case. *West African Pilot,* March 7, 1950. Upon his release in 1953, Okoye returned to the NCNC Youth Association. He was expelled from the party in 1955, readmitted in 1956, and was Secretary General of the Youth Association at the time of writing and a member of the National Executive Committee. He is the author of several pamphlets which espouse revolutionary

were jailed for six to nine months and on April 13, 1950, the government proclaimed the Zikist Movement an unlawful society on the ground that it sought "to stir up hatred and malice and to pursue its seditious aims by lawlessness and violence." A few days later, Dr. Azikiwe, responding to a question by the *Sunday Times*, issued a statement on his relationship to the Zikist Movement: "The Zikist Movement was founded by a group of young Nigerian patriots in 1946, when I was staying temporarily at Onitsha. My name was used without my knowledge and consent. . . . So far as the ideals of the Zikist Movement are concerned, I am in complete sympathy with the Movement and I am proud that my name was considered fit and proper for such veneration."

He drew a parallel between the Zikist Movement and Christianity, an unlawful society identified with Jesus, that was persecuted and driven underground. The methods of the nations of the world have not been blameless. "Why," he asked, "must I declare my stand on the methods of the Zikist Movement simply because that organization bears my nickname (as Christianity bears the nickname of Joshua whom the Greeks called Jesus) even though I am not its founder nor a member?"[109] On May 31, 1950, the NCNC pledged itself to restore the identity of the banned Zikist Movement.

Nduka Eze, acting President of the Zikist Movement, was not ensnared by the police net which depopulated the ranks of the militant Zikists. In mid-1950 he attained a perilous height of personal importance when the sagging Trades Union Congress and the independent Government Workers Union merged with the leftist Nigerian National Federation of Labour to form a unified central organization, the Nigerian Labour Congress, under leftist leadership.[110] In August, Eze led the 18,000-member UNAMAG in an

---

socialism and human freedom: *Some Facts and Fancies* (Yaba: n.d.) ; *African Cameos; Pangs of Progress* (Onitsha: n.d.) ; *Blackman's Destiny;* and *Fullness of Freedom* (Onitsha: n.d.).

[109] *Daily Times*, April 17, 1950. The followers of Azikiwe were not unaccustomed to the use of religious symbolism for political purposes, although it is not a characteristic technique of Azikiwe himself. Coleman has drawn attention to the activities of the National Church of Nigeria, founded at Aba in 1948 as "the religious wing of the Zikist Movement. . . . The National Church was virtually coextensive in its membership and branch organization with the Zikist (and subsequently with the Freedom) Movement. . . . The main objectives of the National Church apparently were the glorification and awakening of racial and national consciousness. As such the Church was not so much a religious enterprise as a strand in the nationalist movement." *Op.cit.*, pp. 302-303.

[110] The three top officers of the N.N.F.L., M. A. O. Imoudu, President, F. O. Coker, Vice-President, and N. Eze, secretary, assumed these posts in the Nigerian Labour Congress.

effective strike against the U.A.C. which yielded, after arbitration, a substantial increase in the cost-of-living allowance for the workers.[111] Four months later, the Nigerian Labour Congress recklessly called a general strike of mercantile workers for which the unions were unprepared. This time the UNAMAG and the Nigerian Labour Congress sustained crushing losses; Eze's career as a labor leader was nipped in the bud and his days of political influence were numbered. In January 1951 he joined the newly formed Freedom Movement led by ex-Zikists who renounced Zikism for the more specific ideology of revolutionary socialism.[112] The Freedom Movement joined with a Marxian study group, known as the People's Committee for Independence, to form a "League" to advise the UNAMAG and to direct the socialist movement in Nigeria.[113] Hopes remained in the revolutionary circle that a base of operations could be secured in the trade unions under the direction of a new left-wing socialist party. But the project appeared to those concerned to hinge on the establishment of a newspaper and this was seen by the small group of left-wing activists to depend on financial support from European communist sources, primarily in Eastern Germany and Czechoslovakia.[114] The scheme collapsed in February 1951 when a

[111] Eze writes that he wired the branch unions of the UNAMAG to down tools on April 2 and that the strike was immediately effective in the Delta and Rivers area (Niger Basin) where the U.A.C. sustained heavy losses of timber, palm oil, and plantation produce. In the Abonema district, Eze writes, the union created a police force of its own which arrested strikebreakers, and formed a union court which levied fines and imposed other penalties on the "white legs." *Op.cit.* In Lagos, Eze and 21 other strikers were arrested for holding an unlawful assembly and fined. *Daily Times*, August 7 and September 21, 1950.

[112] M. C. K. Ajuluchuku, a founder of the Zikist Movement, is reported to have been primarily responsible for the organization of the Freedom Movement. H. R. Abdallah, President of the banned Zikist Movement, and O. C. Agwuna, Vice-President, were elected to the same offices in the Freedom Movement; both of them renounced Zikism and resolved not to affiliate with the NCNC. Plans were made instead to affiliate with the World Federation of Democratic Youth and the International Union of Students (both communist-controlled). Nduka Eze continued his criticism of Dr. Azikiwe as chairman of the Lagos branch of the Freedom Movement; in February 1951, Azikiwe expelled Eze from the NCNC cabinet, a power he had never used previously. Editorials in the *London Daily Worker* supported Eze and condemned Azikiwe as a decadent nationalist leader.

[113] Members of the League included S. G. Ikoku, Ayo Ogunsheye, Francis Ikenna Nzimiro, Amaefule Ikoro, J. Ola Apara, M. O. Ezumah and Nduka Eze. Eze, *op.cit.*

[114] Previously the World Federation of Trade Unions and the French *Confédération Générale du Travail* had made grants to the Nigerian Labour Congress to promote trade union organization. Furthermore the N.L.C. had set up a National Scholarship Board to administer grants from the Central Council of Free German Youth and 24 scholarships were actually granted to Nigerians. *Ibid.* Non-unionists did not like the way funds from abroad were being handled by the UNAMAG executive, nor did they approve the idea, entertained by Eze and the UNAMAG radicals, to form a Communist Party of Nigeria. Marxian

delegate chosen to make arrangements in Europe was seized at the Lagos airport prior to his intended departure.[115] At this juncture the Nigerian Labour Congress realized the futility of reliance upon overseas support and terminated its affiliation with the (communist-controlled) World Federation of Trade Unions. Eze relinquished his post as general secretary of the Nigerian Labour Congress, resigned from the UNAMAG, and faced a prosecution for tax defaulting.[116]

By mid-1951 the Freedom Movement was virtually defunct but the irrepressible, albeit diminishing, hard core of revolutionary left-wing socialists formed a People's Revolutionary Committee which sent a delegation to the Gold Coast. Factional disputes led to the dissolution of this group in September and it was succeeded by the National Preparatory Committee, which made another attempt to create a radical political party with inter-territorial connections. The new group adopted the name of the leading Gold Coast nationalist organization and proclaimed itself the Convention People's Party of Nigeria and the Cameroons.[117] Representatives of the Gold Coast CPP visited Nigeria but no lasting ties were established. Probably the Gold Coast nationalist leader, Dr. Kwame Nkrumah, declined to support a movement in opposition to his friend and colleague,

---

intellectuals in the People's Committee for Independence objected that a Communist Party at that stage would only isolate the Marxists from the broader movement of nationalists and socialists. In fact, alleged communist penetration of the labor movement was denounced by Azikiwe's *West African Pilot* and by the Roman Catholic *Herald*. At this time, Nduka Eze was unable to finance a daily newspaper, the *Labor Champion,* which he founded in Lagos, and was compelled to abandon the venture. Cf. Coleman, *op.cit.,* p. 305.

[115] The individual was S. G. Ikoku, an employee of the Department of Marketing and Export who studied under Harold Laski at the London School of Economics. Ikoku was seized at the airport on a charge of theft from the Department and sentenced to a prison term of six months. Subsequently he became Leader of the Opposition in the Eastern House of Assembly.

[116] Eze has reported the statement of the late Justice Jibowu, a respected conservative, who tried his case: "I am not interested whether this young man is a Communist or has Communist affiliations. The prosecution has failed to make any case against the accused. I therefore discharge and acquit him." "Memoirs of a Crusader." Subsequently the UNAMAG was dissolved into separate local components which never recombined. Eze returned briefly to the NCNC in 1954 but left it finally in 1955, and began his political career anew as a member of the Action Group. He was assigned the task of building the Action Group in his home Division, the Western Ibo community of Asaba, and was widely credited with the Action Group victory in the local government election of 1958, following which Eze became Chairman of the Asaba District Council. Meanwhile he became an influential member of the Action Group Federal Executive; his private activities have been in the field of small business.

[117] Habib Raji Abdallah was President of the Convention People's Party of Nigeria and the Cameroons; Osita C. Agwuna was General Secretary.

Dr. Azikiwe, and the CPP in Nigeria soon expired. Many of the Zikists and radicals returned to the NCNC to continue their agitation within that major party's Youth Association. After 1951 revolutionary socialism and incipient communism ceased to impart tangible momentum to the NCNC or its trade union affiliates. Organized Marxism receded to clandestine intellectual circles, surfacing weakly in 1954 as the United Working People's Party, which is discussed in a subsequent chapter.

The Failure of the National Emergency Committee

After the public hearings at Enugu on the Iva Valley massacre, leaders of the National Emergency Committee, including Dr. Azikiwe, President of the NCNC, and Dr. Akinola Maja, President of the Nigerian Youth Movement, met to explore the possibility of forming a unified political party. Eventually, Dr. Azikiwe and barrister Bode Thomas of the Youth Movement were requested to draft an Instrument of Coalition to formalize the agreements reached in the course of discussions. The Instrument provided for the creation of a Coalition Council and embodied specific principles of conduct: the proposals of the Secretary of State for constitutional reform would be rejected and the N.E.C. would press its demand for immediate self-government; a moratorium would be declared on public statements disparaging the institution of chieftaincy; the development of ethnic group organizations would be encouraged as the most effective means of propagating nationalism among the peasantry; the N.E.C. would be supported by the principal nationalist newspapers. Moreover, the parties agreed that "a dependent country desperately struggling for independence cannot afford the rancour and disunity" generated by electoral competition. Therefore, it was proposed that candidates in the future would be chosen by the coalition.[118]

An occasion arose in October 1950 to test the feasibility of the alliance, namely the election for the new Lagos Town Council—the first election in Nigerian history to be conducted on the basis of universal adult suffrage. The National Emergency Committee appointed a sub-committee of nine (three Nigerian Youth Movement, three NCNC/NNDP, and three Nigerian Labour Congress) to recommend candidates for the 24 elective seats.[119] But the alliance

[118] "Instrument of Coalition of the Nigerian Youth Movement and the National Council of Nigeria and the Cameroons." (Mimeographed.) A leading participant later wrote that the Instrument was regarded as "a masterpiece of draftsmanship. When it was read everyone was satisfied." F. R. A. Williams in the *Daily Service*, April 2, 1951.

[119] Eze, *op.cit.*, Chapter 6.

foundered when Dr. Azikiwe informed the N.E.C. that its slate of nominees was not acceptable to the leaders of the Nigerian National Democratic Party, who insisted upon the inclusion of that party's two perennial standard bearers, Hon. Adeleke Adedoyin and Dr. A. B. Olorun-Nimbe. Neither of these gentlemen were associated with the N.E.C., and both of them had been criticized sharply by it for their failure to support the united front. But the NNDP was adamant, and the parties to the alliance finally agreed to postpone implementation of the Instrument of Coalition until after the Lagos election.

Thereupon the NCNC presented a "triple alliance" consisting of the Nigerian National Democratic Party, the Nigerian Labour Congress, and the Lagos Market Women's Guild. For its part, the Nigerian Youth Movement contested through the medium of its local ally, the Area Councils, under the leadership of Oba Adele II, who was himself a candidate.[120] About 25,000 persons or 21 percent of the registered electorate voted[121] and gave a decisive margin of victory to the NCNC "triple alliance" which won 18 of the 24 seats. Dr. Azikiwe was disqualified on a technicality and Dr. Olorun-Nimbe was chosen first Mayor of Lagos by the elected councillors.[122]

Following its victory, the NCNC proposed to delete the critical election clause from the still pending Instrument of Coalition. It was apparent to the Nigerian Youth Movement that its rival was determined to exploit its great electoral edge. Recriminations between the parties ensued and the Instrument of Coalition never came into effect. Azikiwe's insistence on deletion of the vital election clause

[120] Oba Adele II organized the Area Councils shortly after his installation of 1949. It was based on the *Egbe-Ilu* or town committee which is said to have been formed in 1944 to promote the welfare of the indigenous people of Lagos. The *Egbe-Ilu* included the heads of the numerous tribal societies and Adeniji Adele, then a civil servant, was its first secretary. In 1951 the Action Group adopted the Area Councils as its Lagos affiliate.

[121] The election was contested in eight multi-member wards of three seats each. Voters were required to mark their ballots with an "X" next to the candidates of their choice and officials aided the illiterate voters. Many persons did not vote as they became impatient waiting for long periods of time in the voting queues, and many thousands were reported to have been turned away when the polls closed at 6 P.M. *Daily Times*, October 17, 1950.

[122] Azikiwe's name had been omitted from the voters list compiled from the Lagos census. When the census was taken he had been at a meeting of the Legislative Council in Enugu. His lieutenant, Mbonu Ojike, was chosen Deputy Mayor. Oba Adele II resigned from the Council when it was apparent that his dignity would be eclipsed by an elected mayor. He was widely criticized for having contested in the first place by persons who thought it was indecorous for a reigning *Oba* to seek election. In 1953 the *Oba* was made ceremonial president of the Council.

from the Instrument, which he co-authored, indicates that he did not seriously regard the National Emergency Committee as a vehicle for future political operations. Possibly he and his supporters felt that the N.E.C. would only serve to bolster the influence of the Lagos elite, which might have been expected to decline in the impending era of popular elections. The outcome of the Lagos election would have provided support for that point of view. Furthermore, the Yoruba cultural society, *Egbe Omo Oduduwa*, with its enormous potential for political organization in the Western Region, was closely related to the Nigerian Youth Movement. Azikiwe could not attack the *Egbe* in principle since he had advocated ethnic unity for the Ibos and other nationality groups as a prerequisite to national unity on a federal basis. But pan-tribalism in opposition to the NCNC was another matter. When the *Egbe* was formed by leaders of the Youth Movement, Azikiwe's Yoruba supporters organized the Yoruba Federal Union in a vain attempt to counter its influence. Now that the Youth Movement had suffered a defeat, it might have seemed possible to confine the *Egbe* to cultural interests through the liquidation of its political wing. When Azikiwe encountered Obafemi Awolowo at a pre-election conference of the N.E.C., he was probably unaware that the Ibadan barrister and publisher (Awolowo's *Nigerian Tribune* was founded in 1949) had already initiated a political group that was destined to absorb the Nigerian Youth Movement and eclipse the NCNC in the Western Region.

Nor can it be assumed that the leaders of the NCNC/NNDP rejected permanent cooperation with the Youth Movement for doctrinal socialistic reasons. Had the NCNC/NNDP politicians been willing to share their leadership with the laborites, a leftist mass party might have emerged,[123] and the ensuing ineffectual, sectarian radicalism of the isolated labor-left might have been averted. When the Nigerian Labour Congress was staggered by defeat in the mercantile strike of December 1950, radical labor leaders, including Nduka Eze, were swiftly excluded from positions of control in the "triple alliance." In short, the labor leadership of 1950 was too diffuse and erratic, and the politicians of the NCNC/NNDP were too obdurately ambitious to conclude a durable alliance. Azikiwe, whose influence was based on his commercial press and his leadership of a mass movement, had no commitment to the labor leaders and little sympathy for the extremist element among them. Since 1951, the representation of organized labor in the NCNC Executive has been relatively minor

[123] Nduka Eze shows clearly that they were not willing to do this. *Op.cit.*

85

and confined primarily to the conservative wing of trade union leadership.

Azikiwe could not escape criticism for the failure of the N.E.C. and he reacted with characteristic acumen. In the course of a presidential address to the Ibo State Union at Enugu in December 1950, he declared his intention to retire from politics for five years. He explained that he had been in the forefront of Nigerian politics for sixteen years and thought that other people should have their chance. An individual leader, by his unwillingness to step down at the right moment could bring misfortune to himself and to the nation. Everything considered, he preferred to retire for five years; if his services were needed then he would be prepared to donate them with humility. He was not pessimistic, for he thought that Nigeria could be a free country if Nigerians would follow in the footsteps of other nations, like India, China, Burma, Egypt, and Indonesia. "But," he said, "it is obvious that our people are not ready and I must not impose on an unready people . . . so, I beg leave to take my exit, but I shall come back when my people are ready. That is, if they need me by then."[124] A public debate on the question of Azikiwe's retirement was held in Lagos and the idea was rejected by a reported 700 votes to 24.[125] Subsequently, Azikiwe revoked his decision to retire in response to public opinion and pressure from the Democratic Party. Nigeria was on the threshold of political transformation, and the NCNC was about to change its nature from that of a national movement into a responsible political party within a highly competitive national party system.

[124] *Daily Times*, December 28, 1950.
[125] *Daily Times*, January 8, 1951.

CHAPTER III: REGIONALISM
AND THE EMERGENCE
OF A THREE-PARTY SYSTEM

THIS account of the rise of Nigerian political parties does not review in any detail the related story of constitutional advance.[1] In Nigeria, as elsewhere in emergent Africa under British and French rule, nationalist pressures quickened the pace of constitutional advance which in turn stimulated the development of political parties.[2] The classic Nigerian example is the Constitution of 1946, which gave an enormous if unintentional boost to the newly born NCNC. Largely as a result of intensive agitation by that party, a general review of the constitution was initiated by the government in 1948. Conferences were organized by administrative officials at the village, divisional, provincial, and regional levels, culminating in a General Conference at Ibadan in 1950. As James S. Coleman has observed, "there can be little doubt that the method of constitutional revision did in fact give heavy weight to rural and traditional elements and minimized the influence of urban, educated, and nationalist elements."[3] Needless to say, the method of revision was objectionable to most radical nationalists who wanted an elected constituent assembly.

At the Ibadan General Conference, representatives from the East and West advocated the introduction of ministerial responsibility in the regions and at the Center, a step forward that the Northern delegates did not then feel prepared to take.[4] On other issues the

[1] The authoritative study of Nigerian constitutional development is Kalu Ezera, *Constitutional Developments in Nigeria* (Cambridge: Cambridge University Press, 1960).

[2] See Thomas Hodgkin, "Political Parties in British and French West Africa," *Information Digest, Africa Bureau*, No. 10 (London: August 1953), pp. 13-16; James S. Coleman, "The Emergence of African Political Parties," *Africa Today*, ed. C. Grove Haines (Baltimore: Johns Hopkins Press, 1955), pp. 225-255.

[3] James S. Coleman, *Nigeria: Background to Nationalism* (Berkeley and Los Angeles: University of California Press, 1958), p. 312. Dr. Azikiwe did not attend the Ibadan General Conference because of his fundamental disagreement with the method of review. However, he was a member of the Select Committee of the Legislative Council that considered its recommendations and he wrote a highly critical "Minority Report," objecting to the three-region structure among other proposals. *Ibid.*, pp. 348-349.

[4] Thus on January 12, 1950, Hon. Abubakar Tafawa Balewa declared that the North would not object to the introduction of ministerial responsibility in the East and West, but would not sanction it in the North or the Center "not because we do not like it, not because we lack confidence, but because we want to be

cleavage between northern and southern members was even more acute. The northerners invoked the population principle to demand, and eventually to win, 50 percent representation in the proposed Central Legislature, while the southerners generally favored equality of regional representation. Northern delegates argued for the distribution of central revenues to the regions on a per capita basis, while southerners generally preferred other principles of allocation, e.g., regional need or volume of trade, which were more beneficial to them.[5] Furthermore, Western delegates pressed for revision of the North-West boundary in order to unite the Yorubas of Ilorin and Kabba Provinces with the Yoruba majority of the Western Region.[6] These conflicts impressed Northern leaders with the necessity of forming a political organization to serve their interests in the field of constitutional and parliamentary maneuver. But the Northern political parties do not stem solely or primarily from the constitution-making process; they have deeper roots of a popular and spontaneous nature to which we turn at this point.

The Origin of Political Parties in the North

Embryonic political societies in Northern Nigeria were first organized by educated youth in the public service (government and Native Administration), many of whom were born into privileged families and nearly all of whom were exposed to nationalist thought from southern origins and abroad. Two of the most important early societies were the Bauchi General Improvement Union and the Youth Social Circle of Sokoto. The former was established in 1943-1944 largely through the efforts of Malam Sa'adu Zungur, a dedicated nationalist who was chosen as Federal Secretary of the NCNC by Dr. Azikiwe in 1948.[7] The Youth Social Circle was formed in 1945

---

together." He urged restriction of ministerial responsibility to the East and West for five years. *Proceedings of the General Conference on Review of the Constitution, January, 1950* (Lagos: 1950), pp. 63ff.

[5] This question was referred to a special commission which based its recommendations on four criteria: "Independent Revenues," "Derivation," "Needs," and "National Interests." See *Report of the Commission on Revenue Allocation* (Lagos: 1951).

[6] This matter was referred for settlement to the Governor of Nigeria, who decided, after investigation, that no change in the inter-regional boundary was justified. Colonial Office, *Report of the Commission appointed to enquire into the fears of Minorities and the means of allaying them* (London: 1958), p. 76.

[7] The memory of the late Malam Sa'adu Zungur, who died after a lingering illness in 1958, is revered today by leaders and supporters of the opposition Northern Elements Progressive Union as an inspirational critic of the system of emirate rule. He was born into a Habe family with learned traditions, and was himself

by progressive intellectuals who are now among the leaders of the Sokoto section of the Northern Peoples' Congress.[8] In 1946 nationalists at Kano formed the first non-localized Northern political society called the Northern Elements Progressive Association (NEPA). The General Secretary of the NEPA was Malam Habib Raji Abdallah, who became President of the Zikist Movement in 1947.[9] NEPA was

---

schooled in both English and Arabic. His knowledge of the Qur'an is said to have been extensive and profound; indeed, the writer was told by a highly responsible critic of Sa'adu Zungur's political activities that he was probably the most learned Koranic scholar of his time in the North. He studied to be a medical dispenser at the Yaba Higher College (Lagos) but devoted most of his time in Lagos to nationalist politics and to the reformist Ahmadiyya Movement, which he tried unsuccessfully to introduce among the Muslims of Bauchi. During the early 1940's he taught dispensary attendants at Zaria where he formed the Zaria Friendly Society with Abubakar Imam, editor of *Gaskiya Ta Fi Kwabo* (an official Hausa-language newspaper), and others. The Friendly Society lapsed when Zungur tried to use it as a platform for criticisms of the N.A. system. From 1948 to 1951 he was Federal Secretary of the NCNC, and in 1949 he accompanied Dr. Azikiwe to Europe. Later he supported the NEPU but illness severely limited his activities after 1951.

Sa'adu Zungur and Abubakar Tafawa Balewa, then headmaster of the Bauchi Middle School, now Prime Minister of the Federation, were rival thinkers at Bauchi in the 1940's. Aminu Kano was close to Zungur while Yahaya Gusau, later General Secretary of the Northern Peoples' Congress, a member of the Federal Public Service Commission, and Secretary to the Executive Council of the Northern Regional Government, was close to Balewa. The latter two did not join the Bauchi General Improvement Union but they had been active in the Bauchi Discussion Circle formed upon the suggestion of the Resident in 1943 following the publication of provocative articles by Aminu Kano and others in the *West African Pilot*. Administrative officers are reported to have participated in open forums of the Circle devoted to the discussion of current issues. The Secretary of the Discussion Circle was Mr. Ibiam, a government dispenser, who became a leader of the Bauchi General Improvement Union.

[8] The founders of the Youth Social Circle included Malam Shehu Shagari, MHR, Federal Minister of Economic Development and Research in the first independent government, Alhaji Ahmadu Danbaba, MHR, Administrative Secretary of the Sokoto N.A., and Malam Ibrahim Gusau, *Sarkin Mallamai*, MHR, Head of the Department of Community Development, Sokoto N.A. At first the Circle was regarded with suspicion by administrative officers, but the Sardauna of Sokoto was an early adviser and patron behind the scenes. About the time of the formation of the YSC, a Nigerian Citizens Welfare Association was formed at Sokoto by Malam Muhammadu Sani Dingyadi, now Makaman Sokoto, MHA, N.A. Councillor for Natural Resources and a member of the NPC National Executive. The NCWA may have been conceived as a political party but it never developed.

[9] Early leaders of the NEPA included the following:

Malam Abdurahman Bida, President (Nupe from Bida), then employed as a dispenser at the Kano N.A. Hospital.

Malam Habib Raji Abdallah, General Secretary (Igbirra), then a government employee at Kano who later became President of the Zikist Movement in 1947, a member of the NCNC Cabinet in 1948, President of the Freedom Movement in 1951, and Principal Organizing Secretary of the NPC in 1957. See *supra*, pp. 74-75, footnotes 96, 99, 100.

widely, if somewhat inaccurately, regarded as an auxiliary of the Zikist Movement; it rallied support for the NCNC's pan-Nigerian delegation during the national tour of 1946, which added to the suspicion with which it was viewed in government and Native Administration circles. During the four years of its existence (1945-1949), the NEPA program emphasized political reform, economic development, and educational opportunity for promising Northern students.

It would be difficult to overstate the value of Western education for members of the new political elite of Northern Nigerians.[10] Among the educated few, teachers were pre-eminent; indeed, teacher training was regarded as the most suitable and respectable kind of educational preparation.[11] In 1945 the Nigerian Government sent four Northern teachers, including the future Prime Minister of the Federation, Malam Abubakar Tafawa Balewa, then headmaster of the Bauchi Middle School, to the University of London Institute of Education for a two-year course of professional study. The following year a second group was chosen, including Aminu Kano.

Malam Abba Sa'id, a railway employee.
Malam Abubakar Zukogi, Field Secretary (Fulani from Bida), a forester who later became General Secretary of the NEPU.
Malam Hawaidi, a civil servant from Kano.
Malam Umaru Agaie, President of the Bida branch (Nupe from Bida), later the Secretary of the Northern Nigerian Congress in 1949.

Bida was a cultural crossroad that transmitted currents of southern thought into the North and the prominence of Bida men in the NEPA is an indication of the intellectual advancement of that city's favored youth.

[10] The political value of education in Northern Nigeria greatly exceeded that in Southern Nigeria owing to the appalling retardation of educational development in the North and the consequent dearth of Northerners who were qualified to assume leadership within the legalistic, parliamentary context of the nationalist and reform movements. The "differential impact of Western education" has been discussed by James S. Coleman who observes that in 1947 there were only 251 Northern students in secondary schools, representing 2.5% of the total secondary school enrollment in Nigeria. ". . . . As late as 1951 the 16 million people of the north could point to only one of their number who had obtained a full university degree—and he was a Zaria Fulani convert to Christianity educated in England by Walter Miller." *Nigeria*, pp. 132-140. The references are to Dr. A. R. B. Dikko, who was president of the NPC from 1949-1951, and a famous C.M.S. missionary. See also the Nuffield Foundation and the Colonial Office, *African Education, a Study of Educational Policy and Practice in British Tropical Africa* (Oxford: Oxford University Press, 1953), pp. 47-48, for tables on the growth of primary, secondary, and teacher training education in Nigeria from 1912 to 1947, including comparative statistics on northern and southern educational development.
[11] An impressive number of the top leaders of the North today, including the Premier, the Prime Minister of the Federation, and several senior ministers in the regional and federal governments, are alumni of the elite Katsina Teacher Training College. Theirs is the most cohesive "old school tie" in Nigeria.

In London, several of these teacher trainees organized the Northern Teachers' Welfare Association; Malam Aminu was chosen as secretary and pledged to convene a meeting of all Northern teachers and headmasters upon his return to Nigeria. The first conference of the Northern Teachers' Association, called by the young teacher of the Bauchi Middle School, was held at Zaria in December 1948. By then political ferment in the North was tangible and the teachers' association was viewed by officials and Northerners alike as a political rather than an occupational society. Indeed any organization that assembled educated men for the purpose of serious discussion was politically important and carefully watched by officials.[12]

Three months earlier, on September 26, 1948, Dr. A. R. B. Dikko, the first medical officer of Northern origin, and Malam D. A. Rafih, a senior employee of the Nigerian railways who had been trained in England, held parallel meetings in their respective homes at Zaria and Kaduna to which they invited prominent individuals who were anxious to promote the development of the North. Apparently these two men had not been in communication, were not personally acquainted with one another, and were not even aware of the coincidence of their respective meetings until after the events. On October 3, 1948, Rafih's group at Kaduna formed a society called *Jam'iyyar Mutanen Arewa A Yau* (The Association of Northern People of Today); on October 12, 1948, at Zaria, Dr. Dikko and Malam Abubakar Imam, the influential editor of the Government-published, Hausa-language weekly newspaper, *Gaskiya Ta Fi Kwabo* (Truth is worth more than a penny) organized the *Jam'iyyar Jama'ar Arewa* (Northern Nigerian Congress). Malam Rafih participated in the latter meeting and it was decided to merge the Zaria and Kaduna groups into a single society town as *Jam'iyyar Mutanen Arewa* (then called, in English, the Northern Nigerian Congress, now rendered literally as Northern Peoples' Congress). Sympathetic persons throughout the region were contacted and urged to form local branches in preparation for a general meeting. Among the local groups that agreed to affiliate were the Sokoto Youth Social Circle, a Bauchi group, and a Citizen's Association that was formed at Kano (the largest city in the North, with a

[12] Prominent individuals who attended the first annual meeting of the Northern Teachers' Association at Zaria in December 1948 told the writer that many of the topics and grievances discussed had unmistakably political overtones. The Association elected principal officers as follows: the late Shettima Ajram, President; Abubakar Tafawa Balewa, Vice-President; Aminu Kano, Secretary; Abubakar Imam, then editor of *Gaskiya Ta Fi Kwabo*, Patron and Auditor. By 1950 the Association had become highly influential and was given representation on the Regional Board of Education.

population of some 130,000). On June 26, 1949, the Northern Nigerian Congress held its inaugural meeting at Kaduna. Over 300 delegates attended and officers were elected, including Dr. A. R. B. Dikko as first President.

The founders of the Northern Nigerian Congress emphasized that their association was purely social and cultural; its objective, stated by the President, was to combat "ignorance, idleness, and injustice" in the Northern Region. In fact, the organizers were obliged to remain technically non-political inasmuch as the vast majority of them were either government servants, to whom overt political action was forbidden, or employees of Native Administrations, for whom such action would have been imprudent.[13] Congress leaders were anxious to avoid the fate of the Northern Elements Progressive Association which had been destroyed because of its open political activities by the discharge or transfer of its principal leaders from

[13] An official registration book of the Northern Peoples' Congress for Zaria and Kaduna, with entries from October 12, 1948 to November 26, 1951, includes 135 names. Reliable informants established the occupations of 56% of those listed. The largest number, or 53% of those determined, were employed by the government (57% of the latter were employed by the Gaskiya Publishing Corporation); 30% were employed by various Native Administration departments and 17% were teachers or educational officers.

The initial entry is dated October 12, 1948, the date of the founding of the *Jam'iyyar Jama'ar Arewa* at Zaria, and the first 5 names are as follows: Dr. A. R. B. Dikko (Medical Department), Malam D. A. Rafih Tiyaje (Nigerian Railways), Malam Abubakar Imam (Gaskiya Corporation), Malam Sanusi Maaji (Native Treasury), Malam Yahaya Gusau (Bauchi Middle School teacher). The NPC Secretariat supplied the writer with a list of 16 participants in the Zaria meeting of October 12, 1948, and 30 participants in the Kaduna meetings of the *Jam'iyyar Mutanen Arewa A Yau* of October 3, 1948. The occupations of 36 of those founders were determined thus: 17 government employees, 10 N.A. employees, 7 teachers, and 2 self-employed.

At the inaugural meeting held at Kaduna on June 26, 1949, pro-tem officers were elected as follows:

Dr. A. R. B. Dikko, President (Christian, Fulani, Zaria, Medical Officer);
Malam D. A. Rafih, First Vice-President (Muslim, Fulani, Sokoto, Railways);
Malam Yusufu Maitama Sule, Second Vice-President (Muslim, Hausa, Kano, teacher);
Malam Umaru Agaie, Secretary (Muslim, Nupe, Bida, Gaskiya Corp.);
Malam Isa S. Wali, Assistant Secretary (Muslim, Fulani, Kano, Government Secretariat);
Malam Isa Koto, Financial Secretary (Muslim, teacher);
Alhaji Abubakar Imam, Treasurer (Muslim, Hausa, Zaria, Gaskiya);
Malam Julde, Joint Auditor (Christian, Fulani, French Cameroons, Medical Dept.);
Malam Aminu Kano, Joint Auditor (Muslim, Fulani, Kano, teacher);
Malam Abdulkadir Makama, Publicity Secretary (Muslim, Fulani, Kano, Gaskiya);
Malam Sa'adu Zungur, Adviser on Muslim Law (Muslim, Habe, Bauchi, dispensary teacher).

their positions in the Government and N.A. services. Certainly the Congress was a good deal less radical than the NEPA had been although highly controversial matters, including a resolution on abolition of the Northern House of Chiefs and the question of female membership in the Congress, were debated at length during the inaugural conference.[14] However the Congress leadership was not disposed to affiliate with Dr. Azikiwe's NCNC.[15] Two political aims appear to have motivated a majority of the founders. First, to foster peaceful reform and democratization, in particular abolition of the archaic "Sole Native Authorities." Secondly, to ensure that the inevitable movement for self-government in the North would be led by moderate northerners rather than radical southerners, who were feared by the traditional and educated elites of the North as a potentially oppressive alien power.

The first annual convention of the *Jam'iyyar Mutanen Arewa,* henceforth known as the Northern Peoples' Congress (NPC), was held at Kano, December 25-27, 1949. A district officer, representing the Resident of Kano, who had been invited, admonished the delegates to proceed with prudence and caution. Malam Aminu Kano, then

[14] A leading participant in the inaugural conference of the Northern Nigerian Congress in June 1949 informed the writer that a resolution submitted by Malam Isa Wali on behalf of the Kaduna branch proposed the abolition of the House of Chiefs as a legislative chamber. Many speakers (including Malam Sa'adu Zungur and Malam Aminu Kano) favored the creation of a Council of Elders to include emirs and chiefs with advisory powers only as a substitute for the legislative chamber of chiefs that was bound to involve the chiefs in politics. This debate was reported in newspapers, notably in the "dreaded" *West African Pilot,* arousing the fury of the chiefs and the ire of administrative officials. The Sultan of Sokoto, whose personal blessing was read at the opening session of the conference, sent another telegram before adjournment to withdraw his blessing. Discussion on the content and wording of the proposed constitution, dominated by Malam Sa'adu Zungur, lasted from 4 p.m. to 4 a.m. the next morning with but a two-hour recess for dinner and prayers. It is interesting to reflect that among the most controversial items in the proposed constitution was the question of the eligibility of women for membership in the Congress. Views were equally divided and Malam Sa'adu Zungur was called upon to intervene, as Adviser on Muslim Law. He ruled in favor, citing the arguments of Shehu Usuman Dan Fodio for the admission of women to his classes.

[15] In fact the founders of the Congress may have been influenced by the example of the Yoruba cultural society, *Egbe Omo Oduduwa,* which was technically non-political. An *Egbe* publication indicated the possibility of parallel development in the West and North:

"We are watching the progress of the Hausas with great interest. In many places in the North many responsible Hausas are looking to *Egbe Omo Oduduwa* as a link between the North and the South. This attitude is most inspiring and we on our part are extending a hand of fellowship daily to the Northerners. That is one reason why the Northern People's Conference held at Kaduna on June 26, 1949, has been of much interest to us even though we do not agree with all their decisions, such as abolition of the House of Chiefs." *Egbe Omo Oduduwa, Monthly Bulletin,* Vol. I, No. 8 (August 1949).

headmaster of a government teacher training college in Sokoto, was called upon to reply, and his caustic response is recalled by Northerners today with pride and amusement: "You may tell us to go by camel but we will go by airplane."[16]

In August 1950 a small group of radical youth in Kano organized the first declared political party in the North, called the Northern Elements Progressive Union (*Jam'iyyar Neman Sawaba* in Hausa).[17] The party's ostensible purpose was to operate as a political

[16] There are many extant versions of Malam Aminu's now famous impromptu response, e.g.: "We can move by camel, horse, motor car, or airplane, and will go the fastest way." Another version is the following dialogue:

District Officer: "Learn to walk before you run."

Malam Aminu: "If we fall we will get up and run again."

Officers were elected at the first annual convention as follows (data included for those not listed in footnote 13):

Dr. A. R. B. Dikko, President;

Alhaji Sanda, Deputy President (Muslim, Hausa, Kano, Lagos merchant);

Malam D. A. Rafih, Vice-President, North;

Malam Muhammadu Na-Nifulani, Vice-President, East (Muslim, Fulani, Kano, Enugu merchant);

Alhaji Muktari, Vice-President, West (Muslim, Hausa, Makurdi, Lagos and Freetown merchant);

Malam Yahaya Gusau, General Secretary (Muslim, Hausa, Sokoto, teacher);

Malam Isa S. Wali, Assistant Secretary;

Alhaji Abubakar Imam, Treasurer;

Malam Abubakar Tunau, Financial Secretary (Muslim, Hausa, Sokoto, Gaskiya Corp.);

Alhaji Abdulkadir Makama, Publicity Secretary;

Malam Julde, Joint Auditor;

Malam Aminu Kano, Joint Auditor;

Alhaji Inuwa Wada Kano, Adviser on Education (Muslim, Fulani, Kano, teacher);

Malam Sa'adu Zungur, Adviser on Muslim Law.

[17] The eight foundation members of the Northern Elements Progressive Union were as follows:

M. Abba Maikwaru (Kano, Hausa), President (then president of the *Taron Masu Zunuta* or Friendly Society);

Mr. Bello Ijumu (Kabba, Yoruba), General Secretary;

M. Maitama Sule (Kano, Hausa), teacher;

M. Sani Darma (Kano, Hausa), N.A. clerk;

M. Abdulkadir Danjaji (Kano, Hausa), trader;

M. Ahmadu Bida (an elderly man);

M. Mogaji Danbatta (Kano, Hausa), journalist;

M. (later Alhaji) Abba Kashiya (Kano, Hausa), N.A. cashier.

The founders appear to have had the support of Malam Aminu Kano who was then in charge of the Government Teacher Training College in Sokoto and could not openly join a declared political party at that time, although he did so upon leaving his post less than three months later.

Political thought in Kano had been stimulated by the transfer of the *Daily Comet* (Zik Group) to that city from Lagos. Among the early members of the NEPU were several young men who wrote articles for the *Comet* on political topics. The

94

vanguard within the broader but more conservative Northern Peoples' Congress. Ideologically, the new party was in the tradition of its nominal forebear, the Northern Elements Progressive Association. A "Declaration of Principles" (October 1950) dedicated the new party to the "emancipation of the *Talakawa*" (commoner class) through "reform of the present autocratic political institutions."[18] In December 1950 the Northern Peoples' Congress held its second annual convention at Jos. Adherents of the Northern Elements Progressive Union (NEPU), comprising a majority of the Kano delegation, presented resolutions which are said to have been drafted by Malam Aminu Kano, urging the convention to declare the NPC an explicitly nationalist political party. By that time it was apparent to persons of all shades of opinion that a Northern political party was required to operate the constitutional machinery then emerging from the process of constitutional review. But powerful emirs and certain administrative officers regarded the NPC as a dangerously radical group. Rumors were current to the effect that the emirs and their political associates contemplated the formation of a political party conceived on more conservative lines. Moderate leaders of the NPC surmised that their hopes for the transformation of their cultural organization into a dominant political party were doomed if overtly radical tendencies prevailed. It seems likely that leading Northern politicians had already decided to utilize the NPC providing the radical elements were eliminated.[19] Spokesmen for the Youth Social

---

two prime movers appear to have been Bello Ijumu, who later organized the pro-NCNC Middle Belt People's Party and Malam Maitama Sule, a foundation member of the NPC in 1948, later NPC Chief Whip in the Federal House of Representatives and Federal Minister of Mines and Power in the first independent government. Malam Maitama Sule suggested the name Northern Elements Progressive Union for three reasons: it signified the unity of Northern Progressives, it honored the old NEPA whose members had been victimized by the government for their beliefs, and the initials N.E.P.U. could be pronounced as a single word.

The NEPU has two Hausa names: *Jam'iyyar Neman Sawaba* and *Jam'iyyar Cigaban Arewa. Sawaba*, the party slogan and its popular name, means "freedom."

[18] The root cause of the social and economic degradation of the *Talakawa* (common people) was said to be the "vicious system of Administration by the Family Compact rulers . . . which has been established and fully supported by the British Imperialist Government." *Sawaba Declaration, Northern Elements Progressive Union, Declaration of Principles.* Extracts were published in the *Report on the Kano Disturbances. . . .* May 1953, Northern Regional Government (Kaduna: 1953), Appendix A.

[19] Two of the highest-ranking officers of the NPC told the writer that the need for a political party had been recognized during the period of constitutional review in 1949 and that the decision to utilize the NPC had been confirmed by the experience of the Northern leaders at the Ibadan General Conference. Malam Abubakar Imam, Treasurer of the NPC and editor of *Gaskiya Ta Fi Kwabo*, ridiculed

Circle of Sokoto threatened to withdraw from the NPC if the radical leaders, Aminu Kano and Sa'adu Zungur, were renamed to its central executive committee. Other moderates and conservatives supported that position and secured the adoption of a resolution to the effect that no member of the NEPU could remain as a member of the NPC. Thereupon the NEPU wing of the Kano delegation broke with the NPC, which became a suitable instrument for the use of conservative politicians.[20]

But the transformation did not occur until the latter part of 1951, after the primary voting phase of the first parliamentary election. Conservative northerners were dismayed when prominent members of the administrative elite in several provinces, whose candidatures were supported by emirs, were defeated in direct, open voting by candidates of the NEPU. Conversations were held between the most prominent politicians, notably the Sardauna of Sokoto and Malam Abubakar Tafawa Balewa, and the principal leaders of the NPC, notably Dr. A. R. B. Dikko and Abubakar Imam. On October 1, 1951, it was announced that the Northern Peoples' Congress with "65 branches and over 6,000 members" had been converted into a political party. The published declaration stated that all civil servants, including the General President, Dr. Dikko, had been advised to resign their NPC offices, that Alhaji Sanda, a Lagos merchant, had been elevated from the office of Deputy General President to Acting General President, and that the Sardauna of Sokoto and the Hon.

---

the proposed new conservative party of emirs and politicians as the *Jam'iyyar Sarakuna* (party of the nobility by birth). He is also said to have been among the most articulate opponents of the NEPU at the Jos convention, which gives weight to the opinion that moderates viewed the expunging of radicals from the NPC as an essential part of their program of political action.

[20] Prior to this rupture with the NEPU, the prestige of the NPC in conservative circles had been enhanced by an unusually successful fund-raising drive. The Ibadan General Conference on Review of the Constitution of January 1950 failed to resolve the deadlock produced by the Northern demand for 50% representation in the federal legislature. That demand was reiterated by a joint meeting of the Northern Houses of Chiefs and Assembly in February 1950 and supported by all sections of Northern opinion. Northern leaders, including leaders of the NPC, decided that, if necessary, a delegation would be sent to London to present the Northern case directly to the Secretary of State for the Colonies. For that purpose a fund-raising drive known as *Kurdin Taimaken Arewa* (Money to assist the North, or Northern Self-Development Fund) was launched. However, the Northern demand for 50% representation was ultimately conceded by leaders of the East and West and the fund was applied to its alternative purpose, the provision of scholarships for Northern children to study in the United Kingdom. James S. Coleman has described the K.T.A. as "financially the most successful public collection in Nigerian history." *Nigeria*, p. 363. M. G. Smith reports that the amount raised totalled "more than £40,000." *Government in Zazzau* (London: Oxford University Press, 1960), p. 278.

Abubakar Tafawa Balewa had become members.[21] At this point we may sketch briefly the biographies of these two who were destined to become Premier of the North and Prime Minister of the Federation, followed by a biographical sketch of a third leader, Aminu Kano, who personifies the Northern political opposition.

Alhaji Sir Ahmadu Bello, the Sardauna of Sokoto (knighted in 1959), is a direct descendant of Shehu Usuman dan Fodio, founder of the Fulani empire,[22] a great-grandson of the latter's son and successor, Sultan Bello, the first Sultan of Sokoto, and a first cousin to the incumbent Sultan of Sokoto, Sir Abubakar.[23] He is also related by marriage to the royal family of Kano. The Sardauna was born in 1909 in Rabah (Sokoto Division), where his father was District Head, and educated at the Sokoto Provincial School. Subsequently he attended the Katsina Teacher Training College, and served as a teacher of English and mathematics at the Sokoto Middle School (1931-1934) until his appointment as District Head of Rabah (1934-1938). Upon the death of Sultan Hassan in 1938, Abubakar was elevated to the Sultancy, and Ahmadu, a rival candidate, was appointed Sardauna (the "Leader of War"). He was the first holder of that title to be a member of the Sultan's Council and was assigned to administer the sub-divisional area of Gusau. Several years later (1943-1944) he was convicted by the Sultan's Court for alleged discrepancies in the *jangali* (cattle tax) account under his administration. But the conviction was reversed on appeal to a British High Court, and the Sardauna returned to the Sokoto Native Administration to assume the portfolio of Social Services with responsibility for education and police. Thereafter his relationship with the Sultan improved greatly and there has been little if any evidence of friction between them since that period. In 1945 he quietly supported the formation of the Youth Social Circle; when that group affiliated with the Northern Peoples' Congress in 1948, he was its non-public patron. When the Waziri of Sokoto died in 1949, the Sardauna was chosen to replace him as the Sokoto representative in the Northern House of Assembly, then an advisory chamber. He played a major part in the review of the Constitution of 1949-1950, emerging as an

[21] *Declaration of Jam'iyyar Mutanen Arewa (Northern Peoples' Congress), 1st October, 1951.*

[22] *Supra,* p. 8.

[23] The Sardauna's genealogy is traced and his early life is described in the Hausa-language publication, *Firimiyan Jihar Arewa Na Farko, Sardaunan Sakkwato Alhaji Ahmadu* (Zaria: Northern Region Literature Agency, 1956); and see his recently published autobiography, *My Life* (Cambridge: Cambridge University Press, 1962).

articulate defender of northern views who was acceptable as a regional leader to the emirs and the moderate progressives alike.

Alhaji Sir Abubakar Tafawa Balewa (knighted in 1959), the future Prime Minister of the Federation, was born in 1912 into a Muslim family of Tafawa Balewa, a small town in Lere District of Bauchi Emirate. His tribal origin is Gerawa, a Habe tribal group to which the royal family of Bauchi belongs.[24] Abubakar's father attended to the horses of the Ajiya, the District Head of Lere and a traditional Fulani councillor to the Emir. Abubakar was educated at the Bauchi Provincial School (1925-1928) and attended the Katsina Teacher Training College (1928-1933). After graduation he became a teacher, subsequently headmaster, at the Bauchi Middle School; in 1943 he was one of the founders of the famous Bauchi Discussion Circle. In 1945-1946 he studied for a teacher's professional certificate at the London University Institute of Education. Shortly after his return to Nigeria he was chosen by the Bauchi Native Authority to represent that Native Administration in the Northern House of Assembly and by the latter body as a Northern member of the reconstituted Nigerian Legislative Council. There he disputed the claim of the NCNC London delegation to speak for all of Nigeria and expressed his own belief that independence would not be a feasible object for Nigeria until a significantly greater measure of national unity had been achieved.[25] In 1948 he was elected Vice-President of the Northern Teachers' Association. He was active in the review of the constitution at all levels and emerged as the foremost spokesman

[24] The first Emir of Bauchi was a Habe student of Shehu Usuman dan Fodio who had been given a flag by the latter to prosecute the *jihad* among his people. He did so with the assistance of Fulani lieutenants who became his noblemen upon his installation as Emir. The Bauchi state is ethnically composite, with the Emir-ship vested in a Habe dynasty and most of the senior titles held by Fulanis.

[25] Hon. Abubakar Tafawa Balewa's speech in the Nigerian Legislative Council of March 24, 1947, was cited frequently thereafter as evidence of the necessity of continued British rule to foster the unity of diverse peoples in Nigeria. He was reported to have received a personal message of congratulations from the Governor, Sir Arthur Richards, an arch-opponent of Dr. Azikiwe. Hon. Abubakar Tafawa Balewa's address closed on this contentious note:

"We shall demand our rights when the time is ripe. We do want independence and we shall fight for it if necessary, but I should like to make it clear to you that if the British quitted Nigeria now at this stage the Northern people would continue their interrupted conquest to the sea." *Legislative Council Debates*, First Session, March 24, 1947, p. 212.

See the *West African Pilot*, April 10 and May 12, 1947, for the ensuing controversy over the interpretation given the above statement by the press. In subsequent speeches to the Legislative Council, Balewa developed the theme of unity through toleration, economic interdependence, and political federation. See *Legislative Council Debates*, Second Session, March 1948, p. 453.

of Northern constitutional views at the Ibadan General Conference of January 1950.[26]

In August 1950, Abubakar Tafawa Balewa incurred the hostility of the emirs, and secured his place of honor among the builders of modern Nigeria. At a meeting of the Northern House of Assembly he proposed the appointment of an independent commission to make recommendations for the "modernisation and reform" of the Native Authority system. His memorable address called for the abolition of the institution of the "Sole Native Authority" (whereby the powers of local government were vested in an emir or chief alone, subject only to the authority of administrative officials) as iniquitous and inconsistent with tradition, and for the introduction of a law requiring the emirs and chiefs to act "in Council."[27] All but one of the African members of the Northern House of Assembly voted for the motion, which passed by a single vote over the disapproving official bloc and led to a review and reform of the emirate system.[28] Yet Balewa alone

[26] Although the main theme of Hon. Abubakar Tafawa Balewa's principal address to the Ibadan General Conference was an exposition of the North's immediate demands for 50% representation in the House of Representatives and for revenue allocation on a per capita basis, his longer view envisaged the evolution of a strong central government as the development of the North became roughly even to that of the East and West:

"It is true that we are now trying an experiment never tried in any part of the world, that is the devolution of authority from the centre to the Regions, but I take it that this is merely temporary up to the time when the Regions in Nigeria reach equality. We may have to reverse it when the North can really march with the East and the West, we may have to reverse the recommendation of a regional autonomy and to strengthen the centre and weaken the Regions, but we want a strong regional autonomy for a temporary measure, that is all and nothing more."

Proceedings of the General Conference on Review of the Constitution, January 1950 (Lagos: Government Printer, 1950), pp. 63-69.

[27] Malam Abubakar Tafawa Balewa's "note of warning" to the "Natural Rulers" of the North reveals his keen perception of the political implications of social change: "Our Natural Rulers," he declared, "should realize that Western education and world conditions are fast creating a new class of people in the North. That this new class must exist is certain, and the Natural Rulers, whom the North must retain at all costs, should, instead of suspecting it, try to find it proper accommodation." *Northern House of Assembly, Official Report*, Fourth Session, August 1950, pp. 91-98.

[28] The vote was 20 unofficials in favor, 19 officials opposed. *Ibid.*, p. 98. Subsequently the Governor appointed an official commission (Maddocks-Potts) that reported to a Joint Select Committee of the Northern Regional Council. Among the recommendations that emerged were abolition of the Sole Native Authorities and the establishment of councils at the village, district, and town level, as well as advisory councils at the level of the Native Authority. See the *Report of the Joint Select Committee of the Northern Regional Council*, 1951. The Sole Native Authorities were abolished in 1952 and replaced by Native Authorities-in-Council. See D. A. Potts, *Progress Report on Local Government in the Northern Region of Nigeria* (Lagos: 1953), p. 2. The subsequent development is indicated *supra*, pp. 26-27.

seems to have drawn the resentment of conservative emirs, some of whom endeavored without success to prevent his election to the House of Assembly in 1951.

Malam Aminu Kano, the outstanding radical leader of the North, was born in 1921 into a Fulani clan of Kano (the Genawa) known for men of juristic learning. His father was a scribe and his mother an educated woman who taught him Arabic and initiated his study of the Qur'an at an early age. He learned English at the Kano Middle School, and began training for the teaching profession in 1939, when it was said that the German armies might invade the country and conscript every man without a position. He attended Kaduna College, successor to the famous Katsina Training College, and in 1941 was assigned to the Bauchi Middle School as a practice teacher. There he read widely in the field of history, and became the close friend of Malam Sa'adu Zungur, the foremost critic of the system of native administration in the North. Aminu wrote articles in a similar critical vein, some of which were published in the Hausa-language weekly, *Gaskiya Ta Fi Kwabo,* and others in the *West African Pilot.* He participated in a school dramatic society that produced satirical plays featuring thinly veiled ridicule of the pompous ways of traditional rulers. He was also an articulate member of the Bauchi Discussion Circle to which the headmaster of his school, Abubakar Tafawa Balewa, belonged.[29] We have observed that in 1943-1944, Malam Aminu and Malam Sa'adu Zungur organized the quasi-political Bauchi General Improvement Union, that in 1946 Aminu was a-warded a two-year government scholarship to attend the University of London Institute of Education, that in London he helped found the Northern Teachers' Welfare Association, and that he convened the first annual meeting of the Northern Teachers' Association in 1948, at which time he was elected secretary. The following year he participated in the founding of the Northern Peoples' Congress and was elected to the office of Joint Auditor.

Meanwhile government officials evinced an interest in his career and he appears to have been offered a choice of several attractive

[29] On one occasion Malam Aminu engaged in a debate with a Senior District Officer on the proposition: "That Indirect Rule is the best form of government for Northern Nigeria." Malam Aminu's speech, partly recorded in an old journal, began by granting that Lord Lugard's original aim was commendable but that indirect rule in practice has proved to be "the most exploiting system of colonial administration the world has ever known."

Malam Aminu relates that he utilized original songs, some of which had political overtones, to teach English grammar. One of the most popular was the *Zamani* song, meaning "Today" or "New Time," which encouraged the youth to acquire education and to abandon archaic customs.

positions in the administrative service which he declined, requesting promotion in the teaching field instead. He accepted an appointment as Acting Education Officer in charge of a new teacher training college at Sokoto, but his political interests did not subside with professional advancement; his criticisms of Northern educational policies, published by the Northern Teachers' Association, disturbed the government, and his growing influence in Sokoto troubled the Sultan.[30] Finally Aminu decided that his position in the government service was untenable, and that he might as well resign and devote his full attention to politics. In November 1950 he returned to Kano and joined the NEPU; subsequently he became permanent secretary of the Northern Teachers' Association. By 1951 Malam Aminu was an acknowledged leader of the radical Northern youth; he was chosen Vice-President of the NEPU at its first annual conference of April 1951 and was one of four NEPU candidates from Kano District who were elected to the final electoral college in November 1951 where they were eliminated by supporters of the Emir of Kano and the NPC.[31] Thereafter, Malam Aminu was identified with the causes of electoral reform and political liberty in the North.

The Birth of the Action Group in Western Nigeria

By 1950 the basic outline of the new constitution, to be introduced in 1951, was widely known, and the anti-Azikiwe group among the Yoruba elite contemplated the depressing likelihood that an NCNC government would come to power in the Western Region. Their old party, the Nigerian Youth Movement, was an effective instrument in Lagos only, where it could not match the electoral strength of the Nigerian National Democratic Party, an NCNC affiliate. The logical nucleus of a new political opposition to the NCNC was the pan-Yoruba cultural organization, *Egbe Omo Oduduwa*, which did engage in limited political activities through a political committee and a committee on constitutional reform.[32] Moreover, the *Egbe* had evolved into an effective medium of cooperation between the new elite of the Western Region and the Yoruba chiefs. Among the people of the rural areas and traditional towns of Yorubaland,

[30] One of Aminu Kano's first acts as headmaster of the college was to dismiss the Sultan's "messengers" whose real function was to report to their patron on school activities. He also discovered that certain farmers, whose land had been taken for the school, had been under-compensated and he pressed successfully for additional payments to them.

[31] *Supra*, p. 30.

[32] See *Egbe Omo Oduduwa, Monthly Bulletin*, April 1949, pp. 4-5; also *Egbe Omo Oduduwa, Proposals for 1950 Constitutional Reform* (Lagos: n.d.).

the influence of the chiefs was considerable. As Obafemi Awolowo wrote in 1945, chieftaincy has an "incalculable sentimental value for the masses in Western and Northern Nigeria. This being so, it is imperative, as a matter of practical politics, that we use the most effective means ready to hand for organizing masses for rapid political advancement."[33]

But many chiefs were reluctant to engage openly in politics. In the first place, a chief was an agent of the administration, and it was widely thought, by Africans and white officials alike, that overt partisanship by a chief would constitute an abuse of traditional authority. Secondly, most chiefs feel that their positions are sanctioned by customary laws which prevail "above politics"; customarily, in Nigeria a chief, as a traditional or "natural" ruler, is the "father" of all his people, irrespective of their political affiliations. Many chiefs were prepared to affiliate with the *Egbe Omo Oduduwa* because it was nominally non-partisan, and their participation in the "cultural" activities of the *Egbe* did not invite criticism. Moreover, the chiefs were asked to support the *Egbe* by the most illustrious Yoruba personalities in the business and professional worlds, not a few of whom were identified prominently with political moderation and official respectability.

In the opinion of youthful and radical nationalists, the complexion of the membership of the *Egbe Omo Oduduwa* was too conservative for that organization to serve as a satisfactory base for militant action. Nationalists who wanted to use the *Egbe* for political purposes without being controlled unduly by the conservative elements within its fold, decided that an independent political group was required. On March 26, 1950, Obafemi Awolowo, barrister and publisher, general secretary of the *Egbe* and secretary of its committee on constitutional reform, convened a meeting at his residence in Ibadan which was attended by seven persons in addition to himself and is commemorated as the inaugural meeting of the Action Group.[34] The primary purpose of the Group was to win electoral control of the Western Region in 1951; to that end, professional and educated Yoruba personalities resident in Lagos and Ibadan, who did not accept the leadership of Azikiwe, would be encouraged to "return" to their home areas and organize their people to support their candidatures to the Western House of Assembly.

[33] Obafemi Awolowo, *Path to Nigerian Freedom* (London: Faber, 1947), p. 66.
[34] The founding members of the Action Group, in addition to Obafemi Awolowo, were Abiodun Akerele, S. O. Shonibare, Ade. Akinsanya, J. O. Adigun, Olatunji Docemo, B. A. Akinsanya and S. T. Oredein. All eight are Yoruba from Ijebu, Oyo, or Ibadan Provinces.

"The Action Group," it was stated at the inaugural meeting, "would consist of members of the *Egbe* so the *Egbe* might be able to carry the views of the Action Group across anywhere the *Egbe* existed."[35] At the third meeting of the Action Group, in June, it was reported that the *Egbe* had decided to organize a political group of its own, and the view was expressed that the Action Group should disband in order to avoid duplication of effort and mutually injurious competition. Mr. Awolowo and barrister S. L. Akintola, editor of the *Daily Service* and chairman of the Lagos branch of the Nigerian Youth Movement, argued that a political directorate working within the *Egbe*, but not a part of it, would be more effective than a mere committee of the *Egbe*, and might be expanded eventually to operate elsewhere in Nigeria. It was decided that the Action Group should continue to function in close cooperation with the *Egbe*.[36]

With the exception of Mr. Awolowo, the most influential of the early members of the Action Group was Chief Bode Thomas, the son of a wealthy merchant who studied law in England (1940-1942) and set up a highly successful practice in Lagos, where he joined the Youth Movement and became chairman of the editorial board of the *Daily Service*.[37] Chief Thomas personified the group of Lagos professional men who assumed political leadership in their home divisions in accordance with the Action Group strategy. In 1950 he was installed as *Balogun* of Oyo, an honorary title conferred upon

[35] Minutes of the Inaugural Meeting of the Action Group held at Mr. Obafemi Awolowo's Residence, Oke-Bola, Ibadan, 26 March, 1950. Mr. Awolowo seems to have made this concrete proposal:
"The Central Committee of the Action Group should consist of members from each of the 21 Divisions in the Western Region who were already members of the *Egbe Omo Oduduwa* and were interested in politics. They must be such persons who could be relied upon to carry out a concerted program."
It was agreed that candidates for election to the House of Assembly would be submitted for approval to the Council of the *Egbe* as the Action Group would provide "only the leading thought about the selection of suitable candidates." See Obafemi Awolowo, *Awo: The Autobiography of Chief Obafemi Awolowo* (Cambridge: Cambridge University Press, 1960), pp. 214ff.
[36] Minutes of the Third Meeting of the Action Group held at Mr. Awolowo's Residence, Oke-Bola, Ibadan, 4 June, 1950. Cf. Awolowo, *Awo* pp. 219-221.
[37] Dr. Nnamdi Azikiwe has credited Chief Bode Thomas with having made the first systematic exposition of a theory of regionalized political parties in 1947, soon after the return to Nigeria of the NCNC delegation to London. In the course of an address, Chief Thomas is reported to have proposed the inauguration of regional political parties to "deal exclusively with matters affecting their respective zones. . . . These bodies may join at the top and form a council for Nigeria which will be competent to tackle any matter that may affect the country generally." *Daily Times*, October 11, 1947, quoted in Nnamdi Azikiwe, *The Development of Political Parties in Nigeria* (London: 1957), p. 16. Thomas' idea of 1947 is reflected in the formative meetings of the Action Group in 1950-1951 and in that party's first public announcement of March 21, 1951.

him in recognition of service and merit by the *Alafin* (king) and the traditional councillors of Oyo. At the fifth meeting of the Action Group, Chief Thomas emphasized the necessity for Action Group leaders in the provinces to enlist and utilize the support of chiefs for mass organization. Mr. Awolowo added a point of clarification to the effect that the Action Group had been organized to neutralize the influence of chiefs by encouraging the people to vote for men of their choice in the forthcoming primary elections.[38]

At the sixth meeting, on October 8, 1950, Mr. Awolowo felt obliged to propose the discontinuance of the Action Group for lack of support. If the Action Group disbanded, persons opposed to the NCNC were likely to fall back upon the Central Council of the *Egbe Omo Oduduwa*, where the influence of non-radical professionals, conservative businessmen, and traditional elitists was far greater than within the Action Group. Mr. M. A. Ajasin of Owo argued that a large number of people were not required at the planning stage, and the meeting reached a unanimous agreement to carry on with redoubled efforts.[39] A new high of 27 persons attended the seventh meeting (the fifth had been attended by 20) which decided to invite sympathizers of the Action Group in the non-Yoruba provinces of Benin and Warri to organize a parallel wing.[40] At the ninth meeting

[38] Minutes of the Fifth Meeting of the Action Group held at the *Egbe Omo Oduduwa* Secretariat, Oke-Bola, Ibadan, August 6, 1950.

[39] Minutes of the Sixth Meeting of the Action Group held at Mr. Obafemi Awolowo's Residence, Oke-Bola, Ibadan, October 8, 1950.

[40] "*Mr. Awolowo* replied [in the course of discussion on expansion to the mid-West] that it was true that it was decided at a meeting that the non-Yorubas should be invited to join the group simultaneously. But at a certain stage it was considered yet inopportune as it would be difficult to get people from far distances to attend the Group's meetings because very few people were public-spirited. Another point was that it was originally thought that the A.G. should consist of members from each of the 16 Divisions (who were Yorubas) in the Western Region, who were already members of the *Egbe Omo Oduduwa* and were interested in politics. Another point was that people who were not of Yoruba stock worked on certain peculiar hypotheses. If we called in the Benin and Warri, they might introduce something which would not be acceptable to the Group in view of their claim for Benin-Warri State. He felt that the Yorubas should first weld themselves together so that it might be difficult for other tribes to break through them. It was therefore finally decided that for the time being, we should ensure that the Yorubas were first strongly organized and that the Benins and Warri and other non-Yorubas could be drawn in later. These were the reasons why the Benins and Warri had not yet been invited."

Chief Bode Thomas added that it was only prudent to take steps to avoid the emergence of a strong anti-Yoruba sub-Regional minority in the mid-West. Minutes of the Seventh Meeting of the Action Group held at the *Egbe Omo Oduduwa* Secretariat, Oke-Bola, Ibadan, November 12, 1950.

Chief Thomas consulted with his school chum, the Itsekiri barrister M. E. R. Okorodudu, later Commissioner for the Western Region in the United Kingdom

it was affirmed that in Yorubaland the Action Group should be the "political wing" of the *Egbe Omo Oduduwa*.[41]

In March 1951, after a year's preparation and nine private meetings, the Action Group announced itself to the nation as a "Western Regional Political Organization." A statement was released expressing the "ardent wish" of the founders that a nation-wide organization, acceptable to all sections of the nationalist movement, would emerge, in which event the Action Group would be content to constitute its Western Regional Working Committee. For the time being, the Action Group was pledged to cooperate with the *Egbe Omo Oduduwa*, the *Edo Union* and other ethnic associations in the West. "As far as possible it will use the existing branches of these organizations to foster its own interests and it will in turn use its organizational machinery to enlarge and consolidate the spheres of their influence."[42]

(1954-1958) and with Anthony Enahoro, formerly an editor of Zik Group newspapers, then publisher of the *Nigerian Star* at Warri. In 1950, Enahoro and barrister Arthur Prest, President of the Warri National Union, inaugurated a Mid-West Party, which evolved into the Mid-West section of the Action Group. Thirty-three delegates attended the first meeting of the Mid-West Zone of the Action Group at Sapele on April 21, 1951.

[41] "After a lengthy discussion on the relation between the [Action Group and] the *Egbe*, it was decided that the A.G. should be made the political wing of the *Egbe* and should function as such. That members of the A.G. need not necessarily be members of the *Egbe* provided they embrace the political programme of the *Egbe*." Minutes of the Ninth Meeting of the Action Group at the *Egbe Omo Oduduwa* Secretariat, Oke-Bola, Ibadan, March 4, 1951.

Four of the first ten meetings of the Action Group were held at the *Egbe Omo Oduduwa* Secretariat, Oke-Bola, Ibadan; five were held at the nearby residence of Mr. Awolowo and one at the Ibadan Boys' High School.

[42] *Daily Times*, March 21, 1951, also *Daily Service*, March 21, 1951. The following circular letter was sent to supporters and potential supporters in the Western Region:

The Action Group (Western Zone) Nigeria
Motto: "Freedom From The British Rule"

> The Secretariat
> Action Group
> Oke Ado
> c/o P.O. Box 136
> Ibadan
> 1951

Gentlemen,

1. It would no doubt interest you to hear that for almost a year now a body, comprising of responsible men in the Western Provinces, has been organized under the name Action Group.

2. This Group is meant to be developed into a powerful political party which will be strong enough to win popular mass following in the West, and control the government in the West under the proposed new Constitution.

3. After organizing secretly for almost a year during which it has succeeded in winning the support of leaders of opinion in this region, it has now decided to make

On April 28-29, 1951, the Action Group held its inaugural conference at Owo, which was attended by delegates from both the Yoruba and the Mid-Western (Benin-Warri) zones. Obafemi Awolowo, chairman of the Yoruba section, was elected President, Chief Bode Thomas was elected General Secretary, and three of the four elected Vice-Presidents represented the Bini, Urhobo, and Itsekeri ethnic groups of the Mid-West.[43] On June 10, the new party took a long stride toward the seizure of power in the Western Region. At a joint meeting of the Central Executive Council of the *Egbe Omo Oduduwa* and the leading Yoruba *Obas* (Paramount Chiefs)[44] in Ibadan, the latter pledged their support to the Action Group. The decision of the chiefs was announced by the pre-eminent spiritual *Oba* of the Yoruba people,

---

public appearance, organize branches and enroll members in all town and villages in the West.

4. Membership of the Group is open to farmers, teachers, traders, market-women, black-smiths, carpenters, artisans, tailors, merchants, lawyers, doctors, all alike —no discrimination either religious or otherwise in the Group.

5. The Group believes first and foremost in Unity of all people of Western Nigeria as stepping stones for a prelude to Unity of Nigeria as a whole.

6. It also believes that opportunity of comfortable living, medical attention, and free education should be given all people in the West.

7. These and other programmes of activities which the Group believes in and is prepared to see in operation in the Western Region shall soon be made public.

8. Mr. ....the organizer of the Group in .... Province will start a tour of the .... Province as from .... 1951.

9. A copy of his first itinerary is attached.

10. It will be greatly appreciated if you would kindly form a small committee and help arrange a mass meeting to meet him. Other particulars will be explained when he arrives yonder.

11. If you have a local town Union, your Union could be made the spearhead for the mass meeting is open to all citizens, male or female, educated or illiterate. I repeat—no discrimination.

Yours faithfully,

....

Secretary—Action Group

[43] The officers of the Action Group elected at the Owo Conference of April 28-29, 1951 were as follows:

Obafemi Awolowo, President; Hon. Gaius Obaseki, Vice-President; Chief W. E. Mowarin, Vice-President; Chief Arthur Prest, Vice-President; M. A. Ajasin, Vice-President; Chief Bode Thomas, General Secretary; Anthony Enahoro and S. O. Sonibare, Assistant Secretaries; S. O. Ighodaro, Treasurer; M. A. Ogun, Publicity and Propaganda Secretary; S. L. Akintola and M. E. R. Okorodudu, Legal Advisers; S. T. Oredein, Administrative Secretary.

[44] It was noted in Chapter 1 that an *Oba* in Yorubaland is the sacred or divine king of a traditional state. Technically it is incorrect to render the term *Oba* into English as "Paramount Chief." We do so because *Obas* are normally the administrative equals or superiors to all other chiefs within their local government council areas.

106

Sir Adesoji Aderemi II, the *Oni* of Ife; a concurring statement was made by the *Alafin* of Oyo, traditionally the leading secular ruler of the Yorubas, who was then a patron of the *Egbe* and a benefactor of Chief Bode Thomas.[45]

Clearly, the Action Group was founded with a realistic awareness of the fact that chiefs were destined to play a major role in local and national politics under the Constitution of 1951 which extended the franchise to millions of people on a semi-democratic basis. However, the powers of the Yoruba chiefs of the Western Region were limited by custom, and the chiefs, with few exceptions, were not averse to political cooperation with those members of the new elite who were prepared to observe the traditional proprieties. Most enlightened chiefs realized that a democratic era was at hand, and they preferred to reach an agreement with the able and trusted sons of their communities than to suffer the indignities of disregard by unpredictable politicians who were apt to be less sympathetic to their feelings. These "modern" chiefs readily attached their interests to the interests of the rising class[46] and agreed to assist the Action Group.

By and large the founders of the Action Group were economically independent men of liberal opinions; for the most part they were barristers, businessmen, and teachers in the employ of private schools. (See Table I.) Chief Bode Thomas appears to have been one of the very few early members who were born into comparative affluence. Few of the founders or early activists were wealthy cocoa traders, but they came from areas (and families) which prospered as a result of the lucrative cocoa export trade and their careers in the professional, educational, and business worlds rested largely on the economic basis of agricultural prosperity. Manifestly the Action Group represented the interests of a rising class, and its leadership was determined to control the politically crucial institution of chieftaincy. The achievement of that objective after 1952 will be discussed in Chapter VI. In 1951, members of the Action Group who returned to their home districts in order to stand for the Western House of Assembly, bowed respectfully to the traditional chiefs, took honorary titles (for which

[45] *Daily Times*, June 13, 1951.
[46] P. C. Lloyd, a perceptive student of the changing institution of chieftaincy among the Yoruba, has said that Yoruba chiefs have been obliged to observe modern standards of conduct and ostentation in order to maintain their traditional prestige: " . . . in the 19th century the *oba* expressed his wealth in numerous wives, horses, and generous entertainment; in the 20th century he is expected to live in a large house, own a car and send a son to England." "The Changing Role of the Yoruba Traditional Rulers." *Proceedings of the Third Annual Conference of the West African Institute of Social and Economic Research* (Ibadan: University College, 1956), pp. 58, 60-61.

TABLE I

Inaugural and Executive Members of the Action Group,
26 March 1950-17 December 1953*

(Ethnic Identification, Home [Town and/or Division],
Religion and Occupation)

Obafemi Awolowo - Ijebu Yoruba, Ikenne, Remo - Methodist - Barrister; General
Secretary of the *Egbe Omo Oduduwa*; Legal Adviser to the Ibadan Native
Settlers Union; publisher of the *Nigerian Tribune*; formerly engaged in the
produce trade and motor transport business; formerly Western Provincial Secretary of the Nigerian Youth Movement.

Abiodun Akerele - Oyo Yoruba, Oyo - Christian - Barrister; later *Balogun* of Oyo.

S. O. Sonibare - Ijebu Yoruba, Ijebu-Ode - Christian - U.A.C. Manager (Lagos),
businessman, later Managing Director of the Amalgamated Press.

Ade. Akinsanya - Ijebu Yoruba, Ikenne, Remo - Christian - Manager of the African
Press, Ibadan (*Nigerian Tribune*); subsequently studied law in the United
Kingdom.

J. O. Adigun - Oshun Yoruba - Christian - Editor of the *Morning Star*, Ibadan;
subsequently a Western Region Minister.

Olatunji Dosunmu - Ijebu Yoruba, Iperu, Remo - Christian - *Daily Service* reporter,
later Administrative Secretary of the Action Group.

B. A. Akinsanya - Ijebu Yoruba, Ikenne, Remo - Christian - Medical Department
employee; subsequently a chemist and druggist; and Chairman of the Ikenne
Local Council.

S. T. Oredein - Ijebu Yoruba, Ogere, Remo - Christian - General Secretary, British-
American Tobacco Company Workers, Ibadan; subsequently Principal Organizing
Secretary, Action Group.

S. O. Awokoya - Ijebu Yoruba, Ijebu-Igbo, Ijebu-Ode - Christian - School Principal;
subsequently Minister of Education.

Akintunde Sowunmi - Egba Yoruba, Abeokuta - Christian - Joint Editor, *Morning
Star*, Ibadan; later with the Western Nigeria Information Service Cinema
Division.

S. L. Akintola - Oshun Yoruba, Ogbomosho - Christian - Barrister and journalist;
Editor *Daily Service*; Chairman Lagos branch NYM; later Federal Minister of
Communications and Aviation, and Premier, Western Region.

I. O. Delano - Egba Yoruba, Abeokuta - Christian - Pensioner, author; Administrative Secretary of the *Egbe Omo Oduduwa*.

G. A. Fagbure - Oshun Yoruba, Iwo - Christian - Journalist, *Western Echo*, Ibadan;
later became editor of the *West African Pilot* and a member of the NCNC;
then Information Officer in the Office of the Nigerian Commissioner in the
United Kingdom.

M. A. Ogun - Ijebu Yoruba, Ijebu-Ode - Christian - Public Relations and Advertising business; later an Action Group leader in the Lagos Town Council.

M. A. Ajasin - Yoruba, Owo - Christian - College Principal.

Chief Bode Thomas - Oyo Yoruba, Oyo - Christian - Barrister; *Balogun* of Oyo;
Chancellor of the African Church Organization; later Central Minister of
Transport and Chairman of the Oyo Divisional Council.

E. C. B. Omole - Ibadan Yoruba - Member Ibadan People's Party, 1951.

S. O. Lanlehin - Ibadan Yoruba - Christian - Businessman; member, Ibadan
People's Party, 1951.

D. Ariyo - Ilesha Yoruba - Later an Action Group field secretary.

* See end of Table.

TABLE I (continued)

T. T. Solaru - Ijebu Yoruba, Ijebu-Ode - Methodist pastor; Minister, educator, representative of the Oxford University Press.

Ayotunde Rosiji - Egba Yoruba, Abeokuta - Christian - Barrister; later, Federal Minister of Health.

J. B. Williams -

E. A. Babalola - Ekiti Yoruba - Christian - Educator; became a Minister in the Western Region Government, resigned from the party in 1956 and returned in 1958.

Ayo Okusaga - Ijebu Yoruba, Ijebu-Ode - Christian - Barrister; later, Western Minister of Education.

Rev. E. O. Alayande - Ibadan Yoruba - Christian - Educator.

O. Akeredolu-Ale - Ikeja Yoruba.

A. M. A. Akinloye - Ibadan Yoruba - Christian - Barrister; Western Minister of Agriculture; President, Ibadan People's Party, 1951.

Oba Adetunji Aiyeola, Afolu II - Ijebu Yoruba, Remo (Makun) - Christian.

A. A. Adio-Moses - Yoruba - Christian - Trade unionist; later Labour Officer, Western Region.

Oladipo Amos - Yoruba, Ikorodu - Christian - Publicity Secretary, resigned 1956.

Hon. Gaius Obaseki - Edo, Benin - Christian - Businessman; *Iyase* of Benin; Chairman of the Benin Divisional Council; member of the Governor's Executive Council; leader of the Reformed *Ogboni* Fraternity of Benin.

Chief Arthur Prest - Itsekeri, Warri - Christian - Barrister; Central Minister of Communications.

Chief W. E. Mowarin - Urhobo - Christian - Businessman.

Anthony Enahoro - Edo, Ishan - Christian - Businessman and publisher (*The Nigerian Star*); later Western Minister of Home Affairs.

S. O. Ighodaro - Edo, Benin - Christian - Barrister; later Attorney General, Western Region.

M. E. R. Okorodudu - Itsekeri, Warri - Christian - Barrister; later Western Commissioner in the United Kingdom; resigned from the party in 1958.

D. N. Oresanya - Edo, Benin.

C. O. Evoigbe - Ishan.

E. J. Igenuma - Kukuruku.

P. A. Oladapo - Ondo Yoruba - Christian - Businessman.

A. O. Ogedengbe - Owo Yoruba - Christian - Educator; later Western Minister of Works.

D. A. Oguntoye - Ijesha Yoruba, Ilesha - Christian - Barrister.

Reece D. Edukugho - Itsekeri, Warri - Christian - Merchant.

Chief M. F. Agidee - Western Ijaw - Christian - Timber contractor.

Chief F. J. Okene - Urhobo.

Dr. Akanni Doherty - Lagos Yoruba - Christian - Medical Practitioner; Chairman Lagos branch of the Action Group.

J. A. O. Odebiyi - Egbado Yoruba - Christian - Educator; subsequently Western Minister of Finance.

Rev. S. A. Adeyefa - Ife Yoruba - Christian - Educator.

Dr. Akinola Maja - Lagos Yoruba - Christian - Medical Practitioner and businessman; Chairman of the Board of the National Bank; President of the *Egbe Omo Oduduwa*; formerly President of the NYM.

Chief C. D. Akran - Badagry Yoruba - Christian - retired civil servant; subsequently Western Minister of Economic Planning.

Chief J. F. Odunjo - Egbado Yoruba - Christian - Educator; subsequently Western Minister of Lands.

D. S. Adegbenro - Egbe Yoruba - Muslim - clerk and merchant; subsequently Western Minister of Local Government.

TABLE I (concluded)

Alfred O. Rewane - Itsekeri, Warri - Christian - Businessman; subsequently Chairman of the Western Region Production Development Board.

S. Y. Eke - Edo, Benin - Christian - Businessman (rubber factory).

F. R. A. Williams - Egba Yoruba - Christian - Barrister; subsequently Attorney General, Western Region.

R. A. Fani-Kayode - Ife Yoruba - Christian - Barrister; resigned in 1959.

F. O. Awosika - Ondo Yoruba - Christian - Educator; subsequently Western Minister of Finance and Chairman of the Western Housing Corporation.

Mrs. T. T. Solaru - Yoruba - Christian - Teacher.

Alhaji S. O. Gbadamosi - Ikorodu Yoruba - Muslim - Businessman.

E. A. Sanda -

Sources:

Minutes of the first ten meetings of the Action Group: March 26, 1950; April 23, 1950; June 4, 1950; July 30, 1950; August 6, 1950; October 8, 1950; November 12, 1950; December 10, 1950; March 4, 1951; April 1, 1951.

Report of the Owo Conference, April 28-29, 1951, *Daily Service*, May 2, 3, 1951.

Minutes of the Central Executive Committee, May 26, 1951.

Report of the Benin Conference, December 17-20, 1952.

Minutes of the Central Executive Committee, January 12-13, 1953.

Minutes of the Emergency Meeting of the Executive Committee, March 24, 1953.

Minutes of the Executive Committee, May 1, 1953.

Minutes of the Emergency Joint Meeting of the Executive Committee and the Parliamentary Council, July 1 and July 17, 1953; September 8, 1953.

Report of the Warri Congress, December 15-17, 1953.

they sometimes paid dearly) to enhance their prestige, and easily gained the upper hand over old-fashioned chiefs, most of whom were politically inept. In this way the Yoruba elite outmaneuvered Azikiwe, whose electoral hold on Lagos could not then be shaken.[47]

In vain the NCNC tried to prevent the incorporation of Lagos into the politically uncertain Western Region. The General Conference on Review of the Constitution (January 1950) had recommended the establishment of an independent municipality of Lagos, but the Select

[47] Cf. this passage from a critical yet sympathetic appraisal of Chief Bode Thomas by a Nigerian student in London:

"Nationalists, like Thomas, who had failed to break Azikiwe's hold on Lagos, were encouraged by the post-war prosperity of the provincial areas to seek a future in the virgin political lands of the Sole Native Authorities. [Actually the Sole Native Authority institution had been abolished in the Western Region by 1949.] The authorities were 'democratised' to admit the newcomers. The small fish in the big waters of Lagos politics became big fish in the small provincial waters and the new alliance of Natural Rulers and middle-class professionals summoned the forces of the old to redress the balance of the new.

"Bode Thomas sought and was given the office of Balogun of Oyo not so much because he wanted to head the demands for reform against perhaps the most obscurantist of the First Class rulers in the West as because the road to the Regional and Central legislatures must, for him, as for other anti-Azikiwe Lagos politicians, begin from a Native Authority area." "Bode Thomas—A Chapter of History," *The Nigerian*, No. 3 (London: February 1954), p. 2.

Committee of the Legislative Council, to which the report of the General Conference was submitted, rebuffed Azikiwe and recommended the inclusion of Lagos in the Western Region for administrative and legislative purposes.[48] On this issue, Azikiwe was supported by his old rival, barrister H. O. Davies, a founder of both the Nigerian Youth Movement and the *Daily Service*, who was then an influential member of the *Egbe Omo Oduduwa*. Davies had been a consistent advocate of Nigerian unity; he regarded Lagos as a symbol of the emerging nation and he rejected in principle the proposal to compromise its national character by incorporation within a particular region.[49]

Oddly, the leaders of the Action Group were reluctant initially to include Lagos within the scope of their operations, a reflection of the fact that opposition to the new party within the *Egbe* and the Nigerian Youth Movement was centered in the seacoast capital.[50] However, the major objectives of the Action Group were identical to those of

[48] Recommendations of the General Conference on Review of the Constitution, pp. 232-248; *Review of the Constitution of Nigeria: Dispatch dated the 15th July, 1950 from the Secretary of State for the Colonies*, Sessional Paper No. 20, 1950 (Lagos: 1950); "Minority Reports on the New Constitution," *Nigerian Legislative Council, Debates*, September 1950.

"On the incorporation of Lagos into the Western Region, which the select committee approved, Azikiwe and three other dissenting members argued that 'Lagos representation in the Central Legislature should be direct and unfettered—and not through the Western House of Assembly which must, in turn, select the same Lagos Representatives in that House to the Central Legislature.' Azikiwe's Yoruba critics argue that he opposed the merger of Lagos with the Western Region because he feared that an anti-Azikiwe, Yoruba-dominated, Western House of Assembly would not only freeze him out of the Central House of Representatives (for which it was the electoral college), but would also legislate for Lagos, the main center of his political power and his business enterprises. Actually, in 1952 Azikiwe was excluded from the Central House in this manner." Coleman, *Nigeria*, p. 349.

[49] H. O. Davies emphasized his objection to the Lagos-West merger by resigning from the Nigerian Youth Movement in February 1950. Within a few days a public reconciliation had been effected, but Davies broke finally with the N.Y.M. a year later and formed the Nigerian People's Congress. Davies was also a prominent member of the *Egbe Omo Oduduwa*; at the inaugural conference in June 1948 he was chosen as co-legal adviser (with Bode Thomas) and he was largely responsible for the successful promotion of the *Egbe* Endowment Fund for "Oduduwan scholars." But he opposed the *Egbe* philosophy of regionalism and its utilization for political purposes. In this regard he clashed with Obafemi Awolowo, who had been a follower and admirer of Davies in the Youth Movement.

[50] "After a lengthy discussion on certain complications which were likely to crop up between the *Egbe* and the Action Group, it was decided to leave Lagos out." Minutes of the Inaugural Meeting of the Action Group, March 26, 1950; the decision to omit Lagos was reiterated at the third meeting of June 4, 1950 (Minutes). J. S. Coleman states that the newly formed Action Group "shunned Lagos, partly because of Awolowo's emphatic belief that the capital city was a cesspool of intrigue, petty bickering, and confusion." *Nigeria*, p. 350. The fourth

111

the Lagos Yoruba elite, and leaders of the Youth Movement con-cluded that the political aims of Azikiwe might be thwarted by placing his metropolitan base under the jurisdiction of an anti-NCNC government in the Western Region. At the tenth meeting of the Action Group (March 31-April 1, 1951) an alliance with the Nigerian Youth Movement for electoral purposes was approved.[51] Shortly thereafter, the N.Y.M. was gently put to rest and reincarnated by its leading members as the Lagos branch of the Action Group with a new spirit of mass participation.[52]

The Three-Party System Established

The Committee of National Rebirth

In March 1951, shortly before the Action Group proclaimed its existence, supporters of the NCNC made an extraordinary attempt to recreate the national front which had collapsed in October 1950 with the failure of the National Emergency Committee. Possibly their maneuver had the ulterior purpose of heading off the political drive of anti-NCNC elements under the leadership of Awolowo. The con-veners of the Committee of National Rebirth were Mbonu Ojike and Kingsley Ozuomba Mbadiwe. These two prominent nationalists, born in 1914 and 1915 respectively, were kinsmen—members of the Aro-Ibo tribe from the historic community of Arondizuogu in Orlu Division in the Eastern Province of Owerri. They were among twelve Nigerians who journeyed to the United States in 1938 for higher education.[53] At first they enrolled in Lincoln University—Azikiwe's alma mater; ultimately Ojike earned a B.Sc. at Ohio State University, while Mbadiwe took a B.Sc. at Columbia University and an M.A. at New York University. In America they published books on the nationalist theme,[54] and made significant contributions to the initiation

meeting of the Action Group was abbreviated because Lagos members had requested a week's postponement, indicating an impending change in the A.G., policy of exclusion. Minutes of the Fourth Meeting of the A.G., July 30, 1950.

[51] Minutes of the tenth meeting of the Action Group at Ibadan Boys' High School, Oke-Bola, Ibadan, March 31-April 1, 1951.

[52] The Lagos branch of the Action Group was inaugurated on May 5, 1951. Nearly all of the inaugural members were well-known leaders of the Nigerian Youth Movement. The first 15 names in the membership book are as follows: Dr. Akinola Maja, Chief J. A. Doherty, Chief Bode Thomas, Chief J. A. O. Obadeyi, S. L. Akintola, Arthur Prest, Sir Kofo Abayomi, F. R. A. Williams, Alhaji Jibril Martin, Alhaji S. O. Gbadamosi, M. A. Ogun, Alfred Rewane, Lady Oyinkan Abayomi, S. O. Shonibare, and Ladipo Amos.

[53] On the activities of Nigerian students in the United States during the Second World War, and the influence upon them of American culture see Coleman, *Nigeria*, pp. 242-248.

[54] *Supra*, p. 72 n. 93.

of cultural interchange between Africa and the United States. For that purpose, and to assist African students in the United States, they founded the African Academy of Arts and Research.[55] Mbadiwe, in particular, evinced a deep interest in the promotion of mutually beneficial commercial ties between Africans and American Negroes.[56]

Upon his return to Nigeria in 1947, Mbonu Ojike plunged into the mainstream of militant nationalism, and became general manager of the *West African Pilot*. He wrote an influential Saturday column entitled "Weekend Catechism," he supported the Zikist-oriented National Church of Nigeria,[57] and he urged his countrymen to don African national costumes rather than emulative Western-style clothing. His slogan was "boycott the boycottables" of imperialist culture, for which he was nicknamed the "boycott king." In lectures he explained that he conceived the boycott as part of an economic policy designed to buttress incipient domestic manufacturers.[58] In 1948 Ojike "graduated" from the *Pilot* and founded the African Development Corporation Limited, a general business firm to which many investors, large and small, were attracted.

When K. Ozuomba Mbadiwe returned to Nigeria from the United States, he toured extensively in behalf of the African Academy of Arts and Research, exhibiting a film with which his name was widely associated: "The Greater Tomorrow of the African Peoples." In 1949 Ojike and Mbadiwe were instrumental in the formation of the National Emergency Committee, and in 1950 Ojike, as we have seen, became Deputy Mayor of Lagos. The Committee of National Rebirth which assembled in the Glover Memorial Hall (Lagos) on March 27, 1951, was their conception. Among those in attendance were leaders of the Nigerian Youth Movement and members of the recently surfaced Action Group, including Dr. Akinola Maja, Obafemi Awolowo, and Bode Thomas. But party lines were too indelible to be

[55] Mayor William O'Dwyer of New York City accepted the honorary chairmanship of the African Academy of Arts and Research; the Reverend James H. Robinson, pastor of the Riverside Church in New York, became Chairman of the Board of Directors. K. O. Mbadiwe succeeded Mbonu Ojike as President when the latter returned to Nigeria. The Academy established an Africa House in New York City, for the maintenance of which £1,000 was reported to have been raised by a committee in Lagos. *West African Pilot*, October 27, 1948.

[56] Both Mbadiwe and Ojike lectured extensively in the United States and their speeches were sometimes reported in the *West African Pilot*. Thus Mbadiwe's plea for economic cooperation between West Indians, American Negroes, and Africans, delivered to the 44th Annual Convention of the National Negro Business and Housewives League in Birmingham, Alabama, was reported in the *West African Pilot*, September 29, 1944.

[57] *Supra*, p. 80 n. 109.

[58] *West African Pilot*, October 22, 1948.

erased and neither side appears to have taken the prospect of a merger seriously.[59] After the first meeting, the Youth Movement-Action Group element withdrew from the Committee, which then summoned the NCNC to prepare for the general elections by reviving as a genuine political party based on individual membership.

The third annual convention of the NCNC (Kano) in September 1951 adopted fundamental revisions of organization and policy.[60] Individual membership was instituted, although member-unions retained the right of non-voting representation at meetings of the National Council. The cabinet system was discarded in favor of an elected Central Working Committee of seven national officers; a 28-member National Executive Committee was set up consisting of the Central Working Committee and a seven-member Provincial Working Committee for each of the three regions. It appeared to the

[59] Sir Adeyemo Alakija, President of the *Egbe Omo Oduduwa*, who was asked to serve as chairman of the meeting of March 27, 1951, agreed to do so for five minutes only, after which he handed over to Dr. Azikiwe and departed. He remarked that the "so-called conveners" of the meeting—there were twelve in number, of which he was reported to have been one—had never met to issue invitations. Chief Bode Thomas frankly declared that regionalization was conducive to the best interests of Nigeria and that the meeting was a waste of time. Most of the Action Group-N.Y.M. contingent departed before the end of the meeting. However Obafemi Awolowo remained throughout and made a speech in which he "supported the founding of ethnical political organizations and remarked that unless all existing political organizations in the country were dissolved, no sound Nigeria-wide organization could be formed." *Daily Service*, March 29, 1951. Logically, this was not inconsistent with the announced purpose of the Action Group to become, eventually, the Western Regional Working Committee of a nationwide organization, and Awolowo's interest in the Committee of National Rebirth may have been more serious than that of his political colleagues in the Youth Movement. On the other hand, the Committee may have been regarded by Action Groupers as an attempt to thwart their plans inasmuch as the meeting was announced in the press on March 12, nine days before the Action Group openly proclaimed its own existence (March 21, 1951).

After the departure of most of the Action Group-Youth Movement element, a resolution was adopted calling for the inauguration of a national political organization dedicated to the socialist ideal that would endeavor to achieve self-government in five years. An organizing committee of seven was set up (H. U. Kaine, chairman, K. Balogun, Margaret Ekpo, M. Ojike, M. C. K. Ajuluchuku, K. O. Mbadiwe, and H. O. Davies) that rejected the idea of a new coalition movement and recommended the reinvigoration of the NCNC to carry out the program of National Rebirth. See *West African Pilot*, April 3-14, 1951, especially Minutes of the Meeting of National Rebirth Committee, March 27, 1951, by Ozuomba Mbadiwe, *ibid.*, April 3, 1951, which gives the names of persons in attendance. Five recommendations of the National Rebirth Assembly reported by the Federal Secretary, Kola Balogun, to the Third Annual Convention of the NCNC at Kano in August-September 1951, included: individual membership, election of national officers, independence by 1956, transformation into a political party for electoral purposes, and a socialist commonwealth in the event of freedom. *West African Pilot*, August 31, 1951.

[60] *Daily Times*, September 8, 1951.

delegates that the Action Group had appropriated the principle of federalism for the end of regional separation, and the NCNC ideal of "One Nigeria" seemed to require the abandonment of federalism and the proclamation of unitary government as the constitutional goal of the party.

The Election of 1951: Seeds of Discord

At Kano, the NCNC National Convention selected as candidates to contest for the five Lagos seats in the Western House of Assembly the three perennial standard-bearers of the Nigerian National Democratic Party (NNDP)—Nnamdi Azikiwe, Adeleke Adedoyin and Dr. A. B. Olorun-Nimbe—and two trade unionists, H. P. Adebola, secretary of the Railway and Ports Transport Staff Union, and F. O. Coker, secretary of the Posts and Telegraphs Workers Union. But the Lagos NNDP rejected Coker and insisted upon the popular barrister, T. O. S. Benson[61] The general election was conducted on the basis of three-stage electoral colleges in all Western Regional constituencies save Lagos, where universal adult suffrage obtained. There the five NCNC candidates polled nearly double the number of votes of their Action Group opponents.[62] Under the Constitution, a stipulated number of representatives from each administrative division was to be elected to the Central House of Representatives by and from the Western House of Assembly. The Action Group had claimed 44 of the 75 members elected indirectly from all constituencies but

[61] *Daily Times*, October 18, 1951. F. O. Coker subsequently left the labor field to study law. T. O. S. Benson became a national officer of the NCNC and a federal minister in the first independent government.

[62] The result of the election was as follows:

A. B. Olorun-Nimbe (NCNC)	12,875	J. Martin (A.G.)	6,726
N. Azikiwe (NCNC)	12,711	M. A. Ogun (A.G.)	6,656
A. Adedoyin (NCNC)	12,539	N. A. B. Kotoye (A.G.)	6,651
H. P. Adebola (NCNC)	12,340	H. O. Davies (Nigerian People's	
T. O. S. Benson (NCNC)	12,249	Congress)	884
F. R. A. Williams (A.G.)	7,070	Magnus Williams (Independent)	406
A. Maja (A.G.)	7,005	O. A. Fagbenro-Beyioku (NPC)	269

(*Daily Times*, November 22, 1951).

Obviously the great majority of electors voted straight party tickets, which accounts for the small number of votes for Chief H. O. Davies on the Nigerian People's Congress ticket. Davies withdrew from the Nigerian Youth Movement early in 1951 before its incorporation into the Action Group. On May 1, 1951, the community of Effon-Alaye, Ekiti, conferred on him the title of *Otun*, and three days later he inaugurated a political party, the Nigerian People's Congress. Davies and Azikiwe then negotiated an agreement to cooperate in bringing about an early reform of the Constitution, but the *entente* between their two parties lapsed when the Nigerian People's Congress refused to affiliate formally with the NCNC. *Daily Times*, May 2, 5, and 9, and August 8, 1951. Subsequently Davies became Legal Adviser of the NCNC.

Lagos; if the Action Group majority were to materialize when the House met in January 1952, the NCNC could not organize the Western Government. But the NCNC hoped that in any event its National President, Dr. Azikiwe, would become a leader in the Central Legislature. Prior to the election, Azikiwe declared that he would not accept a ministerial post in "an inferior legislature of the colonial type." His object was an NCNC majority in the regional and central legislatures that would act to "paralyze the machinery of government" and lead to a reformulation of the Constitution.[63]

In the Eastern and Northern Houses of Assembly, the NCNC and the Northern Peoples' Congress respectively were returned with decisive majorities. But the position in the West was not clarified until the first meeting of the Western House of Assembly on January 7, 1952, when 49 members declared for the Action Group.[64] Obviously

[63] "So far as I am concerned, personally, my aim in trying to get a majority in the regional and central legislatures is to firmly entrench the NCNCers in a strategic position where we would create a deadlock and paralyse the machinery of government and thus rip the Macpherson Constitution and usher in a democratic one.

"This means that if we come to power, we shall not only refuse to become ministers, but we shall use our majority to prevent budgets from being passed. . . . I am no careerist and it is clear that salary for ministers can hold no attraction for me; it comes to only one-third or less of my earning. In fact, if I am offered a ministerial post, I will not accept it because I cannot serve in such a capacity in an inferior legislature of the colonial type.

"I speak for myself and those colleagues of mine who see with me on this issue. There are other NCNCers who hold a different view, but if their opinion subsequently prevails that will not make me change my mind about accepting a ministerial post under the Macpherson Constitution because such a decision of mine is fundamental and irrevocable." Statement by Dr. Azikiwe to a newsman before the Lagos election, *Daily Times*, November 23, 1951.

Dr. Azikiwe is reported to have sent a post-election letter to Mr. Awolowo proposing that their two parties form an alliance in the Western Region that would "create such a deadlock . . . as to force the hands of Government to concede us a better constitution whose provisions would make party politics more effective." *West Africa*, December 29, 1951 (quoted in Coleman, *Nigeria*, p. 476, n. 49).

[64] *Daily Service*, January 8, 1952. In reply to persistent NCNC allegations to the effect that the Action Group majority had been "bought over" by that party after the election of 1951, Chief Awolowo made the following declaration on June 2, 1956: "The Action Group came out of the 1951 election with 44 elected members. On the eve of the 1951 election we published a list of our candidates. The NCNC refused to publish a list of theirs; but as soon as the results were declared the NCNC professed to claim most of our members as theirs and to claim a majority. To counter this we procured the signatures of our 44 members on a declaration form and published them in photostatic forms. The NCNC described the signatures as forgeries.

"Some independents who were not sure of the truth sat on the fence, but others who knew the truth declared for us. Before the first meeting of the House of Assembly our 44 members had risen to 49. During the meeting three

the Action Group, led by Mr. Awolowo, would be able to organize the Western Regional Government, but the House of Assembly was required to elect two of the five NCNC representatives from Lagos to the House of Representatives. Mischievously, the Action Group majority voted for Dr. Olorun-Nimbe and Prince Adeleke Adedoyin, neither of whom would decline in favor of their leader, Dr. Azikiwe. In fact, Adedoyin could not be blamed because he had been chosen by the party Executive to go to the Center with Azikiwe. On the other hand, Dr. Olorun-Nimbe had been given the post of Mayor of Lagos. In an attempt to bring their leader into the House of Representatives, the NCNC National Executive Committee asked Dr. Olorun-Nimbe to relinquish his post of Mayor to Adedoyin, also a Lagos Town Councillor, who might then agree to withdraw from the competition for the Central House and open the way for Azikiwe. Neither of the other two elected Lagos members, Adebola or Benson, would have stood in the way of the National President. When Olorun-Nimbe refused to relinquish his Mayoralty, the Democratic members of the Lagos Town Council, led by Mbonu Ojike, Deputy Mayor of Lagos and National Vice-President of the NCNC, tried to buy off Adedoyin by offering him an appointment to the remunerative post of Lagos Town Clerk. Later, a commission of inquiry, appointed by the Western Regional Government, condemned "without reserve" this attempted jobbery.[65] From the standpoint of the party, Adedoyin had behaved honorably; he had been willing to take any post, even the town clerkship of Lagos, in lieu of his rightful seat in the Central Legislature.[66] But Dr. Olorun-Nimbe was expelled from the NCNC, and the Democratic councillors refused to vote his mayoral salary on the ground that his remuneration as a member of two legislative houses was sufficient.[67]

As a result of this bizarre episode, the National President of the

---

members of the NCNC crossed to the Action Group, one of whom crossed back to the NCNC. . . . " Address by Obafemi Awolowo (Mimeographed).

[65] Bernard Storey, *Report of the Commission of Inquiry into the Administration of the Lagos Town Council* (Lagos: 1953), pp. 34-35.

[66] Prince Adeleke Adedoyin left the NCNC and the arena of Lagos politics in 1953. Subsequently he joined the Action Group and became Speaker of the Western House of Assembly as well as a member of the A.G. Federal Executive.

[67] When his one-year term as Mayor of Lagos expired, Dr. Olorun-Nimbe was not re-elected by the councillors. He formed an independent wing of the NNDP which survived tenuously until 1959. In 1954, Dr. Olorun-Nimbe and Madam Ogundimu, leader of a wing of the NNDP Market Women who were loyal to him, went to London to protest the Lagos Executive Development Board's slum clearance project as an unjust violation of the treaty rights of the people of Lagos, but without success.

NCNC was pigeon-holed as the unofficial leader of the Opposition in the Western House of Assembly. But the real victim of circumstance was the Constitution; for it was covered with ridicule by NCNC militants who resolved with greater determination than ever to break it.

The Struggle for Party Government in the East and West

The Macpherson Constitution of 1951 (unofficially so called for the Governor of Nigeria, Sir John Macpherson) was the kind that invites trouble and is virtually made to collapse. In the terminology of colonial constitutions, it provided for "semi-responsible government" at the Center and in the regions.[68] Four Central ministers were appointed by the Governor from among the central representatives of each region; they were not "responsible" to the legislature in the traditional sense, as their appointments could be revoked by the House only upon a two-thirds vote. In the regions, Executive Committees were formed including a majority of Nigerian ministers, selected from the dominant party, in addition to official members (normally the Civil, Legal, Financial, and Development Secretaries) under the chairmanship of the officer administering the government of the region (i.e., the Lt. Governor). Majority leaders in the regional houses were not given any special parliamentary title (e.g., Leader of Government Business), and no provision was made for the separate dissolution of a regional legislature. Obviously the arrangement could not function without cooperatively-inclined, effective party leadership in all regions and mutual forbearance at the Center. Neither of these conditions was adequately achieved and the Constitution collapsed within 15 months.[69]

[68] The official phrase is "responsible government within defined limits." See Martin Wight, *British Colonial Constitutions* (Oxford: Clarendon Press, 1952), pp. 32ff; *The Nigeria (Constitution) Order in Council. S.I. 1951 no. 1172.* This constitution did not invest central ministers with responsibility for the control of departments within the jurisdiction of their portfolios. For the reflections of one central minister on the problems of holding a semi-responsible office see Okoi Arikpo, "On Being a Minister," *West Africa*, July 31-August 21, 1954.

[69] Dr. Azikiwe pointed out that the Macpherson Constitution of 1951 created a "quasi-federation," in which the central government had the right to veto the legislative acts of the regions. Furthermore, he observed, the regional governments had no power to amend legislation within regional competence which had been enacted by the central government before January 1952. The result was a continuing conflict between the central and regional governments, especially the Western Government. See "The Evolution of Federal Government in Nigeria," an address delivered in London on October 14, 1955. From the time of its formation the Action Group has insisted that the regions must be fully competent in matters under

Azikiwe's frank hostility to the Constitution and his determination to bring it down were not shared by a majority of the NCNC parliamentarians, most of whom were inclined to give the constitution a fair if unenthusiastic trial. Eventually a clear difference of opinion crystallized between the NCNC Ministers of the Eastern and Central Governments on the one hand and non-ministerial, national leaders of the party on the other. Nearly all of the ministers held that the Macpherson Constitution deserved a "fair trial," while the national leaders maintained that it was iniquitous and unworthy of consideration. It was uncertain if the national leadership would be able to control the rank and file assemblymen in the Eastern Region inasmuch as all but a few of them had accepted invitations from Dr. Azikiwe to join the NCNC Eastern Parliamentary Party *after* their election as independent candidates.

In October 1952, the Central Working Committee summoned a meeting of the National Executive Committee at Port Harcourt, to which all NCNC parliamentarians were invited as ex-officio members. The 28 official members of the National Executive (comprising seven members from each of the four working committees) favored a declaration of non-cooperation with respect to the Constitution, but they were voted down by a majority of the 115 parliamentarians under the leadership of barrister A. C. Nwapa (of Oguta and Port Harcourt), then Central Minister of Commerce and Industries.[70] That decision was endorsed by a regional conference in the East but repudiated by a subsequent conference of party leaders in the West.[71] In December, a special convention of the party, summoned by the Central Working Committee, met at Jos, in the Northern Region,

---

regional jurisdiction; on this ground the Action Group has always advocated regionalization of the police.

[70] During this period, Hon. A. C. Nwapa was the target of sharp criticisms in the *West African Pilot*. In reply, he declared his "absolute allegiance" to Dr. Azikiwe and alleged that the drive against the Constitution was engineered by persons who failed in the previous election and wanted to try again. He stated further that the Eastern Working Committee, to which none of the regional or central ministers belonged, had decided in favor of a fair trial for the Constitution prior to the meeting of the N.E.C. at Port Harcourt. *Daily Times*, October 14, 1952. An allegation of careerism on the part of the ministers had been made by Dr. Azikiwe in his address to the N.E.C. *Daily Times*, October 30, 1952.

There does appear to have been a rivalry between Nwapa and Mbonu Ojike, who was not elected to the House of Assembly in his home Division of Orlu because the influential Chief F. N. Ezerioha refused to step down in his favor. In part, the Nwapa-Ojike rivalry may have reflected the animosity then prevalent between British- and American-educated Nigerians. On this matter see Coleman, *Nigeria*, pp. 243-247. Nwapa's opponents alleged that the British were grooming him to replace Azikiwe.

[71] *Daily Times*, November 28, 1952.

to review the decision of the National Executive Committee at Port Harcourt. Two distinct but related issues were at stake: the policy of the party with respect to the Constitution, and the authority of the National President vis-à-vis the parliamentary leaders in the Eastern and Central Governments. It was reported that only two members of the Eastern House of Assembly attended the special convention, despite the fact that the NCNC claimed the allegiance of 74 of the 80 members of that House. Dr. Azikiwe opened the convention by declaring that henceforth ministers would "toe the party line or be disciplined."[72] It was expected that the convention would direct the NCNC Central Ministers to resign their portfolios, but the action taken was surprisingly more drastic: three Central ministers, none of whom were present, were expelled from the party.[73]

[72] At the conclusion of his presidential address, Dr. Azikiwe donated £5,000 to the NCNC treasury. *Daily Times*, December 11, 1952.

[73] Dr. Azikiwe told a public meeting in Lagos that the central ministers had been expelled because they sent him an "uncomplimentary" letter refusing to attend the Jos Convention. *Daily Times*, December 19, 1952. The ministers explained their refusal to attend on the ground that certain party leaders had created the "mischievous impression" that, for purely personal reasons, the ministers were loath to break the Constitution. In a letter to the National President the ministers stated that they would stay away from the convention in order to spare embarrassment to those party leaders who were determined to repudiate both the Constitution and the Port Harcourt decision. "Statement by A. C. Nwapa, Minister of Commerce and Industries, Eni Njoku, Minister of Mines and Power, and Okoi Arikpo, Minister of Lands, Survey and Local Development," *Daily Times*, December 20, 1952. In fact, Nwapa was in London for a meeting of the Commonwealth Economic Conference during the Jos Convention. In 1958, the individual who tabled the motion to expel Messrs. Nwapa and Arikpo declared that Azikiwe had been opposed to their expulsion but the action was forced by others, notably M. Ojike and K. O. Mbadiwe. *West African Pilot*, July 29, 1958. Cf. statement by K. O. Mbadiwe, *Daily Times*, April 15, 1953. Another vocal advocate of expulsion was barrister Kolawole Balogun, a founder of the Zikist Movement who studied law in England and returned in 1951 to become National Secretary of the NCNC. Mr. Balogun arrived in Jos while the convention was in session following the refusal of the Government of Kenya to permit his entry into that country to join the legal defence committee for the Kenyan nationalist, Jomo Kenyatta.

Apart from M. C. Awgu, an Eastern Minister without Portfolio, the NCNC members of the Eastern Executive Council did not attend the Jos Convention for the expressed reason that their presence in Enugu was required during the preparation of Estimates for the impending Budget Session of the Eastern House of Assembly. It addition it has been alleged that earlier plans to hold the party convention at Aba in the Eastern Region had been revised by Dr. Azikiwe and his lieutenants for strategic reasons; and that Dr. Azikiwe had a freer hand at Jos than he would have had in the Eastern Region where the hostile Ita Government was then entrenched. See *Proceedings of the Tribunal Appointed to Inquire into Allegations of Improper Conduct by the Premier of the Eastern Region of Nigeria in Connection with the Affairs of the African Continental Bank Limited and other Relevant Matters*, Vol. II (Lagos: 1957), p. 608.

(The fourth Central minister from the Eastern Region, Dr. E. M. L. Endeley, was leader of the Cameroons legislative bloc aligned with the NCNC.) On the constitutional issue, the convention nullified the previous "fair trial" decision of the National Executive Committee, ruling that the Constitution merited no further trial, and that party leaders should adopt positive means to produce its collapse.

When the Jos decisions were revealed, the Eastern Parliamentary Leader, Hon. Eyo Ita,[74] Regional Minister of Natural Resources, issued a statement to the effect that the people of the East received the news of the expulsion of their Central ministers from the NCNC "with great shock." He then summoned a meeting of the Eastern Parliamentary Committee to consider the new situation and decide upon an appropriate course of action. But Azikiwe seized the initiative and called a joint meeting of the Parliamentary Party and the Central Working Committee for the same time and place as the proposed meeting of the Eastern Parliamentary Committee. Fewer than half of the NCNC Eastern legislators attended, the Regional ministers among them; Azikiwe's right to preside was upheld and the Jos decisions were endorsed.[75] Thereupon Dr. Azikiwe proposed to reshuffle the portfolios of the Eastern ministers. His right to do so in consultation with the Parliamentary Leader had been granted by the October meeting of the National Executive Committee at Port Harcourt, but the Jos Special Convention vested the power in the National President and the National Executive Committee irrespective of the wishes of the parliamentary leadership. On the evening of January 29, all nine Eastern ministers, under party direction, signed letters of resignation for submission to the Lt. Governor by the Central Working Committee of the NCNC. During the night, six of them changed their minds; they appear to have learned that they would not be reappointed to the Executive Council and alleged that their resignations had been obtained fraudulently by means of coercion. When Dr. Azikiwe delivered their letters of resignation to the Lt. Governor

[74] Hon. Eyo Ita, a Vice-President of the NCNC since 1948, studied religion and education in the United States where he obtained a Master's degree in education at Columbia University. Upon his return to Nigeria in 1934 he became an avid educator and a pamphleteer for nationalism. J. S. Coleman has described him as "Nigeria's example par excellence of a sensitive individual who returned from abroad with a strong cultural nationalism." *Nigeria*, pp. 218-220. Later he established the West African People's Institute in his home city of Calabar. Professor Ita belongs to a minority ethnic group in the East, the Efik people of Calabar Division.

[75] *Daily Times*, January 5, 1953. See the statement by Hon. J. A. Wachuku, recounting some of these events in *House of Representatives Debates,* Second Session, Vol. II, March 24, 1953, p. 724.

on the morning of the 30th, he was informed that six of the ministers had submitted previous withdrawals.[76]

At this juncture, a clear majority of the NCNC assemblymen supported the national leadership of their party and the House of Assembly passed a vote of no-confidence in the Eastern Government by 60-13. However, the six recalcitrant ministers refused to resign and they rebutted allegations in the House to the effect that the Eastern Government had been unable and unwilling to carry out NCNC policies. (One minister alluded to a possible underlying cause of the crisis in the realm of financial policy which will be discussed in Chapter IV.) Inasmuch as the ministers were expelled from the NCNC, they joined forces with the small opposition party (the United National Party)[77] to insist that any revocation of a ministerial appointment be made as stipulated by the Constitution, i.e., by a two-thirds vote of the House balloting secretly. Hon. J. A. Wachuku (Aba-Ngwa), Deputy Leader of the House, resigned from the NCNC and acted to implement the ministerial strategy by moving the revocation of the appointment of Eyo Ita as Minister of Natural Resources. Azikiwe's parliamentary supporters objected that the motion for revocation rested on the misconception that ministers could remain in office despite a vote of no-confidence. Technically with respect to the Constitution, the so-called "sit-tight" ministers were in the right, and privately they hoped that Azikiwe's two-thirds majority would disappear in secret ballots on individual appointments. In fact, it was reported that the NCNC position was threatened by ethnic and sectional tensions that were likely to be exacerbated if the crisis were protracted. Two groups in particular seemed liable to disaffection: the Efik-speaking minority from Calabar Province who resented the personal attacks to which their respected leader, Eyo Ita, had been exposed,[78] and the 13 Cameroonian assemblymen, most of whom

[76] The six ministers who withdrew their resignations were Eyo Ita, E. I. Oli, S. J. Una, R. I. Uzoma, S. W. Ubani-Ukoma and R. J. E. Koripamo; those who did not were Dr. M. I. Okpara, M. C. Awgu and S. T. Muna. See *Eastern House of Assembly Debates*, Second Session, January 30 to February 23, 1953, Vol. I, for statements by the ministers and other assemblymen. For the reported list of new appointments drawn up by Dr. Azikiwe see *Daily Times*, February 16, 1953.

[77] The United National Party was formed by four independent-minded persons in the Eastern House of Assembly in 1952. Its leader, Hon. Alvan Ikoku (Arochuku) was a distinguished educator who opposed party politics and advocated a national government. Other founding members were Marcus Ubani (Aba-Ngwa), barrister O. O. Ita (Oron) and barrister L. N. Mbanefo (Onitsha), later Chief Justice of the Eastern Region.

[78] Professor Eyo Ita had been a close associate of Dr. Azikiwe and a director of several companies in the so-called "Zik Group." He was notified of his ex-

favored the creation of a separate Cameroons Region, and were inclined to subordinate other issues to the attainment of that particular object.[79] Within the crucial arena of the Ibo State Union, Azikiwe enjoyed a wide margin of support, although the NCNC split was reflected in dissension at the top level.[80]

When motions to revoke the appointments of Eyo Ita and other ministers were put to vote in the House of Assembly, the NCNC members walked out in protest. Furthermore the NCNC assemblymen paralyzed the constitutional system by voting to defeat or defer

pulsion from the NCNC by a letter signed by the National Secretary of the NCNC but widely attributed to Dr. Azikiwe, which was regarded as an aspersion on the Efik people and deeply resented by them. ("Your behavior on the question of your resignation is a shame to you and your race. It is obvious that no self-respecting party can associate with a person like you. You are hereby informed that you have been expelled from the party with ignominy and for life." *Eastern House of Assembly Debates*, Second Session, Vol. I, 30 January to 11 February, 1953, p. 128.)

In protest to the treatment of Ita, the three expelled central ministers withdrew their appeals to the National Executive Committee of the NCNC. Dr. Udo Udoma, President of the Ibibio State Union, resigned from the NCNC as did other assemblymen from Calabar Province.

[79] A notable exception was Hon. N. N. Mbile (Kumba), a staunch supporter of the NCNC who did not favor Cameroonian separation. His colleague Hon. S. T. Muna (Bamenda), Minister without Portfolio, was one of the three ministers who did not withdraw their resignations and expected to be reappointed by Azikiwe.

[80] A. C. Nwapa, Central Minister of Commerce and Industries, held the office of Vice-President of the Ibo State Union, and Jaja A. Wachuku, Deputy Leader of the Eastern House of Assembly, was Principal Secretary of the Ibo State Union. An Ibo State Assembly was held at Owerri immediately following the Jos Convention of the NCNC, but Azikiwe, then President of the Ibo State Union, did not attend and announced that he was not available for re-election. A. C. Nwapa, who had been in the United Kingdom on an official mission during the Jos Convention, did not attend the Ibo State Assembly either, and barrister R. A. Njoku, President of the Eastern Regional organization of the NCNC and a supporter of Azikiwe, was elected to succeed the latter as President of the Ibo State Union.

A few days after the adjournment of the Ibo State Assembly, Eyo Ita summoned a meeting of the Eastern and Central ministers to which Mr. R. A. Njoku and Hon. J. A. Wachuku were invited. It was reported that the ministers passed a vote of confidence in the expelled central ministers, serving notice on the national leaders of the NCNC that the Jos decisions might be challenged by the Eastern parliamentarians when the House of Assembly met. *Daily Times*, December 22, 1952. Both sides worked to gain supporters within the Ibo State Union and it was rumored that the Union might object to the forced resignation of the six regional ministers, most of whom were Ibo. It was even reported that the Union would formally protest disciplinary action taken by the NCNC against its Principal Secretary, Hon. J. A. Wachuku. *Daily Times*, January 31, 1953. Ultimately, Nwapa and Wachuku were repudiated by the Union and relieved of their offices despite Wachuku's warning that the Union's identification with the NCNC leadership would prove embarrassing for both the party and the Ibo people. *Daily Times*, April 27, 1953.

every bill before the House.[81] As a last resort, the Lt. Governor was obliged to use his reserve power of legislation, 'the ultimate proof of colonial rule in a politically advanced dependency, to pass the Regional Appropriations Bill into law. On adjournment day, the expelled ministers (Central and regional) joined with other legislators and supporters who had resigned from the NCNC to form a new party, called the National Independence Party, with Eyo Ita as President. Some ten weeks later, the Eastern parliamentary crisis was resolved by dissolution of the Eastern House of Assembly following the enactment of an amendment to the Constitution permitting the dissolution of the legislature of a single region.

During this period the strain on the Constitution was not confined to the Eastern Region, as events of a less dramatic but nonetheless fateful character transpired in the West. There the ordeal of transitional government took the form of a head-on conflict between a unified majority party, the Action Group, and the British Administration. In Obafemi Awolowo's view, the letter of the Constitution, as construed by conservative officials, was inconsistent with the "spirit or convention of the constitution" as understood by the leaders of the Action Group.[82] The latter alleged that some officials were unable to adjust to the reality of Africans in positions of authority. This and other grievances were expressed at the Benin Conference of the Action Group (December 1952) in the form of a resolution of non-fraternization with Sir John Macpherson, the Governor of Nigeria. It was alleged specifically that certain officials had been promoted to higher ranks in the civil service despite evidence of their efforts to induce chiefs and members of the House of Assembly to oppose key policies of the Action Group.[83] One of the more "revolutionary" of these policies, which appears to have generated considerable emotion, involved the abolition of the title of "District Officer"—a title that embodied the mystique of colonial administration—in favor of the new and symbolically undistinguished title of "Local Government Inspector." Moreover the redesignated officials were assigned roles of guidance rather than direction of the reconstituted and democratized local authorities.[84] As a result of

[81] *Eastern House of Assembly, Debates,* Second Session, Vols. I and II, January 30, 1953, to February 23, 1953.

[82] Obafemi Awolowo, *Awo,* pp. 227-239.

[83] Action Group, "Statement on Non-Fraternization with Sir John Macpherson" (Action Group Secretariat Records, Ibadan). The ban on fraternization with the Governor remained in force for one year until the Warri Congress of December 1953.

[84] Subsequently the highest administrative field office was abolished when the post of "Resident" was eliminated in favor of Local Government Adviser. See

the cumulative effects of friction with the Governor and subordinate officials in the Western Region, Action Group hostility to the tottering Constitution was scarcely less than that of the NCNC. Indeed it was an Action Group maneuver in the Federal House of Representatives that delivered the *coup de grâce*.

The Self-Government Crisis at the Center

Under the Macpherson Constitution, the members of the Central House of Representatives were elected by and from the Regional Houses of Assembly in the ratio of 2:1:1 for the North, East, and West, with the proviso of due representation for each electoral area. With few exceptions, the representatives from each region belonged to the dominant party of the region. When the House of Representatives met for its annual budget session in March 1953, Anthony Enahoro, the Action Group member for Ishan (Benin Province),[85]

L. Gray Cowan, *Local Government in West Africa* (New York: Columbia University Press, 1958), p. 198.

A similar conflict, affecting the civil service, erupted in the Eastern Region in 1955 when the Eastern Legislature refused to appropriate funds to cover expatriation pay for several senior posts. One intended effect was the elimination of a Resident in Calabar Province. The Appropriation Bill was passed over the objection of the Governor, who contended that the omissions altered the terms of service of particular officers to their detriment. He therefore enacted a supplementary appropriation bill on the strength of his reserve power of legislation. Dr. Azikiwe, then Premier of the Eastern Region, denounced the Governor's action as "alien to the spirit of democracy," and sharply criticized the Secretary of State for the Colonies for alleged bias in the latter's explanation of the episode to the British House of Commons. See "Statement made in the Eastern House of Assembly by Dr. the Hon. Nnamdi Azikiwe, Premier of the Eastern Region of Nigeria. . . ." April 19, 1955, printed as *Constitutional Dispute in Eastern Nigeria* (Enugu: 1955).

[85] Anthony Enahoro was born into the leading family of Uromi in Ishan Division in 1923. His great grandfather had been killed by the British and his father spent over twenty years in exile. As a boy he nursed his hatred of the British and became an avid reader of Azikiwe's *West African Pilot*. His nationalist sympathies were particularly aroused by accounts of the Abyssinian war. Later he attended Kings College at Lagos where he became chairman of the Lagos branch of the Nigerian Union of Students. In 1942 he joined the *West African Pilot* as a reporter and in 1944 he was selected to edit the *Southern Nigerian Defender* (Zik Group) at Warri in Delta Province. In 1945, Azikiwe brought him back to Lagos as editor of the *Daily Comet*. Immediately he earned the admiration of young nationalists for his militant support of the workers in the general strike of 1945. In December 1945, he was convicted for having published an article which was held to constitute a seditious libel against the former Governor, Sir Bernard Bourdillon, and sentenced to nine months in prison. In 1947, he made a speech at Warri advising African policemen to disobey orders to shoot African strikers. He was convicted for seditious utterance by an African judge and sentenced again to three years in prison, although the term was reduced to eighteen months by the West African Court of Appeal. He served twelve months during which time he

listed a motion requesting the House to endorse "as a primary political objective the attainment of self-government for Nigeria in 1956." Enahoro's motion gave expression to an Action Group policy, adopted at that party's annual convention of December 1952.

Northern members objected to the specification of a timetable for self-government on the ground that it was first of all necessary for them to obtain the assent of the traditional authorities and other representatives of the Northern people. In fairness to the Northerners, it must be said that self-government in 1956 was not a policy of the Northern Peoples' Congress, as it was the stated policy of the other major parties, and the Central representatives of the NPC might reasonably have objected to being drawn into a binding

---

did gardening, stone breaking, and a good deal of reading. ("Prison," he says, "was my school.")

In October 1948, he agreed to act as chairman of the Zikist Meeting at which O. C. Agwuna delivered his famous address, "A Call for Revolution." Although Enahoro was not himself a member of the Zikist movement, his participation in that meeting resulted in his being sent back to prison for six additional months. At this time he was alienated from Azikiwe by the latter's hostility to the radical Zikists and he left the employ of his patron upon his release from prison in 1949. Returning to the Mid-West, he organized the Mid-West Press Limited, published a daily newspaper, the *Nigerian Star* (1950-1953) and established a short-lived commercial concern. In 1950 he founded the Mid-West Party in collaboration with barrister Arthur Prest which developed into the Mid-West section of the Action Group in 1951. He was elected joint Assistant Secretary of the Action Group at the inaugural Owo Conference of April 1951 and was elected to the Western House of Assembly later that year.

Enahoro is a fine natural speaker and the Action Group sent him to the United Kingdom in 1952 to study parliamentary procedure in the House of Commons and in Belfast, Northern Ireland. At the Benin Conference of December 1952 he moved the resolution for non-fraternization with the Governor of Nigeria and in March his name was attached to the historic motion for self-government in 1956 in the House of Representatives. Under the Constitution of 1954, he became Minister for Home Affairs in the Western Regional Government and Leader of the Western House of Assembly, i.e., the parliamentary deputy of the Premier, Chief Awolowo. In 1955 he was installed by his people as *Adolo* of Uromi. (This is a genuine "traditional" title, rather than an honorary title. In 1958 Chief Enahoro and Chief C. D. Akran were the only "traditional" rulers in the Western Region Executive Council although several other members of the Council held honorary titles and were addressed as "Chief.") His portfolio was broadened in 1957 to include Mid-Western Affairs and his field of competence was extended to embrace foreign policy. By 1958 he was the Action Group's principal foreign policy spokesman and a foremost advocate of that party's principle of close association with the Western powers. He was a delegate to the first two meetings of the All African People's Conference at Accra, Ghana (December 1958), and Tunis, Tunisia (January 1960), and has been a member of the Steering Committee of the Conference since its inception. In December 1959 he was elected to the Federal House of Representatives, where he serves at the time of writing as "shadow" Foreign Minister in the Action Group "Shadow Cabinet."

126

declaration of such consequence without a mandate. When the matter was discussed by the Council of Ministers, the Northern argument was received sympathetically by the six official members and the three Eastern ministers who belonged to the newly created National Independence Party. A majority of the Council, comprising the six officials and the four Northern ministers, passed a resolution to the effect that no minister should speak or vote on the self-government motion in the House. The three ministers of the Eastern National Independence Party abstained, agreeing to abide by the majority decision of the Council, but the four Western ministers dissented emphatically, as they had been instructed by the Parliamentary Committee of their party, the Action Group, to vote solidly for the motion and to express their views openly in the House.[86] The Western position was supported in the Council of Ministers by the fourth Eastern minister, Dr. E. M. L. Endeley of the Cameroons, who declared, however, that the Cameroons members would henceforth adopt an attitude of neutrality with respect to Nigerian party politics.[87]

On March 31st, Enahoro moved his fateful motion for self-government, and the Northern leader, Malam Ahmadu, the Sardauna of Sokoto, offered an amendment replacing the specific date of 1956 with the phrase "as soon as practicable."[88] Malam Ibrahim Imam

[86] Minutes of the Emergency Meeting of the Executive Committee of the Action Group, Lagos, March 24, 1953.

[87] *House of Representatives Debates,* Second Session, March 3-April 1, 1953, Vol. II, pp. 714-715, 1048. Cameroonian members issued the following declaration:

"The only honest course open to Cameroonians is to discontinue any further political party alliance with Nigeria and to maintain a state of benevolent neutrality and independent cooperation." sgd. E. M. L. Endeley, J. T. Ndze, S. A. George, Rev. J. C. Kangsen, Abba Habib, M. Ahmadu Lamido-Mubi. V. T. Lainjo was away in the Cameroons and N. N. Mbile, Secretary of the Kamerun United National Congress, vehemently opposed the break with the NCNC. Subsequently a majority of the Cameroons bloc in the Eastern House of Assembly formally severed their ties with the NCNC and demanded the creation of a separate Cameroons Region. At an all-Cameroons Conference held in Mamfe, May 22-24, 1953, the Cameroons National Federation and the Kamerun United National Congress were merged into the Kamerun National Congress which stood for establishment of a separate Cameroons Region. A minority group of Cameroons assemblymen, under the leadership of Mbile, formed the Kamerun People's Party with P. M. Kale as President, which also supported the creation of a Cameroons Region but emphasized the value of continued association with Nigeria. The KPP was affiliated to the NCNC, which endorsed the Cameroon demand for a separate region, as did the other major parties.

[88] In his speech on the amendment, the Sardauna declared: "Before we commit ourselves to the people we represent in such matters, we must, I repeat, we must seek the mandate of the country. As representatives of the people, we from the North feel that in all major issues such as this one, we are in duty bound to

(Bornu) then proposed a dilatory motion of adjournment. The meeting was recessed for ten minutes during which time the Action Group and NCNC leaders agreed to walk out if the numerically preponderant Northern bloc (constituting 50 percent of the total membership of the House) acted to defer or defeat the substantive motion. When the meeting resumed, Sir Adesoji Aderemi II, the *Oni* of Ife, announced that his resignation as Minister without Portfolio had been submitted to the Governor, an action that was duplicated by the three other Action Group ministers. Ibrahim Imam pressed his dilatory motion, whereupon two southern leaders (Obafemi Awolowo and K. O. Mbadiwe) made vitriolic declarations of policy, after which the Action Group and the NCNC members left the chamber. It was reported that as the Action Group leader, Mr. Awolowo, emerged from the House, he "embraced" and "shook hands with" Dr. Azikiwe, who had witnessed the debate from the gallery.[89] The next day, two of the ex-Action Group ministers made statements in the House, explaining their decisions to resign and alleging that the British officials and the Northern leaders worked together to perpetuate colonial rule.[90] On a motion to adjourn *sine die*, the Sardauna of Sokoto spoke one sentence: "The mistake of 1914 has come to light and I should like to go no further."[91]

---

consult those we represent so that when we speak we know we are voicing the views of the nation. If the Honorable members from the West and East speak to this motion unamended, for their people I must say here and now, Sir, that we from the North have been given no such mandate by our people. No Honourable Member can, therefore, criticize the Northern Legislators for refusing to associate themselves with such an arbitrary motion fixing as it does, a definite date for the attainment of national self-government. We in the North are working very hard towards self-government although we were late in assimilating Western education, yet within a short time we will catch up with the other Regions, and share their lot. We have embarked upon so many plans of reform and development that we must have time to see how these work out in practice. We want to be realistic and consolidate our gains. It is our resolute intention to build our development on sound and lasting foundations so that they would be lasting." *House of Representatives Debates*, Second Session, March 3-April 1, 1953, p. 992.

[89] *Daily Times*, April 1, 1953.

[90] In the course of these statements, Hon. Bode Thomas and Hon. S. L. Akintola divulged the content of discussions and proceedings within the Council of Ministers. *House of Representatives Debates*, Second Session, March 3-April 1, 1953, pp. 1048-1050. Later in the day the Governor made a public broadcast accusing the ex-ministers of having broken the "oath of secrecy which had been taken by members of the Council in order to facilitate discussions." *Daily Times*, April 2, 1953. The ex-ministers argued that the termination of British rule in Nigeria involved a moral obligation which transcended procedural expedients under the Constitution; and see their reply to the Governor. *Daily Times*, April 6, 1953. Also see Okoi Arikpo, "On Being a Minister," *West Africa*, August 14, 1954.

[91] *House of Representatives Debates*, Second Session, March 3-April 1, 1953,

In the wake of adjournment, Awolowo and Azikiwe signed an agreement of cooperation between their respective parties,[92] and a number of statements were issued by various principals among the disputants which bristled with recriminations but served to illuminate the political background to the collapse of the tri-partite balance at the center. The Sardauna of Sokoto alleged that the Action Group had been motivated by a partisan urge to outdo the NCNC as the fore-most nationalist party.[93] Spokesmen for the National Independence Party supported the Sardauna's allegation and suggested further that the self-government motion was a consequence of the breakdown of negotiations between the Northern Peoples' Congress and the Action Group.[94] Mr. Awolowo denied these allegations and explained that the motion had been introduced for principled reasons but that it could not be withdrawn for frivolous ones without injury to his party. He disclosed that negotiations between the Action Group and the Northern Peoples' Congress had been initiated in August 1952 and not, as the National Independence Party insinuated, during the Eastern crisis.[95] These negotiations were interrupted by NPC crit-

---

p. 1053. This was an allusion to the amalgamation of the Protectorates of Northern and Southern Nigeria by the British in 1914.

[92] The initial Action Group-NCNC agreement was reported to have been signed at a joint meeting of the parliamentary committees of both parties. Three stipulations were announced as follows: (1) the motion for self-government in 1956 would be relisted at the next meeting of the House; (2) efforts would be made to ensure that the House would be reconvened for that purpose as soon as possible; (3) the central ministers would be free to speak and vote on the motion when it was made. *Daily Times*, April 4, 1953.

The text of an agreement between the Action Group and the NCNC, signed by their respective presidents prior to the London Constitutional Conference of 1953 was published by the Action Group following the termination of the alliance between the two parties in November 1953. Salient points of the agreement included the following: Federalism was accepted in principle with the temporary assignment of residual powers to the regions. The Central Legislature would either be bi-cameral or would provide for equal representation of Regions in a uni-cameral chamber. The demand for self-government in 1956 would be renewed. Should the North remain implacably opposed, the Alliance would demand that a constituent assembly be called to prepare for self-government in 1956. In the event of the refusal of the Secretary of State for the Colonies to cooperate, the Alliance would summon a constituent assembly of Southern Nigeria, draft a constitution and declare the independence of Southern Nigeria. The question of the status of Lagos would be deferred for the time being pending discussions on the constitution of a self-governing Nigeria. *Daily Times*, November 27, 1953.

[93] *Daily Times*, April 6, 1953.

[94] *Daily Times*, April 4, 1953 and April 25, 1953. The National Independence Party declared that its own neutrality with respect to the motion did not indicate opposition to self-government, but a desire to mediate the dispute between the North and the West.

[95] According to Mr. Awolowo, the Northern leaders did not respond to Action Group efforts to establish a working basis during the budget session of 1952, but the

icisms of the Action Group decision to adopt a policy of non-fraternization with respect to the Governor of Nigeria, but they were resumed in January 1953 and culminated in the conclusion of an agreement of coalition for the pursuit of concerted policies in the regions and at the Center.[96] However, the Northern leaders asked the Action Group to withhold publication of the agreement, and it merely lapsed without formal repudiation when the two parties clashed over the self-government motion in the House of Representatives. The Action Group statements were trenchantly phrased, repeating the party's allegation of a conspiracy against self-government involving the Governor, the "Sardauna Group," and the National Independence Party.[97]

N.P.C. initiated negotiations in Lagos during the session of August 1952. He met the Sardauna again in Kaduna in October and reported his own remarks at that time as follows:

"I stated frankly and categorically that whatever we the present leaders might do at present, the forces of self-government were already abroad; and unless we took the lead and harnessed them into constructive channels towards the end in view, we would all be swept away by the powerful tide that was now unquestionably gathering strength.

"I told him [the Sardauna] that after seeing some parts of the Northern Region, I had no doubt that the Region provided a fertile soil for either Communism or the type of gangster politics being propagated by some political leaders in the country. I also said that I met some of the revolutionary elements in the North. They were certainly not as opulent and influential as people like himself, but they were gathering in momentum and appeared to have a great future.

"I felt, I continued, that it was in the best interests of the North and of the country that neither the Communist type nor the gangster type of politics should gain ascendancy in the Northern Region. For if either of them did, then woe betide all decency, order and good faith in the country. I argued that it was urgent that he should assert his leadership by encouraging the nationalist elements, aligning himself with them, and moulding their efforts." *Daily Times*, April 9, 1953.

[96] The agreement signed by the Sardauna of Sokoto, Abubakar Tafawa Balewa, Obafemi Awolowo, and Bode Thomas was dated February 2, 1953. It was reported by Mr. Awolowo to read as follows:

"Five Northern Ministers, three from the Region and two from the Centre, flew to Ibadan to meet the Western Regional and Central Ministers to discuss ways and means of strengthening Nigerian unity and accelerating its progress and freedom. The meeting decided to establish a coalition between the leaders of the Northern and Western Legislatures with a view to their pursuing a concerted policy both in the Centre and in the Regions. The first meeting of the coalition will be held in Lagos in March, 1953.

"The meeting expressed strong desire to work in cooperation with leaders of the Eastern Region who believe in the achievement of the unity and freedom of Nigeria through honesty, selfless service and orderly progress. The meeting notes that the political atmosphere in the East is clouded with confusion and uncertainty and fervently looks forward to the time when it will be possible to include in the coalition leaders from the Eastern Region." *Daily Times*, April 10, 1953.

At this time the NPC delegation attempted without success to mediate the dispute between the Action Group and the Governor.

[97] *Daily Times*, April 7, 9, 10, 1953.

The aftermath of the central crisis in the Northern Region has been described by James S. Coleman:[98]

"After the adjournment of the House of Representatives the northern members were subjected to insults and abuse by Lagos crowds, and during the ensuing weeks they were ridiculed and strongly criticized by the southern press. Upon their return to the north they determined never to be subjected to such indignities again; within a few weeks they announced an eight-point program which, if implemented, would have meant

[98] Coleman, *Nigeria*, pp. 399-400; and see his analysis of the objections of northern and southern leaders both to the constitutional system of that period and the policies of one another. *Ibid.*, pp. 400-402.

Although the Kano disturbances were precipitated by a meeting of the Action Group, most of whose members in Kano were Yoruba settlers, violence once begun mainly involved the Hausas on one side and the Ibos on the other; the latter were the most numerous ethnic group of southerners and, for the most part, supporters of the NCNC. The report of an official Commission of Inquiry attributed the riots to tribal tensions mainly, holding that persistent criticisms of the traditional and political leaders of the North "had inflamed, or rendered inflammable, public opinion in Kano," arousing the latent hostility between two dissimilar culture groups. Report on the Kano Disturbances, 16th, 17th, 18th and 19th May, 1953 (Kaduna: 1953), pp. 39-40.

Whether or not one accepts the official thesis that the underlying cause of the conflict was inter-tribal or cultural tension it must be admitted that the overt manifestations were primarily tribalistic. Yet there were exceptions to the primary pattern of Hausa-Ibo conflict. The report noted that "many hundreds, possibly thousands, of individual cases" of conduct diverged from the general line of tribal division. *Ibid.*, p. 39. However, the report neglected to mention that Hausas who were sympathetic to the Northern Elements Progressive Union, an ally of the NCNC, rendered great assistance to the beleaguered southerners, a statement that was frequently repeated to the writer by persons of Northern and non-Northern origin in Kano. Several informants who lived through the tragedy expressed the view that political partisanship was a more fundamental cause of the explosion than the official report allows. Some of them suggested that officials were inclined to emphasize the tribalistic aspect of the rioting because it might appear as a more "primitive" type of behavior and therefore reflect adversely on the ability of the people to govern themselves in a modern state. It might be remarked that allegations of this nature with respect to official reports are not uncommon and sometimes captious. But the Kano riot report invites objections by its disparagements of radical groups, in particular the NEPU and its affiliate, the Askianist Movement.

It is not here suggested that inter-party violence is less reprehensible than inter-tribal violence, but the former may entail different explanations than the latter. For example, explanations of inter-party conflict may emphasize the system of government as a source of instability rather than the phenomenon of contact between dissimilar culture groups.

When the Kano riot took place, Dr. Azikiwe was enroute to a meeting of the NCNC in Kaduna. He was advised by officials at Minna to turn back in order to ensure against the repetition of disturbances elsewhere, which he did. Shortly afterward he made a public statement in Lagos on the causes of the disturbances, placing the blame mainly on the Kano Native Administration and official negligence. *Daily Times*, May 25, 1953.

virtual secession of the Northern Region from Nigeria. This action provoked even harsher criticism from the southern press and from Action Group and NCNC leaders. The northern leaders were repeatedly charged with being unrepresentative of their people; they were called 'imperialist stooges'; and they were criticized as having 'no minds of their own.' Leaders of the NCNC and the Action Group then undertook to send delegations to northern cities to campaign for self-government in 1956. One such delegation, led by Chief S. L. Akintola of the Action Group, scheduled a meeting in Kano at the very height of the north-south tension. This led to a chain of events culminating in four days of rioting in the Kano sabon gari which resulted in 277 casualties, including 36 deaths. . . ."[99]

A post-mortem was pronounced by the Secretary of State for the Colonies in the House of Commons: the "closely-knit" federation envisaged by the Constitution of 1951 did not prove workable; therefore the Constitution would be revised "to provide for greater regional autonomy and for the removal of powers of intervention by the centre in matters which can, without detriment to other regions, be placed entirely within regional competence."[100] In these bleak circumstances, delegates representing the major and principal minor

[99] The "eight point program" of the Northern Peoples' Congress, as endorsed by a joint meeting of the Northern House of Assembly and the Northern House of Chiefs, was as follows:

"1. This Region shall have complete legislative and executive autonomy with respect to all matters except the following: defense, external affairs, customs and West African research institutions.

"2. That there shall be no central legislative body and no central executive or policy-making body for the whole of Nigeria.

"3. There shall be a central agency for all Regions which will be responsible for the matters mentioned in paragraph 1 and other matters delegated to it by a Region.

"4. The central agency shall be at a neutral place, preferably Lagos.

"5. The composition and responsibility of the central agency shall be defined by the Order-in-Council establishing the constitutional arrangement. The agency shall be a nonpolitical body.

"6. The services of the railway, air services, posts and telegraphs, electricity and coal mining shall be organized on an inter-Regional basis and shall be administered by public corporations. These corporations shall be independent bodies covered by the statute under which they are created. The Board of the coal corporation shall be composed of experts with a minority representation of the Regional Governments.

"7. All revenue shall be levied and collected by the Regional Governments except customs revenue at the port of discharge by the central agency and paid to its treasury. The administration of the customs shall be so organized as to assure that goods consigned to the Region are separately cleared and charged to duty.

"8. Each Region shall have a separate public service."

Daily Times, May 22, 1953.

[100] *Parliamentary Debates, 5th Session, Vol. 515, House of Commons, Official Report*, May 4-22, 1953, pp. 2263-68.

parties met in London with representatives of the Nigerian Government and the Colonial office during July-August 1953, to redraw the constitution.[101]

The Regionalist Constitution of 1954
and the Separate States Question

We need not dwell on the details of the constitutional conference of 1953 which transformed the structure of Nigerian government from unitary foundations to the existing bases of federalism.[102] It was agreed that residual powers would be vested in the regions; that the majority party leader in each regional legislature would be appointed to the office of Premier; that apart from the Regional Governor, officials of the administration would be excluded from the Executive Councils of the Eastern and Western Regions; that separate elections would be held for the federal legislature, although uniformity of electoral procedures among the regions would not be required;[103] that the North would continue to have 50 percent membership in the central (henceforth "federal") legislature; and that central ministers would continue to be appointed in equal number from the regions. It was further stipulated that a conference to review the constitution would be held within three years. Inasmuch as the Northern delegates refused to alter their policy of self-government "as soon as practi-

[101] Delegates and advisers representing the following parties were certified: the Action Group, the National Council of Nigeria and the Cameroons, the National Independence Party, the Northern Elements Progressive Union, and the Northern Peoples' Congress. In addition there was a delegate and advisers from the Cameroons as well as representatives of the Nigerian and United Kingdom governments. *Report by the Conference on the Nigerian Constitution held in London in July and August 1953*, Cmnd. 8934 (London: 1953), pp. 13, 14.

[102] *Ibid.*, and see Coleman, *Nigeria*, pp. 371-372.

[103] The Action Group dissented from the agreed arrangements for continued use of the indirect system of elections in the North, insisting that the Northern Region should either be divided into smaller regions or be required to institute, in the company of the other regions, a system of direct elections from single-member constituencies. The Action Group Delegation to the Nigeria Constitution Conference, *Minority Report* (London: August 1953) p. 5. The argument for a uniform electoral law based on universal adult suffrage was supported consistently by the National Independence Party.

In 1955, Dr. Azikiwe declared that the Lyttleton Constitution of 1954 preserved the political unity of Nigeria, but that the failure of the Federal Government to institute a uniform system of electoral regulations based on universal adult suffrage "strikes deeply at the root of parliamentary government in Nigeria." He drew a parallel between the situation in Nigeria and that of India in the mid-1930's, suggesting that undemocratic electoral systems in both cases were conducive to the emergence of communal groups and factions rather than stable national parties based on principle. Nnamdi Azikiwe, "The Evolution of Federal Government in Nigeria," an address in London, October 14, 1955.

cable," the conference agreed to accept a declaration to the effect that full self-government with respect to internal matters would be granted to those regions desiring it in 1956.

As James S. Coleman observed, "the 1953 constitutional agreements . . . reflected an ingenious compromise of what had been regarded as intractable positions." The North appeared to come out best, for "the Northern leaders obtained much greater autonomy for the regions, and they really conceded nothing on the issue of scheduled self-government."[104] However, the Action Group-NCNC alliance on federalism did induce the Northern Peoples' Congress to alter its pre-conference stand of separatist or extreme regionalism. Subsequently, it became apparent that the Action Group gained substantially from the fiscal arrangements which were devised to buttress the new federal system. These provided for the allocation of revenue to the regions mainly according to the principle of "derivation," i.e., insofar as possible, revenues were returned to the region of origin. Owing to the relatively great importance of revenue derived from the export of cocoa, grown mainly in the Western Region, the principle of derivation was bound to benefit the West. Its effect on the North was beneficial to a lesser extent, but the East suffered financially from a reduction in its proportionate allocation.[105]

However, it was another issue on which the Action Group-NCNC alliance foundered during the London conference, namely the matter of the position of Lagos in the new constitutional structure. The Action Group was determined to retain Lagos within the jurisdiction of the Western Region, but the Northern delegation objected that in view of its concession to the principle of federalism, it would insist upon the federalization of the national capital, which was also the principal port and main commercial center. This argument reinforced a previous contention of the NCNC, producing a deadlock which the delegates could not resolve. Finally they agreed to ask the Secretary of State for the Colonies to rule on the question and to abide by his decision. The Secretary of State decided in favor of severance, but the Action Group refused to accept his ruling before consultation

[104] Coleman, *Nigeria*, p. 402.

[105] In his study of the financial effects of regionalization, Arthur Hazlewood concluded: "Where regionalization has brought to the West a financial 'gain' of £3.8m., and to the North one of £1.2m., to the East it has brought a 'loss' of between £0.1m. and £0.2m." *The Finances of Nigerian Federation*, reprinted from *West Africa*, August 27, 1955, by Oxford University Institute of Colonial Studies. The basic document is the *Report of Fiscal Commissioner on Financial Effects of Proposed New Constitutional Arrangements* (Lagos: Government Printer, 1953).

with those affected in Lagos and the Western Region.[106] Recriminations over this matter figured prominently in the termination of the
Action Group-NCNC alliance in November 1953.

A resumed constitutional conference was held in Lagos in January
and February 1954. By then the NCNC had won a landslide victory
in the phased general election for the Eastern House of Assembly
(December 1953), securing 72 seats to 9 for the National Independence Party and 3 for the United National Party. (Later these
parties merged to form the United National Independence Party.)
All 13 Cameroons seats in the Eastern House of Assembly were won
by the Kamerun National Congress, which shunned affiliation with
the NCNC and demanded separation from the Eastern Region. At
the resumed conference it was agreed that the Southern Cameroons
should be severed from the Eastern Region and reconstituted as a
quasi-federal territory with its own government.

The establishment of the tri-regional power system in 1954
ushered in a period of renewed and ultimately triumphant advance
to independence. The "big three"—Nnamdi Azikiwe, Obafemi
Awolowo, and Alhaji Ahmadu, the Sardauna of Sokoto—each assumed the premiership of a regional government, while Dr. E. M. L.

---

[106] *Report of the Conference on the Nigerian Constitution, 1953*, pp. 9, 20-22;
Action Group Minority Report, p. 7; Action Group, *Lagos Belongs to the West*
(London: 1953).

The finality of the separation of Lagos from the West was not accepted by
the Action Group until the Constitutional Conference of 1957. At the Fourth
Regional Conference of the Action Group in October 1955, it was decided that
the party's delegation to the forthcoming constitutional conference should not
compromise in its demand for the return of Lagos to the West. If that object were
not achieved the Action Group would work for a greater measure of local
self-government for the municipality. Extreme partisans of the merger favored
consideration of the secession of the Western Region from the Federation if
Lagos were not returned (Minutes of the Fourth Regional Conference of the
Action Group). After the Constitutional Conference of 1957, Obafemi Awolowo,
Federal President of the A.G., told a party congress that discussions on the
Lagos-West merger question had endangered not merely the success of the
conference but the unity of Nigeria. The Action Group, he explained, did not
regard the demand for merger as an end in itself, but as a means only to
remove certain political disabilities of the Lagos people and to eliminate adverse
financial effects on the Western Region which result from the separation. For the
sake of Nigerian unity the Action Group had offered alternative proposals to
the conference which led to an acceptable solution. *Report of the Action Group
National Congress, 1957*, p. 7. At the Calabar Congress of 1958, Chief Awolowo
said, "We have accepted the present position of Lagos in order to make a
lasting contribution to the unity of Nigeria." *Report of the Fourth Annual
Congress*, p. 82.

In his autobiography, Chief Awolowo conceded that Lagos had been a financial
liability to the Western Region and that its severance had been in the region's
best interest. *Awo*, p. 247.

Endeley became Leader of Government Business in the Southern Cameroons. (When the latter territory attained full regional status in 1958, Dr. Endeley was designated Premier.) In every region, the dominant political party derived its popular support mainly from a dominant nationality group—the NCNC in the East from the Ibo, the Action Group in the West from the Yoruba, and the Northern Peoples' Congress in the North from the Hausa. However, these dominant ethnic groups displayed varying degrees of solidarity. In the East, an overwhelming number of the Ibo people rallied to the NCNC; in the absence of inter-party conflict in Iboland, the Eastern NCNC became a turbulent arena of intra-party conflict. In the West, particular sections of the Yoruba people consistently returned NCNC candidates while the Yoruba majority supported the Action Group. Among the Hausas of the North, the Northern Elements Progressive Union, in alliance with the NCNC, persisted as a virile opposition to the Northern Peoples' Congress.

It will be recalled that every region has a dual ethno-geographical makeup—a "regional nucleus" inhabited by the cultural majority and a "peripheral" zone of ethnic minorities. Prior to 1954, the constitutional blueprints of nationalist leaders generally envisaged the creation of states based on the criteria of cultural and linguistic affinity.[107] Therefore it was not without precedent for sub-regional leaders to have asserted demands for separation from the dominant cultural-political groups in the regionalized system of 1954. As early as 1950, sub-regionalism inspired the formation of a Mid-West Party by two future leaders of the Action Group;[108] in 1953 the Benin-Delta People's Party was formed under the Presidency of the *Oba* of Benin to work for the creation of a Benin-Delta State. That object was endorsed in principle by the Action Group in November 1954, following the electoral sweep of Mid-Western constituencies by the NCNC in the federal election of that year.[109] In 1955 the Western House of Assembly unanimously adopted a resolution favoring the creation of a separate state for the Benin and Delta Provinces; and in 1956, the Mid-West State Movement, essentially an adjunct of the NCNC,[110] was formed to spearhead the campaign.

[107] See Coleman, *Nigeria*, pp. 388-390; Awolowo, *Awo*, pp. 167, 176-181.
[108] *Supra*, p. 104, n. 40.
[109] The NCNC won all ten Mid-Western seats in the Federal House of Representatives.
[110] In 1959 the Leader of the Mid-West State Movement, Hon. D. C. Osadebay, MHA (Asaba), was National Legal Adviser of the NCNC and leader of the Opposition in the Western House of Assembly. In 1960 he succeeded Dr. Azikiwe as President of the Nigerian Senate. Mr. Osadebay is also a founding member of

In the Eastern Region, non-Ibo groups in the former provinces of Calabar, Ogoja, and Rivers agitated for separation from the numerically dominant Ibo areas. Here the minority zone is a non-compact belt of culturally diverse peoples who are united only by feelings of hostility to the Ibo-speaking majority. However, a determined effort to unify these minorities was made by political opponents of the NCNC, some of whom left that party during the struggle between its national and parliamentary leaders in 1952-1953. The demand for a Calabar-Ogoja-Rivers State appears to have been made for the first time by a conference of chiefs and representatives from these provinces in December 1953. The COR State Movement was inaugurated at Uyo (Calabar Province) in 1954; it was closely linked to the United National Independence Party[111] and subsequently absorbed by that party's successor, the Eastern wing of the Action Group. Among the Ijaw people of the former Rivers Province and an adjoining Division of Delta Province in the Western Region, the demand for a Rivers State appears to have been more popular than the idea of a COR State; in 1959, the Niger Delta Congress, an outgrowth of the Rivers Chiefs and People's Conference, captured one seat in the Federal House of Representatives.

The NCNC has steadfastly opposed the creation of a COR State, mainly on the ground that its sole rationale is anti-Ibo sentiment.[112] In 1959 an administrative reorganization was effected in the Eastern Region, abolishing the old provinces and devolving wide local government functions to an increased number of new ones based on a

---

the Ibo State Union. His selection as former Leader of the Regional Opposition and Leader of the Mid-West State Movement is a tribute to his personal qualities since the Ibo people of Asaba and Aboh Divisions are a minority in the proposed state. He is also a well-reputed poet of nationalism; see his *Africa Sings* (Ilfracombe: Stockwell, 1952).

[111] The Leader of the COR State Movement is Dr. Udo Udoma, MHR (Opobo), a prominent member of the UNIP and President of the Ibibio State Union.

[112] During the general election campaign of 1957 the NCNC proposed the creation of three states in the East as part of a 14-state plan for Nigeria as a whole. *The People's Mandate (NCNC Manifesto)*, March 1957, p. 21. In a broadcast on the eve of the election Dr. Azikiwe explained the opposition of his party to the Calabar-Ogoji-Rivers State proposal and made this statement: "The right of the people of former Calabar, Ogoja and Rivers Provinces to determine their political future is conceded. It is for them to decide whether they should form a separate state or whether they should be merged with other states; but we frown upon any idea which will lump them together so as to create minority problems where they have not previously existed. For this reason we hold that if the people of former Calabar Province desire to form a separate state we shall support them, and if the people of former Ogoja Province will prefer a separate state we shall support them also. The same holds good in respect of the people of former Rivers Province." Nnamdi Azikiwe, *After Three Years of Stewardship* (Enugu: n.d.), pp. 15-16.

carefully designed system of local representation.[113] This innovation, among others—e.g., the establishment of a regional House of Chiefs—partially offset the COR State appeal, and candidates to the Federal House of Representatives in 1959 who supported the "COR" solution to the Eastern minorities problem were successful in the Ibibio and Efik areas of Calabar Province only.

In the Northern Region, the principal separatist movement is based on the non-Hausa peoples of the six southerly provinces (Adamawa, Benue, Plateau, Kabba, Ilorin, and Niger) where the Hausa language is not universal and Islam is a minority creed. The history of the Middle Belt State movement from the formation of a Northern Nigerian Non-Moslem League in 1949 to the merger of the United Middle Belt Congress with the Action Group in 1957 is reviewed briefly in Chapter VIII. The Middle Belt is the largest, the most populous (about 5 million people), and culturally the most heterogeneous minority area in Nigeria. Persistent support for the state has been concentrated in particular non-contiguous groups, notably the Tiv and the Birom. However, candidates of the United Middle Belt Congress-Action Group Alliance, favoring creation of the state, won about one-third of the Middle Belt seats in the 1959 federal election.

At the constitutional conference of 1957, it was decided that the Secretary of State should appoint a commission of inquiry "to ascertain the facts about the fears of minorities in any part of Nigeria and to propose means of allaying those fears whether well or ill founded." The commission toured Nigeria for several months in 1957-1958, receiving memoranda and taking oral evidence in public and private from individuals, ethnic associations, minority groups, political parties, and government officials. Its report recommended safeguards for minorities other than the creation of new states, on the ground that the minority fears expressed would not be remedied by the creation of a new state in any one of the existing regions.[114]

[113] See *Self-Government in the Eastern Region, Part I: Policy Statements* (Sessional Paper No. 2 of 1957; Enugu: 1957), pp. 19-22.

[114] Colonial Office, *Report of the Commission appointed to enquire into the fears of Minorities and the means of allaying them* (London: H.M.S.O., 1958), p. 87. Other basic documents include the following: *Memorandum submitted to the Minorities Commission by the Central Executive of the Calabar-Ogoja-Rivers State Movement* (Calabar: 1957); *The Case for a Mid-West State by the Mid-West State Movement, Nigeria* (Warri: 1957); "A Written Address by R. A. Fani-Kayode and O. N. Rewane, Counsel for Action Group and Allied Parties to the Commission of Enquiry into Minority Problems in Nigeria" (mimeographed). Lagos and Colony State Movement, *The Case for the Creation of a Lagos and Colony State within the Federation of Nigeria* (Lagos: n.d.); The Citizens Committee for Independence, *The Case for More States* (1957); and the brief but excellent discussion by Coleman, *Nigeria*, pp. 384-396.

In the commission's view it could not be asserted with confidence that broadly based majorities in each of the proposed states actually favored the separatist solution. On the contrary, it seemed likely to the commission that new minority problems might well flow from the creation of new states. Moreover, the new states would be comparatively weak with respect to financial resources and trained administrative manpower. Finally, the commission did not think that tribal separatism should be embodied in the structure of Nigerian government; it envisaged the future security of the minorities in the inevitable shift of political gravity from the regional governments to the federal government, where no single nationality group predominates.[115]

The report of the Minorities Commission was received favorably by the Northern Peoples' Congress and the Eastern and national leadership of the NCNC but deplored as an unrealistic and disappointing document by the Action Group and by spokesmen for the principal states movements. At the renewed constitutional conference of 1958, the Secretary of State for the Colonies expressed the view that "the early creation of new states was not for practical reasons compatible with the request for independence in 1960." However, a complex procedure for the creation of states in the future was incorporated into the Nigerian constitution.[116]

Some critics of the separate state movements have alleged that these movements betray a dangerous tendency of fragmentation along ethnic lines that might result in national disintegration if allowed to run its course unchecked. This view is reflected in the report of the Minorities Commission. In rebuttal it has been said that ethnic

[115] "If . . . in the course of our report we imply that the Regional Governments are more to be feared by minorities than the Federal Government, this proceeds from the fact that in each of the Regions there is at present an assured majority with one main interest; in the Federation, on the other hand, it seems more likely that there will be a balance of interest between different groups . . . the Federal Government is likely to become more important when it exercises for the first time three functions at present reserved to the Governor-General. These are defence, external affairs and ultimate responsibility for law and order throughout the Federation. With the assumption of these powers, the Federal Government will become a far more attractive field for a man of ability and ambition. National leaders will look to the Federal ministries; each of the great national parties will need to win as many votes as it can in the Federal House of Representatives, and it is to be expected that it will therefore consult the interests of its minorities." *Report of the Commission appointed to enquire into the fears of Minorities*, pp. 88-89. Specific recommendations were made to ensure federal control of the police force and the protection of fundamental human rights, in addition to special arrangements for the Mid-Western, Calabar, and Niger Delta areas.

[116] Federation of Nigeria, *Report by the Resumed Nigeria Constitutional Conference, 1958* (Lagos: 1958), pp. 20-21.

separatism served to offset an even more dangerous drift to extreme regionalism, and the new state advocates generally contend that division of the existing regions into smaller units would revitalize government at the center. This point has been argued forcibly by the intellectual and nationalistic leaders of various minorities,[117] and it largely explains the ambivalent, even tolerant, attitude displayed by many progressive nationalists to the use of ethnic prejudice in political propaganda.

Possibly the historic contribution of ethno-sectional opposition in each of the regions has been to the development of a national party system. The Action Group in particular was transformed into a genuine national party, devoid of its secessionist taint of 1955, through the medium of its fight for the cause of the ethnic minorities in the Eastern and Northern Regions. Since 1955 the two-party system in the East has rested primarily on sub-regionalism, with the NCNC dominant in the Ibo areas and the Action Group rising in the non-Ibo areas. The two-party system of the West has rested mainly on sub-regionalism and Yoruba factionalism, with the Action Group dominant in a majority of the Yoruba divisions, while the NCNC controls most of the Mid-West and certain Yoruba strongholds. In the North, a three-party system rests mainly on sub-regionalism in the Middle Belt (Northern Peoples' Congress v. United Middle Belt Congress-Action Group Alliance) and class conflict in the Hausa heartland (Northern Peoples' Congress v. Northern Elements Progressive Union). The following studies of the nature and exercise of political power lie within that general framework of party distribution.

[117] It is significant that only the National Independence Party, which faced the prospect of a minority existence in the Eastern Region, dissented from the decision of the 1953 constitutional conference to vest residual powers in the regional governments. *Report by the Conference on the Nigerian Constitution, 1953*, p. 4.

PART II

STUDIES IN POWER AND CONFLICT

CHAPTER IV: THE NATIONAL COUNCIL OF NIGERIA AND THE CAMEROONS (NCNC) AND THE AFRICAN CONTINENTAL BANK

The Effect of Regionalization on the Leadership Pattern of the NCNC

IT IS important for the reader to visualize the basic framework of the Lyttleton Constitution (so named for Oliver Lyttleton, Secretary of State for the Colonies) of 1954 which determined that for the time being political power would lie primarily in the regions. In the Eastern and Western Regions, fully responsible governments were established: all ministers were chosen from among the members of the regional legislatures; the leader of the majority party in each legislature was designated Premier, and each regional government remained in power on the condition of its retaining the confidence of a majority of the members of the Regional House of Assembly. (It will be recalled that the Legislatures of the West and North were bi-cameral, including upper Houses of Chiefs.) In the East only, individual ministers were subject to dismissal on a vote of no-confidence by the House of Assembly. In the North, as in the other regions, provision was made for the appointment of the leader of the majority party as Premier, "to hold office so long as his administration enjoyed the confidence of the majority in the House of Assembly"; but three *ex-officio* (i.e., British) members were retained in the Executive Council of that region (namely, the Civil Secretary, the Attorney General, and the Financial Secretary). The federal government remained semi-responsible: three *ex-officio* members were retained in the Council of Ministers (the Chief Secretary, the Financial Secretary, and the Attorney General), and provision was made for the appointment of nine ministers—three from among the federal legislators elected in each region; if no one party had a majority in the House of Representatives, federal ministers would be appointed from among "the majority party in the House from each Region"; as in the past, each federal minister was subject to dismissal upon a two-thirds vote of the entire House. The regional governments were assured of full internal self-government within a few years, and it was hoped that a clarification of the spheres of power of the several governments would be conducive to the revival and steady maturation of national unity at the center.

The new constitutional structure coupled with the dissolution of the crisis-bound Eastern House of Assembly obliged the leadership of the NCNC to make decisions that were agreeable to contemplate but laden with perilous implications. Chiefly, it was necessary to determine an appropriate role in government for the National President. The anti-regionalist wing of the party, in particular the radical youth leaders, wanted Dr. Azikiwe to accept a ministerial post in the federal government in anticipation of his eventual appointment as Prime Minister under the next constitution. Before the London conference of 1953, it had been assumed that the regional legislatures would continue to serve as electoral colleges for the central legislature; Dr. Azikiwe was expected to stand for election in his home town of Onitsha and to gain entry into the Federal House of Representatives through the Eastern House of Assembly. But the London conference decided on separate elections for the House of Representatives, and the Secretary of State ruled, as we have seen, to sever Lagos from the Western Region. Inasmuch as the Constitution provided for the appointment of all federal ministers from the regions, excluding Lagos, the anti-regionalists, who thought that Azikiwe belonged in the Center, were not averse to his standing in Onitsha. But they wanted him to contest the federal rather than the regional election; they thought his goal should be a federal office rather than the Premiership of the East. Azikiwe and the party hierarchy decided otherwise.

At the close of the London conference, Azikiwe declared buoyantly that Nigeria had been offered "self-government on a platter of gold." This statement was repudiated publicly by youth leaders who charged that the NCNC delegates had forsaken the constitutional principles of the party without authorization to do so by a party convention or by the National Executive Committee. By what authority, they asked, did the NCNC delegates swing from the principle of unitary government for Nigeria to the Action Group doctrine of Australian-type federalism, i.e., the reservation of residual powers to the regions? Why, they asked, had no serious effort been made to effect a division of the existing regions into smaller states in keeping with a settled doctrine of the NCNC? These departures from NCNC policies by the party's delegation to London were attributed by some to the expedient alliance with the Action Group[1] that was still in force,

[1] The text of an agreement between Awolowo and Azikiwe, concluded prior to the London conference and released subsequently by the Action Group, included the stipulation that residual powers would be vested in the regions. *Supra*, p. 129, n. 92.

although it verged on collapse over the disputed position of Lagos in the Federation. Furthermore, the idea of a Dominion of Southern Nigeria, comprising the Eastern and Western Regions only, which had been mooted by some leaders of the Action Group and the NCNC alike during the Central crisis of March-April 1953, was criticized by the unitarist element in the NCNC as a betrayal of the nationalist ideal of "One Nigeria."

The Eastern Regional election of September-December 1953 (the last general election in that Region to be held under the protracted system of electoral colleges) produced an overwhelming majority for the NCNC which won 72 of the 84 seats. Soon after the election, it was announced that Azikiwe would lead the Eastern Government in order to direct the implementation of NCNC policies. At the Fifth Annual Convention of the NCNC in January 1954, the radical-unitarist viewpoint was rejected with the adoption of a motion endorsing the decisions taken by the NCNC delegates to the previous London Constitutional Conference. Accordingly, the constitutional policies of the party were reformulated to accept the principle of federalism with the provisos that residual powers should be vested in the central government and that additional states or regions should be created.[2] Thereupon, Dr. Azikiwe assumed the portfolio of Local Government in the Eastern Executive Council, and Mbonu Ojike, who was elected to the Eastern House from Orlu Division, became Minister of Works. On October 1, 1954, Azikiwe was appointed Premier of the Eastern Region and Ojike assumed the crucial portfolio of Finance.

In November 1954, direct elections to the Federal House of Representatives were held in the East and West. The NCNC won 32 of the 42 Eastern seats (to 4 by the United National Independence Party, 3 by the Action Group and 3 by independents) and scored an upset victory in the Western Region with 23 seats to 18 for the Action Group. Consequently, the NCNC was entitled to designate six federal ministers—three from the East and three from the West. In the North, the Northern Peoples' Congress won 84 of the 92 seats by indirect elections and designated the three Northern ministers. Before the upset in the West, a parliamentary coalition uniting the Action Group and the NPC seemed probable; but the NCNC emerged with a majority in the Council of Ministers and a coalition of expedience was formed between it and the Northern Peoples' Congress, which controlled the largest bloc of representatives.

[2] NCNC, "Report of the Fifth Annual Convention held at Enugu, January 6-10, 1954," pp. 1, 16. (Mimeographed.)

These events gave rise to conditions which imposed an increasingly severe strain on the internal cohesion of the NCNC. In the first place, Dr. Azikiwe, the National President, as Premier of the East, was burdened with the duties of office in that region, and relatively detached from the work of party management in Lagos and the West. Secondly, the London agreement on a phased advance to national self-government, involving an intermediate stage of regional self-government, dulled the militancy of nationalist agitation; for some, the nationalist struggle led to the perquisites of a ministerial career. Thirdly, the extension of the franchise and the concomitant development of party organization in the provinces drew into active political participation some hundreds of thousands, indeed millions, of people, for whom the goal of national independence was less exigent than other matters of a local nature. Therefore it is important to appreciate the ethnic and sectional characteristics of the NCNC leadership pattern that resulted from regionalization. A few observations will suffice to outline certain considerations that are fundamental to this analysis.

We have seen that in 1953 the Ibo people of the Eastern Region numbered about five million or 61 percent of the regional total. Over the years, Ibo communities have given overwhelming support to the NCNC. Thus in the federal election of 1954, only 2 of the 28 candidates elected from constituencies inhabited mainly by the Ibo people were members of an opposition party.[3] The brief synopsis of Ibo culture in Chapter I draws attention to the unique histories of two particular ethnic groups, namely the Aro and the Onitsha.[4] The Aro, it may be recalled, have keen traditions of commerce which date from their former domination of the slave trade in the hinterland of southeastern Nigeria. The Onitshans migrated to Iboland from Benin; their traditional system of authority, involving a high concentration of power in a sacred chief and his council of titled advisers, is exceptional among the dispersed power systems that typify Ibo indigenous communities. Among the Ibo, as among other Nigerian nationalities, numerous tribal sections and sub-sections have their

[3] Both of them were elected from Aba-Ngwa Division of Owerri Province, where the dominant Ngwa Ibo tribe followed the leadership of its two "favorite sons," barrister J. A. Wachuku (formerly Deputy Leader of the Eastern House of Assembly under Eyo Ita) and Chief Marcus W. Ubani, MHA. Both Wachuku and Ubani were ardent members of the United National Independence Party in 1954 and both returned to the NCNC in 1957. The five other candidates who were elected to the federal house on the platform of opposition parties in 1954 (3 Action Group and 2 UNIP) stood in non-Ibo constituencies.

[4] *Supra,* pp. 15-16.

146

particular customs and traditions which inspire local or sectional loyalties. The Nnewi, the Mba-ise, the Ohafia, the Ngwa, the Ikwerri, etc., exemplify that remarkable "strength of Ibo clan feeling"[5] which sustains the vigor of the ubiquitous Ibo improvement associations and the enthusiasm with which programs of community development based on voluntary communal labor have been pursued.[6] Yet the particularistic spirit of the Aro and the Onitsha people is unique; technically they are non-Ibo or marginally Ibo, and their histories imbue them with a consciousness of particular eminence in the milieu of the Ibo nation. It is in this impalpable but meaningful sense that we may speak of the special leadership roles or propensities of the Aro and the Onitsha. The latter inhabit one traditional home, to which they have given their name, on the east bank of the Niger River, 150 miles from the sea. The Aro, however, are dispersed in several centers as a result of their old "colonization" system; all Aro communities acknowledge the historic and ritual primacy of Arochuku, in Enyong (or Itu) division of the former Calabar Province, once the site of the feared and fabled "God of the Aros." Arochuku lies between the Ibo and the Ibibio nations, and the Aros of Enyong speak the language of both, i.e., Ibo and Efik. Frequently they refer to themselves as Aro-Calabar. Their kinsmen who are descended from the Aro colonists in Iboland are Ibo-speaking and usually refer to themselves as Aro-Ibo.

In contemporary times, Nnamdi Azikiwe is pre-eminent among the many illustrious sons of Onitsha. The Aros, too, have contributed men of great eminence to the political life of Nigeria. Those of Aro-Calabar extraction have been, for the most part, opponents of the NCNC. Thus Alvin Ikoku, the venerable President of the Nigerian Union of Teachers (at the time of writing), was formerly the leader of the tiny band of United National Party assemblymen in the Eastern House of Assembly during 1952-1953; his son, Samuel G. Ikoku, was elected to the House of Assembly from Enyong in 1957 as an Action Group member and was appointed Leader of the Opposition. Among the Aro-Ibo, the two most prominent individuals during the decade prior to independence were Mazi (an Aro title) Mbonu Ojike and Mazi K. Ozuomba Mbadiwe, sons of the leading Aro community in Iboland, Arondizuogu in Orlu Division of the former Owerri Province. In 1948 Ojike and Mbadiwe

[5] See H. Kanu Offonry, "The Strength of Ibo Clan Feeling," *West Africa,* May 26 and June 2, 1951.

[6] See I. C. Jackson, *Advance in Africa* (London: Oxford University Press, 1956).

were among the founders of the Ibo State Union; they were instrumental in the formation of the National Emergency Committee of 1949, initiated the Committee of National Rebirth in 1951, and were trusted lieutenants of Azikiwe during the intra-party conflict of 1952-1953. In 1954 Ojike was Second Vice-President of the NCNC —he was first elected to that office in 1951—and Azikiwe's principal deputy in the Eastern Regional Government. (After the expulsion of A. C. Nwapa and Eyo Ita from the NCNC in 1952 and 1953, as noted above,[7] Ojike was clearly second only to Azikiwe in the NCNC leadership. Eyo Ita, an Efik of Calabar, was First Vice-President at the time of his expulsion. When Azikiwe assumed the leadership of the Eastern Government, care was taken to select the First Vice-President from the Western Region, and Ojike held the highest party office appropriate for an Eastern Minister and an Ibo, albeit Aro-Ibo.) K. O. Mbadiwe was elected to the Federal House of Representatives from Orlu Division in November 1954, and designated Leader of the NCNC Federal Parliamentary Party.

Azikiwe's removal to the East created a leadership vacuum in the Western NCNC that was filled by an ensemble of personalities, no one of whom had a regional stature comparable to that of the Western Premier, Obafemi Awolowo of the Action Group. The top NCNC leaders in the Western Region of 1954-1955 may be classified into three categories. First, there were the leaders of communal-type parties in areas of traditional habitation where the NCNC remained dominant despite Action Group control of the regional government. The outstanding leader of this type was Hon. Adegoke Adelabu of Ibadan (Yoruba), the Federal Minister of Social Services, whose remarkable career is discussed at length in Chapter VII. Other communal party leaders who ranked highly in the Western Regional hierarchy of the NCNC were Chief Humphrey Omo-Osagie, MHR,[8] of Benin (Edo), a vigorous elder of 58, and Hon. J. O. Fadahunsi, MHA,[9] of Ilesha (Yoruba), a businessman and the First Vice-President of the NCNC. The second category comprised those leaders who rose by virtue of the support of cosmopolitan electorates. Of these, the most eminent were barrister T. O. S. Benson, MHR, of Lagos (Yoruba), chairman of the Western Regional Organization Committee, and Chief Festus Sam Okoite-Eboh, MHR, of Warri (Itsekeri-Urhobo), a businessman, National Treasurer of the NCNC, and Federal Minister of Labour and Welfare. The third category

---

[7] *Supra*, pp. 120-122.
[8] Member of the House of Representatives (Federal).
[9] Member of the House of Assembly (Regional).

consisted of organizational intelligentsia, i.e., leaders who persevered within vanguard associations of the nationalist movement and became famous through identification with the nationalist cause. Among the most prominent in 1954-1955 were barrister Dennis C. Osadebay, MHR of Asaba (Western Ibo), Leader of the Opposition in the Western House of Assembly, National Legal Adviser of the NCNC, and a leader of the movement for the creation of a Mid-West state; and barrister Kolawole Balogun, MHR of Oshun (Yoruba), the youthful National Secretary of the NCNC who was appointed Federal Minister of Research and Information.[10] Hon. T. O. S. Benson, mentioned above, belongs to this category also.

For a decade from 1944-1953, Azikiwe led the NCNC from his political and commercial base at Lagos, first as its General Secretary, then as Federal and National President. Over this entire period, he made comparatively little effort to create a disciplined and cohesive organization, comparable to the Action Group under Awolowo, the Convention People's Party of the Gold Coast (later Ghana) under Kwame Nkrumah, or the Guinea section of the *Rassemblement Démocratique Africain* (later the *Parti Démocratique de Guinea*) under Sékou Touré. Possibly the NCNC encompassed too heterogeneous and dispersed a membership to permit effective centralization under the conditions obtaining in Nigeria. Until 1951, the NCNC was a collection of member-unions—tribal unions, trade unions, occupational associations, political parties, etc.—and its rebirth as a direct membership party for electoral purposes at the Kano Convention of that year did not transform its conglomerate structure or fortify its shadowy organization. On occasion, usually in times of crisis, Azikiwe would make speeches on the importance of internal party order and discipline, but he never really subscribed to the concept of the party as an apparatus of organizational control. Sometimes he referred to the NCNC as "a sleeping giant" or people's movement that might founder temporarily but was invincible when aroused to positive action. This writer ventures to suggest that few of his contemporaries will object to the characterization of Azikiwe as a persuasive teacher, an effective propagandist, an able formulator of principles, an astute political tactician, a rugged antagonist, an inspiring personality, but a less than dedicated organizer.

[10] Kolawole Balogun, at the age of 32, was the youngest member of the Council of Ministers. Previously, in November 1953, he was elected by the Lagos electorate to fill Dr. Azikiwe's seat in the Western House of Assembly when the latter resigned to contest for the Eastern House of Assembly. Highlights of Mr. Balogun's earlier career are noted *supra*, p. 120, n. 73.

When Azikiwe went East in 1953, the NCNC's malady of organizational particularism became chronic; local and personal interests acquired greater prominence and the impulse of central direction appeared to grow increasingly feeble. In radical circles, especially in the NCNC Youth Association, militant nationalists deplored the organizational effects of regionalization and lamented the influence of office on those who had risen to the heights of ministerial opulence. An embittering conflict between leaders of the party and leaders of the Youth Association erupted at the sixth annual convention of 1955 in Ibadan. Two youth leaders were disciplined by the National Executive Committee for allegedly disloyal conduct,[11] and their associates circulated an "Appeal to the NCNC Convention Delegates," alleging a betrayal of the unitarist, socialist, and democratic principles of the party by a "monied" group including the National President and other parliamentary leaders. The document was released to the press and two of the authors were tried and expelled by the Convention for having exposed the party to public obloquy.[12] Furthermore a constitutional age limit of 25 years was imposed on the Youth Association in order to render it ineffectual as a center of independent political activity.

As in 1948, Azikiwe appeared to turn his back on the radical youth. They retorted with complaints that the NCNC had abandoned the way of socialist idealism for the treacherous path of bourgeois nationalism.[13] But nationalism is no less turbulent for the active

[11] Nduka Eze, a member of the National Executive Committee, a former leader of the Zikist Movement, and a former secretary of the Nigerian Labour Congress (*supra*, pp. 80-82) was expelled for disloyalty; Adesanya Idowu, the Western Regional Organizing Secretary of the NCNC, was suspended for activities likely to bring the parties into disrepute. *Daily Times*, May 4, 1955.

[12] They were the former Zikist leaders Osita Agwuna and Mokwugo Okoye. *Daily Times*, May 6, 7, 1955. See *supra*, pp. 74-80. Both were readmitted to the NCNC in 1957.

[13] "As a result of frustration . . . many leading party workers like H. R. Abdallah, A. M. Sa'adu Zungur, F. O. B. Blaize, Nunasu Amosu, P. K. Nwokedi, Ikenna Nzimiro and a host of others have left the Party. . . . As ministers, the party leaders have shamefully perverted the policy of the Party and the significant thing about them is their willing collaboration with Imperialism and the betrayal and sacrifice of the Party's forward elements. Government patronage (loans, contracts and scholarships) has been disposed of in a questionable manner and membership of Government boards had depended more on wealth and good connection rather than intelligence and ability. . . . Social amenities (such as schools, hospitals, roads, water supply) have been extended only to favoured areas, contrary to party policy of fair and equal distribution. The open abuses of the Party (e.g. by Ministers Mbonu Ojike and M. I. Okpara during their merry-go-round last year), the National Secretary's blatant misstatements on party policy or the National President's published obloquies against the youngmen, should have earned for them a disciplinary measure; when the monied dominant group

presence of those private or "middle-class" interests which are sometimes identified as a source of stability. In Nigeria, such interests
are mixed with ethnic interests producing, as we shall see, a political
composition of explosive content.

THE STRUGGLE OVER THE ONITSHA INSTRUMENT

In the opinion of the writer, Onitsha township is the fulcrum on
which the politics of the Eastern Region pivots. It is the pre-eminent
center of cultural, professional and educational activity in Iboland
as well as the leading produce market on the Niger River. The great-
ness of Onitsha lies primarily in the civic fusion of two self-conscious
groups of people: the Onitsha indigenes, to whom we have referred,
and the Ibo settler population of some 70,000-80,000 roughly, who
call themselves non-Onitsha Ibos. (In addition there are about 8,000
non-Ibos, mainly Hausa, Yoruba, Nupe, and Kakanda.) The
Onitshans, or indigenes, live mainly in the traditional Inland Town
which is built around the palace of the sacred *Obi* of Onitsha. They
are intensely proud of their cultural heritage and they do seem to

---

intrigues against the ineffectual youngmen (such as the Balogun-Ojike-Mbadiwe-
Onyia plot to unseat Mr. T. O. S. Benson as chairman of the Western Organisation Committee, Ojike-Mbadiwe plot to remove Osita Agwuna as Principal organ-
ising Secretary of the Party, Ojike's intrigue against Dr. S. E. Imoke as President
of the Abakaliki NCNC and his subversive activities against NCNC constituency
branches in the nomination of election candidates, the National President's counter-
plot against the Demo-Delegation to the Gold Coast, Ojike-Balogun plot to prevent
Mokwugo Okoye from occupying an office in the Party H.Q. to which he was
to be appointed by the NEC or the dominant leadership's intrigue to stop Nduka Eze
from contesting the last Federal Elections) they were all 'toeing the party line,'
but when the youngmen make any attempt to defend and sustain the ideals and
policy of the Party they are branded as rebels, bevanites, communists, ir-
responsibles and anything that suits the dominant leadership." From "An Appeal
to the NCNC Convention Delegates," (Sixth Annual Convention of the NCNC,
Ibadan, May, 1955) (Mimeographed) signed by Osita Agwuna, Mokwugo Okoye,
J. E. Otobo, F. M. Yamu Numa "and 56 other NCNC members" (not named).
These four were leading members of the party in 1958.
    After his expulsion by the Annual Convention on May 5, 1955, Mokwugo Okoye
addressed the Convention thus:
    "As I go, I have no bitterness for the party to which I have devoted the best
years of my youth [it will be recalled that Okoye was imprisoned for nearly
three years when the Zikists were repressed in 1950, *supra*, p. 79] but my only
distress is that this hope of Nigeria, unleavened by the buoyant youthful idealism
that had inspired it, is steadily going the way of all flesh—the way of the Chinese
Kuomintang. By your vindictiveness, shallowness and poltroonery, you have lost
some of the noblest characters that a Nigerian nationalist movement has produced
over the years, and amidst the complex conditions of the present I trust that our
country shall yet produce able, true and brave sons and daughters who can effect
her deliberations and usher in the socialist millennium we all visualise today.
Goodbye and good luck!" *Daily Times*, May 7, 1955.

resent the capture of local government in Onitsha by the numerically preponderant population of "strangers" in the name of democracy. This should not be taken to mean that the Onitshans lack the spirit of modern Nigeria. On the contrary, it is unlikely that any ethnic group in Nigeria has produced a greater proportion of learned men (lawyers, doctors, clergymen, teachers, etc.) than the Onitsha indigenes. But their feeling about their little town is something special, and somewhat above argumentation.

The settlers reside in the "Waterside" and other new urban districts of modern Onitsha. Their local loyalties have been summarized by a competent student of Nigerian society as follows:[14] "Their traditional loyalty is to the town of their birth, where they own land and where their relatives live. But they have also a loyalty to Onitsha as a place where they live and have their business, as a cultural centre where most of them were educated, and as a centre of Ibo political and cultural activity."

In 1935 the Inland Town and the Waterside were amalgamated to form the Onitsha Town Native Authority under the *Obi* and his traditional council (the titled *Ndichie*). Shortly thereafter, progressive Onitshan youth utilized the traditional age grades to form an Onitsha Improvement Union which advocated the introduction of enlightened non-traditional members into the *Obi*'s Council. This was done in 1938, but the settler community was not given any representation whatever until 1942. In 1945, members of the various Ibo ethnic associations of the Waterside, including the influential Onitsha Ibo Union (an affiliate of the then Ibo Federal Union), organized a Non-Onitsha Ibo Association. At first, the objectives of the Association were economic—e.g., equal treatment for non-Onitshans in the matter of allocating market stalls, etc.—but its focus soon shifted to the aim of democratic representation in the Onitsha local government.[15] Inevitably, the Onitsha improvement Union and the Non-Onitsha Ibo Association became rival "political clubs," although a majority in each was devoted to the NCNC. Prior to the regional election of 1951, a third faction emerged in

[14] G. I. Jones, *Report of the Position, Status, and Influence of Chiefs and Natural Rulers in the Eastern Region of Nigeria* (Enugu: 1957), p. 31.

[15] In July 1950, a Non-Onitsha Ibo delegation to the Government at Enugu requested the introduction of democratic representation for the Onitsha Town Council. Members of the delegation included P. O. Aneke, President, M. O. Ajegbo, C. C. Mojekwu, P. N. Okeke, T. O. Nwankwo, C. T. Onyekwelu, S. M. Obike, E. O. Ude, H. O. Ngordy. See the Report of the Select Committee (of the Eastern House of Assembly) set up to Enquire into the Petition of the Non-Onitsha Ibo Community resident in Onitsha; and see Jones, *op.cit.,* p. 30.

the name of the NCNC, including elements of both the Onitshan and the non-Onitshan communities. The Onitshan and the composite factions endeavored to agree on a mutually acceptable candidate, but their efforts were undermined by personal animosities. As a result, a non-party candidate of Inland Town origin was elected to represent Onitsha in the Eastern House of Assembly,[16] and the militant non-Onitshans decided to organize for independent political action.

In 1954 the Association agreed with reluctance to accept a reformed local authority—the first Onitsha Urban District Council—including a slight majority of traditional and elected representatives of the Inland Town. Subsequently, disclosures by a non-partisan Onitsha Community League and muckraking articles by an Onitshan barrister, Mr. Chuba Ikpeazu, in the daily *Nigerian Spokesman* (the Onitsha newspaper of the Zik Group), drew the attention of the public to the venal and irregular practices of certain members of the Onitsha Urban District Council. This gave the Non-Onitsha Ibo Association a golden opportunity to renew its campaign for democratic representation. The Onitsha branch of the NCNC, dominated by non-Onitsha Ibos, instructed all members of the Council to resign forthwith. A majority of them complied and the government appointed a Commissioner to inquire into the affairs of the Council. When the inquiry demonstrated misconduct,[17] the Council was dissolved and a Caretaker Committee was appointed including an equal number of Onitsha and non-Onitsha Ibos under the chairmanship of the *Obi* of Onitsha. It was apparent that the Regional Government would prescribe a new Instrument[18] reconstituting the Onitsha Urban District Council and the Onitshans were faced with the prospect of minority representation for the first time.

Onitshan interests were represented by the Onitsha Improvement Union, under the leadership of Hon. P. H. Okolo, MHR, an educator and supervisor of schools for the Roman Catholic Mission; among the leaders of the Union were a goodly number of exceedingly able professional men, notably lawyers. Their case rested on three principles set forth in a memorandum to the Minister of Internal Affairs: (1) the right of "Natural Rulers and Elders" to "substantial

---

[16] The successful candidate, barrister Louis N. Mbanefo, was the first Ibo lawyer and is the present Chief Justice of the Eastern Region.

[17] O. P. Gunning, *Report of the Inquiry into the Administration of the Affairs of the Onitsha Urban District Council* (Enugu: 1955).

[18] An Instrument establishing every local government council is issued by the responsible minister of the regional government under the provisions of the Local Government Law of the region. The Instrument specifies the name, type, area, and constitution of the council concerned.

representation in Local Government Councils"; (2) the right of the "indigenous people" to majority representation in local government councils, however more numerous the "stranger elements" may be; (3) the rule "that no one man should at one and the same time be a member of two Local Government Councils of distinct areas of jurisdiction."[19] The third principle was intended to disqualify settlers who kept a hand in the affairs of their home towns by means of membership in their home town councils. In addition, the Onitshans argued that indigenes are entitled to majority representation on a communal basis to ensure their control of policies with respect to land.

On the other side of the question, the Non-Onitsha Ibo Association comprised an equally impressive array of professional and entrepreneurial talent; the chairman of its central planning committee, barrister M. O. Ajegbo (Obosi Ibo) was destined to become the first Nigerian Attorney General of the Eastern Region in 1958. It should be noted that the Non-Onitsha Ibo cause was supported vigorously by the Obosi, a neighboring Ibo people who were engaged in a protracted litigation against the Onitshans over rights in disputed lands.[20] In addition the Non-Onitsha Ibo cause was supported by most leaders of the Ibo State Union, while the Onitshans solicited regional support among the non-Ibo chieftaincies of Calabar and the Niger Delta. This may account for the Onitshan emphasis on the prerogatives of chiefs in general, and the particular desirability of creating a Regional House of Chiefs as an upper chamber of the regional legislature.

With reservations, the controversy may be characterized in economic terms as a conflict between the interests of land and the interests of commerce. The leadership of the Non-Onitsha Ibo Association was interlocked with that of the influential Union of Niger African

[19] *Papers relating to the Instrument Establishing the Onitsha Urban District Council*, Sessional Paper No. 1, of 1956 (Enugu: 1956), pp. 4-5.

[20] The Obosi-Onitsha dispute has been litigated as far as the Judicial Committee of the Privy Council. Its origin lies in the lease of land by Onitsha people to the Royal Niger (later United Africa) Company in the 19th century. It was a condition of the lease that the rights of Obosi farmers would not be disturbed by the company. In 1900 the Colonial Government assumed possession of all land which had been acquired by the Royal Niger Company. Thereafter, Obosi and Onitshan families asserted conflicting claims to the lands, some of which had been leased to third parties. When the government surrendered certain lands to Obosi claimants, the Onitshans sued for ownership. In Nigerian courts they were granted possession as well as ownership in addition to an injunction against the further alienation of land to third parties by the Obosi. On appeal, however, the Privy Council revoked the judgment of the Nigerian Courts with respect to possession and the dispute was unsettled to the writer's knowledge in 1959.

Traders, which claimed a membership in excess of 2,000 small businessmen.[21] Furthermore, the Association had political connections that were inimical to the NCNC inasmuch as several of its leading members were also members of the United National Independence Party, then the official opposition in the Eastern House of Assembly. Inasmuch as the editors of the *Nigerian Spokesman* (Zik Group) favored the Onitsha Improvement Union, the Non-Onitsha Ibo Association utilized a rival daily, the *New Africa*, published by P. E. Chukwurah, an ardent member of both the Non-Onitsha Ibo Association and the United National Independence Party. In mid-May the press war reached a peak of unprecedented virulence when the *Spokesman* carried an editorial, purported to have been written by barrister Ikpeazu, advising discontented non-Onitsha Ibos to "pack and go" back to their home towns.

Some days later, a delegation of Onitshans urged Dr. Azikiwe, Premier and Minister of Internal Affairs with responsibility for Local Government, to support an amendment to the Instrument that would give non-Onitshans the right to vote but deny them the right to stand for election to the Onitsha Urban District Council. The Premier rejected that extreme proposal on the spot but he gave assurances to the delegation that the regional government appreciated the special traditions of the Onitshans and that local councils would not be permitted to acquire lands compulsorily without express ministerial approval.[22] For weeks Dr. Azikiwe pondered the problem —one of the most difficult he had ever faced, for which no solution was conceivable that would not scathe him politically. He contemplated the strongly worded petitions submitted by both sides and finally announced the decision of the government on August 25, 1955. It provided for: "a Council of thirty-seven members, consisting of the *Obi* of Onitsha as President, twelve traditional members [i.e., *Ndichie*], and twenty-four elected members one of whom shall be chairman." The elected members would represent 18 waterside wards and 3 wards in the Inland Town.[23] Then, like Solon, Azikiwe

[21] The President of the Union of Niger African Traders, Mr. C. T. Onyekwelu, was Chairman of the Onitsha Chamber of Commerce, a prominent Protestant layman and a leading member of the Non-Onitsha Ibo Association. The General Secretary of the Union, Hon. P. N. Okeke, MHA, was also Secretary of the Non-Onitsha Ibo Association. Records of the Non-Onitsha Ibo Association (made available to the writer by a leading member) indicate regular cooperation between its Executive Committee and the Union of Niger African Traders.

[22] Ministerial approval for compulsory acquisitions of land by a local government council is required by the Eastern Region Local Government Law (E. R. No. 26 of 1955), sections 187-194.

[23] *Papers Relating to the Instrument Establishing the Onitsha Urban District Council*, p. ii.

left for England on official business. He had done his level best but could not escape censure.

To the Onitshans, the new Instrument signified the engulfment of their traditional values by the commercialist democracy, an event they knew full well to be inevitable, but hoped nonetheless to delay. The non-Onitshans were furious; by what right, they asked, do the indigenes, comprising a mere 12½ percent of the population, retain better than 40 percent of the Council's membership? They insinuated that Azikiwe, an Onitshan himself, had cynically capitulated to the pleading of his townsmen. In 1953, they said, the non-Onitsha Ibo masses had rallied to him and to the party while certain Inland Town elements equivocated on his candidature to the Eastern House of Assembly. Now, they remonstrated, he had disappointed the majority of his constituents and betrayed the principle of local democracy for which the NCNC stood. In Lagos, they pointed out, the NCNC demanded a wholly elected Council while the Action Group wanted a traditional component of 16 percent; but in Onitsha, a traditional component of one-third had been prescribed by an NCNC government. It was outrageous, they complained, for the NCNC to stand for one principle in Lagos and another in Onitsha. Protest meetings were held, and one mass meeting, called by the Non-Onitsha Ibo Association, actually passed a "vote of no confidence" in the Premier.[24]

The Onitshans were less inclined to condemn the Premier but they were enormously indignant at the role alleged to have been played by certain Eastern ministers, especially Mbonu Ojike, the Minister of Finance, who was known to favor the non-Onitsha Ibo cause in principle. Elections to the reconstituted Onitsha Urban District Council were held during Azikiwe's absence abroad, and Ojike, acting for the Premier, was thought to have been responsible for decisions which were justifiable in themselves but regarded as detrimental to Onitshan interests.[25] Candidates of the Non-Onitsha

[24] In April 1956, Chief Festus Sam Okotie-Eboh, the Federal Minister of Labour and Welfare, conducted an inquiry into the Onitsha dispute at the behest of the NCNC National Executive Committee. His report condemned the utilization of non-party platforms, such as that of the Non-Onitsha Ibo Association, by NCNCers in local elections and sternly rebuked the members of the Association for their "vote of no confidence" in Dr. Azikiwe. NCNC Eastern Working Committee. File No. 26, 22 April 1956; also *New Africa,* April 26, 1956.

[25] For example the registration period is said to have been extended on a request from the Non-Onitsha Ibo Association, and a British Administrative Officer was appointed as Returning Officer for the election in place of the Nigerian Town Clerk who was considered partial to the Onitshans. The writer was told that the "quorum clause" of the Onitsha Instrument (E. R. L. N. No. 207 of 1955,

Ibo Association won 19 of the 24 elective seats (all but the 3 Inland Town seats and 2 seats in the Hausa and Yoruba wards of the Waterside), giving the Association an overall superiority of one in the Council. All 19 signed undertakings of loyalty to the Association, and barrister C. C. Mojekwu, a member of the Association's planning committee, was elected Chairman of the Onitsha Urban District Council.[26] Within a few weeks of the inauguration of the new Council, the local dispute was eclipsed by an episode of enormous political significance to the Eastern Region and the NCNC in which protagonists of the Onitshan and the non-Onitshan Ibo causes were deeply involved.

---

clause 5), which did not require the participation of traditional members, was attributed to Ojike's influence. It was also alleged, probably unfairly, that Ojike and other ministers favorable to the Non-Onitsha Ibo cause opposed the prohibition of dual membership in councils of different jurisdictions in order to protect the interests of non-Onitsha Ibos who were members of councils in their home towns. In December 1955, the Eastern House of Assembly amended the Eastern Region Local Government Law to restrict individuals to membership in one council only, except insofar as an individual might be elected to a higher Council from a lower one within the same jurisdiction. *Eastern House of Assembly Debates,* Second Session, Fifth Meeting, 15 and 16 December 1955, pp. 32-33. (A three-tier system of local, district, and county councils then obtained in the East, with indirect elections to rural district and county councils from subordinate local councils. Urban district councils, as at Onitsha, were elected directly by taxpayer suffrage.) Twelve members of the Onitsha Urban District Council were affected and disqualified. *Daily Times,* January 24, 1956. Later a clarifying amendment was adopted which gave any person holding dual membership 14 days to resign from either council. In support of this amendment, the Minister of Internal Affairs (Dr. Azikiwe) acknowledged that the original amendment had been a source of complaints but denied allegations of bad faith on the part of the government. "I hope," he said, "that no responsible Member of this House will think that these changes have been introduced because of the activities of certain pressure groups, no matter how influential they may appear to be." Hon. P. N. Okeke, Secretary General of the Non-Onitsha Ibo Association, expressed his gratitude to the Minister "for this gesture because we realized that it affected a few people outside Onitsha and that the confusion in Onitsha also affected a large number of Councils. This stopped the working of the council for three months." *Eastern House of Assembly Debates,* Third Session, First Meeting, Vol. II, 20-28 March 1956, pp. 660-661.

[26] At first the *Obi* of Onitsha was designated as Chairman, and the elected leader as Vice Chairman, pending the anticipated revision of the Local Government Law to provide for the designation of the *Obi* as President and the elected leader as Chairman. There was some difficulty in having the "sacred" *Obi* sworn as Chairman which had to be resolved before the Onitshans would agree to participate. One bar to the designation of Onitsha as a municipality is said to be the objection of the Onitsha Improvement Union to the attribution of a "foreign" title, that of Mayor, to the *Obi* and their simultaneous opposition to the assumption of that highly prestigious title by any other person, particularly a non-Onitshan. See *ibid.,* pp. 661-662. In 1958, Onitsha township was still an Urban District Council with County Council powers.

The Eastern Government's Commission of Inquiry into Bribery and Corruption

In August 1955 the Eastern Regional Government appointed a Commission of Inquiry to investigate the extent of bribery and corruption "in all branches of public life" within the region and to propose measures to remedy the evils found. This was widely regarded as an impressively bold earnest of the NCNC's dedication to rectitude in public affairs. Previous governmental inquiries had disclosed grievous misconduct on the part of elected councillors in three of the principal cities of the East.[27] In July 1955, at a meeting of the NCNC Eastern Working Committee in Aba, Dr. Azikiwe deplored the prevalence of corruption in local government. "It does no credit," he is reported to have remarked, "to fill local government bodies and the legislatures of the land with crooks who have stained hands."[28] This comment cut deep into local sensibilities in Aba, where the urban district council had been described as "venal" by the report of an official inquiry.

There is no reason to suppose that the Commission of Inquiry into bribery and corruption was intended to evolve into a political circus. The four commissioners applied themselves with diligence to investigations of alleged bad conduct for three months (November 1955-January 1956). Public sessions were held in various cities, and accusations, some of which were patently malicious, were made against public servants, European and African alike. In order to discredit false reports summarily, the Commission agreed to render public verdicts on individual cases as soon as decisions were reached. Routine cases involved police officials, magistrates, members of scholarship boards, contractors, hospital employees, vehicle inspectors, etc. But the terms of reference under which the Commission operated were as broad as they were vague, and several accusations were entertained respecting the conduct of persons in high places. Two sensational cases involved regional ministers; the Minister of Land was alleged to have been responsible for irregularities in the allocation of urban plots, and the Minister of Finance, Mazi Mbonu Ojike, was alleged

27 R. K. Floyer, D. O. Ibekwe, and Chief J. O. Njemanze, *Report of the Commission of Inquiry into the Working of Port Harcourt Town Council* (Enugu: 1955); P. F. Grant, *Report of the Inquiry into the Allocation of Market Stalls at Aba* (Enugu: 1955); Gunning, *op.cit.*

28 *Proceedings of the Tribunal Appointed to Inquire into Allegations of Improper Conduct by the Premier of the Eastern Region of Nigeria in connection with the Affairs of the African Continental Bank Limited and other Relevant Matters,* Vol. I (Lagos: 1957), p. 383, and *ibid.,* Vol. II, p. 800. (Hereafter referred to as *Proceedings of the Foster-Sutton Tribunal of Inquiry.*)

to have been corrupt during his tenure as Minister of Works in 1954. When the allegation against him was lodged in November 1955, Ojike was acting for the Premier during Dr. Azikiwe's absence abroad.

Ojike's accuser was a fantastic individual who described himself to the Commission as "a native doctor and soap maker." He asserted that he was used by Ojike as an intermediary in a corrupt transaction with an Italian firm of builders and civil engineers. The alleged deal pertained to the construction of the famous Onitsha market, a huge structure on the banks of the Niger River that was erected mainly to accommodate small traders at a cost of some £433,000 to the regional government. Ojike was alleged to have exerted influence to defeat objections to the project within the Eastern Government,[29] and to secure the contract award for the firm of Borini Prono and Company. In return he was said to have been paid one shilling on every pound of the contract's value, while his accuser was said to have been promised one penny on every shilling. The accuser complained that he had not been paid.

Ojike's lawyers contended that the accusation had been trumped up by his political opponents. They pointed out that Borini Prono was a highly reputable firm and that its selection for the contract was approved by a responsible British engineering company and by the former chairman of the Regional Production Development Board. Moreover, the testimonies of Ojike's accuser and of an associate who endeavored to collect the latter's purported share of the graft, were not impressively credible.[30] But the case appeared to have become an incident in the bitter struggle between the Onitshans and the non-Onitsha Ibos which was then rife.[31] This was an ironical twist since

[29] In fact the Onitsha market scheme had been a bone of contention since January 1952, when the Eastern Regional Production Development Board agreed to make a 25-year loan of £500,000 to the Onitsha Native Authority for that purpose. Objections were voiced throughout the region to the effect that £500,000 was an exorbitant and inequitable sum to allocate for a single project. Following a debate in the House of Assembly (*Eastern House of Assembly Debates*, First Session . . . July 1952, pp. 174-206), the Eyo Ita (NCNC) government took steps to reduce the loan to £100,000 but the Board of Onitsha Town sued the Eastern Regional Production Development Board for the full amount. Ultimately, in 1953, the ERPDB accepted a liability for £500,000 as a commitment which had been made and could not be abrogated unilaterally.

[30] Defence counsel pointed out that the accusation dated the alleged deal in 1953, before Ojike had been elected to the Eastern House of Assembly and appointed Minister of Works. The General Manager of Borini Prono admitted having known Ojike's accuser, but denied the allegation.

[31] See reports of the proceedings of the Commission of Inquiry and comments in the *Daily Times* and other newspapers of November 1955-January 1956.

both factions in Onitsha town favored the construction of the new market. Yet Ojike, it will be recalled, was regarded as an opponent of the Onitshan cause with respect to the Instrument establishing the Onitsha Urban District Council; it seemed more than coincidental that his accuser was assisted by several Onitshan lawyers while the Minister was defended by prominent members of the Non-Onitsha Ibo Association.[32]

In this regard, the composition of the Commission of Inquiry itself engendered speculation, however unfairly. The chairman, barrister Chuba Ikpeazu, was an ardent Onitshan who wrote the "pack and go" article of May 20th and led a delegation to the Premier to plead the Onitshan cause. Barrister C. C. Mojekwu was a leading member of the Non-Onitsha Ibo Association who became chairman of the Onitsha Urban District Council. Barrister E. E. Koofrey of Calabar (Efik) was a member of the United National Independence Party; he was appointed to the Commission by Ojike in late August following the departure of Azikiwe for Europe.[33] Mr. J. A. Ita of Calabar (and Ikot Ekpene), a photographer, was a strong member of the NCNC. Speculation was inevitable when the Commission divided on the question of Ojike's guilt—it was affirmed by Ikpeazu and Koofrey, but denied by Mojekwu and Ita. Koofrey's position was especially difficult as he was an old friend of Ojike, who was responsible for his appointment to the Commission. His adverse vote was liable to various unfair interpretations: Ojike had been instrumental in the overthrow of the Eyo Ita Government in 1953, and Koofrey was Ita's townsman as well as a member of the United National

[32] Mbonu Ojike's counsel before the Commission were M. O. Ajegbo, Chairman of the Planning Commission of the Non-Onitsha Ibo Association, later Attorney-General of the East, and barrister G. C. Onyiuke, an adherent to the United National Independence Party.

[33] Initially, the chairmanship of the Commission was offered to Sir Francis Ibiam, a highly respected doctor, later Principal of the Hope Waddell Training Institute of Calabar, President of the University College of Ibadan, and Governor of the Eastern Region. Sir Francis anticipated difficulties with respect to the non-specific terms of reference and declined the offer of appointment. Barrister Ikpeazu, whose fame as a reformer stemmed from his campaign against corruption in the Onitsha Urban District Council, was then chosen by the Eastern Executive Council. Prior to Azikiwe's departure for Europe in August 1955, barrister E. E. Koofrey of Calabar was offered an appointment to the proposed commission to study the position of chiefs in the Eastern Region. A few days later, when Azikiwe had gone, the Acting Premier, Ojike, put Koofrey on the Bribery Commission in the place of barrister O. O. Ita of Oron who was also a member of the United National Independence Party. Subsequently, Azikiwe cancelled the chieftaincy commission and appointed Mr. G. I. Jones of Cambridge, an anthropologist and former district officer, as sole commissioner to inquire into the status of chiefs in the Eastern Region.

Independence Party; the Efik community of Calabar was deeply sympathetic to the Onitshan cause because Calabar township had been inundated by a flow of Ibo settlers and the Efiks desired to vindicate the principle of local control by the indigenous people of traditional communities. Ikpeazu risked similar derogatory imputations when he resolved the deadlock against Ojike by means of his casting vote as chairman and then announced publicly that Ojike had been corrupt. Thereupon, Dr. Azikiwe requested the resignation of the Minister of Finance, and the Commission of Inquiry came to an abrupt halt as the two "minority" members refused to participate any further.[34] Eventually the Eastern Regional Government rejected both majority and minority reports for reasons which will emerge below.

The Commission of Inquiry into bribery and corruption produced a harvest of bitterness which rankled deeply within the NCNC. One of those who were attacked maliciously before the Commission was Effiong O. Eyo of Uyo in Calabar Province (Ibibio), the Government Chief Whip in the Eastern House of Assembly who was also chairman of the strategic Eastern Region Development Corporation (formerly the Eastern Regional Production Development Board). During the Eastern parliamentary crisis of 1953, Eyo was a principal spokesman in the House of Assembly for the national leadership of the party. Since then he had been a close associate of Mbonu Ojike and he felt intensely that the Minister of Finance had been wronged. In December 1955, Eyo was criticized sharply within the NCNC Parliamentary Party by back-bench members who were regarded as militant followers of Azikiwe.[35] The same individuals renewed their criticisms of his administration of the Eastern Region Development Corporation during the budget session of the House of Assembly in March 1956.[36] In April, Eyo asked to be relieved of his offices as Government Chief Whip and chairman of the Development Corporation. He then accused the Premier of grossly abusing his office in connection with the investment and deposit of public funds in a private bank of which Dr. Azikiwe was the principal shareholder.

[34] Ikpeazu's declaration of January 19, 1956, of the guilt of Ojike was the first finding of guilt rendered by the Commission. The following day it was announced that M. C. Awgu, the Minister of Land, had acted improperly but not corruptly in connection with the allocation of certain plots in Enugu. Awgu's case was complicated by his sharp controversy with the Commissioner of Land that we need not examine here. On January 21, 1956, the Premier requested the resignations of both ministers. Apart from the two ministers, only two other persons, both government employees, were declared guilty of corruption.

[35] *Daily Times*, December 14, 15, 1955.

[36] *Eastern House of Assembly Debates*, Third Session, First Meeting, Vol. II, 20-28 March 1956, pp. 385-390.

The Tribunal

Eyo's allegation against Azikiwe can only be appreciated in the light of economic policies and institutional developments which culminated in the transactions to which he took exception. These can be summarized briefly. Shortly after the Second World War, the Nigerian Government created statutory agents known as Commodity Marketing Boards to purchase the four main agricultural export crops (cocoa, palm produce, ground nuts, and cotton) from producers at fixed prices for sale abroad.[37] In addition to their primary function of price stabilization, the marketing boards were authorized to allocate surplus funds for the purpose of agricultural development and research, and Regional Production Development Boards were created to administer grants from the marketing boards. At the end of 1953, marketing board accounts, after the deduction of allocations for development and research, were reported to total £75 million, owing mainly to the rise of world commodity prices relative to the prices paid to producers.[38] This amount was included in the sterling balance (or credit) of Nigeria in the United Kingdom;[39] and that part of it

[37] On the history and rationale of export trade controls in Nigeria, see P. T. Bauer, *West African Trade* (Cambridge: Cambridge University Press, 1954), especially Part 5: "The Statutory Marketing Boards and Their Policies," pp. 263-343; also C. Leubuscher, "The Policy Governing External Trade," *Mining, Commerce, and Finance in Nigeria*, ed. Margery Perham (London: Faber, 1948), pp. 137-175; and David E. Carney, *Government and Economy in British West Africa* (New York: Bookman Associates, 1961).

[38] The International Bank for Reconstruction and Development, *The Economic Development of Nigeria* (Baltimore: The Johns Hopkins Press, 1955), p. 85.

[39] "Throughout the war and the postwar period Nigeria has earned more than it has spent on consumption and domestic investment. The difference between total output and total expenditure of necessity took the form of foreign assets; these have been held as sterling balances in London. At the beginning of 1953, these balances exceeded £150 million, not counting £55 million representing the estimated Nigerian share in the holdings of the West African Currency Board. Most of the balances are funds of the central and regional governments and of native administrations, the Marketing Boards and the Regional Production Development Boards." *Ibid.*, p. 17.
The same authorities assert that "this level of external assets of banking and official and semi-official institutions is quite unusual (over £200 million). In March 1953 not one of the 20 Latin American republics had such reserves. In the independent sterling area only Australia and India had greater assets. South Africa's total gold and foreign exchange reserves were less than two-thirds as large. To look at the assets from another side, they were considerably greater than the investments of expatriate companies in Nigeria; actually they exceed the total of these investments and the Nigerian debt, so that Nigeria is for the moment a net creditor." *Ibid.*, p. 145.
The Ghanaian sterling balance in London is even more impressive, since that smaller country had a credit of more than £200 million, or one-sixth of the total colonial balances in 1957, mainly as a result of the postwar cocoa boom. Anthony

which was not required as working capital was invested in sterling securities including British government savings bonds bearing 3 percent interest. Nigerian leaders contemplated the repatriation of a portion of these sterling balances for the purposes of economic development.

In 1954, as a result of decisions taken at the Lagos Resumed Constitutional Conference and in keeping with the agreements on political and economic regionalization, the four commodity marketing boards were dissolved and their assets were distributed among new all-purpose regional marketing boards according to the principle of derivation.[40] The regional marketing boards were authorized to make grants for development and research generally, rather than for agricultural purposes alone as had been the case previously.[41] £15.1 million was allocated to the Eastern Regional Marketing Board and a law establishing that board authorized it, upon direction of the Eastern Minister of Trade, to make grants within the region to local governments and to statutory corporations.

In mid-1954, Dr. Azikiwe, then Minister of Local Government and Premier-designate, and Louis P. Ojukwu, a wealthy businessman, undertook an economic mission to Europe and North America; their report, submitted to the Eastern House of Assembly in May 1955, included a recommendation for "the creation of a statutory body known as Finance Corporation, which should have wide discretionary powers for stimulating economic expansion."[42] Among its proposed functions were that of investment in business and financial enterprises, loans to and investments in other public corporations, and loans to "hard-pressed" African businesses and

---

Rudd, "Ghana and the Sterling Area," *The Banker*, CVII, No. 374 (March 1957), pp. 166-171. On the sterling balances of Nigeria and Gold Coast in 1953 see D. E. Carney, *op.cit.*, pp. 56-60.

[40] *Report by the Resumed Conference on the Nigerian Constitution held in Lagos in January and February, 1954* (London: 1954), p. 60; The International Bank for Reconstruction and Development, *op.cit.*, pp. 169-170.

[41] This departure was endorsed by the Mission of the International Bank, *ibid.*, p. 88 ("While the present reserves of the boards can be an important source of development capital, we recommend that the boards' contribution be made through long-term loans to government out of that portion of their funds which need not be kept liquid. . . . ") and p. 109; however, the mission warned that in its opinion "the second-line reserves of the Marketing Board in the Eastern Region are insufficient to permit their use for long-term loans during 1955-1960." *Ibid.*, p. 118. The amounts allocated to the regional marketing boards in 1954 were as follows: West—£34.4 million; North—£24.8 million; East—£15.1 million; and Southern Cameroons—£1.2 million. *Ibid.*, p. 170.

[42] *Economic Rehabilitation of Eastern Nigeria*, Sessional Paper No. 6 of 1955 (Enugu: 1955), p. 5.

to public agencies in order to provide employment. To this end it was recommended that the Eastern Regional Marketing Board should make an outright grant of £2 million to the Finance Corporation[43] which in turn should invest substantially in an indigenous bank, so as to control not less than three-fourths of its equity capital.[44] This long range policy had in fact been initiated by the Eastern Region Finance Corporation Law of 1954, which equipped the new corporation with powers to grant loans and subsidies and to acquire "loan or share capital in any government agency, statutory corporation, local government body, co-operative society, or limited liability company."[45]

During March and April 1955, appointments to the board of the Finance Corporation were approved by the Executive Council of the region, and the Marketing Board agreed to a transfer of £2 million. At the inaugural meeting of the Corporation, Mazi Mbonu Ojike, the Minister of Finance, criticized the monopolistic practices of the

[43] *Ibid.*, p. 6.

[44] "We recommend that the Eastern Region Finance Corporation should make a substantial investment in an indigenous bank to enable the Corporation always to control not less than three-fourths of the equity capital of that bank. That done, the Finance Corporation should use the bank for purposes of economic development of this Region. We also recommend the increased use of such bank by the Government of the Eastern Region, the statutory corporations, Local Government bodies and other Government agencies. Provided that the requirements of the Banking Ordinance had been met, such a bank should not only be used as depository for official and semi-official funds, but it should be the nucleus for a central bank envisaged by the International Bank Mission. The strengthening of indigenous banks will facilitate the mobilisation of domestic capital." *Ibid.*, p. 22. The precedent of Japanese industrialization was cited in support of this recommendation. In fact, the entire report, written by Dr. Azikiwe in consultation with Mr. Ojukwu, is based on impressive scholarly research in the fields of public finance and economic development, drawing largely upon American experience. The idea of the Finance Corporation was described as "really a sort of Rooseveltian 'New Deal' transported from across the Atlantic," although the U.S. Reconstruction Finance Corporation Act was also cited.

It should be observed that the International Bank Mission specifically opposed the large-scale transfer of government reserves to African commercial banks on the ground that subsequent decisions by the government to draw upon deposits for expenditures would produce a contraction in the flow of credit. The mission also expressed the fear that "decisions regarding transfers of government deposits to African commercial banks would not always be free from party-political motives." The International Bank for Reconstruction and Development, *op.cit.*, p. 98 n. 12, and p. 159. On this matter there has been a sharp difference in outlook between Nigerian leaders and foreign economic experts.

[45] *Report of the Tribunal Appointed to Inquire into Allegations Reflecting on the Official Conduct of the Premier of, and Certain Persons Holding Ministerial and Other Public Offices in, the Eastern Region of Nigeria,* Cmnd. 51 (London: H.M.S.O., 1957), p. 11. (Hereafter referred to as the *Report of the Foster-Sutton Tribunal of Inquiry.*)

leading expatriate bank, the Bank of British West Africa, and cited with approval the example of the Eastern Regional Development Corporation which had recently made a deposit of £30,000 in the African Continental Bank. He urged members of the Corporation to make a substantial investment in that indigenous bank in order to build up its reserves. Thereupon the Finance Corporation resolved to invest £750,000 in the African Continental Bank and to appoint it as banker for the Corporation.[46] In May, the chairman of the Finance Corporation concluded an agreement with the Acting Chairman of the African Continental Bank, providing for the purchase by the Corporation of 877,000 shares in the bank at a cost of £1 each,[47] giving the Corporation 87.7 percent ownership. The Corporation was empowered to appoint managing agents for the bank and to nominate five directors, while the bank was entitled to nominate four directors, "including the Chairman who shall always be the Founder of the Bank and/or the Governing Director or the nominee of the Founder" and three others to be selected by the latter. The Corporation agreed to persuade its beneficiaries and customers to use the bank as a main depository for their funds and agreed further to purchase at par, i.e., at £1 each, the shares of any shareholder desiring to sell.[48] Those who were familiar with the condition of the bank at that time might well have concluded that the agreement was rather favorable to the owners and directors of the bank. At this point it is necessary to look briefly into the bank's history and its financial position.

In 1944 Nnamdi Azikiwe acquired a small property bank, the Tinubu Properties Limited, to buttress the financial foundations of his newspaper business. A few years later it was renamed the African Continental Bank Limited, and Dr. Azikiwe assumed the offices of "Founder, Governing Director and Chairman." In 1949 the bank's nominal capital was £250,000; all but a small percentage of those shares that were assigned to individuals were held by Azikiwe himself and a few members of his family. Some 55 percent of the shares were held by four companies in the so-called Zik Group of companies, namely Zik Enterprises Limited, publisher of the *West African Pilot*,

---

[46] *Ibid.*, pp. 22-23.

[47] "Pursuant to the agreement, the Bank issued, on the 16th of June, 1955, share certificates for 784,000 Ordinary shares of £1 each and 93,000 Preference shares of £1 each, and on the 21st June, 1955, the Finance Corporation paid to the bank £789,300 which was the full amount owing for the shares taking into account the 10 per cent commission allowed to the Corporation under clauses 9 and 10 of the agreement." *Ibid.*, p. 27.

[48] *Ibid.*, pp. 25-26.

and three firms involved in Azikiwe's publishing business, namely, the African Book Company, the Nigerian Paper Company, and the Nigerian Printing Supply Company. As Dr. Azikiwe owned from 45 to 63 percent of each of these companies his personal control of the bank was assured. The bank itself was one of 12 companies in the Zik Group and its purpose, according to Dr. Azikiwe, was primarily to finance the activities of the Group.[49] After 1949, the Zik Group suffered heavy financial losses, largely attributable to effective newspaper competition from the British-owned *Daily Times* and the *Daily Service,* which was controlled by his political opponents. The companies resorted to extensive borrowing from the bank at low rates of interest, which drained the bank's fund of deposits and reserves. Despite these adversities, the African Continental Bank managed to survive a protracted period of bank failures in the early 1950's during which time some 15 indigenous banks, mainly "mushroom banks" resulting from a boom in speculation, were liquidated.[50]

Nigerian banking was encompassed by regulatory legislation in 1952, when a Banking Ordinance passed by the House of Representatives required banks to obtain a license from the Financial Secretary of the Nigerian Government. Existing banks were permitted three years of grace, until May 1955, to qualify. Among the stipulated requirements were the possession of a nominal capital of £25,000, half of which had to be paid up, a record of satisfactory conduct and an adequate liquidity ratio, i.e., reserves in proportion to deposits, to be determined by the Financial Secretary.[51] In 1952, Dr. Azikiwe requested Eyo Ita, then Leader of the NCNC Govern-

[49] "Dr. Azikiwe has, on more than one occasion, placed on record the fact that the African Continental Bank 'was founded primarily to finance the activities of the Zik Group whilst at the same time protecting the interests of the public so far as it is compatible with banking practice.'" *Ibid.,* p. 7.

[50] "Around the time when the Banking Ordinance was enacted, but not because of it, a series of failures occurred among small indigenous banks which had sprung up in the immediately preceding years. Many of these banks were fraudulent in their conception and operation but others failed from a combination of inexperience, inefficiency and lack of capital. Although losses to depositors were small in relation to total deposits with all banks in Nigeria, the principal failures caused acute distress in certain areas, shook public confidence and even now act as a brake on the growth of the banking habit." *Report by Mr. J. B. Loynes on the Establishment of a Nigerian Central Bank, the Introduction of a Nigerian Currency and other Associated Matters* (Lagos: Federal Government Printer, 1957), p. 10. See also The International Bank for Reconstruction and Development, *op.cit.,* p. 158; W. T. Newlyn and D. C. Rowan, *Money and Banking in British Colonial Africa* (Oxford: The Clarendon Press, 1954), p. 107.

[51] See the critical appraisal of the Nigerian Banking Ordinance in *ibid.,* pp. 230-245.

ment in the Eastern Region, to persuade local government bodies in the East to deposit their funds with the African Continental Bank. The Ita Government did not comply with that request because it was not satisfied with the condition of the bank, and it has been alleged that its refusal was an underlying cause of the Eastern Government crisis of 1953.[52] In any event, the African Continental Bank was denied a license in 1953 because its liquidity ratio of 9.8 percent was far short of the required ratio of 30 percent.

When Dr. Azikiwe became Minister of Local Government in 1954, he made a full disclosure of his financial holdings to the Lt. Governor of the Eastern Region and, in keeping with principles formulated by the Secretary of State for the Colonies on the basis of British practice, he resigned his directorships of the bank and the other companies, and proceeded to appoint his associate of many years standing, Adolphus Kofi Blankson, then Editor-in-Chief of the *West African Pilot* and National Auditor of the NCNC, to act in his stead as Governing Director and Chairman of the bank, and to exercise his privileges as chairman and director of the companies.[53] Although

[52] See the statement by the Minister of Local Government in the *Eastern House of Assembly Debates*, Second Session, 30 January-23 February 1953, Vol. I, p. 21, and the testimony of Mbonu Ojike, Eyo Ita, and Dr. Azikiwe before the Foster-Sutton Tribunal of Inquiry in *Proceedings of the Foster-Sutton Tribunal of Inquiry*, Vol. I, p. 363 and Vol. II, pp. 607, 802-803. Professor Eyo Ita testified that his government balked because the African Continental Bank failed to produce financial statements and other documents relating to the status of the bank. Dr. Azikiwe acknowledged his participation in discussions of the proposed deposits but denied that the government had been brought down because it refused to patronize the bank.

[53] *Report of the Foster-Sutton Tribunal of Inquiry*, pp. 9-11. Mr. A. K. Blankson had been associated with Dr. Azikiwe in the *African Morning Post* (Accra) which Azikiwe edited from 1934 to 1937. He came to Nigeria to help found the *West African Pilot* in Lagos in 1937 and held several positions in the Zik Group organization thereafter. From 1947 to 1951 he was Vice-President of the NCNC and in 1954 he was elected National Auditor. When Dr. Azikiwe appointed Mr. Blankson as Governing Director and Chairman of the African Continental Bank on January 30, 1954, he sent him a letter summarizing the history of the founding of the bank, portions of which were published in a sessional paper of the Eastern Regional Government and are reproduced here for the illumination they shed on the motivations of Azikiwe and other Nigerian nationalists in the lives of whom business and politics have been mingled.

"You will recall, Kofi, that I accepted an invitation from the British Council to visit war-time Britain, in June 1943, as a member of the West African Press Delegation. It is within your knowledge that during my absence our newspaper business suffered financial handicaps.

"On my return from the United Kingdom in October, I decided to increase the price of the *Pilot* to two pence and to seek overdraft facilities from our bankers. I was prepared to offer my properties at 74-76 King George Avenue as collateral.

"I needed a thousand pounds and the properties were worth more than £2,000 according to the Lagos Town Council assessments. They were unencumbered and

an overt role by Dr. Azikiwe in the direction of the bank during its perilous period prior to the investment by the Finance Corporation was not permissible, it is on record that he made informal efforts to facilitate its licensing; thus he attempted to persuade a British bank-

---

I had valid title to them on a leasehold from the Crown for a period of 99 years from 1938.

"You knew that I was frustrated because of the shoddy way and manner the Manager of the Marina Branch of the Bank of British West Africa Limited treated me with rebuff. Not only did he keep me standing in his office, for some minutes, but he was curt and condescending, as if I was seeking a favour. He told me that he could not extend the accommodation sought until he had received a nod from their head office in London.

"Because in my personal capacity I had used that bank since my return from the Gold Coast in 1937, and because it was also one of the bankers of the Zik's Press Limited, the other being the National Bank of Nigeria Limited, of which we are shareholders, I thought that I should have received sympathetic consideration; naturally my pride was hurt and it dawned on me that the struggle for Nigerian freedom had many fronts, and that political freedom was not enough; economic freedom must be won also.

"I returned home and sent a letter to the Manager and predicted that, other things being equal, I would yet found a bank, if for nothing else, to teach alien banks to respect African business on its own right and to reckon with African patronage of banks as a factor in the economy of the country. You will remember that this influenced me to insist that when freedom comes, all banks must be nationalised, and I had to incorporate it in the Party's Manifesto when I drafted it for the Kano Convention in 1951.

"Going back to my experience with the B.B.W.A., you will remember that I told you how I contacted Mr. Rasmussen, my Swedish friend, who collaborated with me and other far-sighted patriots to develop Yaba Estate as a business centre. He sold the Tinubu Properties Limited to me for a nominal figure and I took possession of the share certificates of all the shareholders of that company.

"Although I bought one of the properties belonging to this firm at Victoria Street, I did not hesitate to re-sell it to the proprietors of Alban Pharmacy, who needed that property badly; my real reason for buying the Tinubu Properties Limited was because one of the objects of its memorandum was: 'generally to act as banker for customers and others.' Presto, I set an objective in my business career to become a banker!

"Of course, I had no experience in banking, but I was determined to call off the bluff of alien exploiters who think that because we are a colonial territory, we have no economic power which can force those who benefit from our political bondage to respect us. By 1st September, 1948, you will recall I had managed to accumulate £5,000, by virtually appealing to my father, sister, relatives, friends, and even yourself, to subscribe whatever widow's mite we may have in order to enable us to establish a financial structure which can help to develop our country.

"I can still remember the day we opened the doors of the bank to the public, when, after Chief Imam Tijani had said prayers according to the rites of Islam and blessed the bank and its founders and workers, I spoke briefly and almost tremulously, confidently looking forward to a brighter future but warning that no investor in banking business under present day Nigerian conditions should expect to reap dividends until after the bank had existed for ten years.

"In spite of disappointing experiences we have had the mortification to have, due to the dishonesty, disloyalty, incompetence and general inefficiency of some members of our staff and some of our patrons, most of the latter being our 'fair weather'

168

ing concern to invest in the African Continental Bank and to assume responsibility for its management.[54] These efforts were unavailing, mainly because a balance sheet of March 1954 gave the bank an appearance of insolvency. There is some dispute as to whether or not the bank was in fact insolvent when the Finance Corporation made its investment of more than £¾ million, and whether or not the investment saved the bank and the Zik Group of companies from liquidation.[55] In any event, it is clear that the investment and deposit of £2 million, previously held by the Marketing Board in the form of 3 percent savings bonds, gave the bank a new birth of vitality and the wherewithal to extend large amounts of credit. From an accounting point of view, the value of individual shares increased from

---

friends, I have implicit faith in the future of this bank. We have consolation that quite a number of our staff have been honest and efficient, and many of our patrons have been true to their word. You will notice that many Nigerians, representing several tribes, are now our shareholders. That is something to think about.

"The bank has come to stay and it must. It has played a constructive role in stirring Nigerians to appreciate that the control of money and credit is a nerve centre in any country's economy. In spite of the closing down of so many Nigerian banks, have we not been able to hold our own? And have we not survived the worst financial blizzard in the country's history, along with three expatriate banks and three Nigerian banks?" *Report on Banking and Finance in Eastern Nigeria* (Sessional Paper No. 4 of 1956), pp. 12-13.

[54] The U.K. banking firm approached by Dr. Azikiwe was Martins Bank Limited, which is linked to John Holt and Co., the second largest trading company in Nigeria, after the United Africa Company. *Report of the Foster-Sutton Tribunal of Inquiry*, pp. 16-18, 40; see the affidavit by John A. Holt, *Proceedings of the Foster-Sutton Tribunal of Inquiry*, Vol. 11, pp. 708-710.

[55] "Statements were laid before us to show the position of the Bank and the Zik Group of Companies at 31st March, 1955. From these it was clear that the state of insolvency which then existed throughout the whole organization (with one exception) could only result in the liquidation of the Bank and the Companies in the Group, unless substantial amounts of new capital could be provided. . . . We were told by Dr. Azikiwe and other witnesses, that the question of liquidation would never have arisen as the African Continental Bank possessed 'immeasurable goodwill' which would enable it to raise any capital required in the event of a crisis. . . . The fact remains that no serious attempt was ever made to obtain new capital from any source other than the Finance Corporation." *Report of the Foster-Sutton Tribunal of Inquiry*, p. 30.

Mr. L. P. Ojukwu, the prominent businessman who personally guaranteed overdrafts given by the bank to the Zik Group of companies, emphasized the asset of goodwill in his testimony to the tribunal: " . . . if it were any other Bank—it would have been closed four or five years ago. But it has a goodwill. There is no run on the bank. Even now that a Commission of Inquiry is sitting on the African Continental Bank, you go into the bush, cocoa area, palm belt area, people are streaming in paying their money into the Bank. As a native, born and bred in Nigeria, who knows all about business here, I will pay anything into that Bank because of the goodwill of the people." *Proceedings of the Foster-Sutton Tribunal of Inquiry*, Vol. I, p. 400. And see the testimony of Mr. Akintola Williams, A. C. A., the bank's auditor, *ibid.*, Vol. II, pp. 68off.

nothing to 14s. 10d. each,[56] and the shareholders were entitled to sell to the Corporation at the par value of £1 per share. Moreover, the bank obtained a license from the Federal Government enabling it to stay in business.

In November 1955, Dr. Azikiwe had an interview with the Secretary of State for the Colonies in London; the latter had knowledge of the agreement between the Finance Corporation and the Bank, and is reported to have objected strenuously to a clause which seemed to preserve Dr. Azikiwe's personal rights to be chairman of the bank (following his retirement from public office) and to nominate three other directors. Dr. Azikiwe disclaimed knowledge of the agreement and assured the Secretary of State that he was no longer a director of the bank and had no legal right to resume his former offices; but he conceded to the Secretary of State that if there was an offending clause, such as the latter alleged, it should of course be expunged. Upon his return to Nigeria, statements were issued by Dr. Azikiwe and by the Chairman of the Eastern Region Finance Corporation disclosing the investment and confirming the transfer of all rights and privileges in the bank by Dr. Azikiwe from the time of his appointment as a Minister.

It will be recalled that Mr. E. O. Eyo submitted his resignation as Government Chief Whip and Chairman of the Eastern Region Development Corporation in April 1956. Within a few days of its acceptance by Dr. Azikiwe, he filed a motion to censure the Premier for abuse of office which he amended subsequently to request the appointment of an independent commission of inquiry to report to the House of Assembly. In June the Secretary of State for the Colonies informed the Governor of the Eastern Region that apart from the ambiguous matter of Dr. Azikiwe's reversionary rights in the bank, the transfer "during Dr. Azikiwe's tenure of office as Premier, of a substantial amount of money to a company in which he has rights and interest . . . is, to the best of our knowledge, without precedent here [i.e., in Britain] in modern times."[57] When Eyo's motion came up for debate in the House of Assembly, the Speaker ruled it out of order on the ground that the matter was *sub judice* since Dr. Azikiwe had initiated a libel action against Mr. Eyo for having made public allegations to the effect that the Premier's conduct had been corrupt. But the Governor and the Secretary of State intimated that a formal investigation would be required. Dr. Azikiwe and his colleagues threatened to resign in protest to the "dictatorial"

[56] *Report of the Foster-Sutton Tribunal of Inquiry*, pp. 29-31.
[57] *Proceedings of the Foster-Sutton Tribunal of Inquiry*, Vol. II, p. 780.

attitude of the Secretary of State but they were instructed to remain in office by the National Executive Committee of the party. On August 4, the Secretary of State appointed a Tribunal of Inquiry under the chairmanship of Sir Stafford Foster-Sutton, Chief Justice of the Federation of Nigeria, to inquire into "allegations of improper conduct on the part of Dr. Nnamdi Azikiwe, Premier of the Eastern Region of Nigeria, in connection with the affairs of the African Continental Bank Limited"; "the circumstances in which securities, or the proceeds of securities, belonging to the Eastern Regional Marketing Board were transferred to the Eastern Region Finance Corporation and the circumstances in which such proceeds were invested in or deposited with the African Continental Bank Limited by the Eastern Region Finance Corporation," and other related matters.[58] This required a postponement of the Nigerian Constitutional Conference which had been scheduled to convene in September.

Dr. Azikiwe struck back with vehemence, not at Mr. Eyo, but at the Secretary of State for the Colonies and other persons who were prominent in the City of London. Rising to support a motion in the Eastern House of Assembly which prayed the Federal Government to inquire into an alleged conspiracy by the Bank of British West Africa to create a monopoly of banking throughout the Federation, he declared:[59]

[58] The members of the Tribunal, in addition to the Chairman, Sir Stafford Foster-Sutton, Chief Justice of the Federation of Nigeria, were Joseph Henri Maxime de Comarmond, Chief Justice of the High Court of Lagos and of the High Court of the Southern Cameroons, Vincent Akinfemi Savage, a Chief Magistrate in the Eastern Region of Nigeria, and George Forest Saunders, Fellow of the Institute of Chartered Accountants in England and Wales.

[59] *Eastern House of Assembly Debates*, Third Session, Second and Third Meetings, 22nd to 27th June and 2nd to 8th August, 1956, pp. 209-210; this entire speech was reprinted under the title *Banking Monopoly in Nigeria: Statement made by the Hon. Premier in the Eastern House of Assembly on 8th August, 1956* (Enugu: n.d.). See also the statements by Mr. Alan Lennox-Boyd, the Secretary of State for the Colonies, and others in the House of Commons on July 24, 1956. *Parliamentary Debates, House of Commons, Official Report*, 23 July-2 August 1956, pp. 215-221.

The temper of the time may be gauged from the following matters debated in the Eastern House of Assembly during June 22-27 and August 2-8, 1956: a proposed inquiry into the operations of the Eastern Region Development Corporation, a vote of confidence in the Premier and the regional ministers in connection with the investment of public funds in the African Continental Bank, the alleged "irresponsible and destructive" conduct of the Opposition in the House, a vote of no-confidence in the Governor of the Eastern Region, a proposed Commission of Inquiry into the alleged monopolistic activities of the Bank of British West Africa, and the Commission of Inquiry into the investment of funds in the African Continental Bank. In the course of debate on the last item, the Premier, Dr. Azikiwe, contended that the members of the Tribunal of Inquiry should not be subject to

"The B.B.W.A. (Bank of British West Africa) has always attracted eminent statesmen and colonial administrators to its directorate. After he had retired as Governor-General of South Africa, Lord Milner was elected Chairman of the B.B.W.A. in 1916. It is remarkable that in 1920, he was the Secretary of State for the Colonies. The present Chairman of the B.B.W.A. is Lord Harlech, who was formerly known as W. G. A. Ormsby-Gore. He was Under-Secretary of State for the Colonies in 1922-24, Postmaster-General in 1931, and Secretary of State for the Colonies in 1936-38. He is also Chairman of the Midland Bank which is capitalized at £45,200,000. The qualification share for Directors in the Midland Bank is £6,000. The noble lord is also a Director of the Standard Bank of South Africa whose capital is £10,000,000, and the Yorkshire Penny Bank whose capital is £1,750,000.

"Lord Milverton is a Director of the B.B.W.A. He was formerly Governor of North Borneo, Gambia, Fiji, Jamaica, and Nigeria. He is also a Director of the West Indies Sugar Company Limited, Kamuning (Perak) Rubber and Tin Company Limited. Sir Frank M. Baddeley, former Chief Secretary of Nigeria, is also a Director of the B.B.W.A. Another important figure who is a Director of the B.B.W.A. is Sir Edward Spears who is also a Director of the following companies: Ashanti Goldfields Limited, British Portland Cement Manufacturers Limited, British Bata Shoe Company Limited, and Bibiani Gold Mines Limited.

"Other Directors of the B.B.W.A. are equally important and influential figures, who are well-known in the City. Mr. S. G. Gates is a Director of Westminster Bank Limited and the Tecalemit Limited. Sir Sydney Parkes is Director and late Chief General Manager of Lloyds Bank, Chairman of National Bank of New Zealand, and Chairman of Crosse and Blackwell (Holdings) Limited, who are manufacturers of marmalade and jam which find a ready market in this part of the world. Mr. Ernest Whitley-Jones, who was former Deputy Chairman of the B.B.W.A. is still one of its directors, in addition to being a Director of Lloyds Bank Limited, Premier Investment Company Limited, and Argus Press Limited.

"It is very relevant now for me to disclose the fact that when the Conservative Party were out of office in the United Kingdom, its

---

the authority of the Secretary of State for the Colonies who was cited as an interested person and a witness in a pending libel suit by the Premier against Mr. Eyo. He contended further that the subject matter of the Tribunal was regional rather than federal and that the proposed Tribunal exceeded the aim of Eyo's original motion insofar as it authorized a general investigation into Dr. Azikiwe's relationship with the A.C.B. at all times. *Eastern House of Assembly,* Debates, Third Session, June-August 1956, pp. 223-228; reprinted as *Commission of Inquiry into African Continental Bank: Statement made by the Hon. Premier . . . on 8th August, 1956. . . .* (Enugu: n.d.).

A special convention of the NCNC at Onitsha in late July condemned the Tribunal as a manifestation of imperialism but endorsed a previous decision of the National Executive Committee to the effect that the Premier and the ministers should not resign. A defense fund was inaugurated and preparations were made for leaders of the party to tour the country and explain the stand of the NCNC to the people.

leaders headed by the Right Honourable Sir Anthony Eden, and the Right Honourable the Marquess of Salisbury were Directors of Westminster Bank, which is one of the four banks which own the B.B.W.A. One cannot be a Director of Westminster Bank unless he has shares worth £2,000, so that it is likely that Mr. Eden and Lord Salisbury are still shareholders of Westminster Bank. As is well known Sir Anthony is Prime Minister and First Lord of the Treasury of the United Kingdom; the Marquess of Salisbury is Lord President of the Council and Leader of the House of Lords, and he is also a brother-in-law to Lord Harlech. Another member of the British Cabinet who used to be a Director of Lloyds Bank, which owns the largest block of shares in the B.B.W.A. is the Right Honourable Derick Heathcoat Amory, who is Minister of Agriculture. The Lloyds Bank is capitalized at £74,000,000 and the qualification share for Directors is £5,000, so that Mr. Heathcoat Amory may be presumed to be a shareholder of Lloyds Bank.

"Apart from banks, some members of the British Cabinet used to be Directors of heavily capitalized firms of which they are shareholders. For example, the Right Honourable R. A. Butler, Lord Privy Seal and Leader of the House of Commons, is formerly Chairman of Courtaulds Limited, the company which enjoys monopoly over rayon and textiles. The Right Honourable Harold Macmillan, Chancellor of the Exchequer, was Director of the Monotype Corporation Limited and Chairman of Macmillan and Company Limited, book publishers. The Right Honourable Duncan Sandys, Minister of Housing and Local Government, was a Director of Ashanti Goldfields Corporation Limited and is presumed to be a shareholder of that company now that he is a Minister of State.

"The Right Honourable A. T. Lennox-Boyd, Secretary of State for the Colonies, was a Director of Guinness (Arthur) Son and Company Limited, whose capital is £9,500,000. His wife, Lady Patricia Lennox-Boyd is also a Director of this company, as well as the Right Honourable the Earl of Iveagh (Rupert Edward Cecil Lee Guinness), his father-in-law who is Chairman of this company, which brews Guinness stout which is widely sold in British West Africa. Lord Moyne, his brother-in-law, is also a Director of the Guinness business.

"I have mentioned these illustrious names because Mr. Lennox-Boyd talked of public morality in the House of Commons when he announced that he would appoint a Spanish Inquisition on my biography even when I was in the womb of my mother, as if it is only in Nigeria that we have men holding public offices who held directorships in banking and other business ventures to which they could return after they had had their fling in politics. Now that Honourable Members have had an insight into the personalities who own the banking institutions of the United Kingdom which, in turn, owns the B.B.W.A., they should be able to discern quite clearly that the hand is Esau's but the voice is Jacob's. That being the case, we can now appreciate why the B.B.W.A. must enjoy monopoly wherever it operates, or else the ire of the Molochs of Great Britain will descend upon any person who dares to challenge the banking supremacy of the B.B.W.A. particularly as a depository of Government funds, from which source it earns the bulk of its profits."

The Foster-Sutton Tribunal of Inquiry sat for fifty days during September-November 1956. In the context of this narrative it is neither necessary nor feasible to discuss in detail those technical matters of individual conduct upon which the Tribunal pronounced. Questions were raised about the conduct of Mbonu Ojike, Minister of Finance during the period under review, because he did not bring the matter of the investment to the attention of the Executive Council of the Region until it had been concluded and a license had been issued to the African Continental Bank.[60] Inasmuch as the agreement between the Finance Corporation and the bank was thought to be unduly favorable to the shareholders of the bank, the chairman of the Finance Corporation was criticized for not having ascertained the condition of the bank prior to the investment and for having failed to refer the agreement to the board of the Corporation for approval prior to its execution. With respect to Dr. Azikiwe, the Tribunal found that on one occasion he exerted influence to encourage the deposit of £30,000 in the bank by the Eastern Regional Production Development Board at a time when the liquid assets of the bank were dangerously low. On the crucial issue of whether or not Dr. Azikiwe knew the terms of the Agreement prior to his conversation with the Secretary of State in November 1955, no conclusive evidence was adduced to rebut Dr. Azikiwe's categorical denial. But circumstantial evidence indicated that the investment had been effected by means of collusion involving Dr. Azikiwe, Mr. Ojike, and Mr. Blankson, the Acting Governing Director and Chairman of the Bank. It was established that the board of the African Continental Bank had voted to increase the bank's authorized capitalization from £250,000 to £1,000,000 and to issue a total of 877,000 shares to the Eastern Region Finance Corporation even before the Corporation had been inaugurated or its membership approved by the Executive Council. In fact, the precise terms of the agreement that was signed by the chairman of the Corporation and the Acting Chairman of the Bank on May 20, 1955, were discovered in the minutes of a meeting

[60] Although the Minister of Finance was not required by law to seek the approval of the Executive Council for actions taken in accordance with the provisions of the Eastern Region Finance Corporation Law of 1954, there does appear to have been a "gentleman's agreement" among the ministers to the effect that the Minister of Finance would exercise his powers under that law in consultation. Under examination, the Premier and three other ministers stated that Mr. Ojike had told them about the investment informally, but in general terms only without having specified the amount or the details of the agreement between the Finance Corporation and the bank. *Report of the Foster-Sutton Tribunal of Inquiry,* pp. 27-28; *Proceedings of the Foster-Sutton Tribunal of Inquiry,* Vol. II, pp. 649, 738, 838, 858, 936-937.

of the board of the Bank on March 5th. Dr. Azikiwe admitted having been told informally by the Minister of Finance that an investment of about £½ million would be made, but he denied emphatically that either Ojike or Blankson had ever informed him of the terms of the agreement.[61]

A major portion of the evidence adduced before the Tribunal was relevant mainly to the technical issue of propriety in ministerial conduct. However justifiable it may have been for the Secretary of State to seek to vindicate public moralities in a United Kingdom dependency, there was an element of futility in the Tribunal's task, since the technical proprieties of ministerial conduct were incidental to more fundamental political issues in the light of which Azikiwe's conduct would be judged by laymen in his time and thereafter. The value of the record of the Tribunal to the political analyst lies mainly in the relevance of the evidence adduced to issues upon which the Tribunal could not render a verdict. It seems helpful in this context to consider those political matters under three headings: the role of the African Continental Bank as an instrumentality to effect the nationalist and socialist policies of the NCNC; the role of the African Continental Bank as a political asset to the NCNC; the role of the bank as a political and economic asset to Dr. Azikiwe.

With respect to matters of party policy, the most widely accepted justification for the buildup of the bank was in terms of its expanded capacity to provide credit facilities to African businessmen. British banks operating in Nigeria have a notorious record of reluctance to finance incipient African enterprise.[62] Those who engineered the

---

[61] *Ibid.*, pp. 763-777.

[62] "Since these banks (the Bank of British West Africa and Barclays Bank, Dominion, Colonial and Overseas) came to Nigeria primarily to render services in connection with international trade, their relations have been chiefly with the European trading companies and with the government; their lending to and their business contacts with Africans have been very limited. They have derived their income largely from handling trade remittances and advances against the security of goods entering international trade. They have played virtually no part in developing local African entrepreneurship. Their lending policies in the Gold Coast have been described by Sir Cecil Trevor as 'extremely conservative' and it would seem that the remark applies equally to Nigeria. . . . The economic development of Nigeria will require increased credit facilities, in particular for Nigerians. It is the mission's impression that the European banks, which at present control close to 90% of deposits, will contribute rather little to meeting that demand, at least until they feel that the level of business experience and sense of responsibility of the Nigerian community at large approaches European standards. The task of providing credit to African enterprise and of educating African businessmen to these higher standards of experience and responsibility will therefore largely fall to African banks and governmental lending institutions. As a result the share of the European banks in Nigerian banking is likely to decrease over the years."

transfer of funds from the Marketing Board to the bank via the Finance Corporation testified that the sum involved (£2 million) was many times greater than the comparatively small amount of £125,000 required by the bank to qualify for a license, because the objective was not merely to rescue the bank from impending disaster but to transform it into an effective instrument of economic policy.[63]

It has been argued that the innate conservatism of British banks in Nigeria is attributable to their multiple and intimate relationships with British companies in Nigeria and in the United Kingdom.[64]

The International Bank for Reconstruction and Development, *op.cit.*, pp. 156-157.

W. T. Newlyn and D. C. Rowan observe that "African dissatisfaction with the services provided by the British banks in Nigeria and the Gold Coast is of long standing. It rests upon allegations that the banks act in combination regarding charges and, at the same time, adopt a racially discriminatory credit policy." *Op.cit.*, p. 118. These authorities postulated that banking in Nigeria would evolve from the present "passive" state (i.e., lending does not expand in proportion to the accumulation of overseas assets) to an "active" state of brisk credit with the rise of indigenous banking. *Ibid.*, p. 167. In their opinion, as in the opinion of P. T. Bauer, British banks in West Africa do not discriminate for racial reasons, but they are by virtue of their structures and policies less capable than African banks of providing adequate credit facilities to African businessmen. *Ibid.*, pp. 212-213, and P. T. Bauer, *West African Trade* (Cambridge: Cambridge University Press, 1954), pp. 183-188.

[63] Mr. Ojike explained that the intention of the Government was to make an "investment of sufficient strength" to equip the bank with the means to carry out large-scale lending operations. *Proceedings of the Foster-Sutton Tribunal of Inquiry*, Vol. I, p. 312; see also the testimony of the Chairman and Deputy Chairman of the Finance Corporation. *Ibid.*, pp. 96-97, 181, 191. Mr. Ojukwu, the prosperous businessman and Chairman of the Eastern Regional Marketing Board, who helped formulate and supported the policy, defended it as follows: "My whole idea was that we have suffered a lot. If an African goes to a European bank and asks for a loan, they will give very few people—perhaps they give people with a good fine tie and coat, but they do not know the resources of the African. But if it is an African owned bank, they know our people, know what their worth is and know where they live and they will be able to give them loans in a way that we require." *Ibid.*, p. 398.

[64] "It would probably be beneficial to the economic life of the colony if intra-territorial banking were extended, for it is at present almost impossible for an enterprising African to raise capital through impersonal channels, while an internal banking system, enjoying the confidence of the people, would enable savings, which now lie in sterile hoards, to be used productively. Since intra-territorial banks would be primarily interested in the internal development of the country, they would be more eager to create conditions enabling them to lend to Africans than the extra-territorial banks. These naturally concentrate on external trade; and, to the extent that they are interested in the profitability of existing investments in the United Kingdom, they are probably more anxious to preserve the present industrial structure of Great Britain, by retaining colonial markets for British export goods, than to develop secondary industries in Nigeria and elsewhere, when conditions are favourable for their growth, or initiate complementary changes in the industrial structure of Great Britain. Intra-territorial banks would also probably be more willing to assist in counteracting seasonal and cyclical fluctuations

To the extent that British banking enterprise and British commercial enterprise are inter-dependent, Nigerian policies which aim to eliminate or to restrict the activities of British banking may be regarded as inimical to the interests of British commerce. The Secretary of State for the Colonies gave color to this argument when he objected to a clause in the agreement between the African Continental Bank and the Finance Corporation which required the Corporation to "persuade its beneficiaries and customers to use the Bank as one of the main depositories of its funds." In a letter to the Governor of the Eastern Region, he termed that clause "reprehensible" and warned that "commercial people will not be encouraged to put their money into a country whose Government appears to encourage its Statutory bodies so to discriminate in purely commercial matters."[65] This complaint scarcely evokes sympathy in view of the fact that prior to 1955, two British banks, each one closely related by means of shareholding and interlocking directorates to the major banks of the United Kingdom, enjoyed a near monopoly of the banking business in Nigeria.[66]

---

of economic activity than extra-territorial banks, for the latter can always return their funds to London when investment opportunities in Nigeria are either less profitable or more limited," J. Mars, "The Monetary and Banking System and the Loan Market of Nigeria," *Mining, Commerce, and Finance in Nigeria*, ed. Margery Perham (London: Faber, 1948), p. 208.

[65] *Proceedings of the Foster-Sutton Tribunal of Inquiry*, Vol. II, p. 778. In a statement to the Eastern House of Assembly, Dr. Azikiwe alleged that in the course of his interview of November 10, 1955, with the Secretary of State for the Colonies in London, the latter "made it clear that he had a responsibility in British domestic politics to preserve British colonies for the benefit of British commercial initiative and enterprise." *Banking Monopoly in Nigeria*, p. 8.

[66] The Bank of British West Africa (now the Bank of West Africa), established in 1894, "is partly owned by Lloyds, Westminster, and National Provincial Banks and the Standard Bank of South Africa, and interlocked, by common directors with the Midland Bank, Coutts and Co., and the Yorkshire Penny Bank. The Standard Bank of South Africa has common directors with Lloyds, the Midland Bank, and Westminster Bank, while the National Bank of India, though independent of the 'big five,' owns the share capital of Grindlays Bank, which has total assets equal to half of its own." Barclays Bank, (Dominion, Colonial and Overseas) was "established in 1926 by the amalgamation of the Colonial Bank, the Anglo-Egyptian Bank, and the National Bank of South Africa. . . . " Its varied experience "probably accounts for the greater degree of flexibility in the bank's policy and its apparent readiness to give a trial to unorthodox banking methods." W. T. Newlyn and D. C. Rowan, *op.cit.*, pp. 74-75. The lending policy of Barclays has been regarded as more liberal than that of the B.B.W.A. and a resident director of Barclays, Mr. Leonard Daldry, was appointed to the Nigerian Senate by the Prime Minister in 1960 (see the portrait in *West Africa*, April 16, 1960, p. 425). In 1949, a third expatriate bank, the British and French Bank for Commerce and Industry, affiliated with the Banque Nationale pour le Commerce et l'Industrie, began operations in Nigeria. International Bank for Reconstruction and Development, *op.cit.*, pp. 156-157; see also P. T. Bauer, *op.cit.*, p. 180, and J. Mars, *op.cit.*, p. 185.

The senior and more extensively based Bank of British West Africa was the sole agent of the West African Currency Board and the sole depository of the funds of all government bodies until 1955, when the governments of Western and Eastern Nigeria arranged to transfer a portion of their funds to indigenous banks, the National Bank of Nigeria (generally regarded as a financial ally of the Action Group) and the African Continental Bank respectively.[67] In fact the National Bank of Nigeria had initiated a large scale program of lending as early as 1952, following deposits in that bank of funds totaling £2 million by the Western Regional Production Development Board and the Cocoa Marketing Board;[68] supporters of the NCNC in the Eastern Region were anxious for the African Continental Bank to follow the National Bank's example.[69]

In both the Eastern and Western Regions, the strategy of economic planning involved the repatriation of a portion of the funds belonging to the regional marketing boards which had been invested in British Government securities in London.[70] These repatriated funds were

[67] In March 1955, the Western Regional Government transferred about 45 per cent of its funds to the National Bank of Nigeria. *Western House of Assembly Debates, Official Report*, December 19, 21, and 22, 1956, pp. 58, 135-139. In that same month, the Executive Council of the Eastern Region decided to effect the transfer of certain governmental accounts to the African Continental Bank. *Proceedings of the Foster-Sutton Tribunal of Inquiry*, Vol. I, p. 890.

[68] International Bank for Reconstruction and Development, *op.cit.*, pp. 158-159.

[69] *Proceedings of the Foster-Sutton Tribunal of Inquiry*, Vol. II, p. 764.

[70] As W. T. Newlyn and D. C. Rowan have observed, "It is probable that the policies of the Marketing Boards in accumulating large stabilization funds have further reduced the finance available to Africans. It is significant that, in order to allow the National Bank of Nigeria to finance African Licensed Buyers the Cocoa Marketing Board had to deposit substantial funds with it." *Op.cit.*, p. 217 n.1.

The "costs" of the sterling system to member states of the Overseas Sterling Area are considered by Philip W. Bell, who points out that nearly all increases in the sterling balances of a colony are in effect loans to the United Kingdom. This observation "applies equally well to balances held in the accounts of overseas branches of British banks and to balances held by marketing boards." *The Sterling Area in the Postwar World* (Oxford: Clarendon Press, 1956), p. 274. For a most critical appraisal of the effects of the sterling system see Paul A. Baran, *The Political Economy of Growth* (New York: Monthly Review Press, 1957), who writes:

"Where the situation is nothing short of outrageous—matched perhaps only by what happens to the economic surplus of the oil-producing countries—is in the British colonial empire. These areas, the population of which has undoubtedly the world's lowest per capita income, have been made by Britain's 'paternalistic' government (Labor as well as Conservative) to *support* throughout the entire postwar period the United Kingdom's incomparably higher standard of living. In the years 1945 through 1951 the colonies were forced under innumerable pretexts to accumulate no less than 1 billion pounds of sterling balances. Since these represent the difference between the colonies' receipts from abroad and their payments to other countries, this billion pounds constitutes the colonies' capital *export* to

channelled through indigenous commercial banks contrary to the advice of the World Bank Mission.[71] In both regions public funds were invested in private banks, but the Eastern Regional situation differed from that in the West in certain fundamental respects. First, no minister of the Action Group Government in the Western Region was "a shareholder of the National Bank or of any of its subsidiary or allied companies."[72] Secondly, in 1955 the Western Regional Marketing Board made an investment of £1 million in non-participating shares of the National Bank that did not alter its nature as a privately controlled institution. Dr. Azikiwe defended his government's policy in testimony before the Tribunal, on the ground that the Eastern Region Finance Corporation obtained 87.7 percent ownership and decisive control of the African Continental Bank. Eventually, he assured the Tribunal, the Eastern Regional Government would acquire 100 percent of the shares of the bank and full control of its management in accordance with a declared policy objective of the NCNC to nationalize all banks.[73] That appears to have been the general understanding of party leaders, although the most prominent business personality associated with the NCNC expressed a deviant opinion to the effect that he favored an eventual transfer by sale of all publicly owned shares in the bank to private persons.[74]

Britain! In the measured words of the author on whose excellent paper the above is based, the colonies' 'investment of £1,000 million in Britain does not accord well with commonly held ideas on the desirable direction of capital flow between countries at different levels of economic development. There is a belief that British colonial policy has been pursued with great financial generosity. The colonies' needs were great 'so the British taxpayer came to the rescue.' It is thought that' the United Kingdom, since the war, has given large sums of money to help the colonies. One purpose of this paper has been 'to test the order of thought by the order of things.' " *Ibid.*, p. 231. The author cited is A. D. Hazlewood, "Colonial External Finance Since the War," *Review of Economic Studies* (December 1953), pp. 49ff. "Mr. Hazlewood's first quotation is from the official government publication *Introducing the Colonies* (1949), p. 58." *Ibid.*, p. 231 n. 65.

[71] *Supra*, p. 164 n. 44.

[72] *Western House of Assembly Debates, Official Report*, 19, 21, and 22 December 1956, p. 62.

[73] *Proceedings of the Foster-Sutton Tribunal of Inquiry*, Vol. II, pp. 755-761 and 829.

[74] Mr. Louis P. Ojukwu testified that "the whole idea is that presently most of our people are still sleeping, and my idea is that if we can help them to finance that project and then control three-quarters of the shares there, well after some years if they work very hard Government will be able to take their money and invest it to develop another industry, and the people will pay them back, and then they run their bank, and I do not want to ask Government to go into business enterprises, but our people are sleeping presently and they have got to wake them up. . . . (Q) Is it your idea then, Mr. Ojukwu, that the investment in the bank should be a temporary investment?—(A) That was my idea." *Ibid.*, Vol. I,

At the bar of public opinion in Nigeria, Dr. Azikiwe's case was strong because he stood for such popular principles as liberal credit for African businessmen, a larger share of commercial and financial enterprise for Africans, and for the repatriation of Nigeria's sterling assets to promote economic growth. Probably the division of public opinion and the ambiguity of party policies with respect to the socialization of banking was an additional factor in his favor.

Turning to our second heading—the role of the African Continental Bank as a political asset to the NCNC—it emerges that direct financial assistance by the bank is the lesser of two principal manifestations, and it suffices to note that in 1956 the NCNC was indebted to the bank by £50,000.[75] The more important relationship involves the dependence of the Zik Group of companies on the bank for working capital.[76] Nine of the ten active companies of the Zik Group were devoted to the journalistic and publishing business of Dr.

---

p. 398. This may be described as "Ojukwu's deviation." Mr. Ojukwu, then a member of the House of Representatives and Chairman of the Eastern Region Marketing Board, later Chairman of the Eastern Region Development Corporation and the Nigeria Produce Marketing Company, is a director of ten business firms, mainly European, and a leading proponent of capitalist ideology in the officially socialist NCNC. He collaborated with Dr. Azikiwe in the authorship of the Report of the Economic Mission to Europe and North America (*Economic Rehabilitation of Eastern Nigeria*, 1955) and explained to the Tribunal that his views are reflected mainly in the non-socialist proposals of that largely socialistic document. Ojukwu's "deviation" corresponds in principle with the views expressed in the Report of the International Bank Mission: "While we believe that government policy should emphasize the support and encouragement of private endeavor, we recognize that under present Nigerian conditions government and the public agencies may in some instances have to take the initiative in establishing industrial projects. Such a course can accelerate industrial development, provided two general principles are observed. First, the venture should be operated by experienced management, which in the case of large enterprises would have to be a foreign manufacturer, preferably one willing to contribute to the capital. Second, government should stand ready at all times to sell all or part of its interest to private investors." *Op.cit.*, p. 53. In 1960 Mr. Ojukwu was knighted Sir Odumegwu Ojukwu, K.B.E.

[75] *Report of the Foster-Sutton Tribunal of Inquiry*, p. 34. Mr. E. O. Eyo testified that in July 1955, the NCNC decided to use the African Continental Bank to finance future elections, beginning with the Western Regional election of 1956. *Proceedings of the Foster-Sutton Tribunal of Inquiry*, Vol. I, p. 487. However the NCNC Manifesto for the federal election of 1954 states that the party "is uncompromisingly opposed to the use of such (Nigerian) Banks for the furtherance of party interest, particularly where public funds form part of its resources." *Battle for Unity and Freedom* (Lagos: 1954), p. 11. In cross-examination of Dr. Azikiwe, Dr. Udo Udoma, MHR, expressed the view of the Leader of the Opposition in the Eastern House of Assembly, Professor Eyo Ita, "that it would be wrong for public funds to be made available through banks to Parties." *Proceedings of the Foster-Sutton Tribunal of Inquiry*, Vol. II, p. 888.

[76] The bank bought debentures bearing 2-3% interest in the Zik Group of companies at a total cost of £205,000. See *ibid.*, Vol. II, pp. 754, 830.

Azikiwe and it was remarked that one object of their existence was to protect the assets of the newspapers from libel suits and fines for seditious publications.[77] These companies supported the *West African Pilot* and the five provincial newspapers which constitute the main publicity apparatus of the NCNC; clearly the preservation of these newspapers depended upon the financial solvency of the Zik Group. In his final address, the counsel for the tribunal suggested that the liquidation of the bank, which might have resulted from its failure to obtain a license, would have entailed the collapse of the Zik Group. He conceded that Azikiwe's motive may have been a genuine conviction "that the *West African Pilot,* financed by the bank, was a good thing for Nigeria."[78]

With respect to the third set of issues—those involving the bank as a political and economic asset to Dr. Azikiwe—the Tribunal concluded that he was anxious to retain the financial power inherent in control of the bank and the political power inherent in control of the newspapers.[79] It found that his formal resignation from the offices of Chairman and Governing Director of the Bank and the appointment of Mr. Blankson to those positions was intended "to create an agency, with himself in the background as principal." It was suggested by counsel for the tribunal that if Dr. Azikiwe and his lieutenants were guided by policy interests only, they could have created a state bank by arranging for the transfer of all shares to the Finance Corporation, justifiably without compensation, in return for which the Corporation might have agreed to cancel the substantial liabilities of the shareholders for investments that were not paid up.[80] Mr. Eyo alleged that Dr. Azikiwe had foisted a deviation

[77] *Ibid.*, p. 967. The Zik Group of Companies were identified and described by Dr. Azikiwe in a statement prepared for the Tribunal. They are 12 in number, as follows: The African Continental Bank; the African Book Company; the Comet Press Ltd., publisher of the *Daily Comet* (Kano); the Associated Newspapers of Nigeria, publisher of several provincial newspapers; the Nigerian Paper Co.; the Nigerian Printing Supply Co.; the Nigerian Real Estate Corporation; the West African Pilot Ltd.; Suburban Transport Ltd., distributor of newspapers from Lagos to the provinces; Nigerian Commodities Ltd., a rubber and timber company that was dormant in 1956; the African News Agency Ltd., dormant in 1956; Zik Enterprises Ltd., a holding company which owns lands and buildings of the newspapers. *Ibid.*, Vol. I, pp. 78-79.

[78] *Ibid.*, Vol. II, p. 1018.

[79] *Report of the Foster-Sutton Tribunal of Inquiry,* p. 42.

[80] In March 1955, the African Continental Bank had a nominal capital of £115,935, only £28,276 of which was actually paid up. *Report of the Foster-Sutton Tribunal of Inquiry,* p. 51. Dr. Azikiwe and others testified that for several reasons the outright nationalization of the African Continental Bank was not contemplated in 1955. He intimated that he was willing to surrender his personal shares "even for nothing," but insisted that the creation of a regional state bank was impractical

181

in policy upon the party by introducing the concept "nucleus" of a state bank to describe the African Continental Bank, thereby implying the preservation of a private interest.[81] Dr. Azikiwe replied that he merely anticipated the utilization of a state bank as the "nucleus for a central bank," suggesting that the concept was introduced because the World Bank Mission had expressed strong opposition to the assumption of commercial banking functions by the proposed central bank of Nigeria.[82] Yet it cannot be denied that his retention of the only important private share in the control of the bank (he owned a majority of the shares assigned to individuals and controlling interests in those companies of the Zik Group to which shares of the bank were assigned), gave Dr. Azikiwe a leverage on the business and monied members of the party that was bound to weigh politically.

The most disparaging allegation against Azikiwe intimated that his object was pecuniary gain; it rested on two considerations: the benefits accruing to the shareholders of the African Continental Bank as a result of its agreement with the Finance Corporation, and the payment of arrears of directors' fees following the investment, including a sum of £5,200 to Dr. Azikiwe. Given the decision for practical and political reasons to preserve a private sector in the ownership and management of the bank, it might be argued that the

---

under the existing constitution since banking was a subject on the exclusive federal legislative list and the establishment of a statutory banking corporation in the Eastern Region would require a federal law. The position was clarified by the Constitutional Conference of 1957 which authorized regional governments to own or participate in commercial banks. *Report by the Nigeria Constitutional Conference, May and June 1957,* Cmnd. 207, p. 19.

However, the Chairman of the Eastern Region Finance Corporation, Dr. G. C. Mbanugo, testified that the corporation planned to require those shareholders who were not fully paid up to sell their holdings at par to the corporation which would eventually acquire 100% ownership. *Proceedings of the Foster-Sutton Tribunal of Inquiry,* Vol. I, p. 108.

[81] The phrase "nucleus for a central bank" was first used in the Report of the Economic Mission to Europe and North America by Dr. Azikiwe and L. P. Ojukwu, *Economic Rehabilitation of Eastern Nigeria,* p. 22. Mr. Eyo testified that Azikiwe asked him to insert the sentence "At the risk of being attacked by the Opposition, may I suggest that the African Continental Bank should be the nucleus of our own State Bank" in a speech which he delivered in the Eastern House of Assembly in March 1955. "The policy of the Party was the conversion of the A.C.B. into a State Bank," he testified, "but the phrase 'nucleus of our own State Bank' was Dr. Azikiwe's phrase." Azikiwe denied this assertion. *Proceedings of the Foster-Sutton Tribunal of Inquiry,* Vol. I, p. 505, *ibid.,* Vol. II, pp. 829-830.

[82] *Ibid.,* p. 829; International Bank for Reconstruction and Development, *op.cit.,* pp. 99-100.

financial provisions of the agreement were not unreasonable.[83] Nor was the payment of fees owed to directors of the bank for a period of several years' service improper *per se*. It should be noted that Azikiwe's personal contributions in money and capital equipment to the party and related causes are not inconsiderable (e.g., he donated £5,000 to the NCNC at the Jos Special Convention of December 1952). His private wealth derives mainly from real and tangible property (he estimated its value as £300,000) held by the Nigerian Real Estate Company of which he owns 93 percent. This was the only active company of the Zik Group that did not drain the reserves of the bank; on the contrary, the losses of the publishing companies might have compelled Azikiwe to realize his properties.[84]

Finally, it was said logically in Azikiwe's defense, that if he did actually scheme to enrich himself at the expense of the public, he could not have adopted a "more obvious or fatuous method" than the one pursued; for it was "bound to be known everywhere and inevitably to invite public attack."[85] If he knew that his conduct was discreditable, possibly dishonest, would he have run the risk of sacking his principal accomplice, the Minister of Finance, on the ground that the latter's reputation had been tarnished by allegations of corruption that were in certain respects less damaging than the allegations to which he might have been exposed by counter-disclosures? For an embittered and vengeful Ojike would have been a deadly witness against his vulnerable chief.

It was remarked that as late as March 19, 1956, Mr. Eyo, then Government Chief Whip, welcomed the announcement of the investment in the Eastern House of Assembly. Eyo testified that he had not then been aware of the financial condition of the bank when the investment was made, to which he would have objected had he

[83] Dr. Azikiwe did not know that the shares were considered worthless from an accounting point of view at the time of the investment and would not, in any event, have accepted that appraisal. *Proceedings of the Foster-Sutton Tribunal of Inquiry*, Vol. II, pp. 783-784.

[84] The corollary, of course, is that a bank failure and consequent liquidation of the companies would have resulted in the attachment of Azikiwe's properties by creditors and sureties of the Zik Group. See the *Report of the Foster-Sutton Tribunal of Inquiry*, p. 30. But our point is that Azikiwe was an independently wealthy man whose resources have been used for political purposes. It seems basically false to this writer to say that Azikiwe's political activities were intended in any important or meaningful sense to increase his private wealth. It seems, on the contrary, that he could have become much wealthier than he is, if the accumulation of wealth had been his major object. *Proceedings of the Foster-Sutton Tribunal of Inquiry*, Vol. II, p. 847.

[85] Address to the Tribunal by Sir Frank Soskice, Counsel for Dr. Azikiwe. *Proceedings of the Foster-Sutton Tribunal of Inquiry*, Vol. II, p. 969.

known the material facts.[86] He alleged that Ojike, who boarded with him in Enugu during the budget session of the Eastern House of Assembly in March 1956, after Ojike's removal as Minister of Finance, told him with bitterness of Azikiwe's determination to have the bank licensed at all costs. It was Ojike, he alleged, who advised him subsequently to delete specific references to misconduct by Azikiwe from his motion to appoint a commission of inquiry in order to enhance the prospect of its passage in the House of Assembly.[87] Eyo said that Ojike had given him that advice in May 1956, only eight days before the latter declared in public that he alone, as Minister of Finance, had been fully responsible for the initiation and negotiation of the investment. In his testimony to the Tribunal, Ojike defended Azikiwe and denied reports to the effect that he had collaborated with Eyo to destroy his leader.[88] He testified that he did not inform Azikiwe about the investment in early 1955, that he did not disclose to Azikiwe the terms of the agreement between the Finance Corporation and the bank, and that Azikiwe had not been present at informal meetings of ministers when the investment was discussed.[89] Other ministers corroborated these submissions, and Mr. Blankson, Azikiwe's successor in the bank, testified that from the time Dr. Azikiwe became a minister he refused to discuss matters relating to the bank or the companies with himself.[90] In the end, the Tribunal was unable to conclude that Azikiwe had seen "the actual agreement" before his interview with the Secretary of State.[91]

Ojike's loyalty to Azikiwe in the hour of his leader's ordeal has been attributed to various causes. First, Ojike was a passionate and sophisticated nationalist, for whom the development of African enterprise was a cardinal tenet of belief. When the issue was framed in terms of nationalism versus economic imperialism he was bound to side with Azikiwe irrespective of his personal feelings and previous actions. Secondly, Ojike hoped that the Eastern Government would re-

[86] In March 1956, the Eastern House of Assembly, acting on the advice of the Secretary of State for the Colonies, abolished the Eastern Region Finance Corporation and assigned its assets, liabilities, and functions to the Eastern Region Development Corporation. Mr. Eyo was then Chairman of the Development Corporation and he testified that he was shown a balance sheet of the African Continental Bank for the years ending 31 March 1953 and 1954 by his Chief Accountant, whereupon he proposed an independent audit of the accounts of the bank. *Ibid.*, pp. 478-479, 800-801.   [87] *Ibid.*, Vol. I, p. 482.

[88] *Ibid.*, pp. 341-342, 520-524.

[89] *Ibid.*, pp. 269-346.

[90] *Ibid.*, pp. 36-43.

[91] *Report of the Foster-Sutton Tribunal of Inquiry*, p. 28.

ject the controversial report of the Bribery Commission, that his reputation would be vindicated and that he would be restored to office. Thirdly, it was intimated that Ojike's firm, the African Development Corporation, anticipated financial assistance from the African Continental Bank. Fourthly, he may have been persuaded to stand firm with the party by his close friend and kinsman, the NCNC Federal Parliamentary Leader, K. Ozuomba Mbadiwe, who suffered in anguish as a result of the rift between the men to whom he had been devoted—Azikiwe and Ojike. Finally it has been said that the Foster-Sutton Tribunal was regarded throughout Iboland as a crisis for the Ibo people and that the chiefs and elders of Arondizuogu told Ojike that he must not testify against Azikiwe. On November 28, 1956, hardly two weeks after the Tribunal concluded its public sittings and less than a month before it completed the writing of its report, Mbonu Ojike died at the age of 42 of hypertension resulting from excessive strain.

The Foster-Sutton report conceded "that Dr. Azikiwe's primary motive was to make available an indigenous bank with the object of liberalizing credit for the people of this country" [Nigeria], but added that his conduct as a minister "has fallen short of the expectations of honest, reasonable people." The Tribunal concluded further that "Dr. Azikiwe ought to have relinquished his financial interest in the Bank when the proposal to inject public monies into it was first mooted, and that he was guilty of misconduct as a Minister in failing to do so."[92]

[92] *Ibid.*, p. 42. On December 1, 1951, regulations based on United Kingdom practice and experience for the guidance of Nigerian Ministers were issued by the Secretary of State for the Colonies. His dispatch includes the following advice:

"It is . . . to be expected that when a member of a Legislature is under consideration for appointment as a Minister, he should, if asked to do so, disclose to the Governor or Lieutenant-Governor in confidence a full list of his holdings in stocks and shares in all companies whether or not they are at the time parties to Government contracts; and, in addition, that he should use the strictest discretion in deciding, in circumstances where his private interest and his public duty conflict, whether he can properly continue to hold such stocks and shares. Since Ministers are to receive appropriate remuneration from public funds, I consider it reasonable that they should be called upon at the time of their appointment to divest themselves for their period of office of any outside interests which might conflict with their public responsibilities so far as private businesses and professional practices are concerned, this ruling should in my view be interpreted as requiring a severance of active connection. In the absence of local precedent, persons considered for appointment as Ministers may require some guidance on this subject. I consider that before the name of any member of a Legislature is put before the Legislature for approval as a Minister, he should be asked to disclose, in confidence, details of his business or professional interests to the Governor or Lieutenant-Governor, and it should be for the Governor or Lieutenant-Governor to exercise his discretion

A QUESTION OF FAITH

When the Foster-Sutton findings were released certain leaders of the NCNC thought that Azikiwe should resign to uphold the party's reputation. They recalled that Ojike had been compelled to resign when his honesty was impugned, and that Azikiwe had insisted upon the resignation of Adegoke Adelabu as Federal Minister of Social Services when, as will be seen in Chapter VII, a commission of inquiry found him guilty of misconduct in his capacity as Chairman of the Ibadan District Council. Those who said, "What is good for the goose is good for the gander," thought that Azikiwe should step down. But the vast majority of party leaders throughout the country felt that Azikiwe's resignation would constitute an abdication of nationalistic principles and an irretrievable setback for the NCNC. Moreover, there was little evidence that the people of the Eastern Region had lost faith in their Premier or in the African Continental Bank. On the contrary, local government bodies throughout the Eastern Region passed resolutions to transfer their funds from the Bank of British West Africa to the African Continental Bank in affirmation of their confidence in Azikiwe.[93] If the rank and file of politically conscious Nigerians did not repudiate Azikiwe's banking policy, the leaders of the party could scarcely demand his political capitulation. On January 18, 1957, a joint meeting of the National Executive Committee and the Eastern Parliamentary Party adopted recommendations submitted by the joint (Federal and Eastern) Ministerial Council to the effect that the Eastern House of Assembly should be dissolved and that all incumbent members of the House

---

in deciding on the degree of severance of active connection which will be necessary in each case." *Ibid.*, p. 58.

This statement does not appear to require Dr. Azikiwe to have relinquished his financial interest in the bank, and it was not cited by the Tribunal in support of its finding of misconduct. However, the rules of conduct set forth by the Secretary of State were advertised as being illustrative rather than exhaustive of the principles of comportment expected of high public officials in the service of the Crown.

[93] *Proceedings of the Foster-Sutton Tribunal of Inquiry*, Vol. II, p. 890. Hon. B. C. Okwu, Government Chief Whip in the Eastern House of Assembly, alleged that the tribunal had been set up with the intention to cause a run on the African Continental Bank so that it would be virtually prostrate by the time the inquiry was concluded. *Eastern House of Assembly Debates*, 3rd Session, August 8, 1956, p. 221. Mr. Okwu was instrumental in encouraging local government bodies to make deposits in the A.C.B. while the Tribunal was sitting. In August, the District Council of his home division, Awgu, took the lead. Dr. Azikiwe stated to the Tribunal that there had been no run on the bank because the people had faith in it. *Proceedings of the Foster-Sutton Tribunal of Inquiry*, Vol. II, p. 771.

should be renominated to test public confidence in the government and its policies. To dispel misgivings and uncertainties about the government's intention with respect to the African Continental Bank, it was resolved, with the concurrence of the Premier, that all private interests in the bank should be transferred to the government.[94]

Inevitably, the campaign energies of candidates were mainly absorbed by issues other than the bank question.[95] Two of the most difficult issues for the NCNC were the Calabar-Ogoja-Rivers State question, noted previously,[96] and the question of government policy with respect to parochial schools. In Eastern Nigeria, the Roman Catholic Mission has the largest following among the Ibo people and operates most of the primary schools owned by voluntary agencies—about 75 percent of the total number.[97] On the eve of the election, Dr. Azikiwe disclosed that Catholic schools had received £1.1 million of the £2.3 million which the Eastern Government had allocated for primary education.[98] However, in 1956 the NCNC government adopted an education policy that was resented by the Church; it decided that all primary schools to be established in the future would be owned and managed by local government councils, that public funds would not be used for the construction of new parochial schools and that government education officers would control the assignment of children to schools on the basis of available facilities. An official government newspaper referred to mission schools critically as "centres of dogmatic indoctrination."[99]

Catholic leaders concluded that their church interests were not

[94] Joint Meeting of the National Executive Committee and Eastern Parliamentary Party at Enugu, 18 January 1957, NCNC Eastern Working Committee File No. 10: Entry No. 138; see also *The People's Mandate (NCNC Manifesto)*, March 1957, p. 1.

The ministerial meeting was reported to have been held prior to the publication of the Foster-Sutton report in anticipation of adverse findings. J. H. Price, "The Eastern Region of Nigeria, March 1957," *Five Elections in Africa*, ed. W. J. M. Mackenzie and Kenneth Robinson (Oxford: The Clarendon Press, 1960), p. 109.

[95] J. H. Price's study of the Eastern Region election of March 1957 has some discussion of the issues in addition to cavalier and, to put it mildly, less than objective aspersions on Dr. Azikiwe in the light of the findings of the Foster-Sutton Tribunal of Inquiry.

[96] *Supra*, pp. 137-138.

[97] According to J. H. Price, the Roman Catholic Mission in Eastern Nigeria "has a total membership of 1¼ millions, including 1 million confirmed Catholics and ¼ million catechumens, with 600,000 school children in the primary schools." *Op.cit.*, p. 111.

[98] Nnamdi Azikiwe, *After Three Years of Stewardship* (Enugu: 1957), p. 10.

[99] Quoted from the *Eastern Outlook* in *Eastern Nigeria Today*, published by the Office of the Commissioner in the United Kingdom for the Eastern Region of Nigeria (London: September 1956).

properly respected because Catholic representation in the government was not proportionate to Catholic strength in the Eastern Region or in the NCNC. The general election seemed to afford an opportunity to redress the balance, but nothing could be done at the stage of nominations owing to the decision of the National Executive Committee that all incumbent members should be returned. As a result, *ad hoc* groups associated with the Eastern Nigerian Catholic Council were formed in several constituencies to support independent Catholic candidates.[100] In Onitsha, a spectacular realignment of political groups occurred; overnight the formerly intense ethnic conflict between the Onitsha indigenes and the non-Onitsha Ibo settlers was eclipsed by an inter-denominational row between Catholic and Protestants that persisted well beyond the 1957 election. Although the NCNC returned all of the incumbent members for Onitsha Division—including Dr. Azikiwe, who is a Methodist[101]—evidence of Catholic discontent was apparent in the electoral results.[102]

[100] NCNC records for various divisions indicate that church officials and Reverend Fathers intervened in behalf of anti-NCNC candidates. NCNC Eastern Working Committee/36: Uyo Division and 46: Eket Division.

[101] In 1938, Dr. Azikiwe, at the age of 34, recounted his religious affiliations in a column of his biographical series entitled "My Odyssey" in the *West African Pilot*, August 15, 1938:

"As a Christian, I have been many-sided. At the tender age of nine, I was a Roman Catholic. At the age of ten I became an Anglican. At the age of twelve, I was a Wesleyan Methodist. At sixteen I became a Presbyterian. [It will be recalled that young Azikiwe attended mission schools in Onitsha, Lagos and Calabar; a transfer to another school entailed a change in religion.] At the age of eighteen, I was a soldier of the Lord (Hallelujah!) in the Salvation Army. At nineteen, I left the emotional side of Christianity for the intellectual side. I became a student Bible Expositor under the banner of Russellism (now known as Jehovah's Witnesses!) At twenty-one, I entered the Baptist fold as a staunch believer. At twenty-four, I became a Congregationalist. At twenty-five, I was re-affirmed in the Presbyterian faith. At thirty, I returned to the Methodist faith which is the original church which baptized me. The sacraments of the various churches benefited me thus. I was baptized a Methodist, confirmed a Baptist, took Holy Communion as a Presbyterian, and married as a Methodist. I have narrated these not necessarily to justify my chequered career in the various denominations of Christendom—and there are factors which necessitated these changes from one denomination to another—but to show how my ideas of life have been influenced thereby."

[102] The Onitsha political realignment of 1957 brought together such former opponents as Hon. P. H. Okolo, Chairman of the Onitsha Improvement Union and P. E. Chukwurah, publisher of the newspaper *New Africa*, a former organ of the Non-Onitsha Ibo Association, in their respective capacities of Chairman and Secretary General of the Eastern Nigerian Catholic Council (Onitsha). On the Protestant side, Mr. C. T. Onyekwelu, President of the Union of Niger African Traders, was Chairman of the Convention of Protestant Citizens; among the leading Onitshan Protestants were Dr. Lawrence Uwaechia and the Premier himself.

In March the Eastern electorate returned the NCNC to power with a decisive majority of 64 to 20 in the House of Assembly. Opposition candidates (Action Group and United National Independence Party) won 18 seats out of a total of 30 in the non-Ibo constituencies, mainly, it would appear, on the strength of the separate state issue.[103] Only one independent candidate who was clearly supported by the Eastern Nigerian Catholic Council was successful,[104] but organized Catholic action appears to have made an impression on the NCNC leadership. The right of parents to choose a school for their children on the basis of religious preference was acknowledged and the proportion of Catholic ministers in the new government was increased to about 50 percent.

With the renewal of the NCNC's mandate to govern the East, the way was clear to proceed with the postponed conference to review the Nigerian Constitution. Meanwhile Dr. Azikiwe informed the House of Assembly that he had relinquished, without compensation, his personal shares in the African Continental Bank. In due course, he declared, total ownership of the bank would be acquired by a statutory corporation of the Eastern Regional Government.[105]

For electoral purposes Onitsha Division was a multi-member constituency of 5 seats; every voter was entitled to cast 5 ballots, and the 5 NCNC official candidates were returned. They included 2 Catholics and 2 Protestants in addition to the Premier. Dr. Azikiwe polled 10,000 more votes than any other candidate, but each of the 2 Catholic candidates polled about 15,000 more than each of the 2 Protestant candidates, while 2 Catholics standing as Independents polled nearly identical totals of 23-24,000. Naturally the Protestants, who held a majority in the executive committees of the Onitsha urban district branch and the Onitsha Divisional Organization, accused the Catholics of sabotage, and the Onitsha urban branch expelled 4 Catholic residents of Onitsha who stood as Independents in Onitsha and Awka Divisions. (They were readmitted in 1958.) For over a year the Onitsha branch was crippled by rivalry between Catholic and Protestant factions while prominent citizens and the Eastern Working Committee endeavored to mediate. In November 1958, NCNC candidates won a clear majority in the Onitsha Urban District Council and the election of an Onitshan lawyer as Chairman of the Council by a majority of Non-Onitsha Ibo members seemed to signify the burial of that ethnic hatchet at last. The religious controversy deserves no little credit.

[103] Mr. E. O. Eyo was among the successful Action Group candidates in Uyo Division; he became Opposition Chief Whip in the Eastern House of Assembly.

[104] Hon. P. U. Amaefunah of Awka Division; he was readmitted to the NCNC in 1958. Only one other Independent, a non-Catholic in Afikpo Division, was elected.

[105] *Eastern House of Assembly Debates, Official Report*, April 5, 1957, p. 2 (mimeographed). Cf. *supra*, pp. 181-182 n. 80.

189

CHAPTER V: THE STRUGGLE
WITHIN THE NATIONAL COUNCIL
OF NIGERIA AND THE CAMEROONS

I N THE previous chapter an attempt was made to indicate relationships between several distinct issues and episodes involving substantial competing interests: the issue of democratic versus communal representation in local government, the question of rectitude in the management of public affairs, the great controversy over the African Continental Bank with its far-reaching implications for Nigerian economic development, and the question of public policy with respect to parochial schools. It is not asserted that the investment of public funds in the African Continental Bank became a public issue because of the rift between Azikiwe and his Minister of Finance. Nor is there any logical or clearly demonstrable connection between the Onitsha dispute, the Bribery Commission, and the appointment of the Tribunal of Inquiry by the Secretary of State for the Colonies. Yet the hypothesis of an underlying political relationship derives plausibility from the fact that the struggle within the NCNC grew more intense despite the resolution or denouement of each particular issue. This chapter seeks to indicate the nature of the social forces in conflict through continuation of the narrative.

THE MINISTERS AND THEIR DISCONTENTS

After the Eastern general election of March 1957, a pall of deepening dissension enveloped the national leadership of the NCNC. At a meeting of the National Executive Committee in Lagos on the eve of a special convention of the party, Dr. Kingsley Ozuomba Mbadiwe, a federal minister and leader of the Federal Parliamentary Party, specified several of the roots of discontent.[1] First, Dr. Mbadiwe and others objected strenuously to the fact that two ministers and three parliamentary secretaries of the previous Eastern Government had not been reappointed by Dr. Azikiwe to his new government after the election. The critics deplored these omissions as a breach of faith with those who stood by the party and the Premier during the Foster-Sutton crisis. Secondly, there was a widespread feeling that

[1] NCNC, Report of the meeting of the National Executive Committee held at the Lagos City College, Yaba, Lagos, on April 18, 1957, p. 2. (Mimeographed.) See also the publication of a document purported to have been prepared by a special committee of the Federal Parliamentary Party in April 1957, setting forth grievances against the National President in the *Daily Telegraph* (Lagos), July 16, 1958.

the Eastern Government should publish the controversial reports of its lamented Commission of Inquiry into Bribery and Corruption. Many of those who grieved the untimely death of Mbonu Ojike wanted the majority report, which condemned him, to be debated and rejected by the Eastern House of Assembly in order to clear his name. Thirdly, the Eastern election had thrust into prominence a new militant "youth" auxiliary of the NCNC, known as the Zikist National Vanguard. It was alleged that the Vanguard had been organized as a result of malicious gossip to the effect that certain ministers and their associates were plotting to overthrow the National President. These indignant persons ridiculed the Vanguard as "Zik's own Regiment." Fourthly, it was alleged that the National President had become increasingly "inaccessible" to his party colleagues and that he habitually made politically important decisions without consultation. Finally, there were suspicions of deliberate delay in the implementation of the National President's promise to complete the conversion of the African Continental Bank into a regional state bank, although it was acknowledged that Dr. Azikiwe did transfer his personal holdings in the bank to the government without compensation and that a constitutional amendment was required to permit regional governments to engage directly in banking.

Two days before the meeting of the National Executive Committee, a purportedly deranged man hurled a stone at Dr. Azikiwe in the courtyard of Government House, Lagos, when the Eastern Premier arrived to attend a meeting of the heads of the several Nigerian governments. In his presidential address to the special convention, Azikiwe intimated that his life was endangered by a conspiracy of unnamed "Brutuses and Cassiuses." He reaffirmed his belief in the subordination of parliamentary leadership to the leadership of the party and he proposed, for the sake of equity and increased participation, that parliamentarians and paid members of statutory bodies should be disqualified from holding national or regional offices in the party.[2] These remarks were indicative of the covert but palpable conflict between the National President and the principal national officers.

At the second plenary session of the convention, the annual election of national officers was begun in Azikiwe's absence. The three top officers were returned unopposed: Dr. Azikiwe as National President; Alhaji Adegoke Adelabu, Leader of the Opposition in

[2] National Presidential Address, 1957 NCNC Special Convention. Ref. No. NC/HQ. AD. 73/7. (Mimeographed.)

the Western House of Assembly and Chairman of the Western Working Committee, as First National Vice-President; and Dr. K. O. Mbadiwe, Federal Parliamentary Leader, as Second National Vice-President (succeeding the late Mbonu Ojike). But the meeting broke up in the confusion of a row which erupted during a vote to re-elect Chief Kolawole Balogun, Federal Minister of Research and Information, as National Secretary. Subsequently the convention decided to postpone the holding of further elections until the next annual convention which would take place after the impending all-party Constitutional Conference. A committee was appointed "to investigate the grave allegations in the Presidential Address" and a motion was passed requesting the Governor-General to ensure the safety of the National President and other members of the NCNC delegation to London.[3]

The London Constitutional Conference of May and June 1957 provided for regional self-government with safeguards for the unity and paramount interests of the Federation.[4] The Eastern and Western Regions requested immediate self-government; the North declared that it would ask for self-government in 1959. In the self-governing regions, the reserved and discretionary legislative powers of the Governor were largely eliminated. It was agreed that the Federal House of Representatives would be enlarged to include 320 members —approximately one representative per 100,000 of the population— elected on the basis of universal adult suffrage in all regions save the North, where universal male suffrage was prescribed subject to periodic review. Furthermore the office of Prime Minister of the Federation was created and all official members of the Council of Ministers (i.e., the Civil Secretary, the Financial Secretary, and the Attorney General) were eliminated. It was also agreed that a Federal Senate based on the principle of equality of regional representation would be established after the next general election. Other major political questions, including those relating to the constitutional protection of fundamental human rights, the appellate jurisdiction of the Federal Supreme Court, and the electoral laws of the regional governments, were deferred for consideration by a subsequent resumed conference. A fiscal commission was prescribed to make recommendations on revenue allocation and a commission of inquiry was prescribed to study the complex and related problems

[3] NCNC Special Convention, April 19, 1957, at the Glover Memorial Hall, Lagos (Official Report), p. 5. (Mimeographed.)

[4] See the *Report by the Nigeria Constitutional Conference held in London in May and June 1957*, Cmnd. 207 (London: 1957).

of minority fears, proposals for the creation of additional states, and disputed regional boundaries. On the vexed question of control of the police, an NCNC centralist doctrine seemed to prevail with the decision to vest ultimate responsibility for law and order in the federal government.[5]

Among the members of the NCNC delegation there was a sharp difference of opinion over a proposal to create the office of Deputy Prime Minister of the Federation. This idea seems to have arisen in NCNC circles in anticipation of the appointment of a Northerner as Prime Minister, whose party was restricted in principle to people of Northern origin. It was endorsed by the National Executive Committee of the NCNC[6] and the Northern Peoples' Congress does not appear to have objected. In London, Azikiwe agreed to the appointment of Abubakar Tafawa Balewa of the Northern Peoples' Congress as Prime Minister, but he was less than enthusiastic about the idea of creating the office of Deputy Prime Minister, both on constitutional grounds[7] and on the unstated but reasonably inferred ground that Dr. Mbadiwe was the most likely candidate. The office was not created by the Constitutional Conference.

On the question of independence for Nigeria, a memorandum submitted by the three regional premiers and the Leader of Government Business in the Southern Cameroons requested the United Kingdom Government to undertake to grant independence to the Federation in 1959. The Secretary of State for the Colonies replied that he could not ask the British Government to set a date for independence

[5] The centralist predisposition of the NCNC in comparison with the other parties was evident in a disagreement over the crucial passage of the *Report of the Constitutional Conference* providing safeguards for the future of the Federation. It was provided that "the Governor-General in his discretion and with the approval of the Secretary of State for the Colonies should be empowered to issue such directions to a Region as might appear to him to be necessary for the purpose of ensuring that the executive authority of the Region was not exercised in such a way as to impede or prejudice the performance by the Federal Government of any of its functions or to endanger the continuance of federal government in Nigeria." *Ibid.*, p. 8. The NCNC wanted this power to be vested in the Governor-General in Council, i.e., in the Federal Council of Ministers, but the Action Group and the Northern Peoples' Congress preferred to vest the power with the Secretary of State in order to avoid federal interference in regional matters during the period of transition prior to independence.

[6] NCNC, Report of the meeting of the National Executive Committee, April 18, 1957, p. 3.

[7] Later Dr. Azikiwe declared that his objection was purely constitutional, since a requirement that would oblige the Prime Minister to exercise his powers only with "the knowledge and consent" of a deputy would weaken the office of the Prime Minister. He said that the proposal was criticized severely, and properly, by the Action Group and the United National Independence Party in London. *Daily Times*, June 23, 1958.

until it was seen that Nigeria could "take the strain of Regional self-government," and other problems, especially the minorities question, had been resolved. He affirmed, however, that a resolution for independence by the Nigerian Parliament in 1960 would be considered "with sympathy." Thereupon the regional premiers and the Leader of Government Business in the Southern Cameroons expressed their "disappointment" at the inability of the Secretary of State to agree to a firm date and declared their unanimous resolve to achieve independence for Nigeria "not later than 2nd April, 1960."[8] Following the adjournment of the conference, the Premiers of the North and the West expressed their general satisfaction with the progress achieved, but Dr. Azikiwe voiced his "painful disappointment," and regional self-government was implemented without celebration in the Eastern Region.

Upon his return to Nigeria, Dr. Azikiwe endeavored to alleviate dissension among party leaders in the East. He directed three Eastern ministers to resign their offices in the NCNC Eastern Working Committee—the principal executive organ of the party in the region—on the ground that disagreements among them adversely affected the Eastern Government. He also took steps to settle a particularly serious dispute within the Enugu branch of the NCNC, to which careful attention is devoted in this chapter. Meanwhile a stinging criticism of Azikiwe's national policy was broadcast by two of his principal lieutenants. The background to this verbal revolt was a decision by the Prime Minister-designate, Alhaji Abubakar Tafawa Balewa of the Northern Peoples' Congress, to form a national government that would include the Action Group as well as the NCNC and the NPC. Alhaji Abubakar proposed to form a council of ministers comprising six NCNC, three NPC, two Action Group, and one Kamerun National Congress, in addition to himself. The Action Group accepted Balewa's invitation and the national government was formed with the approval of the National President of the NCNC.[9] On October 11, 1957, Alhaji Adegoke Adelabu, First National Vice-President of the NCNC and Leader of the Opposition in the Western House of Assembly, and Malam Aminu Kano, President-General of the Northern Elements Progressive Union (the major Northern ally of the NCNC), issued a joint statement denouncing the national government "as an unholy alliance of the reactionary forces of regionalism." Their declaration implied that to

[8] Report by the Nigeria Constitutional Conference, pp. 24-27.

[9] In fact, the formation of a national government under Alhaji Abubakar appears to have been proposed by Dr. Azikiwe during the Constitutional Conference of 1957.

all intents and purposes, Dr. Azikiwe had become a regionalist for personal reasons and that the NCNC Federal Parliamentary Party had been compelled against its will "to serve the vested interests of one man at the top."[10] Two weeks later, delegates assembled at Aba in the Eastern Region for the tensely awaited Seventh Annual Convention of the NCNC.

Toward a More Effective Government of the Party

The Annual Convention of October 28-30, 1957, was attended by about 350 delegates, including the representatives of 109 accredited branches, 11 branches of the NCNC Youth Association, 11 branches of the Women's Association, delegates from several branches of the Zikist National Vanguard, about 35 members of the National Executive Committee, and an indeterminate additional number of NCNC parliamentarians, of which there were about 150 in the several legislatures of Nigeria.[11] Non-delegates who belonged to the party were allowed to attend plenary sessions in the open-air hall of the Aba Rex Cinema as observers.

In his presidential address to the convention, Dr. Azikiwe (who was on leave from his official duties as Premier of the East for reasons of health) alluded bitterly to the chronic malady of dissension within the NCNC and to his party's organizational deficiencies. He reiterated his opinion that parliamentarians ought not to be eligible to hold high party office and suggested further that drastic organizational remedies, "even in a totalitarian manner," had become necessary. "Mine," he lamented, "has been the misfortune to lead an undisciplined army." He was appalled by the public condemnation of the national government by the First National Vice-President and the Leader of the Northern Elements Progressive Union. This and other acts of indiscipline, he said, have exposed the inadequacy of the disciplinary powers of the National President under the NCNC Constitution. Therefore he had given notice of an omnibus motion that was framed to equip the National President with various discretionary powers to initiate disciplinary action against individuals, to dissolve party organs, and to revoke the certificates of affiliation of branches or member unions for actions contrary to the ideology, the best interests, or the Constitution of the NCNC.[12]

[10] *Daily Times*, October 12, 1957.
[11] The list of branches represented is appended to the official minutes of the Annual Convention held at Aba, October 28, 29, and 30, 1957. (Mimeographed.)
[12] "Opportunity Knocks at Our Door," an Address delivered at the Annual Convention of the NCNC, October 28, 1957 by the National President. (Mimeographed.)

This proposal did not reach the floor of the convention, but it reflected the mood of the rank and file delegates and it set the tone of subsequent debate. Two days later, a supporter of Azikiwe from the Western Region offered a motion that was less likely to incur principled or technical objections from the floor; it gave to the National President the right to appoint the other eight national officers who would comprise, with himself, the Central Working Committee or inner core of the National Executive Committee. The official minutes of the convention thus report this fateful event in a single paragraph:[13]

"Hon. B. Olowofoyeku's motion seconded by Mr. Adeniran Ogunsanya 'That for a more efficient administration of the Party, the NCNC until the attainment of Independence for the federation of Nigeria adopt a Cabinet System of Government, i.e., the Convention shall elect every year a President who, subject to the approval prior or subsequent of the Convention, shall elect the other officers as he deems fit.' This motion after a long and heated debate, was put to the house and was carried."

The following passages, paraphrased from notes made by the writer during the third plenary session of the convention, indicate the issues involved and may suggest the emotional grip of the unfolding drama.[14]

Barrister Babatunji Olowofoyeku, MHA (Ilesha, Western Region) said that his motion was designed to improve the administration of the party. Clearly the President needed greater power, although the meaning of his address to the convention had been distorted by critics in the press. This motion found a way between the end of effective administration and the danger of dictatorial rule. Discipline, he said, was a problem in the NCNC mainly because of the lack of power in the office of the President. If the party's weakness was due to the personal weakness of the President, we should change the man in office; otherwise we should give him the power he needs. It may be alleged that the NCNC has thrown democracy to the winds; on the other hand it is often alleged that the NCNC is ultra-democratic. We want the party to be ordinarily democratic, and this motion, he said, was restricted at any rate to the period prior to independence.

[13] NCNC, minutes of the Annual Convention, pp. 4-5.
[14] MHA and MHR following the name of individuals noted in the text signify Member of the House of Assembly (Regional) and Member of the House of Representatives (Federal) respectively. The information in parentheses identifies the home city, area, or constituency of the individual and his region.

Barrister Adeniran Ogunsanya, Leader of the NCNC Opposition in the Lagos Town Council (Ikorodu, Western Region) rose to second the motion. He observed that the party had been run under a cabinet system until 1951 and that a good deal had been achieved during that period. It was well known, he remarked, that he had aspired to the office of National Secretary, but he did not think that the party could afford an internal struggle for office at this time. The motion sought unity for an interim period prior to independence; it did not request a permanent amendment to the constitution. If the constitution were followed to the letter, he said, most of those present would probably be declared ineligible to vote inasmuch as their branch affiliations were not paid up.

Chief (barrister) Kolawole Balogun, MHR, National Secretary, and Federal Minister of Research and Information (Oshun, Western Region) said that the vitality of the party made him happy. He acknowledged that those who supported the motion did so with the best of intentions. All of us, he said, have the highest motives and there was no political party without its pros and cons. With all humility, he would speak against the motion. The NCNC, he said, was founded to extend democratic principles. Democracy may be the most difficult system to use but it is the best system known; that is why we are opposed to the communist system. (He intimated that the motion was suggestive of communist practice and there was an uproar from the floor. The National President rose to restore order and said to the speaker: You will have the protection of the chair.) Chief Balogun continued to say that for 13 years the NCNC had followed both the leadership of Azikiwe and the democratic system to the exclusion of any other.

The National President interrupted to inquire whether the speaker meant to imply that the cabinet system was communistic. There was an uproar and the speaker exclaimed that the convention was the place for members of the party to exchange views. The National President declared that he alone would keep order and that he had a right to ask that particular question because some of the members were ministers under a cabinet system of government.

Chief Balogun said that in the case of cabinet government there were well established customs and known rules. But a party was different; the political party, he said, was the father of government. Cabinet government was not the way of the NCNC. If the National President were so much inclined to cabinet government he might have conferred with his colleagues in the party Executive Committee before he delivered his presidential address. (A member exclaimed: Good

197

point!) Few persons, he insisted, exceeded himself in their devotion to the National President. (Shouts of "No!") But, he went on, the cabinet system proposed by the motion was incompatible with the democratic principles of the party and its adoption by the Convention would injure the reputation of the party abroad. He was not able to support it; if it were adopted he would be obliged to re-examine his own position as he had a reputation to uphold.

Dr. Kingsley Ozuomba Mbadiwe, MHR, Second National Vice-President, and Federal Minister of Commerce and Industries (Orlu, Eastern Region), rose in what he termed a very serious mood to offer an amendment to the motion. He wanted to say first that in his years in the party he had never pursued office or high position. Now he appealed to the young men present to guard their senses and listen to reason. If his proposal did not qualify as an amendment it could be taken as a counter-motion; he would leave the decision to the President.

The National President stated that the convention was entitled not to entertain motions or counter-motions which had not been screened previously by the National Executive Committee. Dr. Mbadiwe continued without objection to propose that the convention vote to uphold the system of electing officers until the report of the special committee on reorganization set up by the last special convention had been considered. (This report, prepared by a committee under the chairmanship of Chief H. O. Davies, was submitted too late for distribution to members of the National Executive Committee or consideration by the convention.)[15] Dr. Mbadiwe warned that the party was about to do something that might cost it the next election. He complained about the persistent heckling from the floor and said that it would serve no purpose for every section to heckle the other. The National President remarked that heckling was a familiar part of the parliamentary system. Dr. Mbadiwe observed that the cabinet system had been abandoned by the party in 1951 because it had not been successful, and that certain members of the pre-1951 cabinet had since turned away from the party. Opposition, he said, was innate in the system of parliamentary government, but the cabinet system of party rule allowed no room for opposition within the party. The motion, he said, was contrary to the ideals of the party; its adoption, he warned, would destroy the party.

The National President rose to quell the noise from the floor.

15 Minutes of the Annual Convention, p. 4; also the official Agenda for the National Executive Committee, October 25-26, 1957, stated that the Davies Committee Report had not been submitted for consideration.

Everyone here, he said, had the right to express his views and to give vent to emotion; that was appropriate.

Alhaji Adegoke Adelabu, MHA, First National Vice-President, and Leader of the Opposition in the Western House of Assembly (Ibadan, Western Region), rose to second the amendment by Dr. Mbadiwe. In his view the motion was contrary to the general advance toward democratic practices of election in the country. In the parliamentary system of Great Britain the distinction between government and party was important. Cabinets may be appointed in government, but party leadership should be elected. At any rate, he said, good principles ought to be capable of general application. If the rule of appointment is adopted for the central organization of the party, it should be applied equally to the regional working committees and for that matter to the branches. Then the Action Group might properly charge that the NCNC was an undemocratic organization.

His confidence in the National President, he declared, was great enough to confer upon him any power of life or death. But he had an even greater confidence in the ability of this great country of Nigeria to produce men of his calibre. The common wisdom of the ideologists of the NCNC assembled, he said, is greater than the wisdom of any one man. We have condemned a theory according to which the Governor-General was deemed wiser than all the people. Shall we, he asked, now introduce a similar theory for the government of our party? If the most militant party has no confidence in its duly elected officers, it was in effect telling the Colonial Office that we are not ready to manage our own affairs. In a team of elected officers, he continued, there was a system of balance and mutual restraint. By electing various people as officers of the party it was possible to combine diverse tendencies into a balanced whole and to ensure the due representation of sectional interests. He exclaimed that he would have been welcomed into the camp of the Action Group or the Northern Peoples' Congress as an ally, but that he rejected both tribalism and religion as the basis of party affiliation. He followed Zik because of ideology; let that ideology live on.

Chief J. I. D. Onyia, MHR (Asaba, Western Region), said that the convention had listened to the youth and the middle-aged men; now it should hear the voice of an elder. The cabinet system was used by this party as far back as 1948 when it was adopted with the Freedom Charter at Kaduna. We agreed then that a cabinet system of government for the party was consistent with democracy. The proposal now was for a period of emergency and the party, he thought, was in a state of emergency. He was fed up with the bickering of

199

people who were struggling for ascendancy. The cabinet system was required for the sake of unity and he was vehemently opposed to any amendment.

Barrister Jaja Anchu Wachuku, MHR (Aba/Ngwa, Eastern Region), said that the main point was whether the motion would increase discipline within the party. In form it would merely reinstate the condition that obtained from 1948 to 1951, and it did not constitute a permanent amendment to the Constitution. It would be manifestly improper, he said, to give the National President power to appoint the National Executive Committee, but the motion did no such thing. The President would appoint a cabinet, and the National Executive Committee, as the representative of the convention, would check the National President. He agreed with the First Vice-President that regional leaders ought to have a comparable power to select the people who would work with them, but observed that such an amendment might necessitate the creation of regional executive committees to check the regional leaders. The various needs he said, require clarification. Possibly the mover would accept his suggestion with respect to regional organization in which case he would have no quarrel with the substantive motion.

Mr. Michael E. Ogon, MHA, Government Chief Whip in the Eastern House of Assembly (Ikom, Eastern Region), rose to support the amendment offered by the "chief floor member" (Mr. Wachuku). He remarked that the quarrel in the party was confined to the leadership. Regional leaders did seem to require power to choose their teams on the working committee level. He declared that no man was indispensable to the party. If the National President were not here the party would go on because it lives in its ideological spirit. He noted that Kwame Nkrumah appointed a central committee of the Convention People's Party in Ghana and said that the system might work equally well for the NCNC. The party would give the President the right to choose a cabinet with the understanding that he would choose men who were devoted to its cause.

Other members spoke for and against the motion, including Mr. Mokwugo Okoye, Secretary General of the NCNC Youth Association, who suggested that the President be empowered to appoint his cabinet from among the elected members of the National Executive Committee. At length, the National President observed that three hours had been devoted to the debate and he called upon the mover to wind up. Barrister Olowofoyeku emphasized that his proposal was an emergency measure for a temporary period only, that it amended one section of the Constitution only,[16] and that Mr. Wachuku's amendment to the motion was not relevant, although he would be willing to support another motion by him to the same effect.

At this juncture the National President injected a harsh note of procedure. He recalled a criticism of the National Secretary which he had made during the previous session, to wit, that the National Secretary had improperly assumed the right to endorse and thereby validate cards of admission to the convention. The National Secretary held in defense that he had endorsed the cards of admission for purposes of identification only and not in an attempt to usurp the prerogatives of the President. His supporters in the aisles and "corridors" explained that the National Secretary's justifiable purpose was to prevent the participation of "anarchistic" elements, in particular delegates from numerous branches of the Zikist National Vanguard. Their contention is buttressed by the official minutes of the convention which noted the attendance of an unspecified number of delegates from "various branches" of the Zikist National Vanguard.[17] (The precise number of Vanguard delegates was probably not known to anyone but the total number of those voting did not seem large and they did not appear to influence the proceedings or decisions appreciably. Several members of the Vanguard, wearing red and blue patched shirts, provided a security guard for the National President during the convention.)

The National President stated that he had asked the National Secretary to produce a register of properly accredited delegates but had been told that records were not available. Supporters of the National Secretary were obliged to admit that his position was weakened by the administrative laxness of the National Headquarters. His opponents alleged, mainly in the aisles, that he wanted to obtain both the *de facto* recognition of improperly affiliated branches and the admission of delegates from "paper" branches who would support him and his political associates in voting on matters of policy. The National President even suggested that it was necessary for him to guard against the threat of an administrative *coup,* and that it seemed prudent to require the representatives of branches to produce their certificates of affiliation or their subscription receipts. According to the constitution, branches became affiliated to the National Council upon the approval of the National Executive Committee.

---

[16] *The Constitution, Rules and Regulations of the National Council of Nigeria and the Cameroons* (Lagos: 1955), Article V, Section 3 (a), p. 4.

[17] Minutes of the Annual Convention, Appendix A, p. 2.

Inasmuch as the National Headquarters had countenanced the admission of branches without the formal approval of the National Executive Committee, he might deem it necessary to rule as invalid all receipts dated after the last annual convention of 1955. The alternative course would be to overlook the slipshod administrative practices of the National Headquarters and to rely wholly upon "the good faith of members."

He did not want to accuse anyone of dereliction. He said that he loved Kola (Chief Kolawole Balogun, the National Secretary) and was not trying to destroy him as the latter seemed to think, but that there was a limit to his endurance. As National President he was not going to be pushed around by his officers. His task was to see that the constitution was followed. Unless the Secretary could produce proof that branches represented were properly affiliated and duly accredited he would feel obliged to restrict voting to the members of the National Executive Committee, all parliamentarians, and the delegates of branches that were accredited prior to the annual convention of 1955.

The National Secretary said that he had set up a committee to ensure that people who entered the hall did so only in accordance with the rules. If errors were made, they were unintentional and he would take the blame; but after all, he said, officers are collectively responsible for the conduct of the party. He had given the President a list of branches that very morning and he thought that it was the duty of the President to support his officers who were working for him. Angrily he declared: it is wrong!

The National President said that it was not his purpose to reopen old wounds. He had come to the convention prepared to say that if the members wanted the party to be run in a disorderly manner he would not be a party to it. In politics, he said, you must be a good loser. Just because you lose is no reason to accuse the National President of trying to destroy you. He was not sorry these things were finally happening. Look, he said, at the people on this rostrum: a Parliamentary Secretary, the Leader of the NEPU, the Minister of Transport, the Minister of Information, the Leader of the Opposition in the Western House, the Minister of Commerce, the Director of a Bank, the Minister of Finance, a Chief Whip, an honourable member . . . look. He sometimes wondered what right the party had to say it could lead the nation. He thought that the National Secretary owed himself and the convention an apology and that he should be man enough to apologize so that the convention could carry on with its business.

The National Secretary said that the National President was the father of the party and could punish those of his children who spoke to him in a disrespectful manner. He offered a full and unqualified apology. The National President arose smiling and shook the National Secretary's hand. He ruled that persons holding cards of admission signed by the National Secretary could vote as they were ratified by himself. Mr. Wachuku's amendment was voted on first and defeated by 197-86. Dr. Mbadiwe's amendment lost overwhelmingly on a voice vote. The substantive motion was carried overwhelmingly by voice vote.

The climactic third plenary session of the Aba Convention lasted for eight and one half hours, adjourning *sine die* at 7:30 P.M. after the re-election of Dr. Azikiwe as National President and the election of 35 members of the National Executive Committee. Azikiwe then appointed eight national officers, including new First and Second National Vice-Presidents and a new National Secretary.[18] However, Messrs. Adelabu, Mbadiwe, and Balogun retained their memberships in the National Executive Committee.

If This Be Tribalism. . . .

If the struggle within the NCNC can be attributed to a structural contradiction it was the inconsistency of a unitary party within a federal state. Constitutionally, power in the NCNC is centralized in the National Executive Committee. But regionalism in the Constitution of Nigeria entailed regionalism in the political command of the NCNC. While the Aba Convention gave the National President absolute control over the Central Working Committee, it did not resolve the deeper issue of centralism versus sectionalism in the party.

An indication of persisting tension was given at Aba by the departure of Alhaji Adegoke Adelabu from the convention hall when the motion to adopt a cabinet system was passed. Adelabu was the pre-eminent leader of the NCNC in the Western Region: he was Leader of the Opposition in the Western House of Assembly, Chairman of the Western Working Committee and the undisputed

[18] Dr. Azikiwe did not at this time refrain from appointing parliamentarians to national office. Hon. J. O. Fadahunsi, appointed First National Vice-President, was a member of the Western House of Assembly, and Hon. R. A. Njoku, appointed the Second National Vice-President, was the Federal Minister of Transport. The new National Secretary, Mr. F. S. McEwen, formerly President-General of the Youth Association, was the Principal of Lagos City College (founded by Dr. Azikiwe), General Manager of the *West African Pilot,* and a member of the Lagos Town Council. See the full listing of National Officers and members of the National Executive Committee in Appendix II.

political leader of the great city of Ibadan—the principal NCNC stronghold in the Yoruba section of the Western Region. It was generally conceded that the NCNC could not hold Ibadan against Adelabu, and his reaction was awaited with apprehension.

Similarly, the attitude of Dr. K. Ozuomba Mbadiwe, the Federal Parliamentary Leader, was a matter of great concern. Dr. Mbadiwe was a towering personality in Iboland. He was the main beneficiary of the national outpouring of affection for the late Mbonu Ojike. His dedication to the promotion of African enterprise was not less than that of Ojike and he was an eloquent spokesman for the businessman's point of view, which he reconciled with a professed commitment to socialist ideology (as do Azikiwe and other leaders of both the NCNC and the Action Group). In his capacity as Federal Minister of Commerce and Industries, Dr. Mbadiwe exerted great influence in business circles throughout the country. As Parliamentary Leader, his signal contribution to the harmonious relationship between the NCNC and the Northern Peoples' Congress was widely appreciated in the North, and the Prime Minister of the Federation appeared to regard him as a deputy in fact if not in form. Shortly after the Aba Convention, Dr. Mbadiwe, a practicing Catholic, fasted for two days to prepare his spirit for the trials of decision to come. He then issued a statement in criticism of the Aba proceedings which resulted in the initiation of disciplinary action against him by the Central Working Committee.[19]

Within three weeks of the Aba Convention, Chief Kolawole Balogun, the Federal Minister of Research and Information and ex-National Secretary of the NCNC, declared publicly that the Aba decisions "were null and void because they were not taken by the accredited members of the Convention."[20] Dr. Azikiwe responded to this challenge by directing the National Secretary to initiate disciplinary action against Chief Balogun. After deliberation, the Central Working Committee voted to suspend the Minister subject to a trial by the National Executive Committee.[21] This action was criticized sharply by a "Committee of Elders" in Lagos and by the

19 *Daily Times*, November 7, 8, and 10, 1957.

20 *Daily Times*, November 16, 1957. This was an apparent reference to the presence of an unspecified number of delegates of the Zikist National Vanguard and other observers in the convention hall at the time of voting. *Supra*, p. 201.

21 Chief Kolawole Balogun refused to recognize the competence of the Central Working Committee to "try" him for an alleged breach of discipline. Minutes of the Meeting of the Central Working Committee of the NCNC, November 15, 1957; Minutes of the Meeting of the Central Working Committee of the NCNC, November 29 and December 2, 1957.

secretary of the NCNC Lagos branch, who was suspended forthwith by the branch executive.[22] Dr. Azikiwe decided to summon a special convention of the NCNC to deal specifically with matters of party discipline. Shortly before the meeting of the convention in Enugu, Dr. Mbadiwe appealed to the Executive Committee of the Ibo State Union for mediation.

It will be recalled that the Ibo State Union is the central or "pan-tribal" organization which unites a multitude of voluntary associations formed to foster civic welfare in the local communities of Iboland and in the Ibo settler communities of new urban areas throughout Nigeria. [23] Dr. Azikiwe had been President of the Union from 1948 to 1952, when he declined re-election mainly to escape the political embarrassment which had resulted from his leadership of a "tribal" organization. On one occasion during the Eastern Parliamentary crisis of 1953,[24] the Union was utilized by the NCNC to persuade Ibo people to close ranks behind Azikiwe.[25] Many Ibos objected to this tactic and the political role of the Union diminished when a number of the most prominent Ibo personalities joined the opposition United National Independence Party. Thereafter the leading NCNC politicians of Ibo nationality withdrew from high office in the Union and formal control of the Ibo State Executive passed to the "non-political" Ibo elite, personified by the incumbent President of the Union, Senator Z. C. Obi, a Port Harcourt business-man. However, the Union remained a highly sensitive barometer of Ibo political opinion, especially the opinion of the rank and file

[22] At a meeting held under the auspices of the so-called Elders' Peace Committee, the members of an "alliance" comprising supporters of Mbadiwe and Balogun in the Lagos branch and a faction of the NCNC Lagos Market Women voted to dis-solve the Lagos branch executive. Barrister T. O. S. Benson, NCNC Chief Whip in the House of Representatives and Chairman of the Lagos branch, denied the validity of any action by the Elders' Peace Committee on the ground that it had no place in the constitution of the party. *Daily Times,* January 24 and 25, 1958.

[23] *Supra,* pp. 65, 70; the structure of the Ibo State Union is described in Chapter X.

[24] *Supra,* pp. 122-123.

[25] In April 1953, a meeting of Ibo leaders was convened in Port Harcourt by Dr. Azikiwe, in his capacity as President of the NCNC, to reconcile the parties to the Eastern Regional dispute. (NCNC notice of April 9, 1953, convening a meeting on April 26, 1953, at the home of Chief M. I. Asinobi in Port Harcourt.) All Ibo ministers were invited to attend, and a decision was taken to the effect that their resignations from the Executive Council were in the best interests of the Ibo people and the Eastern Region. To restore harmony in the region, a peace committee was set up under the chairmanship of Mr. L. P. Ojukwu, a prominent businessman. *Daily Times,* May 1, 2, 6, 1953. A number of Ibo leaders and most non-Ibo leaders objected strenuously to the employment of an Ibo committee to deal with political problems affecting the entire region. At this juncture, many non-Ibos decided that the NCNC in the East served the purpose of Ibo domination and transferred their loyalties to the opposition.

of the new middle class. Thus in 1955 the Union supported the demand of the Non-Onitsha Ibo Association for a democratic Onitsha Instrument. During the Foster-Sutton Tribunal of Inquiry the vast majority of Ibo leaders rallied to the NCNC. As a result, the United National Independence Party virtually disappeared from Iboland and from the councils of the Ibo State Union. This did not render the Union subservient to Azikiwe; on the contrary, the Ibo State Executive functioned as a sounding board for grievances against the Government of the Eastern Region and as a center of latent opposition to the Premier.

On January 26, 1958, four days prior to the NCNC's "discipline" convention at Enugu, the Ibo State Union met in Onitsha at the request of Dr. Mbadiwe. Dr. Azikiwe declined an invitation to attend on the ground that it was improper for the Union to mix in party affairs. This criticism of the Union was expressed by Dr. Azikiwe in his presidential address to the party convention.[26] The National Executive Committee took note of the fact that Dr. Mbadiwe had made an appearance before the Central Working Committee at which time he did plead guilty to a charge of having made a public statement that was detrimental to the interests of the party. Inasmuch as the Federal Parliamentary Leader agreed to apologize to the convention, the National Executive Committee was satisfied to recommend a mere vote of censure. It was deemed necessary to postpone Chief Balogun's case owing to his absence on the ground of illness.[27] Alhaji Adegoke Adelabu did not attend and nothing fundamental was resolved by the special convention.

Two weeks later, Yoruba members of the NCNC in Lagos and Ibadan inaugurated "a new cultural organization" called the *Egbe Yoruba Parapo*—to which they gave the non-literal English subtitle "Yoruba State Union." Its President, Alhaji N. B. Soule, a prominent businessman and Trustee of the NCNC, was chairman of the so-called Elders' Peace Committee of Lagos, an organization which had been conspicuous among the supporters of Dr. Mbadiwe and Chief Balogun.[28] Alhaji Adelabu, as General Secretary of the new

[26] Dr. Azikiwe missed the special convention of January 30, 1958, owing to the death of his mother; the presidential address ("Enforcement of Party Discipline") was read by the Second National Vice-President, Hon. R. A. Njoku, who presided.
[27] Minutes of the National Executive Committee Meeting of the NCNC, Enugu, January 29, 1958, pp. 4-5. (Mimeographed.)
[28] Subsequently Dr. Azikiwe revealed that the Elders' Committee of Lagos had recommended the creation of the office of Deputy Prime Minister of the Federation in April 1957. *Daily Times*, June 23, 1958. In addition to Alhaji N. B. Soule, prominent members of the Elders' Peace Committee included his fellow trustee of the NCNC, Mr. M. N. Ugochuku, and Chief H. O. Davies.

cultural group, affirmed both his unshakable loyalty to the NCNC and the "iron determination" of the members of the group to "co-operate with other ethnic groups in the NCNC only on the terms of absolute equality."[29] It seemed as though the formation of an anti-Azikiwe political cartel embracing ethnic associations and local factions within the NCNC had become a distinct possibility. In the West, opposition to Azikiwe was centered in the *Egbe Yoruba Parapo* and the Elders' Peace Committee of Lagos; in the East, increasingly vehement criticisms of Azikiwe by influential leaders of the Ibo State Union were indicative of the discontents of several local factions that were not unified on a regional basis. A particularly intense political conflict between local factions in the Eastern capital of Enugu gave rise to speculation about the formation of a broadly based opposition in the East.

THE ENUGU TANGLE

This study is concerned mainly with the distribution and the exercise of power within and among political parties. Although the focus of inquiry is centered on "power at the top," its scope encompasses lower-level phenomena which produce new leaders and condition the behavior of the men at the top. In the previous chapter we endeavored to indicate a circumstantial relationship between local politics in Onitsha and events of regional, national and international consequence; Chapter VII below is devoted entirely to the nationally significant subject of local politics in Ibadan. At this juncture, attention is drawn to a political struggle in the capital city of the Eastern Region which was interpreted widely as an augury of major opposition to the NCNC in Iboland.

The city of Enugu in Udi Division of the former Onitsha Province is the twentieth-century offspring of the coal mining industry. The mines were opened in 1915, and by 1948 there were 6,000 employees, mostly Udi men (of Ibo nationality), who lived in settlements near the collieries; by 1958 the work force had increased to 8,000.[30]

---

[29] *Daily Times*, February 17, 1958. Opponents of the Elders' Peace Committee in Lagos warned members of the NCNC to beware of the *Egbe Yoruba Parapo*. The officers of that group were announced as follows: President, Alhaji N. B. Soule; Vice-Presidents, Chief H. O. Davies, Mr. Alex Joaquim and Chief J. A. Oshibogun; General Secretary, Alhaji Adegoke Adelabu; Treasurer, Chief P. A. Afolabi; Legal Adviser, Chief Kola Balogun; Auditor, Mr. G. B. Akinyede. *Ibid.*

[30] In 1938 hewers in the Enugu mines were paid an average daily wage of 3s. 2d. *Report of the Commission of Enquiry into the Disorders in the Eastern Provinces of Nigeria*, November 1949 (London: 1950), p. 15. Twenty years later, grade one miners were paid 6s. 9d. per day.

It will be recalled that the massacre of 21 striking miners by police-men in 1949 served to arouse and inflame nationalistic sentiments throughout Nigeria.[31] After the designation of Enugu as the Ad-ministrative Headquarters of the Eastern Provinces in 1938, a "new middle class" of government employees and men of initiative in the professional, business, and service fields, drawn from all parts of the region, settled in the burgeoning city. By 1952 the population of Enugu totalled 62,000, rather more than half of whom were non-indigenous, i.e., non-Udi, settlers who, for the most part, were engaged in commercial activities or government work. By and large, their incomes and living standards were higher than those of the Udi people, most of whom were urban laborers, coal miners and small farmers.

During the Eastern parliamentary crisis of 1953, Enugu business-men formed an "Emergency Committee" which supported Azikiwe against the Eyo Ita government, mainly by raising a fund that was used to keep the wavering members of the House of Assembly in line. Conspicuous among the militant supporters of Azikiwe was the leader of the Enugu branch of the NCNC Youth Association, namely, Malam Umaru Altine, a Fulani cattle dealer from the Northern Province of Sokoto. In May 1953, Malam Umaru was elected President of the Enugu branch of the NCNC with the support of the cosmopolitan Ibo middle class. The following year, an association of indigenous people, called the Udi-Nsukka-Awgu United Front (Nsukka and Awgu are neighboring Divisions), nominated candi-dates to stand for election to the Enugu Urban District Council against the cosmopolitian branch of the NCNC. A majority of official party candidates were elected, and Malam Umaru Altine was chosen by them as chairman of the council. In 1956 Enugu was elevated to the status of a municipality. Prior to the first municipal election, party leaders made an attempt to reconcile the two factions, but the branch executive committee refused to endorse the candidatures of six former councillors who were affiliated with the Udi-Nsukka-Awgu United Front (UNAUF).[32] As a result of the election, 15 seats were won by the NCNC to 10 by the UNAUF, and Malam

[31] *Supra*, pp. 76-77.

[32] The UNAUF lodged a complaint with the NCNC Eastern Working Com-mittee, which appointed a committee to inquire into the selection of candidates. Its report exonerated the branch executive. *Report of an Inquiry into the Selection of Candidates for the Enugu Municipal Elections* by Dr. A. N. Ogbonna, Mr. K. J. M. Okpokam, and Mr. P. G. Warmate, March 1956. NCNC Eastern Working Com-mittee File No. 11:30. Only two members of the 30-member branch executive appear to have been nominated.

Umaru Altine was chosen by his fellow councillors as the first mayor of Enugu.

Meanwhile, a new political luminary emerged in the person of Christopher O. Chiedozie, the proprietor and headmaster of a secondary school, who was the secretary of the Enugu branch of the NCNC and the Deputy Mayor of Enugu. Although Mr. Chiedozie was a non-Udi settler from Awka Division, he assumed the role of spokesman for the Udi political cause. At an election meeting of the NCNC branch on November 10, 1956, Mayor Altine and Dr. G. C. Mbanugo, a prominent non-Udi medical practitioner who was also Chairman of the Eastern Region Finance Corporation, were elected without opposition as President and Vice-President of the branch respectively. When an overwhelming vote was cast to return Mr. Chiedozie as party secretary, the President-elect and the Vice-President-elect walked out, alleging that the hall was "packed" with non-members. Two days later, the Eastern Working Committee under the chairmanship of Dr. Michael I. Okpara, Eastern Minister of Health, supported Altine's declaration that the election of Chiedozie as branch secretary was void, and appointed a committee to inquire into the general management of the branch. The committee approved the decision of the Eastern Working Committee to nullify the branch election on the ground that non-members had participated in the meeting. Its report contained a sharp rebuke to a member of the Eastern House of Assembly who said in public that the conflict in Enugu was related to a higher-level rift between the Premier and supporters of the ex-Minister of Finance, Mbonu Ojike. It was, remonstrated the committee, "heinous and guttersnipe propaganda" to insinuate that some members of the party were anxious to overthrow the National President.[33]

That observation was heavy with the intrigue of its time. The Foster-Sutton Tribunal of Inquiry into the official conduct of Dr. Azikiwe had drawn to a close and its report was in the offing. It was rumored in sections of the press that certain high officials of the NCNC, including Dr. Okpara, Chairman of the Eastern Working Committee and senior minister in the Eastern Government, thought that the Premier should resign in the event of his condemnation by the tribunal. Ill feeling mounted when the Eastern Working Committee suspended Mr. Chiedozie and three of his associates for six months despite a recommendation of conciliation by its committee

[33] *Report of the Committee of Inquiry into the Enugu Branch of the NCNC* by Chief N. O. E. Edozien, Chairman, Hon. P. O. Nwoga, and Hon. B. E. Ogbuagu, November 1956. NCNC Eastern Working Committee File No. 11.

of inquiry. Thereupon, the *Eastern Sentinel*, a Zik Group daily news-paper in Enugu, extended the range of its hostile criticism from the conduct of the NCNC branch executive to the conduct of the officers of the Eastern Working Committee. Nominally, the editors of the Zik Group newspapers enjoy local autonomy and freedom of editorial expression, and it cannot be established that their opinions reflect the personal views of Dr. Azikiwe. But the *Eastern Sentinel's* sustained attack on the Eastern Working Committee did lead to con-jecture that Chiedozie and his associates were backed by the National President.

Under the Eastern Region Local Government Law, local councils are elected triennially and a chairman—styled mayor in the case of a municipality—is elected annually by the councillors. In April 1957, Malam Umaru Altine's support in the Enugu Municipal Council dwindled to the point of his replacement as mayor by Mr. L. B. C. Ezechi, an Udi merchant.[34] In response to this setback, the NCNC branch executive instructed all NCNC councillors to resign im-mediately. Seventeen of them complied, whereupon the Minister of Local Government dissolved the Municipal Council and appointed a caretaker committee pending another election.[35] When Dr. Azikiwe returned to Enugu from the London Constitutional Conference in August 1957, he promised a mass meeting of the Enugu community that he would seek to settle the dispute, and he terminated the sus-pensions of Mr. Chiedozie and his associates. In September he directed Dr. Okpara and two other Eastern ministers to resign their offices in the Eastern Working Committee because their party activities involved them in controversies that were apt to impair the per-formance of the regional government. Then Dr. Azikiwe appointed a special commission of inquiry under the chairmanship of the Acting National Secretary, Mr. F. S. McEwen, General Manager of the *West African Pilot*, to investigate the Enugu dispute and related matters.

The report of the McEwen commission censured the conduct of both the Eastern Working Committee and Mr. Chiedozie.[36] Acting

[34] Minutes of the Annual Meeting of the Enugu Municipality, April 3 and 10, 1957. (Mimeographed.)

[35] The eight remaining UNAUF councillors were just shy of the one-third membership required to form a lawful quorum. Two other councillors attempted without success to withdraw their resignations. See Report of the Sole Commis-sioner, N. Berwick, to the Minister of Local Government, 1957. (Files of the Enugu Municipal Council.)

[36] Report of the Proceedings of the Five-Man Commission of Inquiry set up by the National President of the NCNC, Dr. the Hon. Nnamdi Azikiwe, to In-vestigate Certain Serious Allegations against Party Leaders and Officers in Enugu,

upon its recommendation, the National President instructed an official of the National Headquarters to conduct a new registration of the Enugu branch. It was well understood that the newly registered members would elect a new branch executive committee which, in turn, would select the NCNC candidates for the impending Municipal Council election. For 12 hectic days the roll of members was open for registration; over 4,000 names were entered as each faction did its utmost to register a maximum number of its supporters.[37] In the end it was obvious that the UNAUF faction, now called the Enugu Indigenous Elements Union, had a decisive majority. The non-Udi faction alleged that the registration was rendered null and void by flagrant irregularities and decided to boycott the branch election in protest.[38] On January 31, 1958, a day after the special convention of the NCNC in Enugu, an estimated 3,000 persons, all supporters of the Indigenous Elements Union, mostly members of the politically active UNAUF women's section, elected by unanimous votes a slate of officers headed by the ex-Mayor, Mr. Ezechi, as President and Mr. Chiedozie as Secretary. The non-Udi faction responded by forming a "Stranger Elements Association," resolving to contest the election to the Enugu Municipal Council in opposition to the new official branch of the NCNC.

Undoubtedly the "Stranger Elements" were supported by the vast majority of the Enugu middle class, i.e., the well-to-do businessmen, professionals, and civil servants who were less than enthusiastic about the mass political power of the indigenes and generally disturbed by the demagogic tactics of Mr. Chiedozie. The leading person-

---

with a view to Effecting Peaceful Settlement of Outstanding Disputes Among Them, pp. 17, 18, 23. (Typed copy.)

[37] Both sides alleged the commission of flagrant abuses by the other. The outgoing branch officers charged that lorry loads of people from the countryside were transported into Enugu by the UNAUF. Mr. Chiedozie and the UNAUF leaders retorted that the wealthy backers of the old executive committee had raised a fund of several hundred pounds by means of which they paid the price of registration (1 shilling) and an additional bonus to potential supporters. When it appeared that UNAUF people were tapping the fund of their opponents, the non-Udi leaders adopted the precaution of collecting registration cards from individuals to be held in safe-keeping until the day of the branch election. However, the party official in charge of registration closed the roll when this abuse became flagrant.

[38] On January 30, 1958, the NCNC National Executive Committee directed the National Secretary to conduct a "peace meeting" prior to the branch election. He did so without avail a few hours before the election on January 31, at which time he told the representatives of the rival factions that the re-registration had netted the party several hundred pounds. But, he said, the party was not a mercantile organization and the chief object was the restoration of harmony in Enugu. He declared that the new register was valid despite the use of monetary inducements by the rival groups.

alities in the Stranger Elements Association were prominent businessmen: the ex-Mayor, Malam Umaru Altine; his fellow Northern
cattle dealer, Alhaji Baba Sule (President of the Association);
Mr. D. A. Nwandu, the Managing Director of the largest African
firm of building contractors in the Eastern Region[39] and an executive
member of the Ibo State Union (Vice President of the Association);
Mr. Izuchukwu Areh, a businessman and secretary of the Association
of Eastern Nigerian Civil Engineers and Building Contractors (Secretary). In brief, most of the "people who mattered" in Enugu,
including the leaders of the NCNC Eastern Working Committee
—the principal executive organ of the party in the region—and the
local leaders of the Zikist National Vanguard were hostile to the
NCNC local branch.[40]

Four days prior to the Enugu municipal election of March 3, 1958,
Dr. Azikiwe, his ministers, and the parliamentary secretaries of the
Eastern Government issued a proclamation of their full support for
the official candidates of the NCNC, admonishing the people of
Enugu to refrain from voting for irregular factions. On the eve of
the election the Stranger Elements Association proclaimed itself an
independent political party, called the Association For One Nigeria.
In a nip-and-tuck contest, the Association For One Nigeria defeated
the NCNC,[41] and Malam Umaru Altine, President of the new party,
was elected once again as the Mayor of Enugu.

It is difficult to assert with assurance that any one or another
single factor was mainly responsible for the Enugu struggle of 1958.
The Indigenous Elements/NCNC claimed to stand for the interests
of the underprivileged masses, most of whom were natives of Udi

[39] The Eastern General Contractors had been awarded contracts totalling more
than £300,000 by the Eastern Regional Government during the period 1954-1957.
Schedule of Contracts Other than Ration Contracts Awarded from October 1954-
1957, prepared by the Eastern Region Ministry of Finance. (Typed copy.)

[40] When the NCNC branch executive expelled ten leaders of the Stranger
Elements Association from the party, Dr. G. C. Mbanugo, Acting Chairman of
the Eastern Working Committee, asserted correctly that the expulsions did not
become effective until they had been ratified by higher party organs, namely the
Eastern Working Committee and the National Executive Committee (*Constitution
and Rules of the NCNC*, Rule X, Regulations 4 and 6). Thereupon the *Eastern
Sentinel* insinuated that Dr. Mbanugo and other officials of the Working Committee were actively supporting the candidates of the Stranger Elements Association
in the municipal election. *Eastern Sentinel*, February 28, 1958.

[41] Some 7,018 persons voted in the Enugu municipal election of March 3, 1958,
in 22 contested wards. The NCNC obtained a total vote of 3316 and returned 11
candidates in addition to one unopposed; the Association For One Nigeria had a
total vote of 3166, returning 9 candidates in addition to 2 unopposed. Two successful
independents declared for the Association For One Nigeria, giving it a majority
of 13-12 in the council.

Division. The Association For One Nigeria claimed to oppose in principle the alleged "bossism" of Chiedozie and the attempt of the Udi indigenes to control the government of Enugu merely because it is situated in their homeland. Both the ethnic and the class characteristics of each faction were reflected in their respective slates of candidates and in the pattern of voting. (Thus, 74 percent of the NCNC candidates were natives of Udi, Nsukka, or Awgu Divisions, compared with 22 percent of the AFON candidates; 65 percent of the AFON candidates were identified as businessmen of entrepreneurial rank as compared with 26 percent of the NCNC list; 48 percent of the NCNC candidates were in the petty trade, craftsman, and storekeeper category, compared with 13 percent of the AFON list.[42] The NCNC won all 5 seats in Ogbette or Coal Camp, an Udi mining district, and the AFON won all 4 seats in the non-Udi commercial area of Asata.)

If economic differentiation was as important a factor as this discussion suggests, it is reasonable to suppose that tangible economic benefits were at stake in the municipal election. But that does not appear to have been the case. It was alleged that the party in power could reward its supporters by means of favoritism in contract awards. But regional regulations governing the award of contracts had withdrawn the power of local government councils to make such awards except in the case of petty contracts valued at less than £50.[43] It is not unknown for a council to split up large contracting jobs in order to create petty contracts that it may then award, possibly on a partisan basis. But that kind of petty jobbery was not likely to lure substantial businessmen into a major political campaign involving the formation of a new party.[44] Similarly, the Municipal Council had very little power with respect to the allocation of plots in Enugu[45] and none with respect to taxation, since responsibility for

[42] *Infra*, p. 488, Table 4.

[43] Local Government Tenders Boards Regulations, 1956, E.R.L.N. No. 94 of 1956.

[44] The contracting plums desired by the leading business personalities of the Association For One Nigeria were considerably beyond the limited competence of the Municipal Council to pluck. For example, in October 1957, the Minister of Local Government approved the application of the Eastern General Contractors (whose general manager, one of two principal owners, D. A. Nwandu, became Vice President of the Stranger Elements Association AFON) for the contract to build municipal offices, worth about £25,000. Minutes of the Enugu Urban District Council, Caretaker Council and the Finance and Education Committee, October 25, 1957. (Mimeographed.)

[45] About 95% of the land in the Enugu township is Crown (Government) land and plots are allocated by the Commissioner of Lands with the approval of the Minister of Town Planning. Large tracts of Crown land have been leased to the Municipal Council for specific purposes, e.g., markets, industrial sites, lorry parks,

tax assessment, collection, and appeals had been vested in the Commissioner for Internal Revenue. Market stalls were allocated by a raffling system that was free of partiality. Rates on property, fees, licenses, and the engagement of local staff were subject to the Council's authority, and may have provided patronage opportunities, but not on a scale that was nearly grand enough to provoke a major political effort. In sum it does not appear that either the economic stakes or the patronage ends of the Enugu municipal election were particularly significant.

Yet a more determined effort to defeat the NCNC in Dr. Azikiwe's capital could hardly be imagined. An obvious explanation is in terms of the explosive antagonism between the Udi indigenes and the relatively well-to-do commercial and professional "strangers." Another arguable interpretation conceives the local struggle in the context of a wider contest involving the top leaders of the NCNC in the Eastern Region. There was no doubt that the Association For One Nigeria enjoyed the discreetly advertised sympathy of certain ministers and leaders of the Eastern Working Committee—notably Dr. M. I. Okpara, Minister of Production (formerly Health), who resigned as Chairman of the Working Committee at Dr. Azikiwe's request in September 1957, and his successor, Dr. G. C. Mbanugo. While their support of the Stranger Elements-Association For One Nigeria was not avowed, the position was known in Enugu and made plain editorially by the *Eastern Sentinel*.[46] On the other hand, Mr. Chiedozie and the NCNC-Indigenous Elements had the vigorous support of the *Eastern Sentinel*[47] and the apparent backing of the National President.[48] Persistent attacks on Dr. Okpara by the

---

etc., which may be sub-leased to individuals with the approval of the Commissioner of Lands. Sub-leases are made infrequently and appear to have no political importance.

[46] *Eastern Sentinel*, February 28, 1958.

[47] In 1957 the NCNC Enugu branch executive alleged that the *Eastern Sentinel* refused to publish reports of branch activities in connection with the election campaign of February-March, while it gave prominence to all activities of the Chiedozie group. *NCNC Enugu Information Committee, No. 1: "Eastern Sentinel" Friend or Foe?* In April and May 1957, the *Sentinel* continued its attacks on Malam Umaru Altine, Dr. Mbanugo, and others until the NCNC Principal Organizing Secretary of the Eastern Region felt obliged to make a formal complaint to Mr. A. K. Blankson, the Managing Director of the Associated Newspapers of Nigeria (Zik Group). While Dr. Azikiwe cannot be held responsible for the editorial policies of the Zik Group of newspapers, especially insofar as he had relinquished his directorships to Mr. Blankson, it would seem unreasonable to suppose that units of the Zik Group chain propagated views contrary to those of Dr. Azikiwe for any prolonged length of time.

[48] Mr. Chiedozie's campaign was supported openly by two of Dr. Azikiwe's closest lieutenants in the Eastern Government—Hon. B. C. Okwu, the Minister of

Eastern Sentinel elicited indignant protests by an Owerri Provincial Union[49] and by the influential Bende Divisional Union in defense of its favorite son. These complaints were echoed within the Ibo State Union as were the grievances of the Association For One Nigeria. It is reasonable to assume that the AFON position was regarded with sympathy by NCNC leaders in other urban centers of Iboland, as the majority of those leaders belonged to a socio-economic stratum comparable to that of the founders of the AFON.[50] At Aba in particular, where settler-indigene hostility has been acute, the Udi movement in Enugu might have been viewed as a dangerous precedent.[51] Nor should it be assumed that rural leaders in other divisions were necessarily sympathetic to the Udi cause. Tribal sensibilities are parochial and rural leaders throughout Iboland were as likely to support their kinsmen among the "stranger elements" in Enugu as they were to sympathize with the indigene movement.[52]

This section was introduced with a suggestion to the effect that the Enugu struggle may have been an omen of general opposition to

---

Information, and Hon. M. E. Ogon, the Government Chief Whip. It may be objected that the report of the McEwen Commission of Inquiry was highly critical of Mr. Chiedozie and that Dr. Azikiwe recited these criticisms in the course of his presidential address to the Aba Convention in October 1957. But the Enugu branch election of January 31, 1958 was conducted by the National Secretary with Dr. Azikiwe's knowledge and consent and, as we have seen, the Executive Council of his Government applied the weight of its influence in support of the NCNC-Indigenous Elements in an eleventh hour effort to prevent a "Stranger Elements" victory. In December 1959, Mr. Chiedozie was elected to represent Enugu in the Federal House of Representatives.

[49] NCNC Eastern Working Committee File 18: 57, letter dated 21 May 1957; and *Daily Service*, October 2, 1957; an Owerri Youth Association was reported to have denounced the McEwen Commission of Inquiry into Enugu affairs as a "continuation of the plot of a clique that is out to discredit Dr. M. I. Okpara." *Ibid.*, October 15, 1957.

[50] Data compiled by the writer indicates that more than 60% of all members of the NCNC branch executive committees in Onitsha, Port Harcourt, and Aba, in addition to NCNC candidates for or members of Municipal or Urban District Councils in these cities in 1958 were classifiable as entrepreneurs, professionals, educators, and clerical or managerial personnel. Some 34% were petty tradesmen, craftsmen, and shopkeepers. *Infra*, p. 488, Table 4.

[51] Aba is a new town with a population, in 1953, of 57,787, situated in the homeland of the Ngwa Ibo tribe. In 1958 the writer determined that all members of the Aba NCNC branch executive and the Aba Urban District Council were non-Ngwa. Previously, petitions from townspeople to separate the Aba urban area from the jurisdiction of the Aba-Ngwa County Council had been opposed by Ngwa elements and denied by the government. See R. Coatswith, *Report of an Inquiry into a Proposal to Excise the Aba Urban District from the Aba-Ngwa County* (Enugu: 1954).

[52] The writer reached this conclusion after discussions with influential rural leaders in the former Owerri Province.

the NCNC in Iboland. At the very least it brought into play organized political groups representing substantial social interests which might have been responsive to the appeal of a region-wide opposition.

The Politics of Democracy

Azikiwe's troubles came in buckets in the spring of 1958. The Enugu election in itself was a disconcerting upset; in the light of concomitant adverse developments it assumed the shape of a minor debacle. The greatest setback for the Eastern Government stemmed from an unforeseen financial strain in connection with its program of free primary education, requiring the re-introduction of school fees which had been abolished for all primary grades (Infant I to Standard VI) since January 1957. Briefly, the Eastern Government had appropriated some £2,886,000 for education in the fiscal year 1956-57, but the actual costs of education were, for a variety of reasons, some £2,560,000 greater than the estimates, with the result that the Eastern Government's expenditure on education reached the unprecedent level of 43 percent of its total budget. Moreover, the estimated £6 million that would be required for education in 1958 was beyond the ability of the regional government to provide.[53] Therefore the government decided reluctantly to re-introduce enrollment and tuition fees.

Education is highly prized in Eastern Nigeria, as it is in all of renascent Africa, but school fees weigh heavily on the limited incomes of the farmers and their womenfolk, who trade in the village markets and frequently bear the expense of sending their children to school. One commentator assessed the burden on "a farmer with an average family of four children" in various grades thus:[54]

" . . . the man will be faced with the problem of finding about £10 enrollment and school fees. This of course excludes school books, uniforms and other contributions. Then in addition, he is called upon to pay taxes and rates amounting to at least £2. Nor is this all. Local community projects including new school buildings and upkeep of old ones, roads, maternity centres, etc., will entail a minimum contribution of not less than £5. The implications of all these are that

[53] See the speech by Dr. Azikiwe, Premier of Eastern Nigeria, in the Eastern House of Assembly, February 13, 1958 (*Daily Times*, February 14, 1958). Dr. Azikiwe stated that the Eastern Nigerian expenditure of 43% of its budget for education was higher than that of any country in the world; he declared further that the anticipated primary school enrollment of 1,500,000 was greater than that of any country in Africa.
[54] Kamanu, "Reintroduce Free Education Scheme Stage by Stage," *Daily Times*, February 4, 1958.

the poorest of farmers who lives from hand to mouth will be called upon under the arrangements to provide more than he can ever hope to earn in a year for the education of his children. [In 1953, the average per capita income in the Eastern Region was estimated at £21 per annum.] The immediate effect is that the majority of the children who were poured into the schools last year when the scheme began will be automatically withdrawn much to the discomfiture of parents and the disappointment of the children themselves."

Clearly the government had been less than prudent—not merely in its unfortunate miscalculation of costs, but also in its failure to prepare public opinion for a bitter disappointment. Throughout the region, people reacted in disillusionment with anger. Wrathful crowds of women demonstrated in several towns; in a few extreme cases they were reported to have denounced the NCNC and its program for self-government.[55] Police units were sent to the Eastern Region from Lagos and the Governor-General was obliged to proclaim a state of emergency in nine administrative divisions. At a special session of the Eastern House of Assembly, government spokesmen announced a modification of the schedule of fees but held firm to the principle that increased costs would be defrayed by "assumed local contributions." Some two weeks after the adjournment of the House of Assembly, the NCNC lost control of the Enugu Municipal Council to the Association For One Nigeria, and it would not have been unreasonable for Azikiwe's opponents to presume that the Premier's popularity had begun to wane.

On March 25, 1958, Nigeria was stunned by the accidental death of the 43-year-old Alhaji Adegoke Adelabu; the collision of Adelabu's car with the car of a European on the Lagos-Ibadan highway deprived the NCNC of its principal leader in the Western Region. No other NCNC personality possessed the political stature to occupy the three crucial posts that were held by Adelabu—Leader of the Opposition in the Western House of Assembly, chairman of the NCNC Western Working Committee, and chairman of the powerful NCNC organization in Ibadan (the NCNC-*Mabolaje* Grand Alliance). Adelabu's death created a leadership vacuum in the West which forced the hand of the anti-Azikiwe faction. If Azikiwe's opponents were passive, Adelabu's posts were likely to be assumed or seized by lieutenants of Azikiwe, his name was likely to be appropriated by NCNC propagandists who would depict him as a martyr to the NCNC cause, and the likelihood of an effective opposition to Azikiwe would be

[55] See reports in the *Daily Times*, January 27-February 19, 1958.

diminished. The anti-Azikiwe faction decided to strike while the impression of Adelabu's recent hostility to Azikiwe was fresh.[55a]

Although Azikiwe sent a delegation of Eastern ministers, led by Dr. M. I. Okpara, then Minister of Production and Leader of the Eastern House of Assembly, to Adelabu's funeral, many Ibadan people took umbrage at the failure of the National President to attend personally. Meetings were held between the leaders of the Ibadan NCNC and leaders of the interlocking *Egbe Yoruba Parapo* (Yoruba State Union) and the Lagos Elders' Peace Committee to settle in advance the choice of a successor to the chairmanship of the Western Working Committee. On June 8, Dr. Mbadiwe presided over a meeting of the Western Working Committee at Ibadan; in attendance were Alhaji N. B. Soule, President of the *Egbe Yoruba Parapo*, Chief H. O. Davies, Vice-President of the *Egbe Yoruba Parapo*, who had been National Legal Adviser of the NCNC until the Aba Convention, and Chief Kolawole Balogun, Federal Minister of Research and Information, ex-National Secretary of the NCNC, and Legal Adviser of the *Egbe Yoruba Parapo*. All but a few of Azikiwe's strong supporters in Lagos and the Western Region were conspicuously absent. With the enthusiastic support of the Ibadan leadership, Chief H. O. Davies, a barrister, celebrated figure in the nationalist movement and long-time critic of Azikiwe, was elected Chairman of the Western Working Committee. (Davies, at 53, was but one year younger than Azikiwe; his descent is Ekiti and Ibadan/Oyo Yoruba. It will be recalled that he returned to Nigeria after a period of study in England in 1937, the year of Azikiwe's return from the Gold Coast, and that he was a founder of both the Nigerian Youth Movement and the *Daily Service*.)[56]

[55a] Spokesmen for the NCNC have insisted that Adelabu would never have broken faith with Azikiwe. Fred. U. Anyiam, then Acting National Secretary, reports that Adelabu had disappointed Mbadiwe and commented adversely on the *Egbe Yoruba Parapo* during a meeting of the Western Working Committee at Ijebu-Ode on March 8, 1958. *Men and Matters in Nigerian Politics (1934-58)* (Lagos: 1959), p. 67.

[56] *Supra*, pp. 49, 52-53, 77, 111. Davies was elected chairman of the Western Working Committee by the nearly unanimous vote of 108-3. One distinguished member, Chief S. J. Mariere, MHR (Urhobo) criticized the proceedings on the ground that the meeting was not properly constituted; he explained that he decided to participate only because the psychological effect of not holding a meeting which had been scheduled and improperly cancelled by an unauthorized press release would be detrimental to the party. On the following day, the validity of the election was disputed by the Acting National Publicity Secretary. *Daily Times*, June 10, 1958.

Meanwhile, on June 2, Dr. Azikiwe paid a state visit to the Premier of the Northern Region, Alhaji Ahmadu, the Sardauna of Sokoto, in Kaduna, returning the Sardauna's visit to Enugu of the previous April. The two Premiers were reported to have discussed governmental matters only, but Action Group sources speculated upon the conclusion of a secret pact between Azikiwe and the Sardauna at the expense of radical parties allied to the NCNC in the North.[57] On June 12, the Bornu Youth Movement affirmed the Action Group allegation as it terminated its alliance with the NCNC and the Northern Elements Progressive Union, citing the NCNC-Northern Peoples' Congress negotiation as one reason, and entered into a new pact with the Action Group.[58] On June 13, Azikiwe passed through Ibadan en route to Lagos, pausing in the Western capital to pay his respects at the late Adelabu's grave.[59] He was scheduled to attend a meeting of the National Executive Committee and a conference of the heads of governments in Nigeria, following which he would sail to Europe for a vacation and discussions in connection with the projected new University of Nigeria (established by the Eastern Government) and other official matters.

On the morning of June 14, 1958 he met informally with representatives of the Lagos Market Women's Association, and in the afternoon the NCNC National Executive Committee assembled at the Lagos City College (Yaba), an institution founded by Dr. Azikiwe. In addition to the regular members of the National Executive Committee, invitations to attend (without voting rights) were extended to all NCNC ministers, parliamentary secretaries, members of statutory boards, and certain other prominent leaders in all regions and Lagos. As a result, there were many people in the hall in addition to 34 of the 41 regular members of the National Executive Committee when Dr. Azikiwe called the meeting to order and announced the agenda. Barrister R. A. Akinyemi, Chairman of the Lagos branch of the NCNC Youth Association, asked permission

[57] *Daily Service*, May 31, 1958; also see the *Daily Times*, June 2, 1958.

[58] Communication from the Bornu Youth Movement to the President General of the Northern Elements Progressive Union . . . June 12, 1958. NCNC National Headquarters File.

[59] At the graveside of the late Alhaji Adegoke Adelabu, Dr. Azikiwe announced that the NCNC would provide scholarships for all 15 of his children. The Eastern Premier made "a cash donation of £100 and expressed the desire to be responsible for the education of one of them." *Daily Times*, June 14, 1958. At the June 8th meeting of the Western Working Committee, Ibadan leaders spoke in opposition to Azikiwe's visit to Adelabu's grave, giving as their reason the argument that any disturbance in Ibadan might provide a pretext for the Western Government to suspend the holding of the impending local government election.

to read a petition signed by twelve young men (mostly Ibo), including three leaders of the Aba branch of the Zikist National Vanguard, that was known to demand Azikiwe's resignation as National President of the NCNC and Premier of the Eastern Region. Azikiwe ruled that statements by members would be in order following the presidential address. He then delivered a short sermonish speech, entitled "Before the Darkness Falls," and he admonished everyone to take the title personally—i.e., "Before the darkness falls on me."

The party, he observed, was passing through a troubled time; "the leadership," he said, "is confused and the followership is very much perplexed." At this meeting he trusted that everyone would "forgive and forget the past." He was authorized by the Central Working Committee to announce a general amnesty for all those who had been suspended or expelled within the previous year. In the face of a mounting political offensive by a "ruthless foe"—the Action Group—it was, he said, imperative for all supporters of the NCNC to close ranks. As a result of his "courtesy visit" to the Northern Region, he was in a position to say that his appraisal of the Action Group was shared "by the God-fearing compatriots who constitute the majority among the inhabitants of the North." He thought there was a tendency among youths to overlook the "divine factor" in human affairs; nothing was needed more than prayer, and he closed his speech by reciting a birthday prayer that President Eisenhower broadcast to the American nation in 1953 (from which he took the title of his address) "now known in history as 'Uncle Sam's Prayer.' "[60]

Rarely had Azikiwe delivered a more trivial speech in a less heroic manner,[61] but its effect seems to have been calculated; a few persons who were devoted to the cause of the party and grieved by the course of events were moved to tears. Chief Festus Sam Okotie-Eboh, the Federal Minister of Finance and National Treasurer of the NCNC, proposed an adjournment of the meeting in order to give everyone an opportunity to ponder the President's appeal for reconciliation, but this was voted down. Mr. O. N. Egesi of Aba, the representative of the Ex-Servicemen of the Eastern Region in the National Executive Committee, arose to read two documents calling upon Dr. Azikiwe to resign forthwith from the leadership of

[60] This address was released to the press; see *Daily Times*, June 16, 1958.
[61] He even quoted Cecil B. De Mille, "the producer of that great film, King of Kings, 'that the purpose of this life is understanding of the spirit and not worship before the calf of gold.' " *Ibid.*

the party and the Premiership of the East. The principal document was signed by 31 persons who went on record as having "lost confidence" in the leadership of Dr. Azikiwe; seven specific complaints were listed: the removal of the late Mazi Mbonu Ojike as Eastern Minister of Finance as a result of the Bribery Commission before its report had been received by the Eastern Government; the removal of two Eastern ministers and three parliamentary secretaries following the Eastern general election of 1957, contrary to the spirit in which the Eastern Government had resigned in order to vindicate Dr. Azikiwe despite the fact that the National Executive Committee of the party had not been aware of the events leading to his quarrel with the Secretary of State for the Colonies; the abolition of elective national officers at the Aba Convention; the alleged failure of the National President to support the party's policy on the question of creating additional states; the manner of the abandonment of free primary education in the East; the "rush" to build a university in the East despite the failure of the primary education scheme; the National President's alleged loss of interest in the affairs of the party.[62] The signatories included two federal ministers (Dr. K. O. Mbadiwe and Chief Kolawole Balogun), their parliamentary secretaries, the three trustees of the party (N. B. Soule, M. N. Ugochukwu, and J. Green Mbadiwe), Chief H. O. Davies, chairman of the Western Working Committee, a few prominent Eastern businessmen, including the Vice-President of the Enugu Association For One Nigeria, the Administrative Secretary of the Ibo State Union, and the leader of the strong NCNC branch at Oyo in the Western Region. Yorubas comprised the largest nationality group among the signatories and four of the nine Ibo signatories were identified as Aro-Ibo.[63] Two of the signatories were executive members of the Ibadan branch, but an Ibadan representative stated that the declaration came as a surprise to the Ibadan delegates and did not reflect their point of view.[64]

[62] See "Release No. 1 of the NCNC Reform Committee" and *Daily Times*, June 16, 1958; the second document was printed as "Release No. 2 of the NCNC Reform Committee: A Loyal Address from the Youth of Nigeria to Dr. Nnamdi Azikiwe."

[63] These included Dr. K. O. Mbadiwe, Mr. J. Green Mbadiwe (a trustee of the National Council and prominent businessman), Mr. L. N. Obioha (a very wealthy produce buyer in the East), and Mr. C. N. Obioha (a director of the African Insurance Company and Chairman of the Aba Urban District Council; also a brother-in-law of the late Ojike). The writer assumes it is understood that these ethnic factors are mentioned because they were regarded by those involved as having political significance. He does not intend, by such mention, to detract in any way from the importance of the non-ethnic issues and arguments *per se*.

[64] NCNC, Minutes of the National Executive Committee Meeting held at the

Dr. Mbadiwe and Alhaji N. B. Soule (President of the *Egbe Yoruba Parapo* and a trustee of the NCNC) made brief statements expressing regret that matters had come to this pass. Soule observed that Azikiwe had refused to honor an invitation to meet with a delegation of the Elders' Peace Committee. As Soule and Mbadiwe rose to leave the hall, Azikiwe replied that he had received merely a telegram from the Elders' Peace Committee, in Soule's name, requesting him to meet members of the Committee at Benin in the Mid-West to answer seven allegations. He said that he did respect genuine "elders," like Alhaji Soule and Pa Joacquim, but that most of the members of the Committee were younger than himself and that the Elders' Peace Committee was in any event extraneous to the party organization. Moreover, "when he found out that one of the names on the list of the Elders' Peace Committee was among those eight who were alleged to have plotted against his life in 1957, he did not come."[65] Angrily, Dr. Mbadiwe took exception to Azikiwe's insinuation of attempted murder. He said that the impasse had reached a virtual state of war and he left the meeting with Alhaji Soule, Chief H. O. Davies, Chief Kolawole Balogun, and their supporters. The "loyalists" —a large majority of the National Executive Committee and the invited observers—milled around shaking hands with one another and exchanging words of encouragement. Radical members of the Youth Association interpreted the breach as a vindication of their views and a reversal of their previous defeat by the "bourgeois" ministerial group at the Ibadan Convention of 1955.[66] When the meeting resumed, nearly every speaker urged the National President to cancel his trip abroad and to rededicate himself to militant leadership of the party. At length Azikiwe replied:

He declared that the controversy between Mbadiwe and himself was essentially personal; that his blood was troubling some people and that he had anticipated the attempt on his life of the previous April, although he had been informed to beware of April 18 rather than April 16, when the attack occurred. In December 1956, he said, certain people gave him four months to live. As a student of history, he knew too well that the leaders of mass movements were apt to be killed; he was not self-destructive, and he would not await the blow of the axe like a tree that was about to be cut. He said that on board ship, returning from the London Constitutional Conference of

Lagos City College Hall, Yaba, on Saturday and Sunday, June 14 and 15, 1958, p. 3. (Mimeographed.)

[65] *Ibid.*, p. 4.

[66] *Supra*, p. 150.

1957, he told Dr. Mbadiwe that he believed him to be "after my blood." Mbadiwe, he said, "flatly denied" the allegation; he was prepared to accept a denial covering Dr. Mbadiwe and his relatives, but he thought that inasmuch as "the two of us were Ibo-speaking, we should perform an oath-taking ceremony which Ibo people call 'Igbandu.' I suggested that he should arrange for this event to take place neither at Arondizuogu, his home town, nor at Onitsha, my home town, but that it should be held at a neutral place in Iboland, where we should be represented by four to six relatives each side." Dr. Mbadiwe, he said, has not been willing to agree to perform the "Igbandu" ceremony, and until he does "I shall forever be suspicious of him, even though I concede to him that he and his relatives may be innocent." [These quotations are taken from the press report of a speech delivered by Dr. Azikiwe one week later in which he repeated in substantially identical language his extemporaneous comments of June 14th.][67] Dr. Azikiwe said that he would cancel his plans to go abroad in compliance with the will of the National Executive Committee.

On the following day, the National Executive Committee expelled Dr. Mbadiwe, Chief Balogun, and Chief Davies along with two Federal Parliamentary Secretaries, Messrs. O. Bademosi and O. U. Ndem. It was reported that the three trustees of the National Council had proclaimed their decision to dismiss Dr. Azikiwe from his office of National President, an action for which there was no basis in the Constitution of the NCNC, and they were therefore replaced by the National Executive Committee.[68] The Western Working Committee was dissolved and the Central Working Committee was instructed to supervise a new election of Western Regional officers. For purposes of immediate and vigorous action against the rebel group, a "Strategic

[67] The writer, who was privileged to attend the meetings of the NCNC National Executive Committee on June 14 and 15, 1958, has, in general, refrained from the attribution of statements to particular individuals. Those statements which have been attributed to speakers prior to the departure of Dr. Mbadiwe and his associates are widely known and were reported in the official minutes; the opening presidential address was reported in the press and the remarks attributed to Dr. Azikiwe at this point in the text were, in the main, repeated by him in a public address delivered in Isalegangan Square, Lagos, on June 21, 1958 and reported fully in the *Daily Times* on June 23, 1958, from which the quotations in the text are taken. This speech should be considered in conjunction with Dr. Mbadiwe's statement to the press on behalf of the NCNC Reform Committee, *Daily Times*, June 20, 1958, and the publication of a letter by Dr. Mbadiwe to Dr. Azikiwe dated March 19, 1957 in the *Daily Service*, June, 1958.

[68] The NCNC Constitution vests all movable and immovable property belonging to the party in the trustees of the National Council, who hold office "during the pleasure of the National Executive Committee." Article XI.

Committee" was formed by the National Executive Committee with the Central Working Committee as its nucleus.[69] It was decided that the National President should remain in Lagos for two weeks to consolidate his support in the West, and to participate actively in local and parliamentary election campaigns that were due to be held shortly in Ibadan.

Meanwhile the rebel group proclaimed itself the NCNC Reform Committee with Dr. Mbadiwe as Chairman, Chief Davies as First Vice-Chairman, Chief Balogun as General Secretary and two wealthy businessmen—Alhaji N. B. Soule, the founder of the new Muslim Bank in Lagos, and Mr. L. N. Obioha, an Eastern produce buyer —as Patron and Vice-Patron respectively.[70] Clearly the fate of

[69] Members of the Strategic Committee were as follows: Dr. Azikiwe (National President), Hon. J. O. Fadahunsi (First National Vice-President), Hon. R. A. Njoku (Second National Vice-President), Mr. F. S. McEwen (National Secretary), Hon. Chief F. S. Okotie-Eboh (National Treasurer), Hon. T. O. S. Benson (National Financial Secretary), Mr. A. K. Blankson (National Auditor), Hon. D. C. Osadebay (National Legal Adviser), Mr. Fred U. Anyiam (National Publicity Secretary), Chief O. A. Fagbenro-Beyioku (Secretary of the Marine African Workers Union and an acting national officer), Mr. Adeniran Ogunsanya (a Lagos barrister and President-General of the NCNC Youth Association), Chief H. Omo-Osagie (Leader of the strong NCNC organization in Benin), Hon. J. M. Udochi (a barrister and prominent member of the Western Working Committee from Afenmai), Mr. H. P. Adebola (Secretary of the Railway and Ports Transport Staff Union), Mr. Kehinde Shofola (a Lagos barrister), and Mrs. Keziah Fashina (Chairman of the NCNC Lagos Women's Association). Minutes of the National Executive Committee of the NCNC, June 14 and 15, 1958, p. 7.

[70] The officers and National Executive Committee of the NCNC Reform Committee, chosen at a two-day conference in Glover Memorial Hall, Lagos, in July 1958, follow. (The list of names was published by the *Daily Service*, July 21, 1958; personal data was obtained by the writer.)

Patron: Alhaji N. B. Soule—Yoruba (Oyo), Founder and Managing Director of the Muslim Bank; wealthy merchant; former Trustee of the NCNC.

Vice-Patron: Mr. L. N. Obioha—Aro-Ibo (Okigwe), produce buyer.

National Chairman: Dr. K. O. Mbadiwe—Aro-Ibo (Orlu), ex-Federal Minister of Commerce and Industries.

First Vice-Chairman: Chief (barrister) H. O. Davies—Yoruba (Ekiti-Oyo).

Second Vice-Chairman: Mr. I. R. E. Iweka—Obosi Ibo (Onitsha), engineer.

General Secretary: Chief (barrister) Kolawole Balogun—Yoruba (Oshun), ex-Federal Minister of Research and Information.

Assistant General Secretary: Y. M. Opere—Yoruba, Lagos estate agent.

National Publicity Secretary: U. O. Ndem, MHR—Efik (Calabar), ex-Federal parliamentary secretary.

National Treasurer: O. Bademosi, MHR—Yoruba (Ondo), ex-Federal Parliamentary Secretary.

National Auditor: C. N. Obioha—Aro-Ibo (Aba), Chairman of the Aba Urban District Council, Director of the African Insurance Company.

Members of the National Executive Committee:

Pa Alex Joacquim—Lagos Yoruba, educator, elder and member of the old Nigerian National Democratic Party under Herbert Macaulay.

F. Adeshina—Yoruba, Lagos businessman.

the Reformers hinged mainly on the reaction of the people of the Eastern Region, where Dr. Mbadiwe counted upon the active support of Aro elements generally.[71] It remained to be seen if he would be able to carry other Ibo groups which had been critical of Azikiwe's Administration, in particular, certain discontented elements in Owerri Province, and the influential business elements in the Association For One Nigeria and the Ibo State Union. Within a week, it was obvious that he would not be able to do so. Mbadiwe's defeat in the East was ensured by a multitude of resolutions supporting the Premier which were adopted with bandwagon effect by community organizations at the local level, including local government councils and ethnic group associations. Had these resolutions gone against the Premier, Azikiwe might have fallen. Dr. M. I. Okpara, who was in England on leave and official business, wired his declaration of loyalty from abroad, and returned to Nigeria to support his Premier; the President of the Ibo State Union declared for Azikiwe; the Association For One Nigeria repudiated the Reformers;[72] several

---

M. Thompson—Yoruba, Lagos businessman.
A. G. Oluwo—Yoruba, Lagos businessman and accountant.
S. B. Oni—Yoruba (Lagos), accountant for the African Development Corporation.
A. I. Davies—Yoruba (Lagos), pensioner.
E. B. Etchie—Warri Division, U.A.C. clerk.
S. O. Oyedokun—Yoruba (Oshun), school manager.
E. T. Adewoyin—Yoruba (Ife), produce buyer.
B. A. Adeyemo—Yoruba.
Peter Daramola—Yoruba (Lagos), pensioner.
A. B. Young—Organizing Secretary for the Reform Committee.
P. A. Afolabi, MHA—Oyo Yoruba (leader of the Egbe Oyo Parapo).
S. F. Odumuyi—Yoruba.
J. O. Osibogun—Yoruba (Ijebu-Ode), transporter and real estate owner.
Dr. O. N. Egesi—Ibo, President of the Eastern Ex-Servicemen's Association.
Dr. Iweka—Obosi Ibo (Onitsha), medical practitioner.
Mr. Onwuzulike—Ibo, Enugu businessman.
J. A. Nwanne—Ibo, Deputy President-General of the Zikist National Vanguard.
Chief Jombo—Ijaw (Okrika), pensioner.
B. Dike.
Mr. Onumba—Ibo, trader (Aba).
Mrs. M. Nwugu—Aro-Ibo (Orlu), housewife.

[71] The Arondizuogu Patriotic Union declared its support of the Reform Committee, and a meeting of the chiefs and people of Orlu Division (Dr. Mbadiwe's constituency) on June 21, 1958, comprising Aro and non-Aro elements, passed a vote of confidence in the Federal Minister. *Daily Times,* June 21, 23 and July 4, 1958.

[72] Eventually the NCNC Enugu branch executive was dissolved and Malam Umaru Altine, President of the AFON, became President of the Enugu NCNC; his former opponents, L. B. C. Ezechi and C. O. Chiedozie, became Vice-President and Secretary respectively; the latter was adopted as the Enugu NCNC candidate in the federal election of 1959.

signatories to the so-called "Zik Must Go" document, including a former trustee of the NCNC and a managing director of the largest African contracting firm in Enugu, withdrew from the Reform Committee. It was alleged that a few of those who backed out were under pressure from the African Continental Bank for the repayment of overdrafts, and were threatened with the loss of their property that was mortgaged to the bank.[73]

In June and July, Azikiwe toured the Eastern Region with a party of loyalists from the East and the West, visiting every division and about 40 district council areas. Formal votes of confidence were presented to him in every division save in Orlu, Mbadiwe's constituency.[74] At a meeting in Orlu, with Dr. Mbadiwe present, Dr. Azikiwe renewed his proposal to perform a traditional covenant with his rival. In fairness to Dr. Mbadiwe, he could not accept Azikiwe's offer without giving some color of substantiation to Azikiwe's allegation of his complicity in a plot to assassinate the Premier. As a remedy for the dispute, he remonstrated, the "Igbandu" covenant was neither appropriate nor dignified. In this respect, Mbadiwe's views were seconded by non-Ibo lieutenants of Azikiwe, who objected to any course of action that would transform the controversy into "an Ibo affair."[75] For this reason the NCNC rejected offers of mediation by the Ibo State Union or "Peace Committees" associated with the

[73] The Reform Committee was reported to have objected to the use of the African Continental Bank for partisan ends on the ground that it was a depository of public funds. *Daily Times*, June 18, 1958; *Nigerian Tribune*, June 18, 1958; *Daily Service*, June 25, 1958.

[74] Dr. Azikiwe told a meeting of the NCNC National Executive Committee in Lagos, August 24, 1958, that, as he saw it, the general consensus of the people of the district councils was not that of animosity toward Dr. Mbadiwe as an individual or toward the Reform Committee *per se*, but a feeling that their methods had not been constitutional. That, he remarked, was an important aspect of the situation which foreign commentators did not seem to appreciate. Most of the councils, he said, made token gestures of their feelings by presenting to the delegates symbolic objects, like brooms, disinfectants, bows and arrows, swords ("in fact I collected over 20 swords"), shields (including an historic shrine shield from Oguta), spears, stones, whips ("what the Yorubas call *Koboko*"), canes, a scale, rams ("rams are usually dynamic"), bulls, a cock, and a scepter. It had been, he said, an impressive demonstration by people who are democratic in spirit. Notes on the Meeting of the National Executive Committee of the NCNC at the Lagos City College Hall, Yaba, Lagos, August 24, 1958.

It should be noted that Dr. Mbadiwe's touring party was reported to have been well received in certain towns, but there was no doubt about the overwhelming demonstrations of support for Azikiwe.

[75] This criticism was made by Hon. T. O. S. Benson, NCNC Chief Whip in the House of Representatives and Chairman of the Lagos branch. *Daily Times*, July 9, 1958. Benson toured the Eastern Region with Dr. Azikiwe and played a major role in the conflict with the Reform Committee.

Union. Yet Azikiwe's proposal of a traditional covenant to settle the dispute was politically shrewd, since many people thought that Mbadiwe should accept any genuine offer to bury the hatchet once and for all.

In late June a joint meeting of the Eastern wing of the NCNC Federal Parliament Party and the Eastern Parliamentary Party passed a vote of implicit confidence in Dr. Azikiwe,[76] as did the entire Federal Parliamentary Party a week later. Chief Festus Sam Okotie-Eboh (Warri), Federal Minister of Finance and National Treasurer of the NCNC, was elected to replace Dr. Mbadiwe as Leader of the Federal Parliamentary Party, and the Prime Minister of the Federation was informed of the expulsion from the NCNC of the two Reform Committee ministers (Mbadiwe and Balogun) and their parliamentary secretaries. At first, Dr. Azikiwe stated that his party would not put pressure on the Prime Minister to drop the Reformers from his cabinet; subsequently he declared that the NCNC would "react logically and face the consequences" if the Prime Minister failed to exercise his "discretion" in a reasonable manner.[77] In late July, Dr. Mbadiwe, Chief Balogun, and their parliamentary secretaries, Hons. Ndem and Bademosi, submitted their resignations to the Prime Minister, who accepted them with apparent regret. It was no secret that Alhaji Abubakar Tafawa Balewa had particular admiration for Dr. Mbadiwe,[78] and it was not unreasonable to assume that Dr. Azikiwe's accord with the Premier of the North was a factor in Alhaji Abubakar's decision to accept Mbadiwe's resignation. A tempered antagonism between the Prime Minister and the Premier of the East was evident for some months thereafter.[79]

[76] Two members of the Eastern Parliamentary Party, Hon. S. O. Achara (Okigwe) and Hon. V. K. Onyeri (Port Harcourt) resigned from the regular organization and declared for the Reform Committee. *Daily Service*, June 26, 1958. The party whip was withdrawn from them and from a former minister, Dr. W. N. Onubogu (Onitsha) who was known to support Dr. Mbadiwe. *Daily Times*, June 26, 1958.

[77] *Daily Times*, July 5, 1958; *West African Pilot*, July 11, 1958; the new leader of the NCNC Federal Parliamentary Party, Chief F. S. Okotie-Eboh, apologized to the Prime Minister for the cablegrams which had been sent to three NCNC federal ministers abroad, advising them to return from official tours. *Daily Service*, July 5, 1958.

[78] It was noted that the Prime Minister and two of his Northern colleagues, the Minister of Lagos Affairs, Mines and Power and the Minister of Works, made appearances at Dr. Mbadiwe's farewell party at his ministerial residence. *West African Pilot*, August 18, 1958.

[79] Friction between Alhaji Abubakar and Dr. Azikiwe was obvious in connection with a bizarre incident involving public allegations to the effect that Dr. Mbadiwe and other Reform leaders were implicated in a plot to assassinate the Eastern Premier in late July 1958. On August 2, the Prime Minister informed the House

On July 4, the Reformers inaugurated a newspaper, the *Daily Telegraph*,[80] and in August they launched a new party, called the Democratic Party of Nigeria and the Cameroons, with Dr. Mbadiwe as National Chairman and Chief Kolawole Balogun as National Secretary.[81] By the end of the year, most of the Western leaders had withdrawn from the new party. Some of them returned to the NCNC;[82] others joined the Action Group, as did most of the supporters of the Reform Committee in the non-Ibo areas of the East. Ultimately, the Democratic Party dwindled mainly to the Ibo areas of the East; it contested the federal election of 1959 in Ibo constituencies as a *de facto* ally of the Action Group but all of its candidates, including Dr. Mbadiwe, were defeated.

By the end of 1958, Azikiwe's leadership of the NCNC was unchallenged and his prestige in Nigeria had risen to unparalleled heights. His rapport with the Sardauna of Sokoto, Premier of the North, was evident during the Constitutional Conference of September and October 1958, at which time delegates representing the major Nigerian parties and the United Kingdom reached agreements on formerly unresolved constitutional issues and on a date of independence for the Federation—October 1, 1960. Millions of Nigerians of every class, tribe, and region believed that in the last analysis, Azikiwe had done more than any other man to realize the dream of national independence. It was not forgotten that in 1943 he published a program for independence involving a 15-year period of accelerated tutelage.[83] In 1946, as leader of an NCNC delegation to London, he

---

of Representatives that a thorough investigation would be conducted by the Inspector-General of Police. A week later, he reported that "with the exception of one statement of doubtful reliability, there is no evidence or information whatever to substantiate this story." In the few moments remaining before adjournment of the House, *sine die*, Hon. Jaja Anchu Wachuku, secretary of the NCNC Federal Parliamentary Party, objected vehemently to the Prime Minister's statement and read into the record part of a sworn statement by an individual which purported to corroborate the assassination threat. Dr. Azikiwe criticized the Prime Minister for having ventured to appraise the value of evidence that would certainly be judged by a court. In fact the controversial document was aired thoroughly in a subsequent prosecution of its author, but it would not serve any useful purpose to recapitulate that sensationalistic trial here. For highlights of the above account see *Daily Times*, August 2, and 23, 1958, and subsequent issues; *West African Pilot*, August 11, and 12, 1958.

[80] The writer is informed that Mr. L. N. Obioha, a major financial supporter of the Reform Committee, was the main financier of the *Daily Telegraph* as well.

[81] *Daily Telegraph*, August 11, 1958; see *Democratic Party of Nigeria and the Cameroons, Why We Break From the NCNC* (Yaba: 1958).

[82] Chief Kolawole Balogun returned to the NCNC in 1959 and was appointed by the government of the Federation as its representative in Ghana.

[83] *Political Blueprint of Nigeria* (Lagos: 1943). Supra, p. 56.

submitted a virtually identical proposal to the Secretary of State for the Colonies. His blueprint was rejected by officialdom in 1946, but history honored Azikiwe with the mantle of a prophet. Upon his return to Lagos in November 1958, Azikiwe was welcomed by a throng which observers termed "huge" if not indeed the largest and the most enthusiastic in memory. It may not be amiss to suppose that many people voted for the NCNC in the federal election of 1959 because they considered that Azikiwe deserved a vote of appreciation for his 22-year campaign for Nigerian independence.

However, the intra-party struggle of 1957-1958 did not arise naturally from the movement for national independence. Both sides were stoutly nationalistic, and there is no reason to assume that Mbadiwe at the helm of the NCNC would have adopted national policies of a radically different order than those of Azikiwe. In particular, Dr. Mbadiwe was not less likely to negotiate a coalition agreement with the Northern Peoples' Congress. Nevertheless the struggle did involve a conflict of interests with profound if incipient ideological implications.

The Reform Committee and its successor, the Democratic Party, reviled Dr. Azikiwe as a cynical and reactionary capitalist, whose failure to complete the conversion of the African Continental Bank into a state bank by June 1958 was symptomatic of his alleged political hypocrisy.[84] In principle, the Democratic Party espoused the ideology of socialism;[85] in fact the party rested its main hope on the adhesion of the rising and enlightened class of independent businessmen, professionals, and other educated elements who were less than enchanted by Azikiwe's charismatic personality and less than content with his leadership of the party and his administration of the Eastern Government. It is not less than factual to say that Dr. Mbadiwe appealed mainly to men of substance, that he was greatly

[84] In late June 1958 the Eastern Government opportunely announced that the representative of a British accounting firm had arrived in Enugu to examine the condition of the African Continental Bank in connection with its prospective full nationalization. *West African Pilot*, June 25, 1958.

[85] The socialist principle of the Democratic Party of Nigeria and the Cameroons was stated concisely as follows: "Socialist Ideology: By this it means that the Party will preserve the principle that individual freedom should be completely subordinated to interests of the entire community, with any deductions that may be correctly or incorrectly drawn from socialism. This provides for substitution of co-operative for competitive production, national ownership of land and capital, State distribution of produce, free education and feeding of children and abolition of inheritance. This is quite a laudable ideology that given every chance to survive, will no doubt thrive and aid the enhancement of social advancement in this country in the future." *Daily Telegraph*, August 11, 1958.

admired in Nigerian business circles and that his strategic connections were largely entrepreneurial. The birth of the African Insurance Company in 1958, involving families and individuals who
were prominent in the Reform Committee, was indicative of the
nature of the social interests upon which he relied.[86] Moreover, his
principal supporter in Lagos, Alhaji N. B. Soule, opened the Muslim
Bank (West Africa) in July 1958, during the height of the struggle.

By and large the seriously socialistic wing of the NCNC sided with
Azikiwe. In their view, the National President as a man was in-
corrigibly bourgeois, but as a symbol of the nationalist movement and
as the leader of the NCNC, he was radical, populist, and even worthy
of devotion. It should be clear by now that Azikiwe's career does not
fit easily into the traditional Marxian framework of socio-political
analysis. How does one classify a populist banker whose political
support lies primarily in the peasantry and the working class, and not
in the new elite of which he is supposed to be the epitome? Azikiwe,
as an intellectual, is acutely conscious of the contradictions in his own
life and anxious to demonstrate their essential unity. Thus he inserted a passage in his presidential address to the Aba Convention
that historians and biographers may ponder:[87]

"Let us not make a popular mistake by assuming that a normal
acquisition of wealth is wrong for society. It is not inconsistent with
Socialism for a Socialist through hard and honest work to acquire a
limited amount of wealth to enable him to co-exist successfully with
his capitalist counterparts. It is not the volume of wealth that makes
it obnoxious to the Socialist, but it is the use to which wealth is put
that matters. If some of us had not accumulated wealth in the dim
and distant decade when the oppressor was in his heyday, it would
have been impossible to found this great Party, and it would have
been an idle dream to achieve the measure of political success that has
come our way. Nevertheless, the well-to-do among us must now use
their wealth in a philanthropic manner, if they had not already been
doing so, for it is said: 'Unto whom much is given, much is
expected.' "

[86] The Mbadiwe and the Obioha families as well as D. A. Nwandu of the
Eastern General Contractors were instrumental in the establishment of the African
Insurance Company.
[87] "Opportunity Knocks At Our Door," presidential address delivered at the
Annual Convention of the NCNC, Aba, October 28, 1957. (Mimeographed.)

CHAPTER VI
THE ACTION GROUP: GUIDED LIBERALISM

IN 1945, Obafemi Awolowo, then a 36-year-old law student in London, appraised the political consciousness of his countrymen in bluntly realistic terms:

"Broadly speaking, there are three classes of people in Nigeria. First, the educated classes consisting of the professional men and women, teachers, and clerks; second, the 'enlightened' classes consisting mainly of traders and artisans; and third, the ignorant masses.

"The number of educated persons is put at 2½ per cent. This figure is probably incorrect; it is not unlikely that there are as many as 5 per cent. Of this number only a very small percentage are politically conscious. The rest, together with the enlightened class, are indifferent.

"As for the remaining masses, they are ignorant and will not be bothered by politics. Their sole preoccupation is to search for food, clothing, and shelter of a wretched type. To them, it does not seem to matter who rules the country, so long as in the process they are allowed to live their lives in peace and crude comfort. If they bestir themselves at all, as they do occasionally, it is because they have been unduly oppressed by a tribal chieftain, or outraged by the blunders of an Administrative Officer.

"These three classes are distinctly marked off from one another. The Chiefs, who form the ruling class, live in a world of their own. The illiterate masses have little or no confidence in the educated few, for the simple reason that the latter, in their political activities, are completely out of touch with the former. There is a mutual distrust verging on antagonism between the educated few and the Chiefs. The latter fear that the former are out to oust them from their privileged positions. Furthermore, while most of the illiterate masses detest the person of some individual Chief, they still have superstitious respect for the institution which the Chiefs represent.

"Given a choice from among white officials, Chiefs, and educated Nigerians, as the principal rulers of the country, the illiterate man, today, would exercise his preference for the three in the order in which they are named. He is convinced, and has good reasons to be, that he can always get better treatment from the white man than he could hope to get from the Chiefs, and the educated elements."[1]

[1] Obafemi Awolowo, *Path to Nigerian Freedom* (London: Faber, 1947), pp. 31-32. This appraisal, insofar as it applies to the educated elite, is substantially

As Awolowo expressed the prevailing view of the educated minority among the Yoruba people of Western Nigeria, the root cause of most tensions between Yoruba communities and their paramount chiefs was the excess of power which had been vested in those chiefs by the British in disregard of customary limitations.[2] His prescription for administrative reform and constitutional advance was predicated upon the assumption of political leadership by the educated minority in every ethnic group. Accordingly, he recommended that the unitary government of Nigeria should be federalized, and that each unit or state should be based on the principle of ethnic affinity.[3] "Strictly speaking," he argued, "the political structure of any particular national group is primarily their own domestic concern."[4]

---

confirmed by James S. Coleman, who writes: "The leaders and most of the active supporters of the Nigerian nationalist movement came from the ranks of those who had been most strongly affected by Western influences, and in particular from the Western-educated, English-speaking minority. By the early 1950's, when nationalism was well advanced, this group at most constituted no more than upwards of 6 per cent of the total population of Nigeria. . . . The articulate nationalist elements within the educated category came from a much smaller subgroup consisting mainly of barristers, physicians, teachers, clerks, and skilled laborers and artisans. . . .This subgroup also included journalists, organizational leaders, and a sizable number of traders and businessmen. These active core elements, however, would constitute at most a little more than .5 per cent of the total population of the country. And even in the subgroup, as Premier Obafemi Awolowo pointed out in 1947, 'only a very small percentage are politically conscious.'" *Nigeria: Background to Nationalism* (Berkeley and Los Angeles: University of California Press), pp. 141-142.

[2] Obafemi Awolowo, *op.cit.*, Chapters VI and VII. P. C. Lloyd has observed that British policies deprived the subordinate chiefs of their customary powers to control paramount chiefs or *Obas*: "The chiefs lost their control over their *oba*, and in his new autocratic position he often failed to consult with his council of chiefs. Policies were arranged over their heads; they were merely told of decisions reached by the *oba* and his 'white friend,' the administrator." "The Changing Role of the Yoruba Traditional Rulers," *Proceedings of the Third Annual Conference of the West African Institute of Social and Economic Research, 1954* (Ibadan: University College, 1956), pp. 59-60.

[3] James S. Coleman has observed "that in contemplating the ideal constitution for Nigeria both Awolowo and Azikiwe have repeatedly and consistently argued that the cultural factor should be the ultimate and overriding criterion in the territorial organization of Nigeria . . . the important point is that the two southern leaders have been much closer in their ideas on the ultimate territorial framework than has usually been acknowledged." *Nigeria*, pp. 388-389. Azikiwe's proposal of eight protectorates in the Commonwealth of Nigeria and the Cameroons was made in his *Political Blueprint of Nigeria* (Lagos: 1943) and incorporated into the NCNC Freedom Charter of 1948.

[4] "Strictly speaking, the political structure of any particular national group is primarily their own domestic concern. The others may criticize it in the same way as French and Russians may criticize the British Constitution. But they have no right to try to interfere effectively in the shaping of such a Constitution. But this is exactly what is happening in Nigeria now. The Ibos, for example, unused to

These ideals motivated the founders of the *Egbe Omo Oduduwa* (Society of the Descendants of *Oduduwa*), a "cultural organization" designed by Awolowo and his associates to promote the objectives of the Yoruba intelligentsia. The founders of the *Egbe* hoped that the chiefs would heed benign inducements to modernize and democratize their administrations. Concomitantly, the chiefs would be persuaded to support the cause of pantribal unity and to assist in the political mobilization of the masses. In Awolowo's view, it was fundamental that the chiefs must not be permitted to dominate the people, and he emphasized that the sole legitimate foundation of government under the auspices of the educated minority was the consent of the people, freely and democratically expressed.[5]

---

having chieftains, cannot understand why the *Obas* in Yorubaland or the Emirs in the North should be entitled to the positions they occupy. On the other hand, the autocracy of the Emirs cuts the Yoruba people to the quick. And what is worse, the Ibos and the Yorubas think it is their business actively to work to bring about a drastic change in these Constitutions. This is certainly not the correct attitude. But as long as every person in Nigeria is made to feel that he is a Nigerian first and a Yoruba or Ibo, or Hausa next, each will be justified to poke his nose into the domestic issues of the others. The only thing of common interest to all Nigerians as such, and in which the voice of one must be as acceptable as that of any other, is the constitution of the central or federal Government of Nigeria. The constitution of each national group is the sole concern of the members of that group." Awolowo, *op.cit.*, p. 53.

"Nigeria," wrote Awolowo in 1945, "is not a nation. It is a mere geographical expression. There are no 'Nigerians' in the same sense as there are 'English,' 'Welsh,' or 'French.' The word 'Nigerian' is merely a distinctive appellation to distinguish those who live within the boundaries of Nigeria from those who do not. There are various national or ethnical groups in the country. . . . It is a mistake to designate them 'tribes.' Each of them is a nation by itself with many tribes and clans. There is as much difference between them as there is between Germans, English, Russians and Turks, for instance. The fact that they have a common overlord does not destroy this fundamental difference. The languages differ. The readiest means of communication between them now is English. Their cultural backgrounds and social outlooks differ widely; and their indigenous political institutions have little in common. Their present stages of development vary." He compared the national diversity of Nigeria to that of Europe and concluded that "the best constitution for such diverse peoples is a federal Constitution," exemplified by the Constitution of Switzerland. *Ibid.*, pp. 47-50.

[5] *Supra*, p. 104. In his 1947 volume, *Path to Nigerian Freedom*, Chief Awolowo insisted upon the consent of the people as the only acceptable and secure basis of political institutions, but he implied that the will of the people may be interpreted by the educated minority, pp. 61-64. Later, Chief Awolowo became a strong proponent of universal adult suffrage, before that policy gained general acceptance among the leaders of the Action Group. He is said to have been personally impressed by the iniquities of the indirect election system when he was nearly defeated by the Intermediate Electoral College of Ijebu-Remo Division in 1951. Chief Bode Thomas, who was deputy leader of the Action Group until his death in November 1953, is said to have been deeply apprehensive of the consequences of universal suffrage.

In 1949, Awolowo founded the African Press Limited and initiated publication of the *Nigerian Tribune,* an Ibadan daily newspaper that supported the ideals and policies of the Nigerian Youth Movement. One of his associates in this publishing venture was the pre-eminent spiritual chief of Yorubaland, Sir Adesoji Aderemi II, the *Oni* of Ife, a noted modernist among the traditional rulers. The *Oni* of Ife approved of the organization of the Action Group by Awolowo and his associates in 1950-51 and he was instrumental in arranging a declaration of support for the new party by the *Obas* (paramount chiefs) of Yorubaland prior to the general election of 1951. In 1952, the *Oni* became President of the Western House of Chiefs, a co-ordinate branch of the Western Regional Parliament. (In 1960 he was appointed Governor of the Western Region.) He is entitled to a large measure of credit for the rapport which has prevailed between the Action Group and the traditional rulers of Yorubaland.

Yet the heart of that harmonious relationship is party control over the institution of chieftaincy. This has been secured by various means. First, the chiefs are amenable to social pressures, in particular moral inducements by the illustrious men who compose the leadership of the *Egbe Omo Oduduwa.* In this connection, *Egbe* and Action Group leaders have cemented their relationships with the traditional rulers through the acquisition of honorary chieftaincy titles, a normal procedure for successful men in Yorubaland. Thus Mr. Awolowo became Chief Awolowo in October 1954, following his accession to the Premiership of the Western Region.[6] Secondly, Action Group ideals and policies are propagated at an annual Chiefs Conference under the Presidency of the *Oni* of Ife; the conference maintains regular liaison with the Premier and ministers of the regional government by means of a standing committee, called the Chiefs Council.[7] Thirdly, party control is assured by the ultimate legal sanction of appointment and deposition of chiefs. The social and legal bases of party control over the major chiefs[8] are illumined by the famous case of the *Alafin* of Oyo; the mechanism of control

[6] Premier Awolowo was appointed Lisa of Ijeun by the *Alake* and Chiefs of Abeokuta. *Daily Times,* October 22, 1954. By December 1956, he had acquired seven chieftaincy titles. *Western House of Assembly Debates, Official Report,* December 19, 21, and 22, 1956, p. 40.

[7] This body was given statutory recognition in 1959. *Infra,* p. 445.

[8] A major chief in the Western Region is a person appointed to a "recognized chieftaincy" under the customary law. These include both ruling house chieftaincies and non-ruling house chieftaincies. *Chiefs Law, 1957* (No. 20 of 1957), Parts I and II. In 1958, nine of the major chiefs were designated as "Head Chiefs," or permanent members of the Western House of Chiefs. *Infra,* p. 444, n. 7.

over the minor chiefs may be illustrated by observations drawn from local politics in Benin division.

THE POLITICS OF CHIEFTAINCY CONTROL

Oyo: The Decline of an Old Order

The recent history of Oyo—a traditional town of some 72,000 people—is dominated by the personality and misfortunes of Alhaji Adeniran Aderemi II, the late ex-*Alafin* (king) of Oyo. Unlike the *Oni* of Ife, the ex-*Alafin* of Oyo personified the old-style chief who did not have the experience of Western education and was not "modernist" in outlook. Nevertheless, he did accede gracefully to the democratization of his Native Administration after the Second World War, involving both the alteration of his personal status from "Sole Native Authority" to "President" of the Native Authority Council and the inclusion of a two-thirds majority of elected councillors. In 1948, the ex-*Alafin* was piqued by the founders of the *Egbe Omo Oduduwa,* who evinced a greater apparent respect for his brother *Oba,* the *Oni* of Ife, than for himself. Nevertheless, he was persuaded by Oyo members of the *Egbe Omo Oduduwa* to endorse both the pan-Yoruba cultural society and its political offspring, the Action Group.

At this time, the *Alafin*'s personal relationship with two prominent sons of Oyo who were leaders of the new party, namely Chief Bode Thomas and Mr. Abiodun Akerele, was notably cordial. It is noted in Chapter III that Chief Thomas, a highly successful Lagos lawyer, was honored with the bestowal of a non-traditional chieftaincy title and installed as the *Balogun* of Oyo in 1950; subsequently he became chairman of the Oyo Divisional Council under the Presidency of the *Alafin*. His associate, Mr. Akerele, a law partner of Obafemi Awolowo in Ibadan, was one of the eight original founders of the Action Group. Both men were supported by the *Alafin* in their successful bids for election to the Western House of Assembly in 1951. But in 1952, the *Alafin* revealed a lack of appreciation for the new political order and clashed with Chief Thomas on the question of actual supremacy in the Oyo Divisional Council. Thereafter, the relationship between the *Alafin* and Chief Thomas deteriorated and political tension in Oyo verged intermittently on the point of violence.[9] An impasse was reached when the Action Group-controlled

[9] The *Aremo,* or Crown Prince, of Oyo was a close personal friend of Chief Thomas prior to the rift, when he sided with his father. On one occasion the *Aremo* was convicted on a charge of having instigated an assault on the person of Chief

Oyo Divisional Council voted to reduce the *Alafin*'s salary by £650. In November 1953, Chief Thomas, then Deputy Leader of the Action Group, Central Minister of Transport, and Chairman of the Oyo Divisional Council, died suddenly after a brief illness at the age of 34. His death deprived the Action Group of a remarkably perspicacious and resourceful leader whose counsel would be missed.

Meanwhile, a number of educated men who opposed the Action Group in general or the methods of Chief Thomas in particular, organized the *Egbe Oyo Parapo* (Oyo People's Party) to which a majority of the Oyo townsmen rallied in support of their embattled traditional ruler.[10] The People's Party is reported to have capitalized on latent hostility to the regional government's capitation levy of 10s. 6d. on male adult persons to finance its primary education scheme and its health program.[11] Action Group leaders surmised correctly that the People's Party was destined to become an affiliate of the NCNC. They alleged that the *Alafin* was both the power behind the People's Party and the chief instigator of anti-tax agitation in Oyo. In August 1954, the Oyo Divisional Council suspended the payment of the *Alafin*'s salary on the ground of his alleged collusion with agitators against the regional levy.

On September 5, 1954, a meeting of the People's Party in Oyo was attacked by members of the Action Group; the *Parapos* retaliated and six persons were killed. On September 6, a committee of seven Western *Obas*, including the *Alafin* of Oyo, met with fourteen leaders of the *Egbe Omo Oduduwa* in the Western House of As-

---

Thomas. That conviction was reversed on appeal to the Regional High Court, but the *Aremo*'s salary was terminated by the Oyo Divisional Council and he was banished from Oyo by the government in the interests of public order. Many Oyo people were incensed against the government when the *Aremo* died in exile.

Not all of the traditional chiefs supported the *Alafin*. His chief councillor, for example, the *Bashorun*, sided with Chief Thomas.

[10] The *Egbe Oyo Parapo* (Oyo People's Party) appears to have been inaugurated by sons of Oyo who were resident in Lagos. Its leader, Mr. P. A. Afolabi, headmaster of a Catholic school and educational secretary of the Archdiocese of Lagos, had been a founding member of the Oyo Progressive Union in the 1930's, which may be regarded as the forebear of the People's Party.

The inhabitants of the Oyo rural districts were less inclined to support the *Egbe Oyo Parapo* because of their grievances against the townspeople. For years it had been the practice of town agents to extort tribute from rural farmers in the name of the *Alafin*. British administrators discouraged this practice, but it seems to have been revived during the reign of the ex-*Alafin*, as a result of which the rural people were inclined to regard the townsmen, especially the *Alafin*'s courtiers, as an oppressive class.

[11] Anti-tax agitation against the Education and Health levy was rife in 1953 and 1954 throughout the region. See *Tax Collection in the Western Region, laid on the table of the Western House of Assembly*, February 1954.

sembly at Ibadan. Oyo spokesmen charged the *Alafin* with having conspired against the government and the party in power. It was recorded that Obafemi Awolowo spoke "with strong feelings and with great emotion." He said that the *Alafin* was to blame for the Oyo tragedy and that the government was determined to take action against him. Heretofore, he explained, the government had been patient with the *Alafin* only in consideration of the sensibilities of the *Obas*. But the government's patience had come to an end and the *Obas* had a last chance to save the situation by making an appropriate recommendation. At length, the committee of *Obas* caucused privately and agreed to recommend that the *Alafin* of Oyo should be suspended from his office, removed from the Native Authority Council, deprived of his salary, and banished temporarily from Oyo.[12] Thereupon, the government suspended the *Alafin* from office and banished him from his domain; eventually he was deposed.[13]

This celebrated case created the impression that no chief could stand against the government and survive. Attention was drawn to the fact that regional legislation empowered the "Governor-in-Council," i.e., the Executive Council of the region, to suspend or depose any chief "in the interests of peace, or order or good government." Moreover, specified local government councils were empowered to discover or clarify and declare the customary law con-

[12] Minutes of a Special Emergency Joint Committee Meeting of Western *Obas* and the *Egbe Omo Oduduwa* held at the Western Secretariat, Ibadan, September 6, 1954. (Secretariat files of the *Egbe Omo Oduduwa*, Ibadan.)

[13] The regional government appointed a sole commissioner to inquire into "the causes of tension in Oyo Division." It was alleged by opponents of the *Alafin* that his agents intimidated the farmers of Oyo Division by making illegal demands in the name of the *Alafin* for the payment of traditional tribute. Furthermore, the *Alafin* was accused of venality with respect to the bestowal of chieftaincy titles, of having interfered in the proceedings of native courts, and of having undermined tax collection within his jurisdiction. However, in the opinion of the Commissioner, the evidence adduced did not justify the condemnation of the *Alafin*. On the contrary, the Commissioner concluded that the elderly chief had made a sincere if inept effort to adjust to the new order and he recommended that the *Alafin* be restored to the throne of Oyo. Furthermore he blamed both political parties equally for the fatal disturbances. *Report of a Commission of Inquiry into Disturbances at Oyo by Mr. R. D. Lloyd, Daily Times*, June 8, 1955. This report was objectionable to the government, which was obliged to choose between difficult alternatives: either to permit the return of the *Alafin* to Oyo in virtual triumph or to reject the report of its commissioner. It chose the latter and affirmed its previous decision to banish the *Alafin*, holding that he was primarily to blame for the malevolent practices of his subordinate officials and for the mischievous activities of the Oyo *Parapo*. "Comment on the Lloyd Report by Chief Rotimi Williams, Minister of Justice and Local Government," *Daily Times*, June 8, 1955. The *Alafin* was finally deposed by an executive action of the regional government in 1956. *Western House of Assembly Debates, Official Report*, July 2-6, 1956, pp. 174-175.

trolling succession to traditional offices in their jurisdictions.[14] At Oyo, for example, the customary law of succession to the office of *Alafin* was subject to declaration by the Oyo Divisional Council, a body under Action Group control. It was no surprise when the traditional kingmakers of Oyo eventually elected an Action Group supporter to succeed the deposed *Alafin*.[15]

The deposition of a chief is an extremely unpleasant matter, both for the Government and for the community concerned; it rarely occurs and never without compelling evidence of misconduct on the part of the chief, or without an exigent popular demand.[16] However, a strong party organization in control of a local council can supply a demand for deposition when it is required, as at Oyo in 1956. Since the deposition of the *Alafin* of Oyo, few chiefs in the Western Region have dared to assert their opposition to the Action Group or their political neutrality. In 1958, only one of the 54 members of the Western House of Chiefs was identified as a supporter of the NCNC.[17]

Benin: A Study in the Mechanics of Chieftaincy Control

Under the federal constitution of Nigeria, exclusive responsibility for local government is reserved to the regions. We have noted that, in general, there are two tiers to the structure of local government in the Western Region: (1) local or district councils, elected directly by the people in local government wards, and (2) divisional councils, elected by and from the members of the lower-tier councils. "Invariably," as we have stated in Chapter I, "the party in control of a lower tier council will elect the specified number of its members to

[14] *Comment on the Lloyd Report by Chief Rotimi Williams, loc.cit.* See the Appointment and Recognition of Chiefs Law, 1954, and the Chiefs Law, 1957 (No. 20 of 1957), sections 4 and 22.

[15] Two of the kingmakers, who were NCNC partisans, did not participate in the selection of the new *Alafin* and 1,000 women were reported to have demonstrated in protest. *Daily Times*, July 13 and 14, 1956. Lest the reader be perplexed by the popularity of the ex-*Alafin* in an area under the control of an Action Group council, it should be explained that the ex-*Alafin*'s strength, and that of the *Egbe Oyo Parapo*, was concentrated in Oyo town, while a majority of the Action Group members of the Divisional Council were elected from the "exploited" rural districts. *Supra*, p. 236, n. 10.

[16] The number of cases of deposition of Western chiefs under Action Group rule have been relatively few. Cases are cited in *Western House of Assembly Debates, Official Report*, July 6, 1956, pp. 145ff; and *ibid.*, December 19-22, 1956, pp. 37, 180.

[17] The Commission of Inquiry into Minority Fears observed that "only one member" out of 52 members of the House of Chiefs was "not a supporter of the Action Group." Colonial Office *Report of the Commission appointed to enquire into the fears of Minorities and the means of allaying them* (London: 1958), p. 23.

represent that council in the divisional council." Instruments establishing councils at both levels usually prescribe the inclusion of "traditional members," i.e., chiefs, up to a maximum of one-third of the elected membership. A "traditional member" is designated president while an elected member serves as chairman.

When the new system was introduced in 1952, certain officials hoped that the traditional members would remain neutral in party politics so as to hold the balance of power in closely divided councils where they might be able to exert a stabilizing influence.[18] That was a false hope which did not reckon with the ability of the government party to control the traditional hierarchies. This facet of "party government" may be illustrated further by observations on the aftermath of the Benin local elections of 1958.

Benin Division in the Mid-West is inhabited by an Edo-speaking people called the Bini. The *Oba* of Benin became a supporter of the Action Group in 1955, when he reversed his former hostility, owing partly to the lesson of the *Alafin* of Oyo, and accepted the post of Minister without Portfolio in the Western Regional Government. He is the President of the Benin Divisional Council which comprises 20 "traditional members," elected by colleges of chiefs, and 60 non-traditional members, elected by the six lower-tier councils of Benin Division. Under the Western Region Chiefs Law, designated major chiefs, including the *Oba* of Benin, have virtually absolute powers to confirm the appointments of minor chiefs and to regulate their official conduct.[19] Needless to say, the great majority of minor chiefs follow the *Oba*'s political line, not merely in deference to his authority under regional law, but in reverence to the sacred and traditional ties which bind the chiefs to their *Oba*.

In Benin Division, the Action Group is a minority party; until 1958, it had never elected a majority of the membership of any one of the six local government councils. In order to control the local government councils of Benin, the NCNC must win enough elective

[18] For example, see R. E. Brown, "Local Government in the Western Region of Nigeria, 1950-1955," *Journal of African Administration*, VII, 4 (October 1955), p. 183.
[19] Chiefs Law, 1957 (No. 20 of 1957), section 18. In 1958, Premier Awolowo described the relationship between the *Obas* and minor chiefs as follows:
"It is, I believe, the traditional prerogative of an *Oba* to have the last say in recommending chiefs under him to Government for appointment, suspension and deposition. He is the undisputed ceremonial, spiritual, and political head of the community. He is entitled to be maintained comfortably in office, and to be paid salaries or remunerations commensurate with his status. He has absolute powers in respect to minor chieftaincies." Address to the Chiefs Conference at Benin City, May 1958. (Mimeographed.)

seats to outnumber the Action Group elected members plus their inevitable allies among the chiefs. In the local election of May 1958, the voters of Benin Division reaffirmed their NCNC sympathies by returning NCNC majorities to the Benin City Council and to three of the five rural district councils; one district council emerged with an Action Group majority and another was deadlocked with 20 members for each party when 18 NCNC candidates were disqualified on the ground that their nominations were invalid.[20]

Prior to this time, "traditional members" were included in two of the six lower-tier councils only. Soon after the election, the *Oba* of Benin made proposals to increase the number of "traditional members" in all of the rural district councils, and the government decided to inject a total of 26 chiefs into the several councils.[21] As a result, the Action Group secured control of three rural district councils, including two district councils where its electoral strength was minor, and was able to send a total of 26 elected members from these councils to the Benin Divisional Council where the NCNC had a total of 34. But 19 of the 20 "traditional members" of the Divisional Council declared for the Action Group, giving that party a majority of eleven and control of the Divisional Council despite the fact that it polled about 35 percent of the total vote in the division to 56 percent for the NCNC.[22] This maneuver is illustrated in Table 1.

In the local elections of 1958, the Action Group won elected majorities in 123 out of 165 lower-tier councils throughout the Western Region. The post-election manipulation of chieftaincies which occurred in Benin was exceptional; yet the partisanship of "traditional members" did reverse a decisive NCNC victory in one other locality.[23]

[20] The Local Government Adviser for Benin Division was reported in the press to have told an NCNC delegation that in one case at least the Electoral Officer had acted improperly in disqualifying an NCNC candidate after the close of nominations. *Daily Times*, June 3, 1959.

[21] The *Oba*'s initiative in augmenting the number of "traditional members" was reported to the Western House of Assembly on June 4, 1958, by the Minister of Local Government. *Official Report*, p. 672. In a letter to the Permanent Secretary, Ministry of Local Government, the leader of the Benin NCNC, Chief H. Omo-Osagie, protested that the Local Government Law (Section 7, Subsection 3 c) stipulated that an inquiry should be held to ascertain the wishes of the inhabitants of an area before the composition of a council was altered, not the wishes of an *Oba* merely. *West African Pilot*, June 28, 1958.

[22] *Report on Local Government Elections in the Western Region of Nigeria, 1958*, Sessional Paper No. 7 of 1958, pp. 26-31, 173.

[23] At Ikorodu in Ikeja Division, the NCNC returned 18 members to the local council to 13 for the Action Group. However 6 of the 7 "traditional members" voted with the Action Group to prevent the NCNC from organizing the council. *West African Pilot*, May 15, 1958. In Western Urhobo, the NCNC returned 21 members to the District Council to 20 for the Action Group and 5 Independents.

TABLE I

Council	Election results* NCNC A.G. Ind.			Number of chiefs prior to June, 1958**	Number of chiefs after the injections of June, 1958***	Number and party affiliation of members elected to the Divisional Council****
Benin City Council	33	8	2	9	9	19 NCNC
Iyekuselu Dist. Council	16	27	6	-	4	10 A.G.
Akugbe District Council	20	20	-	-	5	9 A.G.
Iyekeorhiomwan Dist. Council	24	10	1	-	8	8 NCNC
Iyekovia Dist. Council	20	12	2	5	6	7 A.G.
Uhunmwonde Dist. Council	37	4	3	-	3	7 NCNC

Benin Divisional Council

	NCNC	A.G.	Independent
Elected members	34	26	-
Traditional members	-	19	1
Total	34	45	1

* *Report on Local Government Elections in the Western Region of Nigeria, 1958 S.P. No. 7 of 1958.* Figures do not include post-election changes in party affiliation or declarations of Independents for political parties.

** Instruments Establishing the Benin City Council and various District Councils. *Supplement to the Western Regional Gazette* No. 32, Vol. 4, 7 July 1955—Part B, 507ff.

*** *Western Region of Nigeria Gazette* No. 40, Vol. 7, 12 June 1958, Notices 558, 559, 560, 561, 563.

**** Information supplied by the office of the Benin Divisional Council; also *West African Pilot*, September 13, 1958.

NCNC spokesmen have warned in exasperation that voters may not peaceably abide the nullification of an election result by a palpably undemocratic device in the guise of tradition.[24] However, the government party presumes, realistically it would appear, that a moderate quota of traditional representation, to wit, a maximum of one-third of the elected total, is acceptable to the people and that those *Obas* and colleges of chiefs who control the appointments of "traditional members" to councils are sufficiently influential to ensure popular

After the election the 5 Independents declared for the NCNC, while 8 chiefs declared for the Action Group, giving that party a total of 27. Its control of the Council was assured when a disputed traditional seat was filled in the Action Group's favor. *Daily Times*, May 27, 1958.

[24] "It is morally wrong and not supported by law that after election the Action Group should . . . inject traditional members into the Councils . . . turning victory into failure. The Binis will resist it. And my humble advice is that the Action Group should desist from introducing anarchy into Benin Division which may eventually end in disturbances which my party had been endeavoring to avoid." Chief H. Omo-Osagie, "AG Injection in Benin Division," *West African Pilot*, June 28, 1958. In July 1958, the Benin NCNC observed a "day of mourning and fasting" to protest "our political bondage and *Oba* Akenzua's insistence on active participation in party politics." *Daily Times*, July 26, 1958.

consent to the appointments, and gradually to instill in their communities an appreciation for the Action Group. Nor do Action Group leaders equivocate about their conviction that chiefs ought to be partisan supporters of the government party. In May 1958, the Western Minister of Economic Planning, Chief C. D. Akran (one of the two genuine traditional rulers to whom portfolios were assigned in the Western Regional Government), declared as follows to an assembly of the Western Regional Chiefs Conference at Benin City:[25]

"Is it not our bounden duty to guard and guide our people? Have they made us Chiefs in order that we may show complete indifference to the problems which confront them and us? Is it not our duty to help choose those who will govern in our areas? The mere fact that we have a House of Chiefs where members vote on measures presented to them is sufficient to destroy any argument about neutrality. Chiefs vote in their different Councils, and can they escape being called politicians? There is no doubt at all in my mind that Chiefs are politicians since they vote and cannot be indifferent to who rules this country. . . . Chiefs in particular, must make it known to their people what political party they know can rule this country in the best interests of the people. We shall be quite guilty if knowing the fact we hide it from those who look up to us for leadership. . . . It is our clear duty if we love this great country and wish our people well to strain every nerve to see that the Action Group is voted into power in the Federal Government."

ETHNIC, RELIGIOUS, AND SOCIO-ECONOMIC FACTORS AFFECTING THE CONSOLIDATION AND EXPANSION OF THE ACTION GROUP

It will be recalled that the Action Group began as an avowed Western Regional organization. So long as it remained in existence as a distinct regional organization, two alternative courses of development might have been pursued. One possibility involved the negotiation of working alliances with parties in other regions on the basis of reciprocal recognition of operational areas. This possibility was consistent with the initial conception of the Action Group as the potential Western Regional Working Committee of a national organization. It was not a practicable policy insofar as cooperation with the NCNC was concerned, since that party was solidly based in the Western Region and determined to compete with the Action Group

[25] Speech by the Hon. Minister of Economic Planning at the Chiefs' Conference, Benin, May 1958. (Mimeographed.)

for control of the Western government. However, leaders of the Action Group did reach a virtual agreement for cooperation with the Northern Peoples' Congress prior to the "self-government crisis" of 1953, and serious negotiations between these two parties were resumed in 1954.[26] The prospects for an Action Group-Northern Peoples' Congress combination diminished with the formation of an NPC-NCNC Federal Government Coalition in 1955; these prospects became even more remote in 1956 when the Action Group launched a vigorous campaign in Ilorin, a Yoruba-speaking division of the Northern Region.

A second possible course of development for the Action Group within the context of a uni-regional existence involved the repudiation of all organizational links with non-Western regional parties. The adoption of this alternative was contingent upon the pursuit of an unequivocally regionalist policy. It was a feasible alternative if Nigeria emerged as a loose confederation of autonomous regions or in the event of outright secession by the Western Region from Nigeria, an idea that was entertained by a few influential members of the party as late as 1955.[27] But this was a minority view, and the policy of the Action Group has always envisaged the emergence of a durable federation. Inevitably, the growth of effective power at the center induced men of the rising class in Western Nigeria—the social backbone of the party—to turn toward political action on the national plane.

It is recorded that expansion of the Action Group beyond the Western Region was anticipated by Mr. Awolowo and Mr. Akintola (the two top Action Group leaders at the time of writing) at a formative meeting of the party in June 1950.[28] Preparations for an Eastern campaign were initiated in 1953[29] and a decision was taken in 1954 to support the creation of a non-Ibo state in the Eastern

[26] The Sardauna of Sokoto was reported to have conferred with Chief Awolowo in Ibadan in mid-November 1954. *Daily Times*, November 19, 1954, and the *West African Pilot* (November 26, 1954) reported the possibility of an amalgamation of the Action Group and the Northern Peoples' Congress into a Nigerian Peoples' Congress.

[27] Minutes of the Fourth Annual Regional Conference of the Action Group, Ibadan, October 26-28, 1955.

[28] Minutes of the Third Meeting of the Action Group held at Mr. Awolowo's Residence, Oke Bola, Ibadan, June 4, 1950.

[29] In January 1953 the Central Executive Committee of the Action Group discussed the inauguration of a branch in the Eastern city of Port Harcourt. Minutes of the Central Executive Committee of the Action Group, Ibadan, January 13, 1953. Mr. A. O. Rewane, a close associate of Chief Awolowo and his "political secretary," conducted a comprehensive study of the situation in the East and was largely responsible for the successful establishment of an Eastern wing of the party.

Region, comprising the Calabar, Ogoja, and Rivers Provinces. The Action Group won three of the 14 non-Ibo seats in the federal election of 1954 and 13 out of 30 non-Ibo seats in the regional election of 1957 (until 1961 the Action Group had never won an Ibo seat in a parliamentary election); Mr. S. G. Ikoku, an Action Group member for Enyong Division (Aro-Calabar) was appointed Leader of the Opposition in the Eastern House of Assembly. It should be noted that Action Group penetration of the Calabar-Ogoja-Rivers area has been resisted by certain non-Ibo groups who are more sensitive to local ethnic rivalries than to pressures exerted by Ibo migrants. Thus in Ikot-Ekpene Division of the former Calabar Province, Annangs tend to support the NCNC while Ibibios incline to the Action Group. (Both groups are Efik-speaking and support the Ibibio State Union.) In Calabar township, the Action Group is supported by the vast majority of Efiks, while the NCNC is favored by most Quas and practically all Ibos.[30] Needless to say, other factors matter in addition to the ethnic factors under consideration at this point.

Action Group operations in the Northern Region assumed the proportions of a major effort in 1958. The social basis of that effort in the "lower North" or middle belt, where notable success was achieved, will be discussed in Chapter VIII. The federal election of 1959 demonstrated that expansion had become a vital necessity to the Action Group, which obtained more seats in the Northern and Eastern Regions combined than it did in the Western Region, its original and primary base. (The Action Group totals were as follows: West and Lagos: 34—all but one were Yoruba constituencies; East: 14—all non-Ibo constituencies inhabited by Efik-speaking people of the former Calabar Province; North: 25—all in the area of the middle belt.)

In the Western Region, Action Group influence is bolstered by an impressive record of achievements by the Western Regional Government. Among those achievements which are bound to weigh with the electorate are the successful program of free primary education, the expanding medical program including free medical care for children under 18 years of age, the extensive program of loans to farmers and entrepreneurs, and the steady Nigerianization of the senior civil service. In addition, the government party is able

[30] Probably there are no Ibos in the Calabar section Action Group-C.O.R. State Movement Alliance, although Ibos are estimated to total no less than 50% of the population of the Calabar Urban District. Twenty-one officers of the combined Calabar Action Group Divisional Organization and C.O.R. State Movement identified by the writer in 1958 included 15 Efiks, 4 Yorubas and 2 non-Nigerians (with respect to ethnic origin).

to exert influence by means of its control of the chieftaincy apparatus and through the dispensation of patronage. Nevertheless, the influence of the Action Group in the Western Region is limited by ethnic, religious, and socio-economic factors which predispose the people of various communities to reject the regional government party.

Ethnic Bases of Resistance to the Action Group in the Western Region

The greatest ethnic problem of the Action Group in the Western Region lies in the Mid-West, a minority area comprising several nationalities which total somewhat less than 30 percent of the Region's population. The Action Group's electoral record in the Mid-West is singularly poor: it lost all ten Mid-Western seats in the federal election of 1954, 16 out of 20 in the regional election of 1956 and 14 out of 15 in the federal election of 1959.[31] Following the 1954 election, the Action Group endorsed in principle the creation of a Mid-West State and the Western House of Assembly passed a motion to that effect without a dissenting vote.[32] Possibly Action Group leaders were not averse to the excision of this opposition area from the Western Region in order to ensure continued Action Group control of the regional government. Moreover, the Action Group declaration of support for the creation of a Mid-West State enhanced the potential appeal of Action Group candidates to the Mid-Western electorate.

But the Action Group has not been able to capture the leadership of the separate state movement for several reasons. First, Action Group supporters in certain crucial centers, as in Benin City, have included businessmen and professional persons who benefit from their connections with the regional government party, and do not favor the creation of a separate state that is virtually certain to be controlled by the NCNC. Secondly, the Action Group has objected on ethnic and linguistic grounds to the inclusion of various sections of the Mid-West in the proposed state. A controversial objection involved Warri Division, the homeland of the Itsekeri people. In Warri town, party loyalties and tribal interests coincide: the Action Group is identified with Itsekeri interests while the NCNC is identified with Urhobo interests.[33] Thirdly, spokesmen for the Western Regional

[31] In the regional election of 1960, the Action Group gained substantially in Mid-Western constituencies, suggesting a decline of ethnic resistance to it in that area.

[32] Western House of Assembly Debates, June 14, 1955.

[33] The Itsekeri and the Urhobo are related respectively to the Yoruba and the

Government were obliged to rebut allegations of discrimination against the Mid-Westerners before the Minorities Commission of 1957-1958; this created the impression that Action Group enthusiasm for the cause of the Mid-West State was not unreserved.[34] As an interim measure, the Western Regional Government has experimented with a "Welsh solution" for the Mid-West, involving the establishment of a Ministry for Mid-West Affairs and an advisory body called the Mid-West Advisory Council.[35]

Another source of ethnic resistance to the Action Group in the Western Region lies in the historic rivalries which have divided the Yoruba tribes. Thus it is probable that the people of Illa and Ilesha urban districts have voted consistently for the NCNC because Ife, a traditionally rival town, is an Action Group stronghold.[36]

Edo. Partisanship on a tribal basis in Warri town preceded the issue of exclusion from the proposed Mid-West State; it involved the question of communal representation for the outnumbered Itsekeri landowners, the disputed title of the Itsekeri King (*Olu* of Warri), and the distribution of the proceeds of rents from Crown Lands. See P. C. Lloyd, "Tribalism in Warri," *Fifth Annual Conference Proceedings of the West African Institute of Social and Economic Research* (Ibadan: University College, 1956), pp. 99-110; also the study of the 1956 regional election in Warri East constituency by Philip Whitaker, "The Western Region of Nigeria, May 1956," *Five Elections in Africa*, ed. W. J. M. Mackenzie and Kenneth Robinson (Oxford: Clarendon Press, 1960), pp. 86-94. When this writer visited Warri in 1958, shortly after the local government election, he discovered that Urhobos who supported the Action Group on principle in their home districts were apt to support the NCNC in Warri town itself. Similarly, few Itsekeris in Warri town would support the Urhobo-Ibo dominated NCNC, irrespective of their purely political preferences. Action Group candidates for the Warri Urban District Council in May 1958 included 17 Itsekeris, 2 Urhobos and 2 Yorubas; NCNC candidates included 15 Urhobos, 3 Itsekeris and 3 Ibos. The NCNC returned 15 Urhobos and 2 Itsekeris to the 21-member Urban District Council, while the Action Group, a minority party in Warri town, returned 4 Itsekeris only. Itsekeris constitute about 40% of the population of Warri Division which has returned an NCNC member to the Federal House of Representatives in 1954 and 1959, namely, Chief Festus Sam Okotie-Eboh, Federal Minister of Finance and Leader of the NCNC Federal Parliamentary Party. The minister's ethnic identification is both Itsekeri and Urhobo.

[34] *Report of the Commission appointed to enquire into the fears of Minorities,* pp. 29-30.

[35] Steps to create a Mid-West Region were initiated by the federal government after Independence. In 1962 the federal parliament passed a law to amend the Constitution for this purpose. Spokesmen for the Action Group protested vehemently the inclusion of Warri Division and Akoko-Edo, a Yoruba-speaking district of Afenmai Division. But this protest was unlikely to be heeded inasmuch as the Constitution does not permit the legislature of a single region only to block the creation of a new state. Ultimately the creation of a region is determined by referendum in the area concerned. Affirmative action requires the support of at least 60 percent of the registered electorate.

[36] The NCNC persuasion of the Ijesha people (the inhabitants of Ilesha) has been reinforced by a land dispute between themselves and the Ife people. In

Similarly, the Action Group in Ibadan was rejected by the majority of that city's population partly as a result of its early identification with individuals of Ijebu tribal origin. This factor, among others, is appraised in the next chapter which deals with Ibadan politics exclusively.

Resistance to the Action Group in the Western Region on the Basis of Religion

Ethnically inspired opposition to the Action Group among Yoruba people is reinforced by resistance based on religious sensibilities, specifically among Muslims. The 1952 census revealed that there are 2,100,000 Muslims in the Western Region, comprising over 33 percent of the population; more than 96 percent of them live in the Yoruba areas, where the Muslim population is slightly greater than the Christian.[37] Both religions are propagated vigorously among the Yoruba by evangelists, with Islam gaining ground at a more rapid rate. By and large, religious differences lie beneath the surface of Western Regional politics, for the Yoruba people do not, as a rule, divide politically or socially along religious lines.[38]

---

addition the late *Owa* of Ilesha and the *Oni* of Ife were fraternal rivals. It is not without significance that the late ex-*Alafin* of Oyo sought refuge in Ilesha when he was banished from his domain in 1954. The electoral fortunes of the Action Group in Ilesha have improved since the installation of an Action Group supporter as *Owa* of Ilesha in 1957. Conversely recent political trends in Ife have been more favorable to the NCNC.

[37] About 41.4% of the population of the 6 Yoruba Provinces is Muslim; 41.2% is Christian and 17.4% is Animist. Based on the *Population Census of the Western Region, 1952* (Lagos: Government Statistician, 1956), p. 21.

[38] "Neo-Muslims involved in two universalist systems are influenced by the individualistic secular attitudes of the West and a different attitude to religion has made its appearance, the most striking aspect being religion as personal religious allegiance. Many have adopted Islam as a personal religion rather than as a civilization. They are absorbing the specifically religious elements of Islam first and the civilization, which seems to some to be backward and retarding, only to a limited degree. In regions of consolidated Islam, religion is a question permanently closed by birth, but to Neo-Muslims it is an open question about which the individual may hold any opinion and form any allegiance he pleases. Where Western secular influences are strong, as among Yoruba, individual changes of allegiance can take place without causing any outcry from the community, for it is not thought to menace family solidarity or undermine the fabric of society. Many Yoruba families have Muslim, Christian, and pagan members and all join happily in each other's religious festivals, for they are merely acts of social custom like the observance of Christmas in the Western world. . . . Both Islam and Christianity have gained large numbers of adherents, especially Islam, yet neither of these religions hold together the social edifice, they are simply the religious departments of life. Thus the act of joining the one or the other does not undermine the social structure, and the family remains the real cement of Yoruba society." J. Spencer Trimingham, *Islam in West Africa* (Oxford: Clarendon Press, 1959), pp. 221-222.

But there are historic relationships between Christian penetration, Western education, and nationalistic activity in both the political and the economic spheres. Christianity has been the characteristic creed of the rising, Western-educated, business and professional class, which predominated in the vanguard of the nationalist movement. Islam, on the other hand, has been the characteristic religion of the poor and the nonliterates.[39] It has been noted (in Chapter II) that the mass membership of the populist Nigerian National Democratic Party of Lagos during the 1920's through the 1940's was mainly Muslim, while its rival, the Nigerian Youth Movement—a party of the new Yoruba elite—was predominantly Christian. The Action Group, which emerged in the tradition of the Nigerian Youth Movement, was manifestly a movement of the rising class and very few Muslims can be numbered among its early leaders. (Only two Muslims can be identified in a list of 61 inaugural and executive members of the Action Group compiled by the writer from party records for the period March 1950-December 1953.)[40] Only three Muslims can be identified among the writer's tabulation of 33 Western Regional personalities in the Federal Executive Council of the Action Group in 1958, including only one Muslim among the 12 regional ministers;[41] only five Muslims were identified among 75 constituency and divisional leaders of the Action Group in the Western Region whose religions were determined by this writer (out of a list of 110).[42]

In recent years there has been a marked increase in the number of educated and well-to-do Yoruba Muslims, many of whom have joined the Action Group. Moreover, the Action Group has endeavored assiduously to shed its early sectarian coloration.[43] Nevertheless, many Muslims appear to regard the Action Group as an agent of Christian domination. Among the arguable grievances which have been expressed are the alleged neglect of Muslim schools by the

[39] Cf. the observation of Sir W. Ivor Jennings with respect to the social dispersion of Christianity and Buddhism in Ceylon: " . . . Christianity is strong among the wealthier classes, so that political Buddhism has some of the characteristics of a class war." *The Approach to Self-Government* (Cambridge: Cambridge University Press, 1958), p. 109.

[40] *Supra*, pp. 108-110.

[41] *Infra*, p. 528, Appendix IV.

[42] Constituency and Divisional Leaders: Names and Addresses. Action Group Headquarters Secretariat, Ibadan. (Typed.)

[43] Since the Action Group has become the mass party of the Yoruba indigenes in the capital of the Federation (Lagos), Muslims have been predominant among its leadership in that city. Thus in 1958, 17 of the 30 members of the Action Group Lagos Executive Committee were Muslim, as were 20 of the 37 chairmen of the local electoral ward units of the party.

Western Regional Government in its allocation of funds for educational support, the exclusion of Arabic language training from the curriculum of most elementary schools, the relatively small number of government scholarships awarded to Muslim students, the conversion of Muslim children to Christianity as a result of their education in Christian schools, the inadequate representation of Muslims in the Western Region Executive Council and in the Western House of Chiefs, and the belligerent statements of Christian leaders, all of which add up to the general grievance of religious discrimination.[44]

Muslim organizations, other than prayer congregations, in Lagos and the Western Region, include religious fraternities, in particular the Ahmadiyya Movement,[45] cultural-religious societies, and political groups.[46] In July 1957, the representatives of several Muslim groups, both political and cultural, inaugurated a political party called the National Muslim League (*Egbe Musulmi Parapo*).[47] Action Group

[44] See *Speech by Hadji A. R. A. Smith, President General of the Muslim Congress of Nigeria at the Inaugural Meeting of the National Muslim League (Egbe Muslumi Parapo)*, Ibadan, July 28, 1957; The National Muslim League's Memorandum on the Fears of the Muslim Minorities in the Regions (mimeographed); *The Report of the Commission appointed to enquire into the fears of Minorities*, pp. 26-28, which dismissed allegations of discrimination in the field of education as unfounded.

[45] The Ahmadiyya Movement was founded in India by Mirza Ghulām Ahmad (1836-1906), a mystic reformer who was revered by his followers as the Messiah and Mahdi. In 1916, Ahmadiyya was introduced in Lagos, where it appealed especially to young intellectuals. During the 1930's the movement in Lagos split, primarily on the issue of foreign control, and the Ahmadiyya Movement in Islam was formed under the leadership of a distinguished barrister and leader of the Nigerian Youth Movement, Alhaji Jibril Martin. In 1958 there were three main sections of the Ahmadiyya Movement in Lagos. See Humphrey Fisher, "The Ahmadiyya Movement in Nigeria," *African Affairs*, ed. K. Kirkwood (Carbondale, Ill.: Southern Illinois University Press, 1961), pp. 60-88; Geoffrey Parrinder, *Religion in an African City* (London: Oxford University Press, 1953), pp. 78-79; J. N. D. Anderson, *Islamic Law in Africa* (London: H.M.S.O., 1954), p. 224; H. A. R. Gibb, *Mohammedanism* (N.Y.: Mentor Books, 1955), p. 156; Trimingham, *op.cit.*, pp. 230-232.

[46] In 1947, Mr. M. R. B. Ottun, a journalist with the *West African Pilot* and secretary to the Chief Imam of Lagos, inaugurated a Society for Promoting Muslim Knowledge. The chief object of the society was to obtain scholarships for Nigerian students to study at Al-Azhar University in Cairo, Egypt. In December 1948, Yoruba Muslims inaugurated a cultural organization known as the Muslim Congress of Nigeria, which maintained a fraternal relationship with the Moslem Union (Jam'iyyar Islamiyya) of the North. In 1950 a Muslim Welfare Association was organized in Lagos, and in May 1953 Mr. Ottun founded the United Muslim Party as a political wing of the Society for Promoting Muslim Knowledge. Later, a Muslim Central Council was set up in Lagos as a cultural auxiliary of the United Muslim Party.

[47] The delegates to the meeting which established the National Muslim League represented the Muslim Welfare Association, the United Muslim Party (of

leaders appear to have viewed the emergence of a Muslim party in the Western Region with great consternation.[48] In October 1957, Chief Awolowo declared that a political party based on religion was incompatible with the peace and tranquility of the region and could not be tolerated. He announced that his government would "seriously consider the enactment of a law which would make it an offence for any one to exploit religion for political ends."[49]

There is reason to believe that Action Group leaders were wary of the formation of a three-cornered alliance involving the National Muslim League, the Northern Peoples' Congress, and the NCNC of Ibadan led by the fiery Alhaji Adegoke Adelabu, whose loyalty to Dr. Azikiwe might have been doubted after the Aba Convention. In order to offset the influence of the National Muslim League and to dissuade Muslims from affiliation with a sectarian party, prominent Action Group Muslims inaugurated a United Muslim Council.[50] In turn, the National Muslim League, as a protective measure, changed its name to the National Emancipation League (*Egbe*

Lagos), its affiliate, the Muslim Central Council, the International Muslim League, and the Abeokuta Muslim League. In August 1957, an inaugural conference was held at Ijebu-Ode at which Alhaji A. R. A. Smith, a Yoruba businessman and President-General of the Muslim Congress of Nigeria since 1950, was elected President-General of the Muslim League. It is reported that £700 was collected from supporters during the inaugural conference.

The United Muslim Party of Lagos under Mr. M. R. B. Ottun did not affiliate with the National Muslim League on the ground that the new party favored the incorporation of Lagos into the Western Region. In 1958, the U.M.P. made an alliance with the *Egbe K'Oyinbo Mailo* (Society for "Whiteman Should not Quit Yet"), a small anti-Action Group association in Egba Division.

[48] On October 6, 1957, a meeting of the National Muslim League at Ode Omu in Oshun Division was marred by disturbances caused by the intrusion of an Action Group irregular strong-arm squad. A regional minister and the federal treasurer of the Action Group, both Muslims, who attended the meeting in order to explain their party's objection to the formation of a Muslim political party, were credited by the Willinck Commission with having used their influence to mitigate violence, although police were required to restore order. *Report of the Commission appointed to enquire into the fears of Minorities,* p. 16.

[49] Address by the Hon. Chief Obafemi Awolowo . . . at the Emergency Conference of the Action Group, Ibadan, October 12, 1957. (Mimeographed.) In his capacity as Secretary General of the *Egbe Omo Oduduwa,* Chief Awolowo attacked the National Muslim Party at the Tenth Annual Assembly of the *Egbe* at Oshogbo in November 1957. He alleged that the Muslim Party had been organized in hostility to the Action Group and with the intention "to destroy the solidarity of the Yoruba people" which the *Egbe* was designed to foster. *Daily Times,* November 8, 1957.

[50] Leading members of the United Muslim Council were Alhaji A. T. Awelenje of Lagos, President-General; Alhaji D. S. Adegbenro, Western Minister of Local Government; Alhaji S. O. Gbadamosi, MHA, Federal Treasurer of the Action Group; Prince A. Adedemola, A.G. leader in the Abeokuta Urban District Council; Alhaji Yekina Ojikutu, member of the Lagos Town Council.

S'Eru D'Omo—"to make a slave free-born") and dropped its technical religious restriction on membership. It then concluded an alliance with the Northern Peoples' Congress. The National Emancipation League polled less than 1 percent of the total vote in the local government elections of April-June 1958, and failed to win a single seat in the federal election of 1959. But Muslim hostility to the Action Group may have been a factor in the defeat of Action Group candidates in 16 federal constituencies in the Yoruba area—one-third of the total number of Yoruba constituencies in the Western Region.

Socio-Economic Bases of the Action Group and the NCNC

Opposition to the Action Group in Western Nigeria has a socio-economic basis in addition to the ethnic and religious roots previously considered. Three relevant situations of social conflict may be distinguished. The first has been noted in an essay by Peter C. Lloyd;[51] it involves the phenomenon of competition between conservative "old elites" and nationalistic "new elites" in the traditional towns of Yorubaland prior to the emergence of mass political parties. Often elitist conflict of this nature stemmed from the discontents of progressive youth who resented the monopolization of economic privileges by their chiefs and elders, in particular, the prerogatives acquired by chiefs during the period of indirect rule to manage communal lands and forests.[52] Most controversies of this order have been resolved by the Action Group, often with the assistance of mediation by the *Egbe Omo Oduduwa*, to the mutual satisfaction of the old and the new elites alike. There are a few cases of persistent conflict between local elites which sustain inter-party competition, as at Ife,[53] but these are relatively exceptional.

[51] Peter C. Lloyd, "The Development of Political Parties in Western Nigeria," *The American Political Science Review*, Vol. XLIX, No. 3 (September 1955), pp. 705-707.

[52] In specific instances, public indignation was aroused by evidence of mismanagement or corruption on the part of chiefs and their associates. See Obafemi Awolowo, *op.cit.*, pp. 68-69. It seems possible to trace the origins of several existing local parties, i.e., branch organizations, to such popular risings against the old town elites; e.g., a famous conflict occurred at Abeokuta in 1948 when Mrs. Funmilayo Ransome-Kuti led a branch of the Nigerian Women's Union in agitation that culminated in the exile of the *Alake* (king) of Abeokuta. The Union was opposed to taxation of women in Abeokuta by the Native Authority and demanded a reduction of the *Alake's* power. It was supported by a men's organization called the *Majeobaje* (Reformers, literally in Yoruba, "Do not allow it to be spoiled"), while the pro-*Alake* faction was known as the *Atunluse* (literally, "Those who make the country better"). The exile of the *Alake* was terminated in 1950 but the rival organizations merged with the NCNC and the Action Group respectively.

[53] *Infra*, p. 473.

Secondly, situations of conflict between "sons of the soil" or the "natives" of an area and the "strangers" who settle in the burgeoning towns for occupational reasons are familiar in Nigeria. The so-called "detribalized" settlers normally preserve their home-town connections and loyalties through the medium of ethnic unions for "sons abroad"; but their stakes in the new urban communities become ever greater and the pattern of local politics in Nigeria features many instances of discord between indigenes and non-indigenes over land rights and control of local government councils. In this connection, the Eastern Regional cases of Onitsha and Enugu, discussed in previous chapters, may be recalled. A comparable situation obtains in the Mid-Western port city of Sapele (Delta Province), where the indigenous Okpe-Urhobos support the Action Group, while the non-indigenous Ibo settlers, who constitute over one-third of the urban population, generally support the NCNC. It is reasonable to assume that settler-indigene rivalry is a mainspring of Sapele politics, because the Okpe-Urhobos are the only major Urhobo group that does not normally support the NCNC.[54]

In Yorubaland, Lagos provides a classic example of conflict between an indigenous Yoruba community and non-indigenous Yorubas. For about 25 years prior to 1950, Lagos local politics turned on the rivalry between a majority of the Yoruba indigenes and the main body of Yoruba settlers. The settlers provided the greater portion of "polite" society in Lagos that was typically Christian, professional or entrepreneurial, and prosperous. Not a few of the leading citizens of Lagos were founders and supporters of the Nigerian Youth Movement and most of them now support its lineal successor, the Action Group. On the other hand, the Lagos indigenous community, which is predominantly Muslim and traditionalistic, supported the Nigerian National Democratic Party. That party eventually became an affiliate of the NCNC. Thereafter the two

[54] The Western Region Parliamentary and Local Government Electoral Regulations (W.R.L.N. 266 of 1955) permit individuals to vote in districts where they do not reside provided they can establish nativity in the area by virtue of their own or their father's birth. In the past, non-resident Itsekeris and non-resident Okpe-Urhobos have been advised by the Action Group to register and vote in Warri and Sapele respectively under the nativity provision. The writer was informed that in 1958 about 8,000 of the 36,000 Okpes registered as natives of Sapele rather than their own villages in nearby Western Urhobo, which are safe for the Action Group. Itsekeris resident in Sapele normally choose to vote in Warri although they pay rates to the Sapele Urban District Council. Thus an Action Group Itsekeri candidate to the Sapele U.D.C. cast his vote in Warri although he was actually elected to the Sapele council.

principal ethnic groups in the Lagos NCNC were the indigenous Yorubas and the (non-Muslim) Ibo settlers from the Eastern Region.
"Tribal" tensions at Lagos in 1948[55] involved conflict between the Ibo
and Yoruba settler groups, neither of which was traditionalist. Moreover, the Ibo settlers were allied with the greater part of the traditionalist Yoruba community against the main body of Yoruba settlers. The
Action Group became a "mass party" in Lagos in the early 1950's,
when it won over most of the Yoruba indigenes, thanks mainly to
the efforts of the pro-Action Group *Oba* of Lagos.

A third and most significant situation of socio-economic conflict
involves political cleavage between the people of a traditional community and the members of a rising class. In the traditional communities of southern Nigeria, class structure is incipient, and party
competition cannot be ascribed primarily to class struggle. Anthropological studies generally describe communal societies of a
corporate nature, segmented vertically by lineages, and stratified
horizontally by age grades and title associations. Chieftaincies may
be vested in particular families, but the families of kings, chiefs,
elders, and titled men have not been differentiated in terms of social
class. Under these conditions, the adhesion of a rising class to an
unpopular governing party is likely to produce an acute state of
tension between that class and the local community at large.
Benin, the capital city of the Edo people of the Midwest, provides
an illuminating example.

Some years ago, Edo men of wealth and high social status inaugurated a Benin branch of the Reformed *Ogboni* Fraternity, an
exclusive society which had been founded in Lagos by rising class
Yorubas who had been inspired by the example of European
freemasonry.[56] At first, membership in the Lodge was confined to
the town elite, i.e., professionals, businessmen, top clerical employees
of firms, and leading chiefs. Subsequently the Lodge was transformed
by its leadership into a political machine and opened to all officials,
both high and petty. From 1948 to 1951 the *Ogbonis,* under a

[55] *Supra*, p. 70.

[56] The traditional *Ogboni* was a politico-religious institution in historic Yoruba
states. See W. R. Bascom, "The Sociological Role of the Yoruba Cult Group,"
American Anthropologist, 56, No. 1, Part 2 (Memoir 63, January 1944), pp. 64-73;
and Saburi O. Biobaku, *The Egba and their Neighbors, 1842-1872* (Oxford:
Clarendon Press, 1957), p. 6. Founders of the Reformed *Ogboni* Fraternity in Lagos
included the late Sir Adeyemo Alakija, a member of the Governor's Executive
Council, who was also first President of the *Egbe Omo Oduduwa,* and the
Reverend T. A. J. Ogunbiyi. There are reported to have been a few Masons among
those who brought the R.O.F. to Benin as an elitist society.

dynamic leader,[57] dominated the administration of Benin Division to the great chagrin of its traditional ruler, the *Oba* of Benin, and the distress of the people. *Ogbonis* are reported to have controlled the tax system, the markets, the police, the courts, access to the firms, etc.[58] It is said that members of the Lodge violated the law with impunity, and that they enjoyed special privileges in most spheres of political and economic activity. By 1950 *Ogbonism* had become synonymous with oppression. Moreover, the people of Benin identified it with the bugbear of Yoruba domination and their anxieties mounted in 1951 when the principal *Ogboni* leaders affiliated with the Action Group, a new political party under Yoruba control. Meanwhile, non-*Ogbonis* formed a popular party, known as the *Otu Edo* (Benin Community), dedicated to defend tradition and the sacred institution of *Oba*-ship (kingship) against the alleged encroachments of usurpers. In 1951 the popular party swept the *Ogbonis* from office in local government elections, and defeated them soundly in contests for the Regional House of Assembly.[59]

However, the vindication of traditional value by the electorate of Benin Division did not restore the political supremacy of the *Oba*. His attempts to control the *Otu Edo* were frustrated by progressive leaders of that party, for whom the cause of tradition had been an expedient means to further nationalistic and other political ends. Since the *Ogbonis* were partisan to the Action Group, the leaders of the *Otu Edo* resolved to affiliate with the NCNC.[60] The *Oba*

---

[57] For a sympathetic portrait of the *Ogboni* leader see Chief Jacob U. Egharevba, *A Brief History of Hon. G. I. Obaseki, C.B.E., the Iyase of Benin* (Benin: 1956).

[58] See A. N. Nee-Ankrah, *Whither Benin* (Benin: 1951).

[59] This account is necessarily capsulized and simplified. For example, there were members of the royal family among the *Ogbonis*—the *Oba* was himself an early member—and men of wealth in the leadership of the *Otu Edo*. The leading academic authority on Benin political history is the noted ethnologist, R. E. Bradbury of the Benin Historical Project, University College, Ibadan.

[60] The President-General of the *Otu Edo*-NCNC, its chief policy maker, campaigner, and outstanding personality is Chief Humphrey Omo Osagie, MHR, the *Aighobahi* of Benin and Parliamentary Secretary to the Federal Ministry of Finance. Chief Osagie was born in 1896; he entered politics after his retirement from the civil service in 1945, and was elected to the Western House of Assembly in 1947 and 1951. In 1953 he secured the leadership of the *Otu Edo* and led it into affiliation with the NCNC. He was elected as an NCNC member of the House of Representatives in 1954. Since his appointment as Parliamentary Secretary, he has divided his time between Benin and Lagos, but he is always in Benin to lead the *Otu Edo* personally during campaign periods. His residence, Osana House, is the party headquarters and Chief Osagie appears to devote all of his time at home to politics. He is known to the people of Benin familiarly as "B 2" after the license number of his car. Only the *Oba* of Benin, whose car is "B 1" takes precedence over Chief Osagie in the popular scale of public prestige. Chief Osagie, Vice-Chairman of the NCNC Western Working Com-

spurned the thought of affiliation with either national party. His primary interest was the creation of a new state in the non-Yoruba provinces of the Western Region where *Edo* influence would be dominant, and he organized an independent party, the Benin Delta Peoples' Party,[61] to attain that objective. But it is perilous for any major chief to stand against the party in power. In the words of an official report, commenting on the case of the ex-*Alafin* of Oyo, to which we have referred: "The shadow of one great Chief, now deposed and in exile, lies across the foreground of every Chief's outlook today."[62]

In 1955, the *Oba* of Benin reappraised the realities of power in the Western Region and resolved to support the government party. The government endorsed the idea of a Mid-West State in principle, and the *Oba*, in turn, agreed to join the government as a Minister without Portfolio. A small minority of the Benin people who supported the *Oba* against the *Ogboni* menace to his authority now followed him into the Action Group; eventually they organized an *Otu Edo* wing of the Action Group. But the vast majority remained loyal to their communal party, the *Otu Edo*-NCNC. Their reverence for Benin traditions and the institution of *Oba*-ship persisted but they condemned the incumbent *Oba* for his switch to the Action Group, a party that was associated in Benin with *Ogbonism* and privilege.[63]

---

mittee, strongly supported Dr. Azikiwe during the Reform Committee rebellion of 1958.

[61] The Benin-Delta Peoples' Party appears to have been founded in 1953 but its period of greatest activity and influence was 1955 after the *Oba* of Benin failed in an attempt to assert his authority over the *Otu Edo* and sever that party's connection with the NCNC. The *Otu Edo* routed the BDPP in the local government elections of 1955 and swept the polls again in the Regional election of 1956.

[62] *Report of the Commission appointed to enquire into the fears of Minorities*, p. 11.

[63] It is generally acknowledged in Benin that the importance of *Ogbonism* as a political issue has diminished considerably since 1956, but most *Ogboni* Lodge members are still associated with the Action Group. Twenty-four of the forty-two Action Group candidates to the Benin City Council in 1958 were identified to the writer as members of the Reformed *Ogboni* Fraternity. Among 13 leading members of the Action Group Divisional Executive, including the 6 officers, 6 district chairmen, and the Benin City chairman, there were 8 businessmen of moderate to large scale (a rubber-factory owner, 2 rubber plantation owners, 2 transporters, a timber contractor, a wealthy trader and a photographer), a bank manager, a barrister, a president of a cooperative society, and 2 pensioners. Six of the 13 were members of the Reformed *Ogboni* Fraternity. Most informants agree that about 90 percent of the wealthy people in Benin support the Action Group; the writer's list of nine top economic personalities in Benin includes eight Action Groupers, six of whom are also *Ogboni* members, and one NCNCer who is not an *Ogboni* member.

Conflicts between communal interest groups and rising-class interest groups constitute a main root of party competition in certain areas of Yorubaland. The seminal case of Ibadan is discussed in the next chapter. Other cases include Oyo and Ilesha. The *Egbe Oyo Parapo* (Oyo People's Party), which has been noted previously in connection with the banishment of the *Alafin* of Oyo, is comparable to the *Otu Edo* of Benin. Both parties arose to defend the prerogatives of a traditional ruler which were threatened by the representatives of a rising class; both came under the leadership of nationalists who favored affiliation with the NCNC. In Ilesha town where the NCNC is a dominant mass party, the Action Group is supported by business-men and well-to-do persons who were likely to have economic relations with the regional government, e.g., agents licensed by the Western Regional Marketing Board to purchase agricultural products from primary producers, government contractors, and recipients of industrial loans from the Western Region Finance Corporation. Needless to say, party division never corresponds exactly to socio-economic cleavage. But it is significant if the supporters of the Action Group are drawn mainly from among prominent representa-tives of the rising class in areas where popular sentiment is over-whelmingly in favor of the NCNC.

No party in Nigeria has undertaken as systematic an effort to organize the peasantry as the Action Group; for that purpose, the Action Group has utilized chiefs and communal institutions with great effect in various sections of all regions. Nor has any party adopted a more progressive wage policy for all employees, public and private. [64] Yet the backbone of the Action Group, its vital component, is unmistakably the new and rising class. This conclusion emerges from data compiled by the writer on the occupations of Action Group leaders at all levels. Of 149 delegates to the Fourth Annual Federal Congress of the Action Group (Calabar, 1958) whose occupations were determined (out of a total of 214 delegates), the largest group of 30.2 percent were businessmen and traders, followed by 19.5 per-cent educators and 16.1 percent professionals, including 21 lawyers. Similar data compiled for 94 constituency and divisional leaders of the Action Group in the Western Region in 1958 (out of a list of 110) discloses a top group of 37.3 percent businessmen, followed by 24.5

[64] The Action Group government of the Western Region introduced a 5/-per day minimum wage for employees of the region in 1954 and the party has advocated similar action by the federal government. Chief Awolowo has taken the lead in urging the enactment of "a national minimum wage (by the Federal Parliament) not below 5/- which must be paid by all employers of labour in Nigeria." Obafemi Awolowo, *Action Group 14-Point Program* (Ibadan: 1959), p. 10.

percent educators and 21.3 percent professionals, including 19 lawyers.

Assuredly, "rising" or "middle class" leadership typifies the NCNC as well, as we have noted in Chapter V; indeed comparative tabulations of occupational data on the local-level leadership of the Action Group and the NCNC in both the Eastern and Western Regions reveal roughly similar distributions. The chief difference that emerges from a comparison of Tables 2 and 3 is the 15 percent edge that the NCNC holds in the petty trade, crafts, and shopkeeping categories, while the Action Group has a slightly higher percentage in the business, educational, professional, and clerical categories. Wage laborers are virtually excluded from the leadership cadres of both parties; traditional authorities do not appear in force, inasmuch as their affiliations with the parties are normally informal.

Various explanations may be adduced for the conclusion which may be drawn, to wit, that at the time of this study the Action Group was more specifically representative of the interests of the new and rising class than the NCNC. First, the home region of the Action Group from which its leadership is largely derived, namely the Western Region, is the most affluent of the regions of Nigeria (per capita annual income in the West was £34 in 1953 as compared with the national average of £21), with the greatest number of fairly well-to-do citizens[65] and the highest level of professional and educational achievement.[66] Secondly, the bipartisan traditions of the Western Region channel dissatisfied elements, notably anti-tax movements, into opposition groups which may align or affiliate with the NCNC.[67] Vast

---

[65] P. C. Lloyd, op.cit., pp. 694-695.

[66] J. S. Coleman states: "In 1921 educated Yorubas and 'native foreigners' held an overwhelming majority (78 percent) of the positions that required knowledge of the English language, and yet they constituted only 47 percent of the educated group and less than 16 percent of the population of townships." Nigeria, pp. 142-143.

[67] At the time of the federal election of 1954, anti-tax feeling ran high in Oshun Division and the Action Group returned only one of its four candidates to the House of Representatives. At Ikirun, Mr. D. L. G. Olateju, a pensioner and cocoa farmer, organized the Nigerian Taxpayers Association which adopted the name Nigerian Liberal Party and merged with the Nigerian Commoners Party, led by Miss Adunni Oluwole of Mushin (Colony Province). Mr. Olateju was elected on the platform of the Nigerian Commoners Liberal Party, and two candidates were returned by the NCNC, including the National Secretary, Chief Kolawole Balogun. Ultimately the Nigerian Commoners Liberal Party affiliated with the NCNC (and the Northern Peoples' Congress), but its electoral strength declined sharply. By 1956 the Western Region's primary education scheme and its farm loan program had offset the unpopularity of systematic taxation, and the Action Group won all 8 seats for Oshun Division in the Western House of Assembly. In 1958 the A.G. gained control of all district councils in the Oshun Divisional area.

In Ijebu-Remo, the home division of Chief Awolowo, the principal opposition in 1958 was provided by an Ijebu-Remo Taxpayers Association, a small party

TABLE 2

The Occupational Background of Leaders of the Action Group at Local Levels in the Western and Eastern Regions and the Federal Territory of Lagos, 1957-1958

	Number of persons	1. Traditional authorities	*Functionary strata* 2. Senior functionaries (government)	3. Senior functionaries (public and private enterprise)	4. Junior functionaries (government services, and public or private enterprises)*	5. Agents of occupational, cultural, and political associations	*Learned arts and skills* 6. Free professions and scientists	7. Communications and cultural arts—e.g., journalists	8. Educators (teachers and headmasters)**	9. Ministers and teachers of religion	*Profit and wage occupations* 10. Businessmen (finance and entrepreneurship)	11. Petty trade	12. Artisans, craftsmen, shopkeepers, and self-employed	13. Wage laborers and domestic servants***	14. Farmers	15. Unemployed or non-employable****	16. Unknown
Lagos AG Executive Committee: Officers and councillors, 1958	30	2			2	1	7	1		1	13	1	2				
Abeokuta AG Divisional and Central Officers, 1958	11	1			2					1	3		1		3		
Oyo AG Divisional Executive and Southern Dist. Officers, 1958	12					1	2		2	1	4	1			1		
Ife AG Divisional and District Officers, 1958	21				2		3		7		6				3		
Ilesha AG Divisional and Central Officers, 1958	10				4		1				3	2					
Ondo AG Divisional Executive, April 1957	18				1				4		7	3	1		2		

	Total											
Ondo AG N.W. Constituency Exec., October 1956	12			2			1		3		1	5
Owo AG Town and Constituency Officers, May 1958	10	1		2			4		3			2
Benin AG Divisional Officers and District Chairmen, 1958	13			2					8	3		
Sapele AG Branch Executive, 1958	26			3			1		13	9		
Warri AG Div. Executive, 1958	6			1		1	1		3			
Calabar AG and COR State Executive Officers, February 1958	21			3	1	1ᵃ	3	1	7	2	2	1
Uyo AG Divisional Officers, and clan chairmen	12			1			2			6	2	1ᵇ
Totals	202	4	2	23	3	16	1 24	5	73	24	9	17 1
		1.9%	1%	11%	1.5%	7.9%	11.9%	2.5%	36.1%	11.9%	4.5%	8.4%
											16.4%	

* Junior civil servants; junior executives, clerks, and other functionaries in business enterprise; junior military and police functionaries; persons pensioned from these positions

** Government and private schools

*** Government and private employment

**** Domestics, including housewives, students, and other dependents; beggars

ᵃ In addition 7 professionals were co-opted into the Executive

ᵇ Housewife

TABLE 3

The Occupational Background of Leaders of the NCNC at Local Levels in the Eastern and Western Regions, 1957-1958

	Number of persons	Functionary strata					Learned arts and skills				Profit and wage occupations						
		1. Traditional authorities	2. Senior functionaries (Government)	3. Senior functionaries (public and private enterprise)	4. Junior functionaries (Government services, and public or private enterprises)*	5. Agents of occupational, cultural, and political associations	6. Free professions and scientists	7. Communications and cultural arts—e.g., journalists	8. Educators (teachers and headmasters)**	9. Ministers and teachers of religion	10. Businessmen (finance and entrepreneurship)	11. Petty trade	12. Artisans, craftsmen, shopkeepers, and self-employed	13. Wage laborers and domestic servants***	14. Farmers	15. Unemployed or non-employable****	16. Unknown
Enugu NCNC Branch Executive, 1957	31				4	2	3				11	4	4				7
Onitsha NCNC Branch Executive, 1958	42		2		8	1	5		9		8	8	5			2ª	
Port Harcourt NCNC Branch Executive, January 1958	44				1				3		15	9	5	1	1		
Aba NCNC Branch Executive, February 1958	22				2		1		2		7	7	3			1	
Benin NCNC Central Executive, 1958	25								1		17				5		
Ilesha NCNC Officers (District, Divisional), 1958	8				1				2		3	1	1		1		
Oyo NCNC Executive, 1958	18								1	2	2	10			2		
Ibadan NCNC Central Executive Committee, July 1958	38	4			3		4			1	10	12	1		3		
Totals	228	4 1.75%	2 .9%		19 8.4%	3 1.3%	13 5.7%		18 7.9%	3 1.3%	73 32%	51 22.4%	19 8.3% / 30.7%	1	12 5.3%	3 1.3%	7 3.07%

* Junior civil servants; junior executives, clerks, and other functionaries in business enterprise; junior military and police functionaries; persons pensioned from these positions [...]

*** Government and private employment

**** Domestics, including housewives, students, and other dependents; beggars

ª Housewife and unemployed person

numbers of farmers, traders, and workers are drawn into the communal opposition parties of Ibadan, Ilesha, Oyo, and Benin. Thirdly, a large proportion of the manual and clerical workers in new urban areas of the Western Region are settlers from areas where the NCNC is dominant, in particular from Iboland.[68] Finally, the Action Group is the offspring of a prosperous new class and its educated minority. The party's mass appeal lies in the responsiveness of all major social groups to the values of nationalism. It endeavors constantly to reconcile conflicts which could result in mass opposition; its rationale was expressed by a former leader thus:[69] "The Action Group is the party of the masses, with reverence for *Obas*, understanding for the rich, and complete identification with the aspirations of the common man."

At this point we turn to an appraisal of the diverse ideological tendencies within the house of the Action Group.

IDEOLOGICAL TENDENCIES IN THE ACTION GROUP

In July 1957, Chief S. L. Akintola, then Leader of the Action Group Opposition in the Federal House of Representatives, commented with characteristic vividness on the ideological diversity of the Action Group:[70]

"As a member of the Government once told me, when they look around the Opposition from the bench they see some reactionary Members, some middle-of-the-road Members, and they also see some people whom they regard as extreme firebrands. If any group is truly democratic in the sense that they have extreme right and extreme left, and we are not lacking in either, there are also those who travel the middle of the way, then it is the Opposition in the Federal House."

---

composed mainly of petty traders and farmers who are opposed to the Government's local rating policies. See *Rules and Regulations of the Ijebu-Remo Taxpayers Association* (Shagamu: 1957) and the Memorandum of the IRTPA to the Nigeria Constitutional Conference, May 11, 1957. (Mimeographed.) In 1957 this party claimed affiliation with the NCNC (letter from the IRTPA to the Western Working Committee of the NCNC, dated August 20, 1957) but in 1958 the party extended its criticism of rates to opposition to self-government for Nigeria. Action Group candidates were successful in 256 of the 283 local government electoral wards in 1958 as that party won control of all 14 local councils in Ijebu-Remo Division.

[68] J. S. Coleman has calculated that Ibos "constitute more than one-third of the non-indigenous population of the urban centers of the Northern and Western regions." *Nigeria*, p. 76.

[69] Statement by R. A. Fani-Kayode, former Action Group member for Ife in the House of Representatives, *Daily Service*, August 1, 1958.

[70] *Third Annual Federal Congress of the Action Group, Lagos*, July 12, 1957 (Proceedings), p. 20.

The ideological diffuseness of the Action Group is more remarkable than that of the NCNC, inasmuch as the Action Group is a more highly centralized party which has developed into a mass organization from a relatively selective social base. Nevertheless, tendencies may be distinguished among Action Group leaders which may be identified as right, left, and center with respect to the universal yardstick of equalitarianism. Naturally, the practical criteria of ideological distinction in Nigeria are determined by local circumstances. Some American conservatives and an occasional British Tory may wonder that the "right wing" of the Action Group has given consistent support to welfare statist and socialistic policies, including free primary education, free medical care for children, progressive minimum wages, factory legislation, and public enterprise. The views of several wealthy conservatives, highly placed in Action Group councils, with respect to public enterprise may be summarized thus: There is no contradiction between our capitalistic activities or beliefs and our directorships of public enterprises. Public wealth is the chief source of capital in Nigeria and its prudent use will create many opportunities for private enterprise. Besides, public ownership will protect the natural resources of Nigeria from foreign ownership and control.[71]

[71] This should not be taken to imply hostility to foreign investment. On the contrary, the Action Group government is anxious to attract foreign capital and has given assurances of protection. Chief Awolowo has stated the Action Group policy with respect to foreign investment on several occasions. It was well summarized by him in a presidential address to an emergency conference of the Action Group at Ibadan, October 12, 1957, as follows:
"We must not allow foreign monopoly in any field of industrial venture. By this I mean that we must not allow a foreign investor to go it alone. Experience has shown that once a foreign investor has entered a particular field of industrial venture, that field is forever closed to Nigerian entrepreneurs. . . . I have said it on a number of occasions that we are not at all rigid as to the ratio of participation between the Western Regional Government or its agencies and any foreign investor. As a matter of fact, in all cases but one where we have entered into partnership with foreign investors, we have taken minority shares. The one exception is where we have 50% of the shares.
"What we are anxious about is that a foreign investor should always take into partnership in any new venture, either the Government or any of its agencies or private indigenous investors. We all know that the latter class of investors is almost non-existent just now and, until they are forthcoming, it is only fair that the Government, as the trustees of our people, should insist on financial participation in any new industrial venture.
"We in the Western Region are determined to ensure that this is the case, and we hope that the other Governments in the Federation, and in particular the Federal Government, will see to it that no industrial venture is launched in this country in the future unless there is substantial indigenous financial participation either by a Government or its agencies, or by private individuals. Unless this is done now, we would be creating a situation which might lead to serious consequences in the future."

The core element of conservative opinion in the Action Group is a business group of impressive size and affluence in the Western Region, probably the largest and wealthiest compact business group of Africans in Africa. This element includes a considerable number of entrepreneurs, merchants, and bankers, many of whom are strongly nationalistic, largely owing to their past experience of economic and social frustration under the conditions of colonial rule. It may be remarked that Action Group businessmen were not wholly unsympathetic to Dr. Azikiwe during his ordeal of investigation by the Foster-Sutton Tribunal of Inquiry into his relationship with the African Continental Bank.[72] Assuredly, the rise of an African govern-

[72] An Action Group leader of the highest order in Nigerian banking circles told the writer that he had been opposed in principle to the exploitation of the African Continental Bank case by his party for political reasons. Prior to the opening of the Foster-Sutton Tribunal of Inquiry, Chief Awolowo issued a statement in which he declined to recognize the appointment of that Tribunal as "a genuine case of British imperialism versus Nigerian nationalism" and further criticized Dr. Azikiwe for conduct which had resulted in a postponement of the Nigerian Constitutional Conference. *Daily Times*, August 20, 1956. At the Action Group Congress in Lagos, July 12-13, 1957, Mr. E. O. Eyo, A.G. member for Uyo in the Eastern House of Assembly, who was responsible for the initiation of the tribunal and had been the principal witness against Dr. Azikiwe, expressed his "indebtedness to the Action Group" for its assistance during the tribunal: "As most of you must have known, but for the Action Group it would have been absolutely impossible for me to go before the Foster-Sutton Tribunal. For one thing I had not the money to retain the services of a Queen's Counsel from England and I have told my people in Calabar Province I will always feel very indebted to the Action Group and also [to] my lawyers in the Action Group who brought up my case." Report of the Third Annual Federal Congress . . . , p. 50. (Mr. Eyo's chief counsel, barrister Christopher Shawcross, was assisted by three prominent Action Group barristers, namely, A. O. Lawson, R. A. Fani-Kayode, and A. Rosiji. *Proceedings of the Foster-Sutton Tribunal of Inquiry*, II, p. 1023.)

In December 1956, the NCNC Opposition in the Western House of Assembly brought a motion for a royal commission of inquiry into the activities of the Western Region government with reference to several matters including that government's investment into and its relationship with the National Bank of Nigeria Limited. In the ensuing debate, Hon. Alhaji S. O. Gbadamosi, Federal Treasurer of the Action Group, merchant, industrialist and a director of the National Bank, made the following statement:

"Any person who has Nigerian blood in his veins must join forces with any organization which is out to help our businessmen of today to regain their lost position. The National Bank of Nigeria Limited as the leading bank, 100 percent controlled by Nigerians, has dedicated its life to this national struggle. . . . Today the expatriate banks operating in this country have started to accommodate the Nigerian businessman, though in a most restricted form, not because of their love for his emancipation, but because of the competition which the National Bank of Nigeria is offering them. I wish the mover of the motion had come to this world earlier to witness what our businessmen had suffered in the hands of the expatriate banks. Time was when no Nigerian businessman was considered good for credit. My business friends like the late Mazi Mbonu Ojike and the honourable Dr.

ment that would foster the development of African enterprise was in the particular interest of this group. Yet it would be mistaken to assume that the desire for national independence on the part of the most prominent businessmen was contingent upon their anticipations of private gain. Some of those who have contributed most to the Action Group, in money and effort, had become wealthy before the emergence of the party; it was the writer's impression that, if need be, the majority of them would sacrifice their fortunes for the national interest.

Until a few years before independence, the hallmark of conservative thought in the Action Group was Western regionalism, possibly a consequence of the profitable cocoa trade which gave the Western Region per capita and general incomes that were substantially greater than the national averages. Conservatives in the West wanted a federal constitution that would safeguard the dominant position of the new regional elite. For this reason, some of them favored the adoption of a "confederationist" policy in 1953, involving the acceptance of the extreme confederationist Eight-Point Program of the Northern Peoples' Congress.[73] They were supported by several non-conservatives who were federalist in principle but anxious for one reason or another to reach a working agreement with the leaders of the North.[74] From time to time, thereafter, principles of confederation

---

Nnamdi Azikiwe were moved to tears when they considered and experienced what our businessmen suffered in the hands of the expatriate banks. This was one of the reasons why somebody else thought of founding a bank of his own." *Western House of Assembly Debates, 22 December 1956 (Official Report)*, pp. 163-164.

[73] *Supra*, p. 132, n. 99.

[74] At a joint meeting of the Action Group Executive Committee and Parliamentary Council in July 1953, prior to the London Constitutional Conference of July and August, the issue of federation vs. confederation was debated at length.

Chief Bode Thomas, the Deputy Leader, argued that the constitutional conference must not be permitted to fail on any account: "Members," he is reported to have said, "must guard against a repetition of the previous mistake which was made through sentiment. The Deputy Leader admitted his own share of the blame." He warned that the party must accept the 8-point program of the Northern Peoples' Congress or face the prospect of having to submit to the unprogressive rule of the North for three years or more.

"It must be understood," Chief Thomas is reported to have said, "that Britain did not want the success of the Conference. If the Conference should fail a federation must be decided upon in which the North might be called upon to rule the country with Dr. Azikiwe as Prime Minister. And the latter could compromise anything for power."

Chief Awolowo is reported to have observed that confederation would not necessarily lead to disunity as it would give the North a chance to see the benefits of association with the South. On this ground he would approve confederation.

T. T. Solaru thought that acceptance of the Northern plan would thwart the British plan to hold on.

and the policy of cooperation or alliance with the Northern Peoples' Congress have been broadly supported among party leaders,[75] but these principles appear to have been the distinctive contributions of conservative opinion.

The Ideological Center

The dominant tendency in the Action Group lies to the left of the business elite; it includes a majority of the professional men and the teachers, most of the active politicians, and the progressive element among the traditional chiefs. (It should be kept in mind that most of those politicians, professionals, and businessmen who are titled and addressed as "chief" are not chiefs in the sense of being traditional councillors or the heads of traditional states. Thus, seven of the twelve

---

S. L. Akintola spoke for acceptance of the 8-point plan as a practicable solution; he did not think that the party would escape a confederationist approach. Rotimi Williams thought that the federal form was best, but agreed that the Northern proposal would permit the regions to grow increasingly interdependent and predicted that the North would soon discover that secession did not pay; he said there was no point in going without the North.

On the other side, Chief Okorodudu, Mr. Awokoya, and Chief Enahoro spoke forcibly against confederation as a threat to the unity of the country. Enahoro argued that the only remedy for disunity was to dispose of the regional blocs. He predicted that confederation would not crystallize into federation and that all hope of unseating the Northern Peoples' Congress in the Northern Region would be lost. He was supported by Chief Akran.

Mr. Awolowo said the constitution did not fail because of regional representation in the center but because of interference by the center in regional affairs. Direct representation in the center, he said, would not prevent bloc voting.

It was decided at length that the Action Group delegation would press for federation with the understanding that specific powers would be delegated to the center while residual powers would be regional.

Minutes of the Joint Meeting of the Executive Committee and Parliamentary Council of the Action Group, Ibadan, July 16 and 17, 1953.

[75] It was reported that Chief Awolowo urged the inclusion in the constitution of the right of regions to secede from the Federation at the Resumed Constitutional Conference of January 1954. *Daily Times*, January 29, 1954. However, the conference agreed not to include a right to secede. *Report by the Resumed Conference on the Nigerian Constitution, Lagos, January and February 1954*, Cmd. 9059, p. 16. At the Fourth Annual Regional Conference of the Action Group in October 1955, certain elements favored secession if the Federal Territory of Lagos was not returned to the Western Region. Chief Awolowo rejected emphatically the idea of a Dominion of Southern Nigeria, which Dr. Azikiwe had suggested in 1953; he declared that the Action Group was "resolved to have one Nigeria or no Nigeria at all." A committee on the constitution concluded that the idea of a Southern Dominion was untenable and that "if for any reason the Northern Region is unable to remain in the Federation of Nigeria, the West should stand alone." Report of the Proceedings of the Fourth Annual Regional Conference of the Action Group, Ibadan, October 26-28, 1955 (Action Group Secretariat Files, Ibadan).

members of the Western Region Executive Council in 1958 were titled "chief," but only two of them held the titles of traditional rulers.[76] Neither Chief Awolowo, then Premier, nor the Action Group Deputy Leader, Chief Akintola, who became Premier of the West in 1959, is a traditional ruler.) By and large the centrists have been consistent advocates of "true" federation in Awolowo's sense i.e., federation with residual powers, in particular control over local governments, vested in the regions or states;[77] the present Nigerian Constitution is reasonably compatible with their ideal conceptions. Ultimately, they favor the creation of new states based on the principle of ethnic and linguistic affinity. In 1957, Chief Awolowo declared "that every ethnic group in this country, and there may be as many as a hundred of them, should in the long run be constituted into a separate State. That," he said, "is the ideal, and it is in our view a long term project."[78] The Action Group's short-run objective, and its main campaign pledge during the federal election of 1959, is the creation of an additional state from the territory of each of the existing regions.[79] Inevitably, partition of the existing regions would

[76] Chief C. D. Akran, *Aholujiwa II* of Badagry, Minister of Economic Planning, and Chief Anthony Enahoro, *Adolo* of Uromi (Ishan), Minister of Home and Mid-West Affairs.

[77] In his presidential address to the Fourth Annual Regional Conference of the Action Group, October 26, 1955, Chief Awolowo declared: "The foundation for lasting unity has been laid. This new and harmonious situation is due solely to the fact that residual powers are left in the Regions . . . the Northern Region (judging from their past and recent declarations) and the Western Region will not agree to residual powers being transferred to the Centre. The issue will undoubtedly be raised at the forthcoming Constitutional Conference by the NCNC spokesmen. There is no harm in doing so. But if it is pressed to a breaking point, it might spell the end of one Nigeria."
In order to limit the legislative power of the Northern leaders in the Federation, Chief Awolowo suggested that it was "absolutely imperative that provision should be made for an Upper House or Senate in the Centre. All the States would have equal representation in the Upper House, which would have concurrent legislative powers with the House of Representatives except in money matters." However, the Federal Senate which has emerged is empowered only to delay non-monetary bills for six months. The Action Group would now reduce the legislative power of the Northern leaders by effecting the division of the North into additional states.

[78] An address by the Hon. Chief Obafemi Awolowo at the Emergency Conference of the Western Region Action Group, Ibadan, October 12, 1957, p. 7. (Mimeographed.)

[79] Action Group spokesmen maintained that contrary to a declaration by the Secretary of State for the Colonies and the views of Dr. Azikiwe, the demands of the three leading separate state movements could have been granted before independence without postponement of the settled date of October 1, 1960. Obafemi Awolowo, *Action Group 14-Point Program* (Ibadan: 1949), pp. 19-20; and see his presidential address to the Emergency Congress of the Action Group

enhance the power of the federal government *vis-à-vis* the states, and the Action Group has declared its support in principle for a vigorous and effective federal government. In 1959, Chief Awolowo expressed the view that "the Federal Government should, where necessary, take the initiative in proposing national minimum standards even in regional matters, and should go further and create conditions which will make it possible for every Regional Government to attain such standards."[80]

Until 1958, the Action Group adhered strictly in principle to the regionalization of the police on the ground that every region or state in a federation should control the means of enforcing law and order.[81] In this connection, Awolowo has argued that "the regionalization of the police would make it extremely difficult for a totalitarian regime to emerge in Nigeria."[82] In 1958, the Action Group modified its position to accept concurrent jurisdiction over the police with ultimate control vested in the federal government.[83]

---

at Kano, December 12, 1958, pp. 1-8. (Mimeographed.) The issue became academic when the Action Group did not win control of the federal government.

[80] Chief Awolowo went on to say that he was "fully aware that, under the Constitution, the Federal Government cannot in respect of exclusively regional functions, compel a Regional Government to adopt its standards, except in some extreme circumstances." He limited his specific recommendations to planning agencies and agencies which would rely on voluntary inter-governmental cooperation. Obafemi Awolowo, *Action Group 14-Point Program* (Ibadan: June 1959) pp. 27-29.

[81] "Every Government in a federation, it must be re-emphasized, is equal in status to and independent in its sphere of activities from the other Governments in the Federation including the Federal Government. Each Government is responsible for the peace, order and good government of its area. It is a flagrant derogation from that function, and a device devoid of sense or worthy of precedent, to have a Regional or State Government without the physical organ essential and indispensable to the discharge of its primary functions." Presidential address by Chief Obafemi Awolowo to the Fourth Annual Congress of the Action Group at Calabar, April 28-May 2, 1958, Official Report, p. 9. See also his statement on this subject to the Third Annual Congress in Lagos, July 12-13, 1957, Official Report, p. 8.

[82] Presidential address by Chief Obafemi Awolowo to the Emergency Congress of the Action Group, Kano, December 12, 1958, p. 9.

Action Group spokesmen have answered criticisms that regionalization of the police would strengthen the oppressive hand of the Northern rulers by noting that the misuse of police power in the North was due to control by the Native Authorities rather than the regional government, thus:

"The N.A. police in the North should be responsible to the Regional Commissioner of Police and not to the Native Authorities as at present. Similar reforms to the Local Government police have been adopted in the West with the result that local government police have been insulated from local politics." J. A. Ola Odebiyi (Western Minister of Finance) "Problems of Nigerian Federation," *Daily Times*, April 22, 1958, p. 5.

[83] The constitutional agreements of September-October 1958 provide for the establishment of "a single force under an Inspector-General responsible to the

STUDIES IN POWER AND CONFLICT

The social philosophy of Action Group centrism may be described as "principled" welfare statism to distinguish it from the "pragmatic" welfare statism of the right wing. In the decade prior to independence no political party in Nigeria rivalled the Action Group's distinctive emphasis on social and economic planning. For planning was the keynote of the Action Group's inception and has remained a first article of Action Group belief.[84] In 1957 the Action Group Government of the Western Region inaugurated a Ministry of Economic Planning, the only such Ministry of its kind in Nigeria, until the creation of a Federal Ministry of Economic Development and Research in 1960.

At the Calabar Congress of 1958, barrister Ayotunde Rosiji, then Federal Secretary of the Action Group and Federal Minister of Health, suggested that it would be appropriate to describe the ideology of the Action Group as "constructive socialism," which he defined to mean that the objectives of social welfare and economic development should be given precedence over doctrinaire nationalization. He thought that nationalization should be restricted to two circumstances: first, if private capital available to develop a necessary industry is insufficient; secondly, "where the industries concerned are such that unless they are publicly owned the country cannot feel safe. In short," he said, "it is not intended that industries should go into private hands in circumstances where private industrialists can hold the Nation to ransom by reason of the fact that they control the

---

Federal Government." *Report by the Resumed Nigeria Constitutional Conference, September and October, 1958*, pp. 8-9. Yet Chief Awolowo expressed his satisfaction that the agreements "preclude exclusive centralisation" and "provide the Regional Governments with the executive instruments under its immediate control for discharging its responsibility for law and order." Presidential address to the Emergency Congress, p. 9.

[84] At the inaugural meeting of the Action Group, on March 26, 1950, it was decided that responsibility for the initial formulation of various aspects of the Action Group program, statement of policy and manifesto, would be assigned to individual members. (Minutes of the Inaugural Meeting.) At the seventh meeting of October 8, 1950, subjects were assigned to members who were directed to submit memoranda in February 1951. Minutes of the Seventh Meeting of the Action Group. These memoranda evolved into a series of policy papers which formed the basis of sessional papers that were submitted by the Action Group government to the Western House of Assembly in 1952 on various subjects, e.g., education, health, water supplies, cooperatives, agriculture, etc. See Obafemi Awolowo, "The Price of Progress" (Text of a speech in the Western House of Assembly, January 23, 1953). Other papers, e.g., on transportation and communications, were useful to members of the federal government.

In 1955, Premier Awolowo set up an Economic Planning Committee for the Western Region, including some of the best economic minds in Nigeria. This committee was mainly responsible for the production of the basic document on the development of the Western Region. (*Development of the Western Region of Nigeria, 1955-60*, Sessional Paper No. 4 of 1955.)

means of production." But foreign investors, he added, should be encouraged "to contribute their skill and managerial ability to the success of the industries which have been so far established."[85]

Most of the delegates seemed to agree fundamentally with Mr. Rosiji. Barrister A. M. A. Akinloye of Ibadan observed with approval that Rosiji's "constructive socialism" was socialism "not to the left but to the right."[86] At the present time, this philosophy is generally compatible with the principles and interests of the main business group.

It is appropriate to distinguish a centrist tendency of non- or quasi-socialistic radicals who are identified with the militant nationalist policy of "positive action." This tendency in the Action Group is represented by the former Western Minister of Home and Mid-Western Affairs, Chief Anthony Enahoro. It will be recalled that in 1953 Chief Enahoro moved the fateful motion for "self-government in 1956" which provided an occasion for the breakdown and revision of the constitution.[87] At the time of writing, he was chiefly responsible for matters pertaining to foreign affairs in the Action Group Shadow Cabinet (Federal) and a member of the steering committee of the All African Peoples' Conference. He is an eloquent proponent of West African solidarity.[88]

Until December 1959, barrister R. A. Fani-Kayode of Ife, Assistant Federal Secretary of the Action Group, typified the activist, racially militant element. At the Calabar Congress of 1958, he criticized the growing influence of Gamal Abdel Nasser in black Africa on racial grounds and declared that "blackism" would be the dominant ideal in Africa for a century.[89] In July 1958, barrister Fani-Kayode had the distinction of moving the resolution for independence on April 2, 1960, which was supported by all parties in the Federal House of

[85] The Action Group, *Report of the Fourth Annual Congress, Calabar, April 28-May 2, 1958* (Proceedings), pp. 35-36.

[86] *Ibid.*, p. 42.

[87] *Supra*, pp. 125-126.

[88] Chief Enahoro's highly regarded address as Leader of the Action Group Delegation to the First All African Peoples' Congress at Accra, Ghana, in December 1958 called for "the establishment of permanent organizations, both on a continental and on a regional basis." He declared that "the Action Group fully supports the evolution of a West African Federation, with the ultimate objective of an African Commonwealth of States. . . . I ought to add that the Action Group envisages a true federation and not a loose association of States, and we believe that it is not necessary to await the attainment of independence by the various States of West Africa before coming together to discuss the basis and form of a West African Federation."

[89] Journal notes on the proceedings of the plenary sessions of the Calabar Congress; this speech was omitted from the Official Report.

Representatives. In 1959 he lost his seat in the House of Representatives to a candidate who was supported by the *Oni* of Ife, whereupon he resigned from the Action Group and joined the NCNC.

The Left

In June 1952, Marxian intellectuals associated with the People's Committee for Independence[90] met at Abeokuta (Western Nigeria) to frame a strategy for socialist action.[91] It was decided to inaugurate a United Working People's Party, but to defer public announcement until organizational preparations were well advanced. In March 1953, the homes of UWPP members in several towns were raided by the police; a few of the leaders were tried for offences of sedition and fined. The United Working People's Party surfaced defiantly in March 1954, but the social and political conditions for revolutionary action seemed less auspicious in 1954 than previously. It was agreed that it would be more realistic for the members to join one of the two major parties in southern Nigeria.

At a final meeting, a debate on the relative merits of the Action Group and the NCNC ended in stalemate and it was agreed that individual members should join the party of their choice. A majority of them appear to have turned to the Action Group for the following reasons. First, Azikiwe had clashed repeatedly with left-wing radicals since 1949, and they renounced him as an erratic bourgeois leader. Secondly, the Marxists seem to have been impressed by the efficient organization and methodological planning of the Action Group. Thirdly, the UWPP was stronger in the West than in the East; prominent among its members were European-trained scholars and professional men who belonged to the social class of the Action Group elite and for whom the Action Group government could provide opportunities that would give scope to their talents. Finally, some of them believed that the Action Group principle of federalism reflected a deeper appreciation of social forces, in particular, ethnic group

[90] *Supra*, p. 81.

[91] The writer is informed that Dr. Chiaka Anozie was chairman of the meeting; other participants included S. G. Ikoku (now Leader of the Action Group Opposition in the Eastern House of Assembly), Ayo Okusaga (later Western Minister of Education), Ayo Ogunsheye (now Director of Extra-Mural Studies, University College of Ibadan), Dr. Victor Oyenuga (U.C.I.), Dr. Sanni Onibamiro (U.C.I.), Gogo Chu Nzerebe (now Secretary of the Post and Telegraphs Workers Union) and Meke Anagbogu.

Ikoku and Ogunsheye are economists, trained at the London School of Economics; Onibamiro is a medical scientist; Oyenuga is an agriculturalist and Okusaga is a barrister. They are all British educated.

sensibilities, and therefore a more realistic approach to the "nationalities question" than the NCNC principle of unitary government.

The socialists are partly responsible for the national expansion of the Action Group, but their main contribution has been ideological rather than organizational.[92] They have edged the party to the left, becoming Fabian thinkers themselves, in the process. In 1958, left-wing thought in the Action Group emphasized the ideal of African unity and the necessity to create a strong Nigeria that would be able to meet force with force on the African continent.[93]

It is probably true, as one highly placed member of the Action Group has remarked to the writer, that a clear ideological program would split the party from top to bottom. (It will appear presently that this prognostication was verified in substance after independence.) Another high-ranking member suggested that there are many members and some leaders who do not even know that the party houses deeply antagonistic ideological groups. Within the party

[92] See Action Group Bureau of Information, *Action Group Summer School Lectures, 1955,* including: "Imperialist Agents in Dependent Countries" by Obafemi Awolowo, "Idealism and Materialism" by O. Agunbiade-Bamishe, "South Africa—A Threat to Nigerian Security" by R. A. Fani-Kayode; and *Action Group Summer School Lectures, 1956,* including: "The Implications of a Federal Constitution" by Obafemi Awolowo, "The Political Significance of Contradictions" by O. Agunbiade-Bamishe, "The Latest Development in Marxist Ideology" by V. A. Oyenuga, and "Social and Economic Forces in Eastern Region Politics," by S. G. Ikoku.

[93] At the Calabar Congress of 1958, Hon. S. G. Ikoku, Leader of the Opposition in the Eastern House of Assembly, said that the Union of South Africa posed a threat to the security of Nigeria and that an independent Nigeria must be prepared to render material assistance to oppressed Africans. This able speech was omitted from the official report of the Congress. Hon. Ayo Okusaga, Western Minister of Education, disagreed with Chief Awolowo's opinion that Nigeria would have a special "sisterly relation" with Great Britain, "a situation which . . . nothing in our past relationship entitles us to hope for . . . we and the British," he said, "are friendly human beings and no more. We are only brothers in the same general sense that all humanity are brothers. . . . Our natural ties, I say, are with those of our race which surround us in the British and French areas of Africa. It is by union with these people that we can make Nigeria greater if we want to. With the rest of the World that is, Western Democracies and the Soviet Bloc and all the other Blocs alike, our policy should be one of friendly independence whilst remaining in the British Commonwealth. India has done it, we too can do so for our own mutual advantage." Report of the Calabar Congress, pp. 45-46. See also the observations of barrister O. N. Rewane on West African Union and the necessity of dividing Nigeria into smaller states in preparation for the formation of a West African Union. *Ibid.,* pp. 38-39.
Following the Second All-African Peoples' Conference at Tunis in 1959, Mr. S. G. Ikoku, who attended as an Action Group delegate announced that he agreed with the foreign policy of non-alignment advocated by Dr. Azikiwe. *West Africa,* February 20, 1960, p. 215. Subsequently, he joined a socialist group in Eastern Nigeria comprising members of the Action Group and the NCNC alike.

the struggle between the left and the right takes various forms—e.g., "youths" vs. "elders," "organizers" vs. "financiers," "propagandists" vs. "organizers," "ideologists" vs. "non-ideologists," etc. The Action Group has never adopted a doctrinaire ideology. The Benin Conference of 1952 decided not to adopt a particular ideological line, but endorsed several specific proposals formulated by the Parliamentary Council, including self-government in 1956, a federal constitution with residual powers in the regions, and free enterprise with public ownership of basic industries.[94] In practice the Action Group line has fluctuated between Fabian socialism and welfare state capitalism.[95]

[94] *Daily Times*, October 23, 1952, and December 23, 1952; it had been reported that the Benin Conference was likely to adopt an ideology. "The Conference will choose one of four 'isms': either Conservatism, Liberalism, Socialism, or Communism. ... " *Daily Times*, November 22, 1952.

[95] A succinct yet comprehensive statement of the welfare state policy of the Action Group was made by Chief Obafemi Awolowo in his presidential address to the Calabar Congress of 1958:

"As a matter of long-term objective, we believe, as I have said before, in a Welfare State. To this end we envisage, in the field of Education, free education for all our children, from the primary school to the university level, and the total abolition of illiteracy among our adults whatever their age and sex. In normal circumstances, the greatest guarantee of the liberty of the citizen is an educated and enlightened society.

"In the sphere of health, we aim at the introduction of measures designed for the prevention and cure of diseases. The health of the citizens, like their education, is the responsibility of the Government. Because of this we are of the considered opinion that children up to the age of 18 should receive free medical treatment, and that adults should enjoy similar treatment under a Health Insurance Scheme which must be introduced in due course. Good housing, scientifically planned towns or villages, good drainage, slum clearance, the provision of good water in towns and villages—all these and other amenities not mentioned here are essential for the prevention of diseases, and the cultivation of a healthy and vigorous citizenship.

"Nigeria is predominantly an agricultural economy: over 80 percent of our people are engaged in farming. If we are to be reckoned among the truly advanced and prosperous nations of the world we must introduce measures which will considerably reduce the number of people engaged in farming and at the same time absorb those who are displaced from the farmlands. But we must do first things first. It is, therefore, imperative that the efficiency and productivity of the farming population should be increased, and their standard of living raised. This will be done by the introduction of modern and scientific methods of farming throughout the country. The immediate effect of course would be that much fewer people would be required to produce the farm products that we need. To meet the new problem that would be created, progressive industrialisation through the media both of the public and private sectors must be pursued right now, and continued with rapidly increasing tempo in future years. In an underdeveloped country such as ours, where the majority of people are unsophisticated and not investment-conscious, it is the duty of the Government either directly or through its agencies, as a matter of deliberate policy, to stimulate an increase in agricultural productivity, and to finance industrialisation either wholly or, preferably, in partnership with indigenous or foreign entrepreneurs.

"The existence of a Welfare State which we aspire after, implies full employment.

The chief spokesmen for the party on matters of ideology are liberal centrists, notably, Chief (barrister) Awolowo, Chief (barrister) Akintola, Chief (barrister) F. R. A. Williams (the first Nigerian to hold the office of Attorney General, which he attained in the Western Region in 1957, and the leading adviser to the Action Group on legal and constitutional matters),[96] Chief (barrister) Ayotunde Rosiji, and Chief Anthony Enahoro. Several of the important young theoreticians, e.g., S. G. Ikoku, barrister Ayodele Okusaga, and barrister O. N. Rewane, are inclined to the left. With the approach of independence and the decision of the Action Group to expand massively into the Northern Region in order to compete on a grand scale with the Northern Peoples' Congress, all major factions within the party became ardent proponents of liberal democracy, including freedom of speech, due process of law, and the extension of the franchise to

unemployment relief for those temporarily out of work, a national minimum wage for the working class, and general contentment and continually rising standards of living for every section of the community. It is our resolve to achieve all these: in particular to see that every citizen of Nigeria whatever his or her calling, rank, or creed is gainfully employed, and that the resources of the land are exploited for the benefits and edification of all our people.

"All these then in theoretical and practical terms are the short-term and long-term ideals which dominate the approach of the Action Group to any given national problem. In the sphere in which our party is in power, these aims and ideals are not mere idle dreams. In the Western Region they are already being translated into action, as many right-thinking people in and outside this country can testify." The Action Group, *Report of the Fourth Annual Congress, Calabar, April 28-May 2, 1958* (Proceedings), p. 4.

[96] Chief Frederick Rotimi Alade Williams was born in Lagos in 1920; his father was a barrister and he was educated through the secondary school level in Nigeria. He pursued higher studies at the University of Cambridge and became a barrister at the age of 23. Upon his return to Nigeria he took an active part in the Nigerian Youth Movement and in 1952 he was awarded a chieftaincy title by the Alake and Chiefs of Abeokuta. About this time, he became legal adviser to the Action Group. In 1953 he was elected Chairman of the Lagos Town Council. When Chief Awolowo became Premier of the Western Region in October 1954, he invited Chief Williams to become a Special Member of the Western House of Chiefs in which capacity he was eligible for appointment as Minister of Justice and Local Government. In 1957 he became Attorney-General of the Western Region. Probably no person, apart from the Prime Minister and the first three regional premiers, has made a greater contribution to the framing of the Nigerian Constitution than has Chief Williams. In 1958 he was assigned primary responsibility by the Action Group Federal Executive Council for the organization of that party's legal defense system in the Northern Region. He was a member of the Action Group delegation to the first All-African Peoples' Conference of December 1958 and participated in the Conference Committee on Permanent Organization. In 1959 he was one of the first two Nigerians to be appointed as Queen's Counsel; in 1960, following the federal election, Chief Williams relinquished his office as Attorney-General of the Western Region and assumed the post of Permanent Legal Adviser to the Action Group. See the "portrait" in *West Africa*, January 17, 1959, p. 53.

Northern women.[97] (The social and legal conditions obtaining in the North in 1958 which motivated the Action Group's policy of militant libertarianism are elucidated in Chapter VIII.) At the first All-African Peoples' Conference of December 1958, held under the auspices of the Ghanaian government in Accra, the Action Group delegates placed their party in the front rank of spokesmen for the principles of liberal democracy in Africa.[98]

LEADERSHIP IN THE ACTION GROUP

While Obafemi Awolowo was the master builder of the Action Group, his was not the sole compelling personality among the illustrious professional and businessmen who gathered around him in 1950-1951. All accounts verify that men of stature in the professional, business, and educational milieu of the Yoruba elite prevailed upon him to assume the leadership of the new movement in Western Nigeria. In the early period, barrister Awolowo relied greatly upon the advice of a small group of confidants in Lagos, including Chief

[97] In his presidential address to the Calabar Congress of 1958, Chief Awolowo declared that the Action Group was "honor bound" by the agreements of the previous constitutional conference not to reopen the question of female suffrage in the North for the federal election of 1959. "Let us all admit," he said, "with solemn remorse, that we have committed a grievous wrong, and make up our minds, resolutely now, that nothing shall deter us in the future from righting an unpardonable wrong." *Report*, p. 5. This objective, i.e., universal adult suffrage in the North, is shared by the NCNC and its ally, the Northern Elements Progressive Union.

[98] The Action Group representative in the All-African Peoples' Conference Committee on Racialism and Discriminatory Laws and Practices (Committee 2), barrister O. N. Rewane, joined with the representative of the True Whig Party of Liberia and the United Party of Ghana (the Ghanaian Opposition Party) to propose that all independent African States should be advised to give legislative sanction to the Universal Declaration of Human Rights, that African member-states of the United Nations should "use their good offices to secure that the 'Universal Declaration of Human Rights' becomes part and parcel of the fundamental or organic law of all member-states of the United Nations," and that a permanent Commission on Human Rights be set up by the All-African Peoples' Conference "with powers to receive and to report to it progress made in the implementation, as well as any denial, of fundamental human rights in any part of the continent of Africa." Draft Resolution on the Implementation of Human Rights by Mr. Rewane (Nigeria), Mr. Morgan (Liberia) and Mr. Apaloo (Ghana). (Mimeographed.) These proposals were incorporated partially (with respect to the extension and assurance of fundamental rights to the citizens and inhabitants of Independent African States and the creation of a committee of the Conference "to examine complaints of abuse of human rights in every part of Africa and to take appropriate steps to ensure the enjoyment of the rights by everyone.") in the Conference Resolution on Imperialism and Colonialism produced by Committee 1 in which Dr. E. O. Awduche, MHR, Federal Vice-President of the Action Group, participated.

Bode Thomas of Oyo, a barrister of great acumen and elitist pre-possessions, who was chairman of the editorial board of the *Daily Service*. Other members of the inner group included barrister S. L. Akintola (Ogbomosho), then editor of the *Daily Service*, M. A. Ogun (Ijebu-Ode), an advertising consultant and the secretary of the editorial board of the *Daily Service*, S. O. Sonibare (Ijebu-Ode), a businessman, and A. O. Rewane (Warri), a businessman. The trust that Mr. Awolowo reposed in the members of this group was indicated by the inclusion of Messrs. Ogun, Rewane, and Sonibare among his initial appointments to the crucial Western Regional Production Development Board in 1952.

Caucus tendencies in the leadership of the Action Group were evident from the outset. After the election of 1951, the Action Group set up a Parliamentary Council, comprising all parliamentarians in addition to those members of the Central Executive Committee who were not parliamentarians and other co-opted members; its purpose was to coordinate and direct party policies in the regional and central legislatures.[99] The Parliamentary Council elected a Leader—Mr. Awolowo—a Deputy Leader—Chief Bode Thomas—and established a Parliamentary Committee consisting of "the Leader, the Deputy Leader and five members elected by the Council at least two of whom shall not be members of the House of Assembly."[100] This committee designated persons for appointment as ministers in the regional and central governments, and drew up a list of members of the Western House of Assembly who would be elected by that body to sit in the central legislature. All selections of the Parliamentary Committee were ratified by the full Parliamentary Council.[101]

It appeared to certain members that there was a tendency for the Parliamentary Committee and the informal group close to Awolowo to assume *de facto* management of the affairs of the party. Radicals especially were anxious to establish regular procedures and to ensure that the "regionalist-confederationist-minded" business group in Lagos did not exert disproportionate influence in the formulation of policies. At first their objections to the concentration of authority in the Parliamentary Committee were dismissed by the leadership on the ground that the powers of the Parliamentary Committee, especially

[99] Action Group Memorandum on Parliamentary Rules, n.d.

[100] *Ibid.* In addition to Mr. Awolowo and Chief Bode Thomas, the members of the Parliamentary Committee are reported to have included S. L. Akintola, Arthur Prest, and Dr. Akinola Maja (Chairman of the National Bank of Nigeria and Vice-President of the *Egbe Omo Oduduwa*).

[101] Minutes of the meetings of the Action Group Parliamentary Council, December 1, 1951, January 5-9, 1952.

the right to designate regional ministers, were in theory the pre-rogatives of the Leader alone. It was averred that prior consultation between the Leader and a formal committee of the Parliamentary Council on the designation of his ministerial colleagues was an innovation on the democratic side that was unknown in England.[102] But the radical wing kept up its pressure for reform, and proposals were drawn up by Anthony Enahoro which restored the primacy of the Central Executive Committee in the sphere of policy formulation by the exclusion of non-legislators from an enlarged Parliamentary Committee, and by the restriction of that body to the function of drafting legislation in accordance with party policies.[103] Ultimately these efforts ensured the supremacy of the Party Executive over the parliamentary wings.

Enahoro's famous motion of 1953 in the House of Representatives, calling upon the British to grant self-government to Nigeria in 1956, appears to have been related to the inner party conflict between radicals and conservatives. The motion was filed without the knowledge of the Leader or the Deputy Leader and without prior submission to the Parliamentary Council for discussion.[104] However, both the Parliamentary Council and the Executive Committee concluded that the technical breach of the party rules should be overlooked in view of the fact that the motion embodied an overriding policy decision of the Benin Conference, and its withdrawal for any reason might be construed as a betrayal of the nationalist cause. Chief (barrister) Arthur Prest (then Central Minister of Communications), among others, argued within the Executive Committee that it was not wise at that point to alienate the leaders of the North or to provoke them into the adoption of a "Pakistanist" policy.[105] Less than four months later, on the eve of the Constitutional Conference of July-August 1953, other leading members agreed with Prest that a mistake had been made "through sentiment," and that a conciliatory attitude toward the North should be adopted.[106]

At the Warri Congress of December 1953, the "strict" federation-

[102] Action Group Parliamentary Council, Minutes of the Meeting of January 19, 1952.

[103] It was also proposed by Mr. Enahoro that the Parliamentary Committees of the Regional and Central Houses be enlarged to include ministers and additional floor members. Action Group, Memorandum on Parliamentary Party System, submitted by Anthony Enahoro, Assistant General Secretary to the President for consideration of the Parliamentary Committee.

[104] Minutes of the Emergency Meeting of the Executive Committee of the Action Group, March 24, 1953.

[105] *Ibid.*

[106] *Supra,* p. 264, n. 74.

ist-radical wing of the party seized control of key positions in the organization. Their instrumentality for the accomplishment of this *coup* was a so-called "pressure group," three of whose members were elected to high party office, notably barrister Ayotunde Rosiji, who became General (later Federal) Secretary.[107] This appears to have been the last concerted effort by a major faction to alter the distribution of power in the party before independence. It was directed against associates of Mr. Awolowo, not against the leader himself.[108] In 1955, the Federal Executive virtually abolished an Action Group Youth Association which had been formed under the leadership of barrister R. A. Fani-Kayode, MHR (Ife), formerly a member of the pressure group. This association was regarded as potentially subversive of the incumbent party leadership. All organs of the Youth Association above the local level were dissolved and an age limit of 18 years was imposed upon its membership. In 1956, two former leaders of the pressure group, one of whom was a regional minister, resigned from the party, along with another regional minister, when they were not selected by their constituency organizations to contest the regional parliamentary election.[109]

[107] The members of the Pressure Group who were elected to national office in the party at the Warri Congress of 1953, in addition to barrister Rosiji, were barrister R. A. Fani-Kayode, elected as Assistant Secretary in place of Anthony Enahoro, a strong federationist who was not, however, a member of the Pressure Group, and Mr. Oladipo Amos, as Publicity Secretary. Other members of the Pressure Group were S. O. Awokoya, Western Minister of Education, J. A. O. Odebiyi, Rev. E. A. Alayande, M. S. Sowole (then General Secretary, Nigerian Union of Local Authority Staff), Abiodun Akerele, and Arthur Prest, Central Minister of Communications, who had been identified with the confederationists. It is said that prior to his death in November 1953, Chief Bode Thomas had been critical of the Lagos clique and sympathetic to the Pressure Group because of his belief that all decisions should be taken within the executive of the party. It emerges that the Pressure Group was mainly but not exclusively federationist in sentiment and that organizational, possibly personal issues eclipsed the issue of ideology in its animation. The writer is informed that some of those who organized the Pressure Group were disturbed on the eve of the London Constitutional Conference by the publication in the press of the list of Action Group delegates prior to their actual selection by the party executive. This led to allegations that a private clique handpicked the delegation.

[108] At the Lagos Congress of July 1957, Chief Awolowo referred to the experience of the Warri Congress of 1953 to discourage lobbying by members for office:

"The mere fact of lobbying, in my opinion, is sufficient disqualification for anyone who goes about doing it and I would appeal to all Members here with whom lobbying had been done, to disabuse their minds from such an act and when you come here to vote for Officers of the Party you do so because you think that the particular candidate is the candidate of your choice and not someone for whom you are voting because there has been lobbying." Report of the Third Annual Congress, p. 22; and Nduka Eze's rebuttal, *ibid.*, pp. 45-46.

[109] S. O. Awokoya, Federal Minister of Education and Oladipo Amos, Federal

STUDIES IN POWER AND CONFLICT

The Action Group is run absolutely according to the method of collegial discussion and extensive consultation. Its policies are formulated by a process of exhaustive discussion at informal levels before they are considered by the Party Executive or the Parliamentary Council. Chief Awolowo speaks privately to his trusted advisers and to certain chiefs and financial supporters who prefer to participate on an unofficial basis. In 1955 he inaugurated the practice of holding informal "leaders' meetings" at his home in Ikenne, Ijebu Remo Division. The "leaders' meeting" is a Western Regional innovation; it convenes monthly when feasible, and is attended by official party leaders from all divisions in addition to other influential persons. Discussions encompass both immediate problems and long-range policies; no minutes or records are kept and those in attendance are honor bound not to divulge the content of the deliberations.[110]

On several occasions, Chief Awolowo has carried out faithfully decisions that were taken by the Party Executive over his strong objection. For example, he personally opposed the decision to adopt a policy of "free and compulsory" primary education in 1952.[111] In his opinion, compulsion was inadvisable at the time inasmuch as it would alienate those parents who required the assistance of their children in the performance of farm chores; moreover, he warned that a compulsory system would commit the government to expenditures over and above its existing means. Eventually, the Party Executive abandoned compulsion, but until that point Chief Awolowo

---

Publicity Secretary of the Action Group, had been members of the Pressure Group. Awokoya formed the Nigerian Peoples' Party which contested 4 seats without success. Subsequently, Awokoya and E. A. Babalola, former Western Minister of Works, reconciled with the party.

110 The Report of the Secretary to the Fourth Annual Regional Conference, Ibadan, October 1955, notes the holding of 7 monthly meetings of party leaders in the West at the Ikenne residence of the President, beginning in February 1955. At the Lagos Congress of 1957, Chief Awolowo commented as follows on the institution of the leaders' meeting: "There is one point I would like to say to new Members here—we have meetings here and we want to institute similar meetings in the Eastern and the Northern Regions and I will go regularly to conduct such meetings myself. At these meetings we don't have agenda and we don't keep Minutes and the result is NCNC don't know how we operate. Adelabu has said we hold meetings in the night and in the jungle and the NCNC have not been able to find a single record of any decisions made by the Action Group." Report of the Third Annual Congress, p. 57.

111 The First Policy Paper on Education adopted by the Action Group in 1951 stipulated: "Education should be free and compulsory from the age of 5 to 13: that is, Elementary Education of eight years course—Infant I to Standard VI should be free and compulsory." Daily Service, May 12, 1951.

defended the compulsory education bill in public debate and in the House of Assembly.[112]

Another occasion on which the view of the leader was overridden on a major issue of policy involved the decision of the Federal Executive to accept the offer of the Prime Minister-designate, Alhaji Abubakar Tafawa Balewa of the Northern Peoples' Congress, to participate in the national government which the latter formed upon taking office in 1957. It was revealed by the Federal Secretary's Report to the Calabar Congress that this decision was taken by the Federal Executive Council while the President was on leave in Europe during August 1957. "The Federal President," it was reported, "was at every stage kept informed of the trend of events."[113] In fact Chief Awolowo did not favor participation in a national government, mainly because he feared that it would compromise the stand of the Action Group opposition in the North. Although the national government never received his approval within the party prior to its formation, he bowed to the decision of the Executive, and gave it his unqualified support.

Members of the party relate one occasion on which their Leader was unbending. When the Action Group lost the federal election of 1954 in the Western Region, a vocal faction in the Executive favored an attempt to "buy over" a few of the successful NCNC legislators. Awolowo was adamantly opposed; the writer was told by an informant of impeccable reliability that the leader admonished his colleagues not to do anything that would bring disgrace upon the party. "When you have done your best," he is reported to have said at the time, "and things go against you, then your belief in God counts." Following the victory of the Action Group in the 1956 regional election, Chief Awolowo declared: "We have never induced and we will never induce any member of the NCNC to cross to our side. It is grossly immoral to do so."[114] A distinguished colleague has said of Awolowo: "He is so transparently honest and so religious that men are bound to respect him. [His church affiliation is Methodist.] No man is indispensable but he would be difficult to replace. He leads without making people feel that he is leading. When a

[112] *Western House of Assembly Debates*, Second Session, Part I, January 23, 1953, pp. 135ff.

[113] *Report of the Fourth Annual Congress*, p. 17. It is known that Dr. Akinola Maja and Alhaji S. O. Gbadamosi flew to London to confer with the Federal President. And see the correspondence between Alhaji Abubakar Tafawa Balewa and Chief Rotimi Williams published in the *Daily Times*, August 31, 1957.

[114] Statement by Chief Obafemi Awolowo, June 2, 1956.

majority decides against his opinion he concedes, but he tells them to make a note of his dissent, and he has generally been proven right."

The debate on Nigerian policy with respect to military power that he initiated at the Calabar Congress of 1958 provides an insight into Awolowo's mind and his method of leadership. In order to "stimulate" discussion within the party and among the public at large, he posed the alternative policies of Power Politics and Welfare Politics and urged the adoption of a policy of virtual non-armament for the independent state of Nigeria:[115]

"Nations which indulge in power politics have brought perpetual fear and heartache to their people. The underdeveloped ones have brought grinding poverty, unspeakable ignorance and diseases to them as well. It is my submission that Nigeria on its attainment of nationhood should regard power politics as a fell poison, and should eschew it as such."

This recommendation was criticized vigorously, albeit respectfully, by many speakers, the greater number of whom emphasized the necessity during the immediate post-independence period of maintaining a military establishment adequate to ensure the territorial integrity of Nigeria. Pronouncements of this order were so numerous and forceful that the Deputy Leader, Chief S. L. Akintola, said at the conclusion of the debate that he was "quite sure that the Leader, as democratic as he is, will take his cue from what you all have said," and reconsider his position.[116] In response, Chief Awolowo contended that there were "moral" as well as "materialistic" issues involved; "faith in God" was required, and no nation seemed to him to have taken that approach.

"When war broke out in India, it was Gandhi who said that left to him alone, he would have demanded that all the soldiers should be disbanded, the navy should be disbanded, and he would then have organised a large-scale civil disobedience and non-cooperation against the enemy. Of course, the pity of it is that there are not many Gandhis in the world. The point I wish to make is that it is wrong to dismiss the argument about having faith in God even in the matter of the sanctity and security of our nation."[117]

[115] *Report of the Fourth Annual Congress*, p. 13.
[116] *Ibid.*, p. 69.
[117] *Ibid.*, p. 83. Chief Awolowo's summation of the issues of the debate on his address, of which defense policy was one, and his response to all of the major points followed Chief Akintola's remarks directly and appeared to be a wholly extemporaneous performance of remarkable lucidity. The official record of the

Subsequently, Chief Awolowo revised his position publicly and accepted the view of his colleagues that an armed force in being was necessary after independence.[118]

Fabian socialism made a deep impression on Awolowo during his law-school years in London, and the vaguely elitist, really meritocratic, preoccupation of his early thought has not survived his deeper belief in equalitarian democracy.[119] On the contrary, his avowed commitment to socialism has become increasingly emphatic since he assumed the leadership of the federal opposition in 1960. By and large, radical elements in the party, espousing pan-African socialism, have rallied to Awolowo, while the views of members identified with the liberal capitalist persuasion are more frequently expressed by his successor as Regional Premier, Chief S. L. Akintola. This rupture was exposed in 1962 when Premier Akintola and Chief Rosiji, the Federal Secretary of the party, walked out of an annual convention in the face of severe ideologically motivated criticism. With Awolowo's approval, the convention elected as Federal Secretary the left-socialist leader of the Eastern opposition, Samuel G. Ikoku.[120] Subsequently, the Federal Executive Council of the party called upon Akintola to resign as Premier of the Western Region. Upon his refusal to do so, he was dismissed from office by the regional Governor, who named Alhaji D. S. Adegbenro, a supporter of Awolowo, as his replacement.[121] But a determined minority of assemblymen, supporting

---

Congress indicates wrongly that these remarks were made a day later and were therefore prepared, but the writer is certain that they were not prepared.

[118] "I am bound to confess publicly that the cogent arguments of my colleagues, coupled with recent happenings in certain parts of Africa, have since my Calabar pronouncement on the subject, convinced me that a ceremonial army is not enough for Nigeria. To preserve our territorial integrity from violation; to create an atmosphere of security within which our ideal of a Welfare State can flourish; to play a role of honour as a worthy member of the British Commonwealth of Nations and of the United Nations Organization; and to command respect from our immediate neighbors; our new nation must be sufficiently armed for our purposes at any given time." A presidential address at the conference of the Action Group held in Jos, September 9, 1958, p. 3. (Mimeographed.)

[119] Obafemi Awolowo. *Awo: The Autobiography of Chief Obafemi Awolowo* (Cambridge: Cambridge University Press, 1960), pp. 270-271. Cf. *supra*, p. 67, and Kalu Ezera, *Constitutional Developments in Nigeria* (Cambridge: Cambridge University Press, 1960), p. 101.

[120] *West Africa*, February 10-17, 1962, pp. 158 and 187.

[121] The Governor acted after 66 Action Group members, a majority of the House of Assembly, signed a petition expressing their lack of confidence in the Premier. Subsequently, the Governor's action was held unconstitutional by the Federal Supreme Court.

281

Chief Akintola, caused a disturbance in the House of Assembly. Federal police were summoned to restore order in the chamber, and the Prime Minister of the Federation called a meeting of the Federal Parliament which declared a state of emergency in the Western Region. Federal statutes were enacted providing for the suspension of the regional government, the detention of persons likely to provoke breaches of the peace, and the temporary appointment of a Federal Administrator to govern the West.

During the period under review in this study, Chief Awolowo was able to lead the Action Group because he was acceptable to the various major interest groups and ideological wings which compose the party. It has been his particular task to ensure the due consideration of important viewpoints by decisional bodies, whether or not their proponents have been present physically. On occasion he has expressed the conservative viewpoint as his own, as in 1955 when he advocated a unitary North in order to enhance the possibility of cooperation between the Action Group and the Northern Peoples' Congress.[122] His characteristic pronouncements have been democratic in nature and at no time has he attempted to be more than the *primus inter pares*. In the course of extemporaneous remarks to the Calabar Congress of the Action Group, he took note of the recent organization of an "Awo National Brigade" by young militants to counteract the influence of the NCNC's Zikist National Vanguard. The group had been formed without his approval and he appealed to the youth to confine their activities to the limits set by the parent organization. "There is," he observed, "an unavoidable element of personality in politics, but is should not be carried to an extreme."[123]

---

[122] In his presidential address to the Fourth Annual Regional Conference of the Action Group on October 26, 1955, Chief Awolowo enunciated three principles to govern the creation of new states: "very strong desire on the part of the majority of the people of the ethnical group or groups concerned to have a separate Region or State of their own"; financial viability or the ability of the people to raise revenues to run the state; preservation of the unity of homogenous ethnical and linguistic units. He concluded that on the basis of these criteria the Northern Region, for the present, should remain intact. Of the Northern leaders he thought it "only fair to say that they are doing their best according to their light and conscience."

[123] This statement, noted by the writer in his journal, was omitted from the official report of the Fourth Annual Congress, p. 81.

Another statement made by Chief Awolowo in the course of these extemporaneous responsive remarks which was omitted from the official record but should, in the opinion of this writer, be recorded, referred to the views of those members of the party who thought that Nigerian independence should be deferred until the creation of new states had been effected. Chief Awolowo reaffirmed his position, taken in the presidential address, that "we must on no account retreat from our legitimate and long-standing demand for independence." (*Report of the Fourth Annual Congress*, p. 16.) Independence, he reminded the Congress, had been the target of the Action Group since 1951. At that time, he said, the piecemeal independence of regions had not been contemplated. It would be wrong and an act of bad faith to reverse the policy of independence; independence was a matter of courage and courage implied the ability to face known dangers in order to achieve noble purposes. Only the lower animals, he remarked, refuse their freedom and look back into their cages. Should we, he asked, behave no better than the lower animals by refusing to be free? Of course, he conceded, there were dangers inherent in independence which were great and grave. He thought, for example, that an NPC dictatorship would be worse than the Egyptian. But even then, he said, we would continue to fight. Besides, many of us had not always been safe under British control. Members, he said, should not think of a retreat from independence but should set their minds on victory in 1959. "Let us," he urged, "cross the Rubicon into Independence and burn the boat. Nigera is a noble purpose and a venture worth fighting for." Journal notes on the Fourth Annual (Calabar) Congress of the Action Group. May 1, 1958.

CHAPTER VII

IBADAN—A STUDY OF PARTY CONFLICT
AT THE LOCAL LEVEL
IN WESTERN NIGERIA

The Historical and Social Background

I T IS difficult to account for the rise of the Yoruba city of Ibadan as the greatest African city in tropical Africa. It lies astride no river nor historic trade route and it was settled fortuitously by warriors of the Yoruba states of Oyo, Ife, and Ijebu during the inter-tribal wars of the nineteenth century, c. 1829.[1] By 1850 Ibadan had become the principal military base of the Oyo Kingdom; Ibadan armies clashed intermittently with the forces of Ibadan's Yoruba neighbors to the south, namely the Ijebu and the Egba, who controlled the routes of trade to the seaport of Lagos. During most of the nineteenth century, the imperial state of Oyo was under military pressure from the imperial Fulani rulers of the North. Responsibility for the defense of Oyo was assigned primarily to the *Bashorun* of Ibadan—a senior councillor to the *Alafin* of Oyo. As Saburi O. Biobaku has observed, the Ibadan emerged from the period of the Yoruba wars "as the scourge of their neighbors (and) the bulwark of Yoruba defense against the advancing tide of Fulani conquest."[2]

By 1950 the population of the urban and rural areas of Ibadan had risen to nearly 800,000, of whom nearly 460,000 lived within the urban limits. 56.8 percent of the people of Ibadan Division were found to profess Islam, 29.8 percent professed Christianity, and 13.4 percent followed other creeds, mainly animistic and idolatrous.[3] The city of Ibadan exemplifies the two-sector pattern of urban development that is familiar in West Africa. A vast majority of the urban dwellers live in the traditional quarters of the town where the characteristic Yoruba "compound" or family residential unit features the "single-storied dwelling of laterite mud, roofed usually with

---

[1] On the early history of Ibadan see Chief (now *Olubadan*) I. B. Akinyele, *The Outlines of Ibadan History* (Lagos: 1946); Samuel Johnson, *The History of the Yorubas* (London: Routledge, 1921), pp. 223-225; Saburi O. Biobaku, *The Egba and their Neighbors, 1842-1872* (Oxford: Clarendon Press, 1957), p. 14.

[2] *Ibid.*, p. 97.

[3] *Population Census of the Western Region of Nigeria* (Lagos: 1952), pp. 21-22. The religious beliefs and institutions of the Ibadan people are the subject of a book by Geoffrey Parrinder, *Religion in an African City* (London: Oxford University Press, 1953).

corrugated iron."[4] Since Ibadan has become the capital city and economic center of the Western Region, many non-indigenous Nigerians, mainly non-Ibadan Yorubas, have settled there for commercial, professional and other occupational reasons. They reside in the new urban sectors of the city and they have been known, in the jargon of local politics, as "native settlers." Among them, Ijebu Yorubas comprise the most numerous ethnic group. Traditionally, the Ibadan and the Ijebu are fervid rivals; in recent years, the remarkable success of Ijebu cocoa traders has engendered additional resentment on the part of their neighbors.[5] Indeed, the acumen of Ijebu Yoruba businessmen, like that of the Aro-Ibo businessmen in Eastern Nigeria, is proverbial.

Assuredly, ethnic rivalry between the Ibadan and the Ijebu is one of the underlying springs of contemporary Ibadan politics. In the eyes of many of the Ibadan, the "native settlers" are objectionable intruders for several reasons. First and foremost, many of them are Ijebu. Secondly, the settler is apt to be Western-educated and to live more comfortably than the average Ibadan man, who is poor, humble, and without satisfactory regular employment.[6] Thirdly, the settler is likely to be a Christian, whereas the typical Ibadan man is Muslim. (Although the Muslims of Ijebu Province outnumber the Christians by 5 percent of the total population of the province, a majority of those who have settled in Ibadan, including members of the professional and upper social strata, are Christian.) Finally, the "native settler" is identified with the governing elite of the Western Region to whom the once powerful Ibadan people are now subject. These palpable antagonisms rankle in the social background of the most acute political conflict in Yorubaland.

The Traditional Order

The social system of the Ibadan traditional community is unique among the people of the Yoruba states in that there are no royal

[4] K. M. Buchanan and J. C. Pugh, *Land and People in Nigeria* (London: University of London Press, 1955), p. 69.

[5] See the discussion of the economic basis of xenophobia, which refers to the activities of Ijebu businessmen, in P. T. Bauer, *West African Trade* (Cambridge: Cambridge University Press, 1954), pp. 39-40.

[6] Unemployment in Ibadan is sometimes estimated at nearly 50%, particularly in slack farming seasons. In 1958, 53% of all ratepayers in the area of the Ibadan District Council were assessed to pay the minimum rate of £3.5/-. The minimum rate is levied on all male persons 16 years of age and over on the assumption that they earn £50 per annum; male persons with higher visible incomes are assessed at a higher rate. In fact, many individuals earn less than £50 per annum, and the large number of minimum ratepayers is indicative of the extent of unemployment in Ibadan. Statistics from the Rate Office, Ibadan District Council.

lineages with hereditary rights to the kingship. Political authority at the lowest level inheres in the *bale*, or head of the family compound. An important family head—usually the head of a *sib* or several related compounds—may be recognized by the Head Chief or *Olubadan* as a *Mogaji*, a distinctive Ibadan title which connotes the first grade in the hierarchy of Ibadan chiefs. In the old days, the *Mogajis* were military leaders and their authority extended to tribute areas in the countryside. Today, *Mogajis*, who live in town, control family land in the rural districts and their incomes are derived mainly from the sale of cocoa. An average Ibadan man divides his time between the rural district, where he farms the family land, and the town, where he seeks transient employment. He may owe allegiance to a village head as well as to a *Mogaji*, but the *Mogajis* of the town are superior to the village heads whom they appoint. A recognized *Mogaji* may be followed and obeyed by several thousand people in the town and the rural districts, although his own extended family does not normally exceed 300 individuals.

The controlling theory on recognition of *Mogajis* by the Head Chief of Ibadan has been stated as follows:[7] "Once a family has had a chief of any importance, that family cannot be ignored. The chief's successor will be recognized as a *Mogaji*, a Hausa word meaning 'first born.' The *Mogaji* need not, however, be the first born son of the late chief. More often the oldest man in the family will be chosen, but ability and character will be considered."

Nowadays it is alleged that the process of recognition is tainted with the political party bias of the *Olubadan* and the senior chiefs.

There are three chieftaincy grades above the *Mogaji* level: the junior chiefs, the senior chiefs, and the Head Chief or *Olubadan*. Junior chiefs are normally selected from among the *Mogajis*, senior chiefs from the junior grade, and the *Olubadan* from two lines of senior chiefs in alternation.[8] There are no hereditary prerequisites for admission to either line and the Ibadan system of government is "democratic" in the sense that any man may become a *Mogaji* and

---

[7] From a 1938 intelligence report by E. N. C. Dickenson, District Officer, quoted in H. L. M. Butcher, *Report of the Commission of Inquiry into the Allegations of Misconduct Made against Chief Salami Agbaje, the Otun Balogun of Ibadan, and Allegations of Inefficiency and Maladministration on the Part of the Ibadan and District Native Authority* (Lagos: Government Printer, 1951), p. 10, hereafter referred to as the *Butcher Report*.

[8] The hierarchy of chiefs and method of selecting the *Olubadan* were clarified in a declaration of the Ibadan Native Authority in 1946. See E. W. J. Nicholson, *Report of the Commission of Inquiry into the Administration of the Ibadan District Council* (Abingdon: 1956), pp. 83-85, hereafter referred to as the *Nicholson Report*.

rise to the *Olubadan*-ship. In practice, a gerontocracy has emerged because "individuals are promoted from one rank to another, with the result that the Senior Chiefs who become *Olubadan* are usually very old men."[9]

The Old System of Administration

Prior to 1934 Ibadan was subject to the administrative supervision of the *Alafin* of Oyo. In that year an independent Native Authority for Ibadan Division was established, including the present Ibadan and Oshun Divisions. In 1936 the title of the *Bale* of Ibadan was changed to *Olubadan*; subsequently, a separate Native Authority for the Ibadan District was set up, consisting of 11 specified chiefs and 4 councillors elected by an Advisory Board of Quarter Representatives, junior chiefs, and *Mogajis*. The number of councillors so elected was increased to 12 in 1949.[10]

During the period of indirect rule the chiefs and *Mogajis* derived incomes of a "customary" nature which correspond to practices which have been identified elsewhere as tribute, jobbery, and graft. At first, the British countenanced the customary rights of the Ibadan chiefs to exact tribute from towns and villages in the countryside.[11] Until 1952 it was an accepted procedure for aspirants to chieftaincy titles in the tributary towns and villages to bring gifts to the chiefs of Ibadan and to the *Mogajis*, who served as intermediaries between the village headmen and the titled chiefs of the city. Furthermore, the Divisional Appeal Court was located in Ibadan City, and appellants from the districts normally brought gifts in kind to the judicial chiefs when they came to court in the city. In their capacities as native court judges, the junior and senior chiefs controlled the local judiciary, and the system was steeped in graft. Nor were the judges the only offenders. Litigants in the native courts often employed the

[9] *Butcher Report*, p. 10.
[10] Lord Hailey, *Native Administration in the British African Territories*, Part III (London: 1951), p. 121. See also *Ibadan*, published under the auspices of the University College of Ibadan and presented to the Third International West African Conference, Ibadan, December 1949.
[11] These tributary relationships were known collectively as the *Ajele* system. See Biobaku, *op.cit.*, p. 94. S. F. Nadel reported a similar system of royal messengers called "*ajele* (from the Arabic *ajala*, to dispatch)" in the Fulani-Nupe kingdom of Bida. *A Black Byzantium* (London: Oxford University Press, 1942), p. 115. The Agreement of 1893 between the British and the *Bale* and Chiefs of Ibadan is published in Samuel Johnson, *op.cit.*, pp. 654-656. In 1933 a student of the Yoruba, H. L. Ward-Price, observed that there were over 100 towns and villages subject to Ibadan, each of which was represented in the Ibadan General Council by an overlord chosen from among the Ibadan chiefs. *Land Tenure in the Yoruba Provinces* (Lagos: Government Printer, 1933), p. 40.

services of a *Baba-ogun*, or person who would plead the case to the judge in private. In this capacity an influential *Mogaji* might participate in the litigation and share the graft. Inasmuch as most of the judges were illiterate, decisions rendered by them orally in Yoruba were recorded by literate court clerks in English and records of cases for appellate purposes were said to be doctored occasionally by the clerks for a price. In the late 1940's proposals for court reform included both the replacement of illiterate judges by literate judges who could record their own decisions in English, and the establishment of a separate judicial branch of the Native Authority, independent of its executive arm. These proposals were adopted in the 1950's by the regional government in the face of strenuous protests from the *Mogajis* and chiefs.[12]

Finally, the system of tax collection under the old system of administration was grossly inefficient and liable to disturbing abuses. It was described in an official report as follows:[13] "Briefly the system is that each Chief or *Mogaji* has his own roster of payers. Incredible as it may seem, each collector may have payers in any or all of the sixty-six quarters of Ibadan, and the Chiefs assess their importance by the number of payers who pay through them."

The tax collectors were entitled to a rebate of 5 percent on their collections and the *Mogajis* and chiefs were known to "raid" one another for payers. Favoritism rendered the system inequitable, and the *Mogajis* and chiefs were alleged to have dodged payment of their own proportionate taxes with regularity.[14] A revision of the tax system in 1952 deprived the *Mogajis* and chiefs of these offices, but, as we shall see, reform has not effaced the stigma of partisanship from the process of tax collection.

[12] A reformed court system was established in 1954 with the present *Olubadan,* Chief I. B. Akinyele, as the first Chief Judge. The senior and junior chiefs were not excluded from the new system, but attached to the various native courts as paid "assessors" or advisers to the literate judges in matters of native law and custom. The *Mogajis* too were declared eligible for appointment as assessors.

[13] *Butcher Report*, p. 50.

[14] *Ibid.*, p. 53. However, the system had its admirers. In 1937, 14 years before the *Butcher Report*, which has been quoted in the text, Margery Perham commended the Ibadan system of tax collection for its efficiency. She found that the compound heads were "worthy of the trust placed in them. They often err . . . upon the side of virtue." *Native Administration in Nigeria* (London: Oxford University Press, 1937), pp. 182ff. Even today, some officials of the Ibadan District Council and many *Mogajis* seem to think that the old system, for all its deficiencies, was less troublesome than systematic procedures of rate collection have proved to be.

Party Origins Under the Old System of Administration

Party origins in Ibadan may be traced to an association of civic-minded elders which emerged in the 1920's and was known in Yoruba as the *Egbe Agbo O-tan*. This group functioned mainly to advise the Ibadan chiefs on matters of town welfare. In the 1930's educated younger men were stimulated by the addition of literate, elected councillors to the Ibadan Native Authority to organize an association which they called the Ibadan Progressive Union (IPU). A few intellectual members of the IPU formed a study circle which met frequently to discuss significant books and topics of public interest. However, Muslim members of the Progressive Union were disturbed by its overtly Christian tone and they inaugurated a parallel group known as the Ibadan Patriotic Association, which did include a few Christian members in addition to Muslims. Thereafter, the Ibadan Progressive Union waxed increasingly conservative and sectarian. Most of the non-traditional Native Authority councillors were drawn from its membership and they came to be regarded by the people of Ibadan as a privileged and opportunistic clique. In 1941 a Youth Section of the IPU was formed by idealistic younger men who desired to resuscitate the earlier progressive zeal of the Union. But the Progressive Union did not introduce populism to Ibadan.

The first political mass organization in Ibadan was the *Egbe Omo Ibile*, or society of native sons; it emerged in the early 1940's as a coalition of societies, including the Ibadan Patriotic Association and various economic groups—e.g., the butchers guild, the goat sellers, the market women, farmers, traders, etc. The chief spokesman for the *Egbe Omo Ibile* was its nationalistic and intensely ambitious secretary, Adegoke Adelabu. He was born into an Ibadan Muslim family in 1915. His father was a relatively prosperous weaver and trader, and he was educated through the secondary school level in Ibadan. Subsequently, he attended the Yaba Higher College at Lagos under the auspices of a scholarship from the United Africa Company. During a vacation period he studied the system of produce-buying, and wrote an original paper for company officials on the subject of its reorganization. His effort elicited the admiration of the company management and brought him an offer of immediate appointment as an African produce manager. So Adegoke left school, and worked for the next ten years in executive capacities, first for the United Africa Company, later as an inspector in the Government Co-operative Department. In 1946 he turned to private business, and engaged in produce buying, motor transport, and merchandising, in addition to journalism and political organization. It is said that Adelabu's great aspiration was to become secretary of the Ibadan Native Authority Council. Despite the premature termination of his formal education, he read widely and acquired a remarkably facile command of the English language that served his keen intellect and ineffable egotism to near perfection.[15]

[15] The best biographical sketch of Adelabu's early years and intellectual development is his own *Africa in Ebullition* (Ibadan: 1952), which suggests to the reader the explosive mixture of altruistic idealism and aggressive egotism in his volcanic temperament. "I am a deliberate egotist," he wrote, "I do not regret it. I do not apologize for it. I am an artist." In vivid, even purple, prose he defended radical nationalism as the only effective means to implement the "cosmological imperative" of self-government for Nigeria. Although the tract is polemical, unsystematic, and occasionally preposterous, it is on the whole well-written, serious, and insightful. Adelabu distinguished three tendencies within the Nationalist Front: the Materialists, the Intellectuals, and the Spiritualists. "The Materialists fight the Battle of Freedom in order to secure economic advantages." They can be diverted from the cause of freedom by "monetary concessions and an opportunity for increased participation in the joint exploitation of the People." The Intellectuals want freedom but are not prepared to suffer for it. They try to debate the merits of their case with the Imperialists who "humour them by weaving their own sophistic counter-arguments." Ultimately the Imperialists resort to force and the "brilliant orators canter cowardly into their hide-outs." The Spiritual Nationalists alone will not succumb to pain or inducements and are therefore invincible.

Adelabu condemned tribalism and cultural isolationism as the chief impediments to Nigerian unity. He declared himself both a "radical socialist" and "a conscientious, convinced and incurable democrat." He wrote: "I despise the comfortable right-winger bent on protecting his possessions at the expense of the welfare of the masses . . . but I do not hate him. . . . I admit his right to exist and would regard his total liquidation as an invitation to dictatorship of the State Bureaucrat and the Official Planner, and a national calamity." He expressed the hope that the Action Group, which he despised, would develop into a "national Liberal-Conservative Movement . . . serving a useful and necessary national purpose as the Rallying Point for the Aristocracy of Birth, Wealth and Individual Excellence, and the other natural stabilizing forces of Society. . . .

"I am convinced that even now, and more with the achievement of Nigerian Freedom, the National Council will gradually purge its ranks of right-wing pseudo-capitalists and become a genuine Radical Socialist Party of workers, peasants and left-wing Intellectuals. Any genuine opposition party must be rightist in complexion. But it must also be national in outlook. There is room enough for us to hold opposing political views without endangering the Unity of our dearly beloved country and delaying its achievement of Independent National Sovereignty. The North and East are anxiously waiting for the Action Group Mission when it has rechristened itself appropriately, out-grown its self-imposed Provincialism and shed its petticoat of shabby Parochialism."

Like Nnamdi Azikiwe, who wrote the foreword to his book, Adelabu had a deep sense of personal destiny and a desire to identify himself with the historic movement of the African peoples to independence. Yet he declared unabashedly that his ideological principles were wholly relative to his national origin:

"Politically, as a West African in 1952, I am a radical socialist and a fanatical nationalist. This means that in other circumstances, I could have been other things. If I were an Englishman, I would be a Conservative; if French, a De Gaullist; if Russian, a Communist; Indian, on the left-wing of Congress; German, a Nazi; American, an incurable capitalist and South African, a racial bigot. For over a

Adelabu's turbulent political career began in earnest with an event known as the "Agbaje agitation" of 1949-1951.[16] Chief Salami Agbaje, the *Otun Balogun* of Ibadan, was the outstanding literate leader among the senior chiefs and next in line for the *Olubadan*-ship. For several reasons he had become personally obnoxious to a majority of the junior chiefs, *Mogajis*, and their followers. First, he was an energetic advocate of judicial and administrative reform; in particular he espoused separation of the native court system from the executive branch of the Native Authority. Moreover, he was resented for his independence of mind and outspoken criticisms of traditional office holders, for the wealth he had amassed in business, and for his alleged failure to display customary generosity by distributing largesses among the chiefs and people. Finally the chiefs and *Mogajis* feared that as *Olubadan* he would be uncontrollable and likely to introduce pernicious reforms into the system of government. Stories were circulated to the effect that he was not really an Ibadan man, that his acceptance of a building contract from the *Alafin* of Oyo would lead to the renewed subjugation of Ibadan to Oyo, and that his proposal to establish a registry of births and deaths would entail governmental interference with the intimate lives of families.

In December 1949 the junior chiefs and *Mogajis* petitioned the Native Authority to depose Chief Agbaje. Throughout the following year this demand was vigorously pressed in public oratory and in newspaper comment by Adegoke Adelabu. In 1951 the government appointed a commissioner, Mr. H. L. M. Butcher, to enquire into the allegations against Chief Agbaje and related allegations of maladministration on the part of the Ibadan District Council. It is widely thought in Ibadan that the administrative officers utilized this opportunity to expose evils in the Native Administration and to introduce unpopular reforms. Chief Agbaje was absolved by the commissioner, who censured the junior chiefs and the *Mogajis* for their "unhealthy" opposition "to the development of modern and progressive ideas," and made sweeping proposals for reform. Thus the

---

decade I have been trying to pump it into the heads of my contemporaries that political-ism, like religious creed, color of skin or height of body is hardly a matter of choice. Finding my country poor to a miserable degree at an Age when most other countries are gradually graduating into an Industrial Utopia, I see clearly that she simply has not got the opportunity for slow evolutionary development. If she does not catch up in desperate haste with the prevailing modern patterns the rest of the civilized world will go on without her."

[16] The writer's knowledge of this incident is derived from interviews in Ibadan and from the *Butcher Report*, cited in Note 7 above, from which all quotations are taken.

archaic tax system was condemned, and a territorial tax-collection scheme based on the compilation of nominal rolls was proposed and eventually adopted. Moreover, the commissioner recommended that the "large and progressive section" of taxpaying "native settlers" should be given representation in the local government council. Finally he struck at the heart of Ibadan chauvinism by proposing that the Ibadan chiefs be shorn of their traditional authority over the populous towns and villages of the northern districts. The campaign of the petty chiefs and *Mogajis* against Chief Agbaje had boomeranged. Within a year of the Butcher Report, Oshun Division, comprising some 850,000 people, was carved from Ibadan territory,[17] the tax system was revamped, and the number of elected councillors more than trebled.

When the agitation began in 1949, political groups in Ibadan were sharply divided. The Ibadan Progressive Union and its Youth Section both supported Chief Agbaje, while the *Egbe Omo Ibile* under the leadership of its secretary, Adelabu, led the attack against him. (Religion was not a factor inasmuch as Agbaje was a Muslim.) In terms of administrative values, Agbaje's supporters were undoubtedly progressive while his opponents were either conservative or reactionary. However, the administrative progressives were not necessarily progressive with respect to political values. By and large, the older members of the Ibadan Progressive Union were reconciled to the values of British rule. Administrative progressiveness and political conservatism were not inconsistent attitudes; in fact they were the characteristic attitudes of the British officials who required administrative reform to render their government more stable and efficient. The Ibadan Progressive Union Youth were progressive in both administrative and political terms, but their influence was not great and their following was restricted to enlightened and modernistic elements. Both groups favored the tax and court reforms but regretted the loss of Oshun for emotional reasons. Their Ibadan patriotism was aroused by the aggressively vocal campaign that was waged by leading "native settlers" in support of Oshun separation.

It will be recalled that in March 1950, barrister Obafemi Awolowo and other non-Ibadan Yorubas secretly inaugurated the Action Group in Ibadan. Among those affiliated with that embryonic political party were influential nationalists from the Oshun area, such as S. L. Akintola and J. O. Adigun, who were leading the campaign

[17] Oshun is the most populous division in the Western Region; both Oshun and Ibadan Divisions have more than twice the population of any other division in the region.

for Oshun separation. In Ibadan itself, the Oshun cause was supported by two local newspapers that were owned by "native settler" interests associated with the founders of the Action Group, namely the *Morning Star* (edited by J. O. Adigun and A. Sowunmi) and the *Nigerian Tribune* (owned by Obafemi Awolowo). Yet the issue of Oshun separation was a comparatively minor one for most of the "native settlers" who were primarily concerned with two more proximate interests, namely, their right to acquire land in Ibadan on a freehold basis and their right to representation in the local government council. These rights were vigorously advocated by the *Nigerian Tribune* and supported by the pan-Yoruba cultural society, *Egbe Omo Oduduwa*. Barrister Obafemi Awolowo, an Ijebu Yoruba, was General Secretary of the *Egbe Omo Oduduwa*;[18] he was also a legal adviser to the Native Settlers' Union in Ibadan.

In February 1951, the Youth Section of the Ibadan Progressive Union publicly repudiated the claims of the Native Settlers' Union, in particular "the aggressively preposterous and gratuitous demand of the Native Settlers' for perpetual freehold of land and representation in our Council."[19] A bitter press war ensued between the *Nigerian Tribune* and the *Western Echo*, owned by conservative members of the Ibadan Progressive Union, all of whom had supported Chief Agbaje. Prior to the Butcher inquiry, political conservatives in the pro-Agbaje camp, including most of the literate councillors, the older members of the Ibadan Progressive Union and the indigenous Ibadan Christian elite generally, less the IPU Youth Section, had organized an Ibadan Citizens' Committee which appeared to support the Butcher reforms with respect to the internal administration of Ibadan city. But the vigorous assertion of "native settler" demands coupled with the Oshun issue alarmed the Ibadan people of virtually all classes and political persuasions into closing ranks. In March 1951, they formed a United Front Committee encompassing the *Egbe Omo Ibile*, the Ibadan Citizens' Committee, the Ibadan Progressive Union, the

---

[18] "The *Egbe Omo Oduduwa*, whose General Secretary is a Remo man (Ijebu Remo Division) and which is probably under pressure from a powerful Ibadan strangers' lobby, has recently come out for completely abrogating all restrictions as between Yoruba [respecting the sale of lands]. 'The Oduduwa conference resolved that the *Egbe Omo Oduduwa* should take steps to regularize land tenure in Yorubaland so that every Yoruba in the land will be regarded and treated as a native of the place . . . all Yorubas should be free to acquire landed property.' " Quotation from the *Daily Service* of October 29 and November 6, 1951, in C. W. Rowling, *Land Tenure in Ijebu Province* (Ibadan: Government Printer, 1956), p. 53.

[19] *Daily Times*, February 20, 1951.

Ibadan Welfare Association and a farmers' league known as the *Maiyegun*.

The United Front Committee was too factious to survive the general election of 1951. Political radicals, including Adelabu and the Ibadan Progressive Union Youth Section, were determined to terminate the reign of the Ibadan Progressive Union "old guard." They formed an electoral coalition known as the Ibadan People's Party-*Egbe Omo Ibile* Alliance in opposition to a conservative coalition of the Ibadan Citizens' Committee-Ibadan Progressive Union. In campaign oratory, leaders of the Ibadan People's Party-*Egbe Omo Ibile*, in particular Adelabu, denounced the conservatives for their purported connection with such progressive reforms as the withdrawal of governmental powers from irresponsible *Mogajis* and chiefs and the release of Oshun from its tributary dependence upon Ibadan.[20]

At this point a paradox in Adelabu's career may be remarked. In principle, Adelabu was progressive, as his writings indicate; in national politics he was a radical. But in local politics he was too astute and ambitious not to appear as a conservative and a traditionalist. Therefore he was not identified with the administrative reformers of the IPU Youth; he publicly opposed court reform and was discreet in his criticism of the inefficient tax system. On local issues he deferred to public opinion and rarely crossed the narrow views of the petty chiefs. Later, when he became the political boss of Ibadan, he seemed to respect principle less than he loved power. In the pursuit of power he cavalierly abandoned the most elementary rules of good administration and frequently resorted to political jobbery. Throughout Nigeria he was admired for his militant nationalism. His colleagues in the nationalist movement respected him for his ideals; but the people of Ibadan loved him because he was the idiosyncratic personification of their traditional values and their cantankerous hostility to imposed reforms.

In the election of 1951 the Ibadan People's Party won a sweeping victory and returned all six of its candidates to the Western House of Assembly,[21] including the President of the party, barrister A. M. A. Akinloye and the Vice-President, Adegoke Adelabu. Although four of the six were alleged to have signed a pledge of cooperation with

[20] Ibadan People's Party-*Egbe Omo Ibile* Political Bulletin, No. 8.
[21] The elections were held in three stages through primary, intermediate, and final electoral colleges. The Ibadan People's Party-*Egbe Omo Ibile* Alliance claimed to have returned 75 of the 85 members of the final college. Ibadan People's Party-*Egbe Omo Ibile* Political Bulletin, No. 6.

the National Council of Nigeria and the Cameroons, it soon became clear that the Ibadan elected members did not acknowledge any prior political commitment.[22] Both the NCNC and the Action Group endeavored to win their allegiance. At length, five joined the Action Group and barrister Akinloye was appointed Minister of Agriculture in the Western Regional Government; only Adelabu affirmed his loyalty to Azikiwe and the NCNC.

In due course most of the "Westernized," educated element of the Ibadan population followed the leadership of the Ibadan People's Party into the fold of the Action Group. The older leaders of the Ibadan Citizens' Committee and the Ibadan Progressive Union, mainly Christian businessmen, professionals, and ex-councillors, were predisposed by their social connections to affiliate with the party in power. Their influence was brought to bear on their close associates among the wealthy and titled senior chiefs and reinforced by the solicitations of the leaders of the pan-Yoruba cultural society, *Egbe Omo Oduduwa*, in the name of pan-Yoruba unity. But the Ibadan people and the petty chiefs were largely unresponsive to the blandishments of the governing elite. The *Mogajis* and chiefs had suffered reversals which were humiliating if inevitable, and they keenly resented the deprivation of their historic rights and privileges. In the nineteenth century Ibadan flourished as a military state. When the British proscribed war as a source of income, the chiefs demanded an economic compensation. They were given control of the court and tax machinery and allowed to retain their peaceful tributary incomes. Therefore the reforms of the early 1950's appeared to them as a breach of contract. Moreover, the acquisitive "native settlers" were speculating in their lands, and the government of the Western Region, based in Ibadan, had fallen into the hands of an Ijebu, barrister Awolowo, who appeared to abet all of their misfortunes. Adegoke Adelabu emerged from the debacle of 1951 as the hero of an aroused but politically disorganized Ibadan people. They honored him for his refusal to join Awolowo, and it was not long before he mobilized them into an invincible political machine.

[22] Two of the candidates, Mr. S. O. Lanlehin and Mr. A. M. A. Akinloye, President of the Ibadan People's Party, participated in early organizational meetings of the Action Group. (Minutes of the 7th Meeting of the Action Group, November 12, 1950; Minutes of the 10th Meeting of the Action Group, March 31, and April 1, 1951.) Akinloye's association with the Action Group appears to have preceded that with the Ibadan People's Party, since it was reported that he would inaugurate the I.P.P. on June 16, 1951, following his nomination by the Action Group. Other Ibadan personalities who were reported as sympathetic to the Action Group but "noticeably inactive," included Rev. Alayande, S. A. Akinfewa, Mr. Lanlehin, and E. C. B. Omole. *Daily Times*, June 16, 1951.

The Mabolaje

In 1952 a political organization of Adelabu's design, known as the Ibadan Taxpayers' Association, came into existence. Its name dramatized both the general fear of excessive taxation and the resentment of the *Mogajis* to the withdrawal of their tax privileges. Along with the *Mogajis*, the Taxpayers' Association mobilized for political action the largest and most assertive economic grievance group in Yorubaland—the *Maiyegun* League of Ibadan cocoa farmers. (*Maiyegun* may be translated into English from the Yoruba as "World" or "Nation" or "Society Builders.") The *Maiyegun* League had been organized after World War II as a reaction against measures taken by the government to eradicate a cocoa plant virus disease called "swollen shoot" by cutting out the infected trees. Ibadan farmers complained that their plants were being cut indiscriminately by government agents with economically ruinous consequences, and in 1949 the *Maiyegun* petitioned the Colonial Secretary to interdict the practice.[23] Cocoa plant cutting was suspended in 1950 but resumed in 1952 by the Action Group government under the direction of the Minister of Agriculture, Mr. Akinloye, who was also President of the Ibadan People's Party. As a result of this well-intentioned but unpopular policy, many Ibadan farmers were alienated from the regional government.

Most of the farmers are poor, and earn a subsistence living by working the family land in the rural districts. Their interests are entwined with those of the *Mogajis*: on the one hand the *Mogajis* derive their incomes from the sale of cash crops; on the other hand, the farmers are attached to the traditional institution by various ties of an economic and sentimental nature. Thus a man's right to work family land is dependent upon his membership in the kin group, which implies respect for traditional authorities. Furthermore, the *Mogaji* is not merely a political superior but a "papa" to whom the members of the family feel close; there is no consanguinal barrier between the *Mogaji* and the humblest farmer in his compound. Nevertheless, the *Mogajis* and the junior chiefs in town distrusted the *Maiyegun* League because they suspected its leaders of attempting to usurp their traditional authority in the districts. One of their grievances against Chief Agbaje had been his alleged support of the *Maiyegun*. Adelabu accomplished an organizational feat of no mean order by

23 Mr. F. U. Anyiam, former political secretary of the Maiyegun League, later National Publicity Secretary of the NCNC, discussed this problem with the writer. See also K. M. Buchanan and J. C. Pugh, *op.cit.*, p. 151.

welding the petty chiefs, in particular the *Mogajis*, together with the *Maiyegun* into the Ibadan Taxpayers' Association which in 1954 was renamed the *Mabolaje*—officially the NCNC-*Mabolaje* Grand Alliance. The writer is informed that *Mabolaje* means "not to lower or spoil or degrade the honor and prestige of chiefs," or loosely, "to bring back the old glories." In March 1954, elections were held to the reorganized Ibadan District Council, which then consisted of the *Olubadan* as President, 19 traditional members specified by their titles, and 73 elected members from the 43 urban and 30 rural wards of the Ibadan District. The NCNC-*Mabolaje* Grand Alliance won 56 of the elective seats and Adelabu was elected Chairman of the Council.

Probably no politician in Nigeria has ever had organizational power in a local sphere comparable to that of Adelabu in Ibadan in 1954-1958. The nearest approximation to his rule of the *Mabolaje* was the control exercised by Herbert Macaulay over the Nigeria National Democratic Party of Lagos.[24] Adelabu like Macaulay, dictated nominations for elective offices, but his authority was more exclusive than the latter's. When Adelabu organized the *Mabolaje*, he had no well-educated or professional colleagues. It will be recalled that Macaulay was ineligible for public office and that he delegated elective responsibilities to his professional lieutenants, including lawyers, doctors, and business executives. In contrast, Adelabu was the sole authoritative spokesman for the *Mogaji-Maiyegun* combination in the 14-member *Mabolaje* Central Executive Committee, all of whom were illiterate. They trusted him implicitly, endorsed his candidates as a matter of course, and supported his decisions almost without question. It is not surprising that Adelabu could easily revoke decisions taken in his absence by the entire District Council.[25] Every NCNC member of the Council owed his election to Adelabu and the *Mogaji-Maiyegun* coalition that entrusted him with the representation of their interests in English-speaking forums. Adelabu personally selected many of the NCNC candidates for the 1954 local election. In each ward he consulted with the elders and influential persons, found a suitable individual to stand for the party, and assumed full responsibility for the campaign. In the federal election of November 1954, only four candidates were required, Adelabu and three of his nominees. All four were returned and Adelabu was appointed Federal Minister of Social Services, an office that he held concurrently with the chairmanship of the Ibadan District Council.

[24] *Supra*, pp. 47-48.
[25] *Nicholson Report*, p. 99.

His tenure of office was theatrically brief. In April 1955, the regional government decided that there was enough evidence of maladministration to justify an inquiry into the affairs of the Ibadan District Council.[26] A commissioner was appointed who found after investigation that the Council had not been guilty of a general failure of administration but noted eleven specific failures, four of which were regarded as "gross." Culpability for most of the failures was attributed to the Chairman, Mr. Adelabu. It was disclosed that until his appointment as a federal minister, Adelabu held the chairmanships of all of the committees of the Council. The Commissioner remarked: "Mr. Adelabu treats all but a handful of his fellow Councillors with contempt, and spoke contemptuously of them in evidence. He not only dictates policy, but decisions on points of detail. As the Secretary wrote, Mr. Adelabu is in effect the Ibadan District Council in himself, and I believe no decision is made against his will."[27]

If that conclusion were true, the inner core of the *Mabolaje* would not have minded in the least. From their viewpoint, the Council and the parliaments (regional and federal) were Adelabu's responsibility,

[26] Numerous petitions for dissolution of the Council were submitted to the Ministry of Local Government during 1954 and 1955. But the movement for dissolution appears to have begun even before the Council was elected. Two weeks before the local election of March 1954, the Action Group-controlled *Nigerian Tribune* declared that "to vote for NCNC is to vote for corruption" which would lead to "inevitable dissolution." Within two months of the Council's inauguration, the *Tribune* called upon the government to intervene. The commissioner referred to that newspaper's precipitate hostility as "an astonishing thing," and thought that the members of the government who had a controlling interest in the paper ought to have restrained its premature condemnation of the Council. *Nicholson Report*, pp. 7-9.

[27] *Ibid.*, p. 99. It should be recorded that the Nicholson Commission of Inquiry was one of the most difficult and successful investigations of its kind ever to have been carried out in Nigeria. Mr. E. W. J. Nicholson, Town Clerk of Abingdon, "happened to be in Nigeria . . . carrying out certain academic and social duties on behalf of the University College, Ibadan, and the British Council respectively . . ." when he was invited by the Western Government to conduct the inquiry. His report is highly informative, perspicuous, and incisively critical of failings without being captious. He made an unmistakably sincere attempt to appraise objectively the performance and the character of the Chairman of the Council. Despite his derogatory observations, he did not overlook Mr. Adelabu's admirable qualities and he concluded: "He [Adelabu] is a son of the people who has made the best of his opportunities, and one who I believe began his political career with a strong and sincere desire to improve the lot of the toiling masses of his fellow countrymen, particularly his fellow townsmen of Ibadan. I do him the credit to believe that behind the webs of political intrigue and personal gain in which he has become deeply involved, this desire still burns. If he could learn to control his overweening personal ambition and his desire to dominate his fellow men he might yet render great service to Nigeria, perhaps either as a Federal Minister, in which capacity he is surrounded by men of equal calibre, or in some other way." *Ibid.*, pp. 100-101.

and they relied upon him to protect their interests. Probably it made little difference to them that the commissioner discovered three instances in which Adelabu "accepted or negotiated for bribes." Adelabu was not an especially wealthy man,[28] but he was celebrated for his generosity. His conduct must be understood within the social context of prevailing relationships between the rich and the poor. Most of the Ibadan people are poor; their situation is typical of the conditions that obtain in many underdeveloped, non-industrialized countries. There are many more farmers than the cocoa farms actually require and a labor situation exists that is sometimes described as hidden unemployment. During slack seasons there are countless idlers in town, apart from the numerous crippled beggars, who are really, if not technically, unemployed. These people among others attach themselves to the compounds of influential persons, and a man of Adelabu's stature is obliged to accommodate many visitors, petitioners and servitors, some of whom may tax the resources of the household.

Adelabu lived in a large two-storied building of laterite mud and cement in the traditional quarter of Oke-Oluokun. As an eminent Muslim he was polygamous. There were few private rooms in his house and no one was ever unwelcome. Every Saturday at noon party leaders gathered in the area of Adelabu's compound. In October 1957, Adelabu conducted the writer through the various concurrent phases of a weekly meeting. Most of the leaders present were the representatives of their electoral ward committees; they comprised the amorphous Central Working Committee of the *Mabolaje*. In one large room of Adelabu's house the writer was introduced to a number of *Mogajis*, whose adhesion to the party was said to be crucial to its mass support. In another room, the members of the Central Executive Committee were discussing matters of the day. Outside a few hundred members of the party milled around in consultation with various leaders.

No Nigerian leader was closer to his people or more familiar with their thinking than Adelabu. When they rejoiced he danced with them, when they sorrowed he wept, and when they mocked their enemies his was the rudest tongue. His way to power was to dance in the streets to the strains of *Mabolaje* songs that celebrated his name. A Nigerian newspaper editor recalled a visit with Adelabu in these words:[29] "When on his invitation for lunch, I visited him in his

[28] According to his own testimony, Adelabu was worth £20,000 in 1955. *Nicholson Report*, p. 19.

[29] Alhaji Babatunde Jose, "My Friend, Adelabu," *Daily Times*, March 27, 1958.

residence at Ibadan . . . I saw him dancing to song records all in his praise. I asked him why and he told me: 'I am an egotist. I am not ashamed of it. These gramophone recordings praising me are all in the plan for political power. They are played in thousands of houses and my name is constantly in the subconscious memory of those who hear them.' "

His campaign methods were similarly flamboyant; he played on passions and utilized arguments that were typically more opportunistic than constructive. Thus local taxation was the standard butt of *Mabolaje* criticism. Urban building regulations were denounced because the people feared, not without reason, that it would be difficult for a poor man to construct a dwelling of the approved kind in town. Adelabu is reported to have criticized the government's free primary education scheme as premature and to have ridiculed the expenditure of public funds on "Awolowo's schools."[30]

In June 1955 Adelabu was removed from the Ibadan District Council for having accepted a remunerative post at its disposal in violation of the law. The following month he was re-elected and restored to the chairmanship. In August he was convicted for contempt of the Ibadan Native Court and sentenced to six months' imprisonment, but the conviction was reversed on appeal to the Regional High Court. After consideration of the report of the Commission of Inquiry into the Administration of the Ibadan District Council, the Western Regional government announced in January 1956 that the Council would be given an opportunity to "dissociate itself from the wrongful acts" by purging the four guilty councillors including the Chairman. Adelabu was compelled to resign his office as a minister in the federal government by Dr. Nnamdi Azikiwe, the National President of the NCNC, who ruled that no Minister found guilty of corruption should remain in office.[31] It was reported that Adelabu threatened to bolt the NCNC and to withdraw the Ibadan legislators from the party. But the party men balked; 28 NCNC members of the Ibadan District Council challenged him openly and demanded his resignation to save the Council. Finally he agreed to remain in the NCNC but he refused

[30] *Mabolaje* spokesmen sometimes contended that the introduction of free primary education would lower the standard of education in the country. The argument ran: when we paid for it the children did not learn much; now that it is free they will learn nothing. This is a perplexing argument in view of the fact that the vast majority of Ibadan people have not had the benefit of any education and object to the local rates which include an education levy.

[31] Adelabu resigned as Federal Minister of Social Services on January 29, 1956, eight days after Azikiwe had demanded the resignation of two ministers in the Eastern Regional Government on similar grounds. *Supra*, p. 161.

to resign his councillorship.[32] On March 2, 1956, the Western Regional government dissolved the Ibadan District Council and appointed a provisional caretaker council, an action that was endorsed as appropriate by the Premier of the Eastern Region, Dr. Azikiwe. Shortly thereafter Adelabu faced two criminal charges, one of corruption arising from the Commission of Inquiry, and another involving assault in connection with a public disturbance. In both cases he was acquitted, but his chief lieutenant in the Council was less fortunate.[33] Adelabu was prosecuted for minor criminal offenses arising out of his political activities on several occasions between 1954 and 1956,[34] but he was never convicted in a final court, and the people believed that he possessed prowess that protected him from the law.

Despite these tribulations, Adelabu's stature in the national leadership of the NCNC steadily increased. At the Ibadan National Convention of May 1955 he was elected First Vice-President of the party; subsequently, he became chairman of the NCNC Western Regional Working Committee. His personal power within the party may be indicated by the manner in which the NCNC candidates for Ibadan Division were chosen prior to the regional election of May 1956. Initially, Adelabu chose the entire slate of candidates, but a minority group headed by barrister E. O. Fakayode appealed to the National Executive of the party, alleging that the procedure was irregular and dictatorial. The National Executive sent a special committee to Ibadan to arbitrate the dispute. In the course of discussions, Adelabu agreed to set up an advisory committee of local party leaders to supplement the *Mabolaje* Central Executive, but he insisted on retaining an ultimate right of decision in order to protect the overriding popular interests of his dedicated supporters. A compromise on nominations was reached, allowing Adelabu to submit a list of ten names to the arbitrators from which the committee would select the eight party candidates.[35] All but one of those selected (Mr. Fakayode) were among the original choices of Adelabu.

Had the NCNC triumphed in the Western Regional election of

---

[32] The leader of the insurgents, barrister E. O. Fakayode, was criticized harshly by Adelabu, but he survived politically and became an increasingly influential member of the NCNC, as the text will show. See *Daily Times*, January 30, and February 27, 1956.

[33] *Daily Times*, April 19, May 29, and June 19, 1956.

[34] See the speech by A. Adelabu on "allegations of victimisation against non-supporters of the Action Group Party," in *Western House of Assembly Debates, Official Report*, July 6, 1956, pp. 151-154.

[35] Report of Arbitration into Ibadan NCNC Affairs by a Committee of the NCNC, April 26, 1956.

1956, as it won a majority of Western seats in the Federal election of 1954, Adelabu would have become Premier of the West. But the Action Group retained control of the West by winning 48 seats to the NCNC's 32 (including 7 of the 8 Ibadan seats with approximately 70 percent of the 120,000 votes cast), and Adelabu became Leader of the Opposition in the Western House of Assembly. In 1957 he attended the Nigerian Constitutional Conference in London; on his return journey he made a pilgrimage to Mecca which entitled him to be addressed as Alhaji. It will be recalled that in October 1957, he joined with Malam Aminu Kano, President General of the Northern Elements Progressive Union, in a strongly worded criticism of the decision of the National President of the NCNC to participate in a national government, including the Action Group, under the Prime Minister-ship of Alhaji Abubakar Tafawa Balewa. Adelabu felt that cooperation with the Action Group at the federal level would weaken the position of the NCNC Opposition in the Western Region. In late 1957 he tried to make allegations against the conduct of the Western Regional government to the Commission of Inquiry into the Fears of Minorities, but the Commission ruled that its terms of reference covered "minorities of a permanent nature" only, i.e., ethnic and religious minorities, and that representations by "political" minorities could not be considered.[36]

As we have seen, Adelabu clashed with Azikiwe at the Aba Convention of the NCNC (October 28-30, 1957); he opposed the constitutional amendment empowering the National President to appoint the members of the Central Working Committee of the party, and he was not reappointed by Azikiwe to the office of First National Vice-President. In February 1958, he became General Secretary of the newly organized *Egbe Yoruba Parapo* (Yoruba State Union), a center of opposition to Azikiwe. His support was crucial to the aims of Dr. Mbadiwe and the anti-Azikiwe group in Lagos, but fate removed him from the drama before its denouement.

[36] The NCNC-*Mabolaje* Grand Alliance attempted to petition the Commission of Inquiry for the creation of a Central Yoruba State to include the provinces of Oyo and Ibadan. The Commission observed that these two provinces (in addition to Ondo, which produced a similar petition for an Ondo Central State) "contain the main strength of the Yorubas of the NCNC opposition to the Action Group. Although in their hostility there is an element of local and sectional feeling, this is really political opposition on party lines, and for the Opposition to ask for a separate state would make nonsense of parliamentary democracy." *Report of the Commission appointed to enquire into the fears of Minorities and the means of allaying them* (London: 1958), p. 28.

The Death of a Politician

On March 25, 1958, Adelabu travelled to Lagos (a distance of 89 miles from Ibadan) with one Mr. Albert Younan, a 30-year-old Syrian textile merchant whose home and business were established at Ibadan. In the afternoon of that day they drove back; Mr. Younan was behind the wheel and Adelabu in the front seat beside him. At mile 51 from Lagos, near Shagamu in the Ijebu Remo Division, Younan's car smashed into an oncoming car driven by an African chauffeur with two European passengers. Adelabu, at the age of 43, and two of his relatives were killed outright; Younan was hurled from the vehicle and survived; the persons in the other car escaped with injuries.[37] These circumstances have been related because of the ensuing speculation that Adelabu's death was no mere accident. At the coroner's inquest, Younan testified that both Adelabu and himself were interested in a business transaction, the nature of which he would not discuss.[38] The Senior Crown Counsel then asked if the amount involved was £50,000. Mr. Younan refused to disclose the figure but admitted that he travelled to Lagos on the fateful day for financial reasons. Barrister Mojid Agbaje, NCNC member of the Western House of Assembly and counsel for the Adelabu family, produced a letter from Younan to Adelabu, written the day before the accident, in which the textile merchant begged his friend, Adelabu, to rescue him from an undefined predicament. Younan acknowledged that his trip to Lagos on March 25 was related to his textile business but denied that Adelabu had made the journey with him for the same purpose. The Federal Minister of Finance, a high ranking official of the NCNC, was reported to have said that Adelabu "had come down to Lagos specially about top-party matters."[39] But the tone of desperation of Younan's letter to Adelabu and the fact that Adelabu travelled in Younan's car gave rise to suspicions that were virtually confirmed by Younan's counsel at the inquest. In stating his objection to a line of questioning on the relationship between his client and the deceased, the lawyer remarked:[40] "If you ask the question it will lead to certain grave revelations which will not be pleasant to hear.

[37] The writer returned to Ibadan from the Eastern Region the day before Adelabu was killed, hoping to study Ibadan politics and the *Mabolaje* with his cooperation as had been agreed. His lieutenants in the party, remembering the writer's visits to his compound several months before, gave him every assistance and courtesy during a period of intense emotional and political strain.
[38] *Daily Times*, May 30 and 31, 1958.
[39] *Daily Times*, March 26, 1958.
[40] *Daily Times*, May 30, 1958; *Nigerian Tribune*, May 30, 1958.

The late Adelabu was my personal friend and I would not like anything that will bring his memory to disrepute."

The nature of the transactions and relationships alluded to in the court of inquest were not publicly examined, but the writer thinks it admissible to record what was said by many people in private. In anticipation of an NCNC victory in the regional election of May 1956, Adelabu was said to have placed a large order with Younan for togas—i.e., garments printed with Adelabu's effigy, his name, and the possible notation "Premier of the West." While Adelabu's commitment appears to have been informal, Younan went into debt, possibly with the African Continental Bank, to place an order abroad. Of course the sales value of the garments depreciated when an Action Group victory ensured that Awolowo would remain as Premier. Probably Younan's creditors and/or suppliers were demanding payment and he hoped to secure a reprieve through an arrangement of one kind or another that he depended upon Adelabu to help negotiate. It was thought that Younan's hopes were not requited on March 25, and that he drove back from Lagos in a state of extreme depression and anxiety. At the inquest, Younan denied suggestions by the Senior Crown Counsel and Mr. Agbaje that he deliberately attempted to commit suicide because of his failure to obtain the money he needed. It is not improbable that the NCNC barrister wanted to explore the theory that Younan had been the willing instrument of a diabolical plot conceived by Adelabu's political opponents. Subsequently, both drivers were prosecuted; at first Younan was acquitted and the other driver was convicted of negligence; ultimately a High Court Judge imposed a fine on Younan for gross negligence.[41]

When Ibadan heard that Alhaji Adegoke Adelabu was dead an awful gloom came over the stunned city. One newspaper reported that "grief-maddened crowds" surged through the streets looting shops and destroying property.[42] It was unsafe for vehicles or persons to venture into the streets without symbolic green leaves conspicuously displayed in token of mourning. At first the rumor spread that Adelabu had been killed by his enemies in Ijebu-Remo, the home division of Premier Awolowo. Certain leaders of the NCNC appeared to believe this story and may have abetted its propagation, although the *Southern Nigeria Defender* (Zik Group) deplored violence and admonished the people to remain peaceful. But an ugly spirit was

41 Younan and Sons were ordered by the High Court to pay over £6,000 in compensation to the Adelabu family. *West Africa*, May 2, 1959, p. 423.

42 *Daily Times*, March 27, 1958.

abroad and avenging mobs roamed the rural districts, committing some brutal atrocities against defenseless persons who were thought to be part of the Ibadan minority that supported the Action Group. The initial shock of Adelabu's death was followed by terror: "Five hacked to death," reported the *Nigerian Tribune*, "tax clerk killed on active service."

Immediately the regional government enacted a curfew law that was imposed on Ibadan for four days while para-military police reinforcements were rushed to the areas of tension. Before the rioting was finally quelled, at least twenty persons were known to have been killed; more than 1,000 persons claimed about £50,000 for damages to property and more than 600 persons were arrested for riot offences of whom more than 100 were charged with murder. At subsequent trials, statements such as the following were typical of those reported to have been made by accused persons:[43]

" . . . . one S............ and others came to him and told him that all NCNCers would wage war on members of the Action Group at Lakandoro Village."

". . . . members of the NCNC said that because Adelabu was killed by members of the Action Group they would wage war on Action Group members."

" . . . . members of the NCNC said that Action Group members killed Adelabu and that they should be killed."

On a day that seven persons were sentenced to death, the presiding judge rendered in English the literal meaning of a song chanted by the mob on the day of violence: "You people who have conspired together to kill Adelabu, there will be no peace for you."

It will be observed that there was no tribal or sectional basis to these disturbances. Both the perpetrators and the victims of aggression were people from the same districts and villages. Possibly the death of Adelabu actuated rational if illogical grievances against the Action Group that were deep-seated, involving tax assessment and the like. But the fury of the reaction may have stemmed from a pathological intensity of party spirit which was essentially irrational and related to the charismatic personality of Adelabu. There was more than a touch of pathos at the Magistrate's Court where scores of ragged, bewildered farmers were arraigned for trial. Eventually 64 persons were sentenced to death for the atrocities; however, all but a very few of those convictions were reversed on appeal.[44]

[43] *Daily Service*, May 13, 1958.

[44] In April 1959, it was reported that the Federal Supreme Court allowed the appeals of 17 out of 19 persons who had been condemned to death by the Ibadan

Naturally the NCNC-*Mabolaje* Grand Alliance was shaken by the death of its leader. Adelabu had devised the organization to ensure its virtual dependence upon himself. Its governing body, the Central Executive Committee, consisted of 14 members apart from Adelabu: 12 surviving foundation members, who spoke little if any English, including 4 *Mogajis* and 6 leaders of the *Maiyegun* League of farmers, and 2 trusted lieutenants of Adelabu who were members of the House of Representatives and House of Assembly respectively. Two of the foundation members were outstanding personalities: the 70-year-old *Mogaji* Akere, and Mr. Abdulai Alfa Akano Elisinmeta, an Arabic teacher and trader of about 50, who was the party's principal orator and campaign director. Akere's house, situated in the vicinity of the stately Mapo Hall, where the District Council offices are located, was the meeting hall of the Central Executive Committee. On meeting days, the courtyard and ground floor of this compound may have been occupied by several hundred people, while the Executive conferred in a chamber above. Akere's compound is to Ibadan what the old "wigwam" of Tammany Hall was to New York.[45]

Before the founding of the *Mabolaje*, Mr. Elisinmeta had been a militant leader of the *Maiyegun* League. Although he was not himself a farmer, he was a poor man, imbued with a strong sense of sympathy for the peasantry and the working class. The people respected his Koranic learning and delighted in his talent for improvising catchy political songs, mainly in praise of Adelabu and the poor. Adelabu regarded Elisinmeta as his deputy leader. At rallies, Elisinmeta normally spoke first, drawing upon religion and folk beliefs to put the audience in a receptive mood for the diatribes of Adelabu.

In 1956, Adelabu agreed to organize an advisory committee, which became known as the Policy Committee. This committee comprised parliamentarians and a few influential English-speaking leaders in the wards, altogether about 15 persons in 1958. It functioned as a board of strategy, while the Central Executive Committee was responsible for basic policy and party organization. For purposes of nominating both parliamentary and local government candidates, the two com-

---

High Court. The Supreme Court held that the Crown's plea of common intention had not been established. At this time 34 convictions had been reversed. *Daily Times*, April 24, 1959. Nigerian readers may forgive the writer for stating the extraneous fact, for the benefit of some American readers, that the prosecuting attorneys, the defense attorneys, the judges and the justices involved in these cases were either all or nearly all Nigerians.

[45] See Roy V. Peel, *The Political Clubs of New York City* (New York: Putnam's Sons, 1935), p. 32.

mittees merged to form an Election Committee, but the Central Executive Committee alone was the final arbiter. Gradually the distinction between these two groups blurred and in March 1958, prior to Adelabu's death, they were merged permanently into an enlarged 35- to 40-member Central Executive Committee of the NCNC-*Mabolaje* Grand Alliance. In the wake of Adelabu's death the Central Executive Committee became a vortex of intra-party struggle as the older *Mogajis* and *Maiyegun* leaders were obliged to cede greater power to the parliamentarians and educated members. Within a few weeks, the four lawyers in the Central Executive Committee emerged as the leading personalities in the party.

Several factors account for the ascendancy of the lawyers. First, they were prominent in the defense of the many NCNC followers who were arrested during the riots. Secondly, they possessed intellectual qualities and professional talents that are essential attributes of leadership for organized political activity within a parliamentary system. Most of the well-educated and professional men in Ibadan support the Action Group, while those parliamentary and English oratorical skills which Adelabu possessed to a high degree were at a premium in the Ibadan NCNC and most clearly exemplified by the lawyers. Thirdly, the *Mabolaje* required leaders who could maintain the prestige and primacy of the Ibadan branch within the Western Regional Organization of the NCNC. At the time of his death, Adelabu was not only the leader of the *Mabolaje*, but the chairman of the NCNC Western Working Committee and the Leader of the Opposition in the Western House of Assembly. None but the lawyers had the requisite stature to be considered for those positions. Finally, the four lawyers were personable as well as able and ambitious individuals. Thus, Abdul Mojid Fodarin Agbaje, MHA, son of the late Chief Salami Agbaje, was an experienced lawyer of 38 who had been a political associate of Adelabu since the latter's hostility to his father was eclipsed by greater issues. E. O. Fakayode, MHA, had challenged Adelabu's arbitrary leadership on two occasions in 1956, but at the age of 36 he was widely respected for his service to the party and his superior intellect. E. Adeoye Adisa, a dynamic barrister of 40, had returned to Ibadan in December 1956 after seven years of study abroad in Cairo and at London University, where he obtained a Master's degree in Law. Like Adelabu, he lived among the people, identified himself wholly with their interests and attracted a large personal following. R. O. A. Akinjide, a youthful intellectual of 27, was also Publicity Secretary of the *Mabolaje* and one of the rising NCNC politicians in the Western Region.

Apart from the lawyers, the enlarged Central Executive Committee consisted of 4 *Mogajis*, 12 traders, 5 produce buyers, 5 contractors, 2 managerial employees of firms, 2 farmers, and 2 Arabic teachers. Their average age was about 45; Muslims outnumbered Christians by about 4 to 1. (See the writer's tabulation of members of the Central Executive Committee of the NCNC-*Mabolaje* Grand Alliance, July 1958.)[46]

[46] Central Executive Committee of the NCNC-*Mabolaje* Grand Alliance— July 1958

	Foundation Members	*Age*	*Religion*	*Occupation*
1.	Mogaji Akere	70	Muslim	large farm owner
2.	Mogaji Lamo (deceased 1958)	80	Muslim	
3.	Mogaji Ekarun Seriki	50	Muslim	
4.	Mogaji Arijemagba	47	Muslim	
5.	Mr. Abdulai Akano Elisin-meta (Maiyegun leader)	50	Muslim	Arabic teacher and shopkeeper
6.	Mr. Yesufu Mogbonjubola	50	Muslim	Trader
7.	Mr. Alli Oyebanji (Maiyegun leader)	43	Muslim	Produce buyer
8.	Mr. Tolorunnioshe (Maiyegun leader)	45	Muslim	Farmer
9.	Mr. Obadara Atanda (Maiyegun leader)	65	Muslim	Farmer
10.	Mr. Akami Mustapha (Maiyegun leader)	46	Muslim	Arabic teacher
11.	Mr. Yesufu Anifa	40	Muslim	Trader
12.	Mr. Ladde Ogunmola	44	Muslim	Trader
	Deceased Foundation Members			
	Alhaji Gbadamosi Adegoke Adelabu	43	Muslim	Politician and merchant
	Mr. Konipe		Muslim	Farmer
	Mogaji Lawal Adebiyi (possibly not a foundation member)		Muslim	
	Non-Foundation Members Co-opted into the Executive prior to 1958			
13.	Hon. S. L. A. Elliott, MHR	44	Christian	Accounts manager to a firm
14.	Hon. I. Lawal, MHA	40	Muslim	Produce buyer, Leventis
	Non-Foundation Members who entered the Executive via the Policy Committee or by Co-option in 1958			
15.	Hon. L. Ade Bello, MHA	42	Muslim	Contractor
16.	Hon. Adebayo Adeyinka, MHR	36	Muslim	Contractor
17.	Hon. E. O. Fakayode, MHA	36	Christian	Lawyer
18.	Hon. A. M. F. Agbaje, MHA	38	Muslim	Lawyer
19.	Hon. L. S. Salanu, MHA	30	Muslim	Produce buyer
20.	Hon. A. O. Adeshokun, MHA	31	Muslim	Produce buyer
21.	Hon. L. A. Lawal, MHR	30	Muslim	Contractor

Adelabu died less than three months before a formidable group of NCNC personalities, including two federal ministers, Dr. K. O. Mbadiwe and Chief Kolawole Balogun, repudiated the leadership of Dr. Azikiwe and demanded his resignation as President of the party and Premier of the Eastern Region.[47] We have seen that six days before the open break, Chief H. O. Davies, a Lagos barrister whose ethnic origin is partly Ibadan Yoruba, was elected as Chairman of the Western Working Committee with the support of the *Mabolaje* Central Executive Committee. Dr. Mbadiwe presided over the meeting which was attended by Chief Kolawole Balogun and by the President of the newly formed *Egbe Yoruba Parapo* (Yoruba State Union), Alhaji N. B. Soule. The latter, a national trustee of the NCNC and a wealthy merchant of Oyo Yoruba origin, was honored in Ibadan as the patron of the exiled ex-*Alafin* of Oyo[48] and as a stalwart partisan of the NCNC who frequently helped to defray the expense of litigations involving the defense of Adelabu. Soule, Mbadiwe, Davies, and Balogun were among the signatories to the "Zik Must Go" document of June 14, 1958, as were two members of the *Mabolaje* Central

22.	Hon. J. M. Johnson, MHR (Minister of Internal Affairs, Labor and Welfare; former Chairman Ibadan Dist. Council; no longer active in the Ibadan party since moving to Lagos.)	43	Christian	Contractor
23.	Hon. E. Adeoye Adisa, MHA	40	Christian	Lawyer
24.	Mr. R. O. A. Akinjide (Publicity Secretary)	27	Christian	Lawyer
25.	Mogaji Ajingbe	60		
26.	Mogaji Ebo-Olobi (Educated; leader of the Ibadan Tax Payers Assn.)	60		Pensioner
27.	Mr. S. O. Olatunji	38	Christian	Trader
28.	Mr. S. A. Bolarinwa	46	Muslim	Produce buyer, GAIZER
29.	Alhaji K. O. S. Are	45	Muslim	Contractor
30.	Mr. Raimi Dosu	45	Muslim	Trader
31.	Mr. Ashunolowo	40	Muslim	Trader
32.	Mr. Adetunji	46	Muslim	Trader
33.	Mr. Tijani Akinboler	42	Muslim	Trader
34.	Mr. Suberu Larenju	38		Trader
35.	Mr. J. P. Abidogim			Trader
36.	Mr. L. A. Kadri			Trader
37.	Mr. S. Lana			Trader
38.	Mr. Akinpelu			Salesman, GBO

[47] *Supra*, pp. 220-221.

[48] The ex-*Alafin* of Oyo lived in Lagos under the protection—i.e., largely at the expense—of Alhaji N. B. Soule.

Executive Committee. However, barrister Mojid Agbaje declared to the National Executive Committee that the document had taken the Ibadan people "unawares" and did not represent the view of the Ibadan NCNC.[49]

Yet the rebellion against Azikiwe did add to the confusion of the *Mabolaje* Central Executive. Adelabu's recent antagonism toward Azikiwe and lesser considerations—e.g., the absence of the National President from Adelabu's funeral—disposed a majority of the Ibadan leaders to remain at least neutral in the dispute and to endeavor to effect a settlement. But barrister E. Adeoye Adisa, who did not attend the meeting of the Western Working Committee on June 8 (the election of Chief H. O. Davies as Chairman), and barrister R. O. A. Akinjide declared their unequivocal loyalty to Azikiwe and resolved to force the issue on the *Mabolaje* Executive. Barrister Adisa had been nominated by the Central Executive Committee to contest the by-election for Adelabu's seat in the Western House of Assembly; now he determined to make a bid for the vacant chairmanship of the *Mabolaje*. His ambition was resented by a majority of the Central Executive Committee which refused to give him the mantle of leadership. An uneasy truce was observed during electoral campaigns for Adelabu's parliamentary seat and a newly constituted Ibadan District Council.

TURMOIL AND TRANSITION

Since the dissolution of the "Adelabu" District Council in 1956, Ibadan local government had been administered by a Provisional Council of about 25 members including the *Olubadan* as President, several chiefs, and prominent citizens appointed by the Minister of Local Government. Although the Provisional Council discharged its responsibilities commendably, it incurred the disapproval of both major parties. The Ibadan branch of the Action Group complained that the Council was not amenable to party direction while the NCNC regarded it as an Action Group tax machine. Assuredly, the great majority of appointed rate assessors were members or supporters of the Action Group, which is not surprising in view of the fact that effective rate collection requires strenuous effort on the part of the assessors, and those in charge prefer to appoint individuals who are politically trustworthy.[50]

---

[49] Minutes of the National Executive Committee of the NCNC, Lagos, June 14 and 15, 1958, p. 3. The two Ibadan signatories, who soon withdrew from the NCNC Reform Committee (Mbadiwe group), were Alhaji K. O. S. Are, and Hon. L. S. Salami, MHA.

[50] Mr. E. W. J. Nicholson reported that the NCNC Council of 1954-1955

The law provides that all men of 16 or above shall be required to pay a local rate which in 1958 was a minimum of £3.5/- in Ibadan.[51] Evasion is flagrant: in July 1958, the Western Minister of Finance estimated that in Ibadan District 40,000 persons or "at least one in every three of the adult male population of the council area was a rate defaulter."[52] To meet the problem of mass evasion all persons subject to the rate were required to carry their receipts with them at all times. When the rate collection drive was on, usually from December to March, persons who failed to produce their receipts upon the demand of an officer of the Council could be arrested, prosecuted for evasion, and sentenced to pay a fine of £100 or to serve one year imprisonment in default of payment.[53] The law did not explicitly sanction arrests and prosecutions for failure to produce a rate receipt, but the legality of the practice had not, to the writer's knowledge, been challenged in court.[54] Political capital was derived in abundance

---

packed the Tax Unit Committees "exclusively with their own followers or sympathizers . . . to ensure that their policy would be carried out without opposition." He criticized this "mistaken policy" as the source of many accusations of partiality and maladministration. *Nicholson Report,* p. 67.

Under the rating system in force at Ibadan in 1958, unit or ward committees were responsible to a Central Assessment Committee and its decisions could be appealed to a Tax Appeals Board of the Council. During the tenure of the Provisional Council, the Central Assessment Committee was directed by its able chairman, Mogaji S. B. M. Busari, a leading member of the Action Group, and included four Councillors and six *Mogajis,* four of whom were Action Group supporters. Subordinate assessment committees in every ward were responsible for both assessing the incomes of residents and collecting rates levied. Five percent of the amount collected in each ward was returned to the ward committee as remuneration for services. Theoretically ward committee members were recommended for appointment to the Chairman of the Central Assessment Committee by mass meetings in the wards. In fact, most of the members certified to the Council for approval were Action Group supporters. The writer was informed that staunch supporters of the NCNC were normally unwilling to serve as tax collectors for an "Action Group" Council, although the Ibadan (Provisional) District Council was officially nonpartisan.

[51] "Every male person of or above the age of sixteen years liable to a rate upon income shall, if he is not assessed by the assessment committee at a greater sum, be deemed to be in receipt of a total income of fifty pounds and shall be assessed accordingly." Local Government Law, 1957, section 151 (2). Income rates are graduated progressively to a maximum income of £300, for which the Ibadan rate in 1958 was £15.15/-. Employed women and those who earn £50 or more are liable to assessment. Levies on total incomes above £300 per annum are subject to taxation by the Inland Revenue Department. Local government levies, with which this discussion is concerned, are technically designated as rates, not taxes, although the latter term is used popularly or unpopularly as the case may be. Local rates are compiled on the basis of standard service costs which normally include education, street lighting, and water charges.

[52] *Daily Service,* July 7, 1958.

[53] Western Region Local Government Law, 1957, Section 251.

[54] The *Akodas,* factotums and messengers who wear blue uniforms, and participate

STUDIES IN POWER AND CONFLICT

from allegations of arbitrary and discriminatory assessments and the tax issue was kept in a torrid state of readiness for partisan use by the frequent drives against evaders.[55]

Naturally, the impact of rate enforcement was greatest on the mass membership of the NCNC, which stood for the reduction of the burden on the poor farmers and workers.[56] During the local government election campaign of June 1958, taxation themes were pressed to the hilt by the NCNC. Some of the arguments were less than veracious—for example, the assertion that the Provisional Council had voted to impose a new tax of ten shillings on each ram to be slaughtered during the Muslim Greater Beiram Festival. This appears to have been a telling insinuation because the Action Group took pains to refute it vehemently.[57] Audiences at the NCNC campaign meetings were reminded that the election was a contest between the party of the rich and the party of the poor. Another reiterated theme was the redemption of Adelabu; the party spirit of mass meetings was invoked frequently by exclamations of "Ade" (for Adelabu) repeated several times with arms stretched upwards and two fingers extended in the Churchillian manner.

The Action Group had little hope of victory; its burden of per-

---

in the tax drives, are reported to apprehend evaders although they have no legal right to do so. There were about 132 *Akodas* employed by the Council in 1958 under the direction of the Council Secretary who acts through a Senior Head *Akoda*. Individuals arrested on charges of tax evasion cannot be retained in custody without arraignment before one of the customary courts empowered to deal with rate cases. Arrested persons are always given time to produce lawfully obtained receipts.

[55] See petitions submitted to the Governor of the Western Region, the Commissioner of Inland Revenue, the Minister of Local Government and the Secretary, Ibadan (Provisional) District Council, published in the *West African Pilot*, January 27, 28, and 29, 1958.

[56] In the year 1954-1955, the NCNC Ibadan District Council down-graded more than 13,000 persons from a higher bracket (Schedule II taxpayers) to the Flat Rate bracket, as a result of which there was a shortfall in the actual collection amounting to about £27,000 and a decrease in the Council's revenues of nearly £10,500 despite an increase of about 2,500 taxpayers over the preceding year. The commissioner who investigated this phenomenon found "that no real explanation was offered" for the down-grading of 13,286 taxpayers. *Nicholson Report*, pp. 59, 69. It has been thought that property rating would enable the Council to relieve the burden of taxation on the poorer classes and the idea has been accepted by the Council in principle, but it had not been put into effect by 1958 because of many technical difficulties to be overcome including the comprehensive evaluation of all houses in Ibadan.

[57] Within a week of the NCNC victory in June 1958, the Action Group *Nigerian Tribune* advised the regional government to "strip" the Council of its rate-collection power and vest the responsibility in a government agency on the arguable ground that the NCNC had fought the election on an anti-tax platform. *Nigerian Tribune*. June 24, 1958.

suasion was weightier than that of the NCNC and its promises were more ambitious. The Action Group Divisional Leader, Mr. A. M. A. Akinloye, declared that his party, if elected, would bring new industries to Ibadan, construct modern markets, increase the number of agricultural loans for farmers and scholarships for students, and raise the level of public health.[58] The following arguments by Action Group orators at a mass meeting may indicate what the politicians think is in the voter's mind. They are recorded as paraphrased by the writer from notes on a running translation from the Yoruba.

"We are contesting as hard as we can because of the recent riots. The people must not be afraid of the NCNC."

Song (with refrains by the audience):

> The death of Adelabu was not the doing of the Action
>   Group;
> It happened while he was on his way home
> From business in Lagos.

"Adelabu tried to get into power but all his efforts failed. Awolowo is a political giant. Now the NCNC is falling apart without its leader."

Song:

> It was a motor accident that killed Adelabu.
> Pray God will not do that to anyone here.
> On the second day there were riots against the
>   Action Group
> Killing people like animals;
> It is not good to do that; it gains nothing
> And it is not the way to show sympathy.
> You cannot use force or hooliganism to make sympathy.
> Awolowo reported to the Governor and
> The Lord punished the rioters.

"If you vote for the NCNC again, the Council will not last long before it is dissolved again."

"Who does not want money? If you want money vote for the Action Group. It is the party in power; the NCNC is an impoverished party. The NCNC said it would reduce taxes, therefore the Action Group made taxes higher. The Action Group is strong."

"If the people vote for the Action Group all the benefits will be given; but if they remain adamant Ibadan will continue to suffer.

[58] *Nigerian Tribune*, June 14, 1958.

All the advantages have been kept in custody for Ibadan until it votes for the Action Group."

"The Action Group plans to build four secondary schools in Ibadan. Vote for the Action Group and the building will be done."

Both parties campaigned intensively for a period of nearly two weeks.[59] On the day before polling, Action Group and NCNC mass rallies were addressed by their respective national leaders, Chief Obafemi Awolowo and Dr. Nnamdi Azikiwe. An enormous throng turned out to greet the National President of the NCNC who was in the midst of his own campaign against the "NCNC Reform Committee." Azikiwe's tremendous popularity in Ibadan could not be overlooked by the members of the *Mabolaje* Executive Committee. Inwardly they chafed when the Reformers were expelled from the NCNC, but they never took an open stand against Azikiwe, and they confined their complaints to the National President's previous neglect of Ibadan.[60] On June 21 the NCNC won a decisive victory at Ibadan, returning 51 Council candidates to the Action Group's 19.[61] Five days

[59] Campaigning in the rural districts was more difficult and the candidates spent many days visiting the homes and farms of people in their constituencies. The farmers were concerned about loans to finance land improvement. A majority of the members of the Local Loans Boards are Action Group supporters and some NCNC farmers feared to apply for loans under the mistaken impression that their houses could be attached as collateral. The writer noted a disposition to accept taxation as inevitable and an interest on the part of farmers to get their money's worth in benefits. On the whole, people in the districts seemed sceptical about the abilities and intentions of candidates to do them much good, but willing to listen to promises.

[60] It was not until July 17, 1958, that the NCNC-*Mabolaje* Grand Alliance issued a declaration of loyalty to Azikiwe, which stated:

"A Press report of the alleged split in the NCNC-*Mabolaje* Grand Alliance over the crisis is completely false. We are all of one voice on the matter. It was for the NCNC that the illustrious son of Ibadan, the late Alhaji Adegoke Adelabu, laid down his life. The NCNC-*Mabolaje* Grand Alliance had made fruitless efforts to settle the rift. We were never privy to the original memorandum of the Mbadiwe group but immediately it was published we endeavoured to make Dr. Mbadiwe see reason but he refused to be drawn. . . .

"On Tuesday, July 15, representatives of the NCNC-*Mabolaje* Grand Alliance had an interview with the Prime Minister, Alhaji Abubakar Tafawa Balewa, in an effort to arrest the crisis and usher in sanity. All the alleged Ibadan delegations and supporters for the Reform Committee published in Ibadan and in the 'Daily Telegraph' in Lagos are false and without foundation. The NCNC-*Mabolaje* Grand Alliance is deeply convinced that no sane lover of the NCNC will have now any quota of sympathy for the political antics of the Mbadiwe Group." *Daily Times*, July 18, 1958. By this time it was apparent that Azikiwe would not be overthrown.

[61] All told, 85,707 or 47% of those registered in 72 contested wards voted. The NCNC won 51 seats, including one unopposed; its percentage of the total vote was 57%. The Action Group returned 19 candidates with 41% of the total vote, which was 16% higher than its vote in the regional election of 1956. One inde-

later, Mr. Adisa was elected by a large majority to Adelabu's former seat in the Western House of Assembly. This was an interesting contest because Adisa's opponent, barrister Y. L. Akande, was a Muslim from Adelabu's own quarter of town. Adisa, who lives in another quarter, is a Christian, unlike Adelabu, and the contest was heralded by the Action Group as "a challenge to Muslims."[62]

Flushed with success, Adisa led the fight for Azikiwe against the shadow of the Reform Committee in Ibadan. On June 29 the NCNC Western Working Committee reassembled at Ibadan with Azikiwe in the chair. Before his arrival, Reform leaders, including Alhaji N. B. Soule, Chief H. O. Davies, Chief Kolawole Balogun, and Hon. O. Bademosi, had put in an appearance but were firmly requested to leave. The main purpose of the meeting was to elect a new chairman of the Western Working Committee to replace Chief H. O. Davies. When the name of Adisa was placed in nomination, the *Mabolaje* leaders reacted furiously. Azikiwe declared a recess while the Ibadan group caucused. Upon resumption, Dr. Azikiwe announced that he had been informed that party leaders from other sections of the Western Region were content to let the Ibadan branch select a chairman of the Working Committee and that the Ibadan leaders had decided upon barrister A. M. F. Agbaje. Thereupon Agbaje was elected unanimously as Chairman of the Western Working Committee; the following week he was selected by the NCNC as Chairman of the Ibadan District Council and in September he accompanied Azikiwe to London as a member of the NCNC delegation to the Resumed Constitutional Conference.

Adisa's bid for the chairmanship of the Western Working Committee was premature because he did not have control of the *Mabolaje* Executive Committee. Confident of his mass support and determined to seize the leadership of the *Mabolaje*, he accused the Executive junta of betraying the ideals of Adelabu by failing Azikiwe in the crisis. This allegation was echoed by the *Southern Nigeria Defender*

---

pendent was elected, 5 were defeated and 12 candidates of the National Emancipation League were defeated with less than 1% of the total vote. Surprisingly, 3 members of the *Mabolaje* Central Executive Committee, including Alfa Elisinmeta and R. O. A. Akinjide, were defeated, but these were regarded by the party as minor aberrations, since 5 other *Mabolaje* Executive members were elected. Mr. Akinloye, the Action Group leader, and Mr. Lasisi Ajimobi, the Divisional Organizing Secretary, were elected, but the only woman candidate, who contested on the Action Group platform, was defeated. *Report on the Local Government Elections in the Western Region of Nigeria, 1958* (Ibadan: Government Printer, 1958), p. 85 and *Daily Times*, June 23, 1958.

[62] *Nigerian Tribune*, June 14, 1958; Mr. Adisa's margin of victory was 5,801-2,862. *West African Pilot*, June 27, 1959.

(Zik Group), the NCNC organ in Ibadan.[63] Both Adisa and his chief lieutenant, barrister Akinjide, regarded the crisis at the national and local levels as a struggle between the left and the right. Of course the issues were not articulated in these terms, but the two insurgents shared a serious interest in ideology, were socialistic in principle, popularist in attitude, and deeply concerned with the larger issues of African freedom. Thus Akinjide attended the All African Peoples' Conference at Accra, Ghana, in December 1958. Ideologically, Adelabu was closer to Adisa and Akinjide than to his more intimate political associates who controlled the *Mabolaje* Executive. It was his fate to have been diverted by circumstance and temperament from left-wing nationalism to unprincipled bossism. Both legacies were inherited by those who followed in his political footsteps.

Adisa's mass appeal was undeniable and the issue of leadership was forced on the Executive by popular pressure. His claim was supported by two organized sections of the *Mabolaje*: the women's section, that insisted on a strong personality of Adelabu's calibre, and the Taxpayers' Association, an influential mass membership group that was formed in 1957 by *Mogaji* Ebo-Olobi of the Oke-Foko quarter, an educated pensioner, with Akinjide as its legal adviser. In July Adisa's faction held a mass meeting at Adelabu's compound at which his leadership of the *Mabolaje* was proclaimed. Thereupon a majority of the Executive Committee repudiated Adisa, and elected the venerable 70-year-old, non-English-speaking foundation member, Mogaji Akere, as chairman of the party. Actually, the leadership of the Executive was collegial, with Mojid Agbaje, Chairman of the Western Working Committee and the Ibadan District Council, the first among several equals.

Agbaje's political reputation was enhanced during the initial weeks of his tenure as Chairman of the Ibadan District Council. Shortly after its inauguration, the new Council dissolved all of the tax assessment committees, alleging that the members had been appointed irregularly and that they were mainly Action Groupers who might not want the Council to succeed in its collection efforts.[64] Agbaje and the Regional Minister of Local Government negotiated an agreement which provided for a six-man assessment committee in each ward in the proportion of 4 NCNC to 2 Action Group. The Chairman then made a public appeal to NCNC supporters to vindicate the Council by paying their rates. But the future of the Ibadan District Council was uncertain inasmuch as the regional government

---

[63] *Southern Nigeria Defender*, July 16, 1958.
[64] *West African Pilot*, July 25, 1958; *Daily Times*, July 15, 1958.

had given notice of a plan to reorganize Ibadan Division into a city council and several separate rural district councils.[65] (Ibadan Division was among those few exceptional areas in the Western Region where the structure of local government was single-tiered; the Ibadan District Council was equivalent to a Divisional Council, as may be inferred from the fact that its president was a Head Chief, the *Olubadan* of Ibadan.) The NCNC declared its adamant opposition to the plan which it regarded as a stratagem to diffuse and thereby weaken the party's electoral strength, and was anxious to deny the government any opportunity to dissolve the Council for failing to collect rates and then to implement reorganization.[66]

Despite his rising prestige, Agbaje was not a strong candidate for the leadership of the *Mabolaje*. His political style was too reserved for the temper of the Ibadan masses who were accustomed to Adelabu. Nor was he wholly acceptable to the *Mogajis* who had participated in the agitation against his father seven years earlier. Probably he preferred the collegial Executive set-up under the leadership of Mogaji Akere. On the other hand, Adisa did covet the political leadership of Ibadan and all that it implied. In September 1958 a "Peace Committee" of the NCNC National Executive Committee mediated the dispute and produced a tenuous agreement that Adisa should be recognized as Chairman of the *Mabolaje* in response to popular demand. The composition of the Central Executive Committee was then altered to reflect the new balance of power. (The writer was informed authoritatively that the reconstructed Central Executive Committee included 48 members as follows: 10 legislators, 14 councillors, 8 *Mogajis*, 8 members from Mogaji Ebo-Olobi's Taxpayers' Association, and 8 members from the Akere group.) However, the wounds of pride were sore, and the Central Executive Committee was no longer the closely knit unit it had been during the Adelabu era. It was not improbable that the new leader, Adisa, would sweep away the archaic caucus and institute a system of organization at once more democratic, i.e., responsive and responsible to the membership, and more amenable to his personal control.

The factional struggle among Adelabu's political heirs was not

[65] The Ibadan reorganization proposal was made by the Minister of Local Government in December 1957 and endorsed by the *Olubadan* and Chiefs. It came to pass in 1961.

[66] An amendment to the Local Government Law enacted by the Western House of Assembly in June 1958 authorized the Governor in Council to dissolve any local council that fails to discharge its functions and either to appoint a committee of management or an administrator, or to direct that a new election be held. Local Government (Amendment) (No. 2) Law, 1958.

settled when the writer left Nigeria in December 1958, and it erupted in 1959 when the Adisa and the Agbaje factions nominated different slates of candidates to contest the federal election. A special convention of the NCNC appointed a committee under the chairmanship of Hon. T. O. S. Benson, MHR, who had been elected to replace Mr. Agbaje as Chairman of the Western Working Committee, to investigate the dispute and make recommendations with respect to candidates. These were mainly favorable to the Agbaje faction, and the National President ruled that Mr. Agbaje and six of his colleagues were entitled to use the party symbol.[67] As a result, the Adisa faction of the *Mabolaje* severed its relationship with the NCNC, contested independently, and won 6 of the 7 seats in the Ibadan District area.[68] Thereupon the victorious wing of the *Mabolaje* declared its support for the Prime Minister of Nigeria and the Northern Peoples' Congress, a development which had been feared by the Action Group while Adelabu was alive and Muslim political action in the Western Region seemed imminent.[69] Oddly enough, it came to pass under the auspices of a Christian leader of the *Mabolaje* (Mr. Adisa), without religious overtones. Ironically, the NCNC lost Ibadan through a political lapse which alienated supporters of Azikiwe in an election which produced an otherwise impressive revival of NCNC strength in the Western Region. It seems unlikely, however, that the *Mabolaje* will remain permanently estranged from the house of the NCNC.

The Social Basis of Party Competition in Ibadan

Party competition in Ibadan is rooted in a two-fold primary division of Ibadan society—first, an ethnic cleavage between the Ibadan indigenes, who constitute an overwhelming majority of the population, and the Yoruba settlers, especially the Ijebu Yoruba; second, a socio-economic cleavage between the Ibadan indigenous community and the relatively privileged class that has arisen from it. Assuredly, other socio-economic cleavages may be distinguished— e.g., between the traditional Ibadan indigenous community and the

[67] *West African Pilot*, October 14, 1959. From a distance this seemed an odd decision to the writer since Adisa had been in the forefront of the campaign against Dr. Mbadiwe in 1958 and appeared then to have the energetic support of Dr. Azikiwe.

[68] The remaining seat was won by barrister A. M. A. Akinloye of the Action Group, former President of the Ibadan People's Party and former Minister of Agriculture. His perseverance as an Action Group stalwart since 1951 was rewarded by his constituents.

[69] *Supra*, p. 250.

new classes generally, including both indigenous and non-indigenous elements—but, in this writer's opinion, the cleavages of prime political significance are the two described here.

Essentially, the *Mabolaje* of Ibadan is a "communal" membership party, like the *Egbe Oyo Parapo* (of Oyo) or the *Otu Edo* of Benin, which have been discussed previously. There is no register of *Mabolaje* members and there are no regular dues procedures, although the *Mabolaje* leadership has been able to raise considerable sums by popular subscription when required.[70] Ibadan people "belong" to the *Mabolaje* in the sense that they regard it as the embodiment of their social and spiritual values and identify it with the honor of the Ibadan tribe, the sanctity of traditional institutions, and the welfare of the common man. Increasingly the latter interest, an incipient lower-class value, has gained prominence in party pronouncements and in public discussion.

Non-Yoruba settlers in Ibadan mainly support the NCNC and its allies: working-class Ibos, who constitute about one percent of the population of Ibadan, vote for the NCNC as a matter of course without organizational compulsion; most of the 9,000 Hausa people in Ibadan support the Northern Elements Progressive Union and therefore vote for candidates of the NCNC. These elements were part of the NCNC-*Mabolaje* Grand Alliance, which in 1958 comprised such additional satellite or ancillary elements as the NCNC Planning Committee (mainly youths of Yoruba nationality who were not indigenes of Ibadan), an Adelabu National Front (mainly Ibadan youths who followed Adisa), a branch of the Zikist National Vanguard (including members of various ethnic origins), a Taxpayers' Association, and an Ibadan NCNC women's organization. Only the Ibadan Indigenes were identified with the *Mabolaje per se*, which was therefore an Ibadan tribal party, as the federal election of 1959 demonstrated.

As in Benin, Oyo, and Ilesha, the tribal party of Ibadan does not enjoy the support of the traditional chiefs. In Ibadan, as elsewhere in the Western Region, a chief is an Action Grouper virtually by definition. Even Adelabu could not deny that component of traditional life to the government party; in 1955 he failed to prevent the election of the present *Olubadan*, a former chief judge of the reformed Native

[70] When the writer visited Adelabu's compound during a meeting of the *Mabolaje* on Saturday, October 19, 1957, he was introduced by Adelabu to the members of the Central Executive Committee while the latter were counting out a pile of money which had been raised to pay British counsel engaged to represent them before the Minorities Commission.

Court system, who was known to support the Action Group.[71] In April 1958, the writer determined that 33 of the 44 officially recognized *Mogajis* and all but one or two of the 12 senior chiefs were supporters of the Action Group.[72] The Action Group chiefs and *Mogajis* do have political followers who account for a substantial portion of the Action Group vote, but they are not sufficiently numerous to dislodge the *Mabolaje* from its position of dominance in the traditional sector of Ibadan. A plausible explanation of their inability to lead the people away from the *Mabolaje*, in the light of this account, may lie in the persistence of pervasive communal consciousness among the people of Ibadan. Another explanation may lie in the nature of the Ibadan traditional order.

The hierarchy of Ibadan chiefs was not established until the nineteenth century, and the process of selection is more "democratic" in Ibadan than in the other Yoruba states. Any man chosen by his kinsmen as a family head is eligible for recognition as a *Mogaji* and for subsequent advancement to the highest traditional office. Therefore, Ibadan chiefs lack the spiritual status that attaches to the semi-hereditary rulers of those communities which have origins that are embedded in mythical legend. Everyone in Ibadan knows how a chief is appointed, and it is not regarded as particularly admirable to join the Action Group in order to make the grade. Those who do so may acquire title but lose respect.

Similarly, the prestige of religious authorities may be compromised by the taint of political partisanship. For example, in the summer of 1958, NCNC Muslims declared a boycott of the Central Mosque, and elected their own Imam because the incumbent Chief Imam was alleged to be an Action Grouper.[73] It emerges that neither the Chiefs nor the Imams can deliver the vote to the Action Group if they are so inclined. But their influence in concert with effective methods of organization and economic inducements is likely to sustain and intensify party competition in the greatest African city.[74]

[71] *Nicholson Report*, p. 90. Chief I. B. Akinyele, *Olubadan* of Ibadan, is also the foremost historian of Ibadan. *Supra*, p. 284, n. 1.

[72] After the local government election of 1958, the Action Group claimed the support of all 19 traditional members of the Ibadan District Council, including the *Olubadan* and the senior chiefs.

[73] *Daily Times*, June 30 and July 5, 1958; *Nigerian Tribune*, July 5, 1958.

[74] Economic inducements include loans and contracts. It may be observed that nearly all persons appointed to Local Loans Boards in Ibadan Division were thought to be Action Group supporters, as were most government contractors in the Ibadan area. In 1958-1959 the Action Group budgeted nearly £6,500 to finance its operations in Ibadan. Action Group of Nigeria, *Approved Estimates, 1958-1959*. The Action Group demonstrated increasing strength in the regional election of 1960 by winning 6 seats to 10 for the *Mabolaje* (NPC) Alliance.

CHAPTER VIII: PARTY COMPETITION
IN THE NORTHERN REGION

I T HAS been observed, in Chapter III, that the Northern Peoples'
Congress (*Jam'iyyar Mutanen Arewa* in the Hausa language),
at the time of its formation as a cultural organization in 1948-
1949, was conceived as a center of political collaboration for
educated and progressive Northerners. The Congress, it will be recalled, was transformed into a political party in 1951, following the
elimination of radicals who were associated with the Northern Elements Progressive Union (NEPU).[1] Possibly, this development was
the immediate consequence of electoral victories by the NEPU in the
primary stage of a protracted general election through a system of
electoral colleges.[2] At this time, Alhaji Ahmadu, the Sardauna of
Sokoto, and Malam Abubakar Tafawa Balewa, the two most influential politicians in the North, joined the Northern Peoples' Congress.[3] As noted above, the system of indirect elections served to filter
out radical candidates with the result that in all but a few middle-belt
(or lower Northern) constituencies, only candidates favored by the
Northern Peoples' Congress and the Native Authorities, i.e., the
emirs and chiefs, were elected to the Northern House of Assembly
by the final electoral colleges in December 1951. Nearly all of the
members of the House of Assembly from the upper Northern constituencies were, in fact, officials of the Native Administrations. This
result was duplicated in the federal election of 1954.

From 1952 to 1954 effective political power in the North was
exercised by the British officials, the chiefs, and the top NPC
politicians in that order. During that period, the Northern Peoples'
Congress itself was but a shadow of its parliamentary organization,
under the effective leadership of its Vice-President, Alhaji Ahmadu,
the Sardauna of Sokoto, who served as Regional Minister of Works,
Local Government, and Community Development. No other minister
held formal office in the party;[4] the omission of Hon. Abubakar

---

[1] *Supra,* pp. 95-96.   [2] *Supra,* p. 30.
[3] Their biographies are sketched briefly at *supra,* pp. 97-100.
[4] On July 5, 1952, an Emergency Conference of the Northern Peoples' Congress
at Kaduna formalized its conversion into a political party; officers were elected to
replace the civil servants who had resigned, as follows:
Alhaji Sanda—President (Hausa, Kano, Muslim, Lagos merchant)
Alhaji Ahmadu, Sardauna MHA—Vice-President (Fulani, Sokoto, Muslim,
Sokoto N.A.)
Malam Ibrahim Imam MHA—General Secretary (Kanuri, Bornu, Muslim,
Bornu N.A., and contractor)

Tafawa Balewa, then Central Minister of Works, was indicative of the relative unimportance of the extra-parliamentary organization. In April 1954, the Sardauna of Sokoto was elected to the office of General President of the NPC and Malam Abubakar Tafawa Balewa was elected First Vice-President; they held these offices at the time of writing.

Malam Aminu Kano[5] was elected President-General of the Northern Elements Progressive Union (NEPU) at its third annual conference (Bida) of 1953. In 1954 the NEPU entered into its present alliance with the National Council of Nigeria and the Cameroons. The Action Group did not become a ponderable force in Northern politics until the latter 1950's, when it formed alliances with the United Middle Belt Congress and localized opposition parties as we will note below.

This chapter inquires into the social and political background of party development in the Northern Region. As in Chapter VI, the presentation is topical rather than narrative. Sections are included on the social basis of political competition in Hausaland, the influence of communalism on party life in Bornu, ethnic separatism and religious sectarianism in the political movements of the lower North, legal limitations on political activity, and the nature of Northern party leadership.

Alhaji Sa'adu Alanamu MHA—Assistant General Secretary (Yoruba, Ilorin, Muslim, Ilorin N.A.)

Alhaji Abubakar Imam—Treasurer (Hausa, Zaria, Muslim, Gaskiya Corporation)

Alhaji Isa Kaita MHA—Financial Secretary (Hausa, Katsina, Muslim, Katsina N.A.)

Malam Nuhu Bamalli, MHA—Publicity Secretary (Fulani, Zaria, Muslim, Zaria N.A.)

Alhaji Abdulmaliki Okene, MHA—Auditor (Igbirra, Muslim, Igbirra N.A.)

Malam Sa'adu Zungur—Adviser on Muslim Law (Habe, Bauchi, Muslim, Dispensary teacher)

Malam Ibrahim Musa Gashash, MHA—Northern Regional President (Tripolitanian Arab-Hausa, Kano, Muslim, Gaskiya Corporation)

"Foundation of the Northern Peoples' Congress," memorandum prepared for the writer by the Central Secretariat of the Northern Peoples' Congress, December 1957. It will be noted that the officers elected in 1952 included two civil servants who were employees of the government-owned publishing house, Gaskiya Corporation, and Malam Sa'adu Zungur, a radical critic of the N.A. system who was associated with the Northern Elements Progressive Union.

[5] His biography until 1951 is sketched at *supra*, pp. 100-101.

ELITISM AND POPULISM IN THE UPPER NORTH:
THE SOCIAL BASIS OF THE NORTHERN PEOPLES' CONGRESS
AND THE NORTHERN ELEMENTS PROGRESSIVE UNION

In the Sudanic Provinces of the upper Northern Region, the Fulani-dominated Emirate states were genuine class societies before the dawn of the European era. There were two broad social strata: a ruling class or titled aristocracy for which nobility of birth was the supreme qualification, and a non-Fulani subject class of common people (*talakawa* in the Hausa language). The colonial government utilized the ruling class for its own administrative ends, introducing reforms insofar as it was expedient to do so. Under British tutelage, an ever-increasing number of literate functionaries were required to fill executive and clerical jobs in the Native Administrations. Since Western education was acquired mainly by the sons of noblemen and their retainers, the transition from feudal government to colonial administration did not entail any considerable transfer of power and prestige from the traditional ruling class to the depressed class of commoners. Apart from the relatively few commoners who achieved political office through educational merit, most salaried officials (*ma'aikata*) in both the Native Administration and the government services belonged either to noble families or to families bound in customary service to, or dependent upon, the nobility. These officials, including titled office holders (*sarauta*) and their bureaucratic subordinates, constitute the administrative elite of the North. The leadership of the Northern Peoples' Congress is drawn largely from their ranks. Tabulations made by the writer in 1958 indicate that the principal occupations of 62 percent of the members of the NPC National Executive were provided by the Native Administration bureaucracies (Table 1) and that 65 percent of the members of the NPC Executive Committees in eight principal emirates of the North were officials or clerical employees of the Native Administrations (Table 2). In certain emirates visited by the writer in 1958, e.g., Sokoto and Adamawa, the NPC Executive was scarcely more than a committee of the Native Administration.

The Northern administrative elite, which forms the backbone of the Northern Peoples' Congress, differs from the politically dominant new class of southern Nigeria insofar as it is not deeply involved in business enterprise. Unlike the early members of the Action Group in Western Nigeria, the founders of the Northern Peoples' Congress were mostly employees of the Native Administrations or the govern-

TABLE 1

Abstract of Data on the National Executive
Committee of the Northern Peoples' Congress (1958)*

Total number of members	74		
National Officers	12	(16%)	
Ministers (Regional and Federal)	20	(27%)	
Parliamentarians	48	(65%)	
Members of the House of Assembly			32
Members of the House of Representatives			16
Religious distribution:			
Muslim	64	(86.5%)	
Christian	19	(12.2%)	
Unknown	1	(1.3%)	
Tribal Distribution:			
Fulani	24	(32.4%)	
Habe	14	(18.9%)	
Nupe	7	(9.4%)	
Kanuri	5	(6.8%)	
Yoruba	5	(6.8%)	
Other Northern Tribes	12	(16.2%)	
Unknown	7	(9.4%)	
Occupational distribution:			
Present or past employment as an N.A. functionary	51	(69%)	
Primarily employed as an N.A. functionary, at present or in the past	46	(62.2%)	
Members of N.A. Central Councils at present or in the past	21	(28%)	
District Heads, at present or past	10	(13%)	
Experience as teachers	18	(24%)	
Primarily employed as teachers before political careers	5	(7%)	
Businessmen, at present or in the past	20	(27%)	
Independent businessmen			19 (26%)
Business agent			1
Business agent as secondary occupation			2
Barrister	1		
N.A. worker	1		
Labor leader, as secondary occupation	1		
Unknown	1		

* *Infra,* p. 513, Appendix I.

TABLE 2

The Occupational Background of Members of Provincial and Divisional Executive Committees of the Northern Peoples' Congress in 8 Emirates, 1958

Functionary strata = columns 2a, 2b, 3, 4. Learned arts and skills = columns 5, 6, 7, 8, 9. Profit and wage occupations = columns 10–16.

	Number of persons	Parliamentarians	1. Traditional authorities	2a. Native Authority officials and clerical employees	2b. Native Authority executive councillors	3. Senior functionaries (public and private enterprise)	4.* Functionaries in the government services (other than Native Administrations) and firms	5. Agents of occupational, cultural, and political associations	6. Free professions and scientists	7. Communications and cultural arts—e.g., journalists	8. Educators (teachers and headmasters)**	9. Ministers and teachers of religion	10. Businessmen (finance and entrepreneurship)	11. Petty trade	12. Artisans, craftsmen, shopkeepers, and self-employed	13. Wage laborers and domestic servants***	14. Farmers	15. Unemployed or non-employable****	16. Unknown
Sokoto (Provincial and Divisional)^a	30	25		25	6								5						
Adamawa (Provincial)	23	6		21	4								1				1		
Katsina (Provincial and Central Branch)	22	6		21	5								1						
Bida (Divisional)	18	2		7	1		1				1	1	3						
Kano (Provincial)	18	9		12	1								4	2	3	2			
Zaria (Provincial Working Committee)	29	5		18	5		1		1				9b						
Bornu (Divisional)	21	2		5	1								10	4	1		1		1
Bauchi (Divisional)	24	6		18	5						2		1	2					1
Totals	195	61 31.3%		127 65.2%	28 14.3%		2		1		3 1.5%	1	34 17.4%	8 4.1%	4 2%	2	2		1

* N.A. clerical stratum included in the figure for 2a.
** Government, Native Administration, and private schools.
*** Government, Native Administration, and private employment.
**** Domestics, including housewives, students and other dependents; beggars
a Not including Parliamentarians from Gwandu, Argungun, and Yauri
b A few of these may properly belong in Column 11.

ment. As such, they were vulnerable to the imposition of economic sanctions by traditional authorities and officials of the Administration who disapproved of radical or nationalist political activities. Few of them could hope to become full-time trade unionists, like Aminu Kano, who became an official of the Northern Teachers' Association when he resigned his post as an education officer, or Habib Raji Abdallah, the Zikist leader who became an official of the NCNC following his dismissal from the public service. It is not surprising that the Northern Peoples' Congress shied away from the adoption of early proposals to restrict the political power of the Northern chiefs,[6] and embarked upon a more conciliatory and accommodationist policy with respect to chieftaincy than did the Action Group in the Western Region.

In Northern Nigeria, as in the south, non-parochial values and interests motivate the political actions of the educated elite. Among southern Nigerians, it will be recalled, supra-tribal and modernistic values inspired the creation of ethnic group associations at the nationality level, notably the *Egbe Omo Oduduwa* (Yoruba) and the Ibo State Union.[7] In the North, organized pan-tribalism has been important among certain minority peoples of the middle belt only. Leaders of the dominant cultural groups have espoused pan-regionalism rather than pan-tribalism; indeed the Northern Peoples' Congress evolved into a political party from a cultural organization that encompassed many nationalities and tribes. This distinctive phenomenon in the social development of the Northern Region may be attributed in part to the universalist teaching of Islam. In part it may be a consequence of the fear of possible "southern domination" which gripped sections of the progressive Northern elite as well as the chiefs in the early post-war period and resulted in the evolution of a regional political party and a Northern territorial mystique that has no basis in tradition. The professed commitment of the Northern Peoples' Congress to multi-cultural liberalism is crystallized in its motto: "One North: One People Irrespective of Religion, Rank, or Tribe."[8]

[6] *Supra*, p. 93, n. 14.

[7] *Supra*, pp. 64-72.

[8] The motto of the NPC is included in a declaration of aims and objects adopted at the General Conference of December 1952:

"1. Regional autonomy within one Nigeria.

"2. Local Government Reform within a progressive Emirate system based on tradition and custom.

"3. The voice of the people to be heard in all the councils of the North.

"4. Drive for education throughout the whole North, laying due emphasis on the improvement of the social, economic and cultural life of the people.

It follows that cultural themes are relatively minor in pan-regional thought, while political and economic themes are prominent. In fact, a cornerstone of the Northern Regional Government's policy is its program to Northernize its public services, i.e., to replace public employees of southern origin with persons of northern origin.[9] Regional discrimination of this kind is not unfamiliar in the Eastern and Western Regions, where it is less frankly declared and less harshly implemented. Yet Northernization has a psychological significance that is not paralleled in the southern regions, inasmuch as it symbolizes the progressive reduction of the Northern Region's comparatively great deficiency in Western and technical education. Moreover, the Northern aristocracy takes particular pride in its tradition of administrative competence and has deeply resented the past preponderance of southerners in the technical and clerical posts of the public services of the North.

In 1958, 27 percent of the National Executive Committee of the Northern Peoples' Congress and 17 percent of the executive members of the party in eight major emirates were engaged in entrepreneurial activity. (Tables 1 and 2 above.) Nearly all of them were men of non-aristocratic and non-Fulani descent. It may be inferred that the hard core of the NPC comprises an economic elite of humble origin in addition to the emirate functionaries. The social horizon of the commercial elite, like that of the administrative elite, tends to be non-sectarian and pan-regional. Logically, the businessmen have formulated an economic corollary to the doctrine of administrative Northernization. At Kano, the principal city of the North, an influ-

---

"5. Eliminate bribery and corruption in every sphere of Northern life.

"6. Eventual Self-Government for Nigeria with Dominion Status within the British Commonwealth.

"7. Membership of the Northern Peoples' Congress is open to all people of Northern descent, whether as individuals or as a Union or as a political party.

"8. Industrial and economic development of the Northern Region.

"9. One North, one people, irrespective of religion, rank or tribe."

Reproduced in the *Report on the Kano Disturbances*, May 16, 17, 18, and 19, 1953, Northern Regional Government (Kaduna: 1953), p. 45.

[9] The policy of "Northernization" was proclaimed in 1954 and implemented with vigor in early 1958 when the Northern government discharged over 100 clerks of non-Northern origin from the regional civil service and 600 non-Northern daily paid workers from the Public Works Department. The dismissed southern clerks were replaced by Northern graduates of clerical training colleges. Subsequently the government offered to pay gratuities to dismissed workers with 5 years' job longevity. *Daily Times*, January 19 and 25, 1958; *West African Pilot*, September 10, 1958. In August 1958, the Premier of the North told the House of Assembly that a total of 2,148 southerners had been dismissed from the Northern public service since January 1954 and that only 24 southerners remained in the senior echelon of the permanent establishment. *Daily Service*, August 5, 1958.

ential association of businessmen, called the Northern Amalgamated Merchants' Union, was organized in 1956, primarily to pressure the government into providing opportunities for businessmen of Northern origin.[10] Another business group, the Northern Contractors' Union, has lobbied energetically for the adoption of regional laws and local regulations that discriminate against non-Northerners. Its efforts were rewarded in 1958 when the government instructed all Provincial Tenders Boards to prepare new registers of local contractors, excluding contractors of non-Northern origin from all but a few specialized tasks "which are not at present within the scope of contractors of Northern origin."[11]

The political influence exerted by the commercial elite in its own right is difficult to appraise. Traditionally in the Muslim North, affluent merchants do not have high political status.[12] But contemporary developments may be expected to alter the distribution of political power in the North in favor of the entrepreneurial elite. Owing to the recent extension of electoral democracy in the Northern Region, the role and influence of business elements within the Northern Peoples' Congress has become increasingly greater. Charitable merchants who demonstrate piety by giving alms to the poor are immensely popular; often they are more effective as campaigners against the radical Northern Elements Progressive Union than are the officials of Native Administrations. For example, in 1956 Alhaji Ahmadu Dantata of Kano, said to be the wealthiest member of the NPC, possibly the wealthiest Northerner, defeated Malam Aminu

[10] The leading spokesman of the Northern Amalgamated Merchants' Union is Alhaji Ahmadu Dantata, MHA, a general merchant, produce-buyer, transporter and textile company director of considerable wealth. Alhaji Dantata's remarks in the Northern House of Assembly embody the dual themes of economic nationalism and economic regionalism. During the 1957 budget session he deplored monopolization of the wealth of the country by foreigners and submitted a motion to exclude non-Nigerian transport firms from an important sector of the road transport field. He also urged that the government's Northernization policy be extended from the civil service to the economic sphere. *Northern House of Assembly Debates, Official Report*, February-March 1957, pp. 76-77, 361-366 and 387. Alhaji Ahmadu Dantata is a son and the principal heir of Alhaji Alhassan Dantata, of Kano Hausa descent, who acquired great wealth in the kola nut, cattle and ground nut trade. To these interests, transport and textiles were added, producing a family fortune that is widely regarded as the largest in the North.
[11] Notice by the Ministry of Finance, Northern Region, "Provincial Tenders Boards," *Nigerian Citizen*, November 8, 1958.
[12] M. G. Smith observed: "Wealth carries great prestige, but little political weight in traditional terms; this means that a merchant, however successful, is debarred from investing his capital in political office." *The Economy of the Hausa Communities of Zaria*, p. 100.

Kano, the enormously popular President-General of the NEPU, in an election to the Northern House of Assembly.[13]

One explanation for the ascent of non-Fulani businessmen to high office in certain branches of the NPC lies in the fact that they remain *talakawa* (traditional commoners) despite their upward mobility. Generally, the merchants are populist in their social attitudes and sympathetic to the feelings of the people among whom they live. Their influence in behalf of the NPC countervails the NEPU appeal to *talakawa* values, and the successes of the government party in urban areas where radicalism is rife are due in no small measure to the efforts of popular businessmen who devote their energies and material resources to the party. It is a paradox of Northern social development that traditional class consciousness mitigates the intensity of modern class struggle.

Within local units of the Northern Peoples' Congress, a touch of subdued antagonism may be noted in the relationship between administrative and commercial elites. Often the emirate function-aries are men of aristocratic birth and good education who regret the necessity of their growing political intimacy with affluent com-moners; on the other hand, the merchants may resent, inwardly, the tradition which obliges them to kowtow to the titled functionaries.[14] Expedient accommodations which serve their mutual interests are re-flected in methods of party organization at the local level.

At Kano, the most powerful Native Administration and the most affluent business community in the North have been welded together politically by the NPC in opposition to a radical populist movement. The Emir of Kano is a regional minister without portfolio whose political interests are keen and whose political influence is enormous. In 1958 the largest policy-making unit of the Kano NPC was its Parliamentary Committee, comprising some 60 members—all federal

[13] The election in Kano East was one of 19 in the region contested directly on the basis of male taxpayer suffrage. The results were reported as follows: Ahmadu Dantata: 2,119; Aminu Kano: 1,776. *Daily Times*, November 16, 1956.

[14] Rivalry between emirate functionaries and businessmen appeared to be a con-tributing factor to dissension within the Bida branch of the NPC at the time of the writer's brief visit there in 1958. On one hand, there were the exponents of elitism based on administrative talent and education; on the other, were the proponents of political populism, typified by the wealthy but largely uneducated merchants and the subordinate employees of the Native Administration who were prominent in the local executive of the NPC. The N.A. councillors seemed to feel that their educa-tional attainments and titled status entitled them to control the party and to represent Bida in the regional and federal legislatures. The businessmen and employees, who tend to be more popular than the councillors, do not normally seek legislative office for themselves, but they did insist on party control of the nominations. In 1956, two N.A. councillors who failed to obtain the party nomination stood against the official NPC candidate in Bida town, and were soundly defeated.

and regional legislators, in addition to the NPC members of the Kano City and *Waje* (non-traditional area) local government councils. Among the legislators were 8 members of the Emir's Council of 12, a federal minister, two regional ministers, a parliamentary secretary, and several prominent businessmen. Active direction of the party was vested in a Provincial Executive Committee of 13 members resident in Kano City, chosen by the Parliamentary Council, of whom 9 were N.A. officials and 4 were businessmen; they included 5 parliamentarians and 3 presidents of the 4 NPC executive bodies in the geographical sectors (*Fuskar*) of Kano City, as well as the president of the *Waje* sector.[15] In 1957, the Provincial Executive selected 3 leading members of the party to contest for the 3 top offices. All three were subordinate N.A. officials, members of the House of Representatives, aged 37-40, and graduates of a middle school. The mass membership of the party was called upon to ballot and the individual with the highest vote was designated as president, the second highest as vice-president, the third as treasurer. Obviously

[15] Kano Northern Peoples' Congress Provincial Executive Committee, 1958:

Hon. Rilwanu Abdullahi, MHR, Provincial President (Fulani-Abbas, related to the emir; Scribe, N.A. Legal Department)

Hon. Abdulkadir A. Koguna, MHR, Provincial Vice President (Fulani-Yerimawo; *Wakilin Riyoji*, Supervisor Rural Water Supply, N.A.)

Alhaji Garba Bayero, *Wakilin Yamma*, MHR (Fulani; N.A.)

Malam Ahmadu Tijjani Kurawa, MHA (Fulani; N.A. Land Registration Officer)

Malam Aba Ja'afar, *Dan Alkali*, MHA (Fulani; Chief Scribe, Alkali's Court)

Alhaji Mai Anguwa Zango (Fulani; Ward Head, N.A.)

Malam Halladu, President, Waje area NPC (Badare-Niger; trader)

Malam Naduni, President, Fuskar Arewa (Northern Section) (Habe; cattle trader)

Alhaji Umaru, President, Fuskar Gabas (Eastern Section) (Habe; trader)

Alhaji Maikwatashi (Habe; merchant)

Malam Bawa (Fulani; Chief Clerk, *Madaki*'s office, N.A.)

Malam Muhammadu Gidado, President Fuskar Yamma (Western Section) (Fulani; Public Works Department timekeeper, N.A.)

Malam Salihu Mohamed, Provincial Secretary (Fulani; Chief Cashier, N.A.) (Source: Record book of the Provincial Secretary.)

Provincial officers and important organizational individuals not listed above:

Hon. M. B. Baba Darara, MHR, Provincial Treasurer (Nupe; Assistant Treasurer, N.A.)

Alhaji Umaru Gumel, MHR, Provincial Auditor (Pharmacist, N.A. Hospital)

Malam Isa Danballo, President, Fuskar Kudu (Southern Section) (Habe; laundry business)

Alhaji Ahmadu Dantata, MHA, Chairman of the Discipline Committee (Habe; businessman)

Malam Ahmadu Rufai Daura, MHR (Fulani; Manager N.A. Schools)

Malam Ahmadu Tijjani Kurawa, MHA (Fulani; Land Registration Officer, N.A.)

Alhaji Umaru, *Sarkin Fulani Ja'idanawa*, MHA

the vote was intended merely to allocate roles, not power, to trusted agents of the higher N.A. officials.

Businessmen in Kano, who are united in the Northern Amalgamated Merchants' Union, include contractors, exporters and importers, transporters, licensed (groundnut) produce-buying agents, cattle dealers, and others engaged in entrepreneurial activities. By and large they are non-Fulani, mainly Habe or men of North African descent, who are excluded by tradition from the administrative hierarchy—10 of the 12 members of the Emir's Council were Fulani at this writing. Their sense of political deprivation is likely to be keen and the potentiality for discord between the commercial and administrative elites is probably greater at Kano than elsewhere in the North. But the serious threat of populist radicalism has been a powerful incentive to political cooperation, and the businessmen are strongly represented in the party organization. In 1958 Alhaji Ahmadu Dantata, MHA, Treasurer of the Northern Amalgamated Merchants' Union, was chairman of the important discipline sub-committee of the NPC Provincial Executive that included 2 N.A. officials and the 5 *Fuskar* presidents, 4 of whom were businessmen. In fact the pattern seemed to be for commercial elements to predominate in the executive bodies of the *Fuskar* organizations, while administrative elements controlled the Provincial Parliamentary Committee, where businessmen and traders were a minority of about 20 percent, exclusive of local councillors.

Similarly at Zaria, administrative and commercial elements controlled separate sectors of the NPC organization. The Zaria City District Committee of the NPC, under the presidency of a titled N.A. official (*Sarkin Tsapta*), and the vice-presidency of a titled member of the Emir's Council (*Wombai*), was part of a larger Zaria Area organization. In 1957 the Area Executive of 12 persons was under the leadership of a businessman, who was president of the Zaria chapter of the Northern Amalgamated Merchants' Union, and included a majority of privately employed individuals, mostly traders, as well as two women, and only two employees of the Native Administration. The Area Organization was the principal organ of the NPC for the residents of *Sabon Gari* (New Town) and *Tudun Wada* (Pleasant Elevation), cosmopolitian areas where commercial interests are ascendant. At the provincial level, administrative influence was uppermost since two-thirds of the NPC inner executive body or working committee of 29 were N.A. officials or employees; most of the remainder were well-to-do merchants and traders.[16]

[16] Zaria Northern Peoples' Congress, Provincial Working Committee Officers and members (chosen annually by the Provincial Conference), 1958:

An interesting example of social differentiation in party organization is provided by the Katsina branch of the NPC. Katsina town
is divided into two socio-political sectors; an eastern sector, containing
the Emir's palace, his retinue, and the vast majority of persons employed by the Native Administration; and a western sector where
the resident elite is typically commercial and Habe rather than administrative and Fulani. In the eastern sector, Western education is
relatively advanced, owing primarily to the late Emir's sponsorship,[17]

Ma'aji Babba M. Sambo, Patron (Headmaster, Junior Primary School, N.A.)
Malam Nuhu Bamalli, MHR, President (Administrator Zaria City; member of
the N.A. Executive Council)
Malam Sama'ila Ahmed, *Sarkin Tsapta*, First Vice President and President,
Zaria City NPC (N.A. Health Supervisor)
Alhaji Mato, Second Vice President (Trader; Zangon Katab District)
Malam Umaru Idris, Secretary (Clerk, N.A. Veterinary Department)
Malam Lawal Ciroma, Asst. Secretary, Supervisor N.A. Agricultural Department
Malam Sa'idu Zango, MHR, Treasurer (Chief Clerk and Cashier, Sabon Gari,
N.A).
Malam Ahmadu Fatika, MHR, Financial Secretary (N.A. Veterinary Depart-
ment)
Malam Bello Rigachikum, Assistant Financial Secretary (trader)
Malam Ahmadu, *Sarkin Fada*, MHA, Parliamentary Secretary, Ministry of
Finance, Auditor (N.A. Councillor)
Malam Yahaya Mohammad, *Sarkin Sabon Gari*, Legal Adviser
Malam Aliyu Gidado, Publicity Secretary (Senior Dispensary Attendant, N.A.)
Malam Sani Maigano, *Wombai* Zazzau, Vice-President Zaria City NPC (N.A.
Executive Councillor)
Malam Garba Gudu ba Gyara (Taxi owner)
Malam Usman S. Yaroson (Storekeeper, N.A. Veterinary Department)
Alhaji Zakari (trader)
Alhaji Babajo (trader)
Alhaji Asha-huva (trader)
Malam Tankon Mama (contractor)
Malam Bello Usman Zaria (Bursar, Provincial Secondary School, N.A.)
Malam Nuhu Bayero, *Dan Iya Zazzau* (N.A. Councillor for Education and
Finance)
Malam Abba Wachakal (trader)
Sgt. Rilwanu (N.A. Prison Warden)
Malam Sani Sambo, *Wakilin Rayoi Koisa* (N.A. Local Government Secretary)
Malama Asaben Jalo (Adult education teacher for women)
Members of the National Executive Committee:
Alhaji Muhammadu Sanusi, *Sarkin Yaki*, MHA (District Head Zaria City and
N.A. Councillor for Police and Prisons)
Alhaji Shafi'i of Tudun Wada (trader)
Malam Abdul Razaq, Legal Adviser, NPC (barrister)
Alhaji Abore Shani (oil seed mill official)
Source: Minute Book of the Zaria NPC Provincial Executive October 10, 1958.

[17] Emir Muhammadu Dikko, father of the incumbent Emir of Katsina, sent all
of his male children to school and opened a primary school for girls despite the
resentment which many leading men of his day bore to the intrusion of Western
education. His example was followed by many of the noble and courtly families
of Katsina.

while in the western sector English literacy is less prevalent, although some knowledge of Arabic script is not uncommon among merchants.

Organizationally, the Katsina NPC of 1958 was patterned on these primary social divisions. The core and most active unit of the party was the Katsina Central Branch Executive Committee which included 22 members.[18] Persons of Fulani and non-Fulani (Habe) descent were represented in about equal proportions. All but one of them were officials and employees of the Native Administration, 4 were administrative Councillors of the N.A. (i.e., councillors with departmental responsibilities—e.g., Natural Resources, Development, Health, Education), and 6 were parliamentarians. The sole non-N.A. member, a wealthy building contractor, was the only member who did not reside in the eastern sector of town. The President of the Katsina branch, and President of the Provincial Executive, was

[18] Katsina NPC Central Branch Executive:

Officers selected by the Provincial Annual Meeting:

Malam Musa Yar-Aduwa, *Tafida*, President and Provincial President (Fulani; N.A. Councillor for Development and Works)

Malam Abubakar Bauchi, Vice-President (Fulani; N.A. Chief Dispenser)

Malam Ahmadu Bambaiwa, Treasurer (Habe; Scribe to Magajin Garin District, N.A.)

Malam Muazu Katsina, Secretary (Habe; Registrar Chief Alkali's Court)

Malam Garba Bakori, Assistant Secretary (Fulani; Accountant, N.A. Agricultural Department)

Malam Lawal Cirakalu, Financial Secretary (Habe; N.A. PWD Labor Relations Officer)

Malam Ja'afar Daura, Auditor (Habe; Public Works Department, N.A.)

Malam Iro Gawo, Publicity Secretary (N.A. Information Officer)

Parliamentarians:

Malam Hassan Rafin Dadi, *Sarkin Mallamai*, MHR (Habe; N.A. Councillor for Education)

Alhaji Othman Ladan Baki, MHA (Fulani; Supervisor of Works)

Alhaji Muhammadu Dodo, MHA (Fulani; Junior Alkali)

Alhaji Muhammadu Dan Mallam, *Wambai*, MHA (Fulani; N.A. Councillor for Health)

Malam Ismalia, *Sarkin Fada*, MHR (Habe; N.A. Councillor for National Resources)

Alhaji Isa Kaita, MHA, Northern Minister of Education (Habe; ex-N.A. Councillor)

Six members chosen by the Provincial Annual Meeting:

Wakilin Kudu, Ward Head
Wakilin Arewa, " "
Wakilin Yamma, " "
Malam Saidu (Head painter, N.A. Works)
Alhaji Wowo (Habe; building contractor—the only non-N.A. member)
Malam Idi Maska (N.A. Clerk)

Co-opted officers of the Youth Association:

Malam Abdummumini, President, Youth Association (Headmaster, Blind Center)
Malam Suni Adiyalle, Secretary, Youth Association (N.A. Works)

Malam Musa Yar-Aduwa, *Tafida*, then 47 years old and a relative of the Emir. He attended the Katsina Training College and served as a middle-school teacher for 15 years and as an agricultural officer for several years more before his appointment as Assistant Development Secretary of the N.A. and subsequent elevation to the Emir's Council. Following his success in the federal election of 1959, he was appointed to the office of Federal Minister with Responsibility for Pensions, Establishment (Civil Service) and Nigerianization. It was no exaggeration to say that the Katsina Central Branch of the NPC was the Katsina N.A. in another guise.

In the western sector of town, a counterpart organization known as the NPC Youth Association was created to serve as a mass organization for supporters of the party who were not connected with the N.A. There was no age limit on membership in the Youth Association and no person could belong to both the Youth Association and the Central Branch. However, the president and the secretary of the Youth Association (both of whom were employees of the N.A.) were co-opted members of the Central Branch Executive. The following diagram indicates the relationship between the two primary components of the NPC organization and the two main sectors of Katsina town.

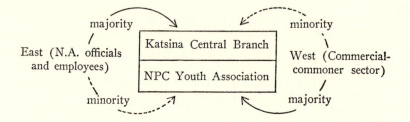

These organizational arrangements facilitate political cooperation between the Northern aristocracy and the wealthy commoners whose adhesion is crucial to the success of the Northern Peoples' Congress. Traditional class distinctions are still observed by the members of the party, but there is an increasing number of cases which illustrate the collapse of customary social barriers before the political coalescence of the administrative and commercial elites.[19] It seems ap-

[19] For example, in the Fulani-Yoruba emirate of Ilorin, the writer learned that traditional authorities of both Fulani and Yoruba descent attend party meetings in the home of the Divisional President of the NPC, who is a Yoruba businessman. A few years ago this would have been improbable.

propriate to suggest that the Northern Peoples' Congress functions institutionally, like the pan-tribal cultural organizations of the non-Northern peoples, to foster the integration of dominant elites on a class basis.[20]

Among the underprivileged masses of Hausaland, radicalism has been persistent among certain occupational groups, notably, petty traders and urban dwellers of comparable status who constitute the rank and file of the populist Northern Elements Progressive Union, e.g., craftsmen, shopkeepers, tailors, butchers, etc. A few observations derived from our analysis of the national leadership groups of the Northern Peoples' Congress and the Northern Elements Progressive Union in 1958 (74 members of the NPC National Executive Committee and 64 NEPU national officers) will disclose the contrast in their respective social compositions. (Tables 1 and 3.) Thus 45 percent of the NEPU officers were petty traders or independent artisans, craftsmen, and shopkeepers; this category was not represented in the NPC Executive, although a few of those listed as businessmen may have been traders of the middle rank. Only 2 members of the NEPU group (the President General and the Secretary of the Women's Wing) had experience in the teaching field, compared with 18 or 24 percent of the NPC Executive. Undoubtedly, a goodly number of teachers and other educated persons throughout the North were either sympathetic to or "quiet" members of the NEPU, but few of them were openly active members in 1958 and none were national officers. While NEPU doctrines appeal to a large number of intellectual and educated Northerners, including many salaried officials of the Native Administrations, most of them are anxious for personal advancement within the system, and therefore are disinclined to bear the onus of identification with a radical move-

[20] In suggesting the emergence of a new class based on the coalescence of the administrative and commercial elites, this writer is not unmindful of the traditional relationships between the Fulani aristocracy and the wealthy Habe merchants, based on the absolute political superiority of the former. However, it is suggested that modern developments tend to increase the political power and to enhance the social status of the business elite. A leading student of Hausa society appears to allude to a similar conclusion:

"On the basis of such consensus as exists we can distinguish, as do the Hausa, three or four social 'classes.' Sometimes the higher officials and the chiefs are regarded as constituting an upper 'class' by themselves, sometimes they are grouped with the mallams and wealthier merchants into a large upper class. The lowest 'class' generally distinguished includes the musicians, butchers, house-servants and menial clients, porters and the poor farmers who mostly live in rural hamlets. The great majority of the farmers, traders, and other craftsmen would, therefore, belong to the Hausa 'middle class.'" M. G. Smith, "The Hausa System of Social Status," *Africa* XXIX, No. 3 (July 1959), p. 249.

ment. Consequently, the number of educated and administratively competent members of the NEPU has always been negligible. Under 5 percent of the NEPU national officers in 1958 were or had been employed primarily by Native Administrations (only one was so employed at that time), compared with 62 percent of the National Executive of the NPC. Similarly, businessmen above the level of petty trade who rely upon the NPC to protect their interests against the competition of southern businessmen, are fewer and much less conspicuous in the NEPU than in the NPC.[21]

It should not be assumed that the working classes of the North,

[21] The following thumbnail sketches of three representative leaders of each party in Zaria (1958) indicate the relationship between party competition and socio-economic cleavage in that city. For the NPC, the first is Malam Nuhu Bamalli, the 42-year-old Provincial President of the party, member of the Emir's Council and Administrator of Zaria City. In 1960 he was appointed to the Nigerian Federal Senate by the Northern Regional Government and to the Federal Cabinet by the Prime Minister as Minister of State in the Ministry of Foreign Affairs. The Senator was a founding member of the NPC at Zaria in October 1948. He is sternly efficient, intellectual, progressive, and aristocratic, with a deep commitment to Northern traditions and a strong appreciation for his own dynastic Fulani heritage. His colleague in the National Executive of the NPC is Alhaji Muhammadu Sanusi, Sarkin Yaki, MHA, a distinguished 52-year-old District Head of Zaria and Senior N.A. Councillor, whose ethnic origin is Habe. The third typical NPC leader is Malam Ahmed Gwadaba, a prosperous merchant of Kano Habe origin, who is the local president of the Northern Amalgamated Merchants' Union.

The outstanding NEPU leader is Malam Gambo Sawaba, a trader who specializes in the sale of incense and lives humbly among the people in the vicinity of the market; he has been elected twice to the Zaria City Council. Second, there is Malam Usman Ango Soba, MHA, a former employee of the N.A. whose father was a district head. He left the Native Administration for farming as a young man, partly as a result of a quarrel with a European official, and he has been a NEPU militant since its inception. Third, is Malam Shehu Marihu, MHA, a former bicycle mechanic of 37 who defeated a regional minister in the 1956 election in Zaria Urban Constituency. Unlike their NPC counterparts these NEPU leaders are occupied primarily in party pursuits. Malam Gambo Sawaba is Provincial Organizer and Regional President of the NEPU; Malam Ango Soba is Regional Secretary and Assistant National Administrative Secretary; Malam Shehu Marihu is constantly engaged in organizing. Both Gambo Sawaba and Shehu Marihu have served terms in N.A. prisons for political offences. The former was sentenced to 2 months in 1956 for political utterances, specifically for alleged abusive language at a public meeting, and for refusal to submit to trial before a Junior *Alkali*. *Nigerian Citizen*, July 14, 1956. (Cases originating with a Junior *Alkali* cannot normally be appealed outside of the Emirate jurisdiction. *Infra*, p. 357.) He served another prison term for a criminal offence in 1959. Hon. Shehu Marihu was sentenced to a total of 5 months in 1957 for various offences, the principal one being an alleged seditious utterance likely to cause a breach of the peace. He is reported to have said that *Alkalis* (Muslim court judges) were NPC and should withdraw from party politics. He served another month in 1958 for having used allegedly abusive language in the course of a political address. *Nigerian Citizen*, December 4, 1957, and November 5, 1958. NEPU sources in Zaria disclosed to the writer that between 1951 and 1957 about 320 NEPU members served prison terms.

TABLE 3

Abstract of Occupational Data on the National Officers, Principal Advisers and Parliamentarians of the Northern Elements Progressive Union (1957-1958)*

Functionaries of the government, Native Administrations, firms, and private associations	13	(20%)	
Civil servants			4
Native Administration			3
Business agents and clerks employed by firms			4
Agents of other associations			2
Lawyers	2	(3%)	
Educators	2	(3%)	
Businessmen (contractors, transporters, produce-buyers, etc.)	11	(17%)	
Petty traders	23	(36%)	
Artisans, craftsmen, and shopkeepers	6	(9%)	
Farmers	2	(3%)	
Unknown	5	(8%)	

* Occupational data was obtained for 59 of the 64 persons listed in Appendix III, *infra*, p. 524.

in general, oppose the government party. On the contrary, the NPC appears to have a larger following among wage laborers, especially employees of the Native Administrations, than its adversary. NEPU leaders concede that it is difficult for the working class to escape the coils of tradition. In the tin mines of the Jos plateau, the largest aggregation of industrial workers in the Northern Region, indeed in all Nigeria, have been organized by the NPC on the basis of an anti-southern appeal that is partially tribalistic and partially economic. Mine workers and independent contractors of Northern origin have resented the monopolization of skilled jobs and positions of authority by educated and technically trained southerners. In 1954 they organized the Northern Mine Workers' Union which appears to have obtained a greater tin-field membership than the older mining unions. Leaders of the NMWU include high officials of the NPC, and the union itself is listed by the NPC central secretariat as an affiliated organization.[22] Another, more typical, case of working-class political

[22] The president of the Northern Mine Workers' Union is Alhaji Isa Haruna, MHR, Regional Vice President and Plateau Provincial President of the NPC. He is an independent contractor for the Bisichi Tin Company, in which capacity he employs labor. In addition he is a camp captain, i.e., a company agent in charge of the resident mining community (company village). In 1959 he was elected to the Federal House of Representatives. The Union Secretary is Provincial Treasurer of the NPC and a company welfare officer. Leaders of the NMWU do not appear to be less disposed than southern trade unionists to bargain vigorously with

orientation is that of the Lokoja Carriers' Union, a river port dockworkers organization that is formally associated with the Lokoja branch of the NPC (in Kabba Province). Most of the carriers are employed by contract agents for the United Africa Company who support the NPC, and they are vulnerable to moral suasion and economic inducements to join the party of their employers.

These observations indicate that the NPC is supported in the first instance by the traditional ruling class, by the Native Administration official and employee occupational class, by wealthy Hausa businessmen, and by the business elite in general. In addition, laborers organized by leaders of the NPC and beggars who live on alms from the rich tend to support the Northern government party. Supporters of the NEPU include a relatively few Fulani, mainly intellectuals and independent traders and a few well-to-do businessmen, in addition to a large number of small traders, craftsmen, and shopkeepers. Scattered intellectuals in the Native Administration and government services evince open support for the NEPU but evidence of mass support for that party among the salaried clerks or organized workers is lacking. Finally, it was apparent in 1959 that the vast majority of urban and rural farmers in the savanna-land emirates favored the NPC, as the Northern government party won the federal elections in all but 6 of the nearly 110 upper Northern constituencies.

The Impact of Communalism on Populism in Bornu

Political party competition in Bornu Division, homeland of the Kanuri people of northeastern Nigeria, illustrates the exploitation of communal sentiment by the dominant political party in its struggle against lower-class radicalism. A brief résumé of party history in Bornu is pertinent.

Organized nationalism probably reached Bornu as it did many other parts of the North, with the NCNC pan-Nigeria tour of 1946.[23]

---

the tin companies. Nor do the contractor-members of the union, who are really employers, appear to dominate its executive organs. It is in the nature of their relationship with the NPC government that the leaders of the NMWU differ fundamentally from the southern trade unionists. While they have never attacked the government's wage and labor policies, a standard tactic of the southern unionists, they have been able to secure government endorsement of their programs in the field of industrial bargaining. Yet it is undeniable that the leaders of the NMWU have loyalties to the companies which may be inconsistent with union obligations, and loyalties to the NPC, an explicitly conservative party, under leadership that would surely desire to channel industrial unionism into non-radical pathways.

[23] There do appear to have been intellectual and occupational groups in Bornu

Dr. Azikiwe was anxious to include a Northerner in the NCNC's 1947 delegation to London and he found an articulate spokesman for Northern nationalism in the person of Malam Bukar Dipcharima, the 29-year-old son of a Kanuri district head. Dipcharima had distinguished himself previously by resigning from his position as a middle-school teacher rather than muffle his criticisms of the administration. From 1948 to 1954, his talents were devoted mainly to managerial duties for the British trading company of John Holt. Meanwhile, the center of the political stage in Bornu was occupied by two able officials of the Native Administration, Shettima Kashim, an education officer, and Ibrahim Imam, the son of a former Chief *Alkali* (judge) and Supervisor of N.A. Works. Both were elected to the Northern House of Assembly in 1951, and chosen by that body as central representatives. Shettima Kashim became a minister in the central government while Ibrahim Imam served as General Secretary of the Northern Peoples' Congress.

Iman's role as an officer of the NPC was ambivalent: within the councils of the party he was known as a radical and a critic of the system of Native Administration that the NPC was pledged to preserve; yet in his capacity as a parliamentarian and publicist, he was a leading spokesman for NPC principles. Thus in March 1953, he moved the famous motion of adjournment in the Central House of Representatives which prevented debate on an Action Group resolution for self-government in 1956.[24] Subsequently, the NPC's eight-point program of May 1953, which called for the abolition of legislative and executive bodies at the Center and for the reorganization of Nigeria as a loose federation of autonomous regions, was submitted in his name to a joint meeting of the Northern House of Assembly and the Northern House of Chiefs. In addition, he played a prominent role in defense of NPC policies at the London Constitutional Conference of 1953. Conceivably, Imam assumed these postures of conservatism mainly because he hoped to retain and extend his influence in the NPC. However, by the 1954 (Jos) Convention of the NPC, he had fallen out with the party leadership, and had resigned from the office of General Secretary.

In 1954, a group of young men in Maiduguri, the capital of Bornu Province, who espoused the principles of the Northern Elements

---

prior to 1946 which gave impetus to political thought and nationalist sentiment. The present Northern Minister of Agriculture, Mallam Mustafa Monguno, was President of a Bornu Literary Society and Secretary of a Young Farmers Union, both of which probably supported the formation of the NPC in 1949-1950.

[24] *Supra*, pp. 127-128.

Progressive Union, organized a counterpart party for Kanuris and other elements indigenous to the province, known as the Bornu Youth Movement.[25] The Bornu radicals launched their new party on a particularist basis mainly because the NEPU was regarded by the ethnically proud Kanuris as a party of the Hausas. Both Bukar Dipcharima and Ibrahim Imam were invited to join; the former declined, but Imam, who appears to have been among the group of initiators, accepted the office of Patron.[26] Among the stated objectives of the party was the creation of a North East State comprising the Bornu, Adamawa, Bauchi, and Plateau Provinces. That proposal was incompatible with the NPC doctrine of a unitary North within a confederated Nigerian state, but it was consistent with the quasi-federal principles of the NCNC-NEPU Alliance, with which the Bornu Youth Movement affiliated.

In the federal election of 1954, Ibrahim Imam was defeated by Bukar Dipcharima, then President of the Bornu NPC.[27] However, the BYM was a rising force, and by 1956 it had become a formidable if not the dominant party in the Yerwa-Maiduguri urban area. (Maiduguri, a small village adjoining Yerwa town, has given its name to the Bornu capital, although Yerwa is the proper name of the urban district.) In November 1956, Yerwa town returned both candidates of the BYM to the Northern House of Assembly, including Ibrahim Imam. As leader of a vastly outnumbered opposition, Imam delivered a series of addresses in 1957 which may be unsurpassed in

[25] The Bornu Youth Movement was proclaimed a political party on July 14, 1954, shortly after its inauguration. The following persons are listed as founders in party records at Maiduguri: Alhaji Sherif (trader, President and organizing secretary of the BYM in 1958); Malam Sanda na Alhaji Hamza (trader); Malam Abba Kano Mattedan (Tripolitanian Arab-Hausa, N.A. Treasury clerk); Mohammed Ben Waffi (Shuwa-Arab-Hausa, N.A. Treasury clerk); Malam Muka Marwa (contractor); Malam Kolo Kamkamba (trader); Malam Lawan Goni (trader); Malam Mai Kyari (trader); Malam Ibrahim Imam (Supervisor of N.A. Works).

[26] Article X of *The Bornu Youth Movement Constitution, Rules and Regulations*, adopted July 14, 1954, stipulates that there shall be one patron who will be elected by the General Meeting of the Movement. Ibrahim Imam has always held this post.

[27] In 1954 the Bornu NPC invited Zanna Bukar Dipcharima to assume the presidency of the party. He accepted, resigned his position as a manager for the mercantile firm of John Holt and Company in Bida, and returned to Bornu where he soon rose to the heights of political eminence. He was prominent in the drive against corruption in the Bornu N.A. and a victor over Ibrahim Imam in the 1954 election to the House of Representatives. At first he served as a junior minister in the federal government; subsequently he was appointed a full minister with the portfolio of Commerce and Industries, which he held in the Independence Government.

Nigerian parliamentary annals for the vigor and breadth of their advocacy of political democracy and civil rights.[28]

Subsequently the fortunes of the Bornu Youth Movement ap-appeared to decline, possibly as a result of the NPC's conscientious effort to extirpate corruption from the Bornu Native Administration. An election to the Yerwa Town Council in October 1957, conducted on the basis of taxpayer suffrage, resulted in a decisive victory for the NPC. During this period there were a number of criminal prosecutions involving members of the BYM.[29] Legal pressures against the BYM reached a peak in December 1957, when Malam Ibrahim Imam was convicted by a Native Court and sentenced to six months' imprisonment for allegedly having accepted a bribe four years earlier during his tenure as supervisor of the N.A. Works Department. However, the Senior Resident of Bornu Province found the conviction unjustified and it was ultimately quashed by a higher court.[30]

A breaking point of political tension was reached in June 1958, when the Bornu Youth Movement withdrew from its alliance with the NEPU-NCNC and entered into a new pact with the Action Group. Among the reasons given by the BYM for its realignment were the alleged intent of the NCNC to effect an alliance with the NPC, the failure of the NCNC to assist minority elements in the North during the presence in Nigeria of the Commission of Inquiry into Minority Fears, allegedly in order to appease the NPC, and the un-equivocal support of the Action Group for the creation of a Bornu State.[31] This maneuver split the lower classes in the Bornu capital city along tribal lines, since the BYM was almost exclusively a Kanuri party and the NEPU was mainly a Hausa party. (The Bornu branch of the Action Group was composed largely of Yoruba settlers in Yerwa town, and the local NCNC was mainly composed of Ibo

[28] See especially the debates on the Public Order Bill, the Confinement of Mallam Saidu Ben Hayatu, the Judicial Committee Motion, Minority Groups, and Devolution of Powers to Provinces, *Northern House of Assembly Debates, Official Report* (Second Legislature), First Session, 1957, pp. 417ff, 493ff, 521ff, 565ff, 841ff, and 1016ff.

[29] Among those sentenced by native courts for political utterances was the Vice President of the BYM, Alhaji Sherif, who was given 12 lashes of the cane and three months' imprisonment. BYM records reveal that 13 members of that party were sentenced by *Alkalis* (Muslim Court Judges) during the period October-November, 1957.

[30] *Nigerian Citizen*, December 12, 1957 and December 21, 1957.

[31] Communication from the BYM to the President General of the NEPU, signed by Ibrahim Imam, Alhaji Sherif, and Malam Basharu, dated June 12, 1958. (NCNC National Headquarters Files.)

341

settlers.) Yet the NPC did not derive unmixed satisfaction from the BYM-NEPU rupture, for it was deeply disturbed by Action Group penetration of the BYM. The Action Group had become the principal opponent of the Northern government party in the Federation of Nigeria, and it was pledged to dismember the Northern Region by creating additional states if it came to power. Moreover, the NPC correctly anticipated that the wealthy and resourceful Action Group would commit the full measure of its organizational and financial capabilities in order to secure a political foothold in the upper North.[32] Political arrests occurred with increasing frequency, and it was reported that the N.A. police did not scruple to interfere with private as well as public meetings.[33] In September, a few days prior to a scheduled visit by Chief Awolowo, Federal President of the Action Group, Maiduguri experienced a rude display of political temper involving the violent deaths of 6 persons.[34] Eleven of the twelve men arrested subsequently for arraignment before the *Shehu's* Court (the *Shehu* is the distinctive title of the Kanuri Emir of Bornu) were members of the NPC, including four high officials of the local organization. Ultimately, it was held that the evidence did not support charges against the party leaders, and they were released.

In Maiduguri, as in other urban centers, the leadership of the NPC exemplifies the crucial balance between traditional-bureaucratic authority and commercialist-popular power. Four of the thirteen members of the NPC Divisional Executive in 1958 were N.A. officials; the other 9 were independent businessmen—i.e., traders of middle and large scale, produce buyers, and transporters.[35] In addition,

[32] After the formation of the BYM-Action Group Alliance, 10 members of the Bornu Action Group were added to the 50-member General Committee of the BYM, including a paid political secretary of the Alliance. In 1958-1959 the Action Group budgeted over £12,000 for its Bornu operations. Action Group of Nigeria, *Approved Estimates, 1958-1959.*

[33] The leader of the BYM, Malam Ibrahim Imam, listed for publication 5 forms of political persecution which he alleged were used against his party: first, "indiscriminate" arrests and imprisonment "on the slightest pretext"; second, ejection of BYM tenants from their homes by NPC landlords; third, the organization of school children by members of the NPC to abuse and stone touring representatives of the BYM/AG throughout the province; fourth, the use of pressure to compel members of the BYM to swear on the Koran that they will renounce that party; fifth, the refusal by district heads to permit the BYM to hold public meetings in their areas of jurisdiction. *Daily Service*, September 15, 1958.

[34] It was reported that a member of the NPC was killed on September 7, 1958, during a scuffle near the home of Ibrahim Imam. On the following day vehicles loaded with partisans of the NPC descended on Imam's compound. The incensed attackers killed 3 persons in Imam's house and 2 other members of the BYM in their homes.

[35] Bornu NPC Divisional Executive Committee, 1958:

4 of the 10 ward presidents of Yerwa town were substantial business-men and 3 others were smaller traders. The NPC has largely overcome ethnic sectarianism at the middle- and upper-income levels by uniting within its fold most of the businessmen (merchants, contractors, transporters, and produce buyers) of diverse Northern tribes (in particular, Kanuri, Shuwa Arab, Hausa, and Fulani) for whom it is profitable to be on good terms with the government and its agent, the Native Administration. Maiduguri merchants are normally munificent in the use of their wealth, populist in their demeanor, and less remote from the poorer people in their manner of life and thought than are the more highly educated officials of the Native Administration, who are identified in the public mind with taxation, the law, and previous scandals of corruption. Heretofore, the Bornu NPC has drawn its parliamentary candidates almost exclusively from the educated ranks of the N.A., but nominations for legislative and local council elections are subject to confirmation by the Divisional Executive Committee where, in 1958, commercial predominance was apparent. At any rate, wealthy merchants were entrusted with the major burdens of party organization, membership recruitment, and finance.

Leaders of the Bornu NPC endeavor to offset the appeals of radicalism to lower-class elements by invoking the communal values of the indigenous people. As in Hausaland, popular businessmen make a crucial contribution; they constitute the most effective social and political link between the N.A. and the common people. Economically,

---

Zanna Bukar Dipcharima, MHR, President (Kanuri; Federal Minister of Commerce and Industry, District Head Yerwa and Councillor in charge of Police)

Malam Bukar Batulbe, Vice President and Acting President (Kanuri; trader and produce buyer, member Northern Region Development Corporation)

Alhaji Ibrahim Isa, Vice President (Hausa; small trader)

Malam Abdullahi Abubakar Ja'afar, MHA, Secretary (Kanuri; Sanitary Inspector, N.A. Medical Department)

Malam Goni Askira, Treasurer (Gazama; trader)

Malam Bulama Boluri, Financial Secretary (Kanuri; N.A. Scribe, Yerwa City Office)

Alhaji Bukar Waziribe, President, NPC Youth Association (Kanuri; Scribe N.A. Revenue Office; member Federal Tax Assessment Committee)

Malam Garba Abba Satomi (Kanuri; large trader and groundnut buyer; member, North Region Cotton Marketing Board)

Alhaji Mustafa Mallam Harunabe (Kanuri; general transport and trading business)

Alhaji Mustafa Alhaji Kazalabe (Kanuri; very large trader in goods and groundnuts)

Alhaji Bukar Ballabe (Kanuri; very large trader in groundnuts, hides, and skins)

Alhaji Salihu Yaro (Hausa; kola nut trader)

Alhaji Umaru na Alhaji Idi (Hausa; kola nut trader)

the business elite is part of the privileged class; culturally, the business-men are well-to-do commoners and thereby persuasive propagandists for the NPC cause among the humble farmers and laborers.

The Kanuri business elite is conspicuous in public meetings and functions of the NPC. In Maiduguri, as in other urban centers of the upper North, political activity is a common leisure-time pursuit, and social rallies in the late afternoon are held frequently by both the NPC and the BYM. These rallies are conducted for the NPC by its Youth Association, which was organized in 1954 to counteract the influence of the BYM. Often the rally takes the form of a mock play; the young men and women are given titles and roles that identify them with the political leaders and eminent personalities of Bornu, e.g., Federal Minister of Commerce and Industry or *Waziri* (Senior N.A. Councillor) for men, the names of female personalities in the royal family for women. The center of attraction at the rally is likely to be decorous traditional dancing performed by young women. These activities not only attract the youths but imbue them with political values and link their moral sensibilities to the party which appears to have the widest social sanction. A party spirit is engendered which may become pathologically intense, since activists may regard their loyalty to the party as an obligation incumbent upon them by virtue of their membership in the community. In 1958 the leaders of the NPC managed to depict the Action Group penetration of Bornu as a threat to the communal interests of the Kanuri people. The Bornu Youth Movement was alleged by leaders of the community to have engaged in an immoral conspiracy with the revolutionary party of an alien tribe. The result was a tragic outburst of inter-party violence in September 1958 that was condemned by all concerned and did not recur during the electoral campaign of 1959.[36]

ETHNIC SEPARATISM AND RELIGIOUS SECTARIANISM IN THE LOWER NORTH

The middle belt or riverain areas of the Northern Region have been defined to include the six southerly provinces of Adamawa, Benue, Plateau, Niger, Ilorin, and Kabba, in addition to southern Bauchi and southern Zaria. The area comprises more than half of the

[36] Three years after the riot of 1958, a correspondent for *West Africa* observed: "Probably nowhere in the Federation is party partisanship as bitter as it is in Maiduguri. A decision of the Maiduguri NPC . . . for example, prohibits contacts of any sort between any NPC supporter and those who support the Opposition, that is, the A.G. and the NEPU. The results of this decision contravene all the teachings of Islam. . . . " *West Africa*, December 9, 1961, p. 1365.

territory of the North and nearly 35 percent of its population—about 5 million people. By and large, the people of the middle belt are either non-Hausa-speaking, non-Muslim or both. Those who do speak the Hausa language are apt to be Christian or animist (e.g., the Birom of Jos Division); the Muslim tribes are apt to speak their own national languages (e.g., the Nupe of Bida and Lafiagi-Pategi Divisions and the Yoruba of Ilorin Division); many other ethnic groups are neither Muslim nor Hausa-speaking (e.g., the Tiv and the Idoma of Benue Province). In this section two lower Northern political movements are discussed briefly—the multi-tribal middle-belt movement and the localized phenomenon of Yoruba irredentism.

The Middle Belt Movement

The ethnic particularism of political movements in the middle belt is mainly a consequence of the area's enormous multiplicity of distinct tribal and linguistic groups. (There are more than 200 linguistic groups in the middle belt.) Probably the earliest non-parochial association of educated elements was the Tiv Progressive Union, formed in 1938 by civil servants among the largest nationality group of the lower North.[37] In 1944 the Tiv Progressive Union became an original member-union of the NCNC; two leaders of the Union, who were elected to the Northern House of Assembly in 1951, were among four members of that House who declared for the NCNC. However, the distinction of having first espoused the cause of a Middle-Belt State belongs to the Birom Progressive Union, organized in 1945 by Mr. Patrick M. Dokotri, partly in order to foster pan-Birom unity and partly to agitate for the payment of fair compensation to the Birom people in return for the use of their lands by British tin-mining companies on the Jos Plateau.[38] Middle-Belt separatism

---

[37] The three principal founders of the Tiv Progressive Union are reported to have been Gaba Nenger, President, Peter Deem Kpuum (later Secretary of the Tiv Farmers Association and MHR, 1955-1959) and E. G. Gundu (later MHA, 1951-1956).

[38] The writer is informed that the six original founders of the Birom Progressive Union were:

Patrick Fom, President, 50 (in 1945), forester, member of the Roman Catholic Mission (RCM)
Patrick Dokotri, Secretary, 25, forester, RCM
Stephen Ajani, 26, mission school teacher, RCM
John Fom, over 30, mission driver, RCM
Lawrence Fom, over 30, agricultural overseer, RCM
Frank Adu, 26, Nurse in a mission hospital, Church Missionary Society.

It will be remarked that five of the original founders of the Union were adherents to the Roman Catholic faith and the Union was initially suspected of having been formed as a center for Catholic indoctrination. Actually, a greater proportion of

assumed organizational form in 1949 following a private member's motion in the Northern House of Assembly which called upon the regional government to restrict the activities of Christian missionaries in the North. A small group of Christian leaders reacted to this potential threat by forming the Northern Nigerian Non-Muslim League with Pastor David Obadiah Vrenkat Lot (Sura) of Pankshin as President.[39] In 1950, the Non-Muslim League was converted into the Middle Zone League in order to emphasize the separatist predilection of its membership. At this time the most active tribal element in the League was the Birom Progressive Union. Two members of that union declared for the NCNC following their election to the Northern House of Assembly in 1951.

In 1953, the leaders of the Middle Zone League resolved upon a policy of cooperation with the Northern Regional Government and entered into an alliance with the Northern Peoples' Congress. Thereupon Hon. Moses Nyam Rwang, MHA (Birom), and Bello Ijumu (a Yoruba from Kabba Province and the first secretary of the NEPU) organized the Middle Belt Peoples' Party as an affiliate of the NCNC. Its largest single component was the Tiv Progressive Union, and a founder of that union, Hon. E. G. Gundu, MHA, became President of the new party. As a result of this break-away, the older but weakened Middle Zone League was confined mainly to Jos Division and the adjoining areas of southern Zaria and southwestern Bauchi. In 1954, both sections of the Middle Belt movement returned candidates to the Federal House of Representatives from their respective areas of strength. An amalgamation was negotiated,

---

its membership was derived from the Sudan Interior (American) and Sudan United (British branch) Missions which have larger followings among the Birom than does the RCM. The Birom Progressive Union was founded two years prior to the installation of the first paramount chief of the Birom (*Sarkin* Birom) and may be regarded as part of the movement for tribal integration. The early career of Moses Rwang Pam of Du village, who became *Sarkin* (or Chief of) Birom in 1947 (later *Sarkin* Jos), is discussed briefly by Tanya M. Baker, "Political Control Among the Birom," *Annual Conference Proceedings of the West African Institute of Social and Economic Research, March 1956* (Ibadan: 1956), pp. 111-119.

[39] The inaugural meeting of the Northern Nigerian Non-Muslim League at Bukuru was proposed by Mr. S. O. James (Yoruba), an employee of the United Africa Company and a Special Member of the Northern House of Assembly. Other founders included Pastor David Obadiah Vrenkat Lot (Sura) of Pankshin who was chosen as President; Johna Assaduhu (Bachama), Sudan United Mission teacher at Numan, field secretary; Musa Kuku (Birom), a transport owner; Mr. Sukumso (Bura) of Biu Division, a transport owner; Pastor Bagaya (Nzit) of Kagoro, Southern Zaria. Subsequently Moses N. Rwang (Birom) was appointed General Secretary.

and on June 10, 1955, the United Middle Belt Congress was formally inaugurated at Kafanchan (Jema'a Division of southern Zaria).

Apparently the leaders of the Middle Belt movement were still inclined to cooperate with the regional government. For in late 1955 Pastor David Lot, President of the United Middle Belt Congress, and Mr. Patrick Dokotri, leader of the Jos Tribal Party (successor to the Birom Progressive Union) accepted appointments in the regional and federal governments respectively, the former as Minister without Portfolio, the latter as Parliamentary Secretary. A new alliance with the Northern Peoples' Congress was concluded, this time with the approval of the Tiv Progressive Union. But Moses Nyam Rwang dissented again and organized an opposition wing.[40] In November 1955, both factions held conferences at Ilorin and there were reciprocal expulsions.

Prior to the regional election of 1956, Lot and Dokotri resigned their governmental positions on the ground that, contrary to their expectations, the alliance with the NPC had not been helpful to the cause of the Middle Belt movement. Concurrently, the Tiv Progressive Union withdrew from its alliance with the NPC. Eleven candidates who were affiliated with one or another UMBC faction were elected to the Northern House of Assembly and a unity meeting was convened which chose Hon. H. O. Abaagu, MHR (Tiv), as President of the re-constructed Congress and Hon. Patrick M. Dokotri, MHR (Jos), as pro-tem Secretary. At the Lafia Conference of January 1957, alternative proposals for alliances with non-Northern parties were considered and two prominent members of the UMBC were expelled for conducting unauthorized negotiations with the NCNC and the Action Group.[41] Hon. Joseph Sarwuan Tarka, MHR (Tiv), was elected President General and Hon. Patrick M. Dokotri, MHR, was returned as Secretary General. Shortly thereafter the leaders of the United Middle Belt Congress perceived the value of an alliance with the Action Group and a formal accord was signed on May 6, 1957, announced in October, and ratified by the Minna Conference of

[40] The Moses Nyam Rwang faction included Hon. H. O. Abaagu, MHR (Tiv) as President; Abdul Ado Ibrahim (Igbira), a former President of the NPC Youth Association, as Secretary General; Bello Ijumu (Yoruba), formerly General Secretary of the Middle Belt People's Party; Johna Assaduhu, MHR (Bachama) of Numan Division.

[41] Malam Bello Ijumu, who favored an Action Group alliance, became Action Group Organizing Secretary for Kabba Province in 1957. Moses Nyam Rwang, who favored an alliance with the NCNC, rejoined the UMBC in 1958 as an organizing secretary for the party in Jos Division, but switched to the NPC in 1959 along with the ex-Leader of the Opposition in the Northern House of Assembly, Bitrus Rwang Pam.

May 1958. Hon. H. O. Abaagu, MHR, disapproved and formed a splinter party, the Benue Freedom Crusade, which aligned with the NCNC until 1959 when it switched to the Northern Peoples' Congress.

It is remarkable that the highly fissiparous Middle Belt movement gained increasing strength for a decade prior to 1960 despite its congenital lack of cohesion. Two factors may add up to a reasonable explanation. First, the Middle Belt movement has been supported consistently by certain fairly large ethnic groups, notably, the Tiv and the Birom, which fear the cultural imperialism and political domination of the numerically preponderant Hausas of the upper North. Secondly, the movement has been supported, openly and clandestinely, by the Christian missions, which are numerous in the lower North. It is difficult to find a Muslim in the Action Group-United Middle Belt Congress Alliance;[42] in many places, as in Numan Division of Adamawa Province, where the Action Group-UMBC is dominant, that party is composed largely of persons who are associated with Christian missions.[43] This factor may account for the precipitous decline of NEPU influence in the lower North and the apparent decision of NEPU leaders to withdraw their support from the Middle Belt State movement. Assuredly, NEPU ideology is non-sectarian and that party did make a good start in the non-Hausa areas in the early 1950's.[44] But the primary strength of the NEPU is among the Hausa people, mainly among the several million inhabitants of Kano, Zaria, Katsina, eastern Sokoto, and adjacent areas, who are universally Muslim and predominantly members of the Tijaniyya brotherhood.[45] In the past, NEPU leaders have been obliged to rebut damaging allegations to the effect that their party was southern-dominated because of its alliance with the NCNC. They may well have concluded that it was hard enough to be radical in the North without the added stigma of association with a political

[42] Probably the only important Muslim personality to have been a leader of the UMBC was Malam Abdul Ado Ibrahim, Secretary General of the Abaagu faction of the UMBC in 1955-1956. Previously, he had been President General of the NPC Youth Association, 1953-1954.

[43] Of the 23 Action Group/UMBC leaders in Numan Division with respect to whom personal data were obtained by the writer in 1958, including all members of the divisional executive and District branch presidents, 22 were Christians associated with the Sudan United Mission, and 8 of them were actually in the mission's employ.

[44] However, in Bauchi Emirate, as in Bornu, the NEPU is confined largely to persons of Hausa heartland origin, while the indigenous supporters of the NEPU are organized by its affiliate, the Habe Tribal Union.

[45] *Infra*, pp. 466-467.

movement in the middle belt that is widely regarded by Northerners as being anti-Muslim. By 1959, NEPU-NCNC influence among the non-Hausa Northern tribes had virtually disappeared apart from exceptional stalwarts, like the Kilba tribe of Adamawa.

It should not be inferred that Christian politicians in the lower North generally support secession, for it is the policy of the Northern Peoples' Congress to adhere to its professed doctrine of "One North: One People Irrespective of Religion, Rank, or Tribe." Four of the sixteen non-traditional members of the Northern Region Executive Council in 1958 were middle belt Christians. A case in point which reveals the non-sectarian and elitist nature of the NPC in the middle belt is that of Igbirra Division in Kabba Province. There the NPC has supported a minority faction of Catholics and Muslims in preference to a purely Muslim majority faction that professes loyalty to the national and regional party leadership. The favored bi-religious faction comprised, in 1958, a majority of both the administrative and the commercial elites of Igbirra Division.[46]

In 1958 the Commission of Inquiry into the Fears of Minorities found that the indigenous inhabitants of the middle belt did have justifiable fears of domination by the regional majority. Yet the Commission concluded that sentiment for the creation of a Middle Belt State was merely sporadic and that legal and political reforms were more appropriate means of allaying minority fears.[47] Its report was criticized bitterly at the Jos Conference of the United Middle Belt Congress-Action Group Alliance of September 1958. In the federal election of 1959, the Action Group based its middle belt campaign

[46] The dominant political party in Igbirra Division is the Igbirra Tribal Union, formed in 1950-1951 to oppose the ex-paramount chief (Atta) of Igbirra and to foster the democratization of the Native Authority. Because the pro-*Atta* party transformed itself into a branch of the NPC, the ITU remained independent. It fought the NPC at the local level but its elected legislators were adopted into the NPC parliamentary parties and one of them, Mr. G. U. Ohikere, was appointed as a minister in the Northern Regional Government. While the ITU mass membership was overwhelmingly Muslim, party and elective offices were held mainly by an educated Catholic elite, trained by the local Roman Catholic Mission schools. In 1957, the Muslim majority repudiated the Catholic leadership and the ITU split on religious lines. Since the ITU legislators and the minister were affiliated with the government party at higher levels, the NPC appeared incongruously to support a Catholic minority in preference to a Muslim majority. In reality, the Catholic elite gravitated into a working alliance with the small elite of educated Muslims in the NPC branch and a bi-religious ITU-NPC organization emerged to contest the federal election of 1959. Its candidate was narrowly defeated by the majority faction of the ITU.

[47] Colonial Office, *Report of the Commission appointed to enquire into the fears of Minorities and the means of allaying them* (London: H.M.S.O., 1958), pp. 71-73.

primarily on the separate state issue, and won 25 seats, or more than one-third of the total in the lower North.

Irredentist Populism in Ilorin

Two administrative Divisions of the lower North, namely Ilorin and Kabba, have been excluded from the Middle Belt State movement on the ground that their inhabitants are Yoruba people and prefer to be merged with the Yorubas of the adjacent Western Region. Ilorin Division is about four times as populous as Kabba and more explosive politically. Roughly 90 percent of the 400,000 inhabitants of Ilorin Emirate (or Division) are Yoruba, but the territory has a dual cultural makeup. The northwesterly districts, known as metropolitan Ilorin, including Ilorin town, are inhabited mainly by Oyo-Yorubas who are predominantly Muslim. This area has been governed directly by a Fulani Emir through his appointed district heads since the Fulani conquest of 1817. In contrast, the southeasterly districts are inhabited by the Igbomina, Igbolo, and Ekiti Yorubas who are mainly Christian.[48] Their customary patterns of chieftaincy survive with modifications resulting mainly from the requirement of subordination to the emir.

Possibly, the difference between Fulani and Yoruba conceptions of chieftaincy has been an underlying factor of political unrest in Ilorin. In the Fulani emirates, horizontal stratification based on class and rank is more important than vertical segmentation based on kinship. Power was vested in relatively despotic emirs and exercised by them through delegation to a ruling class of noblemen and officials. Structural limitations on the powers of emirs were weak in comparison with the customary limitations on the powers of Yoruba kings, who were controlled by chiefs representing the component lineages of the Yoruba states. Although it is not feasible to explore the cultural basis of political ideology in this limited context, it may be supposed that the contrary chieftaincy policies of the Northern Peoples' Congress and the Action Group are attributable in part to the Fulani tradition of absolute monarchy and the Yoruba tradition of limited monarchy. Emirs still rule in the North, assuredly with limitations and through democratized councils under the supervision of government, while *Obas* merely preside in the West. At any rate, it does appear that the absolutism of the Fulani Emir of Ilorin has been

[48] "The Emirs regarded the Ilorins as the metropolitan area and made no serious attempt to convert to Islam the southern tribes, whom they regarded as convenient raiding grounds for slaves and cattle." *Ibid.*, p. 75.

resented by the Yoruba chiefs and people of the non-metropolitan districts.[49]

In the metropolitian districts, the movement for reform of the Native Administration was initiated by educated public servants whose social position was analogous to that of the founders of the Northern Peoples' Congress. At first their criticisms of the Native Administration disturbed the traditional rulers and chiefs of Ilorin, both Fulani and Yoruba.[50] Paradoxically, the conservative chiefs of metropolitan Ilorin were supported by potentially radical Yoruba businessmen, typically non-literate merchants, prosperous traders, weavers, and contractors. They appear to have been hostile to the administrative reformers, including men of Yoruba nationality, because the reform movement was identified with the "Fulani-dominated" administrative elite. In 1954, this element organized the first mass political party in Ilorin, the Ilorin *Talaka Parapo* (Commoners' Party), which leveled criticisms against the reformed Native Administration in the name of tradition.[51] Insofar as the *Talaka*

---

[49] In its survey of fears in Ilorin, the Minorities Commission observed: " . . . it was alleged that under the Northern system an Oba or Chief was either ignored altogether or at best treated as a District Head, nominated by the Emir, liable to dismissal and to retirement on reaching a prescribed age, and in short as a Government servant rather than a hereditary Chief." *Ibid.*, p. 79. A celebrated case upon which this complaint was largely based involved the removal of the *Oloffa* of Offa by the Northern Regional Government in 1957. The premier of the North is reported to have told a delegation of Offa people that the *Oloffa* had been retired in accordance with staff regulations because he was no longer able to do his job as a district head. (*Egbe Omo Oduduwa*, Central Secretariat Files, Ibadan.)

[50] In 1953, the Ilorin Native Authority Council was enlarged to include 49 members elected by and from the traditional title holders of the district and village group councils. (The development of local government in Ilorin since 1913 has been chronicled in an unpublished paper prepared by the staff of the Ilorin N.A. Central Office entitled, "Constitution of Ilorin Native Authority Council.") This innovation was hardly democratic, but it appears to have been introduced in the face of opposition from the traditional authorities.

[51] The following list of foundation members of the Ilorin *Talaka Parapo* was compiled by the writer on the basis of interviews in Ilorin:

Alhaji Sulaiman Maito, MHA, (of Alanamu ward), cattle dealer; now President of the ITP

Jimoh Adelabu (Ajikobi ward), trader and contractor; first Vice President of the ITP; later President of the Ilorin Araromi Congress/NCNC Alliance

Saliman Baruba (Are ward), barber and trader; later ITP/NPC

Yahaya Kannikan (Gambari ward), cattle dealer; later ITP/NPC

Yakubu Olowo (Fulani ward), cattle dealer; later ITP/NPC

Bodinrim Tinko (Gambari ward), machine sewer

Salalu Gedele (Gari ward), agent in the motor park; later NPC

Ma!am Adebimpe Onyiye (Alanamu ward), cloth seller; now Vice President ITP

Dogo Agbogi (Alanamu ward), cloth seller; now Chairman of the ITP

Parapo coupled its commitment to tradition with such popular causes as tax reduction and the suppression of extortionary practices on the part of sanitary inspectors, forest guards, and other petty officials of the administration, it resembled the politically radical but administratively conservative opposition parties of the Western Region (considered in Chapters VI and VII), namely, the *Otu Edo* of Benin, the *Egbe Oyo Parapo* (People's Party) of Oyo, and the *Mabolaje* of Ibadan. But the Ilorin *Talaka Parapo* was more closely identified with commercial interests than any opposition party in the Western Region, owing to the exclusion of businessmen from the governing elite of the North. It is not surprising that the Ilorin *Talaka Parapo* was viewed by the Action Group as a vehicle for its campaign to effect the transfer of Ilorin to the Western Region.

In 1955, Alhaji Yahaya, *Madawakin* Ilorin, a prominent Yoruba personality in the administrative hierarchy of Ilorin and Northern Minister of Health, attempted to negotiate an agreement between the Ilorin *Talaka Parapo* and the Central Executive Committee of the NPC. His effort failed, and Alhaji Yahaya, who remained partial to the *Talaka Parapo*, was relieved of his portfolio and expelled from the government party.[52] In 1956, the Commoners' Party entered into an alliance with the Action Group; thereafter, its criticisms of the Native Administration became more vigorous and its ideological line diverged irrevocably from traditionalism to radicalism. Formerly, the *Talaka Parapo* had espoused the right of chiefs to sit in the Ilorin Town Council—indeed, to constitute a second chamber of that council. But the chiefs of metropolitan Ilorin turned away from the Commoners' Party; possibly they were repelled by the idea of transferring

---

Jima Goroso (Ajikobi ward), Koranic Malam; now party manager, ITP

Alhaji Aremo Alayaba (Alanamu ward), trader

In 1955 the Resident, Ilorin Province, commented as follows on the aims of the ITP: "The Parapo's political objectives have not been fully defined but it is already clear that they aim at 'restoring the former power and authority of the Emir and Chiefs' and at reducing direct taxation. They strongly oppose the present Ilorin Native Authority Council, which, they claim, is not responsive to public opinion." *Provincial Annual Reports for the Year 1955* (Kaduna: 1956), p. 54.

[52] The minister's support of the Ilorin *Talaka Parapo* was not unrelated to his feud with Alhaji Sa'adu Alanamu, the Ilorin Local Government Secretary and President of the Ilorin branch of the NPC. In August 1955, the NPC Executive was reported to have approved an application for affiliation from the ITP (NPC Press Release, Ref. No. NPC NH 214/28, 8 August 1955), but six months later an ITP delegation to Kaduna was admonished by the Sardauna of Sokoto to reconcile with the Ilorin branch of the NPC. This marked the end of Alhaji Yahaya's influence in the government and he was compelled to resign soon afterwards.

Ilorin to the Western Region, where the Action Group government was known to deal harshly with old-style natural rulers.

In June 1956, elections were held to the Ilorin Town Council under regulations providing for taxpayer suffrage at the first of three electoral stages and the participation of traditional members in the latter stages. When the Commoners' Party won a slight majority of the primary seats, it criticized the participation of traditional members as undemocratic and declared a boycott of further elections.[53] Eventually, the regional government conceded direct elections to the Ilorin Town Council. In 1957, the Action Group-Ilorin *Talaka Parapo* Alliance won majorities in the Ilorin Town Council and in 25 of the 33 indirectly elected district and town councils in the division. The Ilorin Native Authority Council was reformed to include 15 nominated members and 50 elected members, chosen by and from the lower-tier councils, under the presidency of the Emir of Ilorin. Thirty-five members of the Council were affiliated with the Action Group-*Talaka Parapo* Alliance.

At this point, social and political tendencies which are fundamental to the modern North began to weigh on the side of the government party. In the Western Region, traditional authorities bow to the political leadership of the rising class of businessmen, professionals, civil servants, educators, and so on. In the North, businessmen generally define their interests in terms of collaboration with the politically dominant chiefs and administrative elite. Normally, the NPC serves to effect a political combination of the administrative and commercial elites on an emergent class basis. This social function of the government party was manifest at Ilorin in 1957 when business elements in the *Talaka Parapo* objected to its policy of transfer to the Western Region, and withdrew from the party. The occasion was provided by the inaugural meeting of the N.A. Council in May 1957, which adopted a resolution for transfer. Hon. Ibrahim La'aro, MHA, a prominent businessman and one of 4 Action Group/ITP candidates who were elected to the Northern House of Assembly in November 1956, formed an independent wing of the *Talaka Parapo* which allied itself with the Northern Peoples' Congress. Subsequently, the Ilorin branch of the NPC acquired a commercial complexion which was hardly less pronounced than its stamp of traditional and administrative approval.[54] On the other hand, irredentism became a

[53] *Annual Report of the Senior Resident, Ilorin, 1956.* (Files of the Provincial Office, Ilorin.)

[54] In 1958, three of the five Ilorin Divisional officers of the NPC were wealthy businessmen; the other two, including a son of the emir, held offices in the Native Administration; and see note 19 above.

nearly exclusive value of the commoner class, defined in terms of economic as well as traditional criteria. Small businessmen remained prominent in the leadership of the *Talaka Parapo*, but that party could no longer be regarded as a movement of the commercial middle class.[55]

The Ilorin and Kabba boundary questions were referred by the London Constitutional Conference of 1957 to the Commission of Inquiry into Minority Fears. In February 1958, the Ilorin N.A. Council and 20 of the 31 District Councils passed resolutions favoring transfer to the West. But the Minorities Commission recommended that no change should be effected in the North-West boundary except as the result of a plebiscite in which 60 percent of those voting favored transfer. Moreover, it was recommended that the plebiscite should be held only if the parties at the Resumed Constitutional Conference would agree to abide by the result.[56] As anticipated, the Northern delegation to the Resumed Constitutional Conference would not agree to a plebiscite before independence. Meanwhile the Northern Regional Government dissolved the Ilorin Native Authority Council and increased substantially the proportion of traditional members in the Ilorin Town Council.[57] In 1959, the government party won a majority of the elective seats in the Town Council (22 out of 34) and all three seats for the metropolitan area of Ilorin in the House of Representatives. (The non-metropolitan seat of Ilorin South was won by the Action Group.) These results attest to the achievements of the Northern Government Party in its

[55] At a meeting with leaders of the Ilorin *Talaka Parapo* in 1958, the writer identified 13 businessmen and traders, 2 craftsmen, 2 Arabic teachers, a school teacher, 2 farmers and 2 political organizing secretaries. The general and ward officers of the party included 6 businessmen and traders, 1 craftsman, 4 Arabic teachers and 1 school teacher.

[56] *Report of the Commission appointed to enquire into the fears of Minorities*, p. 105.

[57] In June 1958, the Northern Regional Government appointed a committee to inquire into the affairs of the Ilorin Native Authority Council. The Ilorin *Talaka Parapo* stipulated, as a condition of its cooperation with the committee, that the inquiry must be public and that members of the Council who might be accused of improper conduct must be given due notice of the charges against them and the right to appear with legal counsel. Upon the rejection of these conditions by the committee, the ITP majority in the Council passed a resolution to boycott the committee proceedings. *Minutes of the Extra-Ordinary Meeting of the Ilorin Native Authority Council held on Friday 13 June 1958 . . . *, pp. 4-5. Subsequently, the government made public findings against the council which it dissolved. *Nigerian Tribune*, July 29, 1958. In 1959, traditional representation in the Ilorin Town Council was increased three-fold from 6 to 18, while its elected representation was reduced from 51 to 34. The intriguing history of administrative and political reform in Ilorin Division is beyond the scope of this discussion, which is confined to the topic of political parties.

drive to win popular support among the Yoruba minority in the Northern Region. As in most other parts of the lower North, the Northern Peoples' Congress of Ilorin has become an ethnically composite party under the leadership of rising- and upper-class elements, while its opposition is ethnically restricted—i.e., purely Yoruba—democratic in principle, and increasingly committed to the affirmation of lower class values.

LEGAL LIMITATIONS ON POLITICAL LIBERTIES

Peaceful opposition to a government party depends, to a great extent, upon the nature of three related systems of authority, namely, the police, the courts, and the criminal law. It is impossible to appreciate either the difficulties faced by opposition parties in the North or the impressive strides which have been taken toward the attainment of political democracy in that region apart from a consideration of these coercive institutions.

In the North, responsibility for the maintenance of law and order in the first instance lies mainly with the Native Authority police, who are generally thought, as the Minorities Commission observed, to be "in sympathy with the NPC."[58] However, the N.A. police forces are rather small for the sizes of the populations they regulate: in 1958 there were approximately 600 N.A. policemen in Sokoto Province, which has a population of 2,650,000, and about 250 in Zaria Province with a population of 825,000; Kano Province, with a population of about 3,400,000 has the largest number of policemen, probably over 1,000. Clearly, traditional authorities do not rely upon the police alone to repress radical tendencies.

There are two systems of courts in the North, as in the other regions, corresponding to the dual system of law. Magistrates' courts are empowered to apply Nigerian statutory law, common law, doctrines of equity, and the laws of England. They are also empowered to invoke native laws and customs when necessary to prevent the commission of injustices.[59] Native courts apply native laws and customs

---

[58] *Report of the Commission appointed to enquire into the fears of Minorities*, p. 60. There are traditional reasons, among others, for the subservience of the N.A. police forces to the ruling nobility. M. G. Smith has drawn attention to the "symbiotic arrangement . . . which allowed selected slaves, as delegates of the ruling class, to exercise certain rights over the common people, and assured the nobility of the loyalty of their slaves and the control of the *talakawa* (common people). It has not been accidental that the great majority of the Native Authority police ('*yandoka*) were until quite recently drawn from among the former slaves of the Emirs." *The Economy of the Hausa Communities of Zaria*, pp. 87-88.

[59] *Northern Region Magistrates' Courts Law, 1955*, N.R. No. 7 of 1955, Section 32.

mainly, but they may be authorized by the Governor-in-Council to enforce particular statutory laws.[60] In fact, jurisdiction had been conferred upon native courts to enforce at least two of the principal statutes regulating political conduct during the period immediately preceding independence, namely, the Criminal Code (Amendment) Law of 1957 and the Public Order Law of 1957. They also enforce rules made by Native Authorities under the Native Authority Law. Furthermore, native-court judges may apply the principles of English law in civil cases when necessary.[61] Finally, during the period under review, cases could be tried by native courts applying native law and customs even though statutory offences were involved.[62] The relative importance of native courts in the process of law enforcement may be inferred from the fact that in 1958 there were only 5 magistrates' courts in the entire Northern Region (Kaduna, Kano, Zaria, Jos, and Ilorin); it was estimated that no less than 80 percent of all criminal cases and 85 percent of all civil cases between Nigerian litigants were adjudicated by native courts.[63]

The distinctive native courts of the North are the Muslim or *Alkali* Courts (*Alkali* is the Hausa equivalent of the Arabic *al-Qādi* or judge) which apply both Islamic law and native laws and customs.[64] Until recently, non-Muslims resident within Muslim areas were subject to the relatively stringent provisions of Islamic law and the authoritarian procedures of Muslim courts. The Penal Code Law of 1960 departed from the territorial principle in granting non-Muslims the right to be tried by any non-Muslim court, including a magistrate's court, rather than an *Alkali*.[65] Non-Muslim

[60] *Native Courts Law, 1956*, N.R. No. 6 of 1956, Section 24.

[61] N.R. No. 6 of 1956, Section 21 (5). Critics of the law have contended that this provision serves to preclude the transfer of cases to magistrates courts on the ground that English law applies. Memorandum by N. A. B. Kotoye, "Spotlight on Justice in the North" (prepared for the Action Group delegation to the Constitutional Conference of 1958), p. 7. (Typed copy.)

[62] N.R. No. 6 of 1956, Section 22.

[63] N. A. B. Kotoye, "Spotlight on Justice in the North," pp. 1-2. This estimate appears to have been conservative. In 1960, it was reported in *West Africa* that "There are at present 756 native courts in the Region handling over 95% of the criminal and civil work coming before the courts including a large number of capital cases." *Ibid.*, September 24, 1960, p. 1071.

[64] Theoretically, Islamic law (the *Shari'a*) does not admit flexible interpretation, but the Maliki school, which prevails throughout West Africa, countenances a flexible judiciary which may apply local customary laws provided they are not inconsistent with the *Shari'a* texts. J. Spencer Trimingham, *Islam in West Africa* (Oxford: The Clarendon Press, 1959), p. 148. Cf. J. N. D. Anderson, *Islamic Law in Africa* (London: H.M.S.O., 1954), pp. 171-172.

[65] *West Africa*, September 12, 1959. The territorial principle with respect to criminal law was stated by the Native Courts Law of 1956 as follows:

native courts exist in emirates and other divisions with Christian and pagan populations, while "mixed" native courts are found in the multi-tribal *sabon garis* (urban residential areas for non-indigenous settlers) of the Northern towns.

Native courts are graded on the basis of their jurisdictions and competences to impose sentences. Junior *Alkalis* preside over lower Muslim courts, typically at the district level. Senior *Alkalis* preside over Grade "A Limited" courts, which lack jurisdiction in homicide cases, while the Emir's Court is Grade "A (Unlimited)." Thus the Emir is the highest judicial as well as the highest executive officer in his jurisdiction. Moreover, he exercises supreme rule-making power in conjunction with his council, and has a legislative role as a member of the Northern House of Chiefs.

Cases that originate with a Junior *Alkali* may be appealed to the Senior *Alkali*, but cannot be appealed beyond the Emir's Court unless a fine exceeding £25 or a term of imprisonment exceeding six months has been imposed.[66] Since most political offences are infractions of Native Authority by-laws, punishable by fines of £25 or less and terms of imprisonment of six months or less, they are usually tried in the Junior *Alkali's* courts and hence are rarely appealed beyond the courts of the Native Authority.[67] Appeals from inferior non-Muslim and mixed courts lie to the Emir's Court which may apply customary law when one or more of the litigants are non-Muslim. Cases originating with the Chief *Alkali* or the emir, or cases which involve sentences in excess of £25 or six months' imprisonment, may be appealed to the Moslem Court of Appeals and the Northern Region High Court.[68] In the past, appellate procedures

---

"In criminal causes the native law and custom prevailing in the area of the jurisdiction of a native court shall be applied by that court to the exclusion of any other native law or custom." N.R. No. 6 of 1956, Section 21 (1).

But the Minorities Commission saw fit to recommend that "Non-Muslims . . . have the option of being dealt with by non-Muslim courts." *Report of the Commission of enquiry into the fears of Minorities*, p. 70. Cf. J. N. D. Anderson, who favored the principle of territorial jurisdiction over "the confusion consequent on every individual being subject to the personal law of his own religion." *Op.cit.*, p. 172.

[66] N.R. No. 6 of 1956, Section 62 (1) (c).

[67] An Action Group lawyer in the Northern Region has characterized the political implication of the limitation on appeals as follows:

"The present provision of the law is a subtle attempt by the N.P.C. Government to break the back of opposition parties in the North by sending their field staff and organizers to continuous short terms of imprisonment and denying them right of appeal to the High Court." N. A. B. Kotoye, "Further Suggestions about Judicial Reform in the North" (prepared for the Action Group delegation to the Constitutional Conference of 1958).

[68] See the *Moslem Court of Appeals Law,* and the *Northern Region High Court Law, 1955.*

have been grossly inefficient owing primarily to the inability of persons convicted by native courts to obtain transcripts without inordinate delays. Occasionally, reversals have been secured on appeal after the petitioner had served his sentence and been discharged.[69]

Until 1955 the Regional High Court was empowered to employ the prerogative writs—mandamus, prohibitions, and certiorari—in order to review decisions of native courts. That power was withdrawn by the Northern Region High Court Law of 1955[70] in what is generally thought to have been a reaction to a decision of the High Court in reversing the conviction of 15 members of the Northern

[69] ". . . we observed that in one case four months had elapsed between the application and the granting of a copy [of orders or proceedings]. Such delays, and the fact that there is no machinery for watching or preventing them, must hinder the lodging of an appeal. One case came to our notice in which the court had refused leave to appeal, although no permission was legally required. In another case, the accused was acquitted by the Muslim Court of Appeal when he had just completed a sentence of six months in prison and had suffered a whipping." *Report of the Commission appointed to enquire into the fears of Minorities*, p. 70.

A Memorandum on Civil Liberties in the North, presented by the Northern Elements Progressive Union to the Rt. Hon. A. T. Lennox-Boyd, Secretary of State for the Colonies, at Kano, Nigeria, January 30, 1957, contained the following statement of appellate problems:

"The right of appeal has almost died simply because of the insurmountable difficulties placed against one's way. Over ten members of this party were jailed last March from two to four years each and also ten others who too, were jailed for some alleged election offences (1 to 4 years) could not proceed with their appeals from both the Chief Alkali's and the Emir's Courts (Kano) to the High Court just because they could not get copies of the proceedings of their cases.

"The case of one Yanbiyu is the most ridiculous. The gentleman has been trying to appeal to the High Court against the sentence of three years passed on him by the Emir's Court. While he was struggling to get copy of proceedings he was found bearing on his person a party badge and some amount of cash in shillings. He was charged with committing a prison offence and was taken before the Emir of Kano and was further sentenced to 1½ years imprisonment. He appealed but was denied having copy of proceedings but was advised to see a lawyer.

"Some weeks later the same Court reduced that 1½ years sentence to six months. He still appeals but has not been supplied with copy of his case without which the High Court cannot accept his appeal and if a month elapses all will be over. This was more than two months ago.

"Now Haliru and seven others; Tsoho and six others; Alhaji Muhammadu and four others who are all serving sentences ranging from two to four years are still waiting for copies or something before appeal."

Possibly, the Muslim Courts have not facilitated appeals because the appellate procedure is alien to Maliki law and resented as an intrusion by the *Alkalis*. In a recent case a judge of the High Court observed:

"It must be understood that the whole conception of a court of appeal is unknown to Maliki law; and the Moslem Court of Appeal is something which is quite new in this system of law." *Kano N.A. v. Marka Yar Jatau Cula, Law Reports of the Northern Region of the Federation of Nigeria, 1958*, Part IV, pp. 97-138.

[70] No. 8 of 1955, Section 27. See the remarks by the Attorney-General of the Northern Region in the *Northern House of Assembly Debates, Official Report*, February-March 1957, pp. 852-853.

Elements Progressive Union. The defendants had been sentenced by an *Alkali* to three months' imprisonment for hurling derisive epithets at leaders of the Northern Peoples' Congress, including the Premier and the Emir of Katsina. An order of certiorari was issued by a High Court judge who reversed the convictions on a technical point of jurisdiction. Leaders of the NPC were furious and were reported to have countenanced the organization of the *Mahaukata* or "Madmen," a belligerent auxiliary that was not above violence in its hostility to the NEPU. Subsequently, the cases of the 15 were reopened before a different *Alkali* who reimposed three-month sentences on the defendants.[71] It may not have been coincidental that the judge who issued the writ and reversed the original convictions was transferred from the Northern judiciary to the High Court of Lagos. In 1958, the Minorities Commission recommended that the right to issue prerogative writs be restored to the Northern Region High Court.

Alkali court procedures have little in common with familiar standards of British due process. Non-Muslims and women appear in *Alkali* courts at a disadvantage. As the Minorities Commission observed, "In theory . . . the evidence of a male Muslim is of greater value than that of a woman, a Christian, or a pagan; indeed, in some traditions the only evidence that is admissible in any degree is that of an adult male Muslim who is regular in his observance of religious duties." Furthermore, "it is open to the court to give a Muslim accused the option of swearing on the Koran that he is innocent; if he accepts this challenge he is discharged, being left, if he is really guilty, to the vengeance of Heaven." Christians and pagans do not have comparable privileges.[72]

Under Maliki law, convictions may be obtained by confession of the accused without confirmatory evidence or by the testimony of two competent, i.e., Muslim, adult male witnesses. Unless it can be shown that at least one of the deposing witnesses is partial, "their evidence is binding on the accused in Moslem Law and there can

---

[71] See *Provincial Annual Report*, 1953, p. 80. The case is *Kano N.A. v. Malam Abba Maikwaru* (1953), popularly known as the Airport Case because the offensive words were uttered at the Kano airport as the leaders of the NPC were departing for the London Constitutional Conference of 1953.

[72] However, it was reported that "some courts . . . admit a similar oath on the Bible or on a fetish. But this is irregular and frowned on by the orthodox." In homicide cases the blood-wit (a compensation in lieu of the death penalty which may be acceptable to the relatives of the deceased) required by Maliki law "if the deceased is a Christian . . . (is) half as much as for a Muslim, while if the deceased is a pagan, the amount is one-fifteenth." *Report of the Commission appointed to enquire into the fears of Minorities*, p. 67. J. N. D. Anderson, *op.cit.*, pp. 197-201.

be no further defence."[73] In principle, *Alkali* court proceedings are open to the public, but the Native Courts Law and orders pursuant to it authorize presiding *Alkalis* to exclude the public under certain conditions. In practice, it is uncommon for members of the public to attend. One student of the system has described the lack of publicity as follows:[74]

"In an Alkali Court the following are . . . invariably present: (1) the Alkali, (2) the Court Scribes, usually two in number, (3) the accused person or defendant, (4) the complainant or plaintiff, (5) witnesses as and when they are called in. No other persons, be they friends or relatives of parties, are allowed in. The Press as a rule are never allowed in and there have been instances when Pressmen have been bundled out from the Alkali Courts in spite of their producing . . . identity cards. The result is that justice, like the civil Administration in the North, is done in secrecy, and the presence of spectators, the Press etc. in a Court which act as a restraint on the excesses of judges are totally absent in an Alkali Court."

Lawyers are barred from Alkali courts, as they are from all native courts in Nigeria. However, this restriction is most ominous in the North where the burden of enforcing criminal law falls mainly on the *Alkalis* and where the circumstances of a day in court are least propitious for the accused. Among the offences of a political nature most frequently tried by the *Alkalis* are utterances tending to provoke public disorder,[75] violations of the conditions imposed by

---

[73] From an affidavit by Malam Muhammadu Sani, Alkalin Kano, in the matter of *Kano N.A. v. Abba Maikwaru* (note 71 above) and quoted in N. A. B. Kotoye, "Spotlight on Justice in the North," p. 3. The *Alkali* is quoted as having stated further:

". . . It is not the practice in Moslem Law to inform accused persons at the end of the case against them that they have been found guilty but they are informed whenever the evidence of each witness is found to be binding on them. When the evidence of two witnesses is found to be binding on them they know that they have been found guilty. It is not the practice of Moslem Law for the *Alkali* to give grounds or reasons for his decision. The accused know the offence of which they have been found guilty because they have been informed of the offence at the commencement of the proceedings." The authorities cited were Mayara, Vol. 1, p. 39 and Tabsira, Vol. 1, p. 42.

[74] N. A. B. Kotoye, "Further Suggestions about Judicial Reforms in the North," p. 2.

[75] A typical case was that which occurred in Argungun Division of Sokoto Province in 1958 when an Action Group organizing secretary was sentenced to 3 months imprisonment by an *Alkali* for making an allegedly false statement likely to cause public alarm. The objectionable utterance was reported to have been a declaration that the Argungun N.A. was corrupt and a suggestion that its merger with another N.A. was or should be contemplated. People were said to have been

permits for political meetings, and utterances which are actionable as slanders against individuals under Muslim law. Permits for meetings are issued by the Native Authorities and normally require the specification of speakers and the subjects to be discussed. Any speaker whose name is not listed on the permit may be prosecuted and imprisoned, as may any authorized speaker who departs from the subjects listed as approved.[76] It has been alleged that certain Native Authorities require that permits be obtained for private political meetings, although it is not likely that this condition has ever been enforced uniformly.[77]

Prohibitions of slander or defamation of character in Muslim law have been stretched by certain Native Authorities and *Alkalis* into virtual proscriptions of any derogatory mention of the names of individuals in political addresses. On occasion public order has been invoked by various N.A.'s as a further justification. Thus during the local election campaign of November 1957 at Sokoto, it was declared illegal to mention the names of the Sultan and the Sardauna, despite the fact that the former is the executive head of Sokoto Division and the latter is Premier of the Region and President of the Government Party.[78] N.A. officials at Sokoto informed the writer that general

---

incensed by the idea of destroying the traditional administrative identity of the N.A. The speaker was sentenced to an additional 2 months for remarks which were construed as having defamed, in general terms, the reputations of members of the NPC. Both sentences were confirmed by the Resident of Sokoto Province. See *Daily Service*, September 23, 1958 and subsequent issues.

[76] Permit violations normally entail penalties of 6 months imprisonment or a £25 fine. See *Kano N.A. Rules and Orders*: "Control of Assemblies." Malam Aminu Kano, President General of the NEPU, testified before the Minorities Commission that members of his party had been imprisoned for permit offences. "He tendered many documents, some of which showed certain conditions to be fulfilled before permits could be granted for meetings. He said he considered this to be a barrier in the way of his party when the NPC was not so restricted. One of the permits issued by the Misau N.A., he said, specifically stated that if N.A. members of NEPU spoke against the Northern Nigeria Government they should be arrested and taken to an alkali court." *Daily Times*, March 3, 1958. The right of the N.A.'s to require the listing of subjects on applications for permits and confinement of the speakers to the subjects listed was upheld by implication in a High Court decision of 1957. The Court reversed a conviction of a NEPU leader for having departed from the list of approved subjects on the ground that her statements did not constitute a departure. *Gambo Amate v. Zaria N.A.* In the High Court of Justice of the Northern Region of Nigeria, February 20, 1957. (Typed transcript of the judgment.)

[77] A formal complaint against the requirement of permits for private political meetings was lodged with the Governor of the Northern Region by an Action Group delegation in September 1958. *Daily Service*, September 2, 1958.

[78] *Daily Times*, November 18, 1957. The Sokoto N.A. defended this action on the ground that political tension results from the abuse of personalities. Malam Aminu Kano, leader of the NEPU, promptly replied that attacks on personalities

STUDIES IN POWER AND CONFLICT

criticisms of institutions, including the N.A. and the *Alkalis*, were permissible although personal attacks would not be tolerated. Yet, in the heat of political oratory the line between general and specific allusions may not be clear; no defense can overcome the adverse testimony of two competent witnesses in a Muslim Court and cases involving minor offences which originate before a Junior *Alkali* cannot be appealed beyond the Grade A native courts. With the enactment of the Criminal Code (Amendment) Law of 1957, the utterance of an "insolent, scurrilous or abusive term of reproach" became a statutory offence, actionable in the magistrates' courts as well as the native courts of all jurisdictions.[79]

It emerges from this review of political rights and authority at the local level in the North that prior to independence, minority and opposition elements lacked the constitutional, structural, and procedural guarantees of liberty that British subjects are wont to regard as fundamental. Prohibitions of provocative and abusive speech embodied in Maliki law and reinforced by the criminal code and by permit requirements have been sufficiently harsh to reduce freedom of expression in the North to a marginal liberty at best. Within his jurisdiction, the emir possesses supreme executive and judicial power in addition to shared legislative powers. The native courts are but instrumentalities of the Native Authority; the *Alkalis,* or subordinate judges in Muslim courts, are nominated by the Emir-in-Council

---

are inevitable in the course of political controversy and that traditional rulers who could not tolerate criticism ought to retire from politics. *Daily Times,* November 19, 1957.

Prohibitions of the mere mention of an official's name is an extreme form of regulation, the enforcement of which is probably haphazard or selective. That such regulations have been enforced is indicated by the following demand contained in an Action Group memorandum to the Governor of the North:

"subject to the provision of the criminal code, there should be no arrests and or trials in the Northern Region for the following:

"(i) the mention or criticism of a Minister of State at any public meeting;

"(ii) the mention or criticism of the N.A. including its staff, judicial officers and Emirs at any public meeting;

"(iii) the singing of party songs;

"(iv) the shouting of party slogans and the participation of women in party rallies." *Daily Service,* September 2, 1958.

In the case of *Gambo Amate v. Zaria N.A.,* cited in note 76, the High Court conceded that her words might constitute "the offence of defamation in Maliki Law or under the Criminal Code" but did not consider the matter since it had not been made the basis of her conviction.

[79] *Criminal Code (Amendment) Law, 1957, Northern Region of Nigeria Gazette,* No. 8, Kaduna, February 7, 1957, Vol. 6, Supplement C, pp. 27-28. In June 1958, an Action Group organizing secretary was convicted of using abusive language against the Premier of the North and sentenced by a magistrate to pay a fine of £20. *Daily Service,* June 25, 1958.

for appointment by the Resident. In practice, the *Alkalis* are political appointees controlled by the emir who generally work closely with the district heads, or principal executive agents of the Native Authority[80] It is notorious that in the rural districts, the district heads and the *Alkalis* together wield virtually absolute political power over the peasantry. Collusive political intolerance on their part renders opposition party activity extremely difficult if not hazardous.[81] The risks of opposition in the North are indicated by the fact that 4 of the 9 persons elected to the Northern House of Assembly in 1956 on the platform of the NEPU or the NEPU-Bornu Youth Movement Alliance (since terminated) have been convicted by *Alkali* courts. Three of them were convicted during their terms of office, two for offences involving political speech entailing prison sentences of less than six months.[82] Finally, the knowledge that conviction by a native

[80] On the techniques of an Emir's control of the Native Judiciary, see M. G. Smith, *Government in Zazzau*, pp. 284-286. The writer is informed that the loyalty of *Alkalis* to the emirs may be ensured by marriage relationships. All title-holders deem it the greatest honor to be related by marriage to the emir; as eminent Muslims they are entitled to a maximum of four wives.

[81] NEPU National Headquarters (Kano) files include the record of a case from Dawakin Kudu District, about 15 miles from Kano City, in which over 30 supporters of the NEPU were imprisoned for a year or more as a result of election campaigning in 1956. It is alleged that the district head, who was himself standing as an NPC candidate, and the *Alkali*, who served as returning officer, saw to the defeat of all NEPU candidates in the primaries. The arrests were said to have been made in the homes of the accused at night. Moreover, the death of a NEPU agent from Kano was noted in Dawaki; oddly, the authorities apprehended the local NEPU president on suspicion of homicide but he was released and no one was prosecuted.

At Ringim, one Mallam Illa, a NEPU member, was arrested for failure to answer a summons from the District Head and sentenced to six month's imprisonment by the Emir of Kano. The NEPU objected without avail on the ground that a district head does not, in theory, have judicial power to issue summonses. NEPU National Headquarters Files, Kano.

An NPC parliamentarian who was also a district head in Kano Province, described his efforts to discourage opposition party activities in a report to the NPC Party Manager as follows:

"When the opponents of my party secured a permit to stage a public lecture in my District I am always careful to allow them a most solitary place to which nobody would care to go, apart from indirect pressure which I assert to make that lecture a total failure, and I do succeed." He went on to explain that as a district head he could not flatly condemn the opposition, but that the influence of a good district head is naturally considerable. (NPC Secretariat Files, Kaduna.)

[82] Hon. Bala Keffi (Kaduna) served 3 months for a political offence in 1955 prior to his election to the House of Assembly; Hon. Haruna Tela (Kaura Namoda, Sokoto) was imprisoned for a month; Hon. Shehu Marihu (Zaria) has been sentenced twice, once for a term of 5 months; Hon. Ibrahim Imam (Yerwa, Bornu) was convicted by an *Alkali* in Bornu for an alleged offence committed 4 years earlier when he was a member of the N.A., but the conviction was quashed by a higher court. (continued)

court may entail an arbitrary punishment, indignities and lashes of the cane, whether "symbolic" or otherwise, cannot be reassuring to the opposition.[83]

In 1958, the Northern Regional Government appointed a mission to study the operation of Muslim law in the Sudan, Lybia, and Pakistan. Its findings were reviewed by a second panel, which included the Chief Justice of the Sudan and a Justice of the Pakistan Supreme Court. The result of this review was the Penal Code Law of 1959 (effective on September 30, 1960—the eve of Nigerian independence), providing a uniform criminal code for the entire region in addition to reforms of the appellate procedures.[84] These reforms,

---

The President-General of the NEPU, Malam Aminu Kano, was convicted twice during the federal election campaign of 1954, once for flying his party's flag on his car in Kano City (thereby comparing himself to the Emir of Kano who alone, with the exception of the British Resident, has the prerogative of flying a flag on his car) and again for publishing articles with alleged "seditious intent." In the first instance he was sentenced to 3 days imprisonment, in the second to a £50 fine. In a letter to sympathetic persons in the United Kingdom, he stated that over 90 members of his party had been imprisoned for wearing party badges and shouting party slogans. Children of seven years of age, he wrote, were arrested by the N.A. police in Kano City for singing NEPU songs. On August 15, 1954, the Emir of Kano caused a proclamation to be issued forbidding all children to shout NEPU songs or to write the word NEPU on their caps or on the doors of their houses. Letter from Malam Aminu Kano to Marjorie Nicholson, the United Nigeria Committee and six members of Parliament, dated September 1954.

The Central Headquarters of the NEPU at Kano supplied the writer with the names of more than 150 persons and a tabulation of about 225 more who were sentenced by native courts in Kano Province for the commission of political offences between the years 1955 and 1957.

[83] "It was explained to us," wrote the Minorities Commission, "that the 'symbolic' lashing is meant to cause disgrace rather than physical pain, but we were not wholly satisfied that the distinction was always carefully observed." *Report of the Commission appointed to enquire into the fears of Minorities. . . . Op.cit.*, p. 69.

An example of arbitrary punishment is contained in a transcript entitled: "The Details of Judgment Passed on Who Were Arrested By 'Yandoka' N.A. Police for Fighting and Cause of Breach of Peace," dated August 29, 1955, under the byline, Walin Kano. Nineteen members of the NEPU were arrested along with 6 members of the NPC. Fourteen of the NEPU accused who had no record of previous arrests were discharged after admonitions and 10 strokes of the cane. Three who had been arrested for one previous offence were sentenced to one year's imprisonment; one person who had a record of 2 previous arrests was given 2 years' imprisonment and one person who had been arrested 3 times previously was sentenced to 3 years' imprisonment. It is not recorded that any member of the NPC was sentenced.

In October 1958, a notorious case of caning was brought to the attention of the delegates to the resumed Nigerian Constitutional Conference in the form of a photograph. The victim was Alhaji Sherif, Vice President and Organizing Secretary of the Bornu Youth Movement, who was sentenced to 80 strokes by an *Alkali* at Gashua, Bornu. It is reported that the incident was discussed informally by delegates; the *Alkali* concerned was reported to have been suspended. *Daily Service*, October 8, 1958, and *Nigerian Citizen*, October 15, 1958.

[84] "In future, no person will be liable to punishment under any native law and

achieved under conservative auspices, were a most hopeful augury for the future of political democracy in the North.

THE SOCIAL ORIGINS AND IDEOLOGICAL ORIENTATIONS OF PARTY LEADERS IN THE NORTH

Social theorists have remarked that status in society may be ascribed or achieved.[85] Briefly, ascribed status connotes an institutional qualification, whereas achieved status is a consequence of character, merit, or talent. Owing to the dependence of the Northern Peoples' Congress on the system of Native Administrations, a single-factor dependence which is not paralleled in southern Nigeria, the distinction between ascribed and achieved status is especially useful in the analysis of party leadership in the North.[86] Leadership status in the Northern Peoples' Congress is ascribed primarily to those in

---

custom, and any punishment imposed by any court in the Region must be by reference to the new Penal Code or some other written law. The High Court, magistrates' and native courts will all administer the same criminal law, although, for some time, native courts will be guided and not strictly bound by the new codes, thereby ensuring that mistakes made in learning the new techniques will not necessarily be fatal to their proceedings. . . . A Native Courts Appellate Division of the High Court will hear appeals from native courts in all matters not within the jurisdiction of the Sharia Court of Appeal, and a Judge of the Sharia Court of Appeal will sit with two Judges of the High Court in this Division. All existing native courts of appeal will be abolished, and in each Province the government is establishing a Provincial Court to hear appeals from the lower-grade native courts. In this way, it is ensured that a litigant will always have a right of appeal to a Regional court. A Judicial Service Commission has been set up in the Region in accordance with the provisions of the constitution, and, in future, appointments to the Regional Judiciary including appointments to the Sharia Court of Appeal and the Provincial courts, will be made by this independent body." "Legal and Judicial Reform in Northern Nigeria," *West Africa*, September 24, 1960, p. 1071.

[85] "Fortunately, human beings are so mutable that almost any normal individual can be trained to the adequate performance of almost any role. Most of the business of living can be conducted on a basis of habit, with little need for intelligence and none for special gifts. Societies have met the dilemma by developing two types of statuses, the *ascribed* and the *achieved*. *Ascribed* statuses are those which are assigned to individuals without reference to their innate differences or abilities. They can be predicted and trained for from the moment of birth. The *achieved* statuses are, as a minimum, those requiring special qualities, although they are not necessarily limited to these. They are not assigned to individuals from birth but are left open to be filled through competition and individual effort. The majority of the statuses in all social systems are of the ascribed type and those which take care of the ordinary day-to-day business of living are practically always of this type." Ralph Linton, *The Study of Man* (New York: D. Appleton-Century Company, 1936), p. 115.

[86] C. S. Whitaker, Jr., analyzes Northern political leadership comprehensively in a forthcoming study. And see R. L. Sklar and C. S. Whitaker, Jr., "Nigerian Political Parties" in the forthcoming volume on "Political Groups in Tropical Africa," edited by James S. Coleman and Carl G. Rosberg, Jr.

high office in the Native Authority system: the higher N.A. officials, i.e., members of Central Native Authority Councils, or Emir's Councils, are more likely than subordinate N.A. officials to hold high party offices. Assuredly, the attainment of high office in a Native Administration may be indicative of personal achievement, but party leadership status is ascribed by virtue of that achievement.[87]

In addition, leadership status in the NPC is ascribed according to ethnic and religious factors which vary from one sector of the North to another. In the numerically preponderant Hausa sector, Fulani birth and the Muslim creed are the most important qualifications of this order.

Six of the seven principal officers of the Northern Peoples' Congress in 1957-1960—all of whom were regional or federal ministers—had high ascriptive status stemming from eminence in the administrative elite. Four of them were members of the Central Native Authority Councils of First Class Emirs: Alhaji Sir Ahmadu Bello, Sardauna of Sokoto, Northern Regional Premier and General President of the Northern Peoples' Congress; Alhaji Sir Abubakar Tafawa Balewa of Bauchi, Prime Minister of the Federation and First Vice President of the Congress; Alhaji Muhammadu Ribadu of Adamawa, Federal Minister of Lagos Affairs, Mines, and Power and Second Vice President of the Congress; Alhaji Aliyu, Makaman Bida, Northern Regional Minister of Finance and General Treasurer of the Congress. Two others were *de facto* members and dominant personalities in their respective N.A. Councils: Alhaji Isa Kaita, Madawakin Katsina, Regional Minister of Education and Financial Secretary of the Congress; Malam Abba Habib, an ex-District Head of Dikwa Emirate, Northern Cameroons Trust Territory, Northern Regional Minister of Trade and Industry and General Secretary of the Congress. The Sardauna of Sokoto and Alhaji Ribadu belong to the traditional, settled-Fulani ruling class of the North; accordingly, their ascriptive status is highest. Makaman Bida is Nupe; he was a teacher and headmaster for 15 years. He is the only NPC officer or minister senior to the Sardauna in age (by 3 years) and with respect to his graduating class in the Katsina Teacher Training Col-

[87] As Sidney Verba has observed, ". . . the status an individual achieves in one situation by his task performance carries over to other tasks. Parsons, Bales and Shils describe the process whereby status accorded an individual on the basis of task achievement will develop into a generalized ascribed status, transferable to other situations. . . ." Verba cites a description of this process by Parsons, Bales, and Shils, which he terms "the development of generalized ascribed leadership status." *Small Groups and Political Behavior* (Princeton: Princeton University Press, 1961), pp. 126-127.

lege; he is the Premier's chief lieutenant in the government and the party. Alhaji Isa Kaita is Katsina Habe (Katsinawa); the Prime Minister of the Federation is Bauchi Habe (Gerawa); Malam Abba Habib is Shuwa Arab. The seventh principal officer,[88] Alhaji Ibrahim Musa Gashash, Regional Minister of Lands and Survey and Northern Regional President of the Congress, is a prominent Kano businessman of Tripolitanian Arab-Hausa extraction. The commercial elite of the North is the "second" component of its emergent dominant class and leadership status in the NPC is ascribed directly according to eminence in the business world.

Of course, the highest ascriptive status in the Northern Region attaches to the most august and powerful traditional rulers, three of whom, namely, the Sultan of Sokoto, the Emir of Kano, and the Emir of Katsina—all Fulani—were regional ministers without portfolio at the time of writing. With respect to the Northern Peoples' Congress, they were the "powers behind the throne" by virtue of their institutional capacities. Within the party organization, their chief spokesman was Alhaji Sir Ahmadu Bello, the Sardauna of Sokoto, whose grandfather and great grandfather were Sultans of Sokoto. Among the principal Nigerian leaders, including the Prime Minister, the presidents of the other major parties and the other regional premiers, the Sardauna is least indebted psychologically to Western culture. Indeed the Sardauna often affects a disdain for "politics" *per se* and probably regards himself as a natural ruler in the temporary service of his people as a politician. It is widely believed that he aspires to become the next Sultan of Sokoto, a position which carries the highest traditional prestige in the Northern system.[89] If he wished

[88] Other members of the National Executive of the Northern Peoples' Congress in the top order of party influence in the period 1957-1960 included, in addition to the seven mentioned in the text, the following: Shettima Kashim, the Waziri of Bornu (Kanuri); Zanna Bukar Dipcharima, Federal Minister of Commerce and Industry (Kanuri-Bornu); Alhaji Inuwa Wada, Federal Minister of Works (Fulani-Kano); Alhaji Aliyu, Turakin Zazzau, Chairman of the Northern Region Development Corporation (Habe-Zaria).

[89] A statement to that effect was issued by the Party Manager of the NPC in 1957 when Alhaji Abubakar Tafawa Balewa was chosen as Prime Minister of the Federation. Yet it is difficult to believe that the Sardauna seriously contemplates permanent withdrawal from active politics; for one thing, the incumbent Sultan of Sokoto is a vigorous man who is only seven years older than the Sardauna. In December 1959, following the redesignation of Alhaji Abubakar as Prime Minister of the Federation, the Sardauna expressed his intention to retire from politics in 1961. Thereupon he was urged to rescind that decision by the National Executive Committee of the NPC and by various delegations. He did so and gave an assurance "that he would continue to serve the people as long as it was necessary or until such time as he was called upon by his party to quit." *Daily Times*, December 30, 1959.

to do so, the Sardauna of Sokoto, as Premier of a region of some 18.8 million people and General President of the political party with the largest representation in the Parliament of the Federation of Nigeria, might attain recognition as a political leader whose power and influence was second to none in Africa.

The criteria of achieved leadership status—e.g., individual merit and personal appeal—are difficult, if not impossible, to tabulate for comparative purposes. Moreover, psychological criteria, which lie beyond the scope of this study, are pertinent. It suffices here to observe that the Sardauna's leadership status is prominently ascribed, although his "achieved" qualifications, notably his executive ability and independence of mind, are impressive. As Premier of the North, the Sardauna fought his battle against recalcitrant British administrative officers under conditions that were possibly more delicate than conditions in other regions.[90] His conduct of these and other matters have earned him the admiration of his followers.

In the case of Alhaji Sir Abubakar Tafawa Balewa, Prime Minister of the Federation and First Vice President of the NPC, leadership status is primarily achieved. The Premier of the North and the Prime Minister of the Federation personify crucial segments of the Northern administrative elite. The Sardauna embodies *sarakuna* or nobility; Balewa is a representative of the *talakawa* or common people. The Sardauna devoted most of his pre-political life to administration. His statements usually reflect the views of the Emirs and the high N.A. officials, who are also the leading politicians.

[90] It is no secret that most NPC leaders were glad to see most of the old colonial officers go. Some of them (the politicians) owed their political advancement to officials who became their "advisers" in the regional government and were either too knowledgeable or patronizing for the comfort of the ministers. Certain high officials of the NPC readily contend that administrative officers who opposed the movement for self-government competed with them for the loyalty of the chiefs, most of whom gave their support in the last analysis to the party. The appointment of a "new style" Governor of the North in 1958 was regarded by the NPC as a signal victory.

It will remain for Nigerian historians to appraise the role of Colonial Administrations. One of the founders of the NPC suggested to the writer that in retrospect the contribution of the controversial Governor of the North, Sir Bryan Sharwood-Smith, to democracy in the North was not inconsiderable. He pointed out that at the Ibadan General Conference of 1950, the Emirs rejected the idea of ministers for the North. "Sharwood-Smith," he said, "persuaded them to accept the idea of Ministers and portfolios. It may have been inevitable, but to go in 7 years from 'we don't want Ministers' to a stage where the Premier can, in effect control the appointment and deposition of Emirs is quite a feat. Before the Emir of Kano knew what happened he was receiving a Christian commoner from the Middle Belt in his home, socially, for equal discussions. The Minister even keeps his shoes on and smokes in the Emir's presence."

Yet his determined espousal of the policy of "Northernization" of the public services has endeared him to the hearts of the growing corps of Northern civil servants. Moreover, he seems to share the admiration of the educated Northern Muslim elite for Arab nationalism, irrespective of British views.[91] Alhaji Abubakar Tafawa Balewa's pre-political experience was chiefly as a teacher and headmaster in the employ of the Bauchi Native Administration. His views usually reflect the opinions of the progressive intelligentsia of the middle administrative echelons, sometimes termed collectively the *ma'aikata* or salaried class. Both the Sardauna and Balewa are accomplished orators and highly competent parliamentarians, but neither is by any stretch of the imagination a leader of the "charismatic" or demagogic type.

At the Jos Convention of the NPC in April 1954, an influential contingent of party regulars, especially the progressive youth, some of whom had been members of the NPC since its inception as a cultural organization, hoped to elect Abubakar Tafawa Balewa as president of the party. But the biases and views of the Emirs weighed heavily against Balewa, and their assured cooperation was thought to require party leadership of the highest aristocratic caliber. Opposition to the Sardauna never reached the convention floor; he was elected unanimously as President, and Balewa was chosen as Vice President. At the Maiduguri Convention of June 1955, it was decided that the stability of the region and the continuity of party policies would best be served by extending the terms of office of the incumbent leadership for 5 years—i.e., until 1960. Thereafter, occasional reports of friction between the Sardauna and Balewa have ruffled the NPC's normally placid exterior.[92] It was thought by some that neither the

[91] The Sardauna of Sokota is reported to have paid a courtesy call on President Gamal Abdel Nasser of the United Arab Republic (then of Egypt) in Cairo in 1956, following his pilgrimage to Mecca in that year. In September 1958, Action Group spokesmen alleged that the NPC had negotiated an agreement with the leaders of the United Arab Republic involving the provision of financial assistance for the Northern government party in the federal election of 1959. This was promptly denied by the Sardauna and the Prime Minister of the Federation in a letter to the Governor-General of Nigeria. *Daily Times*, September 8, 11, 13, 1958. Subsequently, the Prime Minister criticized President Nasser with respect to the latter's association with European communists. *West African Pilot*, September 25, 1958.

[92] In the latter part of September 1957, friction between the Sardauna and the Prime Minister was reported in the Lagos press. The Premier of the North is reported to have told representatives of the Nigeria Broadcasting Corporation that he was happy one of his "boys" had become Prime Minister. However, the possibly offensive word was changed to "lieutenants" for the broadcast. Subsequently, the Prime Minister expressed his pride in having been the one who brought the Sardauna into politics. (The story is that Balewa persuaded the Sardauna to be a candidate for the Northern House of Assembly when the Sokoto seat was vacated by the death of the Waziri of Sokoto in 1949.) The sense of decorum among leaders of the

Sardauna nor the traditional rulers of the North were enthusiastic about the appointment of Balewa to the office of Prime Minister in an independent Nigeria. However, these suspicions were laid to rest in December 1959 when the Northern Premier expressed his un-equivocal support for the continuation of Alhaji Abubakar as Prime Minister of the Federation.

Undoubtedly, Alhaji Sir Abubakar Tafawa Balewa is the leader of the "progressive" wing of the NPC which favors the rapid develop-ment of the Native Authority system into a system of local democracy. In general, the progressives believe that the party should transfer its primary dependence from the Native Administration bureaucracies to the people. Probably, some of the emirs still fear that Balewa's tendencies are radical. His vigorous initiative in the field of Native Authority reform is not forgotten[93] and it is likely that he was not wholly satisfied by the Native Authority Law of 1954 which was largely the fruit of his efforts.[94] There may be a factual basis to the story that conservative Emirs insisted upon Balewa's candidature in the federal election of 1954 because they preferred to advance him "upstairs" rather than to have him in power as a minister in the region.[95] Prior to independence, at least, Balewa's radicalism ap-peared to have been confined to the subject of Native Administration in the North. Politically, his views seem never to have been distant from those of the British; as a minister in the federal government, especially as Prime Minister during the final phase of colonial rule

---

NPC is so high that public manifestations of friction between them are exceedingly rare and relatively mild.

[93] *Supra*, pp. 99-100.

[94] During the intra-party debate on the Native Authority Bill of 1953, progressives argued that all Native Administrations should be constituted by Councils or by Chiefs-and-Council rather than Chiefs-in-Council. ("Chief-and-Council" signifies that decisions of the Native Authority will be taken by a majority vote of the Council with the Chief entitled only to an original and a casting vote in case of a tie; "Chief-in-Council" signifies that the Chief is obliged to consult his Council in all matters but may override the Council subject to the intervention of a higher authority. *Northern Region Native Authority Law*, 1954, Kaduna: Government Printer, 1954, pp. 10-11.) Balewa seems to have inclined to the progressive view. NPC (NHQ) Files, 307: 22 (1953).

[95] Probably it is extreme to infer that the hostility of the Emirs made Abubakar Tafawa Balewa the first Prime Minister of the Federation. It may, however, be observed that he was elected to the House of Representatives by the final electoral college for Bauchi West constituency in Toro on December 21, 1954, despite the fact that he had not been a candidate at the earlier stages. His candidature is said to have been decided upon after a meeting between the Emir of Kano and the Emir of Bauchi at Rimin Zayam. It is thought that he might otherwise have become Regional Minister of Local Government, a portfolio that was held by the Sardauna, in whose loyalty to the emirate system the Emirs were completely confident.

from 1957 to 1960, Balewa gained the reputation of being closer to the British than any other Nigerian leader.

Opposition Party Leadership

By 1958, all opposition parties of any consequence in the North were affiliated with one of the two major parties of southern Nigeria. Affiliates of the NCNC included the Northern Elements Progressive Union and its affiliates, the small Ilorin Araromi Congress and the smaller Middle Belt State Party of Tiv Division. Affiliates of the Action Group included the multi-tribal United Middle Belt Congress, the Bornu Youth Movement (the leader of which, Malam Ibrahim Imam, is introduced above),[96] the Habe Fulani Peoples' Party of southern Bauchi,[97] the Ilorin *Talaka Parapo* (Commoners' Party)-Action Group Alliance,[98] and indigenously based units of the Action Group in Kabba and the upper North. Only the Northern Elements Progressive Union and the United Middle Belt Congress operate on a multi-provincial basis; their respective leaders, Malam Aminu Kano and Hon. Joseph Sarwuan Tarka, represent the causes of Northern radicalism and middle-belt separatism.

It has been observed that the national leadership of the Northern Elements Progressive Union reflects the estrangement of that party from the administrative elite of the Northern Region.[99] Very few of the leaders of the NEPU have high-status family or occupational backgrounds. Ascribed leadership status is therefore much less important in the NEPU than it is in the NPC. Malam Aminu Kano, the pre-eminent leader of the NEPU, has higher ascribed leadership status than most of his colleagues by virtue of his Fulani birth and his pre-political eminence in the field of education. But his unrivalled

[96] *Supra*, pp. 339-341.

[97] The Habe-Fulani Peoples' Party was organized by Malam Ibrahim Dimis in 1957 as a breakaway from the Habe Tribal Union/NEPU Alliance. The HFPP appeared to advocate either a separate Habe Division within Bauchi Province or the separation of the southern districts of Bauchi Division from the rest of that emirate and their inclusion in the proposed Middle Belt State.

[98] The most articulate spokesman for the Ilorin Talaka Parapo/Action Group Alliance was Hon. Josiah Sunday Olawoyin, MHA (Offa Town). Mr. Olawoyin was General Secretary of the League of Northern Yorubas, formed in 1951 to promote the merger of Ilorin and Kabba Divisions with the Western Region. He is administrative secretary of the Offa Descendants Union, a cultural organization that is closely related to the *Egbe Omo Oduduwa* and the Action Group; he is also a close lieutenant of Chief Awolowo.

The Life President of the I.T.P./Action Group Alliance is Hon. Alhaji Sulaiman Maito, MHA, a wealthy cattle dealer and foundation member of the *Talaka Parapo*.

[99] *Supra*, pp. 335-336.

authority within the party is a consequence of his personality and political talent, in addition to the highly centralized organization of the NEPU, which is described in Chapter IX.

At home in Kano City, Malam Aminu lives humbly among the people of Sudawa quarter. His large personal library is an educational incentive to the young men and schoolboys who frequent his home. As a modernist and progressive in Islam he is monogamist in principle, an advocate of female education and the full emancipation of women. While he does practice these ideals he must do so without appearing to offend public moralities. His intellectual commitment to Islam is serious; daily during the month-long Ramaddan observance he reads and interprets the Koran to the people.[100] It is not surprising that he is widely regarded as a religious as well as a political reformer and that many students of the progressive *mallamai* (Koranic teachers)[100a] turn to the NEPU.

Within the wider ambit of the NCNC/NEPU Alliance, Malam Aminu enjoys the universal respect of political idealists and the radical youth. He was personally close to the late populist leader of Ibadan, Alhaji Adegoke Adelabu, and it was in the company of Adelabu at the Ibadan Annual Conference of the NEPU in September 1957 that he repudiated current speculations on a rupture of the NCNC/NEPU Alliance. His tenure in the NCNC National Executive Committee and his personal claim to a major share in the leadership of that party (he was elected First Vice President of the NCNC in 1960) may account in part for the inability of the Action Group to conclude an alliance with the NEPU.

Aminu Kano's public statements often reflect his ideological commitment to democratic and pan-African socialism. In 1955 he contrasted the NEPU and the NPC interpretations of democracy in these terms: "We interpret democracy in its more traditional, radical sense, and that is the rule of the common people, the poor, the illiterate, while our opponents (the NPC) interpret it in its modern Tory sense, and that is the rule of the enlightened and prosperous minority in the supposed interest of the common people."[101]

[100] The writer is informed that Malam Aminu Kano began his practice of reading the Qur'an to the people some years ago in order to counter the influence of Alhaji Nasiru, a conservative mallam of Kano City, who gave the people interpretations of the Qur'an that were inimical to the NEPU cause.

[100a] *Malam* is the polite form of address to an adult male in the upper North. *Malama* is used for women. The plural form, *mallamai*, refers to teachers or learned men. It might be added that *Alhaji* is the form of address to a man who has made the pilgrimage to Mecca.

[101] In this address he commended the regional government for having made

His conception of democracy encompasses individual political liberty and the abolition of the political privileges of special interests or classes, including chiefs. He is a proponent of the concept of unitarian government in Nigeria, comprising provincial rather than regional or sub-regional state units,[102] although his party does support in principle the creation of additional states as a step in the right direction. In principle he is opposed to regional legislatures and to the houses of chiefs in particular. However, he has always regarded the attainment of independence for the Federation of Nigeria as the first object of progressive politics. In that spirit he justified deferment of the Middle Belt State issue until after independence and pledged his party to cooperate with the NPC's program for regional self-government. It would not be out of character for him to seek a de-emphasis of inter-party conflict in order to enhance the stability of his newly independent nation.[103] His relationship with other African

---

progress in the field of education and urged his party to cooperate with the educational program of the government in these words:

"Ignorance breeds apathy, makes people fatalistic and extremely rural and sub-urban-minded. It offers the most obstinate resistance to all efforts of helping the people to improve their livelihood and social status. For think of the poor mother paying a vaccinator a shilling not to vaccinate the child she dearly loves. Think of a farmer who cannot pay his tax and yet designs all means to escape the plough or the improved seeds or modern fertilizer. Ignorance is the root cause of all the evils of our people." Presidential Address to the Fifth Annual Conference of the Northern Elements Progressive Union, 1955.

[102] Aminu Kano's unitarist philosophy of government is based on his confidence in the long-term unity of the Nigerian people and his perception of social change that will render current tribal divisions obsolete. The following statement to the 1957 Annual Conference of the NEPU is illustrative of his belief:

"Nigeria has the good fortune of having large Muslim communities in the North and West as there are pagans in the North and South, and Christians in almost every corner of the country. It is our belief that the overriding factors for unity within a given territory are community of interests, economic problems and the existence of external factors which withhold or threaten full independence of the people of an area. The desire of the people of Nigeria for progress, comfort and freedom is the same all over. The complementary nature of the resources of the different parts of the country emphasizes the need for a single direction of economic development to benefit all people alike.

"It is in the light of this belief that we stand for the unity and ultimate independence of Nigeria. We in Nigeria today, as all of you know, have come to believe that whatever political system may have come to be in the future, the one thing certain is that it will be considerably unlike the system under which most of us have been living. For better or for worse we are for comprehensive changes in the fundamental structure of our society and it will depend on us and on other men much like ourselves what is made of the objective conditions upon which the future state of Nigeria would have to be built."

Presidential Address to the Seventh Annual Convention of the NEPU, Ibadan, September 26, 1957.

[103] In a reply to inquiries from the Fabian Colonial (now Commonwealth) Bureau

nationalists, in particular the Ghanaians, has always been cordial, and he led his party's strong delegation to the first All-African Peoples' Conference at Accra in December 1958.[104] In 1959, Malam Aminu was elected overwhelmingly by the Kano East constituency to the Federal House of Representatives; he is reported to have declined a ministerial appointment, but he accepted the post of Chief Whip of the NCNC/NEPU Alliance and became Chairman of the Alliance Committee on foreign affairs.

In January 1957, Hon. Joseph Sarwuan Tarka, MHR, a teacher and former General Secretary of the Tiv Native Authority Staff Union, then 25 years old, became President General of the United Middle Belt Congress.[105] He had been elected to the House of Representatives in 1954 and was supported for the leadership of the Congress by the Tiv Progressive Union, then the most influential political organization in Tiv Division.

The Tiv, who number about 800,000, are the largest ethnic minority in the Northern Region. Students of the Tiv have drawn attention to their egalitarian, patriarchial, and anti-centrist prepossessions. Tiv egalitarianism was manifest in hostility to the exercise of power by any person.[106] Until the creation of an administrative structure by the British, there were no institutional political authorities among the Tiv.[107] They appear to have responded to

in 1956, respecting NEPU views on the forthcoming Constitutional Conference, the authorized NEPU respondent took note of the threats to national unity and stability resulting from inter-party strife in other new nations and suggested that national solidarity was required during the critical period of transition from colonial rule.

[104] In a brief address to the All African Peoples' Conference, Malam Aminu declared: "This Conference . . . must condemn 'apartheid' and all African Nations in close collaboration with their Asiatic brethren, must take a stand about South Africa; the restoration of the dignity of the 'Black Man' in South Africa is an avowed duty for us all." Address by the NEPU Delegation, Malam Aminu Kano (mimeographed copy).

The Niger section of the *Parti de Federation Africain,* dissolved by edict of the Niger Government in October 1959, is called the *Sawaba* (Freedom) Party. Its symbol, like that of the NEPU and the Ghana Convention Peoples Party, is the black star and its leader, Djibo Bakary, a former Prime Minister of Niger, who opposed the De Gaulle Constitution of 1958, is said to be friendly with Malam Aminu Kano.

[105] Mr. J. S. Tarka had also been General Secretary of the Benue State Peoples' Party. He is a Roman Catholic and holds the title of *Shagbor* of Gboko, which was conferred upon him by his family.

[106] Laura and Paul Bohannan, *The Tiv of Central Nigeria* (London: International African Institute, 1953), pp. 31-37.

[107] Paul Bohannan, "Extra-Processual Events in Tiv Political Institutions," *American Anthropologist,* Vol. 60, No. 1 (February 1958), p. 6.

the introduction of central administrative offices and the initiation of parliamentary elections by observing a principle of alternation among lineage segments in order to prevent the sustained exercise of power by any one section or faction.[108] Prior to the re-election of Mr. Tarka to the House of Representatives in 1959, no Tiv legislator had ever been re-elected to a second term. Mr. Tarka's achievement may be attributed in part to his personal qualities and persistent efforts to inculcate principles of party loyalty, in part to the respect enjoyed by his father and his late grandfather, who served as the heads of administrative divisions, and in part to the support of the leadership of the Tiv Progressive Union.[109]

In several ways, Mr. Tarka typifies the traditional Tiv leader who may unite the people to face external problems but has very limited power in Tivland itself. As President General of the United Middle Belt Congress, he was a delegate to two constitutional conferences in London; he was also a member of the Action Group delegation to the All African Peoples' Conference of December 1958. Yet in 1958, he held no executive office in either the Tiv Progressive Union or the Tiv Divisional Organization of the UMBC; he was not an officer of the Tiv Native Administration and his youth was a traditional mark of low estate. Probably, he was regarded by the Tiv elders as their chief representative abroad. But Mr. Tarka's personal achievement far exceeds that of any former Tiv politician, and leaders of the Tiv UMBC-Action Group Alliance insist that most of the former parliamentarians failed to obtain re-election because their performances did not satisfy their constituents. They maintain that the personality factor has been diminished in importance by party voting and that the Tiv electorate does not object in principle to the return of a worthy representative. This view was substantiated in the federal election of 1959 when Tarka obtained the largest vote given to any candidate in Nigeria as the UMBC-Action Group Alliance swept all 7 seats for Tiv Division.

Until 1959, the United Middle Belt Congress was a fissiparous conglomeration of tribal unions and autonomous local branches, loosely coordinated and subject to no effective central authority.

---

[108] J. G. Wallace, "The Tiv System of Election," *Journal of African Administration*, Vol. 10, No. 2 (April 1958), pp. 63-70.

[109] When the writer visited Gboko, the capital of Tiv Division, in 1958, the Patron of the Tiv Progressive Union, Mr. Ugor Iwoor, a building contractor and motor transport owner, was reported to be the most influential person in Tiv Division politics. Mr. Iwoor had been President of the Tiv Progressive Union for all but 2 years since 1949. Tiv parliamentarians acknowledged that they owed their elections largely to the support of Mr. Iwoor and the T.P.U.

The principal leaders of the Congress, Mr. Tarka included, were primarily local—i.e., divisional or provincial—rather than "Middle Belt" personalities. By virtue of its alliance with the Action Group, the UMBC experienced a new birth of vitality and the Alliance won 25 federal seats in the lower North. The Action Group needed the UMBC to mediate its penetration of the middle-belt area, but the Action Group is a centralized party and its organizational doctrine requires the subordination of regional to central leadership. Consequently, the UMBC shed its separate identity, and its leaders became leaders of the Action Group in their particular areas. Mr. Tarka has since become a Federal Vice-President of the Action Group and, like Aminu Kano, a symbol of national unity through party competition in the North.

PART III

PARTY STRUCTURE
AND SOCIAL STRUCTURE

CHAPTER IX: THE
OFFICIAL STRUCTURES
AND ORGANIZATIONS
OF THE MAJOR POLITICAL PARTIES

I N THIS chapter the official structures and organizations[1] of the major political parties are described mainly on the basis of the following outline:

PRIMARY ELEMENTS

Local level: general membership bodies, including their executive and conciliar organs, constituency organizations, and sub-regional levels of coordination

Regional level: conferences and regional executive organs

National or federal level: conventions or congresses, and national or federal executive organs.

Parliamentary organization: regional and federal

Secretariat organization

---

[1] It may appear that the concepts "structure" and "organization" are used interchangeably. It is more accurate to infer that organization is an aspect of structure, as a number of social theorists have agreed. A. R. Radcliffe-Brown, an exponent of the functional school of thought, has defined these concepts and their relationship thus:

"A convenient use, which does not depart from common usage in English, is to define social structure as an arrangement of persons in institutionally controlled or defined relationships. . . . and to use organization as referring to an arrangement of activities. . . . Within an organization each person may be said to have a *role*. Thus we may say that when we are dealing with a structural system we are concerned with a system of social *positions*, while in an organization we deal with a system of roles." *Structure and Function in Primitive Society* (London: Cohen and West, 1952), p. 11.

In his presidential address to the Royal Anthropological Institute of Great Britain and Ireland, Raymond Firth, a leading "structuralist," observed that "in discussions of social action the notions of structure and of organization are primarily matters of emphasis. They represent different ways of looking at the same body of material; they are complementary, not opposed concepts. Briefly, and crudely, they may be said to stand respectively for consideration of *form*, and of *process* in social life. But neither is precise, either as a theoretical concept or as a definition of an aspect of social reality." "Social Organization and Social Change," *The Journal of the Royal Anthropological Institute*, Vol. 84 (January-December 1954), p. 4.

S. F. Nadel referred with approval to Firth's elaboration of the concept of organization: "The concept most adequately summarizing this operative counterpart to social structure is *organization* as developed by Firth. He speaks of organization in precisely this sense, as being 'complementary' to social structure and as representing, in brief, 'the working arrangements of society,' whereby a group (so-and-so structured) 'is kept in being.'" *The Theory of Social Structure* (London: Cohen and West, 1957), p. 149.

ANCILLARY ELEMENTS

Auxiliary groups: e.g., women's and youth associations
Affiliated parties
Affiliated non-party groups: economic, ethnic, religious, and other interest groups

Studies of British political parties tend naturally to emphasize the parliamentary context of their development and a distinction is sometimes made between the "party," or parliamentary component, and the "organization," or extra-parliamentary component. A similar emphasis on party organization in the parliaments of Nigeria would be rewarding because there are four parliaments (there were five prior to the separation of the Southern Cameroons Trust Territory from the Federation of Nigeria in 1960), all of which have attained high standards of performance. However, this study does not place great emphasis on the parliamentary wings of the Nigerian parties for two principal reasons. First, Nigerian parties have relatively recent non-parliamentary origins which reflect their primary purpose of social mobilization to effect social and political change. Second, the parliamentary wings of the major parties are strictly subservient to the executive bodies of their mass organizations. This is inevitably the case since each major party has at least two parliamentary wings in different legislative chambers of the Federation and confusion would result if the executive committees were not supreme. Furthermore, it should be noted that the writer did relatively little research on the parliamentary parties, and there is much more to be said on that subject than the present study indicates.

Two functions which are internal to the total organization of each party, namely the selection of candidates to contest elections (the nominating system) and the enforcement of party discipline, are treated separately after the structural analysis of each party. Insofar as data permit, these topics are discussed in accordance with the following outlines:

THE NOMINATING SYSTEM

1. *Procedures*
2. *Criteria and requirements of selection*
3. *Degrees of central and local control*
4. *Extra-party control*
5. *Problems in parliamentary and local government elections*

PARTY DISCIPLINE

1. *Offenses*
2. *Procedures*
3. *The application of rules*: regularity and frequency
4. *Remission of penalties*
5. *Legislative group discipline*

Other functions involving administration, recruitment, and publicity are noted under each party's secretariat organization, but data on financial administration is included in a final section for each party.

The first party to be considered in this chapter is the Northern Peoples' Congress, which controls the government of the Northern Region; it had the largest representation in the House of Representatives at the time of independence, and its membership included the Prime Minister of the Federation and a majority of the Council of Ministers.

We then turn to the National Council of Nigeria and the Cameroons —Northern Elements Progressive Union Alliance, which controls the government of the Eastern Region and forms the official Opposition in the West; it had the second largest representation in the Federal House of Representatives. The NPC and the NCNC/NEPU Alliance formed the governing coalition of the Federation at the time of independence. This chapter concludes with a discussion of the Action Group of Nigeria, which controls the government of the Western Region and forms the official Opposition in the Federal, Northern, and Eastern Legislatures.

THE NORTHERN PEOPLES' CONGRESS

In comparison with the other major parties, the Northern Peoples' Congress is "weakly articulated,"[2] widely decentralized, and largely dependent upon the personnel of a non-party administrative apparatus, namely, the Northern system of native administration. However, it has been observed (in Chapter VIII) that administrative elites share control of important branches of the party with assertive commercial elites, a political fusion which may be facilitated by organizational refinements. Inasmuch as data on NPC organization at higher levels is relatively less abundant than in the cases of the other major parties, a compressed outline of structural categories is followed.

[2] Maurice Duverger, *Political Parties*, trans. Barbara and Robert North (London: Methuen and Co., 1954), pp. 41-47.

Primary Elements

Local Level

The Northern Peoples' Congress (NPC) is a "direct," individual membership party based on branches which have been established at various levels of government, e.g., the ward, the village, and the urban or rural districts.[3] In rural areas, mass membership is normally secured on a communal basis with the cooperation of traditional authorities.[4] Branch activities in sub-district areas are coordinated by district committees and the main centers of local party authority are situated at the divisional or the provincial level, depending upon the administrative structure of the province concerned.[5] At the highest effective level of local party authority—provincial or divisional as the case may be—the institution of a regular conference and an executive committee is normal.

The Regional, National, and Parliamentary Organizations

Membership in the Northern Peoples' Congress is restricted in principle to persons of Northern origin. Branches and regional executive bodies have been organized by Northerners in the East, the West, and in Lagos. The Northern Regional organization is overwhelmingly the weightier part.

Supreme authority in the Northern Peoples' Congress is vested in

[3] There were 295 branches listed in the NPC Central Headquarters file in December 1957.

[4] On October 24, 1958, at Konduga in Malari District of Bornu Division, the writer witnessed the inauguration of a "communal membership" branch of the NPC. The day was set aside by the village authorities for ceremonies and festivities in which the entire community participated. Popular young men were elected as branch officers and distinguished elders were chosen as patrons of the party. All proceedings were conducted under the supervision of the District Head of Konduga Malari.

[5] If the province concerned contains a dominant Native Administration or emirate, as in Sokoto and Zaria, the party organization of that administrative division is likely to exercise controlling influence over the organizations of other divisions or emirates in the province. But the pattern is variable, e.g., the Bornu and Kano Divisional organizations did not, in 1958, appear to control the organizations of lesser divisions in those two provinces. Where there is no dominant Native Administration, as in Niger Province, the most effective level of party organization is likely to be the divisional level, unless, as in Plateau Province, the party is particularly strong in one division and relatively weak in others, in which case a provincial executive based on the strong division is apt to control. Cf. the observation by Maurice Duverger: "In general, political articulation tends to model itself upon the articulation of administration in the state: the grouping of the 'basic elements' assumes therefore the pattern of a hierarchical pyramid coinciding with the official territorial divisions. One level often seems preponderant in character, and generally corresponds to the basic administrative area." Maurice Duverger, *op.cit.*, p. 40.

its annual convention, comprising the officers of the Congress and the representatives of its branches.[6] Party records indicate that seven annual and two "emergency" conventions of the Congress were held between 1949 and 1958.[7] Since the Maiduguri Convention of 1955, which extended for five years the terms of those officers who had been elected in 1954, the annual and "emergency" conventions of the Congress have served mainly to enable its leaders to pronounce on matters of party policy.

The National Executive Committee of the Congress comprises the general officers, the Northern Regional officers, an average of four members from each of the twelve (now thirteen) Northern provinces and the two southern regions, chosen by their respective provincial or regional organizations, and all NPC ministers, excluding the four traditional rulers in the Northern Region Executive Council, who are technically not partymen. Day-to-day direction of the party is

[6] Northern Peoples' Congress, *Constitution and Rules* (Zaria: Gaskiya Corporation, n.d.), pp. 3-6. This constitution was adopted by the Inaugural Convention of the Northern Peoples' Congress (then Northern Nigerian Congress) of June 1949, when the Congress was officially a cultural organization. See *supra*, p. 93. Later it was modified to sanction political party activity. It no longer describes the actual or effective organization of the Congress. Conventions of the NPC are normally mass open forums without the strictly regulated attendance which is prescribed constitutionally. Provision is made in the constitution for the following executive organs: an Executive Committee that should meet annually, comprising all officers of the Congress in addition to the President and Secretary of every branch (this corresponds to the present annual convention in theory), a provincial committee in each province, a Central Working Committee and a Parliamentary Committee. The actual organization of the Congress is described in the text.

[7] Annual and emergency conventions of the Northern Peoples' Congress, following the Inaugural Convention of June 26-29, 1949:

December 25-27, 1949: Kano (First Annual Convention of the Congress)

December 1950: Jos (Decision taken that members could not belong to both the NPC and the NEPU.)

July 5, 1952: Kaduna Emergency Convention (Ratification of the decision of Congress leaders to convert the NPC into a political party.)

December 1952: (Adoption of the revised aims and objects of the NPC. See *supra*, p. 326, n. 8.)

April 27-30, 1954: Jos (Election of national officers and preparation for the federal elections.)

June 13-17, 1955: Maiduguri (Extension of the terms of the national officers for five years.)

August 5-6, 1956: Kaduna (Consideration of proposals on the Nigerian Constitution made by a special committee of the Congress in preparation for the London Constitutional Conference.)

September 21, 1957: Zaria Emergency Convention (Confirmation of the commitment of the leaders of the NPC to the achievement of Nigerian independence and the appointment of Alhaji Abubakar Tafawa Balewa as Prime Minister of the Federation.)

January 10-13, 1958: Kano (Confirmation of the policy of Northernization in both the administrative and the economic spheres.)

vested in a Central Working Committee—an *ad hoc* group comprising the national officers, ministers, members of the National Executive Committee, and top-ranking secretariat officials in residence at Kaduna—which may be convened at any time by the General President or an officer acting with his authority. Five of the seven principal officers of the Congress in 1958 were ministers of the Northern Regional government, including the Premier of the North who was General President of the Congress; the other two principal officers, including the Prime Minister of the Federation (First Vice-President of the Congress), were ministers in the federal government.[8] Parliamentary Committees were organized at the regional and federal levels under the chairmanships of the Premier and the Prime Minister respectively, with the usual complement of parliamentary whips and party secretaries. The Federal Parliamentary Party included an executive subcommittee of about 15 prominent back benchers which made recommendations to the Prime Minister concerning appointments to committees of the House, amendments to Government bills, and the disposition of private members' motions.[8a] It has been the practice of the Parliamentary Leaders to convene a joint (regional-federal) parliamentary committee meeting in Kaduna prior to the concurrent budget sessions of the Regional and Federal Legislatures in order to ensure the complementarity of NPC policies. In both legislatures, strict party discipline is imposed by the parliamentary committees.[8b]

Secretariat Organization

In 1957 the National Executive Committee appointed two high functionaries to head the National Secretariat staff, a Party Manager and a Principal Organizing Secretary, full-time officials who were chiefly responsible for administration and recruitment respectively.[9]

[8] *Supra*, p. 366.

[8a] The executive subcommittee of the NPC Federal Parliamentary Committee comprised one member from each of the 12 Northern Provinces, the secretary of the Parliamentary Committee, the Chief Whip and the Deputy Speaker of the House of Representatives, who was the chairman of the subcommittee.

[8b] The writer was informed by an officer of the NPC Regional Parliamentary Committee that members are permitted to speak freely within the Parliamentary Committee where regional ministers are required to defend Government bills against all criticisms. Non-controversial amendments to Government bills are usually moved in the House by their sponsors, but a controversial amendment is generally referred to the Regional Executive Council and will be moved in the House by a minister if it is approved.

[9] The Party Manager was Malam D. A. Rafih, a founder and the first Vice-President of the NPC in 1948-1949. The Principal Organizing Secretary was Malam Habib Raji Abdallah, formerly Secretary General of the Northern Elements Pro-

Hopefully, these officials undertook to strengthen the frail central organization. They circulated memoranda on party reorganization to all officers and branches of the Congress and they instructed all parliamentarians to tour their constituencies twice annually and to submit regular reports to the National Secretariat.[10] A controversial recommendation called for the provision of a secretariat expense fund. These centralizing efforts, intended to lessen the party's dependence upon the bureaucratic and traditional elites of the local Native Administrations, were not favorably received by high party leaders, and the Party Manager resigned in 1958.

ANCILLARY ELEMENTS

In 1958 NPC youth associations and women's sections were prevalent at local levels.[11] Neither of these auxiliaries was then permitted to organize above the provincial level.[12]

A departure from regional isolation was initiated in 1958, when the Congress reversed its policy of non-entanglement with any southern party and invited political parties as well as cultural associations to enter into alliances with the NPC for electoral purposes.[13] This decision reflected a compromise between the views of those who hope to "nationalize" the Congress and those who have resisted proposals to eliminate "Northern" from its name. Probably, the latter associate a regionalist name with the continuation of certain

---

gressive Association (1946-1949), President of the Zikist Movement (1947-1950), and President of the Freedom Movement (1951). The National Secretariat staff included an Administrative Secretary (Malam Garba Abuja), a Publicity Secretary (Malam Abubakar Tugga), three full-time organizing secretaries and nine organizers, four of whom were assigned to Ilorin Province and four to the Middle Belt.

[10] Northern Peoples' Congress: Program of Reorganization, Nos. 1 and 2, dated May 1, 1957; NPC Operational Scheme No. 1, dated May 3, 1957, NPC (NHQ) 190/34; National Secretariat Files, 493: Half Year Parliamentary Reports.

[11] An instance of unusual enthusiasm by one woman organizer was evinced in a report to the Party Manager as follows:

"At Shonga, there is a notable and reputable lady who has a great influence on females; the Galadima . . . called her and talked to her to join the NPC. She was the president of [a] traders social union . . . and changed her society into [an] NPC political party. 100 cards were issued to her freely and 10 badges. . . . She goes on tour of lecture and for enrollment. If Action Group members wish to find a girl or lady to marry, she often advised the fiancee not to agree until he joins the NPC." NPC National Secretariat File, Half Yearly Parliamentary Reports, No. 493.

[12] There seems to have been a regional Youth Association in 1953-1954 under the presidency of Malam Abdu Ado Ibrahim of Igbirra, later secretary of a wing of the United Middle Belt Congress, which displayed radical tendencies and was disbanded.

[13] Nigerian Citizen, December 4, 1957; Daily Times, January 11, 1958.

distinctive policies, notably, vigorous "Northernization" in the spheres of public administration and commercial activity, and the Congress' traditional opposition to female suffrage in the North. In May 1958 the NPC entered into an alliance with the National Emancipation League (formerly the National Muslim League) of the Western Region and Lagos.[14] During the federal election campaign of 1959, the NPC concluded an alliance with the Niger Delta Congress of Rivers Province in the Eastern Region which favored the creation of a separate Rivers State and won a federal seat in Brass Division.

In October 1958 there were ten "tribal unions" registered with the central secretariat as affiliated organizations: five associations of major political significance in non-Hausa areas of the North and five small groups of settlers in Kaduna and Minna. (See Table 1) Affiliates of a non-ethnic nature included an ex-servicemen's union, two student societies, two trade unions, including the important Northern Mine Workers' Union,[15] and a businessmen's association. Other business associations, notably the Northern Amalgamated Merchants' Union and the Northern Peoples' Contractors Union, are probably not recognized officially as affiliated bodies (although they may be regarded as such in certain localities), but their association with the NPC is intimate[16] and the NAMU has been allowed to submit resolutions to annual conventions of the Congress.[17]

THE NOMINATING SYSTEM AND PARTY DISCIPLINE

Theoretically, NPC parliamentary candidates are nominated by divisional or provincial executive committees, depending on which is the more effective unit of party control, subject to the approval of the National Executive Committee.[18] However, the major emirs

---

[14] Agreement of May 30, 1958, between the Northern Peoples' Congress and the National Emancipation League, signed by A. T. Balewa, Vice-President of the NPC (and other officers) and Hadji A. R. A. Smith, President of the NEL (and other officers).

[15] *Supra*, p. 337.

[16] *Supra*, p. 328.

[17] The Northern Amalgamated Merchants Union submitted a six-point resolution to the NPC annual convention at Kano in January 1958 condemning retail trade competition by alien merchants in the North. *Daily Times*, January 10, 1958.

[18] The following extract from a letter from the Secretary of the Central Working Committee to all Provincial Presidents, dated May 7, 1954, indicates the standard procedure for nominations in the federal election of that year:

"I am directed to inform you that there will be a meeting of the Executive of the NPC, of which you are a member, on 22nd and 23rd May at Kaduna.

"You are requested to be in Kaduna not later than May 21st. The meeting is highly important and one of the things to be discussed is the forthcoming General

OFFICIAL STRUCTURES OF MAJOR PARTIES

Table 1: Organizations and Parties Affiliated
with the Northern Peoples' Congress

Tribal Unions

Idoma State Union
Igbirra Tribal Union*
Offa Progressive Union of Ilorin Division
Idah Divisional Union of Igala Division
Biu Divisional Union of Bornu Province
Jami'yyar Bagarmawa (Tchad immigrants in Kaduna)
Chadd Tribal Union (Kaduna)
Igala Tribal Union (Kaduna)
Kabba Divisional Union of Minna

Occupational and Special Interest Groups

Northern Mine Workers Union
Motor Drivers Union, Jos
Northern Transport Owners Union, Zaria
Federation of Northern Ex-Servicemen's Union
University College Ibadan Students (Northern)
Nigeria Union of Great Britain and Ireland (Northern)
A section of the Women's Movement of Nigeria
Odo Ile, Okalle Egbe, Ibadan

Political Parties

North East Convention Peoples Party, Potiskum**
Ilorin Talaka Parapo/NPC***
National Emancipation League ****
Nigerian Commoners Liberal Party*****

Source: Northern Peoples' Congress National Secretariat File.

* *Supra,* p. 349, n. 46.
** At Potiskum in Fika Division (Bornu Province) the effective branch of the NPC is the North Eastern Convention People's Party which was organized in 1953 by Maina Waziri, MHR, the son of the Emir of Fika, to secure the unification of four local tribes: the Karekare, the Ngamo, the Bolawa, and the Ngizima (in order of their numerical size). This proved to be a difficult task for the Karekare and the Ngizima, original inhabitants of the area, incline to the Northern Elements Progressive Union, while the Bolawa and Ngamo (Gamawa), conquering tribes, tend to support the Northern Peoples' Congress.
*** *Supra,* p. 353.
**** *Supra,* p. 250.
***** *Supra,* p. 257, n. 67.

Elections for the new Federal House of Representatives. You are therefore asked to convene a meeting of your Provincial Executive Committee (NPC) and choose names of . . . candidates in your Province for submission to the Central Executive meeting at Kaduna on 22nd May. A most important condition to be strictly observed is that the men you choose must be ACTIVE members of the NPC or strong sympathizers of NPC. Anybody who is neither a member nor a sympathizer will not be accepted or backed by the NPC.

"I am to add that all this must be done in perfect secrecy and you must warn members of your executive against leaking out anything discussed or any name selected. If a selected candidate is not a member of your executive he must not be informed that he has been selected, but if his candidature has been approved by the Central Executive sitting on 22nd May at Kaduna then he may be informed." NPC (NHQ) File No. 306:94.

are known to have dominated the nominating processes in their jurisdictions. Probably, these processes were generally more democratic and consistent with formal party requirements in 1958-1959 than at any previous time. In Zaria, for example, aspirants for nomination were required to submit letters of application to the Provincial Working Committee (of 29 members) along with the endorsements of their respective district committees. Initial selections were made by the Working Committee subject to approval by the full Provincial Executive and ratification by a provincial conference which decided controversial cases.[19] Nevertheless, it seemed highly improbable that any individual who was unacceptable to a major emir would be nominated by the NPC.

Discipline cases and open conflicts among leaders of the NPC are comparatively rare, possibly as a consequence of the wholesale transfer of status and authority from the Northern Region's dominant social institution—the Native Authority system—to the government party. Since the election of the Sardauna of Sokoto as General President in 1954, there have been no rebellions against the leadership and only one discipline case involving a national officer.[20]

PARTY FINANCE

Party finance is an executive matter exclusively in the NPC and it is not discussed at plenary sessions of the annual convention.[21] Un-

---

[19] The writer witnessed two sessions of the Zaria NPC Provincial Conference in October 1958 at which time 6 of the 7 NPC candidates for Zaria Division were nominated. The Conference was attended by several hundred people, including executive members of the party, high officials of the Native Administration, wealthy traders, and a large number of women. Most of the conferees were small traders, farmers, and independent men who attended as delegates for their respective district committees. In one case, the delegates chose an applicant who clearly lacked the support of the provincial leadership.

[20] In 1958, Malam Abdul Razaq, the National Legal Adviser of the NPC, was relieved of his office by the National Executive Committee for having contested a by-election to the Federal House of Representatives in Zaria against the official candidate of the party. He was reinstated as National Legal Adviser in 1959. In 1956, Alhaji Yahaya, Madawakin Ilorin, was asked to resign as Minister of Health in the Northern Regional Government owing to his support of the Ilorin Talaka Parapo. *Supra*, p. 352. Both of these cases were the result of personal conflicts at the local level and neither one involved a threat to the authority of the national leadership of the party.

[21] It was reported that a delegate to the Kano Convention of January 1958 asked for the report of the Financial Secretary following a statement by the General Secretary to the effect that the party was short of funds. "Speaking from the chair, Alhaji Abubakar Tafawa Balewa said he regretted that he ever called on the delegate to speak. If he had known that the delegate would raise the question of funds in public [that is, at the annual convention] he, Alhaji Abubakar, would never have

doubtedly, the financial resources of the NPC have been less ample than those of the other major parties. The Northern government party lacks the backing of a large and affluent entrepreneurial class and it did not have the potential support of an African financial institution until the establishment of the Bank of the North in January 1960.

Revenue is derived from the following sources: enrollment and subscription fees; receipts from the sale of emblems, literature, etc.; levies on the salaries of parliamentarians and members of government boards; donations from wealthy members and supporters; income from public lectures; and social events. Theoretically, one-third of all enrollment fees (2s. 6d.) and subscriptions (1s. monthly) is retained by the branch, one-third goes to the provincial treasury, and one-third is remitted to the National Headquarters. But dues procedures have been spotty and the writer was reliably informed that National Treasury receipts from this source in 1958 were negligible. The writer was also informed authoritatively that parliamentary levies in that year were rated at 5 percent of the salaries of all members of the federal and regional houses, parliamentary secretaries and ministers.[22] These levies were paid directly to the National Treasury which normally returned one-third of the receipts to the provincial treasury of origin, although a greater percentage—sometimes 100 percent—was regularly returned to the Kano Provincial Organization, which has had the highest recurrent expense owing to the large and militant NEPU opposition in that province. Probably, the contributions of NPC parliamentarians and ministers to their party are no less than those made by their counterparts in other parties. They are the main financial donors to their local party organizations; occasionally the contributions of ministers as well as businessmen take the form of capital equipment rather than cash. Prior to the 1959 election, campaign expenditures were defrayed by the provincial organizations with minimal assistance from the Center. But in 1958 the Central Organization supplied each provincial organization with a party van and seemed to assume a more important role in campaign financing.

The National Council of Nigeria and the Cameroons— Northern Elements Progressive Union Alliance

Although the Northern Elements Progressive Union (NEPU) does accept the national leadership of the National Council of Ni-

---

allowed him a say on such a frivolous subject." Ebenezer Williams, "The North Reborn," *Daily Times*, January 27, 1958.

[22] The parliamentary levy was increased to 10% in 1959.

geria and the Cameroons (NCNC),[23] and the President-General of the NEPU, was the First Vice-President of the NCNC and Chief Whip for the NCNC/NEPU Alliance in the Federal House of Representatives at the time of independence, the NEPU scrupulously preserves its separate identity, which it appears to regard as a necessary condition to its continued effective operation in the Northern Region. Another basis of the separate identity of the NEPU may lie in the disparity between the social backgrounds of the NEPU leaders and the social backgrounds of the principal leaders of the NCNC. The former have comparatively minor connections with entrepreneurial interests which preoccupy many of the leaders of the NCNC, and they have little in common socially with the southern bourgeoisie. They might, therefore, be reluctant for ideological reasons to abandon the separate political identity of their party. Finally, the NEPU is a truculent opponent of the Northern Peoples' Congress. It was prepared to cooperate with all nationalist parties, including the Northern government party, to achieve Nigerian independence and to ensure the stability of the new nation, but it does not regard its participation in the Federal Governing Coalition as an obligation to abate the militancy of its opposition in the North. Possibly, the President-General of the NEPU preferred the position of NCNC Chief Whip to a ministerial office in the federal government under an NPC Prime Minister for reasons of this nature. At any rate, the separate identity of the NEPU is politically more convenient for both itself and its partner, the NCNC, than a merger would be, although a degree of amalgamation at the local level in the Northern Region has appeared desirable. In this chapter the distinct organization of the NEPU is discussed after that of the NCNC.

The National Council of Nigeria and the Cameroons: Primary Elements

Local Level

The NCNC has been a "direct," individual membership party since its Third Annual (Kano) Convention of 1951. Branches are formed at various levels of local government, and chapters may be organized at the ward level in urban areas. An amendment to the party constitution in 1959 designated the parliamentary constituency as the appropriate unit of branch organization.[24] The precise number

[23] In 1961 the NCNC changed its name to National Convention of Nigerian Citizens.

[24] National Council of Nigeria and the Cameroons, "Amendments to the NCNC Constitution," Art. IX, Sect. 1 (b). 1959. (Mimeographed.)

of registered branches had not been determined by officials of the National Secretariat in 1958.[25]

Every branch is required to have a committee of management, consisting of "the local branch officers, four representatives from each member-union and ten other members chosen at the general meeting of the branch."[26] In the Eastern municipality of Port Harcourt, where the NCNC is incontestably dominant, the chief concern of the party has been to secure effective control over the Municipal Council. For this purpose a Municipal Committee has been formed, comprising all NCNC elected councillors and specified members of the branch executive committee.[27] The Municipal Committee resolves disputes between party councillors, and carries out the decisions of the party with respect to the annual selection of the Mayor and Deputy Mayor by the Municipal Council. It is widely thought that its major accomplishment has been to guard against corruption in the affairs of the Council.[28]

In Eastern Nigeria, the principal level of sub-regional coordination is the divisional executive committee or divisional conference.[29] In Onitsha, for example, the divisional conference consists of the divisional officers, parliamentarians, two representatives from every local branch, and additional persons of influence, e.g., customary court members and the chairman of local government councils. This broad composition ensures that decisions of the conference will enjoy

[25] In his presidential address to the Eighth Annual Convention of the NCNC at Kano in June, 1959, Dr. Azikiwe stated: "According to the National Secretariat, there are now 315 branches of the NCNC scattered all over West Africa and the United Kingdom as follows: Eastern Nigeria 142, Western Nigeria 126, Northern Nigeria 37, Lagos 1, Ghana 5, Sierra Leone 2, Liberia 1, United Kingdom 1. These branches have a total membership of slightly over 500,000 financially active members." "Sixteen Months to Freedom." (Mimeographed.)

[26] *Ibid.*, Art. IX, Sect. 3.

[27] Port Harcourt NCNC Municipal Branch Minute Book, entries of September 13, 1956 and November 4, 1957.

[28] In June 1954 the Port Harcourt Town Council was dissolved by the government of the Eastern Region for improper conduct on the part of councillors, a few of whom profited as contractors from government loans which had been obtained by the Town Council for building purposes. Its successor, the present Municipal Council, has been subject to close party surveillance and no cases of improper conduct have been alleged. It may be observed that the introduction of party politics at the local government level has frequently been deplored as a source of corruption. Commentators have generally overlooked the influence of high-minded citizens in the nationalist political parties, as in Port Harcourt, where party control of the Municipal Council has had the effect of checking corruption.

[29] The Constitution of the NCNC provides for the formation of divisional executive committees (Article IX, Section 2) but no provision is made for the holding of divisional conferences, which appear to stand on an equal footing with the divisional executive committees.

wide support.[30] Sub-committees of the divisional executive are constituted for special purposes, as for example, to make recommendations to the divisional conference with respect to proposed legislation. In January 1958, the writer was present at a meeting of the subcommittee which discussed the Eastern Government's plan for administrative re-organization that was due for debate in the House of Assembly. Recommendations for the modification and implementation of the government's proposals were made by the sub-committee to the divisional conference, and there is no doubt that Onitsha legislators regarded the ensuing conference resolution as a mandate from their constituency in preparing statements for delivery in the NCNC Parliamentary Council and the Eastern House of Assembly.[31]

Much of the support enjoyed by the NCNC is based on the communal participation of socially cohesive ethnic groups. In Eastern Nigeria, the NCNC benefits from the tendencies of most Ibo people to identify it with their collective interests, as reflected in the bloc vote which netted all 50 Eastern seats in Ibo constituencies for the NCNC in the federal election of 1959. In non-Ibo rural areas of the Eastern Region, party organizers endeavor to enlist communal support through the medium of ethnic group and clan associations.[32] In the Western Region, communal branches have been noted previously among the Edo of Benin, and among the sub-cultural Yoruba groups of Ibadan, Oyo, and Ilesha.[33] The indigenous components of the NCNC in the first three of these towns are known by parochial names which reflect their unique origins: the *Otu Edo* (Edo Community) of Benin, the *Mabolaje* (Do not spoil the dignity of Chiefs) of Ibadan, and the *Egbe Oyo Parapo* (People's Party) of Oyo. In

[30] The writer witnessed a meeting of the Onitsha Divisional Conference on March 2, 1958, that was attended by nearly 150 people. Among the 14 chiefs present were the *Obi* of Nnewi, the *Obi* of Awka Etiti, the *Igwe Ezeokoli* of Nnobi, and the *Igwe Odile* of Obosi. There were at least five school proprietors or headmasters present in addition to several prominent businessmen and professionals. The meeting was addressed at length by the Premier of the Eastern Region, who represented Onitsha in the Eastern House of Assembly.

[31] See the remarks of Hon. E. Chidolue and Hon. P. N. Okeke, which reflect the recommendations of the NCNC Onitsha Divisional Subcommittee on the Government Sessional Paper. *Eastern House of Assembly, Official Report, Second Session, First Meeting, March-April 1958*, pp. 320-323, 365-366.

[32] In Ogoja and Ikom Divisions, the NCNC appears to have depended largely upon clan committees. The Divisional Organizing Secretary at Ikom reported his efforts to strengthen the party by affiliating the following non-traditional organizations: the Ofutop People's Union, the Ibo Union, the Amalgamated Union of Nde-Ofutop-Ukom Clans, the Ofutop Literary Youths Association, the Ukom Clan Union, the Ikom Divisional Union, the Ikom Branch of the Ndagasia Union, and the Boki Group Union. NCNC Eastern Working Committee/30: Ikom.

[33] *Supra*, pp. 253-256.

Ilesha, the NCNC is called simply the *Egbe Akuko* or "party of the cock" in Yoruba. The cock is the NCNC electoral symbol; it is a symbol of the nationalist awakening.

Regional Level

Regional components of the National Executive Committee were created by the Third Annual (Kano) Convention of 1951, but they were dissolved in the wake of the Eastern constitutional crisis of 1953 in order to enhance the unity of the National Council and to ensure the supremacy of its National Executive over potentially autonomistic regional leaders.[34] Following the acceptance of a federal solution to the Nigerian constitutional problem by the NCNC in 1953, the re-establishment of regional working committees was explored by a committee on organization of the Fifth Annual (Enugu) Convention of 1954 and settled by the Sixth Annual (Ibadan) Convention of 1955. The recommendations, embodied in the revised Constitution of the NCNC, prescribed explicit safeguards against the assumption of excessive powers by the leaders of the regional organizations:

"No regional conference or working committee shall implement a decision touching upon national policy without getting the approval of the NEC [National Executive Committee] for the said decision.

"Every regional working committee or conference shall at all times implement the decisions of National Executive Committee.

"The NEC may order the dissolution of a regional working committee which by its activities threatens the unity and harmony of the National Council, and shall as soon as possible, order a new election under the auspices of the NEC or the party. The action of NEC in this respect is subject to appeal to Party Convention without prejudice to the duty of the regional working committee to carry out the order of the NEC in the meantime.

"All party members of the House of Representatives or Regional House of Assembly elected in the region concerned shall be entitled to attend and participate fully in all regional conferences." (NCNC Constitution, Art. VII, 4-7)

The Eastern Working Committee was re-established by a regional conference in 1955 and Dr. Michael I. Okpara, then Regional Minister of Health, was elected to the chairmanship. In September 1957, Dr. Azikiwe, as Premier of the East, directed Dr. Okpara and two of his ministerial colleagues to resign their offices in the regional organization of the party on the ground that political disputes in which they had been involved were inimical to the harmony of the

[34] *Supra*, pp. 118-124.

government. The structure of the Eastern Regional organization is indicated by the composition of delegates invited to attend the regional conference of December 1957 at Onitsha, which elected a new working committee of non-ministerial vintage :[35]

1. All NCNC regional and federal legislators from the Eastern Region.

2. All officers and members of the Eastern Working Committee and Eastern members of the National Executive Committee.

3. Two delegates from each affiliated branch of the NCNC in the Eastern Region.

4. One delegate from each affiliated organization in the Eastern Region, i.e., from each branch of such organization.

In the Western Region, party organization remained fragmentary, although a Western Working Committee, comprising one member from each of 24 administrative divisions, was established under the chairmanship of Alhaji Adegoke Adelabu of Ibadan, the Leader of the Opposition in the Western House of Assembly. Apart from periodic meetings of the Working Committee, no regular conferences were held and the party relied upon a simple "zonal system" of organization, according to which a single prominent personality in every specified zone was assigned responsibility for the conduct of party affairs. In the Northern Region, the NCNC Working Committee, comprising a majority of non-indigenous settlers, was a skeletal body embroiled in persistent factional disputes.

In his presidential address to the Seventh Annual (Aba) Convention of the NCNC, Dr. Azikiwe deplored the lack of a "unified command" in the party and made specific critical references to the irregular procedures of the Eastern and Western Working Committees. He endorsed a particular finding of his special commission of inquiry into the affairs of the party in the Eastern Region to the effect that two delegates of a local branch (the Egede branch of Udi Division) had been wrongfully denied admission to the Second Annual Conference of the Eastern Regional Organization by the officers of the Eastern Working Committee on the spurious ground that the individuals concerned were members of the NCNC branch in the Enugu Municipality. This incident was related to the factional struggle in Enugu, in which, it may be recalled, the officers of the Working Committee were involved on one side and the National President on the other.[36] The National President affirmed emphati-

---

[35] NCNC Eastern Working Committee. Ref. No. NC/E.5 and Minutes of the Regional Conference of the NCNC, Onitsha, December 20, 1957.
[36] *Supra*, pp. 207-215.

cally a controversial ruling of his special commission of inquiry in favor of dual membership, which severely curtailed in principle the power of local leaders over dissident members:[37]

"The Commission is satisfied that once an NCNCer always an NCNCer —unless one resigns, is suspended or expelled; and once an NCNCer in one town always an NCNCer everywhere much more of one's own home town. Besides, it is the prerogative of each local branch of the NCNC to choose its delegates and not for the Regional Working Committee to dictate who should represent a branch."

Officials of the Eastern Working Committee objected to the National President's ruling on the ground that the admission of dual membership was inconsistent with the aim of branch discipline that his commission of inquiry was supposed to restore. But the National President appeared to regard arbitrary intervention by the Regional Working Committee in local affairs as a greater evil to be avoided.

National Level

THE CONVENTION OF THE NATIONAL COUNCIL. The NCNC Constitution provides for two kinds of national conventions—annual and special—both of which embody the supreme authority of the National Council. The right of representation at national conventions is extended to persons in three categories: "(a) Members of the National Executive Committee of the National Council (b) Two representatives from each affiliated branch. (c) All Parliamentarians of the party." (Art. IV, 1) In addition, party rules stipulate that the President and General Secretary of the NCNC Youth and Women's Associations as well as one officer from every branch of both associations may attend as representatives. (Rule IX, Reg. 4, f) That privilege has been extended to the third main auxiliary arm of the party, namely the Zikist National Vanguard. Every accredited representative and member of the convention is entitled to one vote. Except in the case of emergency, the National Secretary must give three months' notice of conventions to all those who are entitled to representation. Special conventions may be convened by the National Executive Committee or the Central Working Committee upon the initiative of either body or upon the request of one-third of the branches of the party. Fifty members, including the national officers, constitute a quorum.

[37] Report of the Proceedings of the Five-Man Commission of Inquiry Set Up by the National President of the NCNC, Dr. the Honourable Nnamdi Azikiwe, to investigate certain serious allegations against party leaders and officials in Enugu with a view to effecting peaceful settlement of outstanding disputes among them." (Typed copy), p. 21. Presidential address to the Seventh Annual (Aba) Convention of 1957. Pp. 17-18. (Mimeographed.)

The powers of the annual or special convention are listed in the Constitution (Art. IV, 6) as follows:

"To amend, repeal, or remake the Constitution.

"To remove from office any officer of the National Council.

"To elect any officer of the National Council provided for in the Constitution.

"To expel any member or member-union from the National Council.

"To dissolve any branch of the National Council.

"To make any levy on the member-unions.

"To decide any appeal against the decision of the National Executive Committee.

"To inaugurate any movement or decree any proceeding in the interests of the National Council and its members.

"To exercise all or any of the powers vested in the National Executive Committee or to direct the National Executive Committee to put such powers or any of them into operation.

"To appoint any sub-Committee or sub-Committees and to invest every such sub-Committee with such powers as may be deemed necessary or advisable and to define their duties.

"To remit for further consideration of the National Executive Committee any decision of that body, and to give such directions in relation thereto as may be deemed expedient.

"It shall govern the National Executive Committee.

"To do such other things whether of the kind before specified or otherwise as may be necessary or desirable in the interest of the National Council or its members."

It is stipulated that "every decision of every Annual and Special Convention shall (be) final and conclusive and shall be binding upon all the branches and shall be accepted by all the branches as the voice of the whole of the members of the National Council." (Art. IV, 7)

Eight annual and five special conventions were held by the National Council during the 12-year span, 1948-1959.[38] Possibly the

[38] The time, venue, and major significance of each of the nine annual and four special conventions between 1948 and 1959 may be tabulated thus:

First Annual Convention, Kaduna, April 1948: This convention was termed the "National Assembly." It adopted the Freedom Charter, which was the outline of a Nigerian national constitution, as the supreme law of the National Council, and empowered the National President to appoint the national officers, termed the Federal Cabinet.

Second Annual Convention, Lagos, April 1949: This convention appears to have been held under inauspicious circumstances in the wake of a sharp controversy between the party leadership and leaders of the Zikist Movement, several of whom

report and discussion of the proceedings of the Seventh Annual (Aba) Convention of 1957 in Chapter V[39] conveys an impression of the free-wheeling spontaneity for which the conventions of the NCNC are generally known.

THE EXECUTIVE COMMITTEE AND OFFICERS OF THE NATIONAL COUNCIL. Article VI of the NCNC Constitution provides for a National

---

had been imprisoned for alleged seditious activities. A decision was taken to introduce individual membership.

Third Annual Convention, Kano, August 1951: This convention transformed the National Council from an indirect into an individual membership party in preparation for the general elections of November 1951. It abolished the cabinet system, whereby national officers were appointed by an elected President, and instituted a system of direct election of officers by the convention. Federalism was abandoned in principle and unitary government for Nigeria was sanctioned as party policy.

Fourth Annual Convention, Lagos, August 1952: This convention, held prior to the Eastern Regional crisis of 1952-53, appears to have been concerned with the unsettled question of whether or not the NCNC should cooperate with the government in giving the new constitution a "fair trial." It was overshadowed by a subsequent meeting of the National Executive Committee, dominated by parliamentarians, that resolved to work within the constitution.

Special Convention, Jos, December 1952: Three central ministers, who were not amenable to control by the party leadership, were expelled and the decision of the National Executive Committee to accept the Macpherson Constitution for the term of a "fair trial" was reversed.

Fifth Annual Convention, Enugu, January 1954: The role of the NCNC delegation to the London Constitutional Conference of July and August 1953 was debated at length and endorsed. In effect the convention approved a return to federalism, although unitary tenets were affirmed insofar as the party stood for the vesting of residual powers in the central government and for the division of the three regions into smaller units or states.

Sixth Annual Convention, Ibadan, May 1955: A revised constitution was adopted providing for the recreation of regional Working Committees. "Radical" members of the NCNC Youth Association were disciplined and expelled for alleged acts of insubordination. Youth Association activities were curtailed by the imposition of an age limit of 25 years.

Special Convention, Oshogbo, April 1956: The main order of business was preparation for the Western Regional election of May 1956.

Special Convention, Onitsha, July 1956: The Premier and ministers of the NCNC government of the Eastern Region were instructed to remain in office and to submit to the Commission of Inquiry appointed by the Secretary of State for the Colonies to inquire into the conduct of the Premier and the affairs of the African Continental Bank. However, the Commission of Inquiry was condemned as a manifestation of imperialism and a threat to the NCNC and the welfare of the country.

Special Convention, Lagos, April 1957: Delegates assembled to discuss the NCNC program for the forthcoming London Constitutional Conference of May and June, 1957. However, the convention was marred by recriminations among the top leaders, by a sharp dispute over the election of officers and by an attempt on the life of the National President that he related to intra-party conflict.

Seventh Annual Convention, Aba, October 1957: A motion that restored the cabinet system of party government was carried after a heated debate. It em-

Executive Committee of 42 members (including national officers);
they meet no less frequently than every quarter and they constitute
the steering committee of the annual or special convention.

"Every decision or order of the National Executive Committee shall
be binding on members, member-unions, and affiliated branches, subject
to appeal to the next succeeding Annual convention, and every member
of the National Council agrees that this Clause shall be of full force or
effect, and that no order or decision of the National Executive Committee
whatever shall be questioned, reversed, controlled, or suspended except
by way of appeal as aforesaid." (Section 7)

Over the years, most major decisions of the NCNC have been
made by full conventions rather than executive action. On occasion,
decisions of the NEC have been overruled by conventions—e.g., the
Jos Convention of 1952 overruled an earlier decision of the NEC to
give the Macpherson Constitution a "fair trial."[40] Meetings of the
NEC are not immune from the air of participant spontaneity that
pervades the party in convention. Some of the famous NEC meetings
have been, in effect, "little conventions," distinguished by a presidential address that is released to the press.

Nine national officers (President, First and Second Vice-Presidents, Secretary, Treasurer, Auditor, Legal Adviser, Publicity Secretary, and Financial Secretary) compose the Central Working Committee[41] which is empowered to manage the affairs of the party
between meetings of the NEC. The Seventh Annual (Aba) Convention empowered the National President, who is elected by the
Annual Convention, to appoint the other national officers, but the
system of annual election for all officers was restored in 1960.
The National President is empowered to make "final and binding interpretations" of any clause of the Constitution (Art. XIII) and to fill
vacancies in the National Executive Committee which would otherwise exist for a period of six months. (Rule VI, 3)

---

powered the National President to choose the National Officers of the party.
The age limit imposed on the Youth Association in 1955 was rescinded.

Special Convention, Enugu, January 1958: The convention met to consider allegations by the National President against leading members of the party at Lagos,
involving fractional organization and public utterances detrimental to the party.
Disciplinary measures initiated by the Central Working Committee and the
National Executive Committee were approved.

Eighth Annual Convention, Kano, June 1959: Preparations were made for the
federal election of December 1959. The party manifesto and the nature of the
understanding between the NCNC and the NPC were discussed at length.

[39] *Supra*, pp. 195-203.   [40] *Supra*, p. 121.

[41] In 1959 two Assistant National Secretaries (for political and financial matters)
were added.

The constitution does not provide for sectional representation in the NEC, but it is customary for members to be selected from the constituent regions and from groups which have been important in the nationalist struggle. At the Aba Convention, 35 members were chosen as follows: 4 Northern Region, 4 Eastern Region, 4 Western Region, 4 Lagos, 2 Southern Cameroons, 3 Parliamentary Leaders (one each from the Federal, Western and Eastern Legislatures), 6 women, 2 NCNC Youth Association, 2 Zikist National Vanguard, 2 Trade Unionists and 2 Ex-Servicemen. Representatives of these several groups caucused separately on the convention floor and submitted candidates to the entire House for approval or decision in the event of competing nominations. The National President was empowered to select additional members to replace any of those who might be appointed by himself to a national office.

The National Executive Committee may appoint sub-committees,[42] and in June 1958, a "Strategic Committee," comprising the nine officers of the Central Working Committee and seven additional members of the party was set up to direct the affairs of the party during the Reform Committee crisis, and to initiate a program of reorganization.[43] This *ad hoc* committee acquired a measure of permanence and assumed responsibility for preparation of the party's policy for the Resumed Constitutional Conference of 1958. Recommendations from the NEC concerning the Nigerian Constitutional arrangements were referred to the Strategic Committee which sifted them for the party's delegation.

Parliamentary Parties of the NCNC

During the final phase of colonial rule in Nigeria, there were three NCNC Parliamentary Parties: the Federal Parliamentary Party formed the federal government in coalition with a more numerous group of legislators belonging to the Northern Peoples' Congress; the Eastern Parliamentary Party provided the government in the NCNC's strong region; the Western Parliamentary Party constituted an Opposition in the regional stronghold of the Action Group. In the Northern House of Assembly, the NCNC was represented indirectly by six members of the Northern Elements Progressive Union, comprising less than 5 percent of the membership of that House. All parliamentary parties were required to select "a Leader,

---

[42] It is required to set up three standing sub-committees for finance, discipline and general purposes.

[43] NCNC National Executive Committee, Official Minutes of the meeting held at Lagos, June 15, 1958, p. 7.

Deputy Leader, Chief Whip, Secretary, Whips and other officers considered necessary to form a Steering Committee." (Rule IV, Regulation 11.)

As in the case of the British Labour Party, the non-parliamentary origins of the NCNC created a "problem of extra-parliamentary control."[44] This gave rise to the Eastern government crisis of 1952 which culminated in victory for those who were committed in principle to centralized extra-parliamentary control. *The NCNC Constitution, Rules and Regulations* of 1955 (in effect at the time of writing) sought to preclude a repetition of the threat of parliamentary autonomy. It was stipulated that "all Parliamentary Parties are subject to guidance of the Central Working Committee in the first instance and are also subject to the scrutiny of the NEC and Party Conventions in that order." Federal and regional ministers are nominated by the National President "in consultation with the NEC and the Parliamentary Party concerned." (Rule IV, Regulations 5 and 7.) In 1958, the supremacy of the extra-parliamentary organization was upheld following the expulsion by the National Executive Committee of the Federal Parliamentary Leader.[45] In accordance with the NCNC Constitutional Rule IV, 3, the Parliamentary Party was required to pass a vote of no-confidence in the Parliamentary Leader in order to effect his deposition. The National President acknowledged that his authority over the Federal Parliamentary Party, to which he did not belong, was external, and he attended the crucial meeting as an observer only.

Under Dr. Azikiwe, the Eastern Parliamentary Party met at the beginning of every session and as often thereafter as required. There was no separate back-bench organization; indeed there were no back-bench caucuses in any Nigerian Legislative House, and any attempt to create one would probably have been regarded by the leadership concerned as a subversive move. Although a generally effective liaison between the government front bench and the back benches was maintained by the Chief Whip and subordinate whips, ambitious and conscientious back-benchers were known to feel that government policies were formulated without sufficient consultation.[46] As in the

---

[44] ". . . the PLP (Parliamentary Labor Party) was in a sense *thrust into* Parliament by the Labour and Socialist movements outside. This raised from the beginning the problem of extra-parliamentary control, and it is important to trace the process by which the PLP established its right to independence of such control." R. T. McKenzie, *British Political Parties* (New York: St. Martin's Press, 1955), p. 385.

[45] *Supra,* pp. 223, 227.

[46] Harold J. Laski made a similar criticism of the Parliamentary Labour Party.

British House of Commons, a member who fails to attend a meeting of the House or to vote with the party when a three-line whip is imposed may be disciplined by the Parliamentary Party. However, the leadership of the NCNC has endeavored to strike a balance between solidarity and tolerance of individual opinion. As a rule, private members may express their opinions on the floor of the House provided they vote with the government on matters of policy.[47] Dr. Azikiwe has taken the position that party government does not require the regimentation of speech in the House; he suggested to his fellow parliamentarians that the accepted right of a private member to criticize the government was the Eastern Region's contribution to the practice of parliamentary democracy in Nigeria.[48]

Secretariat Organization

In 1958 the NCNC maintained a National Secretariat at Yaba (Lagos), and regional secretariats in Enugu, Ibadan, and Kaduna. Administrative secretaries directed small staffs at the National and the Eastern Regional Headquarters, but the principal organizing secretaries of the Western and Northern Regions were responsible for the conduct of both administrative and field activities in their respective areas. Divisional organizing secretaries were employed in the East only where they were required to submit monthly reports to the principal organizing secretary.

Party Rules stipulate that "the National Headquarters shall co-ordinate the activities of the Regional Working Committees" (Rule VIII, 7); the latter are primarily responsible for organization. However, in 1957, central party leaders took the position that inadequate central control had produced failures of party discipline as well as failures of organization.[49] The *West African Pilot* declared frankly that "the party machine, by which we mean the organizational machine, is faulty to an extreme.[50] Shortly thereafter, the

---

"In fact," he wrote, "the whole structure is really an elaborate façade behind which little that is effective really takes place. The meeting of the Parliamentary Party usually lasts for one hour in each week of the session, so that few of its members ever get the chance of serious speech, and the Minister, almost invariably, has the last word." *Reflections on the Constitution* (N.Y.: The Viking Press, 1951), p. 78.

[47] Similarly in the British Labour Party, "it is virtually a conventional rule that, while a member may speak against his party where his conscience is involved, he will refrain from voting against it in the division lobby." *Ibid.*, p. 77.

[48] Journal notes on proceedings of the NCNC Eastern Parliamentary Party, at the Eastern House of Assembly, Enugu, March 12, 1958.

[49] "Proposals for Party Organization," Appendix D to the Official Minutes of the Seventh Annual Convention of the NCNC.

[50] "Above Party and Office," *West African Pilot*, May 12, 1958.

Strategic Committee of the NEC decided to appoint a Territorial Organizing Secretary to coordinate and supervise organizational activities in all regions. In 1959 this office was embodied in the party constitution as National Organizer, a paid official, responsible for the implementation of party policies and the conduct of elections, holding office at the pleasure of the National Executive Committee.[51]

ANCILLARY ELEMENTS

Auxiliary Groups

The NCNC Constitution provides for the organization of a Women's Association, a Youth Association, and the Zikist National Vanguard. These associations are forbidden to present candidates for election or to print separate membership cards. Their local branches are required to accept the guidance of the party executives in their areas. Yet the associations are authorized to have national organizations, and to hold annual conferences. Each of their branches is represented at party conventions by one delegate and their central bodies are represented in the National Executive Committee.

THE NCNC WOMEN'S ASSOCIATION. This auxiliary has operated on a regional basis mainly. Annual conferences of the Eastern Region Women's Organization have expressed the desire of politically conscious women for a greater share in government, especially in the patronage system as members of public boards and corporations.[52] The President of the NCNC Women's Organization in the Western Region at the time of writing was Mrs. Funmilayo Ransome-Kuti, the famous President-General of the Nigerian Women's Union[53] and former Treasurer of the NCNC Western Working Committee. Mrs. Kuti, a school teacher and proprietor, is a leading advocate of the right of women to vote and to stand for election. Her Women's Union has campaigned militantly for the suffragette cause in the North on a non-partisan basis, and she contested for the Federal House as an independent in 1959 when the NCNC refused to adopt her as the official party candidate in Abeokuta. No women contested in the Eastern Region, but the First Vice-President of the Eastern Women's Organization, Mrs. Margaret Ekpo, was appointed as a Special Member of the newly formed Eastern House of Chiefs in 1959.

[51] National Council of Nigeria and the Cameroons, "Amendments to the NCNC Constitution," Article V, Section 6a.

[52] Official Reports of the First and Second Annual Conferences of the NCNC Women's Organization, Eastern Region, July 6, 1956 and May 11, 1957. NCNC Eastern Working Committee File No. 42.

[53] *Supra*, p. 62, and p. 251, n. 52.

THE NCNC YOUTH ASSOCIATION. After the Zikist Movement was declared unlawful in April 1950, radical youth sought alternative channels of expression. Neither the revolutionary Freedom Movement nor its successor, the Convention People's Party of Nigeria and the Cameroons, were able to survive the constitutional and electoral surges of 1951, and the former Zikists decided to return to the fold of the NCNC. They organized the NCNC Youth Association on January 28, 1952,[54] and they played a major role in support of Azikiwe's effort to assert the authority of the NCNC Central Working Committee over recalcitrant ministers in the Eastern and Central governments. Most of them believed strongly in the radical principle of a unitary state, and they were bitterly disappointed when the party leadership agreed to the "regionalist" constitutional departure of 1954. In 1955 moderate and conservative leaders of the party tried to render the Youth Association ineffectual by the imposition of a constitutional age limit of 25 years. But a few die-hard branches of the Youth Association, e.g., the well-organized and highly motivated Port Harcourt branch,[55] resisted the age ban, and their determination was rewarded in 1957 when it was rescinded by the Aba Convention.

THE ZIKIST NATIONAL VANGUARD. This is one of the least well-understood elements of the NCNC. It was maligned in 1958 by the Colonial Office's Commission of Inquiry into the Fears of Minorities as the only "single item" among the grievances and fears of cultural minorities in the Eastern Region that seemed "formidable by itself."[56] That questionable judgment appeared to rest on the Commission's acceptance of an allegation by two federal ministers of the NCNC that the Vanguard was Dr. Azikiwe's "private army." Undoubtedly, these particular ministers were personally disturbed by

[54] See the article by V. Olu Fayemi in the *West African Pilot*, November 19, 1957.
[55] In 1958 the militant Port Harcourt branch of the Youth Association virtually controlled the efficiently managed Port Harcourt Divisional branch of the NCNC. The President of the Youth Association was Second Vice-President of the branch and branch records indicated that all of the members of the branch executive committee were proposed by the Youth Association. In fact, 80% of the members of the branch executive committee were also members of the Youth Association. Furthermore, an influential civic group, the Port Harcourt Rate and Taxpayers Association, was, in reality, an unofficial arm of the Youth Association. Its president was the vice-president of the Youth Association and it was utilized whenever the party required a "nonpartisan citizens" platform, as in January 1958, when a public protest against propaganda for the creation of a separate Rivers State was deemed appropriate during the sitting of the Minorities Commission in Port Harcourt.
[56] Colonial Office. *Report of the Commission appointed to enquire into the fears of Minorities and the means of allaying them* (London: 1958), p. 46.

the existence of the Vanguard. Ethnic minority leaders in the Eastern Region who opposed the NCNC were well aware that the Vanguard had been organized in the course of a struggle between rival NCNC cliques.[57]

[57] The origin of the Zikist National Vanguard is obscured in the mists of intra-party politics. It is reported to have been inaugurated formally on November 16, 1955, to commemorate Dr. Azikiwe's birthday. The National President was then in England on an economic mission and the Eastern Government's Commission of Inquiry into Bribery and Corruption had just begun to hear evidence against the Eastern Minister of Finance, Mbonu Ojike. The first President of the Zikist National Vanguard was barrister Adeniran Ogunsanya of Ikorodu and Lagos, later President-General of the NCNC Youth Association. Mr. Ogunsanya had defended two leaders of the Youth Association during their "trial" by the Ibadan Annual Convention of May 1955, which resulted in their expulsion and in the imposition of the 25-year age ban. (*Supra*, p. 150.) Six months later, Dr. Azikiwe, who approved the disciplinary measures taken against the Youth Association, appeared to sanction the recrudescence of youth militancy in a new organizational guise.

The Vanguard became a principal auxiliary of the NCNC as a direct consequence of the Colonial Secretary's inquiry into the Eastern Premier's connection with the African Continental Bank. Dr. Azikiwe's reputation was tarnished by the report of the Foster-Sutton Tribunal of Inquiry and the National Executive Committee decided that the entire government must resign with the Premier in order to demonstrate its solidarity in the face of an attack upon the conduct of the party leadership in the field of economic planning. Every expedient, including the militant Vanguard, was utilized by the NCNC in its campaign to return the government in the Eastern Region election of March 1957. In January 1957, the Vanguard held its first national convention at Port Harcourt. Mr. Ogunsanya was re-elected President-General in absentia, and the members adopted a plan of campaign financing that was destined to ruin several of them financially and breed bitterness within their ranks.

Eighteen members of the Zikist National Vanguard, representing five branches, accepted loans from the African Continental Bank totalling £5,400. (NCNC National H.Q. File, Statement of Accounts dated March 18, 1958; "Zikist National Vanguard Accounts with the African Continental Bank Limited: Report for the NEC." 1959.) Few of the young men involved had personal means to cover their debts; they planned to devote most of the money to the expenses of the election campaign, and to use the remainder for organizational and commercial purposes. The latter, they hoped, would be remunerative and enable them to repay their loans from the bank. Possibly the motivation of private gain was not absent from their calculations. At any rate, the President-General appears to have regarded the plan as imprudent. He resigned from his office, and was succeeded by the Secretary-General, Mr. Adewale Fashanu, a former Zikist and journalist with the Zik Press. Mr. Fashanu was appointed as Chairman of the Eastern Nigerian Printing Corporation and assumed the private office of political secretary to the Premier of the Eastern Region.

It is reported that £4,571.9.1 was expended during the election campaign and that the debtors were unable to repay their loans to the African Continental Bank which instituted court actions against them for recovery. (*Ibid.*)

Of course the Vanguard personalities involved were chagrined. Some of them had opened accounts with the African Continental Bank on the basis of their loans which had been collected from them by Vanguard officials and used to purchase motor vehicles and campaign equipment. The Vanguard appealed to the Central Working Committee of the NCNC to take over the bad debts as an election expense

The record of the banned Zikist movement plainly shows that the use of Azikiwe's name by a political group is not conclusive evidence of Azikiwe's control.[58] It was not wholly uncharacteristic for leaders of the Vanguard to have been involved in the anti-Azikiwe movement of 1958. Their support of the Mbadiwe group discredited the Vanguard in the eyes of many partymen and strengthened the hand of those leaders, including high officials of the Eastern Working Committee, who were anxious to eliminate the Vanguard, which they regarded as an agent of disunity and confusion.[59] In 1958 it seemed likely that steps would be taken to effect a merger of the Vanguard with the revived NCNC Youth Association, inasmuch as both organizations had identical purposes and overlapping interests. However, their respective leadership groups appeared to guard their organizational positions as jealously as the parliamentarians they

---

or to intercede with the bank (the Managing Director of the African Continental Bank, as National Auditor of the NCNC, was a member of the Central Working Committee) in order to prevent the attachment of the property of the debtors. When the party leadership made no move to liquidate the debt, Vanguard elements became bitterly resentful. In June 1958, three Vanguard leaders from Aba and one from Port Harcourt were among the signatories to the petitions demanding that Azikiwe resign forthwith from the Premiership of the East and the Presidency of the NCNC.

Previously, J. R. Nwachuku, one of the Vanguard signatories to the "Zik Must Go" petition, authored a tract entitled, "The Spirit of the Zikist National Vanguard," which suggested the growing disillusionment of the Vanguard membership. One passage reads as follows:

"What is disorganizing and disintegrating the NCNC today? The Real workers are cast aside *Because They Are Poor*; and the slothful, lazy, grabbing Doctors, Lawyers and Big Businessmen simply step in to purchase with money what they did not work for. What is the spelling of political loyalty today? Money. In this commercial age, everything is purchasable. You may work like a jackass from dawn till dusk for a party; you may sting with the tongues of men and of angels (or demons if you like), you may even give up your body to be burned for your Party, but when the time for the 'Sale' of Office comes, and you have no Money (not charity or Political Conviction, mark you!)—all your exertions profit you nothing." NCNC Eastern Working Committee, File No. 11: 1.

[58] *Supra*, pp. 72-80.

[59] It was alleged that political opportunists formed Vanguard branches in order to overthrow the regular leadership of established branches. For example the secretary of the Okopedi Branch of the NCNC reported to the Principal Organizing Secretary of the NCNC in the Eastern Region that Vanguard organizers entered into an agreement with a dissident wing of the local branch, called a mass meeting and "deposed" the branch leadership. NCNC Eastern Working Committee, File No. 20: Enyong Division. In Bende Division, the Vanguard was organized in opposition to Dr. M. I. Okpara, while the latter was Chairman of the Eastern Working Committee. At Port Harcourt, the local Vanguard was the center of antagonism to an efficient branch organization. At Enugu, the majority of the local Vanguard supported the Association For One Nigeria when that group under settler leadership organized in opposition to the regular NCNC. *Supra*, p. 212.

habitually criticize guard their offices.[60] The Vanguard affirmed its individuality by sending a large delegation to the first All African Peoples' Conference at Accra.

Affiliated Parties

Apart from its major ally, the Northern Elements Progressive Union, which is discussed below, all but one of the parties affiliated with the NCNC in 1958 were local organizations—e.g., the Ilorin Araromi Congress in the North,[61] and the Nigerian Commoners Liberal Party of Oshun Division in the Western Region, whose leader cooperated with the NCNC Federal Parliamentary Party.[62] The principal exception was the Dynamic Party which was granted affiliation by the National Executive Committee in August 1958.

THE DYNAMIC PARTY. This party is the creation of Dr. Chike Obi (Ph.D. Cantab.), a mathematician and lecturer at the University College of Ibadan.[63] Dr. Obi holds that "the only sane ideology for Negro nationalists in general and Nigerian nationalists in particular is the ideology of Kemalism" by which he implies the "total conscription . . . or totalitarian mobilization of all the nation's cultural, spiritual, economic and political resources" in order to ensure the military security and rapid progress of newly liberated African states.[64]

---

[60] "The party has two militant youth wings, the Zikist National Vanguard and the NCNC Youth Association. Their aim is to foster the interest of the party and uphold its principles. What do we find? Both organizations are not at peace with each other. Morbid rivalry. This is undesirable. The two movements must merge into one organization. A move was made in this direction but ran into the bugbear of ambition. It is a necessary step though." "Above Party and Office" Part 3, *West African Pilot*, May 14, 1958.

An annual conference of the regenerated Youth Association in December 1957 passed a resolution prohibiting dual membership in the two rival auxiliaries.

[61] The Ilorin Araromi Congress was inaugurated on December 5, 1956 under the leadership of its founder Mr. Jimoh Adelabu, a founding member of the Ilorin Talaka Parapo (Ilorin Commoners Party) who resigned from that party in October 1956 in opposition to its acceptance of the West merger principle. The Araromi Congress affiliated with the NCNC on May 10, 1958. Another Northern party which may have been allied to the NCNC in 1958 was the Benue Freedom Crusade under the leadership of Hon. H. O. Abaagu, MHR. In 1959 it allied with the Northern Peoples' Congress, and Mr. Abaagu, who lost his seat in Tiv Division, was appointed to the Federal Senate.

[62] *Supra*, p. 257, n. 67.

[63] The Dynamic Party appears to have been organized by Dr. Chike Obi in 1951. The founders are reported to have included S. G. Ikoku, Ayo Ogunsheye, P. O. Balonwu and M. O. Ezumah, all of whom were associated with socialistic movements in the early 1950's.

[64] Chike Obi, *Our Struggle, A Political Analysis of the Problems of the Negro Peoples' Struggling for True Freedom* (Yaba, Lagos: 1955), pp. 52, 56. Dr. Obi's belief in the necessity of a "regimental" state in Nigeria appears to rest on two

Oddly, the first President of the Dynamic Party was Akenzua II, the *Oba* of Benin, who accepted the office in 1954. However, the President was regarded as a figurehead and excluded from membership in the Central Executive Committee of the party.[65] Effective power was vested in the office of the Secretary General, which has always been occupied by Dr. Obi. Branch secretaries are subject to the control of the Secretary General, who may dismiss them at his discretion, and the bylaws which govern the activities of branches require his personal approval.[66]

Heretofore the political influence of Dr. Obi has been minimized by observers, most of whom appear to believe that the Dynamic Party exists on paper only and in the persons of Dr. Obi and a few lieutenants. There is evidence of serious organizational activity in 1955, when the Central Executive Committee decided to campaign against "parliamentary democratic self-government in 1956." On the basis of this appeal, the Dynamic Party sought with candid opportunism to win the support of those intellectuals who did not believe in parliamentary democracy for Nigeria and other persons who did not believe in self-government.[67] Yet, in principle, Dr. Obi is a militant

---

assumptions: first, that a weak Nigeria will be easy prey for aggression from South Africa (*ibid.*, pp. 26-28) ; secondly, that the Negro race will not achieve equal dignity with other races until Negro states have overcome their relative material backwardness. He writes in that vein as follows:

"For the fools who would rather die for their 'democratic freedom of speech' in a colonial country than *LIVE* and help in 'paying the price' in personal restraint and personal discipline for the upliftment of their backward RACE and for the guarantee of REAL DEMOCRATIC FREEDOM for their descendants and probably for themselves—for such fools no amount of light is bright enough for them to see." *Ibid.* p. 36.

"What humiliates us and creates in us painful indescribable feelings, experienced and capable of being experienced only by slighted colonials, is not that we are not advanced at all—we are more advanced than our grand-parents—what makes our souls rebel in this world of RACIAL DISCRIMINATION and its concomitant evils is our backwardness relative to the Anglo-Saxons and other imperialist peoples." *Ibid.*, p. 45.

For an appreciation of this point of view see Isaiah Berlin's discussion of "the search for status" in his *Two Concepts of Liberty* (Oxford: Clarendon Press, 1958), pp. 42-44.

[65] *The Memorandum and Protocols of the Dynamic Party* (Ibadan: 1957), p. 7.

[66] Ordinances of the Dynamic Party, Section II, pp. 14 and 19.

[67] Minutes of the Meeting of the Central Executive Committee of the Dynamic Party, April 3, 1955. These minutes indicate that the use of the term Kemalism to describe the ideology of the Dynamic Party was equally opportunistic and employed to overcome objections by "sentimental critics." They also indicate that the Dynamic Party absorbed the Nigerian Self-Government Fiasco Party; these parties are reported to have "coalesced" prior to the Western Regional election of 1956. Philip Whitaker, "The Western Region of Nigeria, May 1956," *Five Elections in Africa*, ed. W. J. Mackenzie and Kenneth Robinson (Oxford: The Clarendon

if idiosyncratic and controversial nationalist. He is widely respected among supporters of the NCNC and he has served as the secretary to the NCNC delegations to the London Constitutional Conferences of 1957 and 1958. In 1960 he succeeded Dr. Azikiwe, whom he admires greatly, as the member of the House of Representatives for Onitsha urban constituency when the National President of the NCNC became President of the Nigerian Senate. Shortly afterward, Dr. Obi was expelled from the NCNC for his persistent virulent criticisms of party leaders in the federal government, and the affiliation of the Dynamic Party was terminated. In January 1961 he was prosecuted by the federal government for criminal sedition arising from the publication and distribution of a pamphlet in Lagos.[68] For the first time in the new nation's history, the Federal Supreme Court was confronted with a case involving freedom of political speech. It reversed the conviction, finding the prosecution an abridgement of the freedom of expression guaranteed by the Nigerian Constitution.

Affiliated Non-Party Groups

Prior to the Kano Convention of 1951, the NCNC was an indirect membership party based on affiliated member-unions. These were mainly tribal unions, i.e., ethnic group associations organized by educated and progressive persons in various towns and villages throughout Nigeria. Tribal unions formed by "sons abroad" in the new urban areas of southern Nigeria were among the principal centers of cultural enlightenment and nationalist activity during the inter-war and immediate post-war period. Most of the tribal unions which affiliated with the NCNC at the time of its inception in 1944 and during a period of about 10 years thereafter were in fact settler associations domiciled in Lagos.[69]

Press, 1960), p. 26. Dr. Whitaker also reports that Dr. Obi was removed from the leadership of the Dynamic Party in 1956 for having declared his support for immediate self-government for Nigeria on the occasion of the Foster-Sutton Tribunal of Inquiry into the affairs of the African Continental Bank. *Ibid.*, p. 26. However, his removal from the leadership was temporary if it ever was effective.

[68] It is reported that the alleged seditious utterance was contained in a pamphlet written by Dr. Obi, entitled "The People: Facts You Must Know." An objectionable passage reads: "Down with the enemies of the people, the exploiters of the weak and the oppressors of the poor. . . . The days of those who have enriched themselves at the expense of the people are numbered. The common man in Nigeria can today no longer be fooled by sweet talk at election time only to be exploited and treated like dirt after the booty of office has been shared among the politicians." *West Africa*, January 7, 1961, p. 18.

[69] Records of member unions in the National Headquarters of the NCNC list 143 unions, including 120 ethnic group associations, 95 of which had Lagos addresses.

The NCNC Constitution of 1955 provided for two kinds of membership: (a) individual and (b) "associate or organizational membership . . . open to political parties, tribal unions, professional associations, social and literary clubs, etc., as distinct from single persons." (Art. VIII, 1.) However, member-unions were required to affiliate with local branches and their right to independent representation at the National Convention was withdrawn. (Rule III, 2.) Consequently, many tribal unions are formally affiliated with the NCNC at branch and divisional levels, but the National Executive Committee takes cognizance of them only in respect of financial subscriptions, appeals and matters of discipline. (Art. VI, 6; Art. VIII, 8 and 9.) To this writer's knowledge, no member-union of the National Council has ever been expelled by the National Executive Committee.

The Nominating System of the NCNC

Party rules require the Divisional Executive Committees (Constituency Executive Committees in 1959) to invite applications from aspirants for nomination and to submit their selections to the Regional Working Committee concerned. Nominations are then referred to the Central Working Committee and final approval by the National Executive Committee is required before the names of candidates may be published by any branch. In the event of a disagreement, the decision of the National Executive Committee is deemed final. (Rule V, Regulations 1, 8, and 9.)

Five criteria for selection are prescribed. The candidate must have been a member of the party in good standing for not less than two years, he should be "a maximum vote getter," he must be "nationalistic in his ideals and activities," he should have "an unimpeachable record of past performances," and be able to express himself clearly in the English language. (Rule V, Regulation 2.)[70] In many divisions applicants are required to deposit £100 with the Executive; the sum is returned to those who are not chosen. All candidates are required to sign a loyalty pledge formulated by the NEC (Rule V, Regulation 3.)

Nomination is really a function of the local organizations, and the latter jealously guard their rights to choose official party candidates. In general, sons of the soil possess an enormous advantage and the primacy of local control is conceded in principle by the central party leadership.[71] In practice, the NEC exercises much less supervision and

[70] Prior to 1959, at least one Divisional Executive Committee, that of Port Harcourt, nominated its parliamentary candidates on the basis of an allotment of points to every applicant for each of the prescribed criteria.

[71] An exception to the rule of local choice was made in 1957 when the National

control over local executive committees in matters of nomination than do the central executive bodies of the British Labour or Conservative Parties.[72] It rarely proposes candidates to the local organizations, it does not screen candidates prior to their adoption by the divisional executives, and it rarely fails to approve a candidate after his adoption by a local executive. Therefore it is imperative that divisional or constituency executive committees be properly constituted and recognized as legitimate representative bodies by all regular branches in their areas. Improperly constituted executives, i.e., committees which do not obtain periodic renewal by means of election or committees which are but partially representative of their constituency branches, invite factionalism and electoral defeat.[73]

At local council levels, the NCNC has been plagued by the recurrent organizational vice of partially representative branch exec-

---

Executive Committee and the Eastern Parliamentary Party, meeting jointly at Enugu on January 18, decided to dissolve the Eastern House of Assembly, and go to the country on the issue of the conduct of the Premier and the Eastern Government with respect to the African Continental Bank. In order to obtain a full vindication from the electorate, the NEC resolved that all incumbent members of the House of Assembly should be renominated. This ruling was resented in several constituencies where members of the party were dissatisfied with their incumbent representatives, and in Catholic circles generally where a new election was viewed as an opportunity to effect a reversal of government policy with respect to parochial schools by replacing some of the old members with others who were favorable to the Catholic position. (*Supra*, pp. 187-188.) The authority of the NEC was tested at Port Harcourt where the Divisional Executive Committee objected strenuously to the renomination of an assemblyman who had been expelled locally but remained a member in good standing of the Parliamentary Party. The NEC appointed a sub-committee to investigate the dispute and a report was issued which expressed sympathy for the position of the divisional executive but insisted upon adhesion to the ruling of the NEC on the ground that any deviation permitted in one constituency might result in a general upheaval in others where unpopular members had been renominated for the sake of the larger principle at stake in the election. Report of the Committee appointed to investigate the dispute at Port Harcourt under the Chairmanship of Dr. G. C. Mbanugo, NCNC Eastern Working Committee File No. 31 : Port Harcourt.

[72] See R. T. McKenzie, *op.cit.*, pp. 217, 551-553. The power of the NCNC N.E.C. to consider nominations by divisional executive committees and to resolve disagreements is much less absolute than the power of the National Executive Committee of the Ghanaian Convention Peoples Party "to approve candidates for Central Government Elections from lists prepared and submitted by the Constituency Executive Committees." *The Constitution of the Convention Peoples Party of Ghana*, VII, 4.

[73] For example, the NCNC Eket Divisional Executive Committee which made nominations for the May 1958 by-election to the Eastern House of Assembly did not appear to have been representative of the division as a whole and the party was defeated soundly by candidates of the Action Group. Probably the Calabar-Ogoja-Rivers State issue was far a more decisive factor than organization, but there is no doubt that the electoral chances of the NCNC were reduced by an inefficient nominating procedure.

utive committees. A flagrant example in recent years was the Enugu branch executive of 1958 which came under the control of a faction that was unable to secure a majority in the Enugu Municipal Council.[74] Party rules give no instruction to local branches on the conduct of nominations for local elections. In the Enugu controversy, the NEC merely supervised the election to the branch executive committee which was left to its own devices in making nominations for the Municipal Council. The "out" faction was prepared to hazard disciplinary action in order to test its popularity with the electorate. In these circumstances, i.e., in urban areas where factions compete for the control of a single dominant party, an alternative method of nomination would appear to be desirable, but none appeared to be in the offing in 1958.

PARTY DISCIPLINE

In his presidential address to the Aba Convention of 1957, Dr. Azikiwe declared that the powers of the President under the constitution of the party were inadequate to the needs of party discipline. He insisted that presidential powers to suspend members, to dissolve party organs, and to revoke the certificates of insubordinate branches were urgently required. These proposals were sidetracked by barrister Olowofoyeku's famous motion for a "cabinet system" of government involving the appointment of all national officers (or members of the Central Working Committee) by the National President.[75] While this motion did not confer additional powers on the President directly, its effect virtually fulfilled Dr. Azikiwe's request, owing to the fact that party rules stipulate that defiance of constitutional rulings of the Central Working Committee may incur disciplinary action. (Rule X, 1, d.) These rules provide further that publications by members of the party may be actionable if "in the opinion of the NEC or General Working Committee" they constitute "an attack on the party or on a member of the party in party affairs, or (are) calculated to affect adversely the reputation of the party."

In November 1957, following the Aba Convention, two NCNC federal ministers made statements to the press which, in the view of the Central Working Committee, were detrimental to the reputation of the party.[76] Thereupon the Working Committee took action to censure one minister and suspend the other. The party constitution makes no provision for the initiation of disciplinary action by the

[74] *Supra,* pp. 210-212.
[75] *Supra,* p. 196.
[76] *Supra,* p. 204.

Central Working Committee, but the NEC approved both actions, possibly setting a precedent to be followed in future cases.[77] Subsequently, the Special Convention of January 30, 1958, accepted a verbal clarification by the National Legal Adviser to the effect that every organ of the party has the right of trial in the first instance save the convention itself which has the right of appeal only.[78]

The NCNC is widely regarded as a tumultuous party. It is more correct to say that the NCNC has been a vanguard party in a tumultuous era. Most struggles for power within the NCNC have reflected conflicts of interest that run deeper than personality conflict and would have occurred in another form if they had not erupted within the party. By any fair standard the NCNC is distinguished by the quality of stable leadership[79] and by the loyalty of the rank and file of the party to its elected officers, in particular to Nnamdi Azikiwe. Since the First Annual Convention (Kaduna National Assembly) of 1948 and with the exception of the Eastern crisis of 1952-1953, there have been comparatively few cases of disciplinary action involving top level party leaders.[80]

[77] Minutes of the National Executive Committee, Enugu, January 29, 1958.

[78] Yet there have been notable cases in which the convention itself has exercised the right of trial, e.g., the expulsion of the central ministers by the Jos Convention of December 1952 (*supra*, p. 120) and the expulsion of two leaders of the NCNC Youth Association by the Ibadan Convention of May 1955, after a "trial" that is reported to have lasted for five hours. *Daily Times,* May 6, 1955 (*Supra*, p. 150).

[79] Three of the nine national officers in 1958 were members of the NCNC Cabinet in 1947, 5 were national officers in 1954 and 3 others were members of the NEC or prominent parliamentarians at that time. Of the 46 members of the NEC elected at the Fifth Annual Convention of 1954, 26 were still members of the NEC or active party leaders in another capacity in 1958. Of the 10 who were associated with rival parties in 1958, 3 were Northerners who went over to the NPC, one was a Northerner who joined the Action Group, 2 others became leading members of the Action Group and 4 were associated with the Reform Committee of 1958.

[80] M. A. O. Williams, a vice president of the NCNC, was expelled by the Kaduna Convention and readmitted into the party ten years later by the Aba Convention. Three NCNC central ministers were expelled by the Jos Special Convention of 1952; subsequently, A. C. Nwapa was readmitted into the party and appointed to the board of an Eastern statutory corporation; Okoi Arikpo became a leader of the Action Group, and Dr. Eni Njoku, Professor of Botany, University College, Ibadan, became Chairman of the Electricity Corporation of Nigeria and was appointed to the Nigerian Senate in 1960. Most of the 6 Eastern ministers who were expelled from the party in February 1953 following their refusal to resign in obedience to the direction of the N.E.C., appear to have returned to the party. Two radical youth leaders were expelled by the Annual Convention of 1955; subsequently, one of them, Hon. O. C. Agwuna, MHR, was readmitted and appointed as General Secretary of the Zikist National Vanguard; Mokwugo Okoye, an influential author, has since become General Secretary of the NCNC Youth Association. In June 1958, five leaders of the NCNC Reform Committee, led by Dr. K. O. Mbadiwe and Chief Kolawole Balogun, were expelled by

Expelled members may be readmitted by the Party Convention, although a period of probation may be imposed, and members expelled with dishonor cannot be taken back for seven years. (Rule X, 10, 11.) But this rule is not observed in all cases—e.g., the youth leaders who were expelled with dishonor in 1955 were readmitted in 1957. At a meeting of the NEC on June 14, 1958, the National President announced that the Central Working Committee had authorized a general amnesty for all persons who were expelled or suspended during the previous year. At least one member of the NEC questioned the right of the National President or the Central Working Committee to grant a general amnesty, but the issue was merely academic inasmuch as the few individuals affected left the party in the company of Dr. Mbadiwe.

A similar remission of penalties by edict was effected by the leadership of the Eastern Parliamentary Party in 1958. Previously the NEC and the Parliamentary Party had decided that a non-member who contested as an independent candidate and declared for the NCNC following his election might be accepted into the party, but that any member of the party who stood against an official candidate and won would not be admitted into the Parliamentary Party. Mr. P. U. Amaefuna, a member of the party, stood against its official candidate in Awka Division and was elected. Inasmuch as there were extenuating circumstances, the Parliamentary Party leadership decided to admit him into the Parliamentary Party over the protest of the Eastern Working Committee. The latter's only recourse was an appeal to the Central Working Committee which was not pursued since it was unlikely to succeed. Party rules are not categorical on the imposition of extreme penalties for standing against an official candidate and provide for an inquiry into the facts of every case. (Rule V, 5) In matters of discipline, as in other matters, Parliamentary Parties are subject to the "scrutiny" of the NEC and party conventions; the Standing Orders of the Eastern Parliamentary Party merely acknowledge that all cases of disciplinary action imposed on members of the legislature must be reported to the National Executive Committee.[81]

---

the NEC following their repudiation of Dr. Azikiwe. Within three years, Dr. Mbadiwe and Chief Balogun had been readmitted to the party.

[81] Standing orders of the NCNC Parliamentary Party—Eastern Region, Orders 4 and 5.

PARTY FINANCE

Responsibility for the finances of the National Council is vested in three national officers: the National Treasurer, the National Financial Secretary and the National Auditor. In addition, the regional working committees are required by the party constitution to include elected treasurers and auditors. In 1957, the regional organizations did not submit adequate financial statements to the National Treasurer, as a result of which the National Auditor was unable to submit a comprehensive statement of the finances of the National Council to the Seventh Annual Convention, as required by the constitution. The report of the National Auditor was criticized vigorously by members of the Aba Convention, who were disturbed by the deficits and accounting irregularities which had been disclosed with candor in the hope of reform. At length, the National Treasurer was provoked to declare that the financial report was wholly truthful if disappointing.

It was reported that the National Council incurred an expenditure of more than £15,000 for the Eastern General Election of 1957 and nearly £6,000 in connection with the Foster-Sutton Tribunal of Inquiry into the affairs of the African Continental Bank. The "excess of expenditures over revenue stood at £28,864 .5 .10d." Furthermore, "the Party's outstanding liability in respect of [the African Continental] Bank overdraft [amounted] to £97,259."[82] In that statement the dire threat that a failure of the Bank posed for the party was apparent.

In 1956, the National Executive Committee decided to establish a consolidated account to receive payments of all funds collected in the regions. The Eastern Working Committee contributed over £4,000 to the central consolidated fund in order to finance party operations during the bank crisis.[83] However, the regional working committees were authorized to retain an amount equal to their home operating expenses and payments to the consolidated account declined precipitously in 1957. In early 1958, the credit balance of the Eastern Working Committee totalled £520, most of which was committed to the immediate payment of staff salaries.[84]

[82] National Auditor's Report on the accounts of the party (NCNC) for the Period April 1, 1955, to September 30, 1957.

[83] "An Address to the Second Annual Conference of the NCNC in the Eastern Region by Dr. M. I. Okpara, Chairman of the Eastern Working Committee" (Mimeographed), p. 8. The Eastern Region is the electoral and financial core area of the NCNC and the Eastern Working Committee contributed £1,300 to the Western Regional campaign fund of 1956. Report by the Principal Organizing Secretary to the Second Eastern Regional Conference of the NCNC, September 1957.

[84] NCNC Eastern Working Committee Executive Paper No. 2/58: Finance.

In addition to overdrafts on the Bank, the party relied upon four main sources of revenue as follows:

(1) Affiliation fees, membership subscriptions, and dues collections. Branches are required to pay affiliation fees of 21 shillings; member-unions pay affiliation fees of 21 shillings, divided among the National Headquarters, the divisional headquarters, and the branch through which the union registers, in the proportion of 2:1:1; Nigeria-wide organizations pay an entrance fee of 5 guineas to the National Headquarters; individual members purchase cards at the price of 1/- (one shilling) each, of which 6d. is paid to the National Headquarters, 3d. to the divisional headquarters and, 3d. is retained by the branch; monthly dues of 6d. is shared evenly between the branch and the Divisional Executive.[85]

(2) The sale of party constitutions, at 2 shillings each, and other items—e.g., lapel buttons—which netted over £7,000 prior to April 1955.[86]

(3) Levies on the salaries of members of the legislative houses and beneficiaries of patronage. This is the main continuing source of party funds; it amounted to approximately £5,000 in the period April 1955-September 1957. The levy embodies a principle of the nationalist movement: those who are elected to office must not forget that their perquisites are incidental to the cause and they must devote a fixed percentage to the party. Delegates to the Kano Convention of 1951 resolved that elected assemblymen would be required to pay one-fourth of the emoluments of their offices to the party treasury,[87] but that amount was reduced subsequently to 10% to be levied on the salaries of ministers, parliamentary secretaries, assemblymen, representatives, and political appointees to public boards and corporations.[88]

The leaders of the several parliamentary parties were directed to ensure that all members honored their obligations to the party.

Salaries paid to organizational employees, other than office assistants and drivers, varied from £500 p.a. paid to the Principal Organizing Secretary to £180 p.a. paid to divisional organizing secretaries. Auditors Certificate for the Accounts of the Eastern Working Committee, 1956.

[85] NCNC Constitution, Article VIII, 5 and 6; Article IX, 1; NCNC National HQ Circular, Reference No. 90/1.

[86] The party suffered a heavy financial loss when many of the buttons went rusty in storage. National Auditors Report (cited above).

[87] *Daily Times*, September 8, 1951.

[88] Ministerial salaries in 1958 were £3,000; premiers and the Prime Minister were paid £4,000, parliamentary secretaries and chief whips, £1,500 and ordinary members of the houses £800. However, the Eastern Government cut the salaries of the Premier, ministers and parliamentary secretaries by 10% in January 1958.

Many of the members instructed the African Continental Bank to make regular transfers from their private accounts to the party account, a procedure that was recommended by the Finance and Organization Committee of the Fifth Annual Convention of 1954 and adopted by the Eastern Working Committee in 1956. Nevertheless, assemblymen, representatives, and beneficiaries of the patronage system have been notoriously remiss in their obligations to the party, and in 1957 the Auditor of the Eastern Working Committee commented as follows:[89]

"It will be noted that of £8,150 estimated revenue for NCNC members of the Eastern House of Assembly and Statutory Boards, only £5,321 was actually realized. This is because less than half of all the (floor) Members of the House were willing to pay or did pay their 10% party levy. In the case of Parliamentary Secretaries, some of them found it necessary to descend to the level of issuing cheques to the party and writing the Bank the next minute not to honour the cheques. It is therefore necessary to devise a means whereby ungrateful and doubtful members of this party should be disciplined. *Not* more than two members of Statutory Boards and Corporations paid their 10% levies."

In 1957 the parliamentary levy in the East lapsed completely, owing primarily to expenses incurred by all assemblymen in their campaigns for re-election. Members of the several houses complained generally that the levies were evaded regularly by board members who enjoyed the benefits of patronage without the expenses of electioneering. At the Enugu Special Convention of January 1958 a stern resolution was adopted empowering party leaders to "withdraw the Party Whip and patronage from all members who are in arrears for more than six months in respect of the 10% party levy."[90]

(4) Donations by members and supporters of the party. This is a highly irregular and variable source of funds. In 1955, the Eastern Region (NCNC) Finance Committee advised the Working Committee to call upon contractors and other businessmen who were

[89] Auditors Certificate for the Accounts of the Eastern Working Committee for the year ending 31 December 1956.

[90] "Motions intended for the N.E.C. and the Special Convention at Enugu on 29 and 30 January 1958." Subsequently, the West African Pilot commented on delinquencies in the payment of levies as follows:

"The NCNC has a debt of more than £10,000 to collect from its legislators throughout the federation. Very few of them have paid the 10 percent surcharge to the party fund since 1957. Yet these are the very men who expect the administration of the party to function well. You can't run a party without funds and if ministers and legislators who are fattened with the taxpayers' gold won't discharge their obligation to the party, what moral right have they to expect the average member to pay his regular subscription?" "Above Party and Office (3)" *West African Pilot*, May 14, 1958.

sympathetic to the party for donations.[91] Appeals of this nature have been fruitful, but private donors often expect compensations in the way of patronage or contracts which may be embarrassing to responsible leaders of the party.[92] In 1957, the Second Annual Conference of the Eastern Regional Organization attempted to stimulate and regularize donations by providing for the compilation of a "Roll of Honour" that would include the names of persons who contribute "financially and morally above the average."[93] In addition, all members of the party were asked to pay a general levy of £1.[94] Neither scheme was put into effect, but the idea of a £1 levy on all members was adopted by the National Treasury in 1958 in connection with its plan to establish a Central or Omnibus Membership Registry.[95] Initially, the results of the registry scheme were not encouraging.

ELECTORAL FINANCING. The official expenditure of £15,000 on the Eastern Regional election of 1957 hardly indicates the actual cost of that campaign to the party, its candidates or their supporters. Most candidates were allotted £300 by the National Executive Committee while those who stood in riverain constituencies, where the cost of transportation was especially high, were given £400. In a few safe areas, where party organization was strong and the opposition feeble, approved candidates spent little if anything more than their allocations from the central campaign committee. Elsewhere, campaign expenses were as high as £2-3,000, and candidates were obliged to draw upon their private resources or to rely upon financial support from their friends or from partisan tribal unions. Items of expense included transportation, propaganda materials, remuneration of agents, and

[91] NCNC Eastern Working Committee File No. 11:24.

[92] A businessman who had been a heavy donor wrote to the Eastern Working Committee to the effect that he had been overlooked in the distribution of favors. Apart from a small job, he remonstrated, the government had not given him any work for a long time. He was not asking for a contract, but he did think that some self-examination by the party was in order to see if it had been fair to its loyal supporters. NCNC Eastern Working Committee File No. 11:35.

[93] "The Roll will be compiled in three categories. Those who have, in the course of our struggle for self-government, suffered privations by way of imprisonment, fine and/or detention will form a class. Another class will be made up of those who have been arrested, tried and acquitted in courts of law, for political offences as well as those who have, in other ways, suffered other forms of imperialist victimisations either in their employment, business or in private lives as a result of their active participation in the nationalist struggle. A third category will include those who have contributed financially and morally above the average, to the cause of the NCNC." NC/ E.57/213, November 12, 1957; and "Roll of Honour, An Address to the Second Annual Conference of the NCNC, Eastern Region, by Dr. M. I. Okpara, Chairman of the Eastern Working Committee."

[94] Eastern Working Committee NC/ E. 57/221.

[95] Circular letter to all branches, July 15, 1958.

good-will expenditures in the form of entertainment and gifts to villagers. Some of those who did not possess the wherewithal required went into debt in the hope of recouping their losses by means of their future emoluments. By and large, the candidates were drawn from the social strata of persons who could afford to pay the high cost of the campaign.[96]

Publicity is a normal secretariat function, but the NCNC depends almost wholly upon the *West African Pilot* and other commercial newspapers, nearly all of which are members of the Zik Group. This formidable apparatus of opinion formation is discussed in the next chapter.

The Northern Elements Progressive Union

The Northern Elements Progressive Union (NEPU) is a simply structured, highly centralized party based on "direct," individual membership.[97]

Primary Elements

At the local level, NEPU organization does not adhere strictly to the pattern of state administration. In general, there are two effective levels of party organization—the branch, at the urban and rural district level, and the provincial executive. Annual provincial conferences elect provincial committees which, in turn, choose working committees. Supreme authority at the central party level is vested in the Annual Conference (which has never failed to meet) attended by branch representatives and the representatives of local youth and women's sections. "Formerly, the President-General was elected annually, but at the Jos Convention of 1960, M. Aminu Kano was elevated to the position of Life-President. Four party officers are selected by the Life-President, and the others chosen by a committee consisting of one representative from each of the 12 Northern Provinces plus Kano City, over which the Life-President presides. The Life-President also submits a list of candidates for membership of the National Executive Committee to the Annual Conference for its approval.

[96] The writer was reliably informed that candidates in closely contested constituencies in the Western Region spent up to £3,000 of their own money in the federal election of 1954 and the regional election of 1956. One prominent NCNC personality spent about £800 in a successful campaign for election to the Lagos Town Council in 1956. Naturally, those assemblymen and representatives who assume debts during the course of a campaign are apt to resent the imposition of the 10% party levy on their salaries.

[97] The only edition of the NEPU constitution available in 1958 was published in Hausa: *Jam'iyyar Neman Sawaba, Manufa, Sharudda da Ka'idodi* (London: n.d.)

A great deal of party business is in practice conducted by sub-committees, the most important of which are Elections and Finance (chaired by Aminu Kano)."[98] The party maintains a well-staffed and highly efficient National Secretariat in Kano. In 1958 a paid provincial organizer for each of the 12 Northern provinces was appointed on a full-time basis from among the members of the National Executive Committee.

ANCILLARY ELEMENTS

These include the women's wing, the youth association, and several tribal unions. The NEPU women's organization, under the leadership of Malama Gambo Ahmed Sawaba, is a political factor of growing importance in the North.[99] Its chief immediate interest is the campaign for female suffrage in the North. At its Second Annual Conference in July 1958, the Women's Wing resolved to affiliate with the All-Nigeria Women's Union, under the leadership of Mrs. Funmilayo Ransome-Kuti, President of the NCNC Women's Organization in the Western Region.[100]

The NEPU youth movement has a curious history and certain peculiar features. In 1952 youth supporters of Malam Aminu Kano in Kano City organized an auxiliary known as the Askianist Movement—after Askia the Great, a 16th century Songhay king who conquered the old Hausa states and earned a reputation for enlightenment. Possibly the Askianists were inspired by the example of the militant Zikists, but their efforts were comparatively inept and the movement was dissolved in 1954; it was succeeded by a

[98] The writer is indebted to C. S. Whitaker, Jr., for this excerpt which appears in a chapter by the two of us on Nigerian political parties in the forthcoming volume, "Political Groups in Tropical Africa," edited by J. S. Coleman and C. G. Rosberg, Jr.

[99] In 1951-1952 Malama Gambo was trained for politics under the direction of Malam Aminu Kano at the NEPU school for "agitation and propaganda" in Kano. In 1953 she convened the first meeting of the NEPU Women's Wing in Kano but she was arrested with about 200 other women, all of whom were sentenced to a month in prison by an Alkali Court. Malama Gambo was imprisoned on several occasions thereafter and once deported from Kano as an agitator. In 1956 she served half of a six-month prison sentence before her conviction was finally reversed by the High Court of the Northern Region. (See *supra*, p. 361, n. 76.)

[100] Report of the Second Annual Conference of the NEPU Women's Wing held at Jos July 13-16, 1958. Two suffragette resolutions were passed requesting that Northern women be given two seats at the resumed Constitutional Conference and proclaiming a day of fasting by the NEPU women and their sympathizers. But a third resolution requested the regional government "to pass a law prohibiting women from smoking cigarettes in public."

Eleven officers were elected in addition to 4 field secretaries and 5 patrons. Fourteen were Hausa, 3 Fulani, 2 Nupe and 1 Idoma; only 2 were Christians.

highly successful NEPU youth association, known as the *Reshen Samarin Sawaba* ("Freedom Youth Wing," in Hausa).[101] About the same time, religiously inspired youths at Kano under the influence of certain *Mallamai* (Qu'ranic teachers) inaugurated an association known as *Zaharal Haq*, meaning "the Truth is Out." The "Truth" was the NEPU itself, because it stood for freedom and for a purer form of religion that was not corrupted by customary authoritarianism. Youth in their middle teens may have joined "Z-H" following the proscription of political activity on the part of children by the Emir of Kano in August 1954.[102] It has since become a wholly secular youth auxiliary of the NEPU for boys between the ages of 12 and 18. Two other small groups, the *Tab'iunal Haq* ("Those who follow the path") and the *Nujumu Zaman* ("Start of the Day") are linked to the NEPU Youth Association, as is the *Muftahul Haq*, an association for the promotion of Muslim education in Kano City.

Tribal unions comprise a relatively minor component of the NEPU ancillary structure. Five tribal unions were listed by the National Headquarters Secretariat in 1958, one of which, the Habe Tribal Union of southern Bauchi, is an affiliated political party.[103]

THE NOMINATING SYSTEM, PARTY DISCIPLINE, AND FINANCE

Parliamentary candidates of the NEPU are selected by constituency election committees subject to the approval of Provincial election committees, each one meeting under the chairmanship of a provincial

[101] The principal organizer and moving spirit of the Askianist Movement is reported to have been Malam Mudi Spikin, a popular young writer of political songs. His close associates in the movement were Malam S. A. Tanko Yakasai (later Assistant Secretary General and Publicity Secretary of the NEPU) and Malam Mustafa Dambatta (now a journalist with the Gaskiya Corporation). The leaders of the movement conducted a public subscription for the construction of a school but there seem to have been irregularities in accounting which led to the expulsion of the president of the movement in 1954. Thereupon the movement was dissolved and the R.S.S. (NEPU Youth Association) was formed as its successor. Malam Mudi Spikin then organized a short-lived National Liberation Movement; he may have negotiated with the Action Group before he affiliated with the Northern Peoples' Congress in 1954.

[102] The first President of *Zaharal Haq* was Nasidi Kofar Wombai, a leatherworker of about 24 years of age; the incumbent President is Sadi Gambari, a Kano bicycle rentier of about 25 (in 1958).

[103] The other four affiliated tribal unions were the Kilba State Union of Adamawa, the Adamawa Congress, the Katagum Peoples' Union of Bauchi, and the Ngizim-Karekare Tribal Union (GKTU) of Fika Division in Bornu. The last-named union is reported to have been converted wholly into branches of the NEPU in 1958.

organizer who is a paid official of the central organization. All nominations are subject to ratification by the National Election Committee, chosen by the Annual Conference. In 1958 joint NEPU/-NCNC executive bodies, known as supreme councils, were established in the principal urban areas of the Northern Region in preparation for the federal election.[104] Candidates of the Alliance, invariably indigenous Northerners and therefore NEPU members, were chosen by these joint committees, which were also responsible for electoral financing.

Until 1960 the internal life of the NEPU had been relatively placid; the only intra-party conflict of consequence involved an attempt by a former President to replace the NCNC alliance with an Action Group tie, an idea that was rejected at the Lafia Conference of 1954 by an overwhelming vote.[105] Thereafter the need for discipline was minimized by effective centralization of authority buttressed by the immense loyalty and admiration of the rank and file for their leader, Malam Aminu Kano. Rare infractions of party discipline were punished promptly and sternly.[106]

In 1960 NEPU, as an ally of the NCNC, became a partner in the coalition governing the Federation. Inevitably, militant members of the party were offended by this gesture of conciliation toward the Northern Peoples' Congress. For the first time, Aminu Kano was subject to principled criticisms from dedicated members of the party who had been his most ardent admirers. Splits in the party and significant declarations of support for the Action Group were reported. In the regional election of 1961, the NEPU, weakened by disillusionment and dissension, managed to win only one seat in the House of Assembly.

[104] In some cases, as in Jos, the composition of the Joint Executive Committee was based on equality of party representation. Elsewhere, as in Kaduna, there were NEPU majorities. See the *Constitution of the Kaduna Capital Territory (NEPU/-NCNC) Supreme Council* (Kano: 1958).

[105] Malam Abba Maikwaru, then Vice President, was expelled from the NEPU by the Lafia conference for conducting an unauthorized negotiation with leaders of the Action Group.

[106] In 1957 the NEPU National Executive Committee expelled one of the party's most influential parliamentarians, Hon. Isiaku Gwamma, MHA (Jos Town), for a violation of party doctrine. Hon. Gwamma proposed in the House of Assembly that members be given monetary advances by the government for the purchase of private cars. Northern Region House of Assembly Debates, *Official Report*, March 6, 1957, p. 605. In principle NEPU opposes the bestowal of rewards upon legislators, which widens the gap between them and the people and seems to elevate all legislators into the privileged class. There is little doubt that the expulsion of the popular legislator had an adverse effect on the party in Jos, as it lost control of the Jos Town Council shortly thereafter.

The NEPU has no independent source of revenue apart from subscriptions (1 shilling membership fee and 6d. dues monthly); prior to 1959 it did not receive more than token assistance from the NCNC. Its total budget in 1957 was on the order of £4,000.[107]

THE ACTION GROUP OF NIGERIA

The Action Group of Nigeria (AG), which forms the government of the Western Region and the official Opposition in the Federal, Eastern, and Northern Legislative Houses is the best organized, best financed, and most efficiently run political party in Nigeria. With respect to effective central direction, the Action Group ranks with such well organized and highly disciplined parties as the Convention People's Party of Ghana, the Democratic Party of Guinea, and the Malian Party of African Federation.[108] It differs from the latter parties in its relative de-emphasis of personalized leadership, and it adheres rigorously to rules of democratic procedure. Action Group organization is patterned on the British party model as modified by the requirements of Nigerian political strategy and indigenous social institutions.

PRIMARY ELEMENTS

Local Level

The Action Group has been an individual membership party since the time of its founding in 1951. The right of membership is extended to all Nigerians and all persons resident in Nigeria of 16 years or more of age (the age of liability to taxation in all regions). Branches in all regions are established at the basic level of local government—the district or local council in the West, the local or urban county council in the East, and the district or town council in the North. In cities and towns, the "basic element" or mass participation unit is apt to be the chapter or sub-branch in a local government electoral ward while the regular branch meeting includes representatives of the wards.[109] In certain rural areas, as among the Ibibio

---

[107] Auditors Report to the Seventh Annual (Ibadan) Conference of the NEPU, September 1957.

[108] The bitter struggle between the Premier of the Western Region and his party's leadership in 1962 did not seem to require qualification of this appraisal as this study went to press.

[109] For example, in the federal capital of Lagos, the basic membership element was the Action Group unit in each of the 42 local electoral divisions of the 8 primary wards. In 1958 each divisional unit had a chairman, a secretary, and an executive committee which met weekly; a general meeting of the divisional organization was held every month. Control of the party in the Lagos Town Council

people of the Eastern Region, Action Group organization has been adapted to the traditional clan system.[110] Two special cases of local organization involving dependence upon traditional institutions will be examined in the next chapter.

AG organizational policy now prescribes the formation of all branches at the level of the local government electoral ward.[111] In 1958 there was no comprehensive central register of branches.

In the Western Region, branches are coordinated by regional constituency organizations which coincide with one or more local government units. The right to attend meetings of the regional constituency organization is extended to all members of the party who represent their wards in local government councils, all parliamentarians who represent the constituency in the Houses of Assembly and Representatives, all officers of branches in the constituency, candidates to the regional legislature, chiefs "who are interested in the affairs of the party," and 4 to 6 representatives of every local government ward unit.[112] Constituency organizations are required to have officers as follows: President, Chairman, Vice-Chairman, Secretary, Treasurer, and Propaganda Secretary. Federal constituency meetings in the West are limited to the purpose of nominating candidates to the Federal House.

---

was vested in a "Parliamentary Committee," comprising all Action Group councillors, a few traditional members of the Council who were loyal to the Action Group, and several other leaders of the party.

[110] Among the Ibibio people of the Eastern Region, the village is the fundamental unit of social organization. A variable number of villages compose a clan, which has been defined as a "descent group whose members feel they have a common ancestry but who cannot trace this relationship." (G. I. Jones, *Report of the Position, Status, and Influence of Chiefs and Natural Rulers in the Eastern Region of Nigeria*, Enugu: 1957, p. v.) As a rule, Action Group branches in Ibibio areas have been established at the local council level, a level of local government which is intermediary between the village and the clan. In some divisions, party meetings at the clan level were unofficial elements of the party structure. In other divisions, as in the Action Group stronghold of Uyo Division, the clan committee was an official element of the structure of the party and clan officers were elected by the committee. A Divisional Executive Committee comprising representatives of the ten clans of Uyo met under the chairmanship of an influential sub-chief of one of the clans, who was chairman of his clan committee and chairman of the Uyo Taxpayers Association—an unofficial auxiliary which assisted party supporters in appeals against undue assessments, etc. As in the Western Region, where *Obas* (Paramount Chiefs) attend divisional conferences of the Action Group in their ex-officio capacities as patrons of the party, clan heads in the East who support the party are encouraged to attend meetings of their divisional executive committees.

[111] Report of the Committee on Party Organization, Fourth Annual Congress, 1958, p. 1; Action Group of Nigeria, "Constitution, Revised Draft," p. 7, para. 18. (Mimeographed.)

[112] Circular letter No. 2/57, May 17, 1957; "Constitution, Revised Draft," para. 14.

As a rule, party organization corresponds to the administrative system which, in turn, reflects the system of traditional authority. In Western Nigeria, the basic administrative unit of the colonial period was the division, frequently headed by a paramount chief. Heretofore, divisional organization has been the crucial level of local party structure and divisional conferences are prescribed by the Revised Draft Constitution (Para. 12). However, there is an overlap of divisional and constituency organizations and in many areas the latter have surpassed the former in practical importance. In Egba Division of Abeokuta Province, the eclipse of divisional organization by constituency organization corresponds to the relative decline of traditional authority in the local party. Elsewhere, as in Remo, Ikeja, and Ibadan in 1958, the divisional organization was the paramount level of branch coordination. In Ondo Province, a provincial organization met periodically, but that was unique in the Western Region.

Regional Level

The Action Group began as a Western Regional organization and the first general conference of the party at Owo in April 1951 was attended by Western delegates only. All but a very few of the delegates to the Benin Conference of December 1952 were Western Nigerians and national elections were therefore postponed for a year; meanwhile, a caretaker Central Executive Committee was formed by enlarging the Western Regional Executive to include a few representatives from the North and the East.[113] Federal officers were elected at the Warri Congress of 1953 and the demarcation between regional and federal organization was clarified in 1955 by the occurrence of regional conferences in both the East and the West. Membership in the regional conferences is extended to the following persons: "(a) Two Representatives from each Regional Constituency to be chosen by a meeting of representatives of the constituency. (b) All Regional Ministers and all Action Group members of the Regional House of Assembly. (c) All Action Group members of the House of Representatives whose constituencies are located within the Region. (d) In the case of the Western Region, the Chairman of, or the Leader of the Action Group Party in, the Lagos Town Council, together with ten other members to be selected by the District Conference of the Party in Lagos. (e) All members of the Regional Executive Committee. (f) Such other members as may be nominated

113 Action Group, Benin Conference Report, December 17-20, 1952, p. 10.

from time to time by the President of the Party, but who shall not have the right of voting."[114]

The executive committee of the regional organization consists of "(a) The Federal President of the Party. (b) The Chairman of the Regional Conference [who is the Federal Vice-President in that region]. (c) All Regional Ministers or members of the Shadow Cabinet in any Region where the Party is not in power. (d) The Secretary, Treasurer, Publicity Secretary and Legal Adviser of the Regional Conference. (e) The Chairman of each Divisional Conference and Action Group members of Houses of Assembly and House of Representatives in constituencies located within the Region or (in the case of the Western Region) in Lagos. . . . (f) In the case of the Western Region, the Chairman or Leader of the Action Group and one other member of the Party in the Lagos Town Council."[115] It is stipulated that the chairman of the regional conference will preside only in the absence of the Federal President.[116] Technically, the chairman of the regional conference is a federal officer who is elected by the Federal Congress.[117]

In preparation for the 1959 election campaign, zonal organizations, based in part on Action Group policies for the creation of new states, were prescribed for all regions. The zonal organizations in the Western Region coincide with the Yoruba and the Mid-Western sectors of that region. In the Northern Region, 5 zonal organizations were proposed—2 in the Middle Belt area and 3 in the upper North.[118] Two zones were prescribed for the Eastern Region, corresponding to the Ibo and the non-Ibo (or Calabar-Ogoja-Rivers State area) sectors respectively. Zone A comprised 5 areas of 2 or 3 divisions each with a zonal headquarters at Onitsha, while Zone B comprised 4 areas with headquarters at Uyo.[119] In each area of Zone B, a supervisor, who was an elected member of the House of Assembly or the House of Representatives from that area was appointed. Area supervisors met informally with leaders of the divisional units from time to time. A parliamentarian from each zone was chosen as the zonal supervisor and zonal executives were set up consisting of 3 members from every division elected by a divisional conference.

[114] Action Group of Nigeria, "Constitution, Revised Draft," p. 4, para. 9.
[115] *Ibid.*, p. 10, para. 25; and Amendments to the Revised Draft of the Constitution, p. 1, section 28, (a) (2), (c), (g).
[116] Action Group of Nigeria, "Constitution, Revised Draft," p. 10, para. 25.
[117] Amendments to the Revised Draft of the Constitution, Sections 27 and 28 (c).
[118] "Report of the Committee on Party Organization to the Calabar Congress, 1958," pp. 2-3 (mimeographed).
[119] Revised Estimates for the Eastern Region (April 1958-March 1959), pp. 1-2, modified on the basis of additional information.

Federal Level

The Federal Congress of the Action Group consists of: "(a) Two representatives from each Federal Constituency in the country to be chosen at a constituency meeting. (b) All persons who are members of the Party in the House of Representatives. (c) All Regional Ministers who are members of the Party or (in a Region where the Party is not in power) Party members of the Shadow Cabinet in that Region. (d) The Chairman of or Leader of the Action Group Party in the Lagos Town Council and one other member to be selected from among themselves. (e) Members of the Executive Committee of the Federal Congress. (f) Such other members as may from time to time be nominated by the President of the Party, but who shall not have the right to vote."[120] It has been decided that members co-opted by the Congress itself may be given the right to vote.[121]

Strict rules of procedure are enjoined by the party constitution,[122] and have been followed to the letter at congresses under the chairmanship of Chief Obafemi Awolowo. An Action Group Congress is significant chiefly for the promulgation and exposition of party policies rather than their formulation.[123] It provides an opportunity for the

[120] Action Group of Nigeria, "Constitution, Revised Draft," p. 3, para. 7.

[121] Action Group, *Report of the Lagos Congress*, July 12-13, 1957, pp. 20-21.

[122] Action Group of Nigeria, "Constitution, Revised Draft," Third Schedule.

[123] Federal congresses and regional conferences of the Action Group, 1951-1959:

First Regional Conference at Owo, April 28-29, 1951: Inauguration of the Action Group as a Western Regional organization; adoption of a program for the parliamentary election of 1951 and election of party officers.

Second Regional Conference (First National Congress) at Benin, December 17-20, 1952: Report by the President and the Western Minister of Agriculture on their tour of India and other countries; adoption of a motion on non-fraternization with the Governor of Nigeria; decision to press for self-government in 1956.

Second Annual Federal Congress at Warri, December 16, 1953: Election of federal officers marked by the successful maneuver of an informal "Pressure Group" to win election to party offices from incumbents who were regarded as "cliquish," "conservative," or both; termination of the ban on fraternization with the Governor of Nigeria.

Third Annual Regional Conference (possibly a joint meeting of the Central and Regional Executive Committees and the Parliamentary Council) at Ibadan, May 1954: Clarification of policies, e.g., decision to press for the adoption of a 5 shilling minimum wage for employees of the federal government.

Fourth Annual Regional Conference at Ibadan, October 26-28, 1955: Debate on constitutional policies, in particular the matter of new states and the status of Lagos in the Federation; rejection of the idea of a dominion of Southern Nigeria; selection of S. L. Akintola as Deputy Leader.

First Eastern Regional Conference at Aba, November 12-13, 1955: Inauguration of the Eastern Regional organization.

Third Annual Federal Congress at Lagos, July 12-13, 1957: Report on the Consti-

leader to address the country at large and for constituency leaders from all parts of Nigeria to make contact with one another. The Fourth Annual Congress of the Action Group at Calabar in April-May, 1958, was attended by more than 200 delegates, mainly from the Eastern and Western Regions.[124] Plenary sessions were held on each of five consecutive days; the better part of three days was devoted to debate on the presidential address and no fewer than 60 delegates commented on the issues of foreign and domestic policy raised by Chief Awolowo.[125] By and large, these comments from the floor were laudatory although many speakers disagreed with particulars of the address, and most of them, as we have observed, took exception to Chief Awolowo's non-armament proposal with respect to defense policy.[126]

One delegate only struck a discordant note by commenting adversely on the presidential address as a whole. The critic was repudiated by a prominent member of the Action Group from his division. Mr. S. L. Durosaro of Ibadan (barrister and Chairman of the Western Regional Marketing Board) rose to a point of order:[127]

"It is improper to discredit any individual who expresses opinions contrary to the Leader's when we are debating the Leader's Address. It is

tutional Conference, emphasizing the achievement of regional self-government, the A.G. policy for regionalization of the police and the creation of new states.

Emergency Conference of the Western Regional Organization at Ibadan, October 12, 1957: Election of Western Regional members of the Federal Congress; consideration of the threat posed by the activities of the National Muslim League in the Western Region.

Fourth Annual Federal Congress at Calabar, April 28-May 2, 1958: Debate on policies with emphasis on the creation of states, the activities of the party in the North, social policies, and matters of foreign policy and defense.

First Northern Regional Conference at Jos, September 1958: Enunciation of Action Group/United Middle Belt Congress/Bornu Youth Movement policies for the North with emphasis on the aim of creating new states prior to independence.

Emergency Congress of the Action Group at Kano, December 12, 1958: Report on the Resumed Constitutional Conference; reaffirmation of the Action Group positions on the creation of new states before independence and the regionalization of the police.

Fifth Annual Federal Congress at Lagos, September 11, 1959: Preparation for the federal election.

[124] The official list of delegates attending the Congress on April 30, 1958, includes 133 names, but the writer's own tabulation includes about 80 more. See Action Group, *Report of the Fourth Annual Congress*, 1958, p. ii.

[125] The two-day Lagos Congress of July 1957 was devoted largely to debate on the presidential address which occupies most of the 61-page official report.

[126] *Supra*, pp. 280-281.

[127] Action Group, *Report of the Fourth Annual Federal Congress, 1958*, pp. 24-26, 51-52.

equall wrong to dissociate other delegates of his Division with his views when he does not say he is expressing the views of the Division. Our party is not the type where members cringe, kowtow and give slavish respect as if those things, and not merit, are the basis of our appreciation of the Leader's worth."

No major issues of power within the party were debated at the Congress; possibly none were pressing at the time.

Committees were appointed to make recommendations on the following subjects: Finance, Labour and Industrial Welfare, National Independence, Party Organization, Economic Development of Nigeria, and Educational Development of Northern Nigeria.[128] Reports by these committees were referred to the Federal Executive Council for consideration. At its final plenary session the Congress adopted 12 non-controversial resolutions by unanimous votes, all but two of which were proposed by members of the Federal Executive Council. It came to the attention of the Congress, almost incidentally, that the draft constitution of the party had been ratified by the Federal Executive body, acting upon the authority delegated to it by the previous Congress.[129] There was no official report to the Congress on the new party constitution and only a passing reference in the Report of the Federal Secretary to the establishment of a "Federal Working Committee, a body set up under the new Constitution of the Party."[130]

THE FEDERAL EXECUTIVE COUNCIL. This is the principal decision-making unit of the formal party organization. It governs the party between meetings of the Annual Congress and it considers reports submitted to it by committees of the Congress. Membership in the Federal Executive Council is specified as follows: the federal officers, all federal ministers or members of the Federal Shadow Cabinet as the case may be, all regional ministers and members of Regional Shadow Cabinets, the Chairman of or Leader of the party in the Lagos Town Council and one other member to be selected by the members of the party in that Council, and 12 members from every

[128] At both the Lagos Congress of 1957 and the Calabar Congress of 1958, committees were appointed by a selection committee, appointed by the President, composed of 2 members from each region, 1 from Ghana and 1 from Lagos, in addition to a female member at the Calabar Congress. *Report of the Third Annual Congress*, p. 26; *Report of the Fourth Annual Congress*, p. 21.
[129] Journal notes on the Fourth Annual Congress of the Action Group; this matter (the ratification of the Draft Constitution by the Party Executive) was not mentioned in the official Report of the Congress.
[130] Action Group, *Report of the Fourth Annual Congress*, 1958, p. 19.

region to be appointed by the three regional conferences.[131] The Federal Executive Council meets quarterly or as often as necessary. It may delegate functions to the Federal Working Committee which consists of the federal officers, the 3 senior officials of the Headquarters Secretariat and 2 representatives from every region, including all parliamentary leaders of the party. The Working Committee meets monthly in normal circumstances, and directs the administrative and financial activities of the party at both the federal and regional levels.

In 1958, the officers elected were as follows: Federal President, Father of the Party,[132] one Vice-President from each region (the Constitution authorized the Congress to prescribe the number of Federal Vice-Presidents to be elected), Federal Secretary, Assistant Federal Secretary, Federal Treasurer, Federal Publicity Secretary, Federal Legal Adviser, Party Chaplain, and Party Imam.[133]

Prior to July 1957, the Action Group was governed effectively by the Western Regional Executive Committee. The Central Executive Committee did not meet at all between May 1951 and January 1953.[134] It convened once more prior to the Warri Congress of December 1953, while the Western Regional Executive Committee met 14 times in that year, on seven occasions jointly with a committee of Western *Obas* (paramount chiefs).[135] A Federal Executive Committee was established by the Warri Congress of 1953 but regular meetings were not held because the Eastern Regional delegates were either "hand-picked" or employees of the party.[136] However the Eastern delegates to the Lagos Congress of 1957 were genuinely representative of their local organizations and a Federal Executive Council was formed which met twice between that Congress and the

---

[131] Action Group of Nigeria, "Constitution, Revised Draft," p. 8, para. 19.

[132] This office is personal to Dr. Akinola Maja, a medical practitioner, former President of the Nigerian Youth Movement (1944-1951), Chairman of the National Emergency Committee (1949-1950), President of the *Egbe Omo Oduduwa* (Yoruba cultural society) since 1953, ex-Chairman of the Board of Directors of the National Bank of Nigeria, and *Baba Eko* of Lagos.

[133] Action Group of Nigeria, "Constitution, Revised Draft," p. 9. para. 19; Amendments to the Revised Draft of the Constitution, Section 28 (c); *Report of the Fourth Annual Congress, 1958*, p. 76.

[134] Minutes of the Central Executive Committee of the Action Group, Ibadan, January 12, 1953.

[135] Report of the Warri Congress, December 1953 (Central Secretariat Files).

[136] At the Lagos Congress of 1957, Chief Awolowo disclosed that at the Warri Congress of 1953 there were only 3 Eastern delegates who were not party organizing secretaries, and 2 of them were native Westerners. *Report of the Third Annual Congress, 1957*, p. 35.

Fourth Annual Congress of 1958.[137] By then the Federal Executive had displaced the Western Regional Executive as the chief policy-making organ of the party.

Parliamentary Councils

The initial object of the Action Group in 1950-1951 was to win a majority in the Western House of Assembly in order to form the government of the Western Region. Like the NCNC, the origin of the Action Group was extra-parliamentary, but its primary focus, unlike that of the NCNC, was the seizure and exercise of parliamentary power under a colonial constitution. Militant groups of extra-parliamentary nationalists have never been as important in the Action Group as they have been within the fold of its older adversary. Nor had there ever been any conflict of consequence between parliamentary and "organizational" elements of the party before the crisis of 1962.

The Revised Draft Constitution of 1958 provided for the creation of a parliamentary council in every regional legislature, each of which, in conjunction with the executive committee of the regional conference, shall elect a parliamentary leader who shall be Premier if the party is in power, or Leader of the Opposition if the party is the main opposition group. (It is also stipulated that the Federal President of the Party shall preside at joint meetings of the regional parliamentary council and the executive committee of the regional conference.)[138] An Action Group Premier, or Prime Minister of the Federation, is entitled to select his ministerial colleagues (and, to the writer's knowledge, the Leader of the Opposition may select his shadow cabinet). The Constitution provides for a high degree of coordination among the several legislative wings:[139]

"All Action Group Ministers and Members of the Shadow Cabinet in any Legislature where the Party is not in power shall be ex-officio members of all Parliamentary Councils.

"There shall be a Leader of the Party who shall be elected at a joint meeting of all Parliamentary Councils of the Party. He shall hold office for life unless he retires by writing under his hand, or loses an election into the Legislature and the Federal Executive Council.

[137] "Report of the Federal Secretary to the Fourth Annual Federal Congress, 1958," p. 6 (mimeographed).
[138] "Amendments to the Revised Draft of the Constitution," Second Schedule, Section 2.
[139] Action Group of Nigeria, "Constitution, Revised Draft," Second Schedule: Parliamentary Councils, Section 7, as amended.

"There shall be a Deputy Leader of the Party to be appointed in the same manner as the Leader of the Party, and who shall hold office for life."

When Chief Awolowo relinquished the Premiership of the West in 1959 to become a candidate in the federal election and subsequently Leader of the Opposition in the Federal House of Representatives, it was not intended that the redistribution of roles would alter the distribution of authority in the party. Chief Awolowo remained Leader of the Party while his successor as Premier of the West, Chief Samuel L. Akintola, remained as Deputy Leader. These positions are parliamentary offices only, derived from the Westminster model, with the addition of life tenure, provided only that the incumbents retain their parliamentary seats and their memberships in the Federal Executive Council.[140] Chief Awolowo holds the office of Federal President of the Action Group (or President of the Party), for which there is no counterpart in the major British parties.

While there is no constitutional provision for deposition of the Leader or Deputy Leader, it is inconceivable that either one should continue in office following his failure to secure re-election as Leader of the Legislative House to which he belongs, or following a vote of no confidence by the Parliamentary Council to which he belongs or by a joint meeting of the Parliamentary Councils, or following his failure to win an election to a regular party office. In 1962 it was established that the Federal Executive Council could direct the removal of an incumbent from parliamentary office; it voted for the removal of Chief Akintola from the offices of Deputy Leader and Premier of the Western Region.[141] When Chief Akintola defied the decision of the party, he was removed from his office of Premier by the Governor on the ground that he had lost the support of the members of the House of Assembly. Ultimately, the ability of the party organization to impose effective control over parliamentary representatives depends upon the pleasure of the electorate.

Secretariat Organization

The party Secretariat is controlled by the President of the Party through three senior officials who are responsible for organization,

---

[140] The Leader of the British Conservative Party enjoys *de facto* life tenure, while the Leader of the British Labour Party is subject to the formality of annual re-election by the Parliamentary Labour Party when the party is in the Opposition only. R. T. McKenzie, *op.cit.*, pp. 21, 299.

[141] The vote was reported to have been unanimous. Earlier the Western and Mid-West Executive Committees had "decided by 81 to 29 that Chief Akintola should be dismissed." *West Africa*, May 29, 1962, p. 579.

administration and publicity respectively.[142] The Administrative Department, in particular, is the President's office for party management. In 1958 the following table of organization was adopted for the entire country:[143]

	Organization Department	Administrative Department	Publicity Department
Federal Headquarters Secretariat	Principal Organizing Secretary Assistant P.O.S.	Administrative Secretary	Publicity Officer (Party Manager)
Zonal Headquarters	Assistant P.O.S.	Assistant Administrative Secretaries	Assistant Publicity Officers
Constituency Headquarters	Organizing Secretaries		

Table 1 indicates the distribution of organizing and administrative personnel in all Regions.

The typical salary of an organizing secretary was £300 per annum plus increments; field secretaries were paid about half as much.

Since 1956, Action Group field secretaries in the Western Region have been required to tour their areas monthly. Every organizing and field secretary must submit to the Principal Organizing Secretary an Itinerary prior to his tour and a Day to Day Diary upon its completion.[144]

[142] S. T. Oredein, a former secretary of the British-American Tobacco Workers Union, was Principal Organizing Secretary; Olatunji Dosumu was administrative secretary; O. Agunbiade-Bamishe was Party Manager in charge of the Bureau of Information. Oredein and Dosumu were among the eight inaugural members of the Action Group.

[143] "Report of the Committee on Party Organization to the Fourth Annual Federal Congress, Calabar, 1958," p. 3 (mimeographed).

[144] These requirements appear to have been enforced strictly in the Western Region as the following extract from Circular Letter No. 33/56, 24 July 1956, will attest:

"It is observed that you have failed to submit your Itinerary for the months . . . 1956, and your Day to Day Diary for the month of . . . 1956.

"I have to state that unless you comply with my previous instruction on this matter, and your Day to Day Diary and Itinerary are received in this office, on or before 31st of July, 1956, your salary will be withheld."

"(sgd) S. T. Oredein
Principal Organizing Secretary."

The report system was inaugurated in the Eastern Region in 1955, but with less uniform success than in the West, and it seemed to have lapsed.

Table 1*

	Western Region and Lagos	Eastern Region	Northern Region
Organizing Secretaries (including Supervisors and Administrative Secretaries in various field offices).	36	5	124
Field Secretaries	123	21	239
Other field staff (including "organizers", boat boys, messengers, etc.)	36	15	49
Totals, Regional	195	41	412

Total   648 - field staff
               58 - headquarters staff
            706 - total number of Action Group employees

* This tabulation is neither official nor corroborated. It is based on the writer's perusal of the Action Group of Nigeria, *Approved Estimates, 1958/59*.

Action Group diligence in the planning and development of its professional organizing corps has been matched by a concomitant insistence upon the ultimate responsibility of non-paid constituency leaders and parliamentarians for the growth and state of the party. This can be illustrated by an extract from a letter from the Principal Organizing Secretary to a minister in the Western Regional Government. The Principal Organizing Secretary was informed by the Deputy Leader of the Party of numerous complaints alleging that the minister concerned had been guilty of the neglect of his constituency. The P.O.S. wrote to the minister as follows:[145]

"The Deputy Leader feels very much distressed about this, and requests that you should take immediate steps to meet the legitimate desire of the people.
"In the circumstances I am to request you to prepare an itinerary and proceed to your Constituency without any delay. A copy of the itinerary should be forwarded to the Deputy Leader and the Secretariat."

                       "(sgd.) S. T. Oredein
                       Principal Organizing Secretary."

[145] Action Group Constituency File No. 55, 2 August 1957. The principle of non-official responsibility was stated in the Report of the Committee on Party Organization to the Calabar Congress as follows : "It is important to stress that responsibility for organization of the Party rests primarily with party leaders and that the staff are only their agents and tools."

When the Party Executive resolved to launch an all-out organizational drive in the North, prior to the federal election of 1959, ten Western leaders, including ministers, junior ministers and prominent members and chairmen of statutory boards and corporations, were appointed to supervise party organization and the recruitment of local personnel in specific Northern provinces. In short, no Action Group office holder is permitted to stand aloof from the chore work of organization.

Propaganda materials are published continuously by the Action Group Bureau of Information under the direction of the Party Manager. Formerly, the Bureau published a party magazine for private circulation entitled, *The Action Magazine*. Probably the most auspicious efforts at political education undertaken by the Bureau of Information were the Summer School Lectures of 1955 and 1956, some of which were notable for their radical and Marxist orientations.[146]

The main publicity arm of the Action Group, like that of the NCNC, is a privately owned commercial newspaper chain which is discussed in the next chapter.

ANCILLARY ELEMENTS

Auxiliary Groups

There is no constitutional provision for women's or youth organizations, but it is the policy of the party to encourage women's sections at the constituency and local government levels.[147] In 1958, a Western Regional Women's Conference was held and regional officers were elected.[148]

Action Group youth organizations have been localized and limited to youths of 18 years or less since 1955, when party leaders disallowed the attempt of R. A. Fani-Kayode, Assistant Federal Secretary and radical leader of the Ife branch, to set up a regional youth

---

[146] *Supra*, p. 271, n. 92.

[147] "Special efforts must be made to organize women who constitute a large portion of the country's voting strength. The organization should be built round a committee of women drawn from the wards in each constituency. This committee should be responsible for organizing women into the main constituency body of the Party. It will be the duty of members of the committee to organize women's branches in every ward." "Report of the Committee on Party Organization to the Fourth Annual Congress," p. 2 (mimeographed).

[148] "Report of the West Regional Conference of Women, Action Group, Ibadan, 15 March 1958," (mimeographed). The Conference passed resolutions calling for the enfranchisement of women in the North and for the abolition of political parties in the West which were based on religion, among others. The President of the Western Regional Women's Conference was Lady Oyinkan Abayomi, former President of the Nigerian Women's Party of the early postwar era.

organization. In 1958 an "Awo National Brigade" was formed in Ibadan on the occasion of Chief Awolowo's 49th birthday. The Brigade was conceived as a counterpoise to the NCNC's Zikist National Vanguard, but its continuance was discouraged by Chief Awolowo himself at the Calabar Congress.[149]

Affiliated Parties

THE UNITED MIDDLE BELT CONGRESS. Prior to 1959, the fragmentary and amorphous UMBC lacked effective central direction.[150] Its structural bedrock consisted of four principal tribal unions—the Tiv Progressive Union, the Jos Tribal Party (Birom), the Alago Progressive Union (Lafia Division, Benue Province), the Nzit Progressive Union of Jema'a Division (southern Zaria)—and a few strong divisional branches, at Numan (Adamawa), Pankshin (Plateau) and Shendam (Plateau).[151] Elsewhere, as in southern Plateau, Bauchi, Niger, Kabba, and Ilorin Provinces, Middle Belt State sentiment existed but UMBC organization was, at best, incipient.

In view of the congenital fragility of the UMBC,[152] the localization of its leadership, the dependence of the latter on external sources of financing, and the determination of the Northern Government to integrate the middle-belt provinces into a unitary Northern Region, it is doubtful if the UMBC could have survived the adverse recommendation of the Minorities Commission without the support of the Action Group. Withal there were major defections from the party in its strong areas of Jos Division and southern Zaria in 1959. The Action Group alliance gave the UMBC an invigorating infusion of monetary and legal strength in addition to the benefits of systematic organization.[153]

Other political party affiliates of the Action Group in the Northern Region include the Bornu Youth Movement, the Ilorin *Talaka Parapo*

---

[149] *Daily Times,* March 11, 1958; *supra,* p. 282.

[150] In 1958 there were only three general officers of the UMBC: Hon. Joseph Sarwuan Tarka, MHR (Tiv), President General; Hon. Patrick M. Dokotri, MHR (Jos), Secretary-General; and Mr. Isaac Kpuum (Tiv), Financial Secretary and co-editor of the newly founded *Middle Belt Herald,* published by the Amalgamated Press at Jos.

[151] Smaller tribal union associated with the UMBC included the Chamba Progressive Union, the Gwari Progressive Union of Keffi, and the Igala Progressive Union.

[152] *Supra,* pp. 346-348.

[153] Probably the Action Group spent over £50,000 on organizational expenses for the Middle Belt area during the 1958/1959 fiscal year. This was inferred by the writer on the basis of his perusal of the *Action Group Approved Estimates, 1958/1959.*

(Commoners Party) and the Habe-Fulani People's Party of south-western Bauchi.[154]

Affiliated Non-Party Groups

There is no constitutional provision for the affiliation of tribal unions or other non-party groups. Such of the latter as may be linked formally to the Action Group are confined to the local level, e.g., the organized groups of Action Group supporters in the main commodity markets of Lagos.[155]

THE ACTION GROUP NOMINATING SYSTEM

Nominating procedures were regularized in the Western Region prior to the local government and parliamentary elections of 1958-1959. In preparation for the former (local elections) the Principal Organizing Secretary sent directives to organizing secretaries, divisional and constituency leaders, and parliamentarians to assume responsibility for the formation of election committees in every local and district council area. The committees were free to adopt procedures suitable to local circumstances:[156]

"The duty of this [Election] Committee is to call upon the elders or electors of each ward to nominate or present a candidate."

In the event of disagreement, the election committee was advised to appeal to the community elders, e.g., compound heads, for mediation. In those relatively few cases where disputes could not be settled locally, central party leaders were assigned to effect resolutions.[157]

---

[154] *Supra,* pp. 340-342, 351-355, and 371, n. 97.

[155] The AG Lagos secretariat maintains a corps of "market supervisors" (six men in 1958) who encourage the formation of party groups in the various markets, assist in the direction of their activities, and report to party officials on market problems and opinions. In 1958 it was estimated by leaders of both the Action Group and the NCNC that the former enjoyed the support of about 70% of the market women of Lagos. This was attributed in part to the influence of the *Oba* of Lagos and in part to the influence of the Lagos Town Council, then under Action Group control, which regulates market activities. Subsequently the *Oba* declared his neutrality in party politics and the NCNC won control of the Town Council. The Action Group hoped to offset the effects of these reversals by systematic organization in the markets.

[156] Action Group Headquarters, Circular Letter No. 2/58: Local Government Elections, 1958, Directives.

[157] The writer witnessed one settlement in March 1958 in Ishara, Ijebu Remo Division, an Action Group stronghold, where factional groups nominated rival candidates in 10 wards. The Federal Treasurer, Alhaji S. O. Gbadamosi, MHA, who was assigned to settle the dispute, called a mass meeting in every ward, and utilized the official electoral register to call out names and separate the

Nominations for the Federal House of Representatives in the Western Region followed a standard procedure, from which no deviations were countenanced. In July 1958, letters were sent by the Principal Organizing Secretary with the authority of the Federal President to a number of party leaders and prominent members in every federal constituency in the region, appointing them to serve on organizing committees and directing them to select from among themselves a chairman, secretary and additional officers as may be required.[158] Each organizing committee was directed further to convene a meeting of a constituency selection committee based on representation from each local government ward by the Action Group councillor, if the Action Group candidate had been elected in the previous local government election, and by one other man and one woman selected by the ward branch. Persons wishing to be adopted as candidates were advised to send applications in writing to the chairman of the organizing committee, and warned not to accept office as a member of the organizing committee, lest they be disqualified by the Federal Executive Council. A typical selection committee might comprise a few hundred members, and all selections were made by secret ballot. Virtually all Action Group candidates in the Western Region had been nominated by the end of 1958, a full year before the election.

The determination of the party officials to ensure strict adhesion to regular procedures is attested by the case of the nomination of Chief Obafemi Awolowo, Federal President of the Action Group, as the candidate for the Ijebu Remo constituency. The constituency includes 14 local council areas, and the prescribed membership of the Constituency Selection Committee was 632. It was known that Chief Awolowo desired the nomination and that his candidacy to the Federal House was a matter of party policy; there were no other contenders and the result of the Selection Committee meeting was a foregone conclusion. Therefore the Divisional Executive Committee and the Organizing Committee held a joint meeting which resolved to adopt Chief Awolowo and to inform the people accordingly at meetings in every ward. The Principal Organizing Secretary responded immediately rejecting the candidate as adopted:[159]

---

supporters of the rival candidates physically, who were then counted. The candidates with the greater number of supporters were declared the official Action Group nominees. Action Group candidates were returned unopposed in every ward but one, where an independent stood and was defeated.

[158] Action Group, Circular Letter No. 16/58, 25 July 1958, with Directives for Organizing a Constituency Selection Committee.

[159] Action Group Headquarters Secretariat, Federal Constituency Files: Ijebu Remo, No. 207.

"I would refer you to my direction dated 27 July 1958 which clearly set out the way and manner every candidate is to be returned. Permit me to say that it is improper for the Ijebu Remo Executive Committee to assume the duties and functions of the Selection Committee."

Thereupon the Selection Committee was convened and Chief Awolowo was nominated in proper form.[160]

In a few deeply divided constituencies, factional strife persisted, despite democratic procedures, after the selection of an official candidate. With rare exception these disputes were settled by a Protest Committee under the chairmanship of the Federal President.

PARTY DISCIPLINE

So long as the Action Group was primarily a Western Regional party, it remained a tightly knit organization under the direction of men who were, for the most part, bound together by ties of ethnic, class, and ideological affinity. This spirit of socio-political camaraderie was reflected in the "Leaders Meeting" at the home of Chief Awolowo in Ikenne, Ijebu Remo. The first major defection from the ranks of the Western government party occurred in 1956 when two Western ministers and the Federal Publicity Secretary resigned following the failure of their constituencies to adopt them as candidates in the regional election and the refusal of the Federal Executive Council to do so. The first major instance of expulsion occurred in November

[160] In August 1958, the leaders of the Action Group appeared to countenance an exception to regular procedures and normal respect for the chain of party command. Certain high ranking Action Group officials held the view that the incumbent leadership of the Ibadan branch was an inconvertible liability because it was identified by the Ibadan people with the unpopular conservative and elitist element of Ibadan indigenes which had been repudiated in previous elections. Prince Adeleke Adedoyin, Speaker of the Western House of Assembly and a member of the Action Group Federal Executive Council, organized a new party called the *Egbe Atunluse Ibadan* (Ibadan Welfare Association), on the theory that many Ibadan people would join the Action Group if there was an alternative to the incumbent local leadership. Prince Adedoyin, an Ijebu Yoruba himself, did not assume office in the new association, but he directed its activities from his home in Ibadan which he transformed into a political headquarters.

Initially Adedoyin's demarche created a rumpus within the ranks of the Action Group as the *Egbe Atunluse Ibadan* challenged the regular party's right to nominate Action Group candidates for the federal election of 1959. It is extremely unusual for the systematically run Action Group to tolerate factionalism or irregular wings. Yet it was difficult to believe that a member of the Federal Executive Council would attempt to undermine the authority of an established branch leadership in the regional capital without the approval of the Party Leader. His uncharacteristic maneuver was a back-handed tribute to the popular strength of the NCNC/*Mabolaje* Grand Alliance (*supra*, Ch. VII) but it did not succeed and the sole successful Action Group candidate in 1959 was the President of the regular branch organization.

1957, when the Federal Executive Council voted to expel a former Central minister, Chief Arthur Prest of Warri, who had been openly critical of the party leadership for several months. With the growth of the party as a mass organization in the East and the North, its initial cohesion inevitably diminished and, in 1958, a member of the Action Group in the Eastern House of Assembly set a precedent by crossing the carpet to the NCNC.[161] The following year there were a few more defections by legislators elected on the Action Group platform in the North to the Northern Peoples' Congress.

The party constitution broadly defines offenses against the party which may incur disciplinary measures. These include disobedience or neglect of the lawful directives of officers, conduct likely to reflect adversely on the party, and the advocacy of doctrines or views which are contrary to "what the Party has laid down," except at party meetings.[162] Ordinary members are subject to trial for offenses by branch committees; regional and federal officers may be tried by the regional or federal executive bodies only. All appeals terminate with the Federal Executive Council save appeals by members of that Council which may be entertained by the Federal Congress.[163]

Normally, breaches of party discipline are corrected privately through the medium of the Secretariat, and an offending individual is given an opportunity to exculpate himself before the matter is brought to the attention of a disciplinary body for action. In 1957, a junior minister in the Western Regional Government was alleged to have made statements to the press in which he criticized his government for its handling of a local government issue in his division. The Principal Organizing Secretary was directed by the Deputy Leader to warn the individual that public statements by party members attacking the party cannot be tolerated. The offender's utterance seemed to the leadership to indicate that the party had erred in its appraisal of his loyalty to it and he was admonished to make restitution by disclaiming the statement which had been attributed to him in the press. This was done immediately by the individual who claimed that he had been misrepresented, and requested the Principal Organizing Secretary to withdraw the damaging letter from his file as he did not want a bad mark in his record. The matter was thereby closed.[164]

[161] "Federal Secretary's Report to the Fourth Annual Federal Congress, 1958," p. 17.

[162] Action Group of Nigeria, "Constitution, Revised Draft," para. 6.

[163] *Ibid.* First Schedule: "Trial of Offences," as amended.

[164] Action Group Headquarters Secretariat, Constituency File No. 9, August and October 1957.

PARTY FINANCE

Financial responsibility is vested in a Federal Treasurer and regional treasurers. A Finance Committee appointed by the Federal Congress reports to the Federal Executive Council on ways and means of raising funds. Annual estimates are published for private circulation to party members upon approval of the Federal Working Committee and the Federal Executive Council. In the fiscal year 1958-1959, the Action Group budget totalled over £290,000.[165] The writer was reliably informed that expenditures on the federal election of 1959 exceeded £1,000,000.

There are five regular sources of Action Group funds, as follows:

(1) Enrollment fees and monthly subscriptions. Party cards are issued to new members upon the payment of a fee of 1/- which is remitted to the Federal Treasury. Every member is obligated to pay a monthly subscription of 1/- to his local branch treasurer; three-fourths of all subscriptions are remitted to the Federal Treasury.[166] There is no constitutional provision for divisional or constituency revenues, but these bodies are expected to assume, at least in part, the expenses of their operations.

(2) The sale of stores equipment to party members. This item includes "almanacs, flags, handkerchiefs, membership cards, and various publications produced by the Department or Bureau of Information."[167]

(3) Levies on the salaries of legislators and members of statutory boards and corporations. Since 1956, ministerial salaries have been exempt from the normal 10 percent levy—i.e., ministers and junior ministers have been liable to levies on their basic legislative emoluments only, on the ground that a ministerial salary is a professional rather than a political emolument. Moreover ministers are normally expected to defray a substantial portion of the expenses of their divisional and constituency organizations. Parliamentarians and patronage beneficiaries in general have been remiss in the payment of

---

[165] This figure is the writer's estimate based on a perusal of the Action Group of Nigeria, *Approved Estimates, 1958/1959*, and the "Revised Estimates for the Eastern Region (from April 1, 1958-March 31, 1959)." Approved by the Party's Working Committee. The figure is not official.

[166] Action Group of Nigeria, "Constitution, Revised Draft," paras. 5 and 6.

[167] The Finance Committee of the Fourth Annual Congress, Calabar, 1957, expressed concern over the failure of members to purchase and display these items and recommended "that all members of the Party should have the flag of the Party on their cars and wear Action Group brooches at all meetings of the Party. No member should be allowed to bring his car near to a meeting place of the Party unless the car has a Party flag on." "Report of the Finance Committee of the Fourth Annual Congress."

their party levies, and it was reported to the Calabar Congress that indebtedness to the party by members in respect of the 10 percent levy, loans, and purchases of cars from the party, totalled £35,630.[168] The Finance Committee of the Congress recommended the imposition of "stringent" penalties for defaulters including disqualification from the right to stand as a party candidate in any election or the right to serve as a delegate to any party meeting or conference.[169]

(4) Donations. The Action Group relies heavily upon the voluntary financial support of the most affluent and numerous "new middle class" in sub-Sahara Africa, i.e., the commercial and professional class of the Western Region of Nigeria. A Trust Fund was inaugurated at the Benin Conference of 1952, which started slowly but drew increasing support.[170] As the benefits of Action Group government became apparent to the rising class, it responded generously to meet the financial needs of the party. Chief Awolowo has participated actively in fund-raising drives; prior to the 1959 election he travelled extensively throughout the Western Region to solicit funds from potential donors. In addition, there is an informal relationship between party finance and commercial patronage which is discussed below. At this point it suffices to note the remarkable ability of Action Group supporters to make substantial contributions to the party at any time of need. This may be illustrated by a statement on the financing of the £12,000 Headquarters Secretariat in Ibadan contained in the Report of the Federal Secretary to the Lagos Congress of 1957:[171]

"The great significance of this building lies in the fact that all the necessary funds for its erection were collected substantially at the laying of the Foundation Stone of the building and at the formal opening."

(5) A final regular source of Action Group funds is the overdraft or loan facility provided by the National Bank of Nigeria Limited. This aspect of party finance is discussed in the following chapter.

[168] "Report of the Treasurer to the Federal Congress, Calabar 1958," in *Report of the Fourth Annual Federal Congress*, p. 20.
[169] "Report of the Finance Committee of the Fourth Annual Federal Congress."
[170] Report of the Warri Congress, December 1953; the Finance Committee of this Congress proposed to "honour" 1,000 supporters of the party with an annual levy of £5.
[171] Report of the Third Annual (Lagos) Congress, p. 17. Plaques which show the names of persons and organizations who donated to the Headquarters Secretariat fund are displayed prominently in the main meeting hall of the building. All of the "Head Chiefs" in the Yoruba section of the Western Region are included, the exceptions being the ex-*Owa* of Ilesha and the ex-*Alafin* of Oyo, neither of whom was regarded as an Action Group supporter. Other names include those of party leaders, prominent businessmen, distinguished individuals and local groups. The names constitute an abbreviated "Who's Who" in the Western Region.

CHAPTER X: THE UNOFFICIAL
DIMENSION OF PARTY STRUCTURE
AND ORGANIZATION

IT HAS been observed that the major Nigerian parties are "direct" structure types, i.e., that party membership is individual and cannot be obtained by virtue of membership in affiliated social groups.[1] In the preceding chapter, organized non-party groups affiliated formally to the parties at all levels were classified among the ancillary elements of official structure. But the official structures do not include unofficial supporting groups which function as virtual ancillary elements, among them ethnic group associations and informal groups based on social institutions—e.g., chiefs, administrative functionaries, and business groups. This chapter supplies a set of structural categories to facilitate the exposition of relationships between the official party structures and non-party groups which are subject to party control or involved in the performance of party functions—e.g., propaganda, recruitment, finance, nominations of candidates, and the settlement of disputes. The activities of each major party will be examined in the following social spheres: traditional authorities, administrative-governmental (functionary) groups, economic interest groups, ethnic and religious interest groups, and other interest groups. At the end of this chapter, two cases of party penetration into the social structure at the local level will be described. Both of them involve branches of the Action Group. it should be noted, however, that a comparable description of the *Mabolaje* of Ibadan, an NCNC affiliate, is included in Chapter VII, and that the social foundations of local branches of the NPC are examined in Chapter VIII.

TRADITIONAL AUTHORITIES

The institution of chieftaincy persists with unparalleled vigor in the Northern Region. Northern emirs and chiefs exercise executive and judicial powers in their local jurisdictions and the Northern House of Chiefs is a coordinate chamber to the House of Assembly with concurrent legislative powers. (At the time of independence, all other upper houses in the parliaments of Nigeria were limited to powers of delay only.) In 1958, four of the most important chiefs,

---

[1] Maurice Duverger, *Political Parties*, trans. Barbara and Robert North (London: Methuen, 1954), pp. 5-7, 17.

namely, the Sultan of Sokoto, the Emir of Kano, the Emir of Katsina, and the *Aku Uka* of Wukari, were ministers without portfolio in the Executive Council of the Northern Region.[2]

As provided by the Constitution, the power to suspend and depose Northern chiefs in addition to related powers of recognition and grading are vested in the Governor of the region, to be exercised by him in consultation with the Northern Council of Chiefs. This body includes the Premier of the North, those regional ministers who have been appointed from the Northern House of Chiefs, and four additional members of the House of Chiefs, co-opted by the Premier whenever the Council is convened to discuss a specific case.[3] Thus official control over chiefs in the North requires the active cooperation of the leading chiefs themselves. As a rule, emirs and chiefs do not become technical members of the Northern Peoples' Congress, but they support the government party openly and their influence at all levels of party management is enormous.

In the Western Region, traditional authorities generally support the governing Action Group, as noted in Chapter VI. At local levels, it will be recalled that "traditional members" of local government councils—constituting a maximum of one-third of the elected membership—normally vote with Action Group-elected members in order to ensure that party's control of these councils.[4] The ability of the Action Group to organize most of the local government councils is crucial to its control of the Regional House of Chiefs. In every administrative division, traditional authorities are allotted a specified number of seats in the upper legislative chamber. All but the nine permanent members of the House of Chiefs, called the "Head Chiefs," are selected by divisional meetings which consist of prescribed numbers of elected and traditional members chosen by and from the local government councils.[5] The elected members constitute a majority of the divisional meetings and chiefs have occasionally complained about the procedure that invests commoners with virtual

[2] The incumbent *Shehu* of Bornu, 87 years old at the time of writing, and traditional ruler of the Kanuri people, has equivalent status to the top Fulani emirs. Another first-class emir of comparably high status is the Emir of Zaria. The *Aku Uka* of Wukari, a second-class chief, is the most eminent of the middle-belt chiefs historically, inasmuch as the Junkun armies of the 16th century conquered the Hausa states.

[3] *The Nigeria (Constitution) Order in Council*, 1960, Third Schedule, Section 74.

[4] *Supra*, pp. 240-242.

[5] W.R.L.N. 80 of 1956. *Supplement to the Western Region of Nigeria Gazette*, 1956, B 165; *Supplement to the Western Region Gazette Extraordinary*, No. 28, Vol. 5, May 30, 1956—Part B.

control of the composition of their legislative house. However, complaints of this sort are more likely to be made by chiefs who favor the Action Group in areas controlled by the NCNC than by chiefs *per se* in areas controlled by the government party.

It has been noted that in 1958 only one member in 54 in the Western House of Chiefs was identified as a supporter of the opposition party. Nor has that chamber ever obstructed the enactment into law of any bill passed by the House of Assembly. In 1959, its powers were reduced, without public protest on the part of the chiefs, from those of a coordinate legislative chamber to those of an inferior chamber, comparable to the House of Lords in the United Kingdom.[6] At that time, all nine permanent members or Head Chiefs of the Western Region were open supporters of the Action Group.[7]

In 1957, the number of "recognized chiefs"—i.e., persons appointed under the provisions of the Chiefs Law to "recognized chieftaincies"[8]—in the Western Region exceeded 1,500.[9] The vast majority, of course, are so-called "honorary chiefs," rather than authentic traditional rulers. As the *Oni* of Ife (His Excellency, Sir Adesoji Aderemi II, Governor of the Western Region) quipped in a half-serious mood, "In any gathering every third or fourth man is a chief."[10] Although the entire chieftaincy apparatus in the Western Region, unlike that in the Northern Region, is subject to the effective control of the government party,[11] the veritable army of recognized

---

[6] *Report by the Resumed Nigeria Constitutional Conference*, September and October 1958, p. 23.

[7] The Head Chiefs of the Western Region were the following: the *Oni* of Ife, then President of the House of Chiefs, the *Alake* of Abeokuta, the *Oba* of Benin, the *Olubadan* of Ibadan, the *Awujale* of Ijebu-Ode, the *Akarigbo* of Ijebu-Remo, the *Owa* of Ilesha, the *Alafin* of Oyo, and the *Olu* of Warri. In 1959 Sir Adesoji Aderemi II, the *Oni* of Ife, became Governor of the Western Region and Sir Ladipo Ademola, the *Alake* of Abeokuta, was elevated to the Presidency of the House of Chiefs.

In 1960, Akenzua II, the *Oba* of Benin, resigned his office as minister without portfolio and declared his neutrality in politics. Presumably *Oba* Akenzua was influenced by the results of the 1959 election and the certainty that the federal government would initiate procedures to create a Mid-West Region in which a non-partisan *Oba* of Benin would be a logical choice for the office of constitutional Governor.

[8] The Chief's Law, 1957: W.R. No. 20 of 1957, Part II.

[9] "Western Region Notices No. 1141 and 1142," *Western Region of Nigeria Gazette*, No. 58, Vol. 6, December 5, 1957, pp. 673-697.

[10] This comment was made in the course of an address to the Annual Conference of *Obas* and Chiefs in Benin, May 5, 1958, during which the *Oni* "strongly deplored the practice of creating spurious chieftaincy titles, which he called an indiscriminate award to people who merely applied 'ostensibly in return for large fees or for undeserved favours or cheap popularity.'" *Daily Times*, May 6, 1958.

[11] *Supra*, pp. 235-242.

chiefs is a "pressure group" of the first order of influence in the region. The Western Government has provided a sounding board for the opinion of chiefs by instituting an Annual Conference of *Obas* and Chiefs which is utilized by the leading chiefs and by members of the government to persuade the rank-and-file chiefs that Action Group policies merit their enthusiastic support. In 1956, a standing committee of the Annual Conference, called the Council of *Obas* and Chiefs, was set up to advise the government with respect to chieftaincy matters, e.g., the composition of the House of Chiefs and matters of appointment and deposition. In 1959, this council became a statutory body, as agreed by a previous constitutional conference, which the government of the Western Region is obliged to consult "on all matters relating to the discipline of chiefs."[12] The power of decision, however, is vested in the government and not in the Council of Chiefs, as it is in the North.

Chiefs in the Western Region perform honorific functions of procedural and symbolic significance within the emerging political institutions. They constitute a regional "House of Lords"; they preside over and participate in the affairs of local government councils; they have been appointed as public trustees for the preservation of communal rights in land.[13] In all such matters the Action Group Government has given legal expression to the traditional dignities of chiefs without conferring substantive powers over public policy.

In most Ibo areas of the Eastern Region, chieftaincy as a political factor is relatively insignificant. Yet a Regional House of Chiefs was established in 1959, mainly in response to demands from minority ethnic groups, among whom the political role of chieftaincy is greater than it is among the Ibo. These demands were supported by an influential but loosely organized lobby in Iboland, called the Eastern Region Chiefs' Conference. Most of the members of the inaugural Eastern House of Chiefs, from the Ibo and the non-Ibo

---

[12] *Report by the Resumed Nigeria Constitutional Conference held in London in September and October, 1958* (Lagos: Federal Government Printer, 1958), p. 24. It is provided that the Council of *Obas* and Chiefs should consist of "the President of the House of Chiefs, as Chairman and not more than six other members." A two-year term of office is specified for the members of the Council. See also *Western Region of Nigeria, House of Assembly Debates, Official Report, April-May, 1959*, pp. 171-174; *House of Chiefs Debates, Official Report, April-May, 1959*, pp. 39-44.

[13] The Communal Land Rights (Vesting in Trustees) Law of 1958 provides for the appointment of chiefs or local government councils as public trustees for communal land. It stipulates that where traditional authorities in any community have been declared to exist in accordance with the law, they shall be appointed by the minister as "the Trustees of communal rights in respect of that community." (Section 7A.)

areas alike, were NCNC supporters; a number of them had served as unofficial advisers to NCNC delegations to Constitutional Conferences in London. It has been suggested that the resurgence of chieftaincy in the East is attributable in part to the desire of the governing party (NCNC) to use the institution for partisan advantage, as in the North and the West.[14]

Previously, we have noted that in non-Ibo areas of the Eastern Region, branches of the Action Group normally engage the support of traditional authorities at village and clan levels.[15]

Administrative-Governmental (Functionary) Groups

Each of the three major parties has an extensive system of patronage based primarily upon the administrative structure of a regional government. These patronage systems buttress the incumbent party authorities in two familiar respects: first, public officials appointed on a partisan basis tend to support those leaders to whom they owe their positions; secondly, the power to appoint entails control of the institutional and organizational resources at the disposal of government. At the local level in all regions, government party supporters predominate in the local government services. With rare exceptions, officials of the Northern Native Administrations and Native Court judges openly support the NPC. By contrast, local officials in the Eastern and Western Regions, where dual administrative structures do not exist as they do in the North, are required to observe civil service standards of political impartiality. In the East, appointments to the local government service are made by the responsible minister. In the West, appointments to posts in the unified public service and certain customary court appointments are made by the Local Government Service Board, a technically non-partisan agency with powers of promotion, transfer, and discipline. It has been alleged, with some justifiability by opposition spokesmen, that appointments to the local

[14] E. O. Awa, "Local Government Problems in a Developing Country," paper delivered at a conference on representative government and national progress, University College, Ibadan, March 16-23, 1959, p. 8. (Mimeographed.)

[15] *Supra*, p. 423. In his study of "Social and Economic Forces in Eastern Region Politics," S. G. Ikoku, at present the Leader of the Opposition in the Eastern House of Assembly, observed that "the clan head and his council of elders form a sort of 'clearing house' for the clan, while the village and family heads are the real executors of authority within the clan." He added that the clan head may advise the village heads but cannot normally coerce them. "A political party," he concluded, "to be effective, must use the clan as its basis of organisation and must pay great regard to its village organisations. . . . Effective political leadership can only be created by associating the clan leaders and traditional heads with it." Action Group of Nigeria, *1956 Summer School Lectures* (Ibadan: n.d.), pp. 32, 34.

service often reflect the partisan bias of the members of the Board.[16]

At the regional government level, administrative patronage is centered on the three clusters of statutory boards and corporations. The Eastern Regional system is illustrative. Its origin lies largely in the report of the Economic Mission to Europe and North America by Dr. Azikiwe and L. P. Ojukwu in 1954. That report, it may be recalled, recommended the creation of an Eastern Region Finance Corporation to serve as an intermediary for the investment of funds belonging to the Eastern Region Marketing Board in an indigenous bank and the extension of long term loan capital to public corporations.[17] By 1956, four public boards and eight corporations had been established,[18] and 92 persons, other than the chairmen, had been appointed to them; these included a few expatriates, civil servants, and non-party men in addition to a majority of NCNC stalwarts, including legislators. Five of the chairmen served without pay while the others received salaries varying from £600 to £2,000. In addition, nominees of the Eastern Government were appointed to the boards of various statutory bodies of the federal government.[19]

It was demonstrated in 1958 that the leaders of the Eastern Regional Government were prepared to terminate the appointments of board members who opposed them.[20] Moreover, party militants in

[16] Among the superior appointees in the local service in the Western Region are the Secretaries, who normally act as electoral officers in their jurisdictions. Frequently, they are natives of their council areas and it requires both tact and good conscience on their part to preserve a reputation for impartiality. The few electoral officers against whom there were justifiable complaints during the local elections of 1958 fell short of the high standards of impartial performance that were generally maintained.

[17] *Supra*, pp. 163-164. The Report of the Economic Mission recommended specifically "the creation on a large scale of [six named] statutory corporations . . . as essential adjuncts for the stimulation of investments in the Eastern Region." *Economic Rehabilitation of Eastern Nigeria*, Report of the Economic Mission to Europe and North America, by Nnamdi Azikiwe and L. P. Ojukwu (Enugu: 1955), p. 12. The authors recommended further: "These statutory corporations should be owned *in toto* by the Government, without prejudice to the right of any other private or public companies operating within the Region to organise their own enterprises on the same lines and in competition with these corporations. Either the Government or the Finance Corporation should provide the initial equity capital outlay of these statutory bodies. Other investors may provide loan capital or machinery or technical skill or management."

[18] Sports Commission, Library Board, Marketing Board, Scholarship Board, Development Corporation, Finance Corporation, Cinema Corporation, Information Service, Printing Corporation, Pharmaceutical Corporation, Tourist Corporation, and Economic Planning Commission.

[19] *Eastern House of Assembly Debates,* June-August, 1956, Third Session, Second and Third Meetings, pp. 117-120.

[20] The Eastern Regional Government terminated the appointment of Dr. O. N. Egesi to the board of the Cinema Corporation as a result of his active involve-

general feel that the bounties of patronage should be bestowed upon persons of proven fidelity only, and they have objected strenuously to the occasional appointment of a non-party man to the chairmanship of an Eastern Government Board. Appointments outside of the party have been especially controversial when the favored individuals have refused to pay the 10 percent party levy on their salaries that is required of the boardmen as well as parliamentarians.[21] In addition it is widely regarded as inequitable to heap the rewards of patronage upon parliamentarians, who are viewed as a privileged class,[22] and it has been suggested in party councils that every public appointment should be made upon the recommendation of a divisional or branch executive committee in the home area of the appointee, a procedure for which a precedent has been reported.[23] Most of these objections to favoritism and the monopolization of privileges by a select minority as well as most recommendations to democratize and purify the patronage system have been treated by party leaders with gravity. Nevertheless, the top leadership has retained the right to exercise discretion in making appointments outside of the party and from the ranks of parliamentarians, a right which is bolstered by the fact that certain partisan appointments (for which the leadership has been responsible) do not appear to have been defensible in terms of public service.[24]

---

ment in the Reform Committee campaign against the leadership of Dr. Azikiwe. *Daily Times,* July 15, 1958. See *supra,* p. 220.

[21] At the Second Annual Conference of the Eastern Regional Organization, Dr. M. I. Okpara, Chairman of the Eastern Working Committee, declared: "How could the majority of members of boards refuse to pay their 10% levy as do all Ministers and most Assemblymen. This is a serious matter about which a decision must be reached at this conference." "An Address Presented to the Second Annual Conference of the NCNC in the Eastern Region by Dr. M. I. Okpara, Chairman of the Eastern Working Committee" (Port Harcourt: 1955), p. 7. (Mimeographed.)

[22] "Throughout the Region there is too much grumble among Party members about Party patronage. It is not possible that Party patronage should be extended to all at the same time but those who happen to have benefited from the Party should not give the impression that Party patronage is their exclusive right. There are many people who work and sacrifice silently for this Party. What people like that want, is not always appointment to Boards or Public Offices but a simple appreciation for the sacrifices which they make. In many Constituencies, there are complaints about Honourable Members who, once elected to the Legislative Houses, quickly forget those who toiled and sweated with them in order to make it possible for them to win elections." "Report submitted by the Principal Organizing Secretary to the Chairman of the Eastern Working Committee for Presentation to the Regional Conference of the NCNC, Port Harcourt, 6 and 7 September 1957" (mimeographed), p. 6.

[23] Journal notes on a meeting of the Eastern Working Committee at Enugu, February 22, 1958. The agency cited was the Nigerian Broadcasting Corporation.

[24] The Minorities Commission drew attention to the loan of £200,000 made by the Eastern Government to the Eastern Nigeria Printing Corporation, a statutory

A representative example of the utilization of governmental resources for partisan ends is the Eastern Nigeria Information Service. This agency publishes a weekly newspaper, the *Eastern Outlook,* that is for all intents and purposes an NCNC party organ. By contrast, the *Gaskiya* Corporation, a Northern Government instrumentality, publishes biweekly newspapers in Hausa (*Gaskiya Ta Fi Kwabo*—"Truth is worth more than a penny") and in English (the *Nigerian Citizen*) that are noted for their professional standards and traditions of relative objectivity, although they do favor the Northern Peoples' Congress.

In every region, the major instrumentalities of commercial patronage are the regional marketing boards[25] and the regional development corporations. The marketing boards appoint qualified firms and individuals as their certified agents, called Licensed Buying Agents, who purchase controlled crops from middlemen or directly from producers at fixed prices. It has been the policy of all marketing boards under regional government control to license Nigerian agents to compete with the oligopolistic expatriate firms. By 1957, African agents supplied 49 percent of all palm oil sold to the Eastern Regional Marketing Board.[26] Although the licenses are issued on the basis of commercial criteria, the latent asset of political good will cannot be overlooked. In 1958 a political opponent of the NCNC felt the whip of commercial patronage when the Eastern Regional Marketing Board "decided not to reappoint" as a licensed buying agent under its soya bean marketing program, a company headed by an individual who was the Vice-Patron and a principal financial backer of the Democratic Party of Nigeria and the Cameroons. There was little doubt that this decision was in the nature of a political reprisal, inasmuch as the financial position of the company was unquestionably

---

body staffed by political appointees under the chairmanship of the President-General of the Zikist National Vanguard, which "had done no printing." Colonial Office, *Report of the Commission appointed to enquire into the fears of Minorities and the means of allaying them* (London: 1958), p. 41.

[25] It has been observed that in 1954 the assets of several commodity marketing boards were divided among all-purpose regional marketing boards according to the principle of derivation and in keeping with the philosophy of the new federal constitution. The regional marketing boards were authorized to use their funds, varying from £15.1 million to £34.4 million, for unrestricted purposes of economic development. Possibly no single decision in the decade prior to independence has been more fateful for the development of political economy in Nigeria. See the *Report of the Resumed Conference on the Nigerian Constitution held in Lagos in January and February, 1954* (London: 1954), p. 60; *International Bank for Reconstruction and Development, The Economic Development of Nigeria* (Baltimore: Johns Hopkins Press, 1955), pp. 169-170.

[26] Information from the Eastern Ministry of Production.

sound and the Board's action followed an open threat by the Eastern Premier.[27]

Marketing-board funds provide investment and loan capital for the regional statutory corporations, including the development corporations, which undertake agricultural and industrial projects independently and in partnership with other governments or with private interests. In all regions these corporations and their subsidiaries are managed by politically reliable administrators.[28] [29] Funds are also channelled into regional loans boards and finance corporations which make grants to local government authorities, private firms, and individuals. In the Western Region, for example, this function is performed by the Western Region Finance Corporation.[30] Since the

[27] The individual concerned was Mr. L. N. Obioha, the head of Obioha Bros. and Co. In a public speech at Aba during the campaign against the NCNC Reform Committee (later D.P.N.C.), Dr. Azikiwe declared that the government "would be foolish to renew Mr. Obioha's produce buying license in view of the fact that he had joined the Mbadiwe conspiracy to overthrow the Government unconstitutionally." *West African Pilot*, July 26, 1958; *Daily Telegraph*, September 9, 1958.

[28] In 1958 the Eastern Region Development Corporation and the Eastern Regional Marketing Board were under the chairmanship of Mr. L. P. (later Sir Odumegwu) Ojukwu, a transport magnate and director of several firms, including the large British construction company of Costain (West Africa) Limited. He was also Chairman of the Nigeria Produce Marketing Company Limited, an instrumentality of the regional marketing boards which arranges for the sale and export of their produce abroad. Mr. Ojukwu is at the top of the Nigerian business pyramid; he is a son of Nnewi in Onitsha Division, a former NCNC member of the House of Representatives, and a close associate of Dr. Nnamdi Azikiwe.

The chairman of the Western Nigeria Development Corporation was Mr. Alfred O. Rewane, the Political Secretary to the Federal President of the Action Group. The Northern Region Development Corporation was under the chairmanship of Alhaji Aliyu, Turakin Zazzau, an NPC stalwart.

[29] When the Action Group came to power in 1952, reliable party men were appointed to the Western Region Production Development Board (later Western Nigeria Development Corporation) to ensure the implementation of the economic policies of the party. *Supra*, p. 275. Virtually every person who served as a member of the Western Region Production Development Board during the period 1954-57 can be identified as a prominent member or supporter of the Action Group: M. A. Ajasin, MHR (Owo), Rev. S. A. Adeyefa, MHA (Ife), A. Akerele (Oyo), S. O. Lanlehin, MHA (Ibadan), M. S. Sowole (Remo), The Olokpe of Okpe (Sapele), M. A. Ogun (Lagos), A. O. Rewane (Warri), S. O. Sonibare (Director of the Amalgamated Press), W. E. Mowarin (Urhobo), Rev. E. T. Latunde, Chief A. M. Adebule, Prince A. Adedoyin (Remo), S. Y. Eke (Benin), Chief J. O. Kashimawo (Abeokuta), L. Omole (Ilesha), E. A. Sanda, J. O. Odunjo (Egbado). A similar inference may be drawn from a perusal of the members of the Committees of Management, other than officials, for the years 1955-1957. See *Western Region Production Development Board, Annual Report, 1954-1955*; *A. R., 1955-1956*; *A. R., 1956-1957*. Also *Western House of Assembly, Debates, Official Report*, December 1956, pp. 30, 146.

[30] The Chairman of the Western Region Finance Corporation in 1958 was Mr. O. B. Akin-Olugbade; his predecessor was Chief S. L. Akintola (later

business class in every region generally supports the government party, it is not surprising that the vast majority of major loan recipients in the Western Region have been Action Group members or supporters.[31] Smaller loans to farmers and fishermen are made by statutory agents of the Finance Corporation, known as Local Loans Boards. In 1957 there were 209 such boards in existence throughout the Western Region which had made loans to 11,523 persons.[32] In reply to allegations of favoritism in the administration of the loans program, Premier Awolowo stated in the Western House of Assembly that "members have been appointed to all Local Boards largely on the advice of each Local Government Council."[33] Yet it has been alleged that the advice of councils controlled by the NCNC is frequently disregarded, and there is little doubt that the great preponderance of loans board personnel is Action Group in sympathy.[34] Similar observations apply to the loan procedures of the Eastern and Northern Governments.[35] Therefore, in all regions, fledging firms which need loans are likely to cultivate political good will.

Commercial contracts are awarded by the several governments and their statutory corporations. All governments utilize tendering procedures which are strictly monitored by civil servants; but ministers or junior ministers participate, influence filters through the administrative pores, and it is good business to have the right political

---

Premier of the West). The chairman of the Western Region Marketing Board was barrister S. L. Durosaro.

[31] A schedule of loans made by the corporation is appended to the *Second Annual Report and Accounts of the Western Region Finance Corporation, 1956-1957.* See allegations of favoritism by a member of the NCNC in the *Western House of Assembly, Debates, Official Report,* December 1956, pp. 34, 36, and the reply by the Premier listing 13 NCNC supporters who have received government loans and 13 Action Group recipients who have been prosecuted for defaulting on payments. *Ibid.,* pp. 71-73.

[32] *Second Annual Report and Accounts of the Western Region Finance Corporation, 1956-1957,* p. 3.

[33] *Western House of Assembly Debates, Official Report,* December 1956, p. 70.

[34] *Ibid.,* pp. 131, 187, 195. The writer calculated that 50 out of 60 members of local loans boards in 10 urban areas were Action Group members or supporters, including a majority of Action Group members in Benin and Warri, where the local government councils were NCNC controlled. The Commission of Inquiry into the Fears of Minorities noted that certain appointments "bore little relation" to the recommendations of the local councils, but concluded that it was "not satisfactorily proved that the chief qualification for appointment was support of the Action Group." *Op.cit.,* p. 14.

[35] In 1958 the Loans Board of the Northern Region Development Corporation consisted of politically reliable members of the NPC. The writer was informed that preference in the allocation of loans was always given to applicants of Northern origin. In the Eastern Region, loans are handled by a department of the Eastern Region Development Corporation.

connections. Thus, in the Western Region, contracts above the value of £1,000 are awarded by a Regional Tenders Board consisting of three officials and two unofficial members. The writer has calculated that in the period 1951-1957 building contracts exceeding the value of £2,500 each had been awarded by the Regional Tenders Board to 12 African contracting firms, all of which were owned and managed by members or supporters of the Action Group.[36] It should be emphasized again that this does not indicate favoritism as much as it reflects the fact that the overwhelming majority of businessmen in the Western Region support the government party.[37] Government spokesmen have denied categorically that either contractors or the recipients of government loans have ever been required to make donations of 10 percent of the value of such contracts or loans to the Action Group, as alleged by the opposition.[38]

In sum, commercial patronage, including government loans, marketing board licensing, and government contracting, is channelled through public agencies that are quasi-political in nature and composition. In all regions, these agencies serve the political interests of the government party only.[39] At the federal level, the partisan colora-

[36] The names of these firms, derived from the Contract Register, Works and Buildings Division, Western Ministry of Works and Transport (Office of the Chief Architect), were as follows: T. A. Oni and Sons, J. F. Ososami, Adebayo and Olatunbosun, Akinfenwa, Abdulai and Awomolo, Akin-Deko, Foye Builders, Lucas and O'Dwyer, Unity Contractors, Majekadunmi, Idowu Bros., Solan and Sons. T. A. Oni was the most highly rated African contracting firm, i.e., Class "G"; Ososami and Abdulai and Awomolo were rated in Class "F". The writer was able to calculate that contracts totalling £362,415 were awarded by the Western Regional Government between August 1952 and June 1957 to six African firms, the proprietors of which are listed as donors to the Action Group Headquarters Secretariat fund on plaques in the main meeting hall of the Secretariat building at Ibadan. These contracts amount to a shade under 70% of all contracts listed in the Western Region Register of Contracts of the Works Registration Board as having been awarded to African contractors during this period. The firms are: T. A. Oni and Sons, J. F. Ososami, Abdulai and Awomolo, Akin-Deko, Foye Builders (Oyename), and Unity Contractors (J. A. O. Obadeyi).

[37] For allegations of discrimination in the award of contracts and denials by government spokesmen see *Western House of Assembly Debates, Official Report*, December 1956, pp. 36, 113-135, 140-141, 153.

[38] *Ibid.*, p. 203; see allegations by members of the opposition, *ibid.*, pp. 44, 89-90, 118.

[39] During Dr. Azikiwe's campaign against the NCNC Reform Committee in 1958 (*supra*, pp. 223-228), the Eastern Premier was reported to have given his opponents the following ultimatum in the course of an address to the Owerri Urban District Council: "NCNC rebels who fail by today to withdraw their signature from the infamous Mbadiwe document demanding the resignation of Dr. Nnamdi Azikiwe, National President of the Party and Premier of the Eastern Region, may have their property confiscated should they be indebted to the Eastern Government unless they are able to pay up such debts, at once. Others who are members of

tion of loan and contract procedures is not attributable to a single party and the sphere of patronage provided by federal agencies to party leaders is primarily administrative—i.e., the award of jobs—rather than commercial.[40]

ECONOMIC INTEREST GROUPS

The most important relationships in this category involve Nigerian banking institutions. Marketing board funds, channelled into Nigerian banks, have enabled those institutions to extend credit to Nigerian businessmen, notably to Licensed Buying Agents.[41] In 1955 the Eastern Regional Government acquired 87.7 percent of the ownership of the African Continental Bank by virtue of a £750,000 investment; it has since acquired total ownership, including the shares held by companies which are related to the *West African Pilot* and the Zik Group of newspapers—a chain which Dr. Azikiwe founded before the initiation of his career in government.[42] It may be assumed that most of the employees of the African Continental Bank, certainly all of the senior staff, have been members or supporters of the NCNC. In 1958 the Managing Director of the Bank (Mr. Adolphus Kofi Blankson) was National Auditor of the NCNC. He was also Managing Director of the West African Pilot Limited, the Associated Newspapers of Nigeria, and the Comet Press Limited, publishers of the Zik Group of newspapers which constitute the main arm of publicity for the NCNC. Mr. Blankson was Editor-in-Chief of the *West African Pilot* and of the Zik Group generally, while Mr. F. S.

Government Boards or Corporations will be thrown out, while contractors will be blacklisted." *West African Pilot*, July 14, 1958.

[40] For example, the Chairman of the Federal Loans Board in 1958 was a prominent member of the NCNC (Barrister Adeniran Ogunsanya, President General of the NCNC Youth Association and member of the Lagos Town Council). Loans are made upon an investigation by a civil servant, the Director of Commerce and Industry. The board is multi-partisan in its composition and it has not been regarded as a source of commercial patronage.

It is understood, however, that political influence has not been absent from the procedures of the Federal Works Registration Board and the Federal Tenders Board, both of which come under the Federal Ministry of Works, an NPC portfolio since 1954.

[41] W. T. Newlyn and D. C. Rowan, *Money and Banking in British Colonial Africa* (Oxford: The Clarendon Press, 1954), p. 217, n. 1; International Bank for Reconstruction and Development, *The Economic Development of Nigeria* (Baltimore: The Johns Hopkins Press, 1955), pp. 158-159.

[42] In 1958, about 6% of the shares of the African Continental Bank were held by companies of the Zik Group and the remainder were held by individuals, not including Dr. Azikiwe, who had transferred all of his personal holdings in the bank to the Eastern Regional Government without compensation.

McEwen, National Secretary of the NCNC, was General Manager of the *West African Pilot*.

The Zik Group of newspapers[43] are run on a commercial basis and they are not subject to party control. From time to time, leaders of the party have contemplated the extension of official or effective party supervision. In 1957 an *ad hoc* committee of NCNC leaders prepared a memorandum for the National Executive Committee which noted that the "nine Zik Group of Companies engaged in the purchase of printing materials, the printing, publishing, and selling of newspapers, literature, etc." were "indebted to the African Continental Bank to the tune of £300,000 by way of debentures and overdrafts."[44] The committee concluded that no less than £500,000 was required to put the Zik Group of newspapers on a sound financial footing and suggested that such an amount should be raised through the sale of shares in the companies to individuals who were sympathetic to the party. Implicit in this proposal was the idea that the party should both provide for the subsidization and exercise control over editorial policies of the Zik Group of newspapers.

Subsequently the latter proposal was endorsed by a subcommittee of the NEC which advised the National President to spare himself and the party any embarrassment by giving up his personal holdings in the companies.[45] However, the National President, whose financial interests in the Zik Group were controlling, appeared to reject these proposals. On May 14, 1958, exactly one month before the Reform Committee rebellion against the leadership of Dr. Azikiwe, the *West African Pilot* defined its relationship to the NCNC in unequivocal terms:[46]

[43] In addition to the *West African Pilot*, a national daily newspaper, published in Lagos, the local daily newspapers of the Zik Group include the *Eastern Nigerian Guardian* (Port Harcourt), the *Eastern Sentinel* (Enugu), the *Nigerian Spokesman* (Onitsha), the *Southern Nigeria Defender* (Ibadan), and the *Daily Comet* (Kano).

[44] The committee attributed this condition to competition in the newspaper field from the rival Amalgamated Press (Action Group) and from the efficient representative of the *London Daily Mirror's* West African chain, namely the *Daily Times*. Moreover, it was observed that "internal political animosities involved us in a number of libels; and between 1953 and '56 we paid an average of £5,500 a year in court fines for libel and sedition. We did not have the capital to meet the cost of these new developments and heavy court fines and so we had to resort to borrowing." Memorandum on Party Policy prepared by an *ad hoc* committee of NCNC leaders on board the *M. V. Apapa* en route to Nigeria from the London Constitutional Conference of 1957.

[45] Minutes of the meeting of the Committee set up by the National Executive Committee to consider Party Publicity and Finance, October 1957.

[46] "Above Party and Office," Part 3, *West African Pilot*, May 14, 1958.

"We support 100 per cent all that the NCNC stands for. But we cannot live and eat politics all the time. We are a commercial organization, and most members of the party who individually receive our constant support do not reciprocate. This paper must survive either as a commercial concern or political enterprise. But we are the former—at the moment at least—and being so, we intend to maintain our independence whilst upholding the principles of the party."

This declaration left no doubt that persons loyal to Dr. Azikiwe would continue to hold the reins of the "party press," for the time being at least. Moreover, it appeared to obviate a technical objection to the initiation of a rival press by other members of the party. It is known, for example, that Dr. Mbadiwe and others planned to launch a pro-NCNC newspaper several months prior to the inauguration of the *Daily Telegraph* in July 1958. At that time, the only non-member of the Zik Group which supported the NCNC militantly was the *West African Vanguard*, a bi-lingual (English-Yoruba) weekly newspaper, published by NCNC leaders in Ilesha;[47] it was wholly concerned with Ilesha affairs interpreted from an NCNC point of view.

In 1958 there were three African banks in close association with the Action Group. The most important was the National Bank of Nigeria Limited, the oldest existing African bank with the greatest volume of business.[48] Both the Chairman of the Board of Directors (Dr. Akinola Maja) and the General Manager of the bank (Chief T. Adebayo Doherty) were Vice-Presidents of the Lagos branch of the Action Group and influential members of the party hierarchy. Most of the directors and leading shareholders of the National Bank are

[47] The principal backer of the *West African Vanguard* was J. O. Fadahunsi, MHA, First National Vice President of the NCNC and Chairman of the Ilesha Divisional Council. He is the co-proprietor of large trading and transport business in partnership with a leading member of the Action Group, a phenomenon that is rare enough to be noted.

[48] The National Bank of Nigeria Limited was incorporated in 1933 by three promoters, namely, Dr. Akinola Maja, Mr. T. Adebayo Doherty and Mr. H. A. Subair, all of whom became leading members of the Action Group. Dr. Maja and Mr. Subair were leaders of the Nigerian Youth Movement prior to the emergence of the Action Group and were also among the founders of the Service Press in 1938, which published the official organ of the Youth Movement. Dr. Doherty was elected to the Lagos Town Council in 1926 on the platform of the National Democratic Party.

In addition to the National Bank, two smaller banking institutions were supported by the Action Group in 1958, namely the Agbon Magbe Bank Limited and the Merchants Bank Limited. The former was managed and partly owned by Chief M. A. Okupe-Agbonmagbe, a Lagos businessman and chairman of the Action Group in Ijebu-Remo Division. The Merchants Bank was controlled by three persons, two of whom (M. A. K. Shonowo and J. F. Kamson) were associated with the Action Group.

persons of Yoruba descent or "Lagosians" of non-Nigerian descent, who support the Action Group morally and materially.

It is a settled policy of the Action Group to give "financial assistance to indigenous banks so that they may be better able to provide credit facilities to Nigerian businessmen."[49] Government support for the National Bank has taken two main forms: (1) deposits by the Western Government or its agencies—e.g., the Western Region Production Development Board (now Development Corporation) and the Western Region Marketing Board—and (2) direct investments by the Western Region Marketing Board. In 1955 the government of the Western Region deposited 45 percent of its funds in the National Bank[50] and the Western Region Marketing Board invested £1,000,000 in 4% cumulative non-participating preference shares of £1 each.

Critics have alleged that the Action Group has exploited the relationship between the Western Government and the National Bank for purposes of party finance. In 1956 an NCNC spokesman in the Western House of Assembly charged that the bank habitually gives overdrafts to businessmen "in consideration of considerable donations to the fund of the Action Group and its ancillary, the *Egbe Omo Oduduwa.*"[51] Certainly the National Bank has been crucial to the financing of the Action Group. On one occasion, Chief Awolowo characterized the relationship between the bank and the Action Group as "pure and simple, one between banker and customer."[52] Yet this particular "customer," i.e., the party, is chiefly responsible for the

[49] Speech by Premier Awolowo. *Western House of Assembly Debates, Official Report*, December 1956, p. 51.

[50] The negotiation which ended the Bank of British West Africa's "monopoly of Government Banking business" in the Western Region was reviewed by the Western Minister of Finance in the Western House of Assembly on December 21, 1956. The agreement between the B.B.W.A. and the National Bank of Nigeria involved the determination of "geographical spheres of influence for both banks" to be specified by the Western Government. *Ibid.*, pp. 135-139.

[51] *Ibid.*, p. 44, and see the sweeping if exaggerated criticisms made by the late Leader of the Opposition, *ibid.*, pp. 117-119:

"The one million pounds preference share capital supposed to be invested in the National Bank at four per cent was in reality given at an agreed rate of six per cent. The 2 per cent difference goes to the Action Group funds.

"All loan beneficiaries from the Regional Government and its allied agents are compelled to open an account in the National Bank. . . . Most contractors for Government and allied agencies on a specially prepared approved list are required on receipt of jobs to open account in the National Bank from which they pay a ten per cent commission into the Action Group coffers. . . . Many contractors, company directors, transporters are given overdraft facilities in return for large donations to the Action Group and the Egbe Omo Oduduwa."

[52] " . . . . the Action Group is a credit-worthy customer of the National Bank in every sense of the word, and . . . as at 19th of [December 1956] . . . the Action

bank's phenomenal growth and for its vastly enlarged capacity to serve the rising entrepreneurial class. It is not unreasonable to expect the individual beneficiaries of government policies to support the government party. Men of the long purse in Western Nigeria and Lagos have contributed heavily to the Action Group, and their example has been enormously influential among the chiefs and the middle class generally.[53] Nor is it likely that party officials keep tabs on the percentage of individual donations to private capital gains.

For several years prior to Independence, the National Bank was widely regarded as a bulwark of private enterprise and management in the financial structure of Nigeria. However, in 1961, following allegations of insolvency and mismanagement, the Western Regional Marketing Board converted its previous investment of £1 million into equity shares, made an additional investment of £2 million, and assumed total control of the bank. It would appear that the demise of private banking contributed to the eclipse of non-socialist thought in high party councils.

In 1962 a federal commission of inquiry into the financial practices of the Western Regional Government impugned the character of the National Bank's relationship with the Action Group. The bank was alleged to have extended unsecured loans to the Action Group through fictitious accounts and to have concealed the actual indebtedness of the party from a federal examiner.[54] But the main channel of funds for the Action Group between 1959 and 1961 was yet another company, the National Investment and Properties Company Limited, owned in its entirety by four leading members of the party. This company had been created in 1958, ostensibly to develop properties previously owned by the National Bank. Its real purpose, the commission alleged, was to finance the Action Group. Three of the four directors

---

Group's accounts with the Bank are in credit." *Ibid.*, p. 66; also *ibid.*, p. 164. In 1958, the Federal Treasurer of the Action Group reported to the Fourth Annual Congress that the party's account showed "a credit bank and cash balance of £12,228 8s 1d." Report of the Treasurer to the Fourth Annual Congress of the Action Group (*Congress Report*), p. 20.

[53] It is not unusual for several thousand pounds to be raised at a single conference of the Action Group or the *Egbe Omo Oduduwa* (*Supra,* p. 441). Over £3,000 was donated by delegates to the Ninth Annual General Assembly of the *Egbe Omo Oduduwa* in December 1956 (Official Minutes). Delegates at the 11th Annual General Assembly were reported to have donated £2,161. 3s. 5d to the *Egbe* Endowment Fund "in less than 90 minutes," including a donation of £1,000 by Olagbegi II, the *Olowo* of Owo, a regional minister without portfolio. *Daily Service*, November 29, 1958.

[54] *Report of Coker Commission of Inquiry into the affairs of certain Statutory Corporations in Western Nigeria* (Lagos: Federal Ministry of Information, 1962), Vol. I, pp. 55-58, and Vol. II, pp. 1-8.

of the company were prominent businessmen holding high party office—Dr. Akinola Maja, "Father of the Party," Chief S. O. Gbadamosi, Federal Treasurer, and Chief S. O. Sonibare, Federal Publicity Secretary; the fourth, Mr. Alfred Rewane, was the Director of the Western Nigeria Development Corporation and political secretary to Chief Awolowo.

The commission of inquiry disclosed that this company had received loans in excess of £6,000,000 from the Western Regional Marketing Board. Over £2,000,000 more, allocated by the Marketing Board to the Western Nigeria Development Corporation, was also diverted to the company, which realized close to another million pounds from the sale of property to the Western Regional Government at inflated prices, and by other means of questionable legality. During this period, mainly between 1959 and 1961, the company contributed more than £4,000,000 to the Action Group.[55]

Until 1960, the National Bank of Nigeria was the major shareholder in the Amalgamated Press of Nigeria Limited, publisher of the former *Daily Service,* formerly the Action Group's principal organ of the press, the *Nigerian Tribune* (Ibadan), the *Iwe Irohin Yoruba* (a Yoruba language daily newspaper), and several sectional newspapers in the upper North, the Middle Belt, the Mid-West, and the Eastern Region which were inaugurated prior to the federal election of 1959.[56] The Managing Director of the Amalgamated Press was Chief S. O. Sonibare. In 1960, the "Action Group chain" was taken over by a new company, Allied Newspapers Limited, owned substantially by the Nigerian Investment and Properties Company. At this juncture, the NIPC, acting through its subsidiary newspaper company, entered into a 50-50 partnership with a Canadian publisher, Thompson International Limited, to inaugurate the *Daily Express.*[57] Following the disclosures of 1962, this newspaper survived as an independent Action Group organ under the full ownership of its Canadian proprietor.

It is indicative of the pattern of politics in Nigeria that the Democratic Party of Nigeria and the Cameroons, which split away from the NCNC in 1958, was allied with a newly organized bank founded in

[55] The findings of the Report of the Coker Commission of Inquiry, published in four volumes, are summarized in *Sessional Paper No. 4 of 1962* (Lagos: Federal Ministry of Information, 1962).

[56] The Amalgamated Press was formed in 1953 by the merger of the Service Press and the African Press, publisher of the *Nigerian Tribune.* Obafemi Awolowo, founder of the African Press, was an honorary director of the Amalgamated Press until his resignation in 1955, after which he sold his shares. *Western House of Assembly Debates, Official Report,* December 1956, pp. 67-68.

[57] *Report of Coker Commission of Inquiry,* Vol. I, pp. 52-55; Vol. IV, p. 73.

Lagos by the party's Patron, and with a newly established newspaper which has survived the party itself. In 1960, the Northern Peoples' Congress acquired a financial ally in the Bank of the North, inaugurated with the controlling participation of the Northern Regional Government.[58]

In all regions the principal business associations tend to support the regional government party. Among the leading examples are the Northern Amalgamated Merchants' Union and the Northern Contractors' Union, both of which have been noted previously as quasi-affiliates of the NPC, and several Eastern groups allied to the NCNC: the Union of Niger African Traders at Onitsha, the Nigeria Motor Workers' Union (an employer-employee group) at Aba, and the Eastern Nigeria Civil Engineers and Building Contractors at Enugu.[59] In the Western Region and in Lagos a decisive majority of the business community is loyal to the Action Group. Nearly all of the African building contractors listed in the Register of Contractors of the Western Region Works Registration Board can be identified as members or supporters of the Action Group, as can most leading industrialists in the Western Region and most of the Licensed Buying Agents of the Western Region Marketing Board.[60] Action Group influence predominates within the Federation of Civil Engineering Building Contractors (Yaba, Lagos), the African Contractors' Union, the Nigerian Produce Buyers Union, and the Nigerian Motor Transport Union (a motor owners' and employers' association). At local levels, both the Action Group and the NCNC

[58] "The nominal share capital of the Bank is £250,000 which is partly contributed by the Northern Region Development Corporation, Northern Region Marketing Board and indigenous individuals. One of the aims of this Bank is to expand more credit facilities and its policy will no doubt be similar to that of the Banks already established in the country." "Speech by the Premier of Northern Nigeria at the Opening of the Kaduna Branch of the Bank of the North, January 15, 1960." *Northern Nigeria Daily Press Service*, No. 84 (January 15, 1960).

[59] The Eastern Nigeria Civil Engineers and Building Contractors of Enugu was a center of strength for the Association for One Nigeria in 1958. *Supra*, p. 212. Its predecessor, called the Association of Eastern Contractors, appears to have applied continuous pressure on the NCNC Eastern Working Committee to secure business advantages from the Eastern Regional Government. A letter to the Chairman of the Working Committee in 1955 affirmed that the vast majority of Association members were "members, supporters and sympathizers of the NCNC party." NCNC Eastern Working Committee File No. 14: Contractors, 4.

The writer calculated that 37 African contracting firms were listed in the Eastern Government's Schedule of Contracts Other than Ration Contracts Awarded from October 1954-1957. Most of them can be identified as supporters of the NCNC.

[60] Sources of information include the *Second Annual Report and Accounts of the Western Region Finance Corporation, 1956-1957*, and the *Third Annual Report of the Western Region Marketing Board, 1956-1957*, pp. 28-29, 39-40, 52.

have organized groups of market women. The NCNC appears to be stronger than its southern rival in the trade union arena, while the NPC is entrenched in the Northern minefields.

ETHNIC AND RELIGIOUS INTEREST GROUPS

Numerous references have been made in previous chapters to the participation of associations based on ethnic affinity in party politics. These groups are important in the Eastern and Western Regions and in the Middle Belt area of the Northern Region. "In the upper Northern Region, ethnic group associations play a comparatively minor role in politics. Their absence among the Hausa-Fulani may be attributed to alternative bonds of religion and to the multi-tribal span of the traditional Fulani empire."[61] At this point, the two most highly politicized ethnic group associations, which support the NCNC and the Action Group respectively, will be described.

The Ibo State Union is a nationality or pan-tribal association based on the 5.5 million Ibo people of Nigeria, more than 90 percent of whom live in the traditional Ibo areas of the Eastern Region. It has been involved periodically in the internal affairs of the NCNC. The organization of the Ibo State Union is based on the ubiquitous town, clan, and divisional "improvement" unions of Iboland, and the branches of these unions created by "sons abroad" in the new urban areas of commercial towns. Article 3 of the Ibo State Union Constitution (1951) extends membership to all Ibo Unions "at home" or "abroad." In addition, membership is granted to every town, clan, or district in Iboland—e.g., Asaba town, Ututu clan, Northern Ngwa District. Two kinds of membership are prescribed: registered membership (Ibo unions are required to pay a registration fee of two guineas; towns, clans, and districts are required to pay ten guineas), and unregistered membership ("All unregistered Ibo Unions, Towns, Clans or Districts shall be nominal members"). The highest organ of the Union is the Ibo State Assembly, attended by representatives of the various Ibo unions. The latter are graded A, B, and C on the basis of their memberships and allotted 4, 3, and 2 seats respectively; the towns, clans, and districts are allotted 6 seats each. Attendance is reported to vary between 200 and 500 normally, although as many as 1,000 persons are said to have participated on occasion.

The system of representation is even more complicated in practice.

[61] The writer is indebted for this observation to his colleague, C. S. Whitaker, Jr. It appears in a forthcoming jointly written publication.

We have noted that many of the town, clan, and divisional unions have branches "abroad" in the cosmopolitan urban communities. These branches compose the urban Ibo unions which are entitled to four representatives at the Ibo State Assembly. For example, the Port Harcourt Ibo Union consists of many unions, e.g., the Bende Divisional Union, etc., which in turn include lesser unions. It may seem anomalous for a large urban community like Port Harcourt to be restricted to four members, while any rural clan is entitled to six. Yet the urban, educated elements are not overwhelmed in the Ibo State Assembly for two reasons. First, the maximum potential rural attendance is never approached; secondly, the clans are frequently represented by educated sons who reside in urban communities. The closeness of the relationship between city dwellers and their home villages is a fact of prime importance to the process of political communication in Nigerian society.

The effective governing body of the Ibo State Union is an Executive Committee of about forty men, elected for terms of three years by the Ibo State Assembly. At present, no minister of state or ranking officer of the NCNC is a member of the Executive, but eminent Ibos, including ministers of state, are permitted to attend meetings of the Executive as co-opted members. Yet leaders of the Union sometimes insist that it has played no major role in Nigerian politics since the establishment of a genuine party system in 1951.[62] On the other hand, they frequently contend that the Union has a "traditional" role to perform in the settlement of disputes among Ibos. In this connection it may foster Ibo solidarity by resolving quarrels between Ibo politicians before they reach the party level. But the Union failed to resolve a major dispute among Ibo leaders of the NCNC in 1952-1953 and again in 1958. In the former case, the exploitation of the Union for political ends tarnished its claim to be a non-partisan cultural body and infuriated non-Ibos in the Eastern Region, many of whom turned away from the NCNC.[63] Furthermore, NCNC leaders cannot afford

[62] A memorandum submitted by the Ibo State Union to the Minorities Commission in November 1957 contained this statement: "It may only . . . be necessary to say that the political activities of the Union were remarkable only during the period of the country's intense struggle to remove colonial dictatorship. During this period it donated funds to politicians like other organizations in the country to assist them in their struggle for the country's self-government. This was inevitable under a colonial government in which political parties are either weak or non-existent."

[63] In April 1953, a meeting of Ibo leaders was convened in Port Harcourt by Dr. Azikiwe, in his capacity as President of the NCNC, to reconcile the parties to the Eastern Regional dispute. (NCNC notice of April 9, 1953, convening a meeting on April 26, 1953, at the home of Chief M. I. Asinobi in Port Harcourt.)

to acknowledge publicly that the Ibo State Union may perform an occasionally useful role of intra-party conciliation. Historically, the NCNC is as much Yoruba as it is Ibo and it was significant that among the 7 NCNC federal ministers appointed in 1959, Yoruba personalities outnumbered Ibos by 3 to 2. Yet the Ibo constituencies of the East form a solid block of electoral support and the NCNC is acutely sensitive to allegations of "Ibo domination." When the supporters of Dr. Mbadiwe tried to use the Ibo State Executive as a medium of pressure on the National President of the NCNC, Dr. Azikiwe reported his blunt rebuff to the Union to a Special Convention of the party in January 1958, thus:[64]

"I must remark in passing that the Ibo State Union met at Onitsha on Sunday, January 26, at the instance of Dr. Mbadiwe, who requested the convening of this meeting to enable him to air certain grievances against the National President [of the NCNC], who informed the Ibo State Union that although he respected that organization, yet he would not attend this particular meeting, especially if it affects matters which are purely of concern to the party. I hope that this convention will determine the issues involved in accordance with the law and practice of our Constitution."

In the course of debate on the presidential address, a non-Ibo National Officer of the NCNC expressed his enthusiastic appreciation of the National President's statement on the Ibo State Union. Had the National President reacted in any other manner, he observed, critics would allege that the NCNC had a special way to settle disputes between Ibo personalities while non-Ibos were disciplined and thrown to the wolves.[65] When the Ibo State Executive was unable to stem the conflict between Dr. Azikiwe and Dr. Mbadiwe, it announced that neither party would respond to its appeal for a settlement and that it would make no further attempt to intervene. The Ibo State Assem-

All Ibo ministers were invited to attend, and a decision was taken to the effect that their resignations from the Executive Council were in the best interests of the Ibo people and the Eastern Region. To restore harmony in the Region, a peace committee was set up under the chairmanship of Mr. L. P. Ojukwu, a prominent businessman. *Daily Times*, May 1, 2, 6, 1953. A number of Ibo leaders and most non-Ibo leaders objected strenuously to the employment of an Ibo committee to deal with political problems affecting the entire Region. At this juncture, many non-Ibos decided that the NCNC in the East served the purpose of Ibo domination and transferred their loyalties to the opposition.

[64] "Enforcement of Party Discipline," Presidential Address delivered by Dr. Nnamdi Azikiwe at the Special Convention of the National Council of Nigeria and the Cameroons, Enugu, January 30, 1958 (No. E. 144), p. 3.

[65] Journal notes on the proceedings of the NCNC Special Convention, Enugu, January 30, 1958.

bly then passed a vote of gratitude to its Executive for having endeavored to effect a reconciliation.[66] During the 1959 federal election, the Union adopted an official policy of neutrality in the contest between the NCNC and Dr. Mbadiwe's Democratic Party of Nigeria and the Cameroons in the Ibo constituencies.

While the Ibo State Executive has not been amenable to facile manipulation by the NCNC leadership, the lower echelons of the Union—i.e., the town, village, district, and clan unions—work virtually without direction to identify the NCNC with the cause of Ibo welfare. In many instances, town and clan unions affiliated with the Ibo State Union have made up for the organizational failings of the official party organization. For example, the ground swell of mass support for Azikiwe in the summer of 1958, during his struggle with Dr. Mbadiwe, was generated largely by local units of the Ibo State Union. In addition, certain branches of the party, including the strong NCNC organization in Port Harcourt, derive their strength from sub-nationality associations affiliated with the Ibo State Union.[67] Nonetheless, leaders of the party are opposed in principle to organizational reliance on "tribal unions," which they view with mistrust as potentially rival structures of authority. The National Secretary has called such reliance "a lazy man's way of organization." One instance of conflict between the party and a supporting Ibo union, which was most embarrassing to all concerned, occurred in October 1957, when the Bende Divisional Union criticized the Premier for having appointed someone other than its favorite son, Dr. M. I. Okpara, to act as Premier during Dr. Azikiwe's brief leave of absence. Dr. Azikiwe's reaction was prompt and stern: "My dear compatriot," he wrote to the federal secretary of the Bende Divisional Union, "you are playing

[66] *Daily Times*, August 5, 1958. This vote of gratitude was condemned by the *West African Pilot* on the ground that the NCNC "is not an Ibo organization" and that the Union had no right to intervene in party matters. *West African Pilot*, August 6, 1958.

[67] In 1958 numerous ethnic group associations affiliated with the Port Harcourt Ibo Union were represented informally within the official structure of the Port Harcourt NCNC by influential members of the branch executive committee and the executive committee of the Port Harcourt NCNC Youth Association. Among them were the following: the Nnewi Patriotic Union, the Orlu Divisional Union, the Orlu Youth League, the Oguta Union, the Owerri Divisional Union, the Mbasi Clan Union, the Bende Divisional Union, the Ikwerri Development Union, the Okigwe Union, and the Abiriba Improvement Union. The Ibo Union of Port Harcourt, comprising representatives of these and other Ibo associations, coordinates certain of the activities of its affiliates but has no power of direction over them. It does not constitute an effective alternative power structure to the NCNC branch, inasmuch as the latter draws its popular support directly from the people and indirectly from their sub-nationality associations.

with fire and I am in the mood to assure you that fire can burn with disastrous effects."[68]

Among the non-Ibo ethnic group associations which merit designation among the unofficial ancillaries of the NCNC, two Mid-Western organizations have been prominent, namely, the Urhobo Renascent Convention, which has been partisan to the NCNC since 1948,[69] and the Warri Peoples' Party, an Itsekeri group which has favored the inclusion of Warri Division within the proposed Mid-West State.[70]

The leading ethnic group association aligned with the Action Group is the Yoruba nationality association, *Egbe Omo Oduduwa* (Society of the Descendants of *Oduduwa*).[71] Unlike the Ibo State Union, the *Egbe Omo Oduduwa* is a highly centralized organization based on regular branches of the *Egbe* rather than pre-existing or self-subsistent tribal unions. According to the constitution of the society it is the duty of the Central Executive Council to establish branches, and 160 registered branches were reported in 1958.[72] Branches of 40 members or less are represented at an Annual General Assembly by a minimum of 2 delegates and every branch is entitled to an additional delegate for every additional 20 members. The society is governed by a Central Executive Council and officers are elected for two-year terms. Chief Awolowo has been General Secretary since the inauguration of the society; Dr. Akinola Maja, "Father of the Action Group" and Chairman of the Board of the National Bank, succeeded the late Sir Adeyemo Alakija as President of the *Egbe*, and Chief S. L. Akintola, Premier of the Western Region, has been a Legal Adviser. Normally spokesmen for the *Egbe* do not equivocate on the partisanship of the society. At the Ninth Annual General Assembly in December 1956, Chief Akintola is reported to have said that the aims and objects of the *Egbe* and the Action Group are as inseparable as wine and water.[73] Two years later, Dr. Akinola Maja

---

[68] *Daily Times*, October 26, 1957; see also Dr. Azikiwe's Presidential Address to the Seventh Annual Convention, Aba, October 28, 1957, p. 24. (Mimeographed.)

[69] The Urhobo Renascent Convention was organized in Lagos in 1948 by Chief Yamu Numa, who was elected to the Western House of Assembly in 1951. For a time the URC was a member-union of the NCNC.

[70] "Memorandum of the Warri Peoples' Party in behalf of Warri and Western Ijaw People" (to the Minorities Commission), November 1, 1957.

[71] *Supra*, pp. 64-72, 101-112.

[72] Constitution of the *Egbe Omo Oduduwa*, "Branches and District Councils." *Daily Times*, November 29, 1958.

[73] Minutes of the Ninth Annual General Assembly of the Egbe Omo Oduduwa, held at Shagamu, Ijebu-Remo, December 17-19, 1956.

admonished members of the *Egbe* to vote "solidly as a body in the 1959 Federal general elections."[74]

In theory, the *Egbe* is non-partisan and its relationship to the Action Group is wholly unofficial; in practice, its service to the Action Group is beyond compare. The two associations are virtually inseparable in rural areas of Yorubaland. To the average farmer for whom cultural and political interests are indivisible, the distinction between the *Egbe Omo Oduduwa* and the *Egbe Afenifere* (the Yoruba name for the Action Group; literally, "society of the lovers of good things") is too fine to be respected. Neither organization is traditional, their memberships coincide, and both of them are sponsored by the *Obas* (sacred kings) on grounds of Yoruba patriotism.[75] Frequently the *Egbe* is employed to settle disputes between Yoruba personalities, in particular among chiefs, that might otherwise embarrass the Action Group.[76] Occasionally it has been utilized by the pan-Yoruba elite, as in the extreme case of the late ex-*Alafin* of Oyo, to coerce a recalcitrant chief.[77] In general, the *Egbe Omo Oduduwa* functions as a crucial link between the Action Group, the chiefs, and other men of influence to facilitate the implementation of party policies (including policies affecting the position of chiefs), with a minimum of difficulty or resistance.

[74] *Daily Service*, November 28, 1958.

[75] We have seen that Action Group doctrine prescribes a crucial role for *Obas* and chiefs in the political organization of the peasantry. *Obas* are disposed by their cultural interests, especially their interest in the preservation of traditional institutions, to affiliate with the *Egbe Omo Oduduwa*. Their enthusiasm for the Action Group may be enhanced by the notion that the party is but the *Egbe* for elections.

In July 1958, the writer observed a conference of the Action Group Oshun Divisional Organization in the town of Ilobu, near Oshogbo, Western Region. Several hundred delegates and about 25 *Obas* were in attendance, including the *Atoaja* of Oshogbo, the *Olowu* of Iwo, the *Sogon* of Ogbomosho, and the *Timi* of Ede. All of the *Obas* were patrons of the Action Group and their collective presence in customary regalia affirmed the sanction of traditional authority with which the Action Group was endowed. The conference was conducted by the Divisional Leader, Chief S. L. Akintola, then Federal Minister of Communications and Aviation in the "National Government," later Premier of the West. A significant item of business was the report of a committee on the financing of the 1957 Annual Conference of the *Egbe Omo Oduduwa*, a five-day event which had taken place in Oshogbo at a cost of some £4,000, defrayed mainly by the host Oshun section of the *Egbe Omo Oduduwa*. In Oshun Division, the *Egbe* and the Action Group were identical organizations.

[76] For example, it was reported that representatives of the *Egbe Omo Oduduwa* led by President Akinola Maja settled a long standing dispute between Oba Alaiyeluwa Gbelegbuwa II, the Awujale of Ijebu-Ode, on one side and certain Chiefs and people of Ijebu-Ode on the other. *Daily Service*, December 31, 1954. The *Egbe* has not been uniformly successful in the performance of this peacemaking function, as indicated by its failure to prevent a breach between the *Oba* of Lagos and the Action Group in 1958.

[77] *Supra*, pp. 236-237.

None of the other major nationality associations in the Western or Eastern Regions merit designation as unofficial ancillaries of the Action Group, although numerous sub-nationality associations in the Western Region are linked informally to local branches of the party.[78] The quasi-cultural Reformed *Ogboni* Fraternity of Benin is an unofficial adjunct of the Action Group,[79] as are those tribal unions in the middle belt area of the Northern Region which have been crucial to the structure of the United Middle Belt Congress.[80] Other nationality associations, e.g., the Ibibio State Union, the Edo National Union, the Urhobo Progressive Union, and the Ishan Progressive Union, are less highly politicized than the Ibo and Yoruba associations. All of them include informal political groups which support either the Action Group or the NCNC.

In a few cases, associations based on religious affinity are closely related to the major parties. Thus in 1957, leaders of the Action Group in the Western Region formed a United Muslim Council to counter the influence of the National Muslim League (later the National Emancipation League, an ally of the Northern Peoples' Congress).[81] From time to time, leaders of Islamic congregations in southwestern Nigeria have been highly partisan to one party or another, particularly in Lagos and Ibadan. Inter-denominational conflict in the Eastern Region over the issue of public support for parochial schools has ranged the Eastern Nigeria Catholic Council against the Protestant Citizens Convention, although both associations are subject to dominant NCNC influence.[82] We have observed that in the lower Northern Region the separatist United Middle Belt Congress is based mainly on Christian congregations.[83] Among the Muslims of the upper North, there are two numerically important *tariqas* or brotherhoods of the *Sufi* tradition of Islam, namely the *Qadiriyya* and the *Tijaniyya*.[84] A majority of the adherents of each

[78] On the basis of a questionnaire circulated among members of the Western House of Assembly, the writer determined that various Action Group legislators belonged to the following non-party cultural associations: Eruwa Progressive Union, Ifrebumodu Progressive Union (Ibadan West), Egbe "Otun-Oluwa" (Owo), Moba Youngmen Association (Ekiti), Warri National Union, Igbetti Improvement Union (Oyo), Ogbomosho Parapo, Reformed *Ogboni* Fraternity of Oshun, Akoko National Association, Akoko Edo Union (Afenmai), Akure Youth League, Ijebu Parapo of Epe. The Iperu Iwajowa Society was listed among the donors to the Action Group Headquarters Secretariat fund.

[79] *Supra,* pp. 253-255.

[80] *Supra,* p. 435. [81] *Supra,* p. 250.

[82] *Supra,* pp. 187-188. [83] *Supra,* p. 348.

[84] Shehu Usuman Dan Fodio was an ardent follower of *Qadiriyya* and that brotherhood appears to have its largest Nigerian following today in Sokoto Province. The *Tijaniyya* order was embraced by the ruling family of Kano and

support the NPC. But a militant "left wing" of the *Tijaniyya,* known as the *Yan Wazifa,* "is a radical influence in both religion and politics";[85] many of its adherents support the opposition NEPU.

In certain Northern localities, informal groups of orthodox *mallamai* (Koranic teachers) are highly partisan to the NPC. In Kano, for example, conservative *mallamai,* who tend to view the non-indigenous settler population as a threat to religious purity, are said to have been partially responsible for the "tribalistic" riots of 1953.[86] Furthermore they are said to have been instrumental in the organization of the *Jam'iyyar Mahaukata,* or "Association of Madmen," an appropriately named "strong-arm" auxiliary of the Kano NPC, formed in 1953 as a result of a judicial decision which appeared to subvert traditional authority.[87] The contribution of reformist *mallamai* to the NEPU has been noted previously.[88]

OTHER INTEREST GROUPS

Traditionally, representatives of the Nigerian Ex-Servicemen's Union are included in the NCNC National Executive Committee, although the Action Group also enjoys substantial support within that energetic but factional lobby. A Federation of Northern Ex-Servicemen is affiliated with the NPC. The Nigerian Women's Union is led by Mrs. Funmilayo Ransome-Kuti, a greatly respected NCNC personality; in the North, the Women's Union campaigns for the suffragette cause on a non-partisan basis. Finally, all major parties have their supporters among organized groups of students in Nigeria and abroad.

---

enjoys numerical superiority in Kano, southern Katsina, and eastern Sokoto. See J. Spencer Trimingham, *Islam in West Africa* (Oxford: The Clarendon Press, 1959), pp. 97-100.

[85] R. L. Sklar and C. S. Whitaker, Jr., "Nigerian Political Parties" in the forthcoming volume on "Political Groups in Tropical Africa," edited by James S. Coleman and Carl G. Rosberg, Jr.

[86] *Supra,* p. 132.

[87] *Supra,* p. 359. The writer is indebted to C. S. Whitaker, Jr., for his knowledge of the role of the *Mallamai* in the formation of this group.

The *Jam'iyyar Mahaukata* (Association of Madmen) was disbanded in 1954 and reorganized as the Alheri (Good Things) Youth Association. During the federal election campaign of 1954 there were mass arrests of 69 members of the NEPU and 16 members of the *Alheri* Youth Association for various offences involving breaches of the peace. *Provincial Annual Report,* 1954, p. 77. Subsequently, the *Alheri* Youth Association was transformed into the Kano NPC Youth Association.

[88] *Supra,* p. 420.

Two Case Studies of the Relationship
Between Party Structure and Social Structure
at the Local Level

The Action Group Bekwarra Clan and Ogoja District Organization of Ogoja Division, Eastern Region (1958)

The people of Ogoja Division, who number some 207,000, belong to the Ekoi nationality group, which includes a vast number of tribes in the former Ogoja Province of the Eastern Region and in the neighboring Cameroons. Ogoja Division has been described as a "polyglot area where few people can speak any English and where the majority seem to take a pride in being unable to understand any language except that spoken by their particular tribal fragment."[89] It has been reported that a "distinct language" is spoken by each one of the 18 clans in the division.[90] Ogoja Division comprises two administrative districts, namely Ogoja and Obudu, which include 13 and 5 clans respectively. One of the largest clans of the Ogoja District is the Bekwarra Clan,[91] which has a population of about 27,000 and comprises seven village groups of several villages each. The writer was informed that hereditary rights to the chiefships of the villages are vested in particular families, that similar rights to the chiefships (*Ushie*-ships) of the village groups are vested in particular villages, and that the councils (*Ikum-Ushie*) of the village chiefs and the village group chiefs are chosen by the people on the basis of age and intelligence. The clan head (*Ushie Oshen Eguma*) is chosen from a particular village group; his council of advisers includes the seven village group chiefs and representatives of the village group councils.

The Action Group was initiated in Ogoja in 1953 by Chief Iwong I. Morphy, then 23 years old. Chief Morphy, a graduate of a Roman Catholic teacher training college, is "next in line" to both the *Ushie*-ship (head chiefship) of the Bekwarra Clan and the *Ntol*-ship (head chiefship) of the related Nkim Clan.[92] The Bekwarra and the Nkim speak mutually intelligible languages, which is unusual in this Babelian area. Chief Morphy's claim to the *Ntol*-ship of Nkim is

[89] G. I. Jones, *Report of the Position, Status, and Influence of Chiefs and Natural Rulers in the Eastern Region of Nigeria* (Enugu: 1957), p. 49.

[90] S. G. Ikoku, "Social and Economic Forces in Eastern Region Politics," *Action Group of Nigeria, 1956 Summer School Lectures* (Ibadan: n.d.), p. 30.

[91] G. I. Jones refers to the "Bekworra" as a "tribe," which the writer supposes to be technically correct and preferable to the term "Bekwarra Clan" which was used by his informants and is followed by S. G. Ikoku in the study cited in the previous note. Jones, *op.cit.*, p. 49.

[92] Biographical data on members of the Eastern House of Assembly, 1957 (office of the Clerk of the House).

based on patrilineal descent, but he intends to assume the *Ushie*-ship of the much larger Bekwarra Clan instead, to which he has a matrilineal claim.

In 1953, Chief Morphy inaugurated the Ogoja State Union in order to pioneer a method of socially integrated party organization which he calls "environmental control." In 1954, he applied this method to establish the Action Group in the Bekwarra Clan sector. The following year he contested successfully in a by-election to the Eastern House of Assembly and became the first member of the Action Group in that legislature.

Morphy's system of "environmental control" involves the creation of party branches at the village level with the cooperation of family heads. The latter refer all proposals to the village chiefs, who are invited to become ex-officio leaders of their village branches; other village officers of the party are elected by the general membership, a procedure which resembles the customary form of village government. This procedure is repeated at the village-group and clan levels as indicated in the chart on page 471. It will be noted that the clan level organization includes all members of the Bekwarra Local Council who support the Action Group as well as elected members of the Ogoja District Council. Similar organizational programs have been implemented in the other clans of Ogoja District, where opposition to the Action Group was more prevalent than it was among the Bekwarra. In most cases, Morphy's method enabled the Action Group to obtain support at the family compound and village levels in clans where highly influential persons were partial to the NCNC government party.

Chief Morphy presides over the Action Group Ogoja District Executive Committee. Those clan heads who support the party are entitled to membership in this body but they normally defer to other persons who are selected by the clan level party organizations. The District Leader ensures that all clans are represented in the District Executive and that no one of them has disproportionate strength. In 1956, a group of literate youth formed an Ogoja Divisional Union with Morphy's support. However, certain members of this Union, who had been elected on an Action Group platform to the Ogoja District Council, broke with Chief Morphy and supported a rival candidate to the House of Assembly in 1957. In order to channel the political drives of educated youth, Morphy set up a Literate Organization at the district level, which was described to the writer as a "secret" body in 1958. Members were admitted by invitation following private discussions with the District Leader, who ensured that a selected member of the Literate Organization was chosen as secretary of the District Executive Committee. (The writer was informed that in 1958 the District Secretary was a member of the District Executive Committee as a representative of Chief Morphy's patrilineal clan, the Nkim; in fact, he came from Chief Morphy's home village of Ishibori.) The Literate Organization was a temporary measure to control the activities of potentially radical youth, and ease them into the regular organization without offending the communal chiefs.

Chief Morphy has emerged as an eloquent spokesman for his people, who are acutely conscious of their minority status in the Eastern Region. He has served as an adviser to Action Group delegations at the London Constitutional Conferences of 1957 and 1958. At the time of writing, he was Publicity Secretary for the Action Group in the Eastern Region and secretary of that party's Parliamentary Council. His position as leader in Ogoja is the result of his political talents, especially his skill in the field of political organization. Ultimately, his leadership rests upon the implicit trust reposed in him by the chiefs of the Ogoja clans and their followers.

The Action Group Ife Branch Organization of Ife-Illa Division, Western Region (1958)

The Action Group organization at Ife, a Yoruba town in the Western Region, was based on the traditional pattern of family residence and the structure of customary authority. (A few of the characteristic social and political institutions of the Yoruba people are surveyed briefly in Chapter 1.)[93] The basic social unit in Ife is the patrilocal compound, or residential segment of a lineage; compounds normally comprise 200-300 individuals under the leadership of a compound head or *Bale*. Adjacent compounds constitute a sub-ward or "precinct" under a council of compound heads, one of whom is the precinct chief (*Isoro*). Several precincts comprise a main ward, headed by a ward chief (*Bale*) and his council of precinct chiefs. There are six main wards, one of which, namely Modakeke, is inhabited by settlers from Oyo who are not regarded as indigenes of Ife. Until 1960, NCNC influence in Ife was confined largely to the residents of Modakeke ward who resented the traditional rents they were obliged to pay to their Ife landlords. William R. Bascom has reported that the council of the *Oni* (King) of Ife consisted of the five indigenous ward chiefs, three other city chiefs, and eight palace chiefs.[94]

[93] *Supra,* pp. 9-13.
[94] William R. Bascom, "Urbanization Among the Yoruba," *American Journal of Sociology,* LX, 5 (March 1955), p. 450.

The Action Group Bekwarra Clan and Ogoja District Organization

Local Government Structure	Structure of Customary Authority	Official Party Structure	Unofficial Dimension of Party Structure: Ethnic Group Association
District Council (councillors elected for a term of 3 years)		Action Group District: District Leader—member of House of Assembly and prospective *Ushie* of Bekwarra; Representatives of Clan Parties District Secretary	Literate Organization: District Leader and selected members
Local Council (42 councillors elected directly for 3-year terms)	Clan: *Ushie Oshen Eguma* Council of 7 *Ushie* advisers representing the village group councils	A.G. Clan Party: *Ushie Oshen Eguma* 7 *Ushie* Representatives of village group branches All elected councillors, local and district	*The Ogoja State Union*
	Village Group: *Ushie* or chief— hereditary Sub-chiefs— hereditary *Ikum-Ushie*—elected by village group	A.G. Village Group Branch: *Ushie* Village Group *Ikum Ushie* Sub-Chiefs Representatives of village *Ikum Ushie* Other influential people elected by villagers	
	Village: Sub-chief— hereditary *Ikum Ushie*—elected by villagers	A.G. Village Branch: Sub-chief: ex-officio leader Elected officers of branch Mass membership	
	Compound: Family head		

Prior to 1954, the Action Group branch was controlled by a clique of so-called "elders," meaning persons of title and wealth.[95] In that year, Ife youths, who were dissatisfied with the political rule of the dominant elite, formed a counter organization under the leadership of Mr. Remi Ade Fani-Kayode,[96] a 33-year-old Cambridge-educated barrister, whose father had been a magistrate and whose grandfather had been a clergyman. Mr. Fani-Kayode was elected to the House of Representatives in 1954; when his faction secured control of the Ife District Council in 1955, he was elected to the Chairmanship. Meanwhile he and his lieutenants organized intensively in the compounds and the precincts. "Compound stewards" were appointed to enroll members and to secure the support of the customary authorities.

When the writer visited Ife in 1958, the basic party unit was the precinct organization, which accorded with Action Group organizational doctrine inasmuch as the precincts coincide with the local government electoral wards. Most of the precinct chiefs were members of the Action Group and in some instances they were the chairmen of their precinct party units. At the main (traditional) ward level, there were elected party officers and party executive committees. Thus the Ilode ward executive committee was under the chairmanship of a farmer and included three representatives from each of the six precincts. Five of the six main ward chiefs, all of whom were old men, supported the Action Group. In addition, the leaders of most town societies, including associations of market women, were drawn into the organization at the precinct and ward levels as were a majority of the sacred shrine keepers. For example, the chief priest of the *Obatala* shrine was an *Isoro* (precinct chief) and the chairman of the Action Group in his precinct. Influential and respected men of this kind provided an underpinning of communal sanction for the mass organization.[97]

[95] It is frequently the case in Nigeria that "elders" and "youth" are terminological equivalents of the "ins" and the "outs." A "youth" leader of 60 may be showered with praise by those who despise "elders" of 45. Older men who have failed to achieve wealth or social recognition in the form of titles may attach themselves to the cause of a "youth" faction and they may anticipate contract awards and other considerations if the youth party comes to power.

[96] *Supra*, pp. 269-270, 277.

[97] The Action Group organization in Ife appeared to surpass all others in the Western Region in the comprehensiveness of its pattern of relationships to the structure of customary authority. A limited parallel may be drawn with the NCNC mass organization in the nearby town of Ilesha, an NCNC stronghold. (*Supra*, p. 246, n. 36) NCNC chapters were organized in each of the 36 electoral wards of Ilesha, but there are 70 smaller traditional units of government known as "quarters"

The Ife District Council (a local government body) comprised 69 elected members and 23 traditional members, specified by their titles; in 1958 nearly all of the traditional members were declared Action Group supporters and 58 councillors were elected on the Action Group platform. At the district level, there was an Ife Central Executive Committee of the Action Group under the chairmanship of Mr. Fani-Kayode, who was also the Ife-Illa Divisional Leader. The six main wards of Ife town were represented in the Central Executive in proportion to their populations. Among the patrons of the Ife branch were the *Oni* (King) of Ife, three wealthy businessmen, and a distinguished educator, all of whom had been identified with the dominant town elite prior to the "Young Turk" insurrection of 1954. The introduction of direct elections and a liberal franchise gave the radicals an opportunity to seize power through mass organization based on the cooperation of customary authorities at the precinct and compound levels who had been slighted by the old political elite. But in 1959, the *Oni* of Ife, then President of the Western House of Chiefs (he was elevated to the constitutional Governorship of the Western Region in 1960), disavowed Mr. Fani-Kayode and supported a rival candidate for his seat in the House of Representatives. This action split the branch irrevocably and led to the defeat of the incumbent leader, who promptly declared for the NCNC. In 1960 he was elected to the Western House of Assembly and became Leader of the Regional Opposition. It is presumed that the structure of the Action Group Ife branch has been affected substantially by these developments.

---

or "streets" (*Ogbon*), each of which has a headman and a traditional youth leader, known as the *Loriomo*. The writer was informed that *Loriomo* are normally elected by joint meetings of the elders and the youths of the "streets" and that they may be middle-aged themselves. Most of them did not speak English and only two *Loriomo* were elected members of the Ilesha Urban District Council in 1958. Yet the preponderant number of them were said to be NCNC partisans who assisted the party leaders and the councillors regularly at the ward level.

CHAPTER XI: THE SOCIAL BASIS
OF THE PARTY-POWER SYSTEM

THE major Nigerian political parties are unrestricted membership groups—any Nigerian may join the Action Group or the NCNC,[1] any person of Northern origin is eligible for membership in the Northern Peoples' Congress or the Northern Elements Progressive Union. Yet the actual distribution of party strength and the composition of the local affiliates of each party is frequently affected by tendencies toward communal (ethnic or religious) solidarity.[2] Accordingly, it might be instructive at this point to consider what communal solidarity means in psychological terms, as it bears on the nature of mass participation in Nigerian party politics.

Communal and Associational Participation

For this purpose we may take as our starting point the analysis of participation in party politics derived by Maurice Duverger from Ferdinand Tönnies' classic distinction between *Gemeinschaft* (Community) and *Gesellschaft* (Society) :[3]

"The Community (*Gemeinschaft*) has two essential characteristics. First of all it is a social group founded on proximity, neighborhood (Durkheim would say: on solidarity through similarities). It can be a geographical proximity: this is the case for the village, the commune, the parish, the nation. It can be a physiological proximity, a blood relationship (Tönnies insisted a great deal on the community of blood) : here the family is the best example. Finally it can be a spiritual proximity, a kind of consanguinity of minds, which discover a certain nearness and resemblance between themselves. According to Tönnies friendship comes into this category, but it is not a community in so far as it involves an 'elective affinity' based on freedom of choice, for the Community constitutes a spontaneous natural social group, older than the individual. That is the second characteristic of the community. A community is not created, it is discovered. One does not really become a member of a Community: one belongs to it automatically, willingly or unwillingly. One is born into

---

[1] In 1961 this party's name was changed from National Council of Nigeria and the Cameroons to National Convention of Nigerian Citizens.

[2] *Supra,* pp. 244-251, 338-355.

[3] Maurice Duverger, *Political Parties,* translated by Barbara and Robert North (London: Methuen, 1954), pp. 124-125.

a Community and does not escape from it. Being part of one's family, one's village, one's country, and one's race is natural and involuntary.

"The Association (*Gesellschaft*) shows diametrically opposed characteristics. It is a voluntary social group, based on the contract and the adhesion of the members. One joins it deliberately: one could stay out. It is created in its entirety: it does not exist naturally. It is created because it is in someone's interest to create it: instead of being based on neighborhood, geographical proximity, or blood relationship, the Association is based on interest."

In this study, communal participation refers to party alignment on a *Gemeinschaft* basis. Examples which have been discussed in previous chapters include the indigenous elements movement in Enugu,[4] the popular movements of Benin and Oyo,[5] and the *Mabolaje* of Ibadan.[6] Ideally, communal participation implies that the individual member or supporter regards the party as an extension of a social order into which he has been born and to which he attributes spiritual or mystical significance. In his mind and in the minds of others with whom he habitually associates, the party is endowed with the values of that traditional order. Adhesion to the party is virtually automatic for the members of the communal group, so that anyone rejecting the party in spirit may be regarded as having already "contracted out" psychologically. Mere technical or financial membership is relatively unimportant as a token of affiliation. It may be expected, therefore, that parties based on the affirmation of traditional values will utilize traditional institutions for organizational purposes, much, for example, as the *Mabolaje* of Ibadan has utilized the *Mogajis*, or as branches of the Action Group have utilized the sacred *Obas* (traditional kings) of Yorubaland. Indeed, the activities of a party based on communal participation are likely to be interwoven with customary rites and observances which theoretically involve all members of the communal group.[7] Correspondingly, participation is

[4] *Supra,* pp. 207-216.

[5] *Supra,* pp. 253-256.

[6] *Supra,* pp. 296ff.

[7] For example, the previously noted divisional conference of the Oshun Action Group, held at Ilobu in July 1958 (*supra,* p. 465), was a festive occasion for all of the people of that town. Delegates were welcomed to Ilobu by traditional drumming, dancing, and singing. After the formal meeting, most of the town joined in merriment and festivities. The activities of the day were those of a communal group rather than an association of restricted interests. Spiritual sanction was provided by the *Olobu* of Ilobu and his brother *Obas* in attendance, each of whom personified the corporate identity of an Oshun chiefdom. As might be expected, an average citizen of Ilobu would be drawn into the fold of the Action Group by cohesive group values of a spiritual nature.

limited to the corporate social group concerned, i.e., the tribal or sub-tribal community which is indigenous to the specific area. Thus, non-indigenous supporters of the National Council of Nigeria and the Cameroons (NCNC) at Ibadan were members of the NCNC-*Mabolaje* Grand Alliance; they were not members of the *Mabolaje* per se.

Implicit in the concept of communal participation is the ideal of an integrated system of value involving the combination or synthesis of political, spiritual, and cultural values into a unified moral universe similar to the symbolic universe of traditional society.[8] Consequently, the supporters of a communal membership party are apt to view opposition to that party by a member of the community with moral indignation and to punish it as antisocial conduct. It is not improbable that the violence perpetrated by supporters of the Ibadan communal membership party against their political opponents in 1958 stemmed from profound feelings of pietistic wrath.[9]

By contrast, associational participation refers to party alignment on a *Gesellschaft* basis, implying rational, deliberate affiliation, such as that which may be entailed in the affirmation of a political belief or in the pursuit of a personal goal. Ideally, associational participation is motivated by non-traditional and non-sacred interests, even when they are ethnic interests or sensibilities. For example, ethnic-group associations in urban areas are mainly devoted to the accomplishment of non-traditional ends. "Nationality" associations, in particular, exemplify associational participation on a supra-tribal and emergent-class basis.[10] Urban settlers who support a particular political party

[8] "An African ruler is not to his people merely a person who can enforce his will on them. He is the axis of their political relations, the symbol of their unity and exclusiveness, and the embodiment of their essential values. He is more than a secular ruler. . . . His credentials are mystical and derived from antiquity. Where there are no chiefs, the balanced segments which compose the political structure are vouched for by tradition and myth and their interrelations are guided by values expressed in mystical symbols . . . these sacred symbols, which reflect the social system, endow it with mystical values which evoke acceptance of the social order that goes far beyond the obedience exacted by the secular sanction of force. The social system is, as it were, removed to a mystical plane, where it figures as a system of sacred values beyond criticism or revision." M. Fortes and E. E. Evans-Pritchard, *African Political Systems* (London: Oxford University Press, 1940), pp. 16-18.

[9] *Supra*, pp. 304-305. At Benin in 1951 partisans of the popular *Otu Edo* party, in the flush of electoral triumph, inflicted physical punishment upon their hated adversaries of the Reformed *Ogboni* Fraternity. The latter were despised by the people, not merely for their contumely and exploitative conduct, but for their disrespect to the sacred *Oba* (King) of Benin and for their importation of a society from Yorubaland. *Supra*, pp. 253-255.

[10] *Supra*, pp. 64-72.

because they identify that party with the interests of their ethnic group (tribe or nationality) do not thereby exhibit communal participation of a *Gemeinschaft* type. Their political predispositions do not have the same spiritual quality that infuses dedication to a social order which is thought to be sacred. "On the contrary, membership or support may be also contingent on the position of the party regarding issues of social conflict, endemic to the class structure of a commercial town, which affect settlers' interests. Once an individual no longer perceives the social order as sacred, ethnic affinity does not produce communal participation in the *Gemeinschaft* sense."[11]

It is not too much to suggest that participation on the basis of class interest tends to be of the associational type. To be sure, communal and class values may coexist; but in principle they are inconsistent, the former implying a conception of the community as corporate and functionally integrated, while the latter signifies the fragmentation or division of the community into groups of conflicting (perceived) interest.[12] For this reason we classify urban populism in the Northern Region, exemplified by the Northern Elements Progressive Union and the Bornu Youth Movement, as a form of associational participation. Though communal factors doubtless affect the nature of participation of the members and supporters of these parties, class affiliation, as indicated in Chapter VIII, is paramount. In the

[11] R. L. Sklar and C. S. Whitaker, Jr., "Nigerian Political Parties," *Political Groups in Tropical Africa*, J. S. Coleman and C. G. Rosberg, Jr., eds. (forthcoming).

[12] Maurice Duverger holds that "belonging to a social class is a *Gemeinschaft* link." *Op.cit.*, p. 129. But Tönnies appeared to regard associations based on class as being *Gesellschaft* in nature, and to conceive an innate contradiction between class and community. Ferdinand Tönnies, *Community and Society (Gemeinschaft und Gesellschaft)*, translated and edited by Charles P. Loomis (East Lansing: The Michigan State University Press, 1957), pp. 83-84, 101, 256. See also Rudolf Heberle, "Ferdinand Tönnies' Contributions to the Sociology of Political Parties," *American Journal of Sociology*, LXI, 3 (November 1955), pp. 213-220.

Max Weber distinguished between "communal action" and "societal action"; the former, he explained, "is oriented to the feeling of actors that they belong together"; the latter is "oriented to a rationally motivated adjustment of interests." "Class, Status, Party," *From Max Weber: Essays in Sociology*, eds., H. H. Gerth and C. Wright Mills (New York: Oxford University Press, 1946), p. 183. Class consciousness, he observed, may generate communal action. But the idea of communal participation employed in this study implies a psychological commitment to the social order that is typical of traditional or 'folk' societies of Robert Redfield's conception ["The Folk Society," *Sociological Analysis*, edited by Logan Wilson and William L. Kolb (New York: Harcourt, Brace and Co., 1949), pp. 349-366], where the natural and moral excellence, indeed, the sacred quality, of the social order is a collective premise of general opinion. Communal action that stems from class consciousness does not correspond to that state of mentality but, as Weber suggested, it is likely to reflect moral indignation against an order of things that people regard as unnatural and unjust.

Northern Regional areas of traditional class conflict, communal participation has been encouraged and utilized by the Northern government party as a weapon against lower-class populism. In Bornu, as we have noted, the invocation of communal values to achieve the partisan ends of the Northern Peoples' Congress resulted in a tragic outburst of violence.[13] Similarly, in "metropolitan" Ilorin, sustained political tension may be attributed in part to a conflict between class and communal interests.[14]

In all regions, political parties have relied for mass support upon communal participation in areas of traditional habitation. The government party of the Western Region has been notably successful in its endeavor to enlist communal participation by recourse to a systematic program involving cooperation between the party and traditional authorities. Occasionally, organized movements based on communal participation have been antagonistic to a regional government party. This has occurred when the inhabitants of a traditional community have rebelled against the political ambitions of a new and rising class, as in the Western Regional towns of Benin, Oyo, Ilesha, and Ibadan.[15] In the first three of these towns, the rising class was almost wholly indigenous; in Ibadan it was mainly a settler class with an indigenous component. In all four cases, a majority of the rising-class elements affiliated with a government party—the Action Group—which the people at large happened to identify with interests they regarded as being hostile to their communal traditions. In every case, a large majority of the communal chiefs, particularly so the major chiefs, disavowed the local communal party which stood for traditional values, and affirmed their support for the government party, which controls the system of appointment and deposition. Social conflict in these towns, then, was neither a conflict between modern and traditional elements, nor one between higher and lower classes; it was a clash between class and community, a type of social conflict which is more explosive than class conflict since it is the more likely to outrage the moral sensibilities of vast numbers of people.[16]

[13] *Supra*, p. 344.
[14] *Supra*, pp. 350-355.
[15] *Supra*, Chapter VI, passim, and Chapter VII.
[16] Conflicts of interest between emergent classes and the classless communities from which they arise have been a principal source of political violence in Nigeria. The cases of violence in Ibadan, Benin, Oyo, and Maiduguri noted in this study all correspond to the description of class versus community. The notorious Kano riots of May 1953 also appear to have involved a communal factor of importance. The writer is informed that conservative Koranic *Mallams* in Kano City, who viewed the non-indigenous southern population of Kano as a threat to religious orthodoxy,

Rising classes herald the decline of old orders, and, in many parts of Nigeria, they symbolize the transformation of classless communities into class societies. This is evidenced in the tendency of communal partisans to shed their traditional values and to adopt lower-class perspectives, as has happened, for example, in Ibadan and in Ilorin; it was evident in Enugu in 1958, where many of the communal partisans were employed as industrial laborers in the coal mines. As social transition proceeds, psychological distinctions tend to blur. Insofar as political values are fused with the integral group values of a traditional order, they are communal; insofar as they reflect differentiated secular interests, they are associational, i.e., typically class values.

It must be emphasized that communal and associational value systems are ideal types, and that neither type can account fully for the motivations of any particular individual. The concept of communal participation does not apply at all to most of the leaders of communal-membership parties who are drawn from the new and rising class and whose participation is associational in nature.[17] The leaders of

---

were aroused by anti-southern political agitators. Those *Mallams* are said to have played a part in the instigation of the riots.

Other conflicts between tribal or nationality groups which have not appeared to affect the sacred values of a traditional order have been mainly pacific. The Okrika-Kalabari dispute over fishing and settlement rights in the former Rivers Province of the Eastern Region may be an exception. See the *Report of the Commission of Enquiry into the Okrika-Kalabari Dispute* (Enugu: 1950). The Tiv-Hausa riots of 1947 in Makurdi may be another exception, but they were not, to the writer's knowledge, particularly severe. The Itsekeri-Urhobo conflict of 1952 in Warri Division of the Western Region lasted for several days and resulted in serious damage to property, but no reported loss of life. See P. C. Lloyd, "Tribalism in Warri," *Annual Conference Proceedings of the West African Institute of Social and Economic Research* (Ibadan: University College, 1956), p. 100. Finally, tension in Lagos between settlers of Ibo and Yoruba nationality, cited frequently as a prime manifestation of tribalism in Nigeria between 1937 and 1951, was confined to verbal attacks, never, to this writer's knowledge, reaching the point of violence.

[17] The writer has tabulated occupational data on the leadership of the NCNC branches in the Western Region urban districts of Oyo, Ibadan, Ilesha, and Benin (including members of party executive committees and candidates for election to the urban district councils) in 1958, and the Action Group branches in these urban districts (including members of party executives, other than at Ibadan, and candidates for election to the urban district councils, other than at Ilesha) in 1958. (See Tables 4 and 5 below.) These NCNC branches exemplified communal participation in traditional urban communities; the Action Group branches exemplified associational participation. Little difference in the occupational distributions of these two opposing groups of party leaders is discernible. The Action Group has a slight edge in the higher-status occupational categories, while a significantly greater proportion of NCNC leaders are listed as petty traders.

In the case of Ibadan, which has been discussed at length in Chapter VII, the writer did not find that socio-economic differentiation between the top leadership groups of the NCNC and the Action Group was especially marked, although the

communal participation parties are likely to be populist and radically disposed individuals who have attained social, educational, or professional distinction and have rallied to the popular cause either on principle or because of a perceived personal advantage. Owing to the influence of these radical leaders, mass parties based on the communal participation of the Nigerian peasantry have assimilated nationalistic and secularist principles into their codes of traditional values.[18] A prime example is the *Mabolaje* of Ibadan, which was conservative with respect to administrative reform but radical with respect to political nationalism—i.e., the movement for independence.[19]

THE ROLE OF EMERGENT CLASSES

In this study the concept of the emergent or new and rising class refers to an actual social aggregate, engaged in class action and characterized by a growing sense of class consciousness. Its composition is indicated by four objective criteria: high-status occupation (notably professionals, educators, substantial businessmen, and senior

---

Action Group Divisional Executive was a more distinguished club in terms of social prestige than its NCNC counterpart. The former included 3 lawyers, several well-to-do businessmen, 3 proprietors of schools, 2 persons who occupied executive positions on government boards, and the *Iyalode*, or head woman's chief of Ibadan. Cf. "The Central Executive Committee of the NCNC-*Mabolaje* Grand Alliance, July 1958," *supra*, p. 308, n. 46. Socio-economic difference was more conspicuous at the middle-leadership level, which may be inferred from a comparison of the occupational distributions of NCNC and Action Group candidates for the Ibadan District Council in 1958. Seventy-two candidates were certified for each party. Fifty-six percent of the NCNC candidates were petty tradesmen, artisans, craftsmen and shopkeepers; 21% were farmers and 10% were businessmen of entrepreneurial rank. Thirty-two percent of the Action Group candidates were businessmen of entrepreneurial rank (in fact, 22% were contractors) and 10% were teachers, while none of the NCNC candidates were either contractors or teachers. However, it may well have been that NCNC contractors shunned the Council for pecuniary reasons, inasmuch as the NCNC anticipated victory and the Local Government Law, 1957, section 72 (3), forbids a council to enter into a contract with one of its members.

[18] Mass participation of the peasantry in political parties during the pre-independence era may render less likely the subsequent emergence of reactionary movements based on the resurgence of traditionalism. Cf. Rupert Emerson, *From Empire to Nation* (Cambridge: Harvard University Press, 1960), pp. 366-371.

[19] This seemingly incongruous mixture of administrative conservatism and political radicalism may be interpreted another way: radical nationalists require mass support and they will give in to the inhabitants of traditional towns and villages who may favor the persistence of archaic administrative and economic practices for sentimental reasons. Thus it has been reported that the leaders of the nationalistic and progressive Nyasaland African Congress criticized economically sound agricultural rules promulgated by the Colonial government but unpopular among the rank and file of their supporters. Colonial Office, *Report of the Nyasaland Commission of Inquiry* (London: H.M.S.O., 1959), p. 19.

functionaries in the public service and in public or private enterprise), high income, superior education (especially in the cases of professionals, civil servants, and teachers), and the ownership or control of business enterprise.[20] The formation of this class in relation to the development of political parties corresponds to a social process termed by Robert Michels the "amalgam" or "intermixture" of elites.[21]

To illustrate: The nationalistic elites which created and periodically revitalized the NCNC in 1944, 1948, and 1951, consisted mainly of students, educators, journalists, professionals, and businessmen.[22] Elements of like origin created the Action Group in 1950;[23] and the nationalistic elites which created the Northern Peoples' Congress as a cultural organization in 1949 were made up of the northern counterpart to the intellectual and professional strata of the south, i.e., the northern administrative intelligentsia.[24] Subsequently, these militant elites in all three major parties united with less radical leaders who had been more or less indifferent to, or wary of, their political aims. The non-radical elites, particularly those of southern Nigeria, including most chiefs, most high-ranking functionaries of the old Native Administrations, and the rank and file of the trading class,[25] imbibed the heady wine of nationalism; in turn, many of the radicals acquired attitudes and interests akin to those of a privileged class. In power, the nationalistic parties helped to create a new pattern of social stratification. They sanctioned the liberal use of public funds to

[20] Inasmuch as the Nigerian social system encompasses several distinct cultural areas, the results obtained by applying these four criteria will differ from section to section of the country. Thus, the social status of a high administrative functionary in Kano may be comparable to that of a Queen's Counsel in Lagos, although their respective incomes and educational attainments may not be commensurate. Differences between the emergent class of the emirate sector of the upper North (an area of traditional class structure) and the emergent class of southern Nigeria (a traditionally classless area) are marked, and the formation of a modern dominant class in each of these areas is more advanced than the formation of a dominant class for the country as a whole. This analysis is similar to Thomas Hodgkin's discussion of the social origins of African political leaders. *African Political Parties* (London: Penguin Books, 1961), p. 28.

[21] Robert Michels, *Political Parties* (New York: Dover Publications, 1959), pp. 177, 378.

[22] *Supra,* pp. 55-58, 112-114.

[23] *Supra,* pp. 101-110.

[24] *Supra,* pp. 91-94.

[25] Obafemi Awolowo, writing in 1946, characterized the "enlightened" class of traders and artisans as politically indifferent. *Path To Nigerian Freedom* (London: Faber, 1947), p. 31. James S. Coleman has drawn attention to the political awakening of the trading class in his section on the transformation of individual grievances, especially economic grievances, into the "national grievance" which "can be completely eliminated only by national liberation." *Nigeria: Background to Nationalism* (Berkeley and Los Angeles: University of California Press, 1958), pp. 88-89.

promote indigenous private enterprise, while many of their leading members entered upon a comparatively grand manner of life in parliamentary office.[26] To borrow a phrase from Michels, the "Honourable Member" is an *arrivé*, whether or not he was "at first an *arriviste*."[27]

The fusion of elites on an emergent-class basis is evident both in the composition of the executive bodies of the governing parties at all levels, and in the composition of the elective (legislative and local council) bodies which they dominate. How far this process of fusion has gone may be seen in data on the occupational status of members of the top executive bodies of the three major parties which the writer obtained in 1958.

Northern Peoples' Congress: Of the 74 members of the National Executive Committee, 62 percent were clerical employees of Native Administrations (the social equivalent of the professional, managerial, and, to some extent, educated strata in the south), and 26 percent were businessmen of entrepreneurial rank.[28] Ninety-seven percent of them were classified in the administrative, managerial, professional, educational, and business categories.

National Council of Nigeria and the Cameroons: The 71 members of the National Executive Committee, the Eastern and Western Working Committees, in addition to members of ministerial rank in the Eastern and federal governments, were made up of 27 percent professionals, 20 percent educators, and 28 percent businessmen; all told there were 80 percent in the professional, educational, entre-

---

[26] In 1960 there were about 650 legislators in the four parliaments of Nigeria at stipends of £800 per annum, about 55 junior ministers at stipends of £1,500 on the average, and about 75 full ministers at £3,000. In a few cases, ministerial service involved a financial sacrifice by the individual concerned, as in the cases of those barristers whose private practice netted more than £3,000 per annum. For the vast majority of ministers and legislators, however, politics was a channel of rapid upward mobility. This indeed was an underlying cause of the conflict between the leaders of the NCNC and the leadership of the NCNC Youth Association in 1955 (*supra*, pp. 150-151). Ever since, the NCNC Youth Association has pressed for the reduction of ministerial, legislative, and administrative salaries in order to lessen the "income gap" between the privileged class and the poor. See, e.g., *Daily Times*, January 21, 1958.

In the Northern Region, a legislator is a rich man by definition and the Northern Elements Progressive Union, in particular, has been highly sensitive to the danger of losing its leaders or worse still, the convictions of its leadership through victory at the polls. In 1957, a prominent member of the NEPU was actually expelled from the party for having proposed in the Northern House of Assembly that the Northern Regional Government provide monetary advances to enable the members of that House to purchase private cars. *Supra*, p. 421, n. 106. And see Thomas Hodgkin, *op.cit.*, pp. 101-102.

[27] R. Michels, *op.cit.*, p. 206.

[28] *Supra*, p. 324, Table 1.

preneurial, managerial, and senior civil servant (retired) categories. (Table 1.)

TABLE 1

Executive Members of the NCNC (1958): including members of the National Executive Committee, the Eastern and Western Working Committees and members of ministerial rank in the Eastern and federal governments

Abstract of Data

Total number of members	71			
National officers	9	(13%)		
Ministers (regional and federal)	20	(28%)		
Parliamentarians	42	(59%):	27 MHA,	15 MHR

Regional distribution (normal residence):

Northern	5
Eastern	37
Western	22
Lagos	5
Cameroons	2

Tribal distribution:

Ibo speaking	35	(49.3%)	Ijaw	1
Yoruba speaking	19	(26.7%)	Ikom	1
Efik speaking	5	(7%)	Hausa	1
Edo speaking	3		Kanuri	1
Cameroonian	3		non-Nigeria	1
Itsekeri	1			

Religious distribution:

Christian	55	(91.5%)
Muslim	6	

Occupation:

19 professionals: 15 lawyers, 4 doctors (26.8%)
14 educators   (19.7%)
20 businessmen   (28.2%)
4 senior functionaries (private enterprise) and senior civil servants (retired)
57 in professional, educational, entrepreneurial, managerial and senior civil servant categories (80.3%)

Source: Appendix II: National Executive Committee, Regional officers (East and West) and Ministers of the National Council of Nigeria and the Cameroons, 1958.

Action Group: The 66 members of the Federal Executive Council, including the federal officers, regional representatives, ministers in the Western and federal governments, in addition to Western Regional officers, included 30 percent professionals, 18 percent educators, and 21 percent businessmen; there were a total of 74 percent in the professional, educational, entrepreneurial, managerial, and senior civil servant categories. (Table 2)[29]

TABLE 2

Federal Executive Council of the Action Group (1958)
(including national officers, regional representatives,
Western Regional officers, regional and federal ministers)

Abstract of Data

Total number of members	66	
Federal officers	15	(23%)
Ministers (regional and federal)	14	(23%)
Parliamentarians	30	(45%): 24 MHA, 1 MHC, 5 MHR

Regional distribution (normal residence):

Northern	15
Eastern	14
Western	31
Lagos	6

Tribal distribution:

Yoruba speaking	45	(68.2%)	Ijaw	2
Efik speaking	5		Itsekeri	1
Ogoja tribes	4		Nupe	1
Edo speaking	3		Idoma	1
Ibo speaking	3	(4.5%)	unknown	1

Religious distribution:

Christian	49
Muslim	5
Unknown	12 (11 in North probably Christian)

Occupation:
22 professionals: 18 lawyers, 2 doctors, 2 academic degrees (33.3%)
12 educators (18.2%)
14 businessmen (21.2%)
1 retired Senior Civil Servant (1.5%)
49 in professional, educational, entrepreneurial, managerial and senior civil servant categories (74.2%)

Source: Appendix IV: Federal Executive Council of the Action Group.

Thus, by collating these figures, we obtain a fairly distinct occupational profile of 211 top executive members of the three major parties: 84 percent of them fall into the several occupational categories

[29] The composition of the Federal Executive Council of the Action Group is less indicative of the predominance of rising-class orientations in that party than is the leadership of its core area, namely the Western Region. A tabulation of 52 party leaders other than the 66 members of the Federal Executive Council, all but nine of whom were Westerners, disclosed 81% in the professional, educational, entrepreneurial, managerial, and senior civil servant categories. *Infra*, p. 528, Appendix IV.

which have been enumerated as typifying the leading echelons of the new and rising class. (Table 3)

A similar conclusion may be drawn from tabulations of the occupations of Nigerian parliamentarians. A comprehensive tabulation, comprising the memberships of the Northern, Eastern, and Western Houses of Assembly and the Houses of Representatives during the years 1952-1957 has been made by James S. Coleman. His calculations indicated the following conclusions:

"As to occupations, educators and barristers are heavily represented in the southern membership; educators constitute 30 per cent of the eastern and barristers 25 per cent of the western membership in the 1952 House of Representatives. There are no northern members who are barristers. Rather, there is an extremely heavy representation from the native authorities, ranging from 75 to 95 per cent of the total northern membership. . . . The NCNC in the Western Region ranks highest in the number of members drawn from native administrations (81 per cent), the Action Group highest in members engaged in private enterprise (32 per cent)."[30]

These conclusions on the predominance of rising-class leadership apply with equal force at the local level. It has been noted above that 65.2 percent of the local executive leadership of the Northern Peoples' Congress in eight principal emirates in 1958 were officials or clerical employees of Native Administrations, while 17.4 percent were businessmen.[31] Table 4 indicates the occupational backgrounds of the local leadership of government parties in urban areas of the Eastern and Western Regions in addition to the candidates of those parties to local government councils. The present writer has tabulated the occupations of 640 such persons in seventeen urban areas (without correction for the small overlap of local party executive committees and slates of candidates), and the principal finding is that the largest percentage—31 percent—fall in the business column (No. 10),

---

[30] *Nigeria: Background to Nationalism* (Berkeley and Los Angeles: University of California Press, 1958), p. 379. Elsewhere, Professor Coleman has observed that 30% of the combined memberships of the Eastern and Western Houses of Assembly for the period 1952-1957 consisted of teachers and headmasters, that 20% consisted of professional persons, while 27% were engaged in private enterprise. "The Politics of Sub-Saharan Africa," *The Politics of the Developing Areas,* Gabriel A. Almond and James S. Coleman, eds. (Princeton: Princeton University Press, 1960), p. 342. The present writer's tabulation of the occupations of 221 Northern members of the Northern House of Assembly and Federal House of Representatives in 1957 and 1958 respectively, indicates that 78% of them were members of Native Administrations while 15% represented the business, educational, managerial, and other clerical occupations.

[31] *Supra,* p. 325, Table 2.

TABLE 3

The occupational background of the national and federal leaders of the three major political parties, 1958

	Number of persons	1. Traditional authorities	*Functionary strata* 2. Senior functionaries (government); Northern Native Authority officials, clerical employees*	3. Senior functionaries (public and private enterprise)	4. Junior functionaries (government services, public or private enterprises)**	5. Agents of occupational, cultural, and political associations	*Learned arts and skills* 6. Free professions and scientists	7. Communications and cultural arts, e.g., journalists	8. Educators (teachers and headmasters)***	9. Ministers and teachers of religion	*Profit and wage occupations* 10. Businessmen (finance and entrepreneurship)	11. Petty trade	12. Artisans, craftsmen, shopkeepers, self-employed	13. Wage laborers and domestic servants****	14. Farmers	15. Unemployed or non-employable *****
Line 1 NPC (National Executive Committee)	74		46 62%	1 1%			1 1%		5 6.7%		19 26%				1	
Line 2 NCNC (Executive Members)	71	1	1	3 5.6%	5	2	19 27%	1	14 20%		20 28%				1	4
Line 3 AG (Federal Executive Council)	66	1	1		1	1	22 33%	3	12 18%	2	14 21%	4	1	1		1
Line 4 AG additional top level leadership[a]	52	1	1	2 6%	1	2	10 19%		15 29%		14 27%				1	
Lines 1, 2 and 3 (Totals)	211	2	48 22.7%	4 1.9%	6	3	42 20%	4	31 14.7%	2	53 25%	4	1	1	2	5

Columns 2, 3, 6, 8 and 10 total 84.3%.

[a] Including outstanding legislators, parliamentary secretaries of the Western Regional Government, important divisional and constituency leaders, and persons coopted into the Third and Fourth Annual Federal Congresses of 1957 and 1958. Appendix IV.

* This category includes the local government executive grades in addition to the federal and regional services; senior military and police officials and persons pensioned at these ranks are included; all Northern Native Administration officials are included, although many of them may properly belong in the junior functionary strat[a]

** Junior civil servants, junior executives, cle[rks] and other functionaries in business enterpr[ises]; junior military and police functionaries; pers[ons] pensioned from these positions.

*** Government, Native Administration, [and] private schools.

**** Government, Native Administration, [and] private employment.

***** Domestics, including housewives, stude[nts] and other dependents; beggars.

followed by 21.7 percent in the petty trade column (No. 11),[32] 10.3 percent in the clerical column (No. 4), and 10 percent in the professional column (No. 8). All told, the business, managerial, clerical, professional and educational columns (Nos. 10, 3, 4, 6, and 8) total 65.5 percent, while the petty trade and other self-employed occupations (columns No. 11 and 12) total 28.9 percent. Data on the occupational backgrounds of opposition party leaders and candidates in ten urban areas of the Eastern and Western Regions support conclusions of a similar import. (Table 5.) It is significant, however, that the business, managerial, clerical, professional, and educational columns (Nos. 10, 3, 4, 6, and 8) total 41 percent, while those engaged in petty trade and other self-employed occupations (Columns No. 11 and 12) total 38.7 percent, all of which strongly corroborates the suggestion already ventured that the leading elements of the rising class gravitate toward government parties. Finally, the occupational distribution of 480 members of local government councils in Lagos and twelve urban areas of the Eastern and Western Regions (Table 6) indicates 53 percent in the business, managerial, clerical, professional, and educational columns (Nos. 10, 3, 4, and 8) and 32 percent in the petty trade and other self-employed occupations (Columns 11 and 12).

Thus the party system of Nigeria is the focus of interests which have been defined in this study as the constituent interests of a new and rising class. The political predominance of this class has been suggested in previous chapters.[33] Rising-class interests were found to have motivated the organization and activities of the principal pan-tribal or "nationality" movements;[34] they were fundamental to the momentous controversy over the African Continental Bank;[35] they have produced intense conflict within the dominant party of the Eastern Region,[36] altered a traditional class structure in the Northern Region,[37] generated political opposition within communities in areas

[32] The precise boundary between businessmen of entrepreneurial stature (Column No. 10) and petty tradesmen (Column No. 11) or shopkeepers (Column No. 12) is not always clear and the writer does not claim that his classifications, which were made on the basis of personal knowledge and information received from knowledgeable persons or local government sources, are faultlessly accurate or entirely free of arbitrary characterization. These tabulations represent the writer's best effort in a one-man enterprise of some difficulty and it is hoped that the quantity of data has minimized rather than exaggerated the inevitable errors.
[33] Cf. International Institute of Differing Civilizations, *Development of a Middle Class in Tropical and Sub-Tropical Countries* (Brussels: 1955), p. 453.
[34] *Supra*, pp. 64-72.
[35] *Supra*, Chapter IV.
[36] *Supra*, Chapter V.
[37] *Supra*, pp. 323-335.

TABLE 4

The occupational background of the local leadership of government parties and the candidates of government parties to local government office in urban areas of the Eastern and Western Regions, 1957-1958

	Number of persons	Functionary strata					Learned arts and skills				Profit and wage occupations						
		1. Traditional authorities	2. Senior functionaries (government)	3. Senior functionaries (public and private enterprise)	4. Junior functionaries (government services, and public or private enterprises)*	5. Agents of occupational, cultural, and political associations	6. Free professions and scientists	7. Communications and cultural arts, e.g., journalists	8. Educators (teachers and headmasters)†	9. Ministers and teachers of religion	10. Businessmen (finance and entrepreneurship)	11. Petty trade	12. Artisans, craftsmen, shopkeepers, self-employed	13. Wage laborers and domestic servants‡	14. Farmers	15. Unemployed or non-employable§	16. Unknown
Enugu NCNC Branch Executive, 1957	31				3	2	3		2		11	4	4		1		7
Enugu NCNC candidates to Municipal Council, March 1958	23				3						6 (25%)	4	7 } 48%				
Enugu AFON (NCNC) candidates to Municipal Council, March 1958	23				3		1				15 (65%)		3 (13%)				
Onitsha NCNC Branch Executive, 1958	42				4		5		10 (23%)		9 (21%)	7 (17%)				1ᵃ	
Onitsha NCNC candidates to OUDC October 1958	27						6		6		8	6					
Port Harcourt NCNC Div. Branch Exec. January 1958	44			2	8				3		15	9	1	1	1	1ᵇ	
P.H. NCNC Municipal Councillors, January 1958	19			1	1		1		1		13	2					
Aba NCNC Branch Executive February 1958	22				1		1		2		7	7	3				
Aba NCNC UDC Councillors, February 1958	30								2		5	21ᶜ	1			1	
Calabar NCNC UDC Councillors, February 1958	20				7	1			3		2	7					

Organization	Total	(.9%)	(10.3%)	(.9%)	(4.2%)	(10%)	(1%)	(31%)	(21.7%)	(7.2%)	(9.5%)	(.6%)	(1.72%)
Ijebu-Ode AG candidate to UDC, 1958	33					2	1	14	9	3			
Ibadan AG candidate to IDC, June 1958	72		3		5	7	1	23	17	7	8		
Oyo AG Division Executive and Southern District Officers, 1958	12		3	1	2	2	1	4	1		1		
Oyo AG candidates to Eastern Sect. Oyo So. DC, June 1958	30		1	1		3		4	5	6	10		
Ilesha AG Div. & Cent. officers, 1958	10		4		1			3	2	1			
Ondo AG Div. Exec., April 1957	18		1			4		7	3	1	2		
Ondo N.W. AG Const. Exec., October 1956	12		2			1		3		1	5		
Owo AG Town & Const. Officers, May 1958	10	1				4		3			2		
Benin AG Div. officers, Dist. Chairmen, 1958	13		2		1			8			2		
Benin AG cand. Benin City Council, May 1958	42		2			6		8	4	1	21		
Sapele AG Branch Exec., 1958	26		3			13			9	1			
Sapele AG cand. S.U.D.C. May 1958	23		4		1	7			10	1			
Warri AG Div. officers 1958	6		1		1	1			3				
Warri AG cand. W.U.D.C. May 1958	21		8			1	5		6			1[a]	
Asaba AG councillors 1958	16		3			1		2	3	3	7		
Totals	**640 / 2**	6 .9%	66 10.3%	6 .9%	27 4.2%	63 10%	4 1%	198 31%	139 21.7%	46 7.2%	61 9.5%	4 .6%	11 1.72%

* Junior civil servants; junior executives, clerks, and other functionaries in business enterprise; junior military and police functionaries; persons pensioned from these positions.
† Government and private schools.
‡ Government and private employment.
§ Domestics, including housewives, students, and other dependents; beggars.
a Housewife.
b Unemployed.
c Unspecified size of business.

TABLE 5

The occupational background of the local leaders of opposition parties and the candidates of opposition parties to local government office in urban areas of the eastern and western regions, 1957–1958

	Number of persons	1. Traditional authorities	Functionary strata — 2. Senior functionaries (government)	3. Senior functionaries (public and private enterprise)	4. Junior functionaries (Government services, public or private enterprises)*	5. Agents of occupational, cultural, and political associations	Learned arts and skills — 6. Free professions and scientists	7. Communications and cultural arts, e.g., journalists	8. Educators (teachers and headmasters)†	9. Ministers and teachers of religion	Profit and wage occupations — 10. Businessmen (finance and entrepreneurship)	11. Petty trade	12. Artisans, craftsmen, shopkeepers, self-employed	13. Wage laborers and domestic servants‡	14. Farmers	15. Unemployed or non-employable§	16. Unknown
Oyo NCNC Exec., 1958	18				1				1	2	2	10			2		
Oyo NCNC cand. to E. sect. Oyo SDC, June 1958	27				4				3		1	5	6		8		
Ibadan NCNC Cent. Exec. Committee, July 1958	38	4[a]			3		4			1	10	12	1		3		
Ibadan NCNC cand. to Ib. D.C., June 1958	72				6	1	2			1	7	25	15		15		
Ibadan NEL cand. to Ib. D.C., June 1958	12									2	2	1			4		
Ilesha NCNC Dist. & Div. officers, 1958	8								2		3		3				
Ilesha NCNC cand. to Il. U.D.C., 1958	36				4		1					1	1	1	1		
Ijebu-Ode NCNC cand.									7		7	6	8		2		

	*	†	‡		§								c
to U.D.C., 1958	16		1				1		4	7	3			
Ijebu-Ode NEL cand. to U.D.C., 1958	23			4			4	2	3	5	1	1	2	
Benin NCNC Cent. Exec., 1958	25			2		1	1		17				5	
Benin NCNC cand. to Benin C. Council, May 1958	43			1			5		8	10			19	
Sapele NCNC cand. to S.U.D.C., 1958	24			3		1	2		3	10	4	1		
Warri NCNC cand. to W.U.D.C., May 1958	21			1		6	1		2	9	2			
Asaba U.D.C. NCNC Councillors, April 1958	13			6		3				2	1		1	
Calabar AG and COR State Movement Officers February 1958	21			3	1	1[b]	3	1	7	2	2			1[c]
Uyo AG Div. Officers, Clan chairmen	12		1	1			2	1		6	1		1	
Totals	409	4	1	39	2	19	32	10	76	111	48	3	53	1
		.98%		9.55%	.49%	4.65%	7.8%	2.45%	18.6%	27%	11.7%	.7%	12.9%	

* Junior civil servants; junior executives, clerks, and other functionaries in business enterprise; junior military and police functionaries; persons pensioned from these positions.

† Government and private schools.

‡ Government and private employment.

§ Domestics, including housewives, students, and other dependents; beggars.

a *Mogajis*.

b Several professionals were members of a wider Executive Committee.

c Housewife.

TABLE 6

The occupational background of members of local government councils elected on a party basis in Lagos and urban areas of the eastern and western regions, 1957-1958

	Number of persons	1. Traditional authorities	2. Senior functionaries (government)	3. Senior functionaries (public, private enterprise)	4. Junior functionaries (government services, public or private enterprises)*	5. Agents of occupational, cultural, and political associations	6. Free professions and scientists	7. Communications and cultural arts, e.g., journalists	8. Educators (teachers and headmasters)†	9. Ministers and teachers of religion	10. Businessmen (finance and entrepreneurship)	11. Petty trade	12. Artisans, craftsmen, shopkeepers, self-employed	13. Wage laborers and domestic servants‡	14. Farmers	15. Unemployed or non-employable§	16. Unknown
			Functionary strata				*Learned arts and skills*				*Profit and wage occupations*						
Lagos T.C. 1958 (22 AG, 19 NCNC)	41				6	1	6	1	2	1	17	3	4				
Abeokuta U.D.C. March 1958 (50 AG, 11 NCNC)	61				5		2		4	2	24	23					
Ibadan D.C., June 1958 (52 NCNC 20 AG)	71				9	2	2			1	16	19	8	1	14		
Ondo D.C., May 1958 (61 AG 5 NCNC)	66				2				9		28	8	3		16[b]		
Benin City Council, May 1958 (33 NCNC, 8 AG, 2 IND)	43				1				6		11	4	3		18		
Sapele U.D.C., May 1958 (11 NCNC, 11 AG, 2 IND)	24			1	2				2		4	11	3	1			
Warri U.D.C., May 1958 (17 NCNC, 4 AG)	21				2		6		3		2	7	1				

Table (rotated 90° on page):

Council	No.												
Asaba U.D.C., April 1958 (16 AG, 13 NCNC)	29		9				4		2	5	1	1	8
Onitsha U.D.C., November 1958 (18 NCNC, 1 NPC, 1 DPNC, 7 IND)	27		2	1	5		5		6	6	1		
Enugu Munic. Council March 1958 (13 AFON, 12 NCNC)	25		5				2		10	4	4		
Aba U.D.C., 1958 (30 NCNC)	30		1		1	1	2		5	21[a]	1		
Port Harcourt Munic. Council 1958 (19 NCNC, 3 IND)	22	1					1		14	3	2	2	
Calabar U.D.C. 1958 (20 NCNC)	20		7	1			3		2	7			
Totals	480	2	51	5	22	1	43	4	141	121	31	2	56
		.4%	10.6%	1.4%	4.6%		8.95%	.89%	29.4%	25%	6.5%	.4%	11.7%

* Junior civil servants; junior executives, clerks, and other functionaries in business enterprise; junior military and police functionaries; persons pensioned from these positions.

† Government and private schools.

‡ Government and private employment.

§ Domestics, including housewives, students, and other dependents; beggars.

a Unspecified size.

b Cocoa farmer.

of traditional habitation,[38] and mobilized that opposition effectively for nationalistic purposes.[39] The institutional resources at the disposal of those who control the major political parties have been indicated in Chapter IX on official party organization and Chapter X on the penetration by each party into non-party spheres of activity.

THE STRUCTURE OF THE PARTY-POWER SYSTEM

The major Nigerian parties are governed by central executive bodies all of which, in theory, have the last word in matters of policy, nominations, and discipline. During the period under consideration in this study, centralization was most effective in the case of the Action Group, moderately so in the NCNC, and least apparent in the Northern Peoples' Congress. Probably the Northern Elements Progressive Union aimed at a higher degree of centralization than any other major party. But for its alliance with the NCNC, however, the NEPU would lack the institutional resources which accrue to government parties. This is also true of the United Middle Belt Congress, a Northern ally of the Action Group.

The effective power structures of all parties include those non-party groups and institutions which have been classified in Chapter X as unofficial elements of party structure. Thus the Northern Native Authority System, the Northern House of Chiefs, the Loans Board of the Northern Region Development Corporation, the Bank of the North, the Northern Amalgamated Merchants' Union, and certain groups of Koranic teachers are conspicuous in the unofficial apparatus of the Northern Peoples' Congress; the statutory corporations of the Eastern Region, the Eastern Region Marketing Board, the system of Eastern Government contracting, the Ibo State Union, the African Continental Bank, and the Zik Group of newspapers are crucial to the power system of the NCNC; the Western House of Chiefs, the Conference of Western *Obas* and Chiefs, the Local Government Service Board of the Western Region, the Western Region Development Corporation, the Western Region Finance Corporation, the Western Region Marketing Board, the *Egbe Omo Oduduwa* (Yoruba cultural organization), the Reformed *Ogboni* Fraternity of Benin, the United Muslim Council, the National Bank of Nigeria, and the Amalgamated Press of Nigeria are no less important to the power system of the Action Group than are the general membership and executive bodies prescribed by that party's constitution. As a rule, the

[38] *Supra*, pp. 253-256, and Chapter VII.
[39] *Supra*, Chapter VII.

inclusion of non-party groups within the unofficial dimension of a party's structure implies strict party control over their policies and their politically relevant activities. A major reservation to this rule may be allowed with respect to the pre-eminent traditional authorities of the Northern Region, who exercise effective political power within the government party of that region and, to some extent, independently of the party in governmental matters.

In sum, the major institutions of Nigerian society, in particular those institutions which are fundamental to the pattern of social stratification, are closely related to and substantially controlled by the political parties. The only socio-economic interest group of major significance that is not assimilated into the effective structure of the party system is organized labor.[40] Yet the wage labor class (there were

[40] In 1944, the Trade Union Congress of Nigeria, which claimed a membership of 86 affiliated unions, was among the founding member-unions of the NCNC. It will be recalled that Michael A. O. Imoudu, President of the Railway Workers' Union, was associated with Herbert Macaulay and Nnamdi Azikiwe in the leadership of the pan-Nigeria tour of the NCNC during its campaign against the Constitution of 1946. (*Supra*, p. 61.) In 1948, Dr. Azikiwe appointed Michael Imoudu, F. O. Coker, Secretary of the Posts and Telegraphs Workers' Union, and Nduka Eze, Secretary of the Amalgamated Union of the United Africa Company African Workers (UNAMAG) to the NCNC Cabinet. When the Nigerian T.U.C. terminated its affiliation with the NCNC in 1949, these three leaders of the left wing of the labor movement formed the Nigerian National Federation of Labour as an ally of the NCNC. Its successor, the unified Nigerian Labour Congress, under the leftist leadership of Nduka Eze, was a member of the NCNC "triple alliance" which won the Lagos local election of 1950. But the influence of radical labor leaders within the NCNC diminished precipitously when the Nigerian Labour Congress suffered a crushing defeat in the abortive mercantile strike of December 1950. Thereafter the leftist leadership turned away from the NCNC to the lost cause of radical socialism (*Supra*, pp. 80-83.)

Since 1951, the representation of organized labor in the NCNC National Executive has been relatively minor and confined primarily to the conservative wing of the labor leadership. Trade unionists have never been prominent among the leaders of the Action Group, although several trade union leaders are understood to have Action Group sympathies and radical intellectuals with trade union connections are numbered in the Action Group fold. (*Supra*, pp. 270-271.) Nduka Eze, a member of the Federal Executive of the Action Group, is no longer active in the organized labor movement. Oddly, the leading example of trade union alignment with a major political party is provided by the Northern Mine Workers' Union, a virtual instrumentality of the least socialistic or laboristic of the major parties, namely the Northern Peoples' Congress. (*Supra*, p. 337.)

In 1953, a central labor body, the All Nigerian Trade Union Federation, was formed with M. A. O. Imoudu, President of the Railway and Ports Workers' Union, as President, and Gogo Chu Nzeribe, secretary of the Union of Posts and Telecommunication Workers of Nigeria and the Cameroons, as Secretary. The Federation split in 1956 when a group led by H. P. Adebola, Secretary of the Railway Station Staff Union, N. A. Cole, secretary of the Nigerian Union of Nurses, and L. L. Borha, secretary of the Association of Locomotive Drivers, Firemen, and Allied Workers, accused the ANTUF leadership of communist leanings, and formed a rival International Confederation of Free Trade Unions Com-

about 480,000 employed workers in 1958, including some 237,000 trade union members) was integrated with the three-party system on a non-economic basis, owing to the membership of most workers in ethnic-group associations.[41]

---

mittee. ANTUF denied the allegation but refused to affiliate with the ICFTU or, for that matter, with its rival in world labor politics, the World Federation of Trade Unions. In 1957, the ICFTU group formed a new federation, the National Congress of Trade Unions of Nigeria. It has been reported that this body was inaugurated with the support of NCNC leaders, possibly to thwart the attempt by radical leaders of the ANTUF to organize a broadly based Nigerian Labour Party. In November 1955, a committee of the ANTUF had recommended the formation of a labor party, and in March 1956, the Nigerian Labour Party came into existence with Michael A. O. Imoudu as President and S. U. Bassey, secretary of the Municipal and Local Authority Workers' Union, as Secretary. Subsequently, Bassey became secretary of the ANTUF and W. O. Goodluck, secretary of the Lever Brothers and Van Den Berghs Workers' Union and the Nigerian War Department Workers' Union, became secretary of the Labour Party. The leadership of the Nigerian Labour Party is drawn from the left socialist wing of the trade union movement, which favors the formation of an All African Trade Union Federation, as advocated by President Kwame Nkrumah of Ghana and President Sekou Touré of Guinea, in preference to affiliation with the ICFTU, as advocated by Tom Mboya of Kenya. Following a vain attempt to reconcile the rival central organizations in 1959, the ICFTU group became known as the T.U.C. of Nigeria while its opponent was called the Nigerian T.U.C. Another attempt at merger produced the United Labour Congress of Nigeria in 1962, but the anti-ICFTU wing withdrew when the Congress decided to affiliate with that international body.

[41] T. M. Yesufu, a perceptive student of Nigerian political economy, has drawn attention to the conflicting loyalties of the Nigerian worker to his trade union on one hand and his tribal or ethnic group association on the other:

"The worker's own tribal organization, or 'improvement' union in the town provides benefits in desperate cases, financially assists those who want to get married, pays the burial expenses of a deceased parent, makes a present on the occasion of the birth of a new babe, honours the worker elevated to a chieftaincy, and repatriates the destitute. Some tribal organizations award scholarships to the young educated worker or to the children of others. It is this that explains the seeming paradox that whereas the worker will not regularly subscribe to the funds of a trade union (apparently because he is too poor) he does pay regular subscriptions to the funds of his tribal 'union'; and the contributions here are usually higher than those required by the trade union.

"Thus the trade union is caught in a vicious circle: it is deprived of funds because the services which it ought to render are provided by non-industrial organizations supported by the workers, and it cannot provide rival services because it has not funds. The sociological factors are equally impressive. In the tribal 'union' for example, the worker can speak and be spoken to in a language he understands well, against a background of customs and traditions which he comprehends. Those with whom he has to deal can give him that due personal respect to which the African attaches so much importance. In one word, the worker feels that in the gathering of his tribal organization, he truly 'belongs.' In the trade union meeting on the other hand, matters are often discussed against an industrial and economic background which the worker hardly understands; the secretary of the trade union may be of a different tribe; and, if in addition, he belongs to a rival political party, all the seeds of failure have been sown." *Daily Times*, April 14, 1958.

It is commonplace in newly independent and developing countries for the supremacy of party power to be challenged by bureaucratic and military elites. While this possibility cannot be ignored in Nigeria, it does not loom as a proximate threat to the hegemony of the party system. At present, the master institution of colonial rule, namely, the administrative bureaucracy, is in the process of rapid transformation from an expatriate into a Nigerian service;[42] at the federal level and in all regions, the instrumentalities of "Nigerianization"—in particular, the public service commissions and the local government service boards—are controlled by the heads of the several governments. The new bureaucracy is imbued with the British ideal of loyal service to the legitimate and democratically elected governments. Moreover the Nigerian administrative elites, at the time of independence, were psychologically and ideologically indebted to the leaders of the triumphant nationalist movement. This "sentiment of gratitude" (Michels) which civil servants and members of the free professions feel toward the major party leaders tends to guarantee the subordination of bureaucratic power.[43] Thus far, the police and military establishments have not been of any autonomous political significance.[44]

Finally, it does seem likely that the civil judiciary, following the

[42] In August 1960, the Nigerianization officer of the federal government reported that the proportion of Nigerians in senior posts of the federal public service was "60 per cent and the majority of expatriates are on short-term contract" (as paraphrased in *West Africa*, September 3, 1960) ; See the excellent summary of the situation in all regions and in the federal service by Kenneth Younger, *The Public Service in New States* (London: Oxford University Press, 1960), pp. 12-52.

[43] The gratitude of the intelligentsia has been an asset of incalculable worth to Dr. Azikiwe. During his struggle against the Reform Committee of 1958 (*Supra*, pp. 224-228), a barrister of high standing in the NCNC, whose intellectual caliber and independence of mind are widely acclaimed within the party and among its opponents, declared at a meeting of an executive body of the party that he was in the NCNC because Zik was in the NCNC. He remembered the days when an African could "not open his mouth" to his European superiors or express nationalistic opinions without fear of reprisal—e.g., transfer to a distant post. Today, he quipped, a boy goes to the University College for three years, and he becomes an officer of the administration. Zik made that possible, he said, and some of us will always be in Zik's party; "if he falls, we fall." Journal notes of the Meeting of the NCNC Western Working Committee at the Easy Life Hotel, Mokola, Ibadan, June 29, 1958.

[44] It will be recalled that responsibility for control of the para-military police force was a major issue before the Constitutional Conferences of 1957 and 1958. At length, ultimate responsibility for law and order was vested in the federal government with the regional governments participating in a Federal Police Council. *Report by the Nigeria Constitutional Conference, May and June 1957*, pp. 19-20; *Report by the Resumed Nigeria Constitutional Conference, September and October 1958*, pp. 8-11.

In 1960 it was reported that 40 of the 270 officers on active duty in the armed services were Nigerians. Younger, *op.cit.*, p. 37.

example of the most eminent Nigerian jurists and under the protection of constitutional safeguards, will maintain its independence of party control.[45] But the customary courts of the Eastern and Western Regions were not immune from political influence, at least in the matter of appointments, and it was not without some justification that the Native Courts of the Northern Region were regarded as "political courts" by members of the opposition.[46]

The evidence, then, appears to support the conclusion that the party system is the dominant system of power in Nigeria. In the remainder of this chapter the foundations of party competition are appraised and limitations on the power of the political elite are considered.

PARTY GOVERNMENT AND THE POLITICAL BASIS OF OPPOSITION

Thomas Hodgkin has observed that the mass political parties of the colonial African states (the majority of which have recently attained their independence) were preceded by national "movements," "congresses," or "fronts." The typical "congress," he noted, was "a loosely knit, even amorphous, amalgam of local and functional organizations, grouped around a nuclear executive or working committee."[47]

"The terms which these bodies used to describe themselves— 'Congress', 'National Council', 'Convention', 'Rassemblement'—have a certain significance. They imply a notion of universality—the idea that the organization does really express the 'general will', and has a moral right to challenge the legal authority of the Administration on that account."[48]

Partly as a result of the "precipitant" influence of constitutional and electoral reform, the congress-type associations evolved into political parties in the stricter sense.[49] Hodgkin cites the organizational history of the NCNC as a case in point. Here it is suggested that the NCNC in power, like the Action Group and the Northern Peoples' Congress, experienced yet another morphological transformation as it pene-

---

[45] *Report by the Nigeria Constitutional Conference, May and June 1957,* pp. 10-11; Sir W. Ivor Jennings has observed that "the independence and impartiality of the judiciary are not secured by constitutional provisions. These qualities are derived from the independence and probity of the Bar." *The Approach To Self-Government* (Cambridge: Cambridge University Press, 1958), p. 107.

[46] *Supra,* pp. 355-365.

[47] Thomas Hodgkin, *Nationalism in Colonial Africa* (London: Frederick Muller, Ltd., 1956), p. 144.

[48] *Ibid.,* p. 146.

[49] *Ibid.,* p. 148; see also James S. Coleman, "The Emergence of African Political Parties," *Africa Today,* edited by C. Grove Haines (Baltimore: Johns Hopkins Press, 1955), pp. 225-256.

trated deeply into the structure of Nigerian society. As a result, the major party leaders control social institutions which might otherwise limit the extent of party power, and party influence extends as well into many spheres of the individual citizen's daily life. Sigmund Neumann has termed this type of party "the party of social integration" to distinguish it from an antecedent type which he terms the "party of individual representation."[50]

A dominant party of social integration in an industrially under-developed state has a tendency to push its opponents to the wall. This is likely to occur irrespective of the liberal convictions which may be held by the leaders of the dominant party. For the non-coercive forces which attract influential persons to a government party are immeasurably stronger than counter-forces which repel or compete. It has been observed that rising-class personalities in all regions of Nigeria are particularly responsive to the inducements of the parties in power. Commercial patronage, professional preferment, appointments to recognized chieftaincies, etc., are primarily the perquisites of the members and supporters of government parties. How, then, can we account for the existence of vigorous opposition parties in every region?

Several bases of opposition to the regional government parties have been noted previously. These include historical and psychological factors which influence persons who belong to the nationalistic intelligentsia. For example, many persons of professional and intellectual distinction in the Western Region appear to support the NCNC opposition party because they were involved in that party's formation as a nationalist front in the 1940's or because they were opposed to the subsequent cultural nationalism of the *Egbe Omo Oduduwa* and its offspring, the Action Group. The cultural roots of partisanship

[50] Sigmund Neumann, *Modern Political Parties* (Chicago: University of Chicago Press, 1956), p. 404. Ruth Schachter has said of the mass parties of West Africa: "Insofar as they provided a new social framework for people no longer firmly rooted in a stable ethnic tradition, they can be termed 'parties of social integration.' They and their cultural affiliates were interested in everything from the cradle to the grave—in birth, initiation, religion, marriage, divorce, dancing, song, plays, feuds, debts, land, migration, death, public order—not only in electoral success." Among the parties to which she refers specifically in this connection are the National Council of Nigeria and the Cameroons and the Action Group of Nigeria. "Single-Party Systems in West Africa," *The American Political Science Review*, LV, 2 (June 1961), pp. 299-300. The party of "communal participation" which has been described above (*supra*, pp. 474-480) is a special case of the party of social integration based on the affirmation of traditional group values. Parties of associational participation, based upon the affirmation of non-traditional and non-sacred values, are just as likely to be parties of social integration in Sigmund Neumann's meaning.

are more pervasive and fundamental. It will be recalled that there is a predisposition on the part of the urban *talakawa* (commonality) of the North to oppose the dominant party of traditional authority, for the Christians of the Middle Belt to oppose the party of Hausa-Islamic culture, for the Efik and Ibibio people of the East to reject the dominant party of Iboland, for the Edo-speaking people of the Mid-West to oppose the dominant party of Yorubaland, for the Ibadan Yorubas to oppose the dominant party of the Ijebu Yorubas, etc. These factors create tendencies toward organized and vigorous opposition, but they do not ensure its survival or growth. In this writer's view, the vitality of party competition in Nigeria is a consequence mainly of the federal system and other constitutional arrangements.

At the time of independence, each of the three major parties was entrenched securely in the citadel of a regional government while the main regional opposition parties and most of the minor parties were linked to governmental power in coordinate regions.[51] The Nigerian Constitution synthesizes an adjustment of social interests which required the better part of a decade to achieve and provides for the reservation of non-enumerated powers to the regions. Among the reserved powers are the residual powers over local government and chieftaincy, including the power to recognize and depose chiefs and the power to regulate the participation of traditional authorities in local government councils. It is difficult to exaggerate the contribution of these powers to the consolidation of single-party rule in the regions. Nor is it without significance that their reservation to the regions was a vital tenet of the constitutional thought of Obafemi Awolowo and his colleagues among the founders and leaders of the Action

[51] With the possible exception of the small Nigerian Labour Party (*supra*, p. 496, n. 40), those opposition parties which were not affiliated with government parties were ephemeral, insignificant, or temporarily unattached. Four minor parties offered candidates in one or more constituencies in the federal election of 1959: The Igbirra Tribal Union, which won the seat for Igbirra Division, is aligned with the Northern Peoples' Congress (*supra*, p. 349, n. 46). The National Emancipation League in the Western Region, none of whose candidates were successful, is an affiliate of the Northern Peoples' Congress (*supra*, p. 251). The Niger Delta Congress, which won a seat in Brass Division of the Eastern Region, is an ally of the Northern Peoples' Congress (*supra*, p. 386). The Democratic Party of Nigeria and the Cameroons, a breakaway from the NCNC, contested as a *de facto* ally of the Action Group in the Eastern Region but did not win any seats. The *Mabolaje* of Ibadan, which won 7 of the 8 seats for Ibadan Division, was the majority faction of a divided branch of the NCNC. Dr. Chike Obi's Dynamic Party separated from the NCNC in 1960 (*supra*, pp. 406-408), and won five seats in the Eastern Region election of 1961. Minor parties which have contested previous regional and federal elections have been noted elsewhere in this study. *Supra*, p. 135, p. 255, n. 61, p. 257, n. 67, p. 277, n. 109, pp. 345-355.

Group, which formed the government of the Western Region and the federal opposition in the Independence parliament.

Furthermore, the commercial patronage systems, which foster the hegemony of the three major parties in their respective regions of power, stem largely from the regionalization of the former Nigeria-wide commodity marketing boards by the Constitutional Conference of January 1954. At that time, sums varying from £15.1 million to £34.4 million were allocated to multi-commodity regional marketing boards, and the regional governments were authorized to use these funds for general purposes of economic development.[52] Accordingly, they have created statutory corporations and evolved financial policies which have served to consolidate the regional government parties through the enhancement of their capabilities to recruit members of influence and to create fruitful sources of party revenue. Each government party, therefore, has possessed the wherewithal to exploit oppositional tendencies in other regions on the basis of reciprocity. Opposition parties in general have been inclined to look toward the federal government to check the domineering tendencies of the regional governments. Moreover, opposition elements in affiliation with the parties in power in the federal government anticipate federal patronage and opportunities to compensate them for regional deprivation.

At bottom, the stability of the three-party system depends upon each party's effective control of a regional pattern of chieftaincy, local government, and commercial patronage. The loss of such control by a major party would drastically impair its capacity to compete under existing conditions.[53]

The Communal Basis of Democracy

In Nigeria, the power exercised by leaders of the major political parties would appear to derive mainly from the class and communal foundations of those parties and their unofficial ancillary structures. Communal-interest groups generally accept the leadership of emergent and dominant class-interest groups. Conflicts between class- and communal-interest groups have been channelled into party competition, with secularist leaders of emergent class background in control

---

[52] *Supra,* p. 163.

[53] It was too early to assess the consequences of the Western Regional crisis of 1962 (*supra,* pp. 281-282) when this study went to press. Certainly the appointment of a federal administration to govern the region and the ensuing commission of inquiry into the management of regional affairs threatened to undermine the power position of the Action Group.

of the communal membership parties. Hence the political subordination of communal interests to class interests.

Class interests in the emirate areas of the upper North are asserted within a social system that differs profoundly from the social system of southern Nigeria. In the Northern emirates, class structure is endemic to the traditional order, and political authority remains largely in the hands of the traditional ruling class. It has been suggested in this study that an emergent class of Northerners may be distinguished, reflecting the gradual coalescence of the traditional nobility, the administrative functionaries of humble origin, and the commercial elite. Although the businessmen derive from the traditional commonality and tend to exhibit an attitude of benevolence toward the poor, they define their interests mainly in terms of accommodation to the interests of the traditional rulers. Therefore the emergent class tends to assume a power position vis-à-vis the lower classes comparable to the relationship of the traditional rulers to their subjects.

By contrast, the dominant class of the Eastern and Western Regions and the non-emirate areas of the middle belt or lower Northern Region has arisen mainly from communal societies in which class structure is not the traditional form of social stratification and individual achievement is far more relevant to political status than in the emirate areas of the upper North.[54] The new class of southern Nigeria is a phenomenon of modern urbanization. Men of initiative in the spheres of professional endeavor, public service, business enterprise, and education normally reside in the new cosmopolitan towns (or cosmopolitan sections of traditional urban areas) where they occupy the upper levels of the urban class structure.[55] Their motivating values are derived primarily from Western education, their social perspectives are mainly non-traditional, and they support the nationalistic goals of rapid modernization and social reconstruction.

It is often said that the rapid economic development of emergent nations, especially the accelerated industrialization characteristic of such development, imperils the growth of recently implanted democratic institutions. In order to surmount various obstacles to rapid development, e.g., uneconomic traditional patterns of behavior, ethnic particularism, and insufficient capital resources, zealous political leaders may deem it necessary to embrace authoritarian alternatives to democracy.[56] This argument, formulated with cogency in a few

[54] *Supra,* pp. 9-15, 253.
[55] On the emergent class structure of new urban areas in Nigeria see Hugh H. Smythe and Mabel M. Smythe, *The New Nigerian Elite* (Stanford: Stanford University Press, 1960), pp. 102-103.
[56] Rupert Emerson, *From Empire to Nation* (Cambridge: Harvard University

recent studies, appears to depend upon two assumptions: first, that "the mass of the peasantry and the dominant Westernized few" are separated by an immense "psychological gap";[57] secondly, that the political elite is relatively free to introduce any form of government it deems fit.[58]

These forebodings should not be taken lightly in the case of Nigeria, especially if the trends toward political centralization and emergent-class dominance are accurately portrayed in the present study. On the other hand, Western observers may tend to overlook the ways in which African communal traditions qualify the exercise of political power. In southern Nigeria, for example, it is probably true that a vast psychological gulf divides the new elite from the urban masses, but members of the elite also retain a strong sense of identity with the people of their home towns and villages.[59] A successful man of affairs is expected by his people to contribute to the improvement of his home community and to the education of its youth. If he is polit-ically ambitious he must "go home" for election, for a handful of constituencies only are inhabited by Westernized, cosmopolitan majorities, and, with rare exception, Nigerian constituencies are represented by native sons. At home, the *arrivé* is not regarded and does not regard himself as a member of an upper class; he is an eminent son of the soil, bound to the service of his people by tradi-tional pressures and sentimental ties. If he is too aloof or unmindful of customary obligations, he may lose both his chance of election and communal prestige—e.g., the award of a coveted chieftaincy title by the traditional authorities.

The communal orientation of Nigerian politics, involving a high

---

Press, 1960), pp. 289-90, 371; Seymour Martin Lipset, *Political Man* (New York: Doubleday, 1960), p. 68; *Economic, Social, and Political Change in the Under-developed Countries and its Implications for United States Policy* (A Study prepared at the request of the Committee on Foreign Relations, United States Senate, by Center for International Studies, Massachusetts Institute of Tech-nology; Washington: Government Printing Office, 1960), pp. 36-37.

[57] Emerson, *op.cit.*, p. 366; Lipset, *op.cit.*, p. 66; *Economic, Social, and Political Change in Underdeveloped Countries*, pp. 26-32.

[58] Emerson, *op.cit.*, pp. 277-281; *Economic, Social, and Political Change in Underdeveloped Countries*, pp. 36-37.

[59] Smythe and Smythe, *op.cit.*, pp. 99-100, 109-111. This study does draw at-tention to the "vast gulf between a member of the elite and the masses of his countrymen." But it is focused on the new urban areas of southern Nigeria and does not reiterate uncritically the broad generalization of a great psychological gap between the elite and the mass which is questioned here. Nor does it overlook the fact that urban dwellers of class distinction acknowledge special bonds of loyalty and obligation to their ethnic-group associations in the urban areas which comprise persons of all classes. *Ibid.*, p. 167.

degree of mass participation in the evolution and implementation of public policies, has been noted frequently in this study. It is consistent with traditional political practices of major cultural groups,[60] and it is reflected in party organization and activities at the local level. The assiduity with which members of the political elite, including ministers of state and parliamentarians, keep their ears to the ground and seek continuously to justify public policies to their constituents would seem to suggest that the hypothesis of a great psychological gulf between the "elite" and the "masses" requires re-examination.

An indication of the strength of communal pressure in Nigerian politics is the priority given to welfare programs over industrial programs in the Nigerian economy. All parties base their appeals to the electorate on welfare-state principles, and the several governments of the Federation, in particular the regional governments, devote substantial and increasing proportions of public expenditure to the accomplishment of welfare programs: the provision of schools, hospitals, maternity centers, water-supply systems, communications systems—in short, the things that the rural people want and demand from their representatives. In a sense, the welfare state is a cultural imperative of communal society; industrialization at the expense of welfare would require the repudiation or disregard of communitarian principles which have been affirmed repeatedly by Nigerian political leaders.[61]

Similarly, an authoritarian regime, imposed upon the people by a

[60] *Supra,* pp. 11, 14.

[61] For example, an official Review of the Development Plan of the Western Region, 1957, rebutted the criticism that social services had been given excessive support to the detriment of "economic services" with the following observation by W. A. Lewis and A. Martin:

"India's small expenditure on health and education distinguish her sharply from other progressive governments, especially from the programs of the new nationalist governments in Ceylon, in the Gold Coast, and in Nigeria. In reply to the contention that economic expenditure should precede social service expenditures, politicians in these countries reply both that health and education expenditures are necessary for increasing the output of commodities, and also that it is just as important to get rid of illiteracy and of disease as it is to provide more steel or cloth. Some West African politicians explain the difference mainly in terms of political structure. India, they say, is ruled by her upper classes, in a situation where caste and class differences are pronounced. Her rulers do not have to take much account of what the masses themselves think they want. West African society, on the other hand, is nearly classless. The masses have great political influence and they make it clear that they value expenditure on health and education more than any other kind of government expenditure. In the final analysis there is no 'model' which can show what government expenditure ought to be, without taking into account of differing political pressures." "Patterns of Public Revenue and Expenditure," quoted in Review of the Development Plan, 1957 (Files of the Ministry of Economic Planning, Western Region).

minority, would be inconsistent with communal traditions and might therefore be highly unstable. African leaders, including leaders of the emergent single-party states, appear to endorse this view and seek to ground their "party-states" in majoritarian principles. African proponents of the single-party system have argued that communal traditions reconcile respect for human dignity with social solidarity, and that insofar as communal traditions are observed, the intrinsic worth of the individual will not be forgotten in the drive for national integration and development.[62] Communal traditions in Nigeria reinforce the democratic tendencies of a competitive party system based on free elections and constitutional guarantees of civil liberty.

Postscript on the Independence Coalition

In December 1959 the center of political gravity shifted from the self-governing regions to the government of the Federation. Two of the three regional premiers—Chief Obafemi Awolowo, Premier of the West and Federal President of the Action Group, and Dr. Nnamdi Azikiwe, Premier of the East and National President of the National Council of Nigeria and the Cameroons (NCNC)—resigned their regional offices and were elected to the Federal House of Representatives, as were their principal lieutenants in the Northern Region, Mr. Joseph Sarwuan Tarka, President General of the United Middle Belt Congress (UMBC/Action Group) and Malam Aminu Kano, President General of the Northern Elements Progressive Union (NEPU/NCNC) respectively. Alhaji Sir Ahmadu Bello, the Sardauna of Sokoto and General President of the Northern Peoples' Congress (NPC), remained in office as Premier of the North. (It will be recalled that some 54 percent of the Nigerian people live in the Northern Region.) In the Western Region, Chief Awolowo was succeeded as Premier by the Deputy Leader of the Action Group, Chief Samuel Ladoke Akintola;[63] in the Eastern Re-

[62] In this vein, Julius K. Nyerere, first President of Tanganyika, a libertarian, and an advocate of the one-party system, has observed that the member of a traditional African community "saw no struggle between his own interests and those of his community. . . . He never felt himself to be a cog in a machine. There could not be this all-embracing, all-powerful modern concept of society which could 'use' him as a cog." "Africa Needs Time," *The New York Times Magazine*, March 27, 1960, p. 85.

[63] Chief Samuel L. Akintola was born in 1910 at Ogbomosho in Oshun Division. He served as a teacher at the Baptist Academy of Lagos and edited the *Nigerian Baptist* until 1943, when he became the editor of the *Daily Service* (Lagos), then the official organ of the Nigerian Youth Movement. In 1946 he went to England where he studied public administration and law; in addition he was largely responsible for the continued activities of the London branch of the *Egbe*

gion, the successor to Premier Azikiwe was his colleague in the Eastern Government, Dr. Michael Iheonukara Okpara.[64] Both choices were logical, popular, and conducive to the efficient implementation and rational extension of party policies affecting the development of Nigeria.

In certain respects, the three-cornered electoral contest of 1959 for the House of Representatives was politically anomalous. The Action Group and its allies campaigned against the Northern

---

Omo Oduduwa (Yoruba cultural society) following the return to Nigeria of its founder, barrister Awolowo. In 1950 barrister Akintola resumed his editorial responsibilities on the *Daily Service* and became chairman of the Lagos branch of the Nigerian Youth Movement. Concomitantly, he was active in the formation of the Action Group (*supra*, pp. 103-110) and in the agitation of Oshun Division for separation from the Ibadan divisional government (*supra*, pp. 292-293); subsequently he became the Oshun Divisional Leader of the Action Group. Throughout the decade prior to independence, Chief Akintola represented his party at the national level of Nigerian government. He served as Central Minister of Labour (1952-1953), Leader of the Opposition in the Federal House of Representatives (1954-1957), and Federal Minister of Commerce and Aviation in the national government of 1957-1959. In 1955 he was chosen as Deputy Leader of the Action Group. Probably his popular following in the Western Region is second only to that of Chief Awolowo. His rapier wit has enlivened innumerable parliamentary meetings and he is celebrated for his remarkable facility of expression, in particular for his talent as an interpreter of complex issues of public policy to people in all walks of life. See the "portrait" of Chief Akintola in *West Africa*, January 9, 1960.

[64] Dr. Michael I. Okpara was born in 1920 in Bende Division of Owerri Province. He studied medicine at the Yaba Higher College of Lagos and practiced briefly as a government medical officer and private doctor. In 1949 he was arrested for having made an allegedly seditious utterance at a meeting of the Zikist Movement in Umuahia in connection with the shooting of coal miners by the police at Enugu (*supra*, p. 77). Shortly thereafter he joined the New Africa Party, which had been formed by barrister Jaja A. Wachuku; eventually the New Africa Party was incorporated into the NCNC and Dr. Okpara was among the handful of successful candidates in the Eastern general election of 1951 who stood on the party platform. He became a minister without portfolio in the regional government and sided with Dr. Azikiwe during the Eastern crisis of 1953. (*Supra*, pp. 119-124.) Subsequently he served in the Eastern Regional Government as Minister of Health (1954-1957), Minister of Production (1958-1959), and Minister of Agriculture (1959-1960). In addition he has been Leader of the Eastern House of Assembly and chairman of the NCNC Eastern Working Committee (1955-1957). At the time of his elevation to the Premiership, he was regarded as a moderate socialist with strong associations among the intellectual and business leaders of the region. See the "portrait" of Dr. Okpara in *West Africa*, January 23, 1960.

Although Dr. Okpara has been a trusted lieutenant of Dr. Azikiwe, they have clashed on occasion and the former has been criticized trenchantly by radical and left wing elements within the party. (*Supra*, p. 214.) Yet his career indicates that he was groomed for the Premiership by Dr. Azikiwe, even during their "family quarrels," and his advance to the top would appear to refute the allegation that Dr. Azikiwe could not abide independent-minded colleagues of high intellectual caliber.

Peoples' Congress in the Northern Region and against the NCNC in the Eastern and Western Regions. The NCNC fought the Action Group in the East and West and supported the Northern Elements Progressive Union, which campaigned vigorously against the Northern Peoples' Congress. Yet it was understood that an "accord" existed between the leaders of the Northern Peoples' Congress and the leaders of the NCNC that was expected to mature into a coalition government for the Federation after the election. Observers may have been puzzled by the ability of these two parties to cooperate notwithstanding the NCNC's overt support of a radical Northern party, namely the Northern Elements Progressive Union. The explanation lies partly in the fact that the Northern leaders view the NEPU as a legitimate opposition which reflects a familiar and traditional social cleavage. Furthermore, the NEPU did virtually spring from the Northern Peoples' Congress in 1950,[65] and to some degree, NEPU leaders share the *weltanschauung* of progressive elements in the NPC. Moreover, there are many progressive civil servants of Northern origin who work for the Northern and federal governments, forming a bridge of personal rapport between the Northern government party and the NEPU opposition.

By contrast, the Action Group has been stigmatized in the North as an alien threat to traditional value, despite that party's effort to recruit Northern cadres in all provinces of the region. Action Group spokesmen, like those of the NEPU, campaigned for liberalization of the Northern systems of law and administration. Unlike the NEPU, Action Group efforts were most effective in the lower North and its principal ally, the United Middle Belt Congress, is primarily a non-Muslim movement. Action Group leaders favored the creation of a new state in the minority sector of each region prior to independence in addition to an alteration of the North-West boundary in order to transfer the Yorubas of Ilorin Division to the Western Region.[66] These proposals envisaged a potential reduction of about 35 percent in the population of the Northern Region; a corresponding reduction of Northern influence in the federal government was implied, and the Northern leaders declared their absolute refusal to part with "an inch" of Northern territory. They were appeased by the NCNC, in particular by Dr. Azikiwe, who held that it was impossible to create new states prior to independence without an anguishing postponement of the overriding nationalist goal, and that the question of new states should, for that reason, be deferred until independence had been achieved.

[65] *Supra,* pp. 94-96.   [66] *Supra,* pp. 350-355.

As anticipated by most observers, the Northern Peoples' Congress emerged from the election with a strong plurality—142 seats out of 312, all but one of them in the Northern Region. The NCNC/NEPU Alliance ran second with 89 and the Action Group garnered a total of 73, including 25 seats in the lower North (one-third of the total in that section).[67] Prior to the election it had been speculated that Dr. Azikiwe would be supported by the Sardauna of Sokoto to lead a coalition cabinet with an NPC majority. But the NPC insisted upon the reappointment of its First Vice President, Alhaji Sir Abubakar Tafawa Balewa, as Prime Minister of the Federation. For several days the makeup of the government remained in doubt as the Action Group offered to participate in a coalition under the National President of the NCNC on the condition that the NCNC would agree to the creation of a new state in every region.[68] This offer was rejected by the NCNC,[69] and an NPC-NCNC Coalition Government was formed, comprising 10 NPC ministers and 7 NCNC ministers with Alhaji Sir Abubakar Tafawa Balewa as Prime Minister.[70]

[67] See E. Awa, "The Federal Elections in Nigeria, 1959," *Ibadan*, A Journal published at University College, No. 8 (March 1960), pp. 5-7; and K. W. J. Post, "The Federal Election: an Outside View," *ibid.*, pp. 7-9. Also the excellent reportorial article entitled "Nigeria Elects 1960 Independence Parliament," *Africa Special Report*, Vol. 4, No. 12 (December 1959), pp. 3-4.

[68] *Daily Times*, December 22, 1959.

[69] Dr. Azikiwe disclosed that within the NCNC "two schools of thought emerged after prolonged discussion. One school conceded that a coalition between the NCNC-NEPU Alliance with the Action Group would no doubt produce an efficient Government, but it was stressed that majority opinion in the Western Region would frown against such a coalition. Moreover, it was obvious that if the Alliance agreed to a coalition with the Action Group, then there might be a crisis within the Party with the Westerners probably breaking away. . . . The other school agreed that a coalition between the Alliance with the NPC would also produce an efficient, but with it, a stable Government: yet a strong body of influential opinion severely criticized such a coalition. Warnings were given that the NEPU might feel frustrated in view of its traditional struggle with the NPC. It was feared that this might create a schism in the Alliance."

Eventually, it was decided that in view of the past hostility of the Action Group to the NCNC, the entrenchment of Fundamental Human Rights in the Constitution, which the courts were bound to protect, and the cordial personal relationships obtaining between leaders of the NPC and NCNC, "the NEPU leaders should be persuaded to modify their attitude and give the NCNC a fair chance to work out a *modus vivendi* for the three parties, namely: NPC, NCNC and NEPU, in the interest of national solidarity." *Daily Times*, December 23, 1959.

[70] The Independence Government of October 1, 1960, included 23 members, as follows:

Alhaji Sir Abubakar Tafawa Balewa (NPC, Bauchi), Prime Minister and Minister for Foreign Affairs and Commonwealth Relations

Alhaji Muhammadu Ribadu (NPC, Adamawa), Minister of Defence

Chief Festus Sam Okotie-Eboh (NCNC, Warri), Minister of Finance

Mr. R. A. Njoku (NCNC, Owerri), Minister of Transport and Aviation

Chief Obafemi Awolowo assumed the Leadership of the Opposition and Dr. Azikiwe resigned from the Federal House of Representatives to assume the honorific position of President of the Nigerian Senate. Eventually it was announced that the Prime Minister had recommended him to the Queen for appointment as Governor-General of Nigeria upon the retirement of the popular and respected Sir James Robertson in November 1960. Under the Nigerian Constitution, few substantive powers are vested in that office, which symbolizes the relationship between Nigeria and the British monarchy. In preparation for his assumption of an office above party politics, Dr. Azikiwe resigned from the National Presidency of the NCNC. His successor, elected by a party convention in September 1960, was Dr. M. I. Okpara, Premier of the East. At the center, the NCNC Federal Parliamentary Party remained under the leadership of the party's influential National Treasurer and Federal Minister of Finance, Chief Festus Sam Okotie-Eboh.[71]

Alhaji Muhammadu Inuwa Wada (NPC, Kano), Minister of Works and Survey

Mr. J. M. Johnson (NCNC, Lagos), Minister of Labour

Malam Zanna Bukar Dipcharima (NPC, Bornu), Minister of Commerce and Industry

Mr. Aja Nwachuku (NCNC, Afikpo), Minister of Education

Alhaji Shehu Shagari (NPC, Sokoto), Minister of Pensions

Alhaji Usman Sarki (NPC, Bida), Minister of Internal Affairs

Malam Maitama Sule (NPC, Kano), Minister of Mines and Power

Mr. T. O. S. Benson (NCNC, Lagos), Minister of Information

Alhaji Waziri Ibrahim (NPC, Bornu), Minister of Health

Mr. Olu Akinfosile (NCNC, Okitipupa), Minister of Communications

Malam Musa Yar'Adua (NPC, Katsina), Minister of Lagos Affairs

Mr. Jaja Anchu Wachuku (NCNC, Aba), Minister of Economic Development

Dr. T. O. Elias (NCNC), Attorney-General and Minister of Justice

Mr. M. T. Mbu (NCNC, Ogoja), Minister of State in the Ministry of Defence for Navy

Senator Dr. M. A. Majekodunmi, Minister of State in the Ministry of Defence for Army

Senator Dr. E. A. Esin (NCNC), Minister of State in the Ministry of Foreign Affairs and Commonwealth Relations

Senator Malam Nuhu Bamalli (NPC), Minister of State in the Ministry of Foreign Affairs and Commonwealth Relations

Mr. M. A. O. Olarewaju (NPC, Ilorin), Minister of State in the Prime Minister's Office

Mr. J. C. Obande (NPC, Idoma), Minister of State in the Prime Minister's Office

Chief H. Omo-Osagie (NCNC, Benin), Minister of State in the Ministry of Finance without Cabinet Rank

West Africa, October 15, 1960, p. 1175.

[71] Chief Festus Sam Okotie-Eboh was born in 1912 in the former Warri Province. He was first employed as a Baptist schoolteacher; later he became an accounts manager for an English shoe company which sent him to Czechoslovakia for the study of business administration. He became fluent in the Czech language and

The independence government was the outcome of a maneuver at the top of the Nigerian power system that did not greatly affect the condition of the base. Thus in August 1960, the Western Regional Government dissolved the Western House of Assembly and the Action Group was returned to power by the electorate with a parliamentary majority of about 2:1.[72] Possibly an NCNC-Action Group coalition at the center would have jeopardized the unity of Nigeria inasmuch as the Northern leaders might not have been willing to tolerate a denial of executive power in view of their large plurality in the federal legislature. However, the Prime Minister declared that his party was prepared to form the opposition if the NCNC and the Action Group reached an agreement of coalition.[73] This affirmation of loyalty to the Federation by the Federal Leader of the Northern Peoples' Congress seemed to attest to the viability of the Nigerian party system as it neared the impending strains of independence. Some of the post-independence issues that were expected to test the cohesion of the coalition government seemed likely to invite a spirit of compromise and phased resolution—e.g., the rate of extension of liberal democracy to the awakening North, the method of advance toward pan-African unity, and the relationship of Nigeria with non-African powers.[74]

---

witnessed the *coup d'état* of 1948; it is said that this experience turned him against communism. Subsequently he acquired wealth in the rubber export trade and became a school proprietor. He was elected to the Western House of Assembly in 1951 and the Federal House of Representatives in 1954, serving as Federal Minister of Labour and Welfare until 1957 when he became the first Nigerian to hold the crucial portfolio of finance in the federal government. In 1958 he was elected to succeed Dr. K. O. Mbadiwe as leader of the Federal Parliamentary Party. He is close to the Prime Minister and was reported to have been most instrumental in the prevention of an NCNC-Action Group coalition following the federal election of 1960. *New York Times*, December 21, 1959. Chief Okotie-Eboh is regarded as a proponent of the welfare-capitalist philosophy and close association with the Western powers. This may have weakened his bid for the Presidency of the NCNC in 1960, inasmuch as the majority opinion in the NCNC is socialist and neutralist.

[72] It was noted that the Action Group appeared to gain in former NCNC strongholds, including Ibadan and the Mid-West, which gave the NCNC overwhelming majorities in the previous federal election, while the NCNC increased its strength in sections which had been regarded as safe for the Action Group.

[73] *West Africa*, December 19, 1959, p. 1097.

[74] Foreign policy was a major issue in the campaign of December 1959. The Action Group favored Nigeria's outright alignment with the West; the Northern Peoples' Congress ruled out "neutrality" and called for "increasing friendship with the United States of America"; the NCNC espoused a policy of non-alignment. In 1960 it did seem that the NCNC had influenced its coalition partner in the field of foreign policy, as the Prime Minister declared that his government would pursue a policy of non-alignment without neutrality. In addition, the government of the Federation accepted a loan from Israel, which had previously enjoyed

Other issues, involving conflicts of social interests, including demands for the creation of new states within the Federation, were likely to provide the irreducible content of party competition and political tension for an indefinite period of time.

In Nigeria, class, communal, and ideological affinities transcend party alignments. Yet it does seem fair to infer from this study that the Northern Peoples' Congress is mainly "rightist" and "centrist," while the Northern "left" is identified primarily with the Northern Elements Progressive Union and radical affiliates of the Action Group. In southern Nigeria, the membership of each of the two major parties spans the ideological spectrum. It has been observed that before independence, liberal and entrepreneurial elements were predominant within the executive and unofficial decision-making bodies of the Action Group, which may account for that party's initial advocacy of alignment with the Western powers in international politics. Inevitably the role of the Action Group as the official Opposition in the Federal, Northern, and Eastern Parliaments was an attraction for idealists and grievance groups to enter its fold, thereby strengthening the influence of radical elements and producing a swing to the left. It was virtually predictable that the more conservative wing of the Action Group would be loath to support an increasingly radical opposition to the federal government. But Chief Awolowo, supported by party militants, was determined to steer a leftward course, guided by the lights of socialism, neutralism, and pan-Africanism. His deputy, Chief Akintola, became the spokesman for a conservative minority which was defeated within the party during the crisis of 1962.[75] Akintola and his supporters then inaugurated the United People's Party in opposition to the majority faction of the Action Group.

These developments may portend a general realignment of political forces according to ideological lights. It seemed likely that the Action Group's new look would appeal strongly to the Nigerian intelligentsia, especially the politically conscious youth. Meanwhile, in 1961, the inauguration by young socialists of a proto-party, the Nigerian Youth Congress, appeared to offer a meeting ground for radical followers of all three major parties.[76] But the youth wings of the NCNC

notably more cordial relations with the Eastern and Western Regional Governments than with the government of the Northern Region. The Israeli loan was accepted despite the adoption of a resolution against it in the Northern House of Assembly.

[75] *Supra*, pp. 281, 431.

[76] The president and founder of the Nigerian Youth Congress, organized in 1960,

questioned the purposes of the Youth Congress and prohibited dual membership.

Within the main body of the NCNC, the political drives of entrepreneurial and other potentially conservative class-interest groups were checked temporarily in 1958. At least that opinion was expressed by radical and socialistic members of the National Executive Committee at the climax of a bitter intra-party struggle. By Independence Day, October 1, 1960, however, moderate and entrepreneurial elements appeared to have regained substantial control of the party organization.[77] Their former leader and nemesis, a man of unplumbed depth and unparalleled popularity, withdrew from the arena of active politics, waiting, perhaps, for the wheel to turn.

---

is Dr. Tunji Otegbeye, a medical doctor in Lagos. The Congress is supported by a less radical Nigerian Youth Council which includes organizational affiliates, e.g., student and teacher groups, throughout the country. See Sam C. Sarkesian, "Nigerian Political Profile," Master's thesis, Department of Government, Columbia University, 1962.

[77] It should be noted that a rapprochement on the personal level between Dr. Azikiwe and Dr. K. O. Mbadiwe, President of the Democratic Party of Nigeria and the Cameroons (*supra*, p. 228) was announced in December 1960. Subsequently, Dr. Mbadiwe was appointed Adviser on African Affairs to the Prime Minister, readmitted to the NCNC, elected to the Federal House of Representatives, and restored to a position of cabinet rank in the federal government. Few persons in Nigerian public life have been as dedicated to the promotion of private enterprise as Dr. Mbadiwe and Chief F. S. Okotie-Eboh, his successor as Federal Parliamentary Leader of the NCNC.

APPENDIX I

THE NATIONAL EXECUTIVE COMMITTEE OF THE NORTHERN PEOPLES' CONGRESS, 1958

(Name, party office, government office, ethnic identification, home division and/or province, religion, and occupational background*)

NATIONAL OFFICERS

1. Alhaji Sir Ahmadu Bello, Sardaunan Sokoto, MHA—General President—Premier of the North—Fulani—Sokoto—Muslim—N.A. Councillor and District Head (teacher)

2. Alhaji Sir Abubakar Tafawa Balewa, MHR—First Vice President—Prime Minister of the Federation—Gerawa (Habe)—Bauchi —Muslim—teacher and headmaster (N.A. Councillor)

3. Alhaji Muhammadu Ribadu, MHR—Second Vice President—Federal Minister of Mines, Power and Lagos Affairs—Fulani—Adamawa—Muslim—N.A. Councillor and District Head (teacher)

4. Malam Abba Habib, MHA—General Secretary—Northern Minister of Trade and Industry—Shuwa Arab—Dikwa (Bornu, Northern Cameroons Trust Territory)—Muslim—N.A. (District Head) (teacher)

5. Alhaji Aliyu, Makaman Bida, MHA—General Treasurer—Northern Minister of Finance—Nupe—Bida (Niger)—Muslim—N.A. Councillor (teacher and headmaster)

6. Alhaji Isa Kaita, Madawaikin Katsina, MHA—General Financial Secretary—Northern Region Minister of Education—Hausa—Katsina—Muslim—N.A. Councillor

7. Malam Umaru Agaie—Publicity Secretary (Niger Provincial Secretary)—N.A. Liaison Officer, Niger Province—Nupe—Bida—Muslim

8. Malam Abdul Razaq—Legal Adviser—Yoruba—Ilorin—Muslim —barrister

9. Alhaji Ibrahim Musa Gashash, MHA—Northern Regional President—Northern Minister of Land and Survey—Tripolitanian Arab and Hausa—Kano—Muslim—businessman

10. Alhaji Isa Haruna—Northern Regional Vice President—Hausa (Jos)—Muslim—Contractor, company agent, and labor leader

* Secondary occupations are listed in parentheses. N.A. denotes Native Administration.

11. Mr. Michael Audu Buba, Wazirin Shendam, MHA—Northern Regional Secretary—Northern Minister of Social Welfare and Co-operatives—Shendam (Plateau)—Catholic—N.A. Councillor

12. Alhaji Muhammadu Inuwa Wada, MHR—National Organizer —Federal Minister of Works—Fulani—Kano—Muslim—N.A.

PROVINCIAL REPRESENTATIVES

(those in parentheses have been listed above)

Adamawa

13. Malam Bello Malabu, Madawaki, MHA—Fulani—Muslim— N.A. (Councillor) (teacher)

14. Malam Idirisu, Tafida, MHA—Provincial President—Fulani-Hausa—Muslim—N.A. Councillor, District Head (teacher)

15. Alhaji Abdullahi Dan Buram Jada, MHA—Northern Minister of Animal Health, Forestry and Northern Cameroons Affairs— Fulani—(Adamawa Trust Terr.)—Muslim—N.A. District Head (Alhaji Muhammadu Ribadu, MHR No. 3 above)

Bornu

16. Shettima Kashim, Waziri—Kanuri—Muslim—N.A. teacher (Councillor); subsequently constitutional Governor of the North

17. Zanna Bukar Dipcharima, MHR—Provincial President—Federal Minister of Commerce and Industry—Kanuri—Muslim—N.A. Councillor, (teacher and business agent)

18. Malam Bukar Batulbe—Provincial Vice President—Kanuri— Muslim—businessman

19. Malam Yunusa Mai-Haja, MHA—Kanuri—Muslim—Nguru— trader

Bauchi

20. Malam Usman Katagum—Divisional President—Galambawa (Habe)—Bauchi—Muslim—N.A. worker (engine turner)

21. Malam Yakubu Wanka, Waziri—Fulani—Bauchi—Muslim— N.A. Councillor

22. Malam Hamza Gombe, MHR—Fulani—Gombe—Muslim— N.A.

23. Malam Muhammadu Kabir, Ciroman Katagum, MHA—Northern Minister of State—Fulani—Katagum (Bauchi)—Muslim— N.A. District Head

24. Malam Abubakar Garba, Madaki, MHR—Fulani—Bauchi— Muslim—N.A. District Head and Councillor (teacher)

Benue

25. Alhaji Ari—Provincial President—Muslim (Makurdi)—businessman

26. Malam Mijin Yawa—Provincial Secretary—(Makurdi)—Muslim—trader

27. Mr. J. C. Obande, MHR—Idoma—Christian—businessman—subsequently Federal Minister of State

28. Malam Ibrahim Sangari Usman Wukari, MHR—Parliamentary Secretary, Federal Goverment—Junkun—Wukari—Muslim—N.A.

29. Mr. Benjamin Akiga Sai Gboko—National Organizing Secretary—Tiv—Christian—N.A. Education Officer (preacher)

Ilorin

30. Mr. M. A. O. Olarewaju, MHR—Yoruba—Christian—Ilorin—N.A.—subsequently Federal Minister of State

31. Malam Sani O. B. Okin, MHR—Divisional Vice President—Yoruba—Muslim—Ilorin—N.A.

32. Malam Buari Edun—Divisional and Provincial President—Yoruba—Ilorin—Muslim—businessman

Kabba

33. Peter S. Achimugu, P.C.—Igala—Christian—contractor

34. Mr. George Uru Ohikere, MHA—Northern Minister of Health—Igbira—Catholic—mission teacher (N.A.)

35. Mr. Samuel Aliyu Ajayi, MHA—Yoruba—Kabba—Christian—business (N.A.) (teacher)

Kano

36. Malam Rilwanu Abdullahi, MHR—Provincial President—Fulani—Muslim—N.A.

37. Malam Maitama Sule, MHR—Chief Whip, Federal Parliamentary Party—Hausa—Muslim—teacher—subsequently Federal Minister

38. Alhaji Shehu Ahmed, Makaki, MHA—Deputy President Northern House Assembly—Fulani—Muslim—N.A. Councillor (teacher)

39. Alhaji Ahmadu Dantata, MHA—Hausa—Muslim—businessman

Katsina

40. Alhaji Usman Liman, Sarkin Musawa, MHA—Chief Whip, Northern House of Assembly—Fulani—Muslim—N.A. District Head

41. Alhaji Othman Ladan Baki, MHA—Fulani—Muslim—N.A.

42. Malam Muhammadu Bashar, Wamban Daura, MHA—Fulani—Muslim—N.A. District Head
(Alhaji Isa Kaita, MHA, No. 6 above)
43. Malam Musa Yaraduwa, Tafida—Provincial President—Fulani—Muslim—N.A. Councillor—subsequently Federal Minister

Niger
44. Malam Baba Nahanna-Dama, MHA—Provincial Treasurer and Minna Divisional President—Hausa—Gwari (Minna)—Muslim—N.A. (company agent)
45. Alhaji Abdu-Anache, Magajin Garin Kontagora, MHA—Fulani—Kontagora—Muslim—N.A. Councillor
(Malam Umaru Agaie, No. 7 above)
46. Malam Ibrahim Muku—Nupe—Bida—Muslim—N.A.
47. Malam Hassan, Makaman Abuja, MHA—Nupe—Abuja—Muslim—N.A. Councillor
48. Malam Hayatu—Provincial President—Nupe—Bida—Muslim—businessman

Plateau
(Alhaji Isa Haruna, Provincial President, No. 10 above)
49. Alhaji Alin Iliya—Hausa (Jos)—Muslim—businessman
50. Malam Mohammadu Dan Karfalla—Hausa (Jos)—Muslim—businessman (N.A.)
51. Chief J. Y. Dimlong *Pankshin*, MHR—President of N.A. Council

Sokoto
52. Alhaji Abubakar, Madawaki, MHA—Hausa—Muslim—N.A. Councillor (teacher)
53. Malam Sani Dingyadi, Makama, MHA—Hausa—Muslim—N.A. Councillor (teacher and headmaster)
54. Malam Aliyu, Magajin Garin Sokoto, MHA—Provincial President—Fulani—Muslim—N.A. Councillor
55. Malam Bello Alkamawa, MHR—Muslim—N.A.—ex-Provincial Secretary

Zaria
56. Malam Nuhu Bamalli, MHR—Provincial President—Fulani—Muslim—N.A.—subsequently Federal Senator and Minister of State
57. Alhaji Muhammadu Sanusi, Sarkin Yaki, MHA—Hausa—Muslim—N.A. Councillor (teacher)
58. Alhaji Shafi', Tudun Wada—Nupe—Muslim—trader
(Malam Abdul Razaq, No. 8 above)

59. Alhaji Abore Shani—Bui-Babur—Muslim—treasurer Bui N.A. (NRDC)

Eastern Region
60. Malam Moman Tailor—Muslim
61. Alhaji (Chief) Sule, Enugu—Muslim—trader
62. Alhaji Baba Gire—Muslim—trader
63. Chroma Zubairu—Muslim—trader

Western Region
64. Alhaji Sanda—Hausa—Muslim—(Lagos)—trader and businessman

Kaduna Division
65. Alhaji Zakari—Hausa—Muslim—businessman—Divisional President

OTHER MINISTERS (REGIONAL AND FEDERAL)

66. Alhaji Ahman, Galadiman Pategi, MHA—Northern Minister of Health—Nupe—Lafiagi-Pategi (Ilorin)—Muslim—N.A. (Councillor)
67. Alhaji Abdullahi Maikano Dutse, MHA—Northern Minister of Local Government—Fulani—Kano—Muslim—N.A.
68. Malam Mustafa Monguno, MHA—Northern Minister of Agriculture—Kanuri—Bornu—Muslim—N.A.
69. Malam Shehu Usman, Galadiman Maska, MHA—Northern Minister of Internal Affairs—Sokoto—Muslim—N.A.
70. Malam Mu'azu Lamido, Magatakarda of Sokoto, MHA—Northern Minister of State—Sokoto Divisional President—Fulani—Muslim—N.A.
71. Mr. Daniel Ogbadu, MHA—Northern Minister of State—Igala—Christian—N.A.
72. Mr. Abutu Obekpa, MHA—Northern Minister of State—Idoma—Christian—N.A.

OTHER INDIVIDUALS OF MINISTERIAL STATUS, PROBABLY MEMBERS OF THE EXECUTIVE

73. Malam Bello Dandago, Sarkin Dawaki Maituta Kano, MHR—Deputy Speaker, Federal House of Representatives—Fulani—Muslim—N.A. District Head
74. Alhaji Aliyu, Turakin Zazzau—Chairman of the Northern Region Development Corporation—Hausa—Muslim—N.A. Councillor (teacher)

APPENDIX II

EXECUTIVE MEMBERS OF THE NATIONAL COUNCIL OF NIGERIA AND THE CAMEROONS,

including members of the National Executive Committee, the Eastern and Western Working Committees, and members of Ministerial rank in the Eastern and Federal Governments, November, 1957-August, 1958

(Party office, government office, ethnic identification, home town, district or division, religion, and occupational background)

1. Dr. Nnamdi Azikiwe—National President—President of the Senate (Premier of the East)—Onitsha Ibo—Methodist—Journalist and businessman; subsequently Governor-General of Nigeria.

2. Hon. J. O. Fadahunsi, MHA—First National Vice-President—Ijesha Yoruba—Protestant—businessman (teacher)

3. Hon. R. A. Njoku, MHR—Second National Vice-President—Ibo—Owerri—Catholic—Federal Minister of Transport—barrister (teacher)

4. Mr. F. S. McEwen—National Secretary—Chairman, Lagos Town Council—West Indian—Protestant—Lagos—General Manager *West African Pilot* (educator)

5. Chief F. S. Okotie-Eboh, MHR—National Treasurer—Federal Minister of Finance—Itsekeri-Urhobo—Warri—Protestant—businessman—Leader of the Federal Parliamentary Party

6. Mr. A. K. Blankson—National Auditor—Ghanaian—Lagos—Protestant—General Manager—African Continental Bank—Editor-in-Chief *West African Pilot* (journalist and company director)

7. Hon. D. C. Osadebay, MHA—National Legal Adviser—Leader of the Opposition—W.H.A.—Western Ibo—Asaba—Protestant—barrister (author); subsequently President of the Senate

8. Hon. T. O. S. Benson, MHR—National Financial Secretary—Federal Minister of Information (former Chief Whip)—Yoruba—Ikorodu-Lagos—Protestant—barrister

9. Mr. F. U. Anyiam—National Publicity Secretary—Ibo—Orlu—businessman

Northern Region Representatives

10. Malam Aminu Kano, MHR—Life National President of the NEPU—Fulani—Kano—Muslim—educator

11. Malam Ibrahim Imam, MHA—Leader of the Bornu Youth Movement—Kanuri—Maiduguri—Muslim—businessman; subsequently Action Group Leader of the Opposition in the Northern House of Assembly

12. Mr. R. D. Nyamsi—Chairman Kano Waje Council—Bandam— French Cameroons—contractor

13. Mr. C. A. J. Nwajei—Ibo—Kano barrister—Legal Adviser to NEPU

Eastern Region

14. Hon. C. C. Mojekwu, MHR—Legal Adviser, Eastern Working Committee—Ibo—Nnewi—Protestant—barrister

15. Hon. M. E. Ogon, MHA—Provincial Commissioner—Ogoja— Chief Whip, E.H.A.—Boki—Ikom—Catholic—educator

16. Hon. Jaja A. Wachuku, MHR—Speaker-designate of the Federal House—Vice-Chairman of the Eastern Working Committee— Ibo—Aba—Ngwa—barrister; subsequently Federal Minister of Economic Development, Federal Minister of Foreign Affairs, and Chairman of the U.N. Conciliation Commission in the Congo

17. Hon. J. O. Ihekwoaba, MHA—Orlu—Port Harcourt—Ibo— transport owner and produce buyer

18. Mr. F. I. Okoronkwo—Chairman, Aba branch—Ibo—Owerri— Catholic—book dealer

19. Mr. W. K. Anuforo—President, Port Harcourt branch—Ibo— Owerri—Catholic—educator

Western Region

20. Chief H. Omo Osagie, MHR—Vice Chairman, Western Working Committee—Parliamentary Secretary to the Federal Minister of Finance—President *Otu Edo* (Benin) Edo—Benin—retired civil servant

21. Chief S. J. Mariere, MHR—Urhobo—Protestant—business manager (teacher)

22. Chief Kolawole Balogun, MHR—Nigerian Minister to Ghana— former Federal Minister and National Secretary; Yoruba—Oshun— barrister

23. Hon. A. M. F. Agbaje, MHA—ex-Chairman Western Working Committee—Chairman Ibadan District Council—Yoruba—Ibadan— Muslim—barrister

24. Hon. Babatunji Olowofoyeku, MHA—Chairman Ilesha District Council—Yoruba—Ijesha—Protestant—barrister

Lagos

25. Mr. Adeniran Ogunsanya—President General NCNC Youth Association—Chairman Federal Loans Board—Yoruba—Ikorodu—barrister

26. Chief O. A. Fagbenro-Beyioku—member of the Senate—Secretary Lagos—NCNC—Yoruba—Lagos—Secretary, Marine African Workers' Union and other unions

Cameroons

27. Hon. N. N. Mbile, MHA—Vice President Kamerun Peoples' Party—former Cameroons Minister of Works—Balondo—Kumba—businessman—plantation owner (trade unionist and journalist)

28. Hon. P. N. Motomby-Woleta—ex-MHA—former Secretary K.P.P.—Bakwerri—Victoria—Clerk, Cameroons Development Corporation

Parliamentary Leaders

29. Dr. K. O. Mbadiwe—ex-Minister of Commerce—subsequently leader of the Democratic Party of Nigeria and Cameroons—Aro-Ibo—Orlu—Catholic—businessman

30. Alhaji Adegoke Adelabu, MHA—deceased—former Leader of the Opposition, W.H.A. and Chairman of the Western Working Committee—Ibadan—Yoruba—Muslim—businessman (company agent and civil servant)

31. Dr. M. I. Okpara, MHA—Eastern Minister of Production—Ibo—Bende—Protestant—medical practitioner; subsequently Premier of the East and National President of the NCNC

Women's Association

32. Mrs. Margaret U. Ekpo—Vice President, Eastern NCNC Women's Association—member Eastern House of Chiefs—Efik—(Aba) businesswoman

33. Mrs. Iheukumere (North)

34. Mrs. Felicia Obua (West)—Secretary Western Women's Association—Ibo (Sapele)

35. Mrs. Keziah Fashina (Lagos)—Chairman NCNC Lagos Women's Association—Yoruba

36. Mrs. R. Nzirmiro (East)—Ibo (Port Harcourt)

37. Miss Mary Ededem (Calabar)—member Eastern Region Tourist Corporation—Efik—hotel owner

N.C.N.C. Youth Association

38. Mr. V. Olu Fayemi—Assistant Secretary, Y.A.—Yoruba—accountant

39. Mr. J. A. Egwu—Vice President, Y.A. (Onitsha)—Ogoja—Ibo—pharmacist

Zikist National Vanguard

40. Mr. Adewale Fashanu—President-General, ZNV—Chairman Eastern Region Printing Corp.—Yoruba—Catholic—journalist and civil servant

41. Mr. V. K. Onyeri, MHA—Vice President, ZNV—Aro-Ibo—Port Harcourt—Catholic—businessman

Labour

42. Mr. H. P. Adebola—Yoruba—Ijebu-Ode—Muslim—General Secretary, Railway and Ports Transport Staff Union

43. Mr. Ibezim Obiajulu—Assistant Secretary Lagos, NCNC—member War Department, Workers' Union—Ibo—clerical employee

Ex-Servicemen

44. Dr. O. N. Egesi—subsequently, Democratic Party of Nigeria and Cameroons—Ibo—Aba—businessman

45. Mr. Adebayo Adeyinka, ex-MHR—Ibadan—Yoruba—Muslim—contractor

OFFICERS OF THE EASTERN WORKING COMMITTEE

46. Dr. G. C. Mbanugo—Chairman—(former Chairman, Eastern Finance Corporation)—Ibo—Obosi (Onitsha)—medical practitioner (Hon. J. A. Wachuku—Vice Chairman, No. 16 above)

47. Hon. S. O. Achara, MHA—Secretary—Aro-Ibo—Okigwe—Methodist—businessman—member of the DNPC

48. Hon. D. N. Abii, MHR—Assistant Secretary—Ibo—Owerri—Catholic—educator—Executive Member Ibo State Union

49. Mr. S. E. Obinwanni—Treasurer—Secretary Udi Divisional NCNC—Ibo—Enugu (non-Udi)—contractor (Hon. C. C. Mojekwu, MHR—Legal Adviser, No. 14 above)

50. Dr. E. A. Esin—Auditor—Member of the Senate—ex-Regional Minister—Oron (Calabar)—medical practitioner—subsequently Federal Minister of State

Officers of the Western Working Committee
(elected June 29, 1958)

(Hon. A. M. F. Agbaje, MHA—Chairman, No. 23 above)

(Hon. T. O. S. Benson, MHR—subsequently Chairman [1959] No. 8 above)

(Hon. Chief H. Omo Osagie, MHR—Vice Chairman, No. 20 above)

51. Hon. C. O. Komolafe, MHR—Secretary—Ilesha Yoruba—Ilesha—Protestant—educator

52. Hon. E. O. Fakayode, MHA—Assistant Secretary—Ibadan—Yoruba—Christian—barrister

53. Mrs. Funmilayo Ransome-Kuti—Treasurer—President Western NCNC Women's Association and Nigerian Women's Union—Yoruba—Abeokuta—Protestant—educator

54. Hon. J. M. Udochi, MHR—Auditor—Edo (Etsako)—Afenmai—Catholic—barrister—subsequently Ambassador to the United States

55. Mr. Ogunbiyi—Legal Adviser—Ijesha Yoruba (Ilesha)—barrister

56. Mr. R. O. A. Akinjide, MHR—Publicity Secretary—Ibadan—Yoruba—Christian—barrister

Other Federal Ministers (1958)

57. Hon. Joseph M. Johnson, MHR—Federal Minister of Labour and Welfare—Lagos—Yoruba—Catholic—businessman

58. Hon. Aja Nwachuku, MHR—Federal Minister of Education—Afikpo—Ibo—Anglican—educator

Other Eastern Regional Ministers (1958)

(Dr. M. I. Okpara—Minister of Production [later Agriculture and Premier], No. 31 above)

59. Hon. I. U. Akpabio—Minister of Internal Affairs—Annang—Ikot Ekpene—Methodist—educator

60. Dr. S. E. Imoke—Minister of Finance—Ibo—Afikpo—medical practitioner

61. Hon. E. Emole—Minister of Town Planning—Ibo—Bende—barrister

62. Hon. P. O. Ururuka—Minister of Transport—Ibo—Aba—Catholic—educator

63. Hon. B. C. Okwu—Minister of Information—Ibo—Awgu—Catholic—educator

64. Chief A. N. Onyiuke—Minister of Local Government—Ibo—Awka

65. Hon. R. O. Igwuagwu—Minister of Justice—Ibo—Okigwe—educator

66. Hon. P. O. Nwoga—Minister of Agriculture—Ibo—Owerri—Catholic—educator

67. Hon. J. U. Nwodo—Minister of Commerce—Ibo—Nsukka—Catholic—civil service

68. Hon. G. E. Okeke—Minister of Education—Ibo—Onitsha-Ihiala—educator

69. Hon. E. P. Okoya—Minister of Health—Ijaw—Brass—educator

70. Hon. E. A. Chime—Minister of Welfare—Ibo—Udi—civil servant

71. Hon. O. U. Affiah—Minister of Works—Annang—Abak—farmer (registered nurse and dispenser)

APPENDIX III

NATIONAL OFFICERS, PRINCIPAL ADVISERS, AND PARLIAMENTARIANS OF THE NORTHERN ELEMENTS PROGRESSIVE UNION, 1957-1958

(Ethnic identification, home division and/or province, religion, and occupational background)

1. Malam Aminu Kano—President General and Financial Secretary—Fulani—Kano—Muslim—teacher (writer)
2. Malam Yerima Balla—Deputy President General—Kilba—Adamawa—Christian—contractor
3. Malam Abubakar Zukogi—Secretary General—Fulani—Bida (Niger)—Muslim—forester
4. Malam Tanko Yakasai—Assistant Secretary General—Hausa—Kano—Muslim—tailor
5. Malam Adamu Jajire—Assistant Secretary General—Muslim—trader
6. Malam A. Salihu Nakande—Treasurer General—Muslim—transport owner
7. Alhaji Ibrahim Babanta—Assistant Treasurer General—Muslim—trader
8. Malam Ibrahim Heebah—Administrative Secretary General—Muslim—party official
9. Hon. Usman Ango Soba, MHA—Assistant Administrative Secretary General—Zaria—Muslim—farmer
10. Malam Lawan Danbazau—Legal Adviser (Muslim Law)—Fulani—Kano—Muslim—trader
11. Mr. C. A. J. Nwajei—Legal Adviser (English Law)—Ibo—Christian—barrister
12. Malam Ade Gusau—Joint Auditor—Muslim—clerk (business firm)
13. Malam Isa Bule—Joint Auditor—Fulani—Katsina—Muslim—N.A. Veterinary Department Head
14. Malam Mamuda—Welfare Officer—Muslim—trader
15. Alhaji Barba Yerwa—Assistant Welfare Officer—Muslim—transport owner
16. Malam Sani Darma—Chief Party Organizer—Muslim—business firm employee

17. Malam M. R. I. Gambo Sawaba—Propaganda Secretary and Northern Regional President—Hausa—Zaria—Muslim—trader
18. Malama Gambo Ahmed Sawaba—Women's Organizer—Nupe— rents houses
19. Malama Takano—Women's Organizer—Hausa—Kano—Muslim—trader
20. Malam Sani Gule Kano—R.S.S. Representative—Kano—Muslim—trader

Finance Committee

(Malam Sani Darma, No. 16 above)
21. Malam Shehu Satatima—groundnut buyer
22. Malam Tanko Waziri—Hausa (Jos)—Muslim—bicycle rentier
23. Malam M. K. Ahmed—business clerk
24. Malam Abdulkadir Danjaji—Muslim—trader
25. Hon. Abdulmumini—Fulani—Katsina—Muslim—ex-District Head (farmer and business agent)

Organizing Committee

(Malam Lawan Danbazau, No. 10 above)
26. Malam Babba Dan agundi—transport owner
(Malam Sani Darma, No. 16 above)
(Hon. Abdulmumini, No. 25 above)
27. Malam Uba na A. Alkasim—Kano Provincial President—Kano —Muslim—rope trader
28. Malam Salisu Tatta—trader
29. Malam Ibrahim Baban Dije—gardener

Provincial Organizers

ADAMAWA: (Malam Yerima Balla, No. 2 above)
30. BAUCHI: Malam Lamin Sanusi—also Liaison officer with tribal and trade unions—Muslim
31. BENUE: Malam Yahaya Sabo—also Deputy Chief Organizer— farmer
32. BORNU: Malam Garba Kano—Hausa (Bornu)—Muslim
ILORIN and KABBA: (Malam M. K. Ahmed, No. 23 above)
KANO: (Malam Tanko Yakasai, No. 4 above)
KATSINA: (Salisu Tatta, No. 28 above)
33. NIGER: Malam M. B. Yunusa—also Deputy Chief Organizer
PLATEAU: (Malam Tanko Waziri, No. 22 above)
SOKOTO: (Malam Lawan Danbazau, No. 10 above)

ZARIA: (Malam M. R. I. Gambo Sawaba, No. 17 above)
KADUNA: Malam Adamu Dankutu

Advisers (other than those named above)

34.	M. A. Sango	—UAC agent
35.	Malam Sa'adu Zungur	—dispensary teacher
36.	Alhaji Sheikh Gombe	—trader (ex-agricultural officer)
37.	Malam Shehu	—government employee
38.	Yahaya Abdullahi	—government employee
39.	Barrister Adesi	—lawyer
40.	Alhaji Inuwa Kasuwa	—trader
41.	Alin Kohte	—hotel owner
42.	Malam Idi Carpenter	—carpenter
43.	Malam Idi Yari	—trader
44.	Malam Abba Zakar Nguru	—trader
45.	Malam Mohammed Achichi	—transport owner
46.	Bala mai awo Kaduna	—businessman
47.	Alhaji Aminu Tiya	—trader
48.	Danladi Tudun Nufawa	—trader
49.	Baballiya Manager	—trader
50.	Isa Yaro	—trader
51.	Malam Umaru Orante	—trader
52.	Umaru Mai turare	—perfume seller
53.	Alhaji Alin Chindo	—trader
54.	Madam Rakiya mai tuwo	—hotel proprietor
55.	Alhaji Ahmed Trader	—trader
56.	Alhaji Ahmed Kan tudun Mad	—trader

Special Committee Members other than mentioned above

57. Malam Ibrahim Dan Sekondi—member Lagos Town Council —Hausa—Muslim—trader
58. Malam Shehu Kakale
59. Malam Ramalan Garba
60. Madam Ladi Shehu—Secretary of the Women's Wing—Nupe—Christian—teacher

N.E.P.U. members of the Northern House of Assembly

61. Malam Ibrahim Mahmud, MHA (Misau-Bauchi)—Muslim—ex-N.A. Supervisor of Works
(Malam Abdulmumini, MHA, Katsina, South Central, No. 25 above)

62. Malam Haruna Tela, MHA (Kaura Namoda, Sokoto)—Hausa—Sokoto—Muslim—tailor
63. Malam Shehu Marihu, MHA (Zaria Urban)—Hausa—Zaria—Muslim—motor mechanic
(Malam Usman Ango Soba, MHA, No. 9 above)
64. Malam Bala Keffi, MHA (Kaduna)—Muslim—contractor

APPENDIX IV

THE FEDERAL EXECUTIVE COUNCIL
OF THE
ACTION GROUP OF NIGERIA, 1957-1958

(Party office, government office, ethnic identification, home town, district or division, religion, and occupational background)

1. Chief Obafemi Awolowo, MHR—Federal President and Leader of the Party, Leader of the Opposition in the Federal House of Representatives, (Premier of the Western Region), Ijebu Yoruba—Remo—Methodist—barrister

2. Chief Dr. J. A. Doherty—Federal Vice President, Western Region —President Lagos A.G.—Lagos Yoruba—Christian—medical practitioner

3. Dr. A. O. Awduche (ex-MHR)—Federal Vice President, Eastern Region—Ibo—Onitsha—Christian—medical practitioner

4. Alhaji Sulaimanu Maito, MHA—Federal Vice President, Northern Region—Yoruba—Ilorin—Muslim—cattle trader

5. Hon. Ayotunde Rosiji, MHR—Federal Secretary, (formerly Federal Minister of Health)—Egba Yoruba—Abeokuta—Christian —barrister

6. R. A. Fani-Kayode (ex-MHR)—Assistant Federal Secretary, Ife Yoruba—Christian—barrister—resigned from the party in December 1959; subsequently Leader of the NCNC Opposition in the Western House of Assembly

7. Hon. R. T. Alege, MHR—Assistant Federal Secretary, Northern Region—Yoruba—Kabba—Christian—musician

8. Alhaji S. O. Gbadamosi, MHA—Federal Treasurer—Yoruba—Ikeja—Muslim—businessman (merchant and industrialist)

9. Mr. S. O. Shonibare—Federal Publicity Secretary, Western Regional Publicity Secretary—Ijebu Yoruba—Ijebu-Ode—Christian—Managing Director of the Amalgamated Press and businessman

10. Chief F. R. A. Williams, MHC—Legal Adviser, (formerly Attorney General and Minister of Justice, Western Region)—Egba Yoruba—Abeokuta—Christian—barrister

11. Hon. A. M. A. Akinloye, MHR—Legal Adviser, Western Region, Ibadan Yoruba—Christian—barrister (formerly Western Minister of Agriculture)

12. Mr. A. Adeoba—Legal Adviser, Eastern Region—Ekiti Yoruba —Port Harcourt—Christian—barrister

13. Reverend E. O. Alayande—Party Chaplain—member WRPDB—Ibadan Yoruba—Christian—principal grammar school
14. Malam M. S. Yabagi—Party Imam—Bidda—Muslim
15. Chief Dr. Akinola Maja—Father of the Party—Lagos—Yoruba—Christian—medical practitioner, and businessman (Chairman of the Board of the National Bank)

Western Regional Members

16. Chief Akintoye Coker—Western Region Commissioner in the U.K.—Egba Yoruba—Abeokuta—Christian—barrister
17. Chief Anthony Enahoro, MHR—(former Minister of Home and Mid-Western Affairs, Western Region)—Ishan Edo—Christian—journalist and businessman
18. Chief T. A. Odutola, MHA—Ijebu Yoruba—Ijebu-Ode—Christian—businessman (industrialist and insurance business)
19. Chief G. Akin-Deko, MHA—Western Minister of Agriculture and Natural Resources—Idanre Yoruba—Akure—Ondo—Christian—businessman (contractor)
20. Hon. M. A. Ajasin, MHR—Vice President, Western Regional A.G.—Yoruba—Owo—Christian—college principal
21. Prince Adeleke Adedoyin, MHA—Speaker, Western House of Assembly—Ijebu Yoruba—Remo—Christian—barrister
22. Hon. S. A. Tinubu, MHA—Parliamentary Secretary Ministry of Trade and Industry—Yoruba—Oshun—Christian—teacher
23. Hon. S. O. Ighodaro—Attorney General, Western Region (1959)—Benin Edo—Christian—barrister
24. Mr. C. A. Fajemisin—Ijesha Yoruba—Ilesha—Christian—barrister and businessman
25. Mr. O. N. Rewane—Itsekiri—Warri—Christian—barrister
26. Nduka Eze—Chairman Asaba District Council—Western Ibo Asaba—Christian—businessman

Eastern Regional Members

27. Hon. S. G. Ikoku, MHA—Leader of the Opposition, Eastern House of Assembly—Aro—Arochuku—Christian—economist
28. Hon. E. O. Eyo, MHA—Chief Whip, E.H.A.—Ibibio—Uyo—Christian—businessman
29. Hon. A. J. U. Ekong, MHR—(former Parliamentary Secretary Federal Government)—Ibibio—Uyo—Christian—teacher
30. Prince R. N. Takon (ex-MHR)—Ikom—Ogoja—Christian—business agent and trader
31. Hon. Okoi Arikpo, MHA—(ex-Central Minister)—Obubra—Ogoja—Christian—barrister

32. Hon. S. J. Una, MHR—(ex-Eastern Minister)—Ibibio—Uyo—Christian—Lecturer, UCI (Chemistry)

33. Hon. J. A. Agba, MHA—Ogoja—Christian—teacher

34. Hon. Revd. Okon Effiong, MHA—Efik—Calabar—Christian—Secretary to the Obong's Cabinet

35. Chief Okim Okwa Abang—Ikom—Ogoja—farmer (big)

36. Mr. George Lawson—Ijaw—Degema—trader

37. Miss R. T. Brown—Ijaw—Bonny—Degema—Port Harcourt

38. B. E. Mbalu—Port Harcourt—trader

Northern Regional Members

39. Hon. J. S. Olawoyin, MHA—Ilorin; Igbolo—Offa—Christian—Administrative Secretary, Offa Descendants Union

40. Chief D. O. Sanyaolu—Yoruba—Kano—trader

41. D. A. Adesina—Yoruba, Jos—trader

42. M. O. Ikongbe—Idoma—Oturkpo—President of the Oturkpo Native Court

43. A Olu Pinnock—Yoruba—Zaria—U.A.C. employee

44. J. S. Tejuoso—Yoruba—Zaria—trader

45. G. B. Olowu—Yoruba—Katsina—tailor

46. Alfa K. S. Oba—Yoruba-Nupe—Minna—teacher

47. D. L. Ogunmade—Yoruba

48. Omoniyi Olanipekun—Igbolo Yoruba—Offa—trader

49. Peter Onu—Ibo—Zaria—trader

50. Alex Peters—Yoruba—Zaria

Other Action Group Ministers, Western Region

51. Hon. S. L. Akintola, MHA—Deputy Leader of the Party (former Federal Minister of Communications) Premier of the Western Region—Yoruba—Ogbomosho—Oshun—Christian—barrister and journalist, teacher

52. Chief C. D. Akran, MHA—Aholujiwa II—Minister of Economic Planning—Yoruba—Badagry—Christian—civil servant

53. Hon. Alfred O. Ogedengbe, MHA—Minister of Works—Yoruba—Owo—Christian—teacher

54. Chief J. A. O. Odebiyi, MHA—Minister of Finance—Egbado Yoruba—Christian educator—General Secretary, Western Regional Organization

55. Hon. Ayo Okusaga, MHA—Minister of Education—Ijebu Yoruba—Ijebu-Ode—Christian—barrister

56. Chief J. O. Oshuntokun, MHA—Minister of Lands and Labour—Ekiti Yoruba—Christian—educator

57. Hon. J. O. Adigun, MHA—Minister of Health and Social Welfare—Yoruba—Oshun—Christian—journalist

58. Alhaji D. S. Adegbenro, MHA—Minister of Local Government —Egba Yoruba—Abeokuta—Muslim—clerk and businessman (merchant)

59. Hon. A. O. Adeyi, MHA—Minister of Trade and Industry—Oyo Yoruba—Oyo—Christian—educator

Lagos Town Council

60. Mr. A. O. Lawson—Leader of the Party in the L.T.C., formerly Chairman of the L.T.C.—Lagos Yoruba—Christian—barrister

61. Mr. M. A. Ogun—Ijebu-Yoruba—Ijebu-Ode—Christian—public relations and advertising business

62. Hon. L. J. Dosunmu, MHR—Lagos Yoruba—Muslim—barrister

Western Regional Officers, 1958

63. Mr. S. L. Durosaro—Chairman, Western Regional Marketing Board—Ibadan Yoruba—Christian—barrister—Assistant General Secretary

64. Mr. S. Y. Eke—Assistant General Secretary, Constituency Leader—Benin—Edo—Christian—businessman (rubber factory)

65. Chief Mrs. Olu Solaru (late)—Assistant General Secretary—Yoruba—Christian—teacher

66. Mr. S. O. Lanlehin—Treasurer—member WRPDB—Ibadan Yoruba—Christian—businessman

Other important persons who were likely to be members of the Federal Executive, either as Shadow Cabinet members in various Legislatures or by virtue of their prominence and inclusion in some other way:

Legislators

1. Chief V. Duro Phillips, MHR—(former P.S. Federal Minister of Health)—Ijebu Yoruba—Ijebu-Ode—Christian—barrister

2. Chief T. T. Solaru, MHR—Ijebu Yoruba—Ijebu-Ode—Christian —clergyman and representative Oxford University Press

3. Chief S. Jaja Amachree, MHA (East)—Ijaw—Degema—Christian—civil servant

4. A. G. Umoh, MHA (East)—Enyong—schoolmaster

5. Hon. O. O. Ita, MHA (East)—Oron—Calabar—barrister

6. Chief I. I. Morphy, MHA (East)—Ogoja—Catholic—teacher

7. Hon. J. G. Ekunrin, MHA (North)—Igbomina—Yoruba—Ilorin—Christian—AG organizing secretary

8. Malam Ibrahim Imam, MHA (North)—Kanuri—Bornu—Patron Bornu Youth Movement—Muslim—businessman

9. Malam Basharu, MHA (North)—Kanuri—Bornu—Muslim—trader and motor transport owner

10. Hon. J. S. Tarka, MHR (North)—Leader of the UMBC—Tiv—Christian—educator and trade unionist

11. Mr. Patrick Dokotri (ex-MHR, North)—General Secretary, UMBC—Birom—Catholic—N.A. employee

Parliamentary Secretaries, Western Region, 1958

12. S. O. Sogbein—Yoruba—Egba—Christian—teacher

13. Chief G. Ekwejunor-Etchie—Itsekeri—Christian—businessman (timber merchant)

14. A. O. Akingboye—Yoruba—Okitipupa—Christian—teacher

15. E. O. J. Bamiro—Ijebu—Yoruba—Ijebu-Ode—Christian—educator

16. Z. A. Opaleye—Egbado Yoruba—Muslim—educator

17. J. A. O. Ogunmuyiwa—Yoruba—Oshun—educator

18. E. A. Idowu—Badagry—Yoruba—trade unionist (?)

19. O. Oye—Edo—Afenmai—Christian—teacher

20. D. A. Ademiluyi—Ife Yoruba—Christian—printer

21. J. L. Tifase—Ondo Yoruba—Akure—Christian—businessman (general contractor)

22. J. E. Babatola—Ekiti Yoruba—Christian—teacher

23. S. A. Tinubu—Oshun Yoruba—educator

24. O. A. Adedeji—Chief Whip, W.H.A.—Ibarapa Yoruba—Ibadan—Christian—farmer

Members Co-opted into the Calabar and Lagos Congresses

25. B. O. Olusola—member WRPDB—Ekiti Yoruba—barrister

26. Mr. O. B. Akin Olugbade—Chairman W. R. Finance Corporation—Yoruba—Egba—barrister

27. Chief J. F. Odunjo—member WRPDB, (former Western Minister)—Egbado Yoruba—Christian—educator

28. Chief F. O. Awosika—Chairman W. R. Housing Corporation, (ex-Central and Regional Minister)—Ondo Yoruba—educator

29. Mr. A. O. Rewane—Chairman, WRPDB—Itsekeri—Warri—businessman (timber, etc.)—Political Secretary to ex-Premier

30. Chief E. O. Okunowo—Ijebu Yoruba—Ijebu-Ode—businessman (import-export)

31. Dr. Oni Akerele—Oyo Yoruba—Lagos—Medical practitioner

32. Chief J. E. Odiete—Urhobo—Warri—barrister
33. Chief J. A. Ajao—Oyo Yoruba—Lagos—businessman (import-export)
34. Mr. I. O. Ajanaku—Ijesha Yoruba—Ilesha—businessman (transport, etc., produce)
35. Mr. Lawrence Omole—Ijesha Yoruba—Ilesha—businessman (transport, etc., produce)
36. Dr. A. S. Agbaje—Ibadan Yoruba—medical practitioner, U.C.I. Hospital
37. M. A. K. Shonowo—Yoruba—Lagos—businessman (transport)
38. Prince A. Adedemola—Leader AG in Abeokuta UDC—Egba—Yoruba—Muslim—businessman
39. Rev. S. A. Adeyefa—Ife Yoruba—Christian—educator
40. W. J. Falaiye—Ondo Yoruba—Akure—business manager—former Chairman Akure Divisional Council
41. O. Oduyoye—Yoruba
42. Dr. V. A. Oyenuga—Yoruba—Lecturer U.C.I. (agriculture)
43. Chief D. O. A. Oguntoye—Yoruba—Christian—barrister
44. Mr. A. F. Alli
45. Madam C. A. Onabolu
46. Mr. Olatunji Anthonio
47. Mr. Olusoji Sobande—Egbe Yoruba
48. Rev. S. A. Banjo—Yoruba—Christian—educator and minister

Other Outstanding Divisional and Constituency Leaders

49. Mr. F. O. Akenzua—Benin—Edo—Christian—barrister
50. Chief R. D. Edukugho, MHA—Itsekeri—Warri—Christian—businessman
51. Chief M. A. Okupe—Ijebu Yoruba—Remo—banker (Agbonmagbe Bank)
52. Oba Adetunji Aiyeola, MHR—Ijebu Yoruba—Remo

BIBLIOGRAPHY

First Part: Selected Titles Cited in This Study

I

GENERAL

Almond, Gabriel A., and Coleman, James S. (eds.) *The Politics of the Developing Areas.* Princeton: Princeton University Press, 1960.

Baran, Paul A. *The Political Economy of Growth.* New York: Monthly Review Press, 1957.

Bell, Philip. *The Sterling Area in the Post-War World.* Oxford: Clarendon Press, 1956.

Berlin, Isaiah. *Two Concepts of Liberty.* Oxford: Clarendon Press, 1958.

Duverger, Maurice. *Political Parties.* Translated by Barbara and Robert North. London: Methuen, 1954.

Emerson, Rupert. *From Empire to Nation.* Cambridge: Harvard University Press, 1960.

Firth, Raymond. "Social Organization and Social Change," *The Journal of the Royal Anthropological Institute of Great Britain and Ireland,* Vol. 84 (1954), pp. 1-20.

Heberle, Rudolf. "Ferdinand Tonnies' Contribution to the Study of Political Parties," *American Journal of Sociology,* LXI, No. 3 (November 1955), pp. 213-220.

International Institute of Differing Civilizations. *Development of a Middle Class in Tropical and Sub-Tropical Countries: General Report.* Brussels: 1955.

Jennings, Sir W. Ivor. *The Approach to Self Government.* Cambridge: The University Press, 1956.

Laski, Harold J. *Reflections on the Constitution.* New York: The Viking Press, 1951.

Linton, Ralph. *The Study of Man.* New York: D. Appleton-Century Co., 1936.

Lipset, Seymour Martin. *Political Man.* New York: Doubleday, 1960.

McKenzie, R. T. *British Political Parties.* New York: St. Martin's Press, 1955.

Mackenzie, W. J. M. *Free Elections: An Elementary Textbook.* New York: Rinehart, 1958.

Michels, Robert. *Political Parties.* An unabridged and unaltered republication of the English translation first published in 1915. New York: Dover Publications, 1959.

Nadel, S. F. *The Theory of Social Structure.* London: Cohen and West, Ltd., 1957.

Neumann, Sigmund (ed.). *Modern Political Parties.* Chicago: University of Chicago Press, 1956.

Radcliffe-Brown, A. R. *Structure and Function in Primitive Society*. London: Cohen and West, Ltd., 1952.

Redfield, Robert. "The Folk Society," in Logan Wilson and William L. Kolb (eds.), *Sociological Analysis*. New York: Harcourt, Brace and Co., 1949.

Tönnies, Ferdinand. *Community and Society (Gemeinschaft und Gesellschaft)*. Translated and edited by Charles P. Loomis. East Lansing: The Michigan State University Press, 1957.

United States Senate, Committee on Foreign Relations. *Economic, Social, and Political Change in the Underdeveloped Countries and Its Implications for United States Policy*. A Study prepared at the request of the Committee on Foreign Relations, United States Senate, by the Center for International Studies, Massachusetts Institute of Technology. Washington: Government Printing Office, 1960.

Verba, Sidney. *Small Groups and Political Behavior*. Princeton: Princeton University Press, 1961

Weber, Max. "Class, Status, Party," in H. H. Gerth and C. Wright Mills (eds.), From *Max Weber: Essays in Sociology*. New York: Oxford University Press, 1946.

Wight, Martin. *British Colonial Constitutions*. Oxford: Clarendon Press, 1952.

II

AFRICAN POLITICS AND SOCIETY

All-African Peoples' Conference. "Conference Resolution on Imperialism and Colonialism." Accra: December 1958. (Mimeographed.)

All-African Peoples' Conference. "Resolution Submitted for Adoption by Committee No. 2 on Racialism and Discriminatory Laws and Practices." Accra: December 1958. (Mimeographed.)

All-African Peoples' Conference. "Draft Resolution on the Implementation of Human Rights submitted to Committee No. 2 by Mr. Rewane of Nigeria, Mr. Morgan of Liberia and Mr. Apaloo of Ghana." Accra: December 1958. (Mimeographed.)

Anderson, J. N. D. *Islamic Law in Africa*. (Colonial Research Publication No. 16.) London: H.M.S.O., 1954.

Apter, David E. *The Gold Coast in Transition*. Princeton: Princeton University Press, 1955.

Austin, Dennis. *West Africa and the Commonwealth*. London: Penguin Books, 1957.

Bauer, P. T. *West African Trade: A Study of Competition, Oligopoly and Monopoly in a Changing Economy*. Cambridge: Cambridge University Press, 1954.

Buell, Raymond Leslie. *The Native Problem in Africa* (2 vols.). New York: Macmillan, 1928.

Carney, David E. *Government and Economy in British West Africa.* New York: Bookman Associates, 1961.

Coleman, James S. "The Emergence of African Political Parties," in C. Grove Haines (ed.), *Africa Today.* Baltimore: Johns Hopkins Press, 1955.

Cowan, L. Gray. *Local Government in West Africa.* New York: Columbia University Press, 1958.

Davidson, Basil, and Ademola, Adenekan (eds.). *The New West Africa.* London: Allen and Unwin, 1953.

Davis, John A. (ed.) *Africa Seen by American Negroes.* Paris: Présence Africaine, 1958.

Elias, T. O. *Government and Politics in Africa.* London: Asia Publishing House, 1961.

Fage, J. D. *An Introduction to the History of West Africa,* 2nd ed. Cambridge: Cambridge University Press, 1961.

Fortes, M. and Evans-Pritchard, E. E. (eds.) *African Political Systems.* London: Oxford University Press, 1940.

Hailey, Lord. *Native Administration in the British African Territories: Part III. West Africa: Nigeria, Gold Coast, Sierra Leone, Gambia.* London: H.M.S.O., 1951.

Hodgkin, Thomas. *African Political Parties.* Harmondsworth: Penguin Books, 1961.

Hodgkin, Thomas. *Nationalism in Colonial Africa.* London: Frederick Muller, 1956.

Hodgkin, Thomas. "Political Parties in British and French West Africa," *Information Digest, Africa Bureau* (London), No. 10 (August 1953), pp. 13-16.

Kilson, Martin L. "Nationalism and Social Classes in British West Africa," *The Journal of Politics* (May 1958), pp. 368-387.

Mackenzie, W. J. M., and Robinson, Kenneth. *Five Elections in Africa: A Group of Electoral Studies.* Oxford: Clarendon Press, 1960.

National Congress of British West Africa. *The Humble Petition of the National Congress of British West Africa to King George V by its Delegates now in London, 19 October, 1920; Resolutions of the Conference of Africans of British West Africa, Accra, 11-29 March, 1920; Report of Proceedings of a meeting in London between the League of Nations and Delegates of the National Congress of British West Africa, 8 October, 1920.* Colonial Office Library (London), West African Pamphlets, Vol. III, No. 107.

Newbury, C. W. *The Western Slave Coast and Its Rulers.* Oxford: The Clarendon Press, 1961.

Newlyn, W. T., and Rowan, D. C. *Money and Banking in British Colonial Africa.* Oxford: Clarendon Press, 1954.

Nuffield Foundation and the Colonial Office. *African Education: A Study of Educational Policy and Practice in British Tropical Africa.* Oxford: University Press, 1953.

Nyerere, Julius K. "Africa Needs Time," *The New York Times Magazine*, March 27, 1960, pp. 19, 84-85.

Padmore, George. *Pan-Africanism or Communism? The Coming Struggle for Africa*. London: Denis Dobson, 1956.

Roper, J. I. *Labour Problems in West Africa*. London: Penguin Books, 1958.

Rothchild, Donald. *Toward Unity in Africa: A Study of Federalism in British Africa*. Washington, D.C.: Public Affairs Press, 1960.

Schachter, Ruth. "Single Party Systems in West Africa," *The American Political Science Review*, Vol. LV, 3 (June 1961), pp. 294-307.

Trimingham, J. Spencer. *Islam in West Africa*. Oxford: Clarendon Press, 1959.

United Kingdom, Colonial Office. African Studies Branch. "A Survey of the Development of Local Government in the African Territories Since 1947," *Journal of African Administration*, IV, 4 (October 1952), pp. 52-67.

United Kingdom, Colonial Office. *Report of the Nyasaland Commission of Inquiry*. Cmnd. 814. London: H.M.S.O., 1959.

Wallerstein, I. "Ethnicity and National Integration in West Africa," *Cahiers d'Etudes Africaines*, No. 3 (October 1960), pp. 129-139.

Wraith, Ronald E. *Local Government*, rev. ed. London: Penguin Books, 1956.

Younger, Kenneth. *The Public Service in New States*. London: Oxford University Press, 1960.

Second Part: Selected Titles Concerning Nigeria Cited in this Study or Consulted in its Preparation

I

HISTORICAL, SOCIAL, ECONOMIC, AND POLITICAL CONDITIONS IN NIGERIA

A

Selected Official Publications

PUBLICATIONS OF THE GOVERNMENT OF NIGERIA TO 1954

Butcher, H. L. M. *Commission of Inquiry into the Allegations of Misconduct made against Chief Salami Agbaje, the Otun Balogun of Ibadan, and Allegations of Inefficiency and Maladministration on the Part of the Ibadan and District Native Authority*. Lagos: 1951.

Fisher, J. L. *Report on the desirability and practicability of establishing a Central Bank in Nigeria for promoting the economic development of the Country*. Lagos: 1953.

Robinson, G. G. *Commission of Inquiry into the Okrika-Kalabari Dispute.* Enugu: 1950.

Story, Bernard. *Commission of Inquiry into the Administration of the Lagos Town Council.* Lagos: 1953.

Proceedings of the General Conference on Review of the Constitution, January, 1950. Lagos: 1950.

Legislative Council of Nigeria Debates, 1924-1951.

House of Representatives Debates, 1952-1954.

PUBLICATIONS OF THE GOVERNMENT OF THE FEDERATION OF NIGERIA

Annual Report of the Federal Land Department, 1956-57. Lagos: 1958.

Department of Commerce and Industries. *Handbook of Commerce and Industry in Nigeria.* Lagos: 1957.

Department of Labour. "Memberships of the All-Nigeria Trade Unions Federation and the National Council of Trades Unions of Nigeria." (Mimeographed.)

Federal Information Service. *Who's Who of the Federal House of Representatives.* Lagos: 1958.

Federal Works Registration Board. "Register of Federal Contractors as of 1 July, 1958." (Mimeographed.)

First Annual Report of the Federal Loans Board, 1 July 1956 to 30 June 1957. Lagos: 1957.

Lagos Local Government Ordinance, 1959 (Supplement to Official Gazette No. 71, Vol. 46, 19th November, 1959—Part D).

Loynes, J. B. *Report on the Establishment of a Nigerian Central Bank, the Introduction of a Nigerian Currency and other Associated Matters.* Lagos: 1957.

National Economic Council. *Economic Survey of Nigeria, 1959.* Lagos: 1959.

Report by the Ad-Hoc Meeting of the Nigeria Constitutional Conference held in Lagos in February 1958. Lagos: 1958.

Report of the Resumed Nigeria Constitutional Conference held in London in September and October, 1958. Lagos: 1958.

Report of the Constituency Delimitation Commission, 1958. Lagos: 1958.

Tribunal to Inquire into Allegations of Improper Conduct by the Premier of the Eastern Region of Nigeria in connection with the affairs of the African Continental Bank Limited and Other Relevant Matters. Proceedings; with the Minutes of evidence taken before the Tribunal, August-November, 1956 (2 vols.). Lagos: 1957.

Report of Coker Commission of Inquiry into the affairs of certain Statutory Corporations in Western Nigeria (4 vols.). Lagos: 1962.

Comments of the Federal Government on the Report of Coker Commission of Inquiry into the affairs of certain Statutory Corporations in Western Nigeria. Sessional Paper No. 4 of 1962.

The Economic Program of the Government of the Federation of Nigeria, 1955-60. Sessional Paper No. 2 of 1956.

The Role of the Federal Government in Promoting Industrial Development in Nigeria. Sessional Paper No. 3 of 1958.

Report of the Commission to Make Recommendations about the Recruitment and Training of Nigerians for Senior Posts in the Government Service. Lagos: 1948.

Phillipson, Sir Sidney, and Adebo, S. O. *Nigerianization of the Civil Service.* Sessional Paper No. 4 of 1954.

Gorsuch, L. H. *Report of the Public Services of the Governments in the Federation of Nigeria, 1954-55.* Lagos: 1955.

Statement of policy on the Nigerianization of the federal public service and the higher training of Nigerians, 1956-60. Sessional Paper No. 4 of 1956.

Views of the Government of the Federation on the Interim report of the Committee on Nigerianization. Lagos: 1958.

First Report on the Federal Public Service Commission. Lagos: 1958.

Parliamentary Debates, 1954-

PUBLICATIONS OF THE REGIONAL GOVERNMENTS

The Eastern Region of Nigeria

Banking Monopoly in Nigeria. Statement made by the Hon. Premier in the Eastern House of Assembly on 8 August, 1956.

Commission of Inquiry into African Continental Bank. Statement made by the Hon. Premier in the House of Assembly on 8th August, 1956, during a Debate on a Motion to appoint a Judge of the High Court of the United Kingdom and Independent Persons to serve in a Commission of Inquiry to investigate the relations of the Hon. Premier with the African Continental Bank. 1956.

Coatsworth, R. *Report of an Inquiry into a proposal to excise the Aba Urban District Council from the Aba-Ngwa County.* Enugu: 1955.

Cobb, F. P. *Commission of Inquiry into the Administration of the Affairs of the Igbo-Etiti District Council.* n. d.

Floyer, R. K., Ibekwe, D. O., and Njemanze, J. O. *Commission of Inquiry into the Working of the Port Harcourt Town Council.* Enugu: 1955.

Grant, P. F. *Report of the inquiry into the Allocation of Market Stalls at Aba.* Enugu: 1955.

Gunning, O. P. *Report of the inquiry into the administration of the affairs of the Onitsha Urban District Council.* 1955

House of Chiefs in the Eastern Region. E.R. Official Document No. 1 of 1959.

Jones, G. I. *Report of the Position Status, and Influence of Chiefs and Natural Rulers in the Eastern Region of Nigeria.* Enugu: 1957.

Papers Relating to the instrument establishing the Onitsha Urban District Council. Sessional Paper No. 1 of 1956.

Report on banking and finance in Eastern Nigeria. Sessional Paper No. 4 of 1956.

Report on the proceedings and recommendations of the Eastern Region summit conference held in Enugu, July 9, 10, 11, 1956. Sessional Paper No. 5 of 1956.

Swaisland, H. C. *Report of an inquiry into the affairs of the Eastern Ngwa District Council.* 1955.

University of Nigeria. Official Document No. 2 of 1958.

Economic Rehabilitation of Eastern Nigeria. Report of the Economic Mission to Europe and North America. Sessional Paper No. 6 of 1955. Enugu: 1955.

Development Programme, 1958-62. Official Document No. 2 of 1959.

Revised Development Programme. Official Document No. 13 of 1960.

Annual Reports of the Eastern Region Development Corporation, 1955-1956, 1956-1957.

Ministry of Finance. "Schedule of Contracts other than Ration Contracts Awarded from October 1954 through 1957." (Typewritten.)

Second Annual Report of the Eastern Regional Marketing Board, 1 January 1956-31 December 1956.

Self Government in the Eastern Region, Part I: Policy Statements, Sessional Paper No. 2 of 1957.

————, Part II: Data and Statistics. Official Document No. 1 of 1958.

House of Assembly Debates, 1947-

The Northern Region of Nigeria

Hudson, R. S. *Commission Appointed to Advise the Government on Devolution of Powers to Provinces. Provincial Authorities. Report by the Commissioner.* Kaduna: 1957.

Ilorin Native Authority Central Office. "Constitution of Ilorin Native Authority Council." (Typewritten.)

Kano Native Authority Rules and Orders. 1949.

Law Reports of the Northern Region of the Federation of Nigeria. 1956. 1957.

Native Authority Law of 1954. Kaduna: 1954.

Northern Regional Legislature Who's Who, 1957. Kaduna: 1957.

Pott, D. A. *Progress Report on Local Government in the Northern Region of Nigeria.* Kaduna: 1953.

Proposal for Self-Government of the Northern Region of Nigeria. Kaduna: 1958.

Provincial Annual Reports, 1954-1957.

Report on the Kano Disturbances, 16th, 17th, 18th and 19th May 1953. Kaduna: 1953.

Policy for Development, 1955-1956.

Statement of Policy on the Development Finance Program, 1955-60.

Social and Economic Progress in the Northern Region of Nigeria. Zaria: 1957.

Annual Reports of the Northern Region Development Corporation, 1956—

Progress Report on the Development Finance Programme of the Northern Region, 1955-60.

Ministry of Finance. "Northern Region Works Registration Board. Register of Northern Region Contractors, No. F. 2130B." (Mimeographed.)

Regional Council. *House of Assembly Debates,* 1947-51.

——. *House of Chiefs Debates,* 1947-51.

Legislature. *House of Assembly Debates,* 1952-

——. *House of Chiefs Debates,* 1952-

The Western Region of Nigeria

Annual Reports on the Working of the Public Service Commission, Western Region. 1956-1960.

Statement by the Hon. the Premier Chief Obafemi Awolowo on the Regional civil service. 1958.

Annual Report of the Ministry of Justice and Local Government, Western Nigeria. 1957-1958.

Iles, C. E. *Report of an Inquiry into the Affairs of the Asaba U.D.C.* 1956.

Law Reports of Cases Decided in the Federal Supreme Court and the High Court of the Western Region. 1957.

Lloyd, R. D. "Report of a Commission of Inquiry into Disturbances at Oyo." *Daily Times,* June 8, 1955.

Local Government in the Western Provinces of Nigeria, 1939-49: a factual record of political developments during the last ten years. Lagos: 1950

Local Government Manual. Ibadan: 1957.

Nicholson, E. W. J. *Commission of Inquiry into the Administration of the Ibadan District Council, Report.* Abingdon: 1956.

Report on the Activities of the Midwest Advisory Council together with Statements of Government Action in the Midwest. Sessional Paper No. 3 of 1960.

Speeches at the Western Region Chiefs Conference, May 1958, by the Premier, the Minister of Justice, F. R. A. Williams, the Minister of Economic Planning, Hon. C. D. Akran, the Minister of Home Affairs, Hon. A. Enahoro, Chief S. U. Enosegbe II, MHC, the Onogie of Ewohimi. (Mimeographed.)

Self Government for the Western Region. Sessional Paper No. 3 of 1955.

Tax Collection in the Western Region, 1953-54. 1954.

Development of the Western Region of Nigeria, 1955-60. Sessional Paper No. 4 of 1955. 1956.

Progress Report on the Development of the Western Region of Nigeria, 1955-60. Sessional Paper No. 4 of 1959.

Western Region Development Plan, 1960-65. Sessional Paper No. 17 of 1959.

Western Region Production Development Board, Annual Reports. 1954-1957.

Western Region Finance Corporation, Annual Reports and Accounts. 1957-1959.

Western Region Marketing Board, Annual Reports.

Works Registration Board. "Register of Contractors, December 1957." (Mimeographed.)

House of Assembly Debates, 1947-

House of Chiefs Debates, 1952-

PUBLICATIONS OF THE COLONIAL OFFICE, UNITED KINGDOM

Commission Appointed to Enquire into the Fears of Minorities and the Means of Allaying them. Report. Cmnd. 505. London: 1958.

Commission of Enquiry into the Disorders in the Eastern Provinces of Nigeria. Report. Col. No. 256. London: 1950.

Constitutional Progress in the Federation of Nigeria. No. R 3172, November 1955.

Enquiry into the Cost of Living and the Control of the Cost of Living in the Colony and Protectorate of Nigeria. Col. No. 204. London: 1946.

Facts About the Federation of Nigeria. No. R 3222, February 1957.

Nigeria, 1953. London: 1955.

Nigeria, 1955. London: 1958.

Report by the Conference on the Nigerian Constitution held in London in July and August, 1953. Cmnd. 8934. London: 1953.

Report by the Resumed Conference on the Nigerian Constitution held in Lagos in January and February, 1954. Cmnd. 9050. London: 1954.

Report by the Nigerian Constitutional Conference held in London in May and June 1957. Cmnd. 207. London: 1957.

Report of the Fiscal Commissioner on the financial effects of the proposed new constitutional arrangements. Cmnd. 9026. London: 1953.

Report of the Fiscal Commission for Nigeria. Cmnd. 481. London: 1958.

Report of the Tribunal appointed to inquire into allegations reflecting on the Official Conduct of the Premier of, and certain persons holding Ministerial and other Public Offices in, the Eastern Region of Nigeria. Cmnd. 51. London: 1957.

B

Studies, Commentaries, and Non-Official Documents

Adelabu, Adegoke. *Africa in Ebullition.* Ibadan: n.d.

Agwuna, Osita C. *Inner Party Criticism* (for members and branches of the NCNC). Nos. 1 and 2. Lagos: 1954.

———. *Go With the Masses: Studies in Essential Tactics in National and Colonial Struggles.* Enugu: n.d.

Agwuna, Osita; Okoye, Mokwugo; Otobo, J. E.; and Yamu Numa, F. M. "An Appeal to the NCNC Convention Delegates." Ibadan: 1955. (Mimeographed.)

Ahmadu, Bello, The Sardauna of Sokoto. *My Life.* Cambridge: Cambridge University Press, 1962.

Ajisafe, Ajayi K. *The Laws and Customs of the Yoruba People.* Lagos: 1946.

Akintoye, O. A. *Self Government for Nigeria.* Lagos: n.d.

Akinyede, G. B. A. *The Political and Constitutional Problems of Nigeria.* Lagos: 1957.

Akinyele, Chief I. B. *The Outlines of Ibadan History.* Lagos: 1946.

Akpan, Ntieyong U. "Chieftaincy in Eastern Nigeria," *Journal of African Administration,* IX (July 1957), pp. 120-123.

———. *Epitaph to Indirect Rule.* London: Cassell and Co., 1956.

Aluko, S. A. *The Problems of Self-Government for Nigeria, a Critical Analysis.* Devon: Stockwell, 1955.

Anyiam, Fred. U. *Men and Matters in Nigerian Politics (1934-58).* Lagos: 1959.

Arikpo, Okoi. "On Being a Minister," *West Africa,* July 31-August 21, 1954.

———. *Who are the Nigerians?* Lagos: n.d.

Awa, E. O. "Local Government Problems in a Developing Community (Nigeria)." Paper delivered at an International Conference on Representative Government and National Progress, Ibadan, March, 1959. (Mimeographed.)

Awolowo, Obafemi. *Path to Nigerian Freedom.* London: Faber, 1947.

———. *The Price of Progress.* An Address to the Western House of Assembly. Ibadan: 1953.

———. *Some Aspects of our Economic Problem.* An Address delivered to the Lagos Chamber of Commerce. Ibadan: 1955.

———. Statement of June 2, 1956 following the general election in the Western Region. (Mimeographed.)

———. *"I Am On My Way. . . ."* Speeches on Nigerian Unity. Ibadan: 1957.

———. *Forward to a New Nigeria.* Speeches at the Nigerian Constitutional Conference and other occasions. London: 1957.

———. Statement by the Honourable the Premier Chief Obafemi Awolowo on the Regional Civil Service. Ibadan: 1958.

———. *Awo: The Autobiography of Chief Obafemi Awolowo.* Cambridge: Cambridge University Press, 1960.

———. Presidential Address at the Fourth Annual Regional Conference of the Action Group, Ibadan, 26 October 1955. (Mimeographed.)

———. Presidential Address at the Emergency Conference of the West-

ern Region Action Group, Ibadan, 12 October, 1957. (Mimeographed.)
———. Presidential Address at the Fourth Congress of the Action Group, Calabar, 28 April 1958. (Mimeographed.)
———. Presidential Address at the Conference of the Action Group held in Jos, 9 September 1958. (Mimeographed.)
———. Presidential Address at the Emergency Congress of the Action Group held at Kano on 12 December 1958. (Mimeographed.)
———. Presidential Address at the Sixth Congress of the Action Group. Lagos, 11 September 1959. (Mimeographed.)
Azikiwe, Ben N. "Nigerian Political Institutions," *Journal of Negro History*, XIV (July 1929), pp. 328-340.
Azikiwe, Nnamdi. *Liberia in World Politics*. London: 1934.
———. *Renascent Africa*. Accra: 1937.
———. "My Odyssey," *West African Pilot* (installments from July 26, 1938 to June 1939.)
———. *Land Tenure in Northern Nigeria*. Lagos: 1942.
———. *Economic Reconstruction of Nigeria*. Lagos: 1942.
———. *Taxation in Nigeria*. Lagos: 1943.
———. *Political Blueprint of Nigeria*. Lagos: 1943.
———. *Suppression of the Press in British West Africa*. Onitsha: 1946.
———. *Assassination Story: True or False*. Onitsha: 1946.
———. *"Before Us Lies the Open Grave."* London: 1947.
———. *Constitutional Dispute in Eastern Nigeria*. Statement in the Eastern House of Assembly. Enugu: 1955.
———. "The Evolution of Federal Government in Nigeria." An address at a public meeting arranged by the Nigerian Union of Students, London, October 14, 1955.
———. *After Three Years of Stewardship*. An address. Enugu: 1957.
———. *The Development of Political Parties in Nigeria*. London: 1957.
———. "Opportunity Knocks at Our Door." Presidential Address at the Annual Convention of the NCNC, Aba, October 28, 1957. (Mimeographed.)
———. "Enforcement of Party Discipline." Presidential Address at a Special Convention of the NCNC, Enugu, 30 January, 1958. (Mimeographed.)
———. "Sixteen Months to Freedom." Presidential Address at the Annual Convention of the NCNC, Kano, 1959. (Mimeographed.)
———. *Respect for Human Dignity*: Inaugural Address Delivered by His Excellency, Dr. Nnamdi Azikiwe, Governor-General and Commander-in-Chief, Federation of Nigeria. Enugu: 1960.
———. *Zik: A Selection from the Speeches of Nnamdi Azikiwe*, edited by Philip Harris. Cambridge: University Press, 1961.
Azinge, Bialichi; Adeoba, Adetunji; and Akintola, Omodele. "Nigeria's Dilemma and Way Out." (Mimeographed.)
Baker, T. M. "Political Control Amongst the Birom," *Fifth Annual Conference Proceedings of the West African Institute of Social and Economic Research*. Ibadan: 1956, pp. 111-119.

Balogun, Kolawole. *My Country Nigeria*. Lagos: 1955.

Bascom, William R. "The Sociological Role of the Yoruba Cult Group," *American Anthropologist*, New Series, XLVI, i., Part 2, Memoir 63, 1944.

————. "Social Status, Wealth and Individual Differences Among the Yoruba," *American Anthropologist*, 53, No. 4, Pt. 1 (October-December 1951), pp. 490-505.

————. "Urbanization Among the Yoruba," *American Journal of Sociology*, LX, 5 (March 1955), pp. 446-454.

Biobaku, Saburi O. *The Egba and Their Neighbors, 1842-1872*. Oxford: The Clarendon Press, 1957.

————. *The Origin of the Yorubas*. Lagos: Federal Ministry of Information, 1955.

Bohannan, Laura and Paul. *The Tiv of Central Nigeria*. London: International Africa Institute, 1953.

Bohannan, Paul. *Tiv Farm and Settlement*. Colonial Research Study No. 15. London: 1954.

————. "Extra-Processual Events in Tiv Political Institutions, *American Anthropologist*, Vol. 60, No. 1 (February 1958).

Bradbury, R. E. *The Benin Kingdom and the Edo-Speaking Peoples of Southwestern Nigeria together with a section on the Itsekeri by P. C. Lloyd*. London: International Africa Institute, 1957.

Bretton, Henry L. *Power and Stability in Nigeria*. New York: Praeger, 1962.

Brown, R. E. "Local Government in the Western Region of Nigeria, 1950-1955," *Journal of African Administration*, VII (October 1955), pp. 180-187.

Buchanan, K. M., and Pugh, J. C. *Land and People in Nigeria*. London: University of London Press, 1955.

Buchanan, Keith. "The Northern Region of Nigeria: The Geographical Background of its Political Duality," *The Geographical Review*, XLIII, 4 (October 1953), pp. 451-473.

Burns, Alan. *History of Nigeria*, 5th ed. London: Allen and Unwin, 1955.

Calabar-Ogoja-Rivers State Movement, Central Executive Committee. *Memorandum submitted to the Minorities Commission*. Calabar: n.d.

Calabar Union of Great Britain and Ireland. *Memorandum for the Establishment of COR (Calabar, Ogoja, and Rivers) State*, edited by Eyo B. E. Ndem. London: 1957.

Citizens' Committee for Independence. *Forward to Freedom: Constitutional Proposals for a United Nigeria*. Publication No. 1. Ibadan: 1957.

————. *The Case for More States*. Memorandum Submitted to the Minorities Commission. Publication No. 2. Ibadan: 1957.

Coker, Increase. "Report on the Nigerian Press, 1929-1959." (Mimeographed.)

————. *Seventy Years of the Nigerian Press*. Lagos: 1952.

Coker, S. A. *The Rights of Africans to Organize and Establish Indigenous*

Churches Unattached to and Uncontrolled by Foreign Church Organizations. Lagos: 1917.

Cole, Taylor. "Bureaucracy in Transition: Independent Nigeria," *Public Administration* (Winter 1960), pp. 321-337.

———. "The Independence Constitution of Federal Nigeria," *South Atlantic Quarterly*, Vol. LX, No. 1, pp. 1-18.

Cole, Taylor and Robert O. Tilman (eds.). *The Nigerian Political Scene.* Durham: Duke University Press, 1962.

Coleman, James S. *Nigeria: Background to Nationalism.* Berkeley and Los Angeles: University of California Press, 1958.

Comhaire-Sylvain, Suzanne. "Le Travail des Femmes a Lagos, Nigérie," *Zaire*, 5 (May 1951), pp. 475-502.

Cook, A. N. *British Enterprise in Nigeria.* Philadelphia: University of Pennsylvania Press, 1943.

Crowder, Michael. *A Short History of Nigeria.* New York: Praeger, 1962.

Davidson, A. McL. "The Origins and Early History of Lagos," *Nigerian Field*, 19 (April 1954), pp. 52-69.

Davies, Chief H. O. *Nigeria: Prospects for Democracy.* London: Weidenfield and Nicolson, 1961.

Dike, K. Onwuka, *Trade and Politics in the Niger Delta, 1830-1885.* Oxford: The Clarendon Press, 1956.

Eastern Region Development Corporation Workers' Union, *First Annual Conference, Secretary's Annual Report.* Aba: n.d.

Egbe Omo Oduduwa. Constitution. (Mimeographed.)

———. *Proposals for 1950 Constitutional Reforms.* Lagos: n.d.

———. *Monthly Bulletin*, 1948-1949.

———. *A Yoruba Symposium prepared in honour of the Sixth General Assembly of the Egbe Omo Oduduwa.* Ibadan: 1953.

———. Headquarters Secretariat Records, including minutes of the Annual General Assemblies.

———. Minutes of a Special Emergency Joint Committee Meeting of Western Obas and the Egbe Omo Oduduwa held at the Western Secretariat, Ibadan, 6 September 1954.

Egesi, O. N. Nigerian Ex-Servicemen's Union, Eastern Region. A Memorandum on Conditions of Ex-Servicemen in the Eastern Region. (Mimeographed.)

Egharevba, Chief Jacob U. *A Brief History of Hon. G. I. Obaseki, C. B. E., the Iyase of Benin.* Benin: 1956.

Elias, T. Olawale. *Nigerian Land Law and Custom,* 2d. ed. London: Routledge and Kegan Paul, 1953.

———. *Groundwork of Nigerian Law.* London: Routledge and Kegan Paul, 1954.

———. *The Nature of African Customary Law.* Manchester: Manchester University Press, 1956.

———. *Makers of Nigerian Law.* Reprinted from *West Africa*, November 19, 1955-July 7, 1956. London: 1956.

Enahoro, Anthony. Speech to the All-African Peoples' Conference, Accra, December 1958.

Enahoro, Peter. "Wizard of Kirsten Hall," *Sunday Times*, November 9, 1958, pp. 12-13.

Epelle, Sam. *The Promise of Nigeria*. London: Pan Books Limited, 1960.

Eze, Nduka. "Memoirs of a Crusader." (Typewritten.)

Ezera, Kalu. *Constitutional Developments in Nigeria*. Cambridge: Cambridge University Press, 1960.

Fisher, Humphrey J. "The Ahmadiyya Movement in Nigeria," *African Affairs*, edited by Kenneth Kirkwood. Carbondale: Southern Illinois University Press, 1961.

Forde, Daryll. *Efik Traders of Old Calabar*. London: Oxford University Press, 1956.

————. *The Yoruba-Speaking Peoples of South-Western Nigeria*. London: International Africa Institute, 1951.

————, (ed.). *Peoples of the Niger-Benue Confluence*. London: International African Institute, 1950.

————, and Jones, G. I. *The Ibo and Ibibio-Speaking Peoples of South-Eastern Nigeria*. London: International African Institute, 1950.

Fowler, W. "Some Observations on the Western Region Local Government Law, 1952," *Journal of African Administration*, Vol. V (1953), pp. 119-123.

Frodin, Reuben. *A Note on Nigeria*. A publication of the American Universities Field Staff. West African Series, Vol. IV, No. 6, 1961.

Green, M. M. *Ibo Village Affairs*. London: Sedgwick and Jackson, 1947.

Greenberg, Joseph H. "Some Aspects of Negro-Mohammedan Culture-Contact Among the Hausa," *American Anthropologist*, Vol. 43, No. 1 (1941).

————. *The Influence of Islam on a Sudanese Religion*. Monograph of the American Ethnological Society. New York: J. J. Augustin, 1946.

————. "Islam and Clan Organization Among the Hausa," *Southwestern Journal of Anthropology*, Vol. 3, No. 3 (1947), pp. 193-211.

Gunn, Harold D. *Pagan Peoples of the Central Area of Northern Nigeria*. London: International African Institute, 1956.

————. *Peoples of the Plateau Area of Northern Nigeria*. London: International Africa Institute, 1953.

Harris, Philip J. *Local Government in Southern Nigeria*. Cambridge: Cambridge University Press, 1957.

Hazlewood, Arthur. *The Finances of Nigerian Federation*. Oxford University Institute of Colonial Studies Reprint Series No. 14, 1955.

Hodgkin, Thomas. *Nigeria Perspectives, An Historical Anthology*. London: Oxford University Press, 1960.

Hogben, S. J. *The Muhammedan Emirates of Northern Nigeria*. London: Oxford University Press, 1930.

Ibadan. Published under the auspices of the University College of Ibadan and presented to the Third International West African Conference. Ibadan: 1949.

Ibo State Union. Constitution. 1951.

————. Constitutional Proposals, 1949.

————. Memorandum submitted by the Ibo State Union to the Minorities Commission, November, 1957, with extracts from the minutes of Ibo State Assemblies. (Mimeographed.)

————. Memorandum to the Minorities Commission including Address of Ibo Counsel at Calabar and Port Harcourt and the Important Events in the Making of History of Ibo-land, 1841-1958. Port Harcourt: 1958.

Ikoku, S. G. "Social and Economic Forces in Eastern Region Politics," *Action Group of Nigeria, 1956 Summer School Lectures.* Ibadan: 1956, pp. 28-38.

Ikoli, Ernest. "The Nigeria Press," *West African Review,* XXI, No. 273 (June 1950), pp. 625-627.

Imam, Abubakar. "The Problems of Northern Nigeria as the Natives See It. Account of an Interview with Lord Lugard." (Typewritten.)

International Bank for Reconstruction and Development. *The Economic Development of Nigeria.* Baltimore: The Johns Hopkins Press, 1955.

Investment in Education. Report of the Commission on Post-School Certificate and Higher Education in Nigeria. London: 1960.

Ita, Eyo. *The Assurance of Freedom.* Calabar: 1949.

————. *National Youth Renaissance.* Calabar: n.d.

————. *Sterile Truths and Fertile Lies.* Calabar: 1949.

————. *Crusade for Freedom.* Calabar: 1949.

————. *A Decade of National Education Movement.* Calabar: 1949.

Jackson, I. C. *Advance in Africa.* London: Oxford University Press, 1956.

Johnson, J. M. "Address by the Hon. J. M. Johnson, Minister of Labour, to the First Annual Conference of the Trades Union Congress, Nigeria, on 22nd April, 1960," *Ministry of Labour Quarterly Review,* Vol. I, No. 4 (March 1960), pp. 39-42.

Johnson, Samuel. *The History of the Yorubas,* edited by Dr. O. Johnson. London: Routledge, 1921.

Jones, G. I. *Report of the Position, Status, and Influence of Chiefs and Natural Rulers in the Eastern Region of Nigeria.* Enugu: 1957.

Kano, Malam Aminu. Statement on the Founding of the Northern Elements Progressive Union. (Typewritten.)

————. Presidential Address to the Fifth Annual Conference of the Northern Elements Progressive Union. 1955.

————. Presidential Address to the Seventh Annual Conference of the Northern Elements Progressive Union, Ibadan, 26 September 1957.

————. Address by the N.E.P.U. Delegation to the All-African Peoples' Conference, Accra, December 1958. (Mimeographed.)

Kirk-Green, A. H. M. *Adamawa: Past and Present.* London: Oxford University Press, 1958.

Kotoye, N. A. B. "Spotlight on Justice in the North." Prepared for the Action Group Delegation to the Resumed Constitutional Conference of 1958. (Typewritten.)

——. "Further Suggestions About Judicial Reform in the North." Prepared for the Action Group Delegation to the Resumed Constitutional Conference of 1958. (Typewritten.)

Lagos and Colony State Movement. *The Case for the Creation of a Lagos and Colony State within the Federation of Nigeria.* Lagos: n.d.

Lloyd, Peter C. "Craft Organization in Yoruba Towns," *Africa,* XXIII (January 1953), pp. 30-44.

——. "Cocoa, Politics, and the Yoruba Middle Class," *West Africa,* January 17, 1953.

——. "The Integration of the New Economic Classes into Local Government in Western Nigeria, *African Affairs,* Vol. 52, No. 209 (October 1953), pp. 327-34.

——. "Action Group and Local Government," *West Africa,* November 7 and 14, 1953.

——. "The Traditional Political System of the Yoruba," *Southwestern Journal of Anthropology* 10 (Winter 1954), pp. 366-384.

——. "The Yoruba Lineage," *Africa,* XXV (July 1955), pp. 235-251.

——. "The Development of Political Parties in Western Nigeria," *American Political Science Review,* Vol. XLIX, 3 (September 1955), pp. 693-707.

——. "The Changing Role of the Yoruba Traditional Rulers," *Proceedings of the Third Annual Conference of the West African Institute of Social and Economic Research.* Ibadan: University College, 1956.

——. "Tribalism in Warri," *Fifth Annual Conference Proceedings of the West African Institute of Social and Economic Research.* Ibadan: University College, 1956.

——. *Yoruba Land Law.* London: Oxford University Press, 1962.

Losi, J. B. O. *History of Lagos.* Lagos: 1921.

Lucas, J. O. *Oduduwa: A Lecture.* Lagos: 1949.

Lugard, Sir Frederick. *The Dual Mandate in British Tropical Africa,* 4th ed. London: William Blackwood, 1929.

Macaulay, Herbert. *Justitia Fiat: The Moral Obligation of the British Government to the House of Docemo of Lagos.* London: 1921.

——, and Pearse, S. Herbert. "Views of the Lagos Auxiliary of the Anti-Slavery and Aborigines Protection Society upon the Present Policy of His Majesty's Government with Regard to Lands in Lagos and the Rights of the White-Cap-Chiefs and private owners." Colonial Office Library (London), West African Pamphlets, Vol. III, No. 74.

Marris, Peter. "Slum Clearance and Family Life in Lagos," *Human Organization,* Vol. 19, No. 3 (Fall 1960), pp. 123-128.

Martin, Anne. *The Oil Palm Economy of the Ibibio Farmer*. Ibadan: University College Press, 1956.

Mbadiwe, Kingsley Ozuomba. *British and Axis Aims in Africa*. New York: Malliet, 1942.

McEwen, F. S. Speech by the Leader of the NCNC Delegation to the All-African Peoples' Conference, Accra, December 11, 1958. (Mimeographed.)

Meek, C. K. *Land Tenure and Land Administration in Nigeria and the Cameroons*. Colonial Research Study No. 22. London: 1957.

———. *Law and Authority in a Nigerian Tribe*. London: Oxford University Press, 1937.

Mid-West State Movement, Nigeria. *The Case For a Mid-West State*. Warri: n.d.

Nadel, S. F. *A Black Byzantium, The Kingdom of Nupe in Nigeria*. London: Oxford University Press, 1942.

Nee-Ankrah, A. W. *Whither Benin*. Benin City: 1951.

Nigeria Union. *1955 Summer School Papers*. London: 1955.

"Nigerian Prospects," *Pan Africa* (October-December 1947).

Niven, C. R. *A Short History of Nigeria*, 2d. edition. London: Longman's, Green and Co., 1940.

———. *A Short History of the Yoruba Peoples*. London: Longman's, Green and Co., 1958.

Nwachuku, J. R. "The Spirit of the Zikist National Vanguard." NCNC Eastern Working Committee Files No. 48:1. (Mimeographed.)

Obi, Chike. *Our Struggle*. Lagos: 1955.

Offonry, H. Kanu. "The Strength of Ibo Clan Feeling," *West Africa*, May 26-June 2, 1951.

Odiete, J. E. *Problems of Nigerian Minorities*. Lagos: n.d.

Ofakansi, Chuma. *Has Zik any Political Ambition?* Enugu: n.d.

Ojike, Mbonu. *My Africa*. New York: John Day, 1946.

———. *I Have Two Countries*. New York: John Day, 1946.

———. *Guide To Federal Elections*. Kano: 1954.

Ojo, Chief S. *Short History of Ilorin*. Shaki: 1957.

Okoye, Mokwugo. *Fullness of Freedom: A Gaze at Socialist Horizons and Some Fragments of Radical Wisdom*. Onitsha: n.d.

———. *Some Facts and Fancies*. Yaba: n.d.

———. *Pangs of Progress*. Onitsha: n.d.

———. Speech to the All-African Peoples' Conference, Accra, December 8, 1958. (Mimeographed.)

Omo-Ananigie, P. I. *The Life History of M. A. O. Imoudu*. Lagos: 1957.

Onyia, J. I. G. *Review of the Constitution of Nigeria for 1950*. Aba: 1949.

Orakwue, Jerry I. *Onitsha Custom of Title-Taking*. Onitsha: 1953.

Orizu, A. A. Nwafor. *Without Bitterness*. New York: Creative Age Press, 1944.

Ottenberg, Simon. "Ibo Receptivity to Change," in William R. Bascom and Melville J. Herskovits (eds.), *Continuity and Change in African Cultures*. Chicago: University of Chicago Press, 1959.

———. "Improvement Associations Among the Afikpo Ibo," *Africa*, XXV (January 1955), pp. 1-27.

Ottenberg, Phoebe V. "The Changing Economic Position of Women among the Afikpo Ibo," in William R. Bascom and Melville J. Herskovits (eds.), *Continuity and Change in African Cultures*. Chicago: University of Chicago Press, 1959.

Overseas Economic Surveys. *Nigeria: Economic and Commercial Conditions*. London: H.M.S.O., 1957.

Parrinder, E. G. *Religion in an African City*. London: Oxford University Press, 1953.

———. *The Story of Ketu, An Ancient Yoruba Kingdom*. Ibadan: University College Press, 1956.

Perham, Margery. *Native Administration in Nigeria*. London: Oxford University Press, 1937.

———, (ed.). *The Native Economies of Nigeria*. London: Faber, 1946.

———. *Mining, Commerce, and Finance in Nigeria*. London: Faber, 1948.

———. *Lugard: The Years of Authority, 1898-1945*. London: Collins, 1960.

Prest, A. R., and Stewart, I. G. *The National Income of Nigeria, 1950-51*. Colonial Research Studies No. 11. London: H.M.S.O., 1953.

Protest Committee of Nigerian Youths. *Politics Without Bitterness*. Umuahia Ibeku: n.d.

Rowling, C. W. *Land Tenure in Ijebu Province*. Lagos and Ibadan: 1956.

Royal Institute of International Affairs. *Nigeria: The Political and Economic Background*. London: Oxford University Press, 1960.

Sarkesian, Sam C. "Nigerian Political Profile: The emerging political interest groups." Master's thesis, Department of Government, Columbia University, 1962.

Schwab, William B. "Kinship and Lineage Among the Yoruba," *Africa*, XXV, 4 (October 1955), pp. 352-374.

Sklar, Richard L. "The Contribution of Tribalism to Nationalism in Western Nigeria," *Journal of Human Relations*, Vol. 8 (Spring and Summer 1960), pp. 407-418.

Smith, A. R. A. *Speech at the Inaugural Meeting of the National Muslim League (Egbe Muslumi Parapo), Ibadan, July 28, 1957*. Ijebu-Ode: 1957.

Smith, M. G. *The Economy of Hausa Communities of Zaria*. Colonial Research Studies No. 16. London: H.M.S.O., 1955.

———. *Government in Zazzau, 1800-1950*. London: Oxford University Press, 1960.

———. "The Hausa System of Social Status," *Africa*, XXIX, No. 3 (July 1959), pp. 239-252.

Smythe, Hugh H. "Nigeria's 'Marginal Men,'" *Phylon*, Vol. 19, No. 3 (1958), pp. 268-276.

———. "Social Stratification in Nigeria," *Social Forces*, Vol. 37, No. 2 (December 1958), pp. 168-171.

———, and Smythe, Mabel M. *The New Nigerian Elite*. Stanford: Stanford University Press, 1960.

Stapleton, G. Brian. *The Wealth of Nigeria*. London: Oxford University Press, 1958.

Thomas, Isaac B. *Life History of Herbert Macaulay*, 3rd edition. Lagos: n.d.

"Tribal Rivalries Within Islam," *The Times of London*, June 4, 1958, p. 11.

Utchay, T. K. Education Missionary Society. "Petition to the Convention of the NCNC holding at Aba, October, 1957." Aba: 1957.

Uwaifo, H. Omo. "My Past Public Performances in Benin." Benin City: 1955.

Uwanaka, Charles U. *Zik and Awolowo in Political Storm*. 4th edition. Lagos: 1955.

Uzo, Timothy M. *The Pathfinder, A Test of Political Ideals and an Interaction of Facts, Politics and Common Sense in Nigeria*. Lagos: 1953.

Wallace, J. G. "The Tiv System of Election," *Journal of African Administration*, X (April 1958), pp. 63-70.

Ward-Price, H. L. *Land Tenure in the Yoruba Provinces*. Lagos: 1933.

Wheare, Joan. *The Nigerian Legislative Council*. London: Faber, 1950.

Yeld, E. R. "Islam and Social Stratification in Northern Nigeria," British Journal of Sociology, XI, No. 2 (June 1960), pp. 112-128.

C

Selected Official Publications and Commentaries Concerning Electoral Laws and Elections in Nigeria

Federation of Nigeria. *Report by the Ad Hoc Meeting of the Nigerian Constitutional Conference held in Lagos in February 1958*. Lagos: 1958.

———. *Report of the Constituency Delimitation Commission, 1958*. Lagos: 1958.

Federal Electoral Commission. *Report on the Nigeria Federal Elections, December, 1959*. Lagos: 1960.

The Eastern Region of Nigeria. *The Eastern House of Assembly Electoral Regulations, 1955*. E.R.L.N. No. 9 of 1955.

———. *Report on the General Election to the Eastern House of Assembly, 1957*. Sessional Paper No. 1 of 1957. Enugu: 1957.

———. *Report on Eastern Nigeria General Election, November, 1961*. Enugu. 1962.

The Northern Region of Nigeria. *The Northern House of Assembly (Elected Members) Electoral Regulation, 1956.* N.R.L.N. 249 of 1956.

The Western Region of Nigeria. *The Parliamentary and Local Government Electoral Regulations, 1955.* W.R.L.N. 266 of 1955.

————. *Report on the Holding of the 1956 Parliamentary Election to the Western House of Assembly, Nigeria.* Ibadan: 1957.

————. *Report on Local Government Elections in the Western Region of Nigeria, 1958.* Sessional Paper No. 7 of 1958. Ibadan: 1958.

————. *Report of the Western Region Constituency Delimitation Commission, 1959.* Ibadan: 1959.

Colonial Office, United Kingdom. "Report of the First General Election to the Western House of Assembly: General Elections, 1951," *Colonial Reports—Nigeria, 1951.* London: 1953.

Lloyd, Peter C. "Some Comments on the Election in Nigeria." *Journal of African Administration,* IV, 3 (July 1952), pp. 82-92.

Whitaker, Philip. "The Preparation of the Register of Electors in the Western Region of Nigeria, 1955-56." *Journal of African Administration,* IX (January 1957), pp. 23-29.

————. "The Western Region of Nigeria, May 1956," and Price, J. H. "The Eastern Region of Nigeria, March, 1957," in W. J. M. Mackenzie and Kenneth Robinson (eds.), *Five Elections in Africa.* Oxford: Clarendon Press, 1960.

Prescott, J. R. V. *A Geographical Analysis of Elections to the Eastern House of Assembly, March 1957,* University College of Ibadan, Department of Geography. Research Notes No. 10, June 1957. Ibadan: 1957.

Awa, Eme. "The Federal Elections in Nigeria, 1959," *Ibadan,* No. 8 (March 1960), pp. 4-7.

Post, K. W. J. "The Federal Election: an Outside View," *Ibadan,* No. 8 (March 1960), pp. 7-9.

"Nigeria Elects 1960 Independence Parliament," *Africa Special Report,* Vol. 4, No. 12 (December 1959), pp. 3-4.

Dent, M. J. "Elections in Northern Nigeria," *Journal of Local Administration Overseas,* I, 4 (October 1962), pp. 213-224.

II

Documents and Publications of Nigerian Political Parties

Main sources are listed here rather than specific documents and publications, many of which have been cited in footnotes.

Action Group of Nigeria. Headquarters Secretariat Files, Ibadan.

Minutes of meetings of various executive bodies.

Reports of the Proceedings of Regional Conferences and Federal Congresses.
Reports and memoranda submitted to various conferences and congresses.
Reports and memoranda submitted to officers of the Action Group.
Constituency organization files.
Day to day diaries and reports of field secretaries.
Circular letters issued by the Headquarters Secretariat.
Election Manifestos and Policy Papers.
Publications of the Bureau of Information.
Approved and Revised Estimates, 1958.

Action Group of Nigeria

Minutes and Reports of the meetings of sub-regional conferences and executive bodies.
Action Group of Nigeria. *Constitution*. Ibadan: n.d.
————. Proposals for a Draft Constitution of the Action Group. 1957. (Mimeographed.)
————. Revised Draft Constitution of the Action Group. 1958. (Mimeographed.)
————. Amendments to the Revised Draft of the Constitution. 1958. (Mimeographed.)
————. *Democratic Socialism: Being the Manifesto of the Action Group of Nigeria for an Independent Nigeria*. Lagos: 1960.
————. *Minority Report to the Nigeria Constitutional Conference*. London: 1953.
————. *Lagos Belongs To The West*. London: 1953.
————. *Summer School Lectures*, 1955 and 1956.
————. S. T. Oredein. *A Manual on Action Group Party Organization*. Ibadan: n.d.

Bornu Youth Movement. Secretariat Records. Maiduguri.

Democratic Party of Nigeria and the Cameroons. Why We Break from the NCNC. Lagos: 1958.

Dynamic Party. The Memorandum and Protocols of the Dynamic Party. Ibadan: 1957.
————. Ordinances of the Dynamic Party. (Mimeographed.)
————. Minutes of the Central Executive Committee, April 3, 1955. (Mimeographed.)

Ijebu-Remo Tax and Ratepayers Association. Rules and Regulations. Shagamu: 1957.
————. Memorandum of the I.R.T.P.A. to the Secretary General, Nigeria Constitutional Conference, 1957. (Mimeographed.)

National Council of Nigeria and the Cameroons. National Headquarters Secretariat Files, Lagos.

Minutes of meetings of various executive bodies.
Reports of the Proceedings of Annual Conventions.
Reports and memoranda submitted to Annual Conventions.
Reports and memoranda submitted to National officers.
Records of branches and member unions.
Circular letters to branches.
Kumuyi, R. A. The Problems of the National Headquarters. (Typewritten.)
Information Bureau. *NCNC News Bulletin*, 1952.
Election manifestos and policy papers.

NCNC. Eastern Working Committee Secretariat Files, Enugu.

Reports of the meetings of regional conferences and various executive bodies.
Reports and memoranda submitted to regional conferences and regional officers.
Branch and divisional organization files.

NCNC. Northern Working Committee

Minutes of the Northern Wing of the NCNC, Kafanchan, 13 April 1957.
Memorandum to the N.E.C. at Aba, October 1957.

NCNC-Mabolaje Grand Alliance. Secretariat Records, Ibadan.

NCNC. Onitsha Divisional Organization. Report of the sub-committee of the Divisional Executive Committee on the Government. Sessional Paper No. 2 of 1957, March 1958. (Mimeographed.)
NCNC. Port Harcourt Divisional Branch. Minute Book and Records.
NCNC. Memorandum Submitted by the Delegation of the National Council of Nigeria and the Cameroons to the Secretary of State for the Colonies on the 11th August 1947. (Mimeographed.)
NCNC. *The Constitution of the National Council of Nigeria and the Cameroons.* Lagos: 1945.
———. *The Constitution, Rules and Regulations of the National Council of Nigeria and the Cameroons.* Lagos: 1955.
———. "Amendments to the NCNC Constitution," 1961. (Mimeographed.)
———. Eastern Parliamentary Party. Standing Orders. (Mimeographed.)
———. Constitution of Kaduna Capital Territory (NEPU/NCNC) Supreme Council, October 1958. (Mimeographed.)
———. Youth Association Draft Constitution, 1958. (Mimeographed.)
NCNC Reform Committee. Releases 1-3, June 1958. (Mimeographed.)

National Muslim League (Egbe Musulmi Parapo). Constitution, Rules and Regulations. Abeokuta: 1957.

———. Memorandum on the Fears of the Muslim Minorities in the Regions, December 1957. (Mimeographed.)

Northern Elements Progressive Union. National Headquarters Secretariat Files, Kano.

Reports of various conferences.

Auditors Report to the Seventh Annual Conference, September 30, 1957. (Mimeographed.)

Officers of the NEPU, September 1957-September 1958. (Mimeographed.)

Names of NEPU Members who were convicted and sentenced by the Native Courts in Kano Province, 1954-1957. (Typewritten.)

Election manifestos.

Memorandum of the Northern Elements Progressive Union to the Secretary of State for the Colonies, July 1952. (Mimeographed.)

Delegation to the United Kingdom, 19 December 1955. Memorandum. (Mimeographed.)

Memorandum on Civil Liberties, presented to Rt. Hon. A. T. Lennox-Boyd, Secretary of State for the Colonies, at Kano, Nigeria, 30 January 1957. (Mimeographed.)

NEPU. *Jam'iyyar Neman Sawaba, Manufa, Sharudda da Ka'idodi.* Kano: n.d. (Constitution and Rules.)

———. *Sawaba Declaration of Principles.* Kano: 1950.

———. "Sawaba Creed: Why I Join the Sawaba Crusade." n.d.

Northern Peoples' Congress. Central Headquarters Secretariat, Kaduna

Records of members, branches, and affiliated organizations.

Communications with branches.

Half-Yearly Parliamentary Reports.

Proposals for party organization.

Records of the proceedings of conferences and minutes of meetings (mainly in Hausa).

Election manifestos.

Memorandum on the Foundation of the Northern Peoples' Congress. (Typewritten.)

Northern Peoples' Congress. "Declaration of Jam'iyyar Mutanen Arewa (Northern Peoples' Congress), 1st October, 1951."

———. *Constitution and Rules.* Zaria: Gaskiya, n.d.

United Middle Belt Congress

Report of the Convention held in Lafia, January 15-17, 1957.

Minutes of the Conference at Kafanchan, 26 August 1957.

Memorandum on the Creation of a Separate Middle Belt Region, 1956.

Memorandum on Constitutional Reform, 1957. (Mimeographed.)

Minutes of a Meeting Between the Action Group and the UMBC, April 19, 1957.

United Middle Belt Congress. Constitution and By-Laws. Ilorin: 1955. (Mimeographed.)

———. Draft Constitution, 1957. (Mimeographed.)

United Muslim Party. Representations on the Nigerian Constitutional Conference, May 23, 1957. (Mimeographed.)

———. Letter to the Prime Minister of the Federation from M. R. B. Ottun, July 17, 1958. (Mimeographed.)

———. Memorandum on the Creation of a Lagos Region submitted to the Resumed Constitutional Conference, September 1958. (Mimeographed.)

Warri Peoples' Party. Memorandum to the Minorities Commission in behalf of Warri and Western Ijaw Peoples, 1957. (Mimeographed.)

III

NEWSPAPERS AND MISCELLANEOUS SOURCES

Nigerian Newspapers in publication during the writer's research in Nigeria:

Dailies

Daily Comet. Comet Press Ltd., Kano (Zik Group).

Daily Service. Amalgamated Press, Lagos.

Daily Telegraph. United Nigeria Press, Lagos.

Daily Times. Nigerian Printing and Publishing Company, Lagos.

Eastern Nigeria Guardian. Associated Newspapers of Nigeria, Ltd., Port Harcourt (Zik Group).

Eastern Sentinel. Associated Newspapers of Nigeria, Ltd., Enugu (Zik Group).

Eastern States Express. Ikemesit Co. Ltd., Aba.

New Africa. New Africa Press, Ltd., Onitsha.

Nigerian Daily Standard. Old Calabar Press Ltd., Calabar.

Nigerian Spokesman. Associated Newspapers of Nigeria Ltd., Onitsha (Zik Group).

Nigerian Tribune. Amalgamated Press, Nigeria, Ltd., Ibadan.

Southern Nigeria Defender. Associated Newspapers of Nigeria Ltd., Ibadan (Zik Group).

West African Pilot. West African Pilot Ltd., Lagos (Zik Group).

Weeklies

Eastern Outlook. Eastern Nigeria Information Service, Enugu.

Gaskiya Ta Fi Kwabo. Gaskiya Corporation, Zaria (twice weekly—Hausa).

Irohin Yoruba. Amalgamated Press of Nigeria, Ltd., Lagos (Yoruba).
Nigerian Citizen. Gaskiya Corporation, Zaria (twice weekly).
Sunday Times. Nigerian Printing and Publishing Co., Lagos.
West African Vanguard. Ilesha (English—Yoruba).
Eastern Nigeria Today. Published Monthly by the Office of the Commissioner in the United Kingdom for the Eastern Region, London.

Other Sources

Nigeria Year Book, 1958. Lagos: Nigerian Printing and Publishing Company, 1958.
The Nigerian. (London), Nos. 1-3 (October 1953-February 1954).
West Africa. Published weekly by the West Africa Publishing Company, Ltd., London.
Who's Who in Nigeria. Lagos: Nigerian Printing and Publishing Company, 1956.

IV

OTHER BIBLIOGRAPHIES

Coleman, James S. "A Survey of Selected Literature on the Government and Politics of British West Africa," *American Political Science Review,* XLIX (December 1955), pp. 1130-1150.
———. *Nigeria: Background to Nationalism.* Berkeley and Los Angeles: University of California Press, 1958. Pp. 481-496.
Conover, Helen F. *Nigerian Official Publications, 1869-1959: A Guide.* Reference Department, Library of Congress. Washington, D.C.: 1959.
Harris, John. *Books About Nigeria: a select reading list.* Ibadan: University College Press, 1959.
Hazlewood, Arthur. *The Economics of "Under-Developed" Areas: An Annotated Reading List of Books, Articles, and Official Publications,* 2d edition. London: Oxford University Press, 1959.
Perry, Ruth. *A Preliminary Bibliography of the Literature of Nationalism in Nigeria.* London: International African Institute, 1955.
United Kingdom, Colonial Office. *Government Publications, Sectional List No. 34,* Revised to 30th November 1958. London: H.M.S.O., 1958.

INDEX

Abaagu, H. O. 347f, 406n
Abang, Okim Okwa, 530
Abayomi, Dr. Kofororola, 52n, 53, 54n, 112
Abayomi, Lady Oyinkan, 112, 434
Abba Habib, 127n, 366f, 513
Abba Kano Mattedan, 340n
Abba Kashiya, 94n
Abba Maikwaru, 94n, 421n
Abba Sa'id, 91n
Abba Zakar Nguru, 526
Abdu-Anache, Alhaji, 516
Abdul Ado Ibrahim, 347n, 348n, 385n
Abdul Razag, 388n, 513
Abdulkadir Danjaji, 94n, 525
Abdulkadir A. Koguna, 330n
Abdulkadir Makama, 92n, 94n
Abdullahi Dan Buram Jada, 514
Abdullahi Maikano Dutse, 517
Abdulmaliki Okene, 322n
Abdulmumini, Hon., 525
Abdurahman Bida, 89n
Abidogim, J. P., 309n
Abii, D. N., 521
Abore Shani, 517
Abubakar, *Madawakin* Sokoto, 516
Abubakar, Sultan of Sokoto, 97
Abubakar Garba, 514
Ababakar Imam, founding of NPC, 91f; office in NPC, 94n, 322n; NPC as political party, 95n, 96
Abubakar Tafawa Balewa, alliance with National Emancipation League, 386n; in Bauchi, 89, 98; biographical sketch, 98-100; constitutional views, 87n, 99; cooperation with Action Group, 130n; critic of NCNC, 98; Independence Government, 508; joins NPC, 96f, 321; leadership status and style, 366, 368f; and *Mabolaje,* 314n; National Government, 194, 279, 302; and Native Administration reform, 99f, 370; and Northern Teachers' Association, 91n; on party finance, 388n; political thought, 370f; Prime Minister, 20, 193, 370, 383n, 508; relationship with Dr. Azikiwe, 227; relationship with Sardauna of Sokoto, 367n, 369f; teacher training, 90; Vice President of NPC, 322, 513
Abubakar Tugga, 385n
Abubakar Tunau, 94n
Abubakar S. G. Zukogi, 64n, 90n, 524

Achara, S. O., 227n, 521
Achimugu, Peter S., 515
Action Group, 19, 20, 228; alliances, 129, 138, 219, 244n, 322, 347-49, 352f, 435f, 507; appeal to Marxian intellectuals, 270f; in Benin, 239-42, 255; in Bornu, 342; branches, 422f; caucuses, 275f, 278; and chiefs, 106f, 234-38, 265f, 241f, 443-45, 465n; conferences, 106, 126, 272, 424; conflict with British, 124; congresses, 268, 277, 280, 426-28; control of West, 116; cooperation with NPC, 129f, 243, 264, 282; discipline, 438f; effective power structure, 494; ethnic resistance to, 245-47; executive council, 424-30, 439; expansion of, 242-44; factions, 277, 281f, 511; federalist doctrine, 266f; finance, 440f, 457f; founders, 107-10; in Ibadan, 295, 312ff; ideological tendencies, 261-74; in Ife, 470, 472f; inauguration of, 103-7; in Lagos, 112, 253, 436; leaders, 274-83: *duties,* 434: *Occupational backgrounds,* 483f, 486-91; membership, 422; Mid-West section, 104; and Mid-West State movement, 136, 245f; and National Bank of Nigeria, 178, 455-58; nominating system, 436-38; official structure and organization, 422-41; in Ogoja, 468-71; opposition of socio-economic groups to, 251ff; parliamentary councils, 275f, 430f; patronage system, 450-52; policy on new states, 136-40, 349f, 507; policy on police, 267; radicalism, 269-71; regionalism, 264f; relationship to *Egbe Omo Oduduwa,* 102-5, 234, 236f, 464f; religious resistance to, 247-51; secretariat, 431-34; socio-economic basis, 256-61; supremacy of party executive, 276, 431; and United Muslim Council, 250; use of customary institutions, 422f; welfare statism, 262, 268; women's organization, 434; youth organization, 277, 434f; zonal organization, 425
Action Magazine, 434
Adamu Dankutu, 526
Adamu Jajire, 524
Ade Gusau, 524
Adebiyi, Lawal, 308n
Adebola, H. P., 115, 117, 224n, 495n, 521
Adedeji, O. A., 532

561

DE 5 '67				
DE 19'67				